The Sphere of Influence
The Heliocentric Perversion of the Gospel

[K]eep that which is committed to thy trust, avoiding profane and vain babblings, and oppositions of science falsely so called: Which some professing have erred concerning the faith. Grace be with thee. Amen. (1 Timothy 6:20-21)

Edward Hendrie

Copyright © 2019-2022 by Edward Hendrie
Fifth Edition. All rights reserved.
Paperback ISBN: 978-1-943056-06-4
Hardcover ISBN: 978-1-943056-07-1
Ebook   ISBN: 978-1-943056-08-8
EdwardHendrie@gmail.com

Other books from Great Mountain Publishing®
- 9/11-Enemies Foreign and Domestic
- Solving the Mystery of BABYLON THE GREAT
- The Anti-Gospel
- Bloody Zion
- What Shall I Do to Inherit Eternal Life?
- Murder, Rape, and Torture in a Catholic Nunnery
- Antichrist: The Beast Revealed
- The Greatest Lie on Earth
- The Greatest Lie on Earth (Expanded Edition)
- The Damnable Heresy of Salvation by Dead Faith (Expanded Edition)
- Vaccine Danger: Quackery and Sin
- Hoax of Biblical Proportions
- Rome's Responsibility for the Assassination of Abraham Lincoln

Available at:
www.antichristconspiracy.com
https://greatmountainpublishing.com
www.911enemies.com
www.mysterybabylonthegreat.net
www.antigospel.com
https://play.google.com
www.barnesandnoble.com
www.amazon.com

Edward Hendrie rests on the authority of the Holy Bible alone for doctrine. He considers the Holy Bible to be the inspired and inerrant word of God. Favorable citation by Edward Hendrie to an authority outside the Holy Bible on a particular issue should not be interpreted to mean that he agrees with all of the doctrines and beliefs of the cited authority. All Scripture references are to the Authorized (King James) Version of the Holy Bible, unless otherwise indicated.

Table of Contents

Introduction 1

1   Debate With Professor Know-It-All 8

2   The Bible Describes a Flat Immovable Earth 24

3   Why Is it Important? 54

4   Heathen Doctrines Born From Heliocentrism 81

5   Corruption of the Gospel Was Prophesied 105

6   The Occult Origins of Heliocentrism 109

7   The Myth of Gravity 141

8   Heliocentric Keystone of New World Order 151

9   Conspiracy To Silence Flat Earth Believers 166

10   Gatekeepers in the Church 178

11   The Creation Gospel 194

12   Pastors Fired for Preaching Flat Earth 225

13   Pastoral Intolerance of the Flat Earth 230

14   Leaning on Their Own Understanding 262

15   The Nicolaitans 274

16   Anatomy of a Deception 298

17   Knowing God's Eternal Power and Godhead 305

18	On the Broad Highway to Hell	321
19	Salvation Through the Gospel of Creation	329
20	Slippery Slope	355
21	He Saw No God There	365
22	Creation Science Hall of Shame	373
23	Implying God Lied	431
24	Casting Aside the Sword of the Spirit	442
25	Moonlight Discredits Heliocentric Creationists	450
26	Shedding Moonlight on Guile	458
27	Caught Speaking Lies	469
28	It's All a Matter of Perspective	484
29	Swindle At Bedford Canal	501
30	Superstition Passing as Science	528
31	PBS Caught Red-Handed Using Video Fakery	568
32	Propaganda Misfire by National Geographic	576
33	NASA Christians?	586
34	All or Nothing	593
35	Houston Has a Problem	608
Endnotes		621

Introduction

This book is a sequel to *The Greatest Lie on Earth (Expanded Edition): Proof That Our World Is Not a Moving Globe*.[1] This book will primarily focus on the infiltration into the church of the superstitious myth of heliocentrism and how that infiltration has served to undermine the gospel. For purposes of continuity and clarity, the principal biblical concepts discussed in the *Greatest Lie on Earth* are repeated herein, before being expanded upon. But in order to understand the scientific evidence supporting a flat, stationary earth one will need to read *The Greatest Lie on Earth*, in which is explained the physical proof.

Heliocentrism is not true science. It is a spiritual deception, and that deception is with a purpose. In 1887, an occult publication, *Lucifer*, revealed that the satanic scheme behind the heliocentric mythology is to deceive the masses to reject the infallible truths of the Holy Bible and embrace the lie that there is no God.

> We date from the First of January, 1601. This era is called the Era of Man (E.M.) to distinguish it from the theological epoch that preceded it. In that epoch the Earth was supposed to be flat, the Sun was its attendant light, revolving about it. Above was Heaven, where God ruled supreme over all potentates and powers, below was the kingdom of

the Devil, Hell. So taught the Bible. Then came the NEW ASTRONOMY. It demonstrated that the Earth is a globe revolving about the sun; that the stars are worlds and suns; that there is no 'up and down' in space, VANISHED THE OLD HEAVEN, VANISHED THE OLD HELL; the earth became the home of man. And when the modern Cosmogony came, the Bible and the Church, as infallible oracles, had to go, for they had taught that regarding the universe WHICH WAS NOW SHOWN TO BE UNTRUE IN EVERY PARTICULAR.[2]

The modern science of heliocentrism is based more on religious superstition than it is empirical observation. Indeed, scientific observations that allegedly support heliocentrism are plugged into religious dogma before they are then accepted as science. That is not hyperbole. For example, Johannes Kepler first postulated the generally accepted scientific theory today that the planets travel in ellipses around the sun. Paul Sutter, who is an astrophysicist at Ohio State University, the chief scientist at COSI Science Center, and host of Ask a Spaceman, RealSpace, and COSI Science Now,[3] explains that Johannes Kepler based his theory of planetary motion on his superstitious religious beliefs.

> Kepler penned a work in defense of the Copernican model, but not on physical or mathematical grounds — Kepler's argument was religious. He said that since the son of God was at the center of the Christian faith, the sun ought to be at the center of the universe. Ergo, heliocentrism.[4]

Nicolaus Copernicus' heliocentric model could not adequately explain the motions of planets. Kepler solved that problem by constructing his theory that the planets do not travel around the sun in circular orbits but rather elliptical orbits. Who exactly was Kepler? Sutter explains that "Kepler's day job was as the court astrologer for the Holy Roman Emperor. Yes: astrologer. Horoscopes and stuff."[5] The Holy Roman Emperor Rudolf II (1552-1612) was King of Hungary, Croatia, Bohemia, and Archduke of Austria. Emperor Rudolf II was a devotee of occult arts and sciences.

That means that Kepler, the great scientist who came up with the theory of planetary elliptical motion that is still used today to explain heliocentrism, was a heathen astrologer. Kepler plugged his observations into his superstitious belief in astrology and presto-chango his religious beliefs became the laws of planetary motion that are still accepted today as irrefutable scientific facts.

Kepler was already sold on the heliocentric model. He accepted heliocentrism on religious grounds. Kepler then constructed his new system of planetary motion on his religious beliefs. As an astrologer, Kepler was looking for a way to predict the future on earth by explaining the motion of the planets. Sutter explains:

> Kepler wasn't just looking for a handy fitting formula; he was searching for signs of the divine. He was convinced that the heavens, being naturally closer to God, contained a sort of perfection not seen on Earth since the Garden of Eden. What's more, if he could deduce the divine geometry of the heavens, he could look for similarities here on Earth to help predict the future.[6]

Kepler had constructed his heliocentric model on his heathen religious beliefs. "His new system wasn't just a mathematical convenience, but a window into the mind of God and the hidden order of the universe."[7] Kepler was a heathen, and he constructed his heliocentric model upon his understanding of his heathen god. Kepler's science was not science at all. It was a reflection of his pagan religious beliefs and his false god. Heliocentrism is profane science that is based upon a heathen religious belief. But it is taught in schools and believed in churches today as though it is objective science. It is the false science warned of by God in the Bible. "O Timothy, keep that which is committed to thy trust, avoiding profane and vain babblings, and oppositions of science falsely so called:" (1 Timothy 6:20)

Heliocentrism is religious dogma masquerading as science. When a long-standing plan of deception spanning generations has been sold to the masses, any exposure of that conspiracy by revealing the truth is considered utterly preposterous, and the speaker is attacked as a raving lunatic. That is where we are today with the heliocentric model taught in schools. Anyone who reveals the truth of the flat, stationary earth is reviled as a madman. The heliocentric model of a spinning, orbiting, spherical earth is unsupported by real science; it is only supported by pseudoscience. The science fiction of heliocentricity has taken on the status akin to a sacrosanct religious dogma. Anyone who challenges that dogma is a heretic.

Heresy has come to mean "[a] fundamental error in religion, or an error of opinion respecting some fundamental doctrine of religion." But that is not the entire meaning. *Noah Webster's 1828 American Dictionary of the English Language* explains that "[i]n Scripture and primitive usage, heresy meant merely sect, party, or the doctrines of a sect, as we now use denomination or persuasion, implying no reproach."[8]

Heresy is all a matter of perspective. As Noah Webster explains: "an opinion deemed heretical by one body of Christians, may be deemed orthodox by another."[9] The devil considers God's doctrines to be heresy. So if the minions of the devil accuse you of being a heretic, you could consider that a good thing. Indeed, Jesus said as much in Matthew 5:11-12, where he stated that when the minions of the devil revile you and accuse you falsely for Jesus' sake you should consider that a blessing and rejoice. Paul stated that the gospel of Jesus Christ that he preached was called heresy by the Jews. "But this I confess unto thee, that after the way **which they call heresy**, so worship I the God of my fathers, believing all things which are written in the law and in the prophets:" (Acts 24:14)

Heresy could be evil if the heretical belief is against the doctrines of Christ. But sometimes the person leveling the charge of heresy is doing so in order to protect a long-established erroneous belief or practice from being exposed as such. One must step back and consider the merits of the alleged heresy and see if it is a righteous belief or an evil belief. The word "heresy," therefore, can describe something evil (e.g., Galatians 5:19-20) or it can represent something good (e.g., Acts 24:14). If someone speaks against a doctrine of God, that opposition to the truth is an evil heresy; but if someone speaks against a lie that through tradition has become the established orthodoxy, that opposition to the lie is a good heresy. Whether heresy is good or bad, all depends on the nature of the established orthodoxy that is being confronted by the alleged heresy. If the established orthodoxy is erroneous, then it is good to speak against that error (i.e., it can be good to be accused of being a heretic).

A commentator on the *Flat Earth Ministry* blog explains:

> Heretics were the good guys – the heroes who stood against all odds in confronting the powerful establishment. We have been taught to think negatively about heretics, but that was wrong. With the correct definition of "heresy," we can understand that it is NOT right to suppress independent thought. We should not support the establishment (any establishment) which

suppresses the freedom of conscience. And we should be grateful to all the heretics who had the guts and moral courage to stand against this tyranny in the past.[10]

Speaking against a lie that has become an orthodox belief brings with it a responsive attack from the high priests who spring into action to protect the erroneous religious (or scientific) dogma that is being questioned. The *Flat Earth Ministry* commentator explains:

> Inevitably, the High Priests of whatever topic points a finger at the heretic who questions traditional beliefs. The heretic is looked upon with suspicion, and the people all think, "He must be a bad guy or else no one would have accused him of anything." The heretic is rejected ostensibly because of doctrine, but in reality, it was because he refused to join, and thus sanction their conspiracy. The doctrinal issues in question are not allowed to be questioned because truth is not their objective – rather, they seek power through cohesion. That is the way the educational system and government works.[11]

The heresy of a flat and stationary earth, however, will not be characterized as a heresy by the heliocentric gatekeepers. To do so would reveal the religious nature of heliocentricity. So the heresy of a flat and stationary earth must be couched not in religious terms, but rather in scientific terms. One who believes the earth is flat is not called a heretic, instead, he is called a lunatic. Such lunatics (i.e., heretics) must be ridiculed, scorned, and shouted down.

God has always inspired righteous "heretics" in ages past to confront the evil that had become the orthodoxy of their era, including Abraham, Moses, David, the prophets, Paul, etc. Jesus Christ, himself, was viewed as a heretic by the Jews who plotted his death. John 8:37-56; 10:24-33; 11:53. Jesus explained that he did not come to make peace with the errors of orthodox Judaism. Jesus was not preaching unity with error; he came to speak against it and divide from it.[12]

> Suppose ye that I am come to give peace on earth? I tell you, Nay; but rather division: For from henceforth there shall be five in one house divided, three against two and two against three. The father shall be divided against the son, the son against the father; the mother against the daughter, and the daughter against the mother; the mother in law against her daughter in law, and the daughter in law against her mother in law. Luke 12:51-53.

As disciples of Jesus Christ, we are likewise called on to speak against the lies of this world, though we be persecuted as heretics. "And have no fellowship with the unfruitful works of darkness, but rather reprove them." (Ephesians 5:11) We are not to go along to get along. "Preach the word; be instant in season, out of season; reprove, rebuke, exhort with all longsuffering and doctrine." (2 Timothy 4:2) We will suffer persecution for following Jesus Christ and speaking the truth. Christ Jesus explained: "Remember the word that I said unto you, The servant is not greater than his lord. If they have persecuted me, they will also persecute you; if they have kept my saying, they will keep yours also." (John 15:20) But take comfort in words of the Lord:

> Blessed are ye, when men shall revile you, and persecute you, and shall say all manner of evil against you falsely, for my sake. Rejoice, and be exceeding glad: for great is your reward in heaven: for so persecuted they the prophets which were before you. (Matthew 5:11-12)

1   Debate With Professor Know-It-All

This author engaged in an email debate with a couple of professors who believe in the heliocentric model. One of those heliocentric professors in the email debate proudly displays his academic and professional credentials below his valediction in each email as: MBA, CADC-II, NCAC-I, ICADC, S.A.P., Ph.D. In the account of our communications below, he will remain unnamed. The professor argued in the email exchange that the earth casts a curved shadow on the moon during a lunar eclipse. He argued that the curved shadow proves that the earth is a sphere. I presented the professor and the others in the email string with photographic evidence of a daytime lunar eclipse. A daytime lunar eclipse precludes the earth's shadow from being the cause of the lunar eclipse. Indeed, a daytime lunar eclipse is impossible under the heliocentric model. The proof of the daytime lunar eclipse is presented in this author's book *The Greatest Lie on Earth*. Below is one of the photographs I shared with the professor.

Figure 2: December 10, 2011, Daytime Lunar Eclipse Viewed from Madison, Wisconsin

The professor contested the authenticity of the photographs of the daytime lunar eclipse. He claimed that the pictures are not those of a daytime lunar eclipse, but rather hoaxes that actually depicted moon phases.[13] In response, I provided him with video proof of the daytime lunar eclipse that occurred on December 10, 2011, taken from East St. Louis, Illinois, Madison, Wisconsin, and Southern New Mexico.[14] The Madison, Wisconsin and Southern New Mexico videos were time-lapse videos of the daytime lunar eclipse showing the moon being progressively eclipsed.

An entire lunar cycle takes approximately 29.5 days. Moon phases take approximately two weeks to wane from a full moon to a new moon and another two weeks to wax back again to a new moon. But the time-lapse videos show the shadow progressing downward over the illuminated moon and finally eclipsing it within approximately one hour. The hour long eclipses were time-lapse compressed to less than two minutes on one case and a few seconds in another, and were, clearly, not of moon phases. The time-lapse videos are proof that the daytime lunar eclipse pictures I provided the professor are genuine and not pictures of a moon phase, as claimed by the professor.

The video of the daytime lunar eclipse taken from East St. Louis was a narrated real-time video. The videographer of the daytime lunar eclipse filmed at East St. Louis was not a believer in a flat, stationary earth and, indeed, tried (unconvincingly) to explain the daytime lunar eclipse phenomenon under the heliocentric model. The video and time lapse proof was still not sufficient for the professor. He responded by suggesting that I was "a nut," "a dum dum," "stupid," and "a hoaxer," who has never studied the Bible or astronomy.[15]

I added to the proof by presenting data to the professor from NASA[16] and TimeandDate.com[17] that in fact there was a lunar eclipse on December 10, 2011, as narrated in the video I provided to him. The TimeandDate data further proved that both the sun and moon were above the horizon during the lunar eclipse.

The moon and sun calculators on TimeandDate.com indicate that there was a lunar eclipse on December 10, 2011 and the still partially eclipsed moon set on December 10, 2011, in Madison, Wisconson, at 7:18 a.m.[18] TimeandDate.com reveals that the sunrise in Madison, Wisconsin, on December 10, 2011, took place at 7:17 a.m.[19] So, here we have the verified data that the sun and eclipsed moon were both above the horizon at the same time from 7:17 a.m. until 7:18 a.m., just as depicted in the photographs I sent him, which also appear in my book, *The Greatest Lie on Earth*.

A daytime lunar eclipse is an impossibility under the heliocentric mythology. To have a daytime lunar eclipse both the sun and moon must be above the horizon. Such a configuration precludes the shadow of the earth being the cause of the eclipse. The pictures of the December 10, 2011, daytime eclipse from Madison, Wisconsin (and other locations) appearing in *The Greatest Lie on Earth* show clearly that the dark area on the moon is moving from the top-down. That would exclude a light refraction explanation given by the orthodox scientific community. Astronomer's call a daytime lunar eclipse a selenelion.[20] But a daytime lunar eclipse (selenelion) should be impossible under the heliocentric model, where the earth is supposed to be the source of the shadow and the cause of the eclipse. The diagram below, which I sent to the professor, illustrates the impossibility of a daytime lunar eclipse under the heliocentric model.

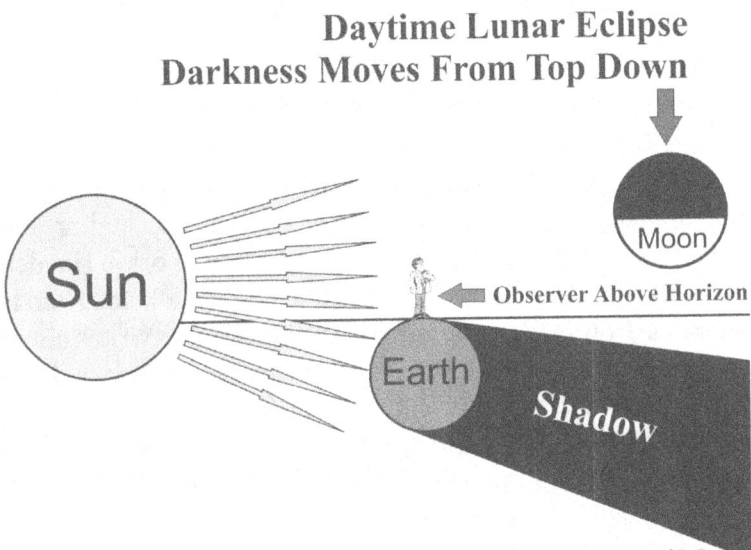

Under the heliocentric model, it is impossible for a daytime lunar eclipse to be caused by the earth's shadow.

Joe Rao, writing for Space.com explains the impossibility of the December 10, 2011, daytime lunar eclipse under the heliocentric model.

> For most places in the United States and Canada, there will be a chance to observe an unusual effect,

one that celestial geometry seems to dictate can't happen. The little-used name for this effect is a "selenelion" (or "selenehelion") and occurs when both the sun and the eclipsed moon can be seen at the same time. But wait! How is this possible? When we have a lunar eclipse, the sun, Earth and moon are in a geometrically straight line in space, with the Earth in the middle. So if the sun is above the horizon, the moon must be below the horizon and completely out of sight (or vice versa). And indeed, during a lunar eclipse, the sun and moon are exactly 180 degrees apart in the sky; so in a perfect alignment like this (a "syzygy") such an observation would seem impossible.[21]

According to Joe Rao's biography posted on the Simon & Schuster website, he is an on-camera meteorologist, an author, and serves as an instructor and guest lecturer at New York's Hayden Planetarium. The director of the venerable Hayden Planetarium is the famous astrophysicist Neil deGrasse Tyson. Rao writes about astronomy for Natural History magazine, the Farmer's Almanac, Space.com, as well as many other publications. Rao was voted "Best Local Television Personality" by the readers of Westchester Magazine. Rao was nominated for an Emmy in 2004, 2006, 2010, 2014, and 2016.[22]

What is Rao's explanation for this seemingly impossible event under the heliocentric model? Rao claims that light refraction explains the phenomenon of a daytime lunar eclipse. "[I]t is atmospheric refraction that makes a selenelion possible."[23] Indeed, Rao claims that "[a]tmospheric refraction causes astronomical objects to appear higher in the sky than they are in reality."[24] The problem with Rao's explanation is that it is untrue. This author addresses the deceptive light refraction explanation in detail in *The Greatest Lie on Earth (Expanded Edition)*. That book proves that light refraction, in actuality, has the opposite effect.

Light refraction makes the apparent height of distant objects drop in elevation and thus causes landmarks to be harder to see. Rao has reversed the real effect of atmospheric refraction in order to support the heliocentric model. Furthermore, the fact that the shadow for the daytime lunar eclipse travels from top to bottom impeaches the light refraction explanation.

The table below is a reconstruction of a table prepared by Joe Rao and posted with his article. It shows the information gathered by Rao for the sunrise and moonset times at different cities. Rao determined that at those cities both the sun and moon could be seen at the same time above the horizon during the lunar eclipse on December 10, 2011.

Below is the pertinent part of the actual caption for the table containing the information posted on Space.com by Joe Rao:

> **This table shows the local times of sunrise and moonset, along with the percentage of the moon's diameter that is within the dark umbral shadow at the time of moonset, for 11 selected cities. An asterisk (*) indicates that totality has already occurred and that the moon is emerging from the umbral shadow.**[25]

City	Time Zone	Sunrise	Moonset	Percent Covered
Chicago	CST	7:05 a.m.	7:06 a.m.	28.9%
Dallas	CST	7:17 a.m	7:18 a.m.	45.4%
Winnipeg	CST	8:14 a.m.	8:17 a.m.	TOTAL
Denver	MST	7:08 a.m.	7:11 a.m.	TOTAL
Phoenix	MST	7:20 a.m.	7:23 a.m.	TOTAL
Helena	MST	8:00 a.m.	8:04 a.m.	*94.3%
Calgary	MST	8:27 a.m.	8:33 a.m.	*61.9%
Los Angeles	PST	6:46 a.m.	6:50 a.m.	TOTAL
San Francisco	PST	7:13 a.m.	7:17 a.m.	*81.1%
Portland	PST	7:38 a.m.	7:44 a.m.	*47.5%
Vancouver	PST	7:55 a.m.	8:01 a.m.	*24.2%

The bottom line is that the earth's shadow does not cause a lunar eclipse, and the daytime lunar eclipse on December 10, 2011, is proof of that fact. The chart above is a reconstruction of the chart that Rao posted along with his article on Space.com and documents that the sun and moon were both above the earth's horizon during the lunar eclipse on December 10, 2011. That configuration of the sun, moon, and earth impeaches the heliocentric model.

I presented the professor the confirmation from TimeandDate.com, but he did not care to address the evidence. Instead, he made another *ad hominem* attack on me and alleged that my belief that the shadow of the earth does not cause a lunar eclipse is indicative of mental illness.[26] Then, in a later email, the professor made an admission that he accepted that daytime eclipses occur after all. It seems that he realized that he could not maintain his untenable position in light of such overwhelming evidence to the contrary.

If the professor admitted that daytime eclipses occur, he would have to, necessarily, admit that the shadow of the eclipse is not cast from the earth. I pressed him on that point, and he responded that "a day time lunar eclipse does not mean what you think it means."[27] I responded by asking him to "tell me what does a daytime eclipse mean to you?"[28] He refused to answer that question. His silence on that issue speaks volumes. There is only one logical explanation for a daytime lunar eclipse, and that is it is **NOT** the shadow of the earth that causes the eclipsed moon. If it is not the shadow of the earth causing the lunar eclipse, one leg for the proof of heliocentrism is knocked out. The professor knew that; hence, his refusal to answer.

Since he would not respond to the TimeandDate data, I sent the professor an email pointing his attention to the time lapse video I sent him previously and how it proves that the pictures of the daytime lunar eclipse on December 10, 2011, were in fact pictures of an eclipse and not moon phases as he claimed.

> You claimed that the pictures I showed you were fake. You claimed that they were not pictures of daytime eclipses but instead pictures of moon phases being passed off by me as pictures of eclipses. I sent you the link below that is a time lapse of the daytime lunar eclipse showing the moon being progressively eclipsed. Moon phases take two weeks to go from a full moon to a new moon. The time lapse shows it happening within one hour. The time lapse is proof that it is not a moon phase as you claim.[29]

The professor responded: "Already addressed your mistake/lie... What escapes me is why you continue, when proven wrong? God doesn't believe in a flat earth so why do you?"[30] He claims that I have been proven wrong, but he provided absolutely no proof of any kind. Apparently, as a professor he thinks that his pronouncement that things are so is to be taken as proof in and of itself. The professor knows full well that the photographs are legitimate. How could he not? I presented unimpeachable proof. But he simply cannot allow it to be known to me or any of the other three people on the email string that he believed the legitimacy of the photographs. He pretends that his mere allegation is sufficient proof in and of itself.

The professor proudly displays his hifalutin academic degrees. That is all well and good, but there is a downside to that for him. With all of his academic achievement, which demonstrates his intellectual acumen, he cannot claim ignorance. So, when he is presented with irrefutable evidence that the earth is stationary and flat, we can only conclude that he knows the truth revealed by the evidence, and therefore he is only pretending not to believe that the earth is stationary and flat. Since his hifalutin degrees preclude ignorance, that makes him a liar and a fraud.

Such men populate higher education. They have made accommodation for lies.

Max Planck was one of the most noted scientists of the last century. He won the Nobel Prize in Physics in 1918. He revealed the cult like belief system in the scientific community. He stated that "anybody who has been seriously engaged in scientific work of any kind realizes that over the entrance to the gates of the temple of science are written the words: Ye must have faith. It is a quality which the scientist cannot dispense with." So-called "scientists" today are more akin to witch doctors, who have mesmerized the superstitious tribe to believe their booga-booga nonsense.

The professor, in his email exchange with this author, revealed just the kind of religious superstition spoken of by Max Planck. The professor's mere pronouncement was to be taken as proof itself. The professor's dissimulation was in full view in our email exchange regarding the daytime eclipses. I presented him progressively increasing proof that daytime lunar eclipses take place, but he pretended to dismiss the proof. I say "pretended" because nobody with his apparent intellectual acumen could ignore the proof of daytime lunar eclipses. And, it turns out, his later admission that daytime lunar eclipses exist, proves that he was only pretending not to accept the proof of daytime lunar eclipses. He must have realized that his pretended position was irrational in the face of the proof I presented. After his admission, the professor was faced with having to admit the ultimate conclusion that the daytime lunar eclipses prove that eclipses are not caused by the shadow of the earth. That, he would not do. He refused to answer my question on that point. He would not acknowledge the logical implications of his admission. He knew that if he did he would have to admit that daytime lunar eclipses render impossible that the shadow of the allegedly spherical earth is the cause of an eclipse. That would put him on record questioning the legitimacy of the heliocentric model.

The professor asked me in an email: "Would you please provide a comprehensive list of Bible scriptures that teach us about the Flat Earth?" I responded to his email with the biblical authority he requested.[31] First, he claimed that he never saw my email. It is possible that he missed it. Another professor in the email string forwarded him my previously sent email with the biblical authority for a flat earth in it. After the moment he received that forwarded email with the biblical authority for a flat earth, he stopped communication for three months and he never raised the issue again, even though the debate continued with another professor on that same email string, and even though he had been courtesy copied on the emails in the continuing email debate.

Three months after ceasing all communication with this author, the esteemed professor made a reappearance. He sent an email to several other professors and included me in the email string. He sent a camera image taken of the screen on the back of the seat in front of him that showed the air route from San Francisco, California, to Qingdao, China, for the aircraft on which he was a passenger. The professor wrote in the email:

> Also, I watched the display and looked out the cabin window periodically. It was my observation that we flew North to China until we went over the pole and then we were flying South to China. On a flat Earth, how is it possible to be flying North and then South to the same destination?[32]

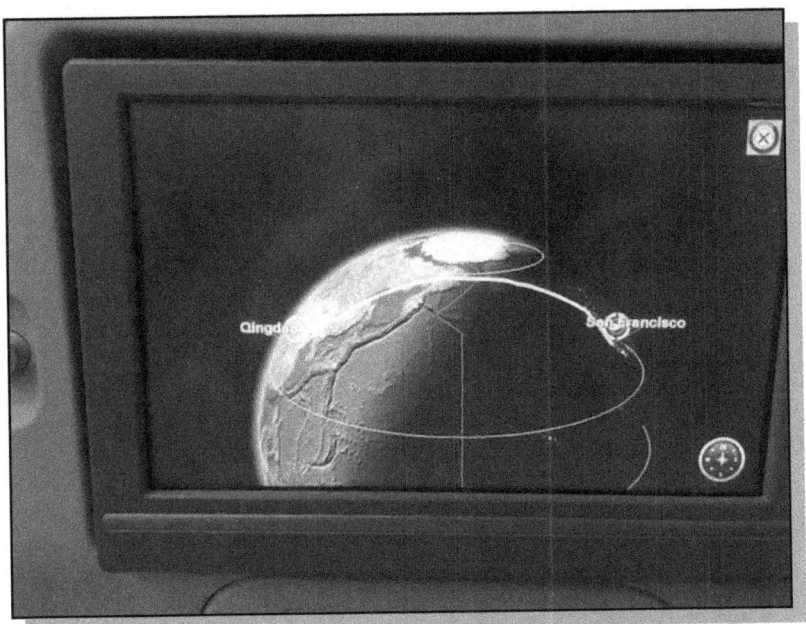

Figure 4: Image of flight path from San Francisco to Qingdao attached to email sent by the professor.

In response to the professor's email, I sent him the graphic and caption below, showing the route on a flat earth and explaining why the direction of travel changed from being northwest to southwest. When comparing the route on the spherical earth depicted in his picture with the route on the flat earth, it is clear that the flight path makes no sense if the earth were a sphere, but it makes perfect sense if the earth is flat. In the spherical earth photo, the plane can be seen to travel from San Francisco northbound to just south of the arctic circle before arcing toward Qingdao. When we look at that same route taken on a flat earth, we find the plane is traveling along the shortest distance between San Francisco and Qingdao, which is a straight line on the flat earth.

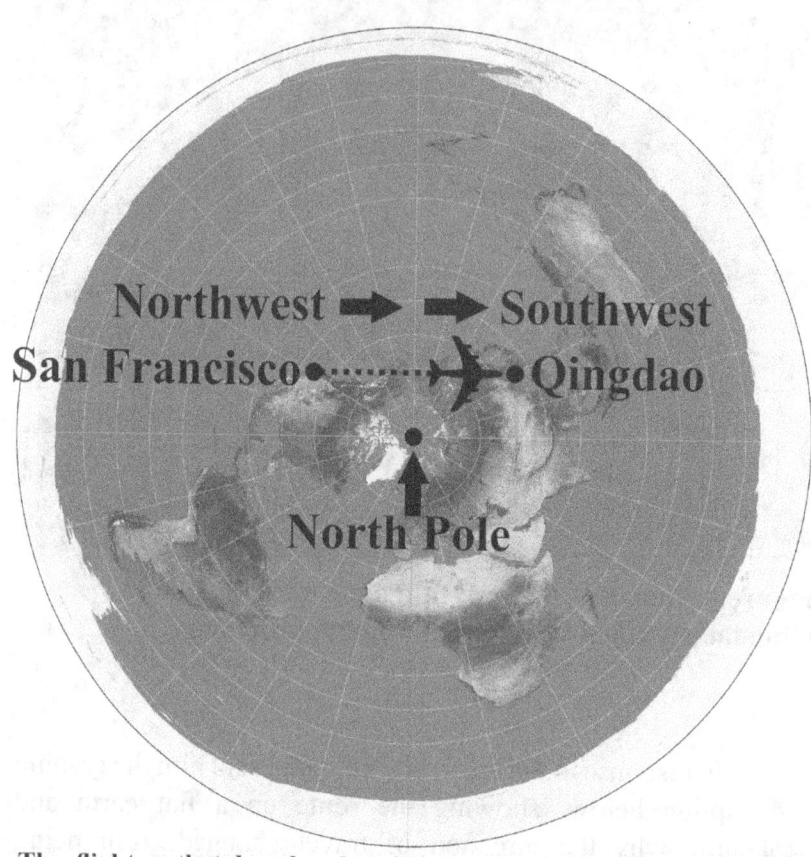

The flight path taken by the airline from San Francisco toward Qingdao can be seen to be a straight line on the flat earth. On that straight flight path, the plane starts out in a northwest bound direction and that straight path direction slowly becomes southwest bound. That happens because the plane is passing the North Directional Pole. At the beginning of the flight, the plane is traveling northwest toward the North Pole, but once it passes the North Pole it is traveling southwest away from the North Pole.

    The strange arc for the flight path as appeared on the image of the back seat screen is because the earth is in reality flat. When the flat earth is made to look like a sphere, the straight flight path appears curved. The shortest distance between two points is a straight line. The flight path taken by the plane was a straight line over the flat earth. The straight flight path that was flown on the flat earth appeared to be curved when that flight path was plotted on an earth that was preternaturally transformed into a sphere. Airline routes over the flat earth are explained in greater detail in this author's book, *The Greatest Lie on Earth (Expanded Edition)*.

The professor's *ad hominem* attack on me is evidence of psychological projection. That is a defense mechanism in which the person defends himself against a negative characteristic by attributing it to others. In the professor's case, he fears that if he were to publically accept the truth of the flat earth he would be denounced as a lunatic. So, he attacks others who espouse belief in a flat earth as lunatics as a way of covering for and compensating for his fear. It is a smokescreen to end any further discussion on a subject that is uncomfortable for him.

The professor is, quite simply, afraid to be objective and honest with the facts. He knows that his academic career is at stake. He has come to love big brother. He submissively accepts all the pablum coming out of academia, because he is afraid not to. He is ruled by fear. He is part and parcel of the problem in universities today, which are turning out obedient sycophants who cannot think for themselves.

What is notable is that the professor claims to be a Christian. Indeed, he proudly proclaims below his valediction in each email that he is on the "Faculty & Mission Team, Vietnam Bible Institute." It is not a surprise when I found out he was an adherent to the Arminian error, which fits very comfortably with his heliocentric theology of a far-off god.[33] The professor is symptomatic of those in the church today. People have been conditioned to accept the science fiction of heliocentricity, which is something that is not allowed to be questioned. Heliocentrism is a religious superstition masquerading as science. God warned us to avoid the "opposition of science falsely so called." 1 Timothy 6:20. Yet, the church has not avoided the "opposition of science falsely so called;" it has embraced it. The churches have welcomed heliocentrism and treated it as a sacrosanct religious dogma. Indeed, any effort to expose the error of heliocentrism is met with rebuke, charges of heresy, and ostracization from the church.

Ignorance of the reality of daytime lunar eclipses ensures that people will buy hook-line-and-sinker the lies of heliocentric science. The scientific community cites to lunar eclipses as proof of heliocentricity but keep secret that daytime lunar eclipses impeach entirely the fact that lunar eclipses prove heliocentricity.

Even those who see through many heliocentric lies cannot bring themselves to abandon the spherical earth, in part, due to their ignorance of daytime lunar eclipses. For example, Sam Adams, pastor of Independence Baptist Church in Belleview, Florida, is a geocentrist. That means that he accepts that the earth is stationary and is at the center of the universe. He is correct about that. But he mistakenly maintains that the earth is spherical.

He supports his correct opinion that the earth is fixed and is not moving on the scientific proofs like the Michelson/Morley experiment. But where he does not see scientific support, he rejects contrary biblical statements. Where profane science disagrees with the Bible, the so-called science wins. Thus, he rejects the flat earth. One basis for his rejection of the flat earth is the modern scientific explanation for the phenomenon of lunar eclipses.

That approach by Adams of accepting scientific dogma over the authority of God's word has caused him to opine in a sermon he gave on November 8, 2015, that belief in a biblical flat earth is "completely untenable and fraught with disinformation."[34] He states that it is "absolutely absurd" to believe in a flat earth. He considers flat earth to be a mass deception akin to NASA's moon landing deception.[35] Adams thinks that belief in a flat earth is a "collateral attack on the true science of geocentricity."[36] Notice that his concern is over what he believes is "true science." He is defending, not the Bible, but rather profane science.

> [The flat earth theory is] disproven by those same laws of physics that I mentioned earlier, gravity, inertia, centrifugal force, etc. **It is also disproven by clearly observable phenomenon such as lunar eclipses.** That's also, I believe, completely disproven by the scriptures which I plan to show later probably in the next message.[37]

Adams claims that lunar eclipses prove that the earth cannot be flat with the sun and moon hovering over it. As we have seen, the reality of a daytime lunar eclipse completely impeaches his argument.

On November 29, 2015, Adams revisited the issue of the flat earth.[38] But Adams spent almost the entire sermon misrepresenting scientific arguments. He makes a general defense of an alleged biblical description of a spherical earth by arguing that the Bible repeatedly references the sun rising and setting. He cites Mark 16:2; Malachi 1:11, 4:2; Ecclesiastes 1:5; Psalm 19, 50:1, 113:3; Isaiah 45:6, 59:19. Those passages describe the sun's rising and setting over the earth. But those passages do not impeach the truth of a flat earth. Adams completely avoided any passages that clearly describe a flat and stationary earth. His sermon was a coverup. Adams revealed more about himself by what he left out of his sermon than by what he included in it.

2 The Bible Describes a Flat Immovable Earth

It has been the accepted dogma of so-called "science" that the earth is a globe spinning faster than the speed of sound as it orbits the sun at approximately 80 times faster than the speed of a rifle bullet. The sun, in turn, is supposed to be hurtling through the Milky Way galaxy at more than 500 times faster than the speed of a rifle bullet. The Milky Way galaxy is, itself, alleged to be racing through space at a speed that some scientists claim is over 1,000 times faster than the speed of a rifle bullet.

God's word, however, states that the earth is fixed and does not move. "Fear before him, all the earth: the world also shall be stable, that it be not moved." (1 Chronicles 16:30) Indeed, the earth cannot be moved. "The LORD reigneth, he is clothed with majesty; the LORD is clothed with strength, wherewith he hath girded himself: the world also is stablished, that it cannot be moved." (Psalms 93:1).

Notice that the immovable earth is closely associated with the praise and glory of God Almighty. They are inseparable concepts. In Psalms 93:1 we read that the LORD is clothed with majesty and strength, just as the world is stable and cannot be moved. If the earth is movable, then it impeaches the majesty and strength of God. Just as the earth is "stablished" that it cannot be moved so also is the eternal throne of God. *See* Psalms 93:2. Indeed, God links the immovable earth with his eternal throne; for in the very next verse after Psalms 93:1 God explains: "Thy throne is established of old: thou art from everlasting." (Psalms 93:2) So, if the earth can be moved, so also, God's throne cannot be eternal. A movable earth impeaches God's eternal throne.

In the book of Isaiah God states that in the day of his anger he will remove the earth out of her place. That means that the earth is not shooting through space faster than a speeding bullet, it is fixed in a place, and it is from that fixed place that God will one day remove it. "Therefore I will shake the heavens, and the earth shall remove out of her place, in the wrath of the LORD of hosts, and in the day of his fierce anger." (Isaiah 13:13)

A spherical, spinning earth subtly undermines the awe in which we should hold God. We should fear and be in awe of God, because by his command he created a world that is fixed and held fast. "Let all the earth fear the LORD: let all the inhabitants of the world stand in awe of him. For he spake, and it was done; he commanded, and it stood fast." (Psalms 33:8-9) If the earth is not understood to have been created by God's command to stand fast, and it is instead thought to be careening through a vacuum of space, man will have nothing to fear from God and will not be in awe of him. That is why Satan and his minions push the spinning, orbiting, spherical earth. The nature of God's creation by his command of a fixed earth is the basis for our fear and awe of him. If there is no fixed earth held fast by God's command, then there is no God of which to be in fear and awe.

Psalms 104.1-5 makes it clear that God laid the foundations of the earth and stretched forth the heavens just as he is clothed with honor and majesty. The concepts of God's majesty and a stable immovable earth are inseparable. If the earth moves and spins, then the God of the Bible cannot exist. However, a stable immovable earth confirms the existence of God.

> Bless the LORD, O my soul. O LORD my God, thou art very great; thou art clothed with honour and majesty. Who coverest thyself with light as with a garment: who stretchest out the heavens like a curtain: Who layeth the beams of his chambers in the waters: who maketh the clouds his chariot: who walketh upon the wings of the wind: Who maketh his angels spirits; his ministers a flaming fire: Who laid the foundations of the earth, that it should not be removed for ever. (Psalms 104:1-5)

The omnipotent reign of God can only be adequately understood if one first understands that God made a stationary, flat earth. In fact, Christians are called upon to tell the heathen that the LORD reigns and we are to also tell them that the world shall not be moved.

> O worship the LORD in the beauty of holiness: fear before him, all the earth. Say among the heathen that the LORD reigneth: the world also shall be established that it shall not be moved: he shall judge the people righteously. (Psalms 96:9-10)

Why are Christians not telling the heathen that the earth shall not be moved today? Because of the pride of life. Christians today are afraid of being labeled a "flat earther," which the devil and his minions have propagandized people to associate with being ignorant. It is a time-honored practice of the devil to use the sinful flesh as a lever to quiet Christians.

God "laid the foundations of the earth, that it should not be removed for ever." Psalms 104:5. What kind of foundation is there in a spinning earth careening through space? Such a spinning, moving earth cannot be said to have any foundation. If there is no foundation, there is no God, since God stated he laid the foundations of the earth. The heavens prove the existence of God, as they demonstrate his skill as the creator. In Psalms 19:1 it states that the heavens declare the glory of God and the firmament shows his handiwork. Part of the glory of God and his handiwork is the fact that the earth is stationary and the sun travels in a circuit over the earth.

> The heavens declare the glory of God; and the firmament sheweth his handywork. Day unto day uttereth speech, and night unto night sheweth knowledge. There is no speech nor language, where their voice is not heard. Their line is gone out through all the earth, and their words to the end of the world. In them hath he set a tabernacle for the sun, Which is as a bridegroom coming out of his chamber, and rejoiceth as a strong man to run a race. His going forth is from the end of the heaven, and **his circuit unto the ends of it**: and there is nothing hid from the heat thereof. (Psalms 19:1-6)

It is the sun that travels in a circuit, not the earth. What is a circuit? It is a continuous circular route that starts and ends in the same place. Some might argue that the circuit of the sun is the sun's revolutions around the Milky Way galaxy. The problem with that interpretation is that Psalm 96:10 states "the world also shall be established that it shall not be moved." If the earth cannot be moved, yet the sun is careening through space, that means that the sun would be flying away from the earth.

The earth was created on the first day. Genesis 1:1. The sun was not created until the fourth day. Genesis 1:14-19. That means that the earth could not have been spinning on its axis and orbiting around the sun for the first three days, since the sun had not yet been created. Clearly, the earth was stationary.

The earth started its existence "without form, and void." Genesis 1:2. God then gave the earth form, and that form was flat. We know that because the waters God created had to have been flat, just as they are today. Indeed, "God moved upon the face of the waters." Genesis 1:2. As the face on a clock is flat, so also is the face of the water on the earth flat. It is a fact that the surface of all water at rest is flat and level.

> In the beginning God created the heaven and the earth. And the earth was without form, and void; and darkness was upon the face of the deep. And the Spirit of God moved upon the face of the waters. (Genesis 1:1-2)

In common parlance, the height of the surface of a body of water is called the water "level," because it is understood that the surface of all water at rest is flat and level. The oceans cover 71% of the earth's surface. It is impossible for the earth to be a sphere when 71% of its surface is covered by water, which necessarily must be flat and level. The very existence of the oceans proves that the earth must necessarily be flat.

We know that there was water covering the earth upon its creation because God states that "darkness was upon the face of the deep." God describes his movement over the face of the waters, and since the surface of all water at rest is flat and level, the earth must have been flat from the beginning.

In Genesis 1:2 God moved upon the face of the necessarily flat water. There is simply no other way to interpret that passage but to mean that the earth created by God began as flat water. Read carefully how God describes the water in Genesis 1:2 before moving upon the face of it. God stated that "the earth was without form, and void; and darkness was upon the face of the deep." (Genesis 1:2) Notice that there was darkness upon the **face of the deep**. Once again we have the face of the water (the surface of which can be nothing but flat) described as having a face (i.e., it was and is flat).

A face is the front side of an object or a person's head. We often talk of the face of a coin, clock, or building. The word face is never used to describe a sphere. A sphere is a round ball and thus cannot have a front; it, therefore, cannot have a face. In conclusion, God did not move upon spherical waters, since a sphere does not have a face, water cannot form a "deep" on the side of a sphere, and water is always flat. God moved upon the face of flat waters.

The *Math is Fun* website is a mathematics website for students from Kindergarten through 12th grade.[39] It is based upon the New York State Education Curriculum.[40] It is reviewed for accuracy by "Les Bill Gates, Graduate of Oxford University with an Honours degree in Mathematics, and a post-graduate Certificate in Education,"[41] and "David Sevilla, Doctorate in Mathematics."[42] The *Math is Fun* website states that a face could be "any of the individual flat surfaces of a solid object."[43] Thus, because a sphere has no flat surface, **a sphere cannot have a face**. This is confirmed by the *Math is Fun* website, which states, in pertinent part, that a sphere has **"one surface (not a 'face' as it isn't flat)."**[44]

As defined by the Merriam-Webster Dictionary, a face in geometry is "any of the plane surfaces that bound a geometric solid. A cube is a solid with six square faces."[45] That means that **a face in geometry must be a plane (flat) surface**. The Merriam-Webster Dictionary further defines Face as "the principal flat surface of a part or object."[46] The *cK-12* education website states that "[a] face is any flat surface."[47] **Since a sphere does not have a flat surface, it has no face.** Physicist Atul Kumar Kuthiala,

MSc., (Hons.), explains that "[i]n solid geometry a face is understood to be a flat or a planar surface that forms part of the boundary of the solid object under consideration. As such a Sphere has zero faces."[48] It is clear that in geometry a face must be a flat surface. While a cube has six square faces, a flat, circular plane with water on it has only one face, the face of the water, just as stated in the Bible. That means that when the Bible describes how "the Spirit of God moved upon the **face of the waters**" (Genesis 1:2) that completely covered the earth, it is describing a flat surface, not a sphere because a sphere cannot have a face.

God then separated the waters using the firmament. He gathered the waters under the firmament. Since the entire earth under the firmament was covered in water at this point, the earth had to be flat.[49] That is because when water fills a container, it always conforms to the shape of its container and the surface of the water at rest in that container is always flat and level.[50]

> And God made the firmament, and divided the waters which were under the firmament from the waters which were above the firmament: and it was so. And God called the firmament Heaven. And the evening and the morning were the second day. (Genesis 1:7-8)

It was after that point in God's creation that God gathered the waters together in one place to let the dry land appear.

> And God said, Let the waters under the heaven be gathered together unto one place, and let the dry land appear: and it was so. And God called the dry land Earth; and the gathering together of the waters called he Seas: and God saw that it was good. (Genesis 1:9-10)

Most of the earth's surface is covered by water. Since the

surface of all water that is at rest is flat and level, that can only mean one thing; the earth is flat.

God summarizes his creation of a flat earth in 2 Peter 3:4-6. Notice that the earth is described as standing out of the water and in the water. And then, in reference to the great flood described in Genesis, God states that the earth overflowed with water. The earth must be an upright container for it to overflow with water. The earth certainly could not be a sphere. The outside of a sphere cannot contain water. Water takes on the shape of its container, but the surface of the water at rest is always flat and level. Certainly, the earth has undulations with valleys and hills both above the water and beneath the water. But in order for the earth to overflow with water, the earth would need to be formed into a kind of spread out vessel upon which the water could be contained. A worldwide flood over the whole earth would result in a flat and level surface, which could only happen on a flat earth.

> And saying, Where is the promise of his coming? for since the fathers fell asleep, all things continue as they were from the beginning of the creation. For this they willingly are ignorant of, that by the word of God the heavens were of old, and the earth standing out of the water and in the water: Whereby the world that then was, being overflowed with water, perished. (2 Peter 3:4-6)

Gravity did not (and does not today) exist, because there is no need for gravity. The waters, grass, herbs, and trees, which were all created in the first three days, are all held to the earth by their density. How and why would the earth suddenly on the fourth day transform into the shape of a ball, begin spinning on its alleged axis, and then start orbiting the sun? What was the force that began the alleged spinning and orbit? Why is that transformation and movement not mentioned in the Bible?

It is only if the earth were a sphere would it be necessary for gravity. Where was the alleged force of gravity before the earth supposedly turned into a ball and started spinning? Gravity was not necessary before the alleged transformation of the earth into a spherical spinning ball. How did it spring into existence? Gravity does not spring into existence upon spinning spherical objects on earth. The earth and the objects on the earth obey the same laws of physics. So if gravity were truly real on earth, spinning spherical objects on earth should develop their own gravity, but they do not. Objects do not develop gravity on earth, because gravity is a myth, and so is a spherical spinning earth.

God's creation of heaven and earth is part and parcel of his creative powers, which he demonstrates every day when he forms each person in the womb. If people lose sight of God as the creator of all things, then any sin, including abortion, can be justified. It is important for people to understand the nature of God's creation because it reveals his character. In Isaiah 44:24 God states that he alone stretched forth the heavens and spread abroad the earth. A ball is not spread out. You spread out things that are flat, like a flat bedspread. God spread out the earth and he stretched forth the heavens above the earth.

> Thus saith the LORD, thy redeemer, and he that formed thee from the womb, I am the LORD that maketh all things; that stretcheth forth the heavens alone; that spreadeth abroad the earth by myself. (Isaiah 44:24)

The account of creation in Genesis refutes the commonly held view of a spherical earth that is surrounded by an endless vacuum of "space." In Genesis 1:6 we read that "God said, Let there be a firmament in the midst of the waters, and let it divide the waters from the waters." A firmament is something that is hard. Indeed, in Job the firmament is likened to a strong, molten looking glass. "Hast thou with him spread out the sky, which is strong, and as a molten looking glass?" (Job 37:18) A looking glass is a highly polished reflective surface.

The firmament divides the waters, which means that there is water above the firmament in heaven. Indeed, all one needs to do is look skyward to see the blue water that is above the firmament. The blue sky is not the atmosphere as claimed by scientists; the blue sky is the water above the canopy of the firmament. "Praise him, ye heavens of heavens, and ye waters that be above the heavens." (Psalms 148:4) God placed the sun, moon, and stars in the firmament.

> And God said, Let there be lights in the firmament of the heaven to divide the day from the night; and let them be for signs, and for seasons, and for days, and years: And let them be for lights in the firmament of the heaven to give light upon the earth: and it was so. (Genesis 1:14-15)

When God flooded the earth he opened the windows of heaven to let out some of the water that was above the firmament.

> In the six hundredth year of Noah's life, in the second month, the seventeenth day of the month, the same day were all the fountains of the great deep broken up, and the windows of heaven were opened. (Genesis 7:11)

God formed the foundation of the earth from the beginning. "Of old hast **thou laid the foundation of the earth**: and the heavens are the work of thy hands." (Psalms 102:25) God laid the foundation of earth immovable forever. "Who laid the foundations of the earth, that it should not be removed for ever." (Psalms 104:5) Please note that God laid the foundations of the earth, which does not at all suggest a globular earth. "**Mine hand also hath laid the foundation of the earth**, and my right hand hath spanned the heavens: when I call unto them, they stand up together." (Isaiah 48:13) The foundation is stated to be pillars. "He raiseth up the poor out of the dust, and lifteth up the beggar from the dunghill, to set them among princes, and to make them inherit the throne of glory: for **the pillars of the earth are the LORD'S, and he hath set the world upon them**." (1 Samuel 2:8) We see that the pillars are the LORD'S. We learn that in Psalms 75:3, that God is holding them up. "The earth and all the inhabitants thereof are dissolved: I bear up the pillars of it. Selah." (Psalms 75:3)

Those who promote the heliocentric model often cite to Job 26:7 to suggest that passage implies that the earth is floating in space. "He stretcheth out the north over the empty place, and hangeth the earth upon nothing." Job 26:7. But a careful reading of Job in the context of the whole Bible indicates that God is making the point in Job that the earth is not hung on anything. The earth is supported from underneath on pillars, which are borne by God. Psalms 75:3. Hanging something suggests that it is being supported from above. To hang means to suspend from above. The earth is not suspended from above, it is supported from below on pillars. It is literally hanging from nothing, just as the passage in Job states. God is bearing the earth upon pillars from underneath, he is not hanging the earth on anything.

What are the pillars that form the foundation of the earth? One could infer that it is the seas. "The earth is the LORD'S, and the fulness thereof; the world, and they that dwell therein. **For he hath founded it upon the seas, and established it upon the floods.**" (Psalms 24:1-2) God has repeatedly referred to the earth as being founded upon water. "To him that **stretched out the earth above the waters**: for his mercy endureth for ever." (Psalms 136:6) God states that he stretched out the heavens over the earth, which suggests a flat earth. "I have made the earth, and created man upon it: I, even my hands, **have stretched out the heavens**, and all their host have I commanded." (Isaiah 45:12) Notice that the earth is "stretched out" above the waters. A flat earth could be said to be "stretched" out, but such an expression would preclude a globular earth.

Indeed, underwater cinematographer Mike deGruy (1951-2012), while filming for the BBC documentary called *Blue Planet*, discovered a super-saline and dense underwater lake at the bottom of the ocean.[51] He was in a submarine and tried to descend the submarine down into the underwater lake. But the lake was so dense that his submarine bounced off the surface. When his submarine bounced off of the surface, it sent visible ripples that could be seen underwater emanating toward the shore of the underwater lake. Please understand that deGruy was already underwater and he saw the very dense underwater lake that was so dense that the fluid from the lake acted like water would act on the surface in the atmosphere. Could this super-saline and dense underwater lake be evidence that the pillars supporting the earth are made of super saline dense water?

Nowhere in the Bible does God state that the earth is a globe. In fact, God expressly states that the face of the earth is a circle. "**It is he that sitteth upon the circle of the earth**, and the inhabitants thereof are as grasshoppers; that **stretcheth out the heavens as a curtain, and spreadeth them out as a tent to dwell in**:" (Isaiah 40:22) A circle is two-dimensional and flat. That does not mean that the earth is two dimensional, as the earth certainly has depth. Rather, it means that the earth has a face that is a flat circle. Amos 9:6. It is "the circle **of** the earth." A globe, on the other hand, is a three-dimensional ball. Isaiah knew the difference between a ball and a circle. *See* Isaiah 22:18. If Isaiah meant ball in Isaiah 40:22, he would have said ball. He did not say ball, because the earth is not a ball. There can be no confusion here. God is stating that the face of the earth is a flat circle and the heavens are spread like a tent over that circle.

A circle is not the same as a ball. A circle is a flat plane whose circumference is equidistant from the center.[52] Indeed, when people refer to a ball they never call it a circle. Can you imagine a player asking his soccer teammate to pass him the "circle?" Nobody confuses a circle with a ball, and you can be sure that God knows the difference. The earth is described by God as a circle (i.e., a flat plane) in the Bible because it is true. "[L]let God be true, but every man a liar." Romans 3:2.

Kent Hovind is a famous creation lecturer and opponent of the theory of evolution. He is also a Christian heliocentrist. Hovind denies that the earth is flat. In reference to the circle mentioned in Isaiah 40:22 he states: "I taught geometry for 15 years. A circle does not exist. A circle is a purely imaginary construct. If its got any height at all, it's now a cylinder."[53] Hovind is trying to make the point that Isaiah 40:22 is actually referring to a sphere because a circle is purely imaginary. Hovind's argument has no merit.

A circle is not imaginary, as claimed by Hovind. Circles do exist. A circle is a geometric figure where all points on the circumference are equidistant from the center and on the same plane.[54] Hovind must know the real definition of a circle, since he claims to be an expert in geometry, having taught it for 15 years. He also must know that the real world definition of a circle precludes the circle in Isaiah 40:22 from being a sphere. That seems to be why he has constructed a definition that a circle is nonexistent in the real world and completely imaginary. Hovind is saying that God used a word (circle) in Isaiah 40:22 that describes something that does not exist and is purely imaginary to describe a supposedly spherical earth.

Hovind's definition of a circle means that a circle cannot simply be a circle; it must be something else, like a sphere or a cylinder. Hovind is using clever sophistry to confuse the issue. Hovind would probably agree that a cylinder is not a circle, but he must also agree that the face of the cylinder is a circle. The face of the cylinder exists. It can be touched and measured. It is not imaginary. The circle of the cylinder is flat circular face just like the circle of the earth.

Hovind is not arguing that the circle of the earth in Isaiah 40:22 is a cylinder. Hovind is, instead, arguing that in that passage the circle of the earth is a reference to a sphere. Hovind is a geometry expert, and so he knows that a sphere cannot be a circle because a circle requires all points to be on the same flat plane. Yet Hovind still argues that the circle in Isaiah 40:22 is a sphere. But God did not say he sits upon the sphere of the earth in Isaiah 40:22. God describes the flat circular face of the earth in Isaiah 40:22. A circle necessarily has a flat face. In geometry, a face is any of the individual flat surfaces of a solid object.[55] A circular face must necessarily be flat. Since a sphere has no flat surfaces and hence no face,[56] a sphere cannot be the circle of the earth referenced in Isaiah 40:22.

Hovind is also ignoring the context of the passage in Isaiah 40:22. Notice that the language in Isaiah 40:22 describes "the circle OF the earth." That means that the surface of the earth is a circle. The surface of the earth is a flat plane with the circumference equidistant from the center.

Let us examine the phrase used in Isaiah 40:22 closely. God calls the earth "the circle." According to the pertinent part of the definition in the Merriam-Webster Dictionary, "the" is "used as a function word to indicate that a following noun or noun equivalent is definite."[57] So God is calling the earth "the circle" to indicate that he is identifying the earth as a particular circle; it is the earth's particular circle. We know that because God follows with the words "of the earth." So, the particular circle is being identified as "of the earth." What does "of" mean? The pertinent part of the definition in the Merriam-Webster dictionary for "of" states that it is "used as a function word to indicate belonging or a possessive relationship."[58] That means that the circle mentioned in Isaiah 40:22 belongs to and is possessed by the earth. The surface of the earth is a circle. The earth's surface is flat with all points on the same plane equidistant from the center. Thus, Isaiah 40:22 describes a particular circle that God "sitteth upon." It is the earth's circle. Isaiah 40:22 is not saying that the earth is a sphere that looks like a circle when viewed from above, as claimed by Hovind; the passage is saying that the earth's surface is, in fact, a circle, and it is that circle on the surface of the earth upon which God sits. "The" circle in Isaiah 40:22 is "of" the earth. In essence, it is the earth's circle that God sits upon. A circle is not a globe. God is not sitting upon a spinning globe.

Matthew Stucky is just another of the many charlatans who attack those who believe that the earth is flat. He claims that the Bible teaches that the earth is a sphere. Stucky is on the ministry staff at Verity Baptist Church, Sacramento, California. Tellingly, behind the pulpit at Verity Baptist Church is a large screen depicting a spherical earth. It was not surprising to find that Verity Baptist Church expressly rejects the sovereign grace of God depicted in the gospel and instead ascribes to the Arminian error of a helpless god.[59] That fits in nicely with their heliocentric theology, which necessarily requires their god to be far-off and impotently wringing his hands hoping that men will exercise their sovereign will to believe in him. Stucky's first argument for why God used "circle" to describe the earth instead of "sphere" in Isaiah 40:22 is as follows:

> Well here's the thing about this the word sphere; even though that word came in the 14th century, the word circle was much more common. In our common vernacular every single person knows circle. In today's world, everybody knows sphere, but at the time maybe not everybody knew sphere like they knew circle.[60]

Stucky just made that up. People throughout the ages knew what a sphere was. His statement to the contrary is just conjecture on his part; he qualified his conclusion with a very big "maybe." In Isaiah 22:18, the prophet Isaiah used the word ball, which soundly impeaches Stucky's argument.

In Stucky's next argument, he claims that when God described the circle of the earth in Isaiah 40:22, he did not mean to describe the earth as being flat and circular, as the word circle would denote. Stucky claims that God was instead conveying the meaning of a sphere. Stucky proudly proclaims that he is a former Math teacher. Our math expert, Stucky, thinks that "honestly there's not much of a difference between a sphere and a circle."[61] He is so discombobulated that when explaining how a circle and a sphere are the same, he actually reveals their significant differences.

In his attempt to explain how a circle is like a sphere, Stucky admitted that a circle, by definition, is flat. But he would not allow the word "flat" pass his lips. Instead, he tried to obfuscate what a circle is by calling it "two-dimensional." Stucky pointed to a circle he had drawn and stated that "the definition of a circle is this: you take the center point of a two-dimensional object and every point along the outside is equidistant from the center."[62] What Stucky, in essence, conveyed is that a circle requires that every point on its circumference be equidistant from the center and on the same plane. Thus, Stucky correctly defined a circle as requiring a flat surface, but he would not use the word flat to describe a circle.

But Stucky thinks that "a sphere is pretty much the same thing" as a circle. How can a sphere be "pretty much the same thing" as a circle when a sphere is a ball, and by definition, cannot be flat? A sphere and a circle are mutually exclusive shapes. A circle cannot be a sphere, and a sphere cannot be a circle. But that inconvenient fact did not stop Stucky from concluding that a circle and a sphere are essentially the same thing:

A sphere is pretty much the exact same thing, the only difference is it's three dimensions. So you take a three-dimensional object, and you take the center of that object and every point along the surface is equidistant from the center. So, basically, a sphere is a three-dimensional circle, and a circle is a two-dimensional sphere.[63]

Stucky's claim that there is not much difference between a circle and a sphere is nonsense. He tried to cloak that nonsense in sophistry by avoiding the word flat to describe a circle. But his sophistry cannot survive the slightest scrutiny. To suggest that a three-dimensional ball is basically the same as a two-dimensional (flat) circle is silliness. Indeed, in his effort to describe how they are the same, he was required to explain that a sphere has a third dimension that is not present for a circle. That is a significant difference.

Stuckey will not say the word flat when describing a circle because he knows it destroys his argument, and so he opts to call a circle two-dimensional. But that does not change the fact that for a circle to be a circle, it must be flat. And for a sphere to be a sphere, it cannot be flat. Stucky tries to ignore that elephant in the room and with a wave of his hand announces that a circle and a sphere are "pretty much the same thing." But they are not the same thing. They are quite different. They are mutually exclusive on the very point in contention, whether the earth is flat. A circle is flat, and a sphere is not flat. It is that simple. When God describes the circle of the earth in Isaiah 40:22, he is describing a flat earth.

Stucky's irrational explanation is like trying to equate a two-dimensional (flat) picture of an automobile and the three-dimensional automobile itself. It is silly to suggest that there is not much difference between the two by explaining that the picture is a two-dimensional (flat) actual automobile, whereas the physical automobile itself is a three-dimensional picture. Try explaining to a baseball pitcher that he can use a flat circle instead of an actual baseball because they are really the same thing. It is absurd to claim that a circle is just a two-dimensional (flat) ball which is equivalent to the ball itself, which is just a three-dimensional circle. Stucky's argument is preposterous.

Ironically, Stucky reveals that his reason for preaching on the spherical earth is to put to bed the foolishness of the flat earth. He states that it's important that "we don't make ourselves look kind of foolish."[64] Well, Stucky failed at that. Romans 1:22 seems to apply to Stucky: "**Professing themselves to be wise, they became fools.**" Romans 1:22.

Another, often overlooked, phrase in Isaiah 40:22 is the description of God stretching and spreading the heavens like a curtain as a tent in which the inhabitants of the earth can dwell. In the context of Isaiah 40:22, the heavens are viewed as a tent that is being pitched over flat ground.

The heliocentric model of a spherical earth makes no sense. Imagine pitching a tent over a massive spherical boulder. Once the tent is wrapped around the boulder as required by the heliocentric model, there would be no room to dwell in it. It would not act as a tent. It would be more like a sack to completely envelop the boulder. But Isaiah 40:22 makes no mention of a sack. If the boulder is completely enveloped in the tent (i.e., sack), as envisioned by the heliocentric model, it could not be affixed to the ground as a place of dwelling. That would preclude a tent. A tent cannot completely envelop a spherical boulder, as would be required under the heliocentric interpretation of the passage, with the heavens surrounding the earth. A tent cannot completely envelop a sphere. To envelop a sphere, you would need to put it in a sack. Now, add the heliocentric requirement of a spinning earth, and we enter a whole new realm of balderdash. A heliocentric interpretation of Isaiah would require the heavens to be represented like a sack, and not a tent, and at the same time, that sack would need to envelop a spinning, spherical earth. That makes no sense. That is not what the passage says.

In the Bible, it states the following about wisdom: "I was there: when he set a compass upon the face of the depth." (Proverbs 8:27) Notice God set a compass upon the face of the depth. What does compass mean in that context? Certainly, a compass is a directional instrument, but the word compass means more than that. Compass also means a circular boundary; the limit or boundary of a space, and the space included; encircle; to surround; to inclose on all sides; a circular course.[65] A compass is a flat circular boundary. In Proverbs 8:27 we have God encircling the seas with a boundary. That can only happen on a flat earth. The boundary of the seas is the ice rim of Antarctica. The globular myth is that one can circumnavigate the globe by going around Antarctica because it is believed to be a continent in the southern most part of a spherical earth. The globular earth myth does not have a circular boundary for the seas, as stated in Proverbs 8:27. "Let God be true, but every man a liar." (Romans 3:4)

God's creation of a stationary earth is a testimony to his truth. In Psalms 33:4-9 we find that just as "the word of the LORD is right," so also "he spake, and it was done." In the same way, "all his works are done in truth," so also "he commanded, and it stood fast." Just as his word is true, so also does the earth, that was created by his word, stand fast.

> **For the word of the LORD is right; and all his works are done in truth.** He loveth righteousness and judgment: the earth is full of the goodness of the LORD. By the word of the LORD were the heavens made; and all the host of them by the breath of his mouth. He gathereth the waters of the sea together as an heap: he layeth up the depth in storehouses. Let all the earth fear the LORD: let all the inhabitants of the world stand in awe of him.

For he spake, and it was done; he commanded, and it stood fast. (Psalms 33:4-9)

In Psalms 33:4-9 David explains that all of God's works are done in truth. God's creation of an immovable earth that stands fast testifies to God's truth. God spake his truth and through that true and sure word he created a fixed earth. Just as the earth is fixed and stands fast, so also is God's word true. If the earth is moving, it means that God's word is variable and cannot be true. The mythology of a spinning, orbiting earth calls into question the truth of God's word. If the earth is orbiting and spinning that means that the Bible, which is God's word, cannot be true. But a spinning, orbiting earth is a lie, and God's creation of an earth that stands fast testifies to his truth.

Five verses later, in Psalms 33:14, God describes his reign over what can only be a flat earth. David segues from explaining that the earth stands fast to, five verses later in Psalms 33:14, explaining that God looks upon all the inhabitants of the earth from his habitation. Where is God's habitation? God's habitation is in heaven. God's throne is heaven and the earth as his footstool. "Thus saith the LORD, **The heaven is my throne, and the earth is my footstool**: where is the house that ye build unto me? and where is the place of my rest?" (Isaiah 66:1) Footstools are not spherical. God can only look over the inhabitants of the earth from one location if the earth is flat. So, within five verses in Psalms 33 we have God describing a stationary, flat earth.

God states that he looks upon all the inhabitants of the earth from one location, his place of habitation in heaven. "From the place of his habitation he looketh upon all the inhabitants of the earth." (Psalms 33:14) It is not possible for God to look upon all of the inhabitants of the earth on a globe from one location; those on the backside of the earth would be hidden from view. People might argue that God is all-powerful and therefore can do anything. Yes, but Satan is not all powerful. In Matthew 4:8 and

Luke 4:5, the devil took Jesus up to a high mountain and showed him all the kingdoms of the world. The devil did not take Jesus around the world on a tour of the kingdoms. The devil showed him all of the kingdoms from one point on a high mountain. How could the devil have shown all the kingdoms of the world from a single spot on a high mountain on a globular earth? Such an event could only be done on a flat earth.[66]

Some argue that Satan showed Jesus a vision of the kingdoms of the world and thus the event is no proof that the earth is flat. The problem with that argument is that it would not be required for Satan to take Jesus up to a high mountain to show him a vision of the kingdoms of the supposed spherical earth. Satan could have done that from where they were standing. There was a reason Satan took Jesus up to an "exceeding high mountain;" and that reason was to show Jesus the kingdoms of the world that span the flat earth.

When Jesus returns to earth, everyone will see him in the sky. "Behold, he cometh with clouds; and **every eye shall see him**, and they also which pierced him: and all kindreds of the earth shall wail because of him. Even so, Amen." (Revelation 1:7) Jesus will return physically "with clouds." That is a fulfillment of the prophecy in Mark 13:26 that Jesus will physically return "in the clouds." That would only be possible on a flat earth. If the earth were a globe those on the back side of the globe could not see him. Some may argue that the prophecy of Jesus' return in Revelation 1:7 would be worked out by God in some miraculous way so that everyone on the supposed spherical earth will see his return. That view is impeached by Acts 1:9-11, where God makes clear that Jesus will return to earth from heaven just as he ascended from earth to heaven. The only way that every eye on earth could see Jesus' descent from heaven in that manner is on a flat earth.

> And when he had spoken these things, while they beheld, he was taken up; and a cloud received him

out of their sight. And while they looked stedfastly toward heaven as he went up, behold, two men stood by them in white apparel; Which also said, Ye men of Galilee, why stand ye gazing up into heaven? this same Jesus, which is taken up from you into heaven, shall so come in like manner as ye have seen him go into heaven. (Acts 1:9-11)

The Bible prophesies that the stars will fall to the earth. "And the stars of heaven fell unto the earth, even as a fig tree casteth her untimely figs, when she is shaken of a mighty wind." (Revelation 6:13) The prophecy of the stars falling to earth would be ridiculous if the stars were enormous suns, millions of light-years away. Of course, that is the point of modern cosmology, to refute the truth and authority of the Bible. If the modern cosmology were correct, a single star would engulf the earth if it struck the earth. Modern so-called science serves to undermine the word of God.

God pours water upon the "face of the earth." "It is he that buildeth his stories in the heaven, and hath founded his troop in the earth; he that calleth for the waters of the sea, and poureth them out upon **the face of the earth**: The LORD is his name." (Amos 9:6) Everyone knows that when speaking of objects, "face" is the flat visible side of an object. For example, we commonly speak of the face of a clock. Never is a ball or globe referred to as having a face. We would never refer to a baseball as having a face. Indeed, it cannot have a face, it is a ball. Face implies the front of an object. Persons have faces, which is because a person's face is considered the front of his head, which is not at all like the back of his head. The front of a persons face is not perfectly flat, but it must be somewhat flat for a person to have binocular vision. The two eyes are lined up on a single plane. A man's face has peaks (the nose) and valleys (eye sockets), just as the face of the earth has peaks and valleys. Even with the irregular surface, a person's face is generally viewed as somewhat flat. Indeed, in Numbers

22:31 we find that Balaam "fell flat on his face." A spherical earth cannot have a face, because there is no front to a globe. However, both God and man refer to the face of the earth, which denotes that the earth is flat. "Thou sendest forth thy spirit, they are created: and thou renewest **the face of the earth**. (Psalms 104:30)

Indeed, God describes the earth in Job 38:14 as being "turned as clay to the seal." The tradition of placing a seal on documents using clay dates to antiquity. The wet clay was flattened under pressure using a seal, which was a hard die, called a signet. The signet was pushed into the clay. This was often done to authenticate royal decrees. The clay then dried with the positive impression from the negative image on the royal signet left visible in the flat pressed clay. The clay image itself was known as the seal. All such seals were necessarily pressed flat.

God calls the process, of creating the clay seal of the earth, being "turned." The word turn in this context is pregnant with meaning. Turn means "to form; to shape,"[67] and "to transfer."[68] That is what happens when the image on the signet is pressed against the clay. That process shapes the clay and transfers the image from the signet to the clay. Turn also means "to reverse the sides or surfaces of: invert."[69] And that is what we see in the positive image left in the clay from the negative image on the signet. Turn has yet another meaning: "to cause to move in a circular course,"[70] "to cause to move around an axis or a center."[71] In the context of a clay seal as described in Job 38:14, it implies that the flat clay seal is being "turned" into a circle. Thus, God's description of the earth being "turned as clay to the seal" clearly describes a flat earth, and it suggests that it is a circle. *See also* Isaiah 40:22, God "sitteth upon the **circle** of the earth."

Tyler J. Doka of Great Harvest Baptist Church in Long Island, New York, makes the point that the heliocentric model with an ever-expanding infinite space with distant galaxies and stars is contrary to God's purpose in creating the heavens and earth.[72] God states in Isaiah 45:18 that God made the earth for a purpose, to be inhabited. The purpose of the visible stars in the firmament (as with the sun and moon) is to "be lights in the firmament of the heaven to divide the day from the night; and let them be for signs, and for seasons, and for days, and years." Genesis 1:14. *See also* Psalms 8:3; 136:9. God did not create the earth or the luminaries in the firmament in vain.

> For thus saith the LORD that created the heavens; God himself that formed the earth and made it; he hath established it, he created it not in vain, he formed it to be inhabited: I am the LORD; and there is none else. Isaiah 45:18.

But it seems that the alleged distant stars and galaxies under the heliocentric model serve no purpose; heliocentrism has them being created in vain. Indeed, the heliocentric model has new stars being born all the time. Dr. Amelia Saintonge, who is on the faculty in the Department of Physics and Astrophysics at the University College London alleges that "there are about 100 billion stars being born and dying each year, which corresponds to about 275 million per day, in the whole observable Universe."[73]

The claim of billions of stars being created and dying each year contradicts the word of God. In the Bible, God unequivocally states that "the heavens and the earth were finished, and all the host of them." Genesis 2:1. All the stars were made by God on the fourth day of creation. Genesis 1:16. God "finished" making stars on that day. According to God, there would be no more stars made. Indeed, if the purpose of the stars is for signs and for seasons and for days and years, what is the point of new stars? If it were true that new stars are being created and those new stars are being matched by star deaths, such alleged occurrences would only cause confusion; the stars would be simply vanity. If what Dr. Saintonge said is true, celestial navigation using a sextant would be impossible. The very fact that for centuries the same stars have been observable in the night sky and can to this day be used for precise celestial navigation impeaches the claim of modern astrophysics that there are hundreds of millions of stars dying and being replaced by new stars each day.

God has numbered and named the stars. "He telleth the number of the stars; he calleth them all by their names." Psalms 147:4. The claim that 275 million stars per day are dying and those star deaths are matched by 275 million stars born each and every day contradicts the Bible, where God finished creating all the host of heaven on the fourth day of creation, and God has numbered and named each one of them. But it seems that the point of modern astrophysics is to contradict the Holy Bible.

If new stars are being created, that means that God did not finish his work of creation and rest on the seventh day, as reported in Genesis 2:1-2.

> **Thus the heavens and the earth were finished, and all the host of them. And on the seventh day God ended his work which he had made; and he rested on the seventh day from all his work which he had made.** (Genesis 2:1-2)

That is of utmost importance regarding our salvation. That is because God explains that the rest he enjoyed on the seventh day of creation is the same rest into which he welcomes his elect. *See* Hebrews 4:1-16.

> For he spake in a certain place of the seventh day on this wise, And **God did rest the seventh day from all his works. And in this place again, If they shall enter into my rest. Seeing therefore it remaineth that some must enter therein**, and they to whom it was first preached entered not in because of unbelief. (Hebrews 4:4-6)

Jesus proclaimed regarding his propitiation on the cross, "it is finished." John 19:30; *see also* John 17:4. Jesus Christ's works of creation and atonement were finished from the foundation of the world. Hebrews 4:3. God has thus provided a rest for his elect. **"There remaineth therefore a rest to the people of God."** (Hebrews 4:9) That rest was ordained by God before the foundation of the world. Ephesians 1:4.

Jesus explains that all of the "law of Moses" and the writings of the prophets and the psalms that were written of him must be fulfilled. Jesus then brought his disciples to understand that the fulfillment of the law of Moses and of the prophets and the psalms was that he must suffer and rise from the dead for the remission of the sins of his elect.

> And he said unto them, These are the words which I spake unto you, while I was yet with you, that all things must be fulfilled, which were written in the law of Moses, and in the prophets, and in the psalms, concerning me. Then opened he their understanding, that they might understand the scriptures, And said unto them, Thus it is written, and thus it behoved Christ to suffer, and to rise from the dead the third day: And that repentance and remission of sins should be preached in his name among all nations, beginning at Jerusalem. (Luke 24:44-47)

Where do we find in the law of Moses a prophecy of the death and resurrection of Jesus Christ? It is found in the Ten Commandments of God given by Moses in Exodus.

> Remember the sabbath day, to keep it holy. Six days shalt thou labour, and do all thy work: But the seventh day is the sabbath of the LORD thy God: in it thou shalt not do any work, thou, nor thy son,

nor thy daughter, thy manservant, nor thy maidservant, nor thy cattle, nor thy stranger that is within thy gates: For in six days the LORD made heaven and earth, the sea, and all that in them is, and rested the seventh day: wherefore the LORD blessed the sabbath day, and hallowed it. (Exodus 20:8-11)

The sabbath in Exodus is a prophecy regarding the sabbath rest provided by Jesus Christ. Notice in Exodus that the reason for celebrating the weekly sabbath was that God "rested on the seventh day." That rest into which God entered after he finished his creation is the same sabbath rest into which God's elect are welcomed. Hebrews 4:9-10.

If new stars are still being created, as the heliocentric model provides, that means that God did not finish his creation of the heavens and the earth and all the host of them. Thus, if God did not finish his work of creation, God has not rested from his work of creation. Therefore, there can be no salvation for God's elect because our salvation is based upon entering into God's rest.

There remaineth therefore a rest to the people of God. For he that is entered into his rest, he also hath ceased from his own works, as God did from his. (Hebrews 4:9-10)

The heliocentric mythology of new star creation subverts the word of God, which states that he "ended" creating the heaven and the earth; it was "finished;" God then rested from all the work that he has done. *See* Genesis 2:1-2. Thus, under the heliocentric mythology, God did not end his creation, it was not finished, and thus there is no rest into which God can welcome his elect. The heliocentric mythology vitiates the salvation rest promised in the Bible.

Joshua 10:12-13 poses a real problem for the Christians who believe in a heliocentric model of a rotating earth orbiting around the sun. In Joshua 10:12-13, God caused the sun and the moon to stand still. In order for Christians to hold to heliocentricity, they must necessarily call God a liar, because God moved Joshua to give a command to both the sun and the moon to stand still in Joshua 10:12-13; whereby God stopped both the sun and moon in their motion across the sky.

> Then spake Joshua to the LORD in the day when the LORD delivered up the Amorites before the children of Israel, and he said in the sight of Israel, Sun, stand thou still upon Gibeon; and thou, Moon, in the valley of Ajalon. And the sun stood still, and the moon stayed, until the people had avenged themselves upon their enemies. Is not this written in the book of Jasher? So the sun stood still in the midst of heaven, and hasted not to go down about a whole day. (Joshua 10:12-13)

God states clearly in the passage that the sun stood still. The passage does not say that the earth stopped spinning. "Scientists" claim that the earth is spinning at 1,000 miles per hour at the equator and that motion of the earth accounts for the path of the sun across the sky. If that were the case, the event in Joshua could never have happened. Any vehicle coming to a sudden stop at 1,000 miles per hour would kill all the passengers aboard. It would be a bloody mess. The same would happen on a supposedly spinning earth. A sudden stop of the supposed spin of the earth would have killed every living thing on earth. God would have killed the very army of Israel that he was helping. That makes no sense.

It was not the earth that stopped spinning. God did just what he said he did; he caused the sun to stop and stand still in the sky. Joshua did not command the earth to stop spinning. The passage states that Joshua commanded the "Sun, stand thou still." God moved Joshua to command the sun to stop and "the sun stood still" by the power of God. Indeed, God states that it "hasted not to go down about a whole day." That means that ordinarily the sun would be hasting to go down, but in this particular case, it did not. The sun is ordinarily in motion, coming up and going down. On that day, God stopped the sun's usual motion in the sky. To suggest otherwise is to call God a liar.

God's intention in helping Israel was to stop the sun. Stopping the moon was not helpful to Israel. However, once God stopped the sun, he also stopped the moon, because God wanted to keep the motions of the sun and moon synchronized. The synchronization of the sun and moon is part of God's creation. God made the sun and moon to be "lights in the firmament of the heaven to divide the day from the night; and let them be for signs, and for seasons, and for days, and years." Genesis 1:14. He made the sun to rule the day and the moon to rule the night. Genesis 1:15-16. In order to keep that purpose intact, once God stopped the sun, it was necessary for God also to stop the moon.

Notice also that Joshua ordered the sun to stand still upon Gibeon and the Moon, to stand still in the valley of Ajalon. The sun could not be said to be "upon Gibeon" if the sun were more than 100 times larger than a spherical earth and 93 million miles away in distant outer space, as it is portrayed under the heliocentric model. Furthermore, the heliocentric model puts the moon 240,000 miles away from a globular earth in distant outer space, which would preclude it from being "in the valley of Ajalon" as stated by God in Joshua 10:12-13. The sun and moon both must be much smaller than and closer to the flat earth in order to stand still over the areas in which they were located in Joshua, chapter 10.

Scientists acknowledge that it is the moon that moves over the earth. They wrongly opine that it is orbiting around a spherical earth. If God were stopping the sun by stopping the spin of the earth, the "scientific" view of the independently moving moon would require that the moon keep moving in its supposed orbit around the spherical earth. But that is not what happened. God stopped the moon in that same way he stopped the sun; he stopped it in its usual circuit over a stationary, flat earth.

3 Why Is it Important?

It seems that the first question asked by church pastors who do not want to discuss the flat earth is: "what difference does it make what shape the earth is?" They take the position that whether God created a flat earth or a spherical earth is of no significance to them because it does not impact the truth of the gospel. They don't even believe what they are saying because after announcing how irrelevant to the gospel belief in a flat earth is they will then preach against belief in a flat earth as being a damnable heresy. They often do so in the most vitriolic fashion, with language that is full of pejorative jargon and *ad hominem* attacks, sometimes reigning down curses from their god on those who would teach that the earth is flat.

For example, a minister identified as Brother Jesse Michael preached a sermon at Steadfast Baptist Church of Fort Worth, Texas, titled *The Flat Earth Heresy Exposed.* Michael explained that he was preaching with the permission of the pastor, who is Jonathan Shelley. It is notable that Steadfast Baptist Church has had Steven Anderson as a guest preacher. Steven Anderson is a strident opponent of God's creation of a flat, stationary earth. "Can two walk together, except they be agreed?" Amos 3:3. During Michael's sermon, Michael went into a vitriolic tirade against those who believe that the Bible depicts a flat earth. He described the belief in a flat earth as a dumb, idiotic, foolish, ridiculous, retarded, heretical doctrine. That is a problem for Michael because he is calling God's word dumb, idiotic, foolish, ridiculous, retarded, and heretical. Michael believes that all people who teach the flat earth are cursed and are leading people to hell. That does not sound to like the opponents of the belief in a flat earth think it is irrelevant. Michael preached in pertinent part:

> God strictly commands us not to do anything that will lead unsaved people from believing the word of God. ... If they are causing people to believe that the Bible is dumb, it's idiotic, it's foolish, there's a curse upon that person. ... Let's say someone hears about a flat earth, and let's say that they grew up in a kind of secular home, you know what they are gonna think, oh wow, the Bible teaches flat earth, that's ridiculous. I better stay away from those Baptist weirdos. I'd better get my education at the university. ... People who lead people away from the truth to this flat earth heresy have a curse upon them. If you're stuck in that category and you're an idiot that holds its retard doctrine, you better repent, and you better stop that, because you're gonna lead people straight to hell.[74]

Michael cites two Bible passages that he then applies to those who preach the earth is flat.

> Thou shalt not curse the deaf, nor put a stumblingblock before the blind, but shalt fear thy God: I am the LORD. (Leviticus 19:14)

> Cursed be he that maketh the blind to wander out of the way. And all the people shall say, Amen. (Deuteronomy 27:18)

Michael claims that preaching about a biblical flat earth

will dissuade a person from believing the gospel because they will think that the idea that the earth is flat is ridiculous and decide that they want no part of such a dumb, idiotic, foolish, ridiculous, and retarded religion. But Michael has it backward. The passages he cites (Deuteronomy 27:18 and Leviticus 19:14) seem to apply to him because he is concealing the truth about creation. He is telling the spiritually blind to wander the wrong way. The curse that Michael thinks God will bring upon those who teach the biblical doctrine that the earth is flat is, in fact, a curse that God will bring upon him. Michael, like Haman, is being cursed by God with the curse that Michael intends for those who believe the biblical account of the flat earth. *See* Esther 7:10.

Michael wants to remove the foolishness of the gospel. He fails to realize that the gospel indeed appears foolish to the lost world. "For the preaching of the cross is to them that perish foolishness; but unto us which are saved it is the power of God." (1 Corinthians 1:18) Lying about the gospel to make it palatable to the unsaved is not the answer. The world must hear the entire unvarnished gospel. Michael does not understand that the gospel is spiritually discerned. "[T]he natural man receiveth not the things of the Spirit of God: for they are foolishness unto him: neither can he know them, because they are spiritually discerned." (1 Corinthians 2:14) If Michael thinks that the clear statement in God's word that the earth is flat is foolishness, what does that say about him? "For after that in the wisdom of God the world by wisdom knew not God, it pleased God by the foolishness of preaching to save them that believe." (1 Corinthians 1:21).

Michael is quite apparently a free-will Arminian. An Arminian is one who follows the doctrines of Jacobus Arminius (1560-1609). Jacob Arminius is the standard bearer for a Jesuit inspired false gospel wherein salvation is not by God's sovereign election but rather by the free will of man. Arminius was an admirer of a Jesuit priest named Luis de Molina, who promoted a false doctrine of Semi-Pelagianism, which eventually became renamed and popularized as Arminianism. Most established "Christian" churches today preach that false Arminian gospel.

Michael is typical of those who don't understand God's sovereign grace. We are saved by God's grace through faith in Jesus Christ. Arminians wrongly believe that the free will of man authors faith. However, the Bible expressly states that Jesus is the author and finisher of our faith. Hebrews 12:2. Faith is "not of ourselves; it is the gift of God." Ephesians 2:8. In the gospel of John, God clearly states that power to believe in Jesus Christ unto salvation is given by God. All who are saved and become sons of God "were born, <u>not</u> of blood, <u>nor</u> of the will of the flesh, <u>nor</u> of the will of man, but <u>of God</u>." (John 1:12-13) Case closed.

The Bible depicts a flat, stationary earth. If that depiction is thought to be wrong, then it undermines the credibility of all other provisions of the gospel. The heliocentric fable of a spinning earth orbiting a giant fireball sun creates a misunderstanding of God's creation. To misunderstand God's creation causes a concomitant misunderstanding of the characteristics of God. God has shown man his character through his creation. If man has a misunderstanding of God's creation, he will have a misunderstanding of who God is. Paul explains this in his letter to the Romans:

> [T]hat which may be known of God is manifest in them; for God hath shewed it unto them. For **the invisible things of him from the creation of the world are clearly seen, being understood by the things that are made, even his eternal power and Godhead**; so that they are without excuse. (Romans 1:19-20)

Jesus is God. Jesus created all things in heaven and on earth. There is nothing that has been created that Jesus did not create.

> For **by him were all things created, that are in heaven, and that are in earth, visible and invisible**, whether they be thrones, or dominions, or principalities, or powers: **all things were created by him, and for him**: And he is before all things, and **by him all things consist**. And he is the head of the body, the church: who is the beginning, the firstborn from the dead; that in all things he might have the preeminence. (Colossians 1:16-18)

If one believes in a creation that does not exist, he also necessarily believes in a creator that does not exist. It is essential, therefore, to have an accurate understanding of God's creation. God did not make a movable, spherical earth. A Jesus who creates a spherical, moving earth is a different Jesus from the real Jesus in the Bible. *See* 2 Corinthians 11:3-4. To misunderstand the creation causes those with such misunderstanding to in turn misunderstand the character of Jesus. If one believes in the heliocentric creation, he will necessarily believe in a heliocentric creator. A heliocentric creation does not exist. So also, a heliocentric creator does not exist. A heliocentric creator is a false god. We have been warned to avoid the preaching of a false gospel, which presents a false Jesus.

> But I fear, lest by any means, as the serpent beguiled Eve through his subtilty, so your minds should be corrupted from the simplicity that is in Christ. For if he that cometh preacheth **another Jesus**, whom we have not preached, or if ye receive another spirit, which ye have not received, or **another gospel**, which ye have not accepted, ye might well bear with him. (2 Corinthians 11:3-4)

Just because someone uses the name of Jesus does not mean that they are believers in the true Jesus. If the Jesus they invoke is not the Jesus of the Bible, they are worshiping in vain. Heliocentric "Christians" reject the Jesus of the Bible who is the creator of a flat and stationary earth, which is his footstool over which he presides from his abode in heaven above the firmament. They, instead, conjure in their hearts a different Jesus who created a spinning ball earth floating in outer space, which thus cannot be Jesus' footstool. They worship a false Jesus. Their worship is in vain. They are not unlike the Muslims who believe in a Jesus, but their Jesus is not the Jesus of the Bible. Muslims believe in a false Jesus who does not, will not, and cannot save them.

The Muslims believe that Jesus was a great prophet, but they reject him as the son of God. That is similar to heliocentric "Christians" who reject the Jesus of the Bible who created a firmament, above which is his heavenly abode that is over the flat and stationary earth. The Quran is the primary religious text for Muslims. The Quran is believed by Muslims to have been given by revelation from the Angel Gabriel to Muhammad. The Quran at Sura 23:91 states in reference to Jesus that "**no son did Allah beget**," and again at Sura 17:111: "All the praises and thanks be to **Allah, Who has not begotten a son**." Allah is the god of Islam. In the Quran at Sura 4:171 it states that Allah did not have a Son. Sura 4:171 adds to the blasphemy by stating that Jesus is a mere messenger of Allah.

The Bible identifies Jesus as the only begotten Son of God. "For God so loved the world, that he gave **his only begotten Son**, that whosoever believeth in him should not perish, but have everlasting life." (John 3:16) "In this was manifested the love of God toward us, because that **God sent his only begotten Son** into the world, that we might live through him." (1 John 4:9) Jesus, the Father, and the Holy Spirit are all one God. "For there are three that bear record in heaven, the Father, the Word, and the Holy Ghost: and these three are one." (1 John 5:7)

The Bible states clearly that "[w]hosoever denieth the Son,

the same hath not the Father: but he that acknowledgeth the Son hath the Father also." 1 John 2:23. Muslims reject the Jesus of the Bible. They reject the son and so they have not the Father. They reject the God who can save them and instead worship a heathen god who cannot save. That same analysis can be done for the Hindu Jesus, the Mormon Jesus, the Catholic Jesus, and the heliocentric Jesus. They are all false Christs and their devotees worship them in vain.

The Bible states that "The heavens declare the glory of God; and the firmament sheweth his handywork." Psalms 19:1. The Bible makes it clear that there is firmament over the earth. And above the firmament is God's throne surrounded by brightness. Ezekiel 1:25-28. The heliocentric outer space is supposed to be full of darkness. That implants in the minds of men that the heaven of the Bible is a myth and there is no God.

According to the heliocentric model there is no glorious brightness surrounding God on his throne in heaven above the firmament. Instead, where God's throne is supposed to be, above the firmament, heliocentrists say there is instead just an empty, weightless, vacuum of black nothingness. The heliocentric model presents an empty vacuum with no heaven and thus there is no God. But the Bible states that God is above us in heaven, watching over man. (Job 22:12; Ecclesiastes 24:5; Psalms 14:2 & 33:13) God states that "heaven is my throne." (Acts 7:49) But Satan has used the "science falsely so called" of heliocentrism to remove God in the minds of men from his throne and replace the glorious abode of God with a dark and hostile empty vacuum. "The LORD is in his holy temple, the LORD'S throne is in heaven: his eyes behold, his eyelids try, the children of men." (Psalms 11:4) "Heaven is my throne, and earth is my footstool." (Acts 7:49)

This false heliocentric Jesus is at the core of many false doctrines. Satan uses the subtle strategy of first undermining the authority of the Bible by introducing the concept that God does not mean what he has said in the Bible about the flat earth he has created. Once that seed is planted in the minds of the congregation, the (beguiled and beguiling) pastor can then undermine what God has said about faith and doctrine. Under this rubric where duped (or unscrupulous) pastors portray the scriptures as having meaning other than the expressed words, doctrine becomes malleable.

In Jeremiah 31:37, God states:

> Thus saith the LORD; If heaven above can be measured, and the foundations of the earth searched out beneath, I will also cast off all the seed of Israel for all that they have done, saith the LORD. Jeremiah 31:37.

Notice that this is God speaking in that passage, so please take heed. Frank Hall, pastor of Sovereign Grace Assembly in Kannapolis, North Carolina, explains how that passage in Jeremiah reveals the importance of God's creation of a flat, stable earth.

> All who know the grace of God in truth fully understand that all of God's elect shall be saved with an everlasting salvation; that must be settled at the outset, if we are to enter into the hope of this text. None of God's Israel, not a single one, can or will be lost—period. Understanding this, we move on to notice the two impossibilities stated by God's Spirit through Jeremiah: the impossibility of measuring the heavens and the impossibility of searching out the foundations of the earth. Because those two things are impossible this final thing is impossible, the casting off of Israel for all that they have done. God says by Jeremiah, "If anyone can measure the heavens or find out the foundations of the earth, I will send every one of my elect to hell."

But God does not state this as if it were actually possible; it is stated to demonstrate to us that it is impossible. The heavens cannot be measured, and the foundations of the earth cannot be found out; therefore, God's people are absolutely secure beneath the precious blood of Jesus Christ. This is the doctrine of the text—rejoice in it.[75]

Some might argue that the passage at Jeremiah 31:37 refers to Israel and not God's elect church. The passage identifies the elect as the "seed of Israel." Who is the seed of Israel? It is the church. The church is the body of Christ for whom he died. For a detailed discussion of that truth, read this author's book, *Bloody Zion*.

In Christ, there is neither Jew nor Gentile; we are all one by faith in Christ. God promised to Abraham that his seed will not only be the recipient of God's blessing, but also the source of that blessing. "And in thy **seed** shall all the nations of the earth be blessed." Genesis 22:18. How can it be that the seed is both the source and the recipient of the blessing? In Galatians 3:16: "Now to Abraham and his **seed** were the promises made. He saith not, And to seeds, as of many; but as of one, **And to thy seed, which is Christ**." Jesus Christ is the seed that is the source of the blessing. All who believe in Jesus Christ, are the recipients of the promises as the spiritual children of God. All who believe in Jesus Christ are Abraham's spiritual seed, and heirs according to the promise of the coming Christ given to Abraham. "And if ye be Christ's, then are ye Abraham's seed, and heirs according to the promise." Galatians 3:29.

Jesus Christ's church is his body, which cannot be divided into Jew and Gentile. 1 Corinthians 1:13. For a kingdom divided against itself cannot stand. Mark 3:24. The seed of the promises to Abraham is Christ and those who have the faith of Christ, his church, not fleshly Israel.

> But before faith came, we were kept under the law, shut up unto the faith which should afterwards be revealed. Wherefore the law was our schoolmaster to bring us unto Christ, that we might be justified by faith. **But after that faith is come, we are no longer under a schoolmaster**. For ye are all the children of God by faith in Christ Jesus. For as many of you as have been baptized into Christ have put on Christ. **There is neither Jew nor Greek, there is neither bond nor free, there is neither male nor female: for ye are all one in Christ Jesus. And if ye be Christ's, then are ye Abraham's seed, and heirs according to the promise.** Galatians 3:23-29.

A Jew who believes in Jesus as Christ becomes a new creation. He is no longer a fleshly Jew. He becomes a spiritual Jew, a Christian. "For in Christ Jesus neither circumcision availeth any thing, nor uncircumcision, but a new creature." Galatians 6:15.

The Bible makes clear that the old covenant made to fleshly Israel has vanished away, being replaced by the new covenant of faith in Jesus Christ. "In that he saith, A new covenant, he hath made the first old. Now that which decayeth and waxeth old is ready to vanish away." (Hebrews 8:13) Why would God reinstate something in which he has said would vanish away and in which he has had no pleasure? "In burnt offerings and sacrifices for sin thou hast had no pleasure." Hebrews 10:6.

The fig tree symbolizes fleshly Israel. That fig tree will never again bear fruit.

> And seeing a fig tree afar off having leaves, he came, if haply he might find any thing thereon: and when he came to it, he found nothing but leaves; for the time of figs was not yet. And Jesus

answered and said unto it, **No man eat fruit of thee hereafter for ever.** And his disciples heard it. . . . And in the morning, as they passed by, they saw the fig tree dried up from the roots. And Peter calling to remembrance saith unto him, Master, behold, the fig tree which thou cursedst is withered away. Mark 11:13-14, 20-21.

The olive tree symbolizes spiritual Israel. "Can the fig tree, my brethren, bear olive berries? either a vine, figs? so can no fountain both yield salt water and fresh." James 3:12. The answer is no! Fleshly Israel will never bear spiritual fruit for God. The spiritual fruit only comes from the spiritual olive plant, the church.

As we have already seen, the blessings of God do not flow to the physical seed of Abraham but rather to his spiritual seed. We know that Jesus is the seed of Abraham. Galatians 3:16. All who believe in Jesus are heirs of the promise given to Abraham. Galatians 3:23-29. Obedience to God is the result of salvation, not the cause of it. Ephesians 2:8-10. Just as with Abraham, who believed God and it was accounted to him as righteousness, so too for all others who believe God it is also accounted unto them as righteousness. Galatians 3:6-9.

A true Jew is the spiritual seed of Abraham, not the physical seed.

> For he is not a Jew, which is one outwardly; neither is that circumcision, which is outward in the flesh: But he is a Jew, which is one inwardly; and circumcision is that of the heart, in the spirit, and not in the letter; whose praise is not of men, but of God. Romans 2:28-29.

> Not as though the word of God hath taken none effect. For they are not all Israel, which are of

> Israel: Neither, because they are the seed of Abraham, are they all children: but, In Isaac shall thy seed be called. That is, They which are the children of the flesh, these are not the children of God: but the children of the promise are counted for the seed. Romans 9:6-8.

The eternal blessings of Abraham flow to all who believe in Jesus Christ. God's kingdom is a spiritual kingdom, not an earthly kingdom. His children are spiritual children, not earthly children. In God's kingdom, there are no distinctions between Jew or Gentile. "There is neither Jew nor Greek, there is neither bond nor free, there is neither male nor female: for ye are all one in Christ Jesus. And if ye be Christ's, then are ye Abraham's seed, and heirs according to the promise." Galatians 3:28-29.

Fleshly Israel of the Old Testament is a temporal type of the spiritual Israel of the New Testament, which is the church.

> But with many of them God was not well pleased: for they were overthrown in the wilderness. **Now these things were our examples, to the intent we should not lust after evil things, as they also lusted.** 1 Corinthians 10:5-6.

> **Now all these things happened unto them for ensamples: and they are written for our admonition, upon whom the ends of the world are come.** 1 Corinthians 10:11.

Thus, the prophecies regarding Israel had both temporal and spiritual fulfillments. The distinction between temporal Israel and eternal Israel is explained clearly in R. B. Yerby's book *The Once and Future Israel*. First, there is the temporal, earthly fulfillment and then there is the spiritual fulfillment. 1 Corinthians 15:46.

The scriptures teach us that in all of God's dealings with mankind, from the time of Adam, we may discern the same divine principle at work, namely, "first the natural, then the spiritual." (1 Cor 15:45-46) God has progressively revealed his purpose through, first, his dealings with the natural Israel and, second and finally, his dealings with spiritual Israel. (There is no scriptural basis for the regressive idea that God's dealings will again be centered exclusively on natural Israel at some future date.)

Because God's dealings follow the sequence of first the natural, then the spiritual, it is easy to see and understand that the same progression applied to his people and his promises. The natural people of Old Testament Israel enjoyed the natural fulfillment of the promises made to them, and saw the promises invalidated through sin and unbelief. Likewise, the spiritual people of New Testament Israel, the followers of Jesus Christ, have received, are receiving and will receive all spiritual fulfillments of the promises.

* * *

[In Galatians 4:21-31] as in many other New Testament passages, Paul skillfully defeated his adversaries with their own ammunition. He took the "foolish Galatians" who desired to be under the law (Gal 4:21) right into the thick of Old Testament Law, into Genesis, the first book of Moses, to prove a spiritual truth with natural types. The early church recognized the need for spiritual authority to support their doctrines (for them, of course, the scriptures were the writings we today call the Old Testament) and therefore, under the inspiration of the Holy Spirit, they quoted freely from the Old Testament.

In the fourth chapter of Galatians, as elsewhere, Paul proved his point through the superior understanding God gave him of the true meaning of the Old Testament scriptures. He said that the story of the two sons of Abraham was more than just a prominent part of the history of the Jewish people. It was, he said, an allegory (Gal. 4:24), that is, a story in which the people and events were symbols or types standing for some greater truth (Gal. 4:24).

The allegory speaks of two women and their two sons who were fathered by Abraham. Hagar, the bondwoman and the mother of Ishmael who was "born after the flesh" (Gal 4:23), typifies natural Jerusalem. Sarah, the freewoman and the mother of Isaac, the child of promise (Gal 4:23, 28), typifies the church which is spiritual Jerusalem. The children of natural Jerusalem are in bondage (Gal. 4:25), as are all who are unsaved, but the children of the church, the heavenly Jerusalem, are free (Gal. 4:26). Those who are in bondage, who are not born again are only "born after the flesh" (Gal. 4:29) cannot possibly be God's people. Therefore, the scriptures "cast out"(Gal 4:30) the natural Jerusalem and her children after the flesh, and identify the heirs as the believers in Christ who are the children of promise (Gal 4:30).

* * *

Paul was constantly in trouble with the Jews

because his spiritual interpretations of the Old Testament scriptures warred with their natural interpretation. Our onetime Pharisee had come to see clearly that "the things that are seen are temporal, but the things which are not seen are eternal" (2 Cor 4:18) but his former colleagues could not believe that their highly vaunted institutions were ready to "vanish away" (Heb 8:13).

* * *

Because the Lord Jesus "endured the cross, despising the shame" (Heb 12:2) spiritual Israel hears a better voice than the voices heard by natural Israel (Heb. 1:1, 2), and we have, among other things, a better Priest (Heb. 4:15), a better priesthood (Heb. 5:6), a better hope (Heb. 7:19), a better covenant (Heb. 8:10), a better Tabernacle (Heb. 9:11), a better altar (Heb. 13:10), a better sacrifice (Heb. 9:14), a better country (Heb. 11:16), and a better city (Heb. 12:22).[76]

The history of natural Israel is one of continual sin intermixed with periods of repentance until God finally finished with them according to his foreordained plan. There is a spiritual Israel, the church, to whom the blessings flow. God's true Israel is and always was the church. The church contains the children of the promise. "Now we, brethren, as Isaac was, are the children of promise." (Galatians 4:28) The church is the Israel of God. "For in Christ Jesus neither circumcision availeth any thing, nor uncircumcision, but a new creature. And as many as walk according to this rule, peace be on them, and mercy, and upon the **Israel of God.**" (Galatians 6:15-16) The church is the temple of God. "Know ye not that ye are **the temple of God**, and that the Spirit of God dwelleth in you?" (1 Corinthians 3:16) The church is God's holy nation inheriting the promises made by God in Exodus 19:5-8. **"But ye are a chosen generation, a royal priesthood, an holy nation, a peculiar people**; that ye should shew forth the praises of him who hath called you out of darkness into his marvellous light." (1 Peter 2:9)

God does not have a plan of salvation for fleshly Israel that is any different from the plan of salvation he has for Gentiles. Salvation is by grace through faith in Jesus Christ for all. There is one body of Christ, his spiritual Israel, made up of Gentiles and the remnant of fleshly Israel.

> Even when we were dead in sins, hath quickened us together with Christ, (by grace ye are saved;) And hath raised us up together, and made us sit together in heavenly places in Christ Jesus: That in the ages to come he might shew the exceeding riches of his grace in his kindness toward us through Christ Jesus. For by grace are ye saved through faith; and that not of yourselves: it is the gift of God: Not of works, lest any man should boast. For we are his workmanship, created in Christ Jesus unto good works, which God hath before ordained that we should walk in them. Wherefore remember, that ye being in time past Gentiles in the flesh, who are called Uncircumcision by that which is called the Circumcision in the flesh made by hands; That at that time ye were without Christ, being aliens from the commonwealth of Israel, and strangers from the covenants of promise, having no hope, and without God in the world: But now in Christ Jesus ye who sometimes were far off are made nigh by the blood of Christ. **For he is our peace, who hath made both one, and hath broken down the middle wall of partition between us; Having**

abolished in his flesh the enmity, even the law of commandments contained in ordinances; for to make in himself of twain one new man, so making peace; And that he might reconcile both unto God in one body by the cross, having slain the enmity thereby: And came and preached peace to you which were afar off, and to them that were nigh. For through him we both have access by one Spirit unto the Father. Now therefore ye are no more strangers and foreigners, but fellowcitizens with the saints, and of the household of God; And are built upon the foundation of the apostles and prophets, Jesus Christ himself being the chief corner stone; In whom all the building fitly framed together groweth unto an holy temple in the Lord: In whom ye also are builded together for an habitation of God through the Spirit. (Ephesians 2:5-22)

Christ did not in any way provide some exclusive plan for the Jews. He stated that the gospel was to be preached to "all nations." Luke 24:47. The only difference for the Jews was that the preaching of the gospel should start at Jerusalem. Romans 1:16; Acts 18:5-6. It was to start with the Jews, but that does not mean it is to end with the Jews in some post-Christian era. The Old Testament has prophecies of the church of God consisting of both believing Jews and Gentiles. Amos 9:11-12; Hosea 1:10; 2:23. The Old Testament prophecies regarding salvation to both the Jews and Gentiles together are explained in Acts 15:13-17; 26:22-23; Romans 9:23-26; and 1 Peter 2:10.

The New Testament writers, being inspired by God, clearly understood that the church is the Israel of God and is the object of the promises made to Israel by God in the Old Testament.[77]

Paul said that believers are:

"The children of God" (Romans 8:16).
"The Household of God" (Ephesians 2:19).
"The children of Abraham" (Colossians 3:7).
"Abraham's seed" (Galatians 3:29).
"The Children of promise" (Rom. 9:8, Galatians 4:28).
"A peculiar people" (Titus 2:14).
"The elect of God" (Colossians 3:12).
"Heirs of God"(Rom. 8:17).
"Heirs according to the promise" (Galatians 3:29).
"The temple of God" (1 Cor 3:16).
"The circumcision" (Philippians 3:3).
"The Israel of God" (Galatians 6:16).

Peter said that believers are:

"A chosen generation" (1 Peter 2:9).
"A royal priesthood" (1 Peter 2:9).
"A holy nation" (1 Peter 2:9).
"A peculiar people" (1 Peter 2:9).

James said that believers are:

"Heirs of the kingdom" (James 2:5).

John said that believers are:

"The sons of God" (John 1:12).
"Kings and priests unto God" (Revelation 1:6).
"The new Jerusalem" (Revelation 3:12).
"The Holy city (Revelation 21:2).

The letter to the Hebrews said that believers are:

"The people of God" (Hebrews 4:9).
"Mount Sion" (Hebrews 12:22).

"The city of the living God" (Hebrews 12:22).
"The heavenly Jerusalem" (Hebrews 12:22).

The Jews are our enemies because they are antichrist. Romans 11:28. Jews hate Christ and Christians. Those that are born after the flesh will always persecute those born after the spirit. Galatians 4:29. The spiritual children of God, however, are to love them and pray for them. "But I say unto you which hear, Love your enemies, do good to them which hate you, Bless them that curse you, and pray for them which despitefully use you." (Luke 6:27-28) God has chosen a remnant of Jews for salvation. We should preach the gospel to the lost world, including the Jews. We, however, should not think that a Jew is any different in God's plan than a Catholic, a Muslim, a Hindu, a Buddhist, a Satanist or any other follower of one of Satan's heathen religions.

Salvation for all is by the grace of God through faith in Jesus Christ. If a Jew repents of his antichrist religion and believes in Jesus, then he is saved. Once saved, a Jew will not continue in his Talmudic practices any more than a Catholic will continue his Catholic practices or a Satanist will continue his satanic practices once they are saved. All believers in Christ become spiritual Jews, who are Christians. Romans 2:28-29.

Loving our enemies does not mean that we should condone the pagan practices of the Jews, Catholics, Muslims, or other heathens. Rather, we are called by God to reprove them. "And have no fellowship with the unfruitful works of darkness, but rather reprove them." (Ephesians 5:11)

Jeremiah states without equivocation that "if heaven above can be measured" then also God will cast off his elect. God's point is that it is as impossible for him to cast off his elect as it is to measure the heavens. Modern science claims to have done the very thing that God states is impossible. Modern science claims to know precisely the measured distance from the earth to the moon

(238,855 miles), the measured distance to the sun (92,960,000 miles), the measured distance to the star Alpha Centauri (4.367 light-years), the measured distance to the Andromeda Galaxy (2.537 million light years), the measured distance to the Galaxy MACS0647-JD (3.3 billion light years). By the way, a light-year is a unit of measure based upon how far light travels in one year. The speed of light is approximately 186,282 miles per second. Frank Hall explains what it means to accept those false scientific claims to be true:

> They claim to know the precise distances to the stars, the celestial landmarks by which they measure from one end of the heavens to the other. They have sent satellites, spaceships, space shuttles, probes, astronauts, and space stations into orbit around the earth, so they say. They have been beneath the earth, and they have searched out the foundations below. They have done precisely what God says is impossible on both accounts; they have achieved the very things that must result in the everlasting damnation of God's elect.[78]

The impossibility of searching out the foundations of the earth establishes the security of God's elect. Just as it is impossible to search out the foundations of the earth, so also it is impossible for God's elect to be lost. But modern scientists claim to have searched out the foundations of the earth. They claim to have done exactly what God says is impossible. If that is true, then God will cast off his elect. The myth of heliocentrism is an affront to God, to God's elect, and to the gospel.

The Lord God rhetorically asks Job where was he when God stretched a line upon the earth and laid and fastened the foundation of the earth?

Where wast thou when I laid the foundations of the

earth? declare, if thou hast understanding. Who hath laid the measures thereof, if thou knowest? or who hath stretched the line upon it? Whereupon are the foundations thereof fastened? or who laid the corner stone thereof. (Job 38:4-6)

Notice the precision of the language. Such an earth described in Job could only be stationary and immovable. God "laid" and "fastened" the foundations. He did so upon a "cornerstone." God is describing a fixed, stationary earth. The earth cannot be a spinning, orbiting globe careening through space. If the cornerstone described by God for the earth is not sure and stable, how can Jesus Christ, whom God describes as the cornerstone for our salvation, be sure and stable? "Wherefore also it is contained in the scripture, Behold, I lay in Sion a chief corner stone, elect, precious: and he that believeth on him shall not be confounded." (1 Peter 2:6) If people consider God's creation, which reveals his character (Romans 1:19-20), to be established on an unstable cornerstone, there is nothing that can prevent people from considering the creator himself, Jesus Christ (Colossians 1:16-18), to be an unstable cornerstone upon which to place their faith.

God further revealed in Psalms 104:5 that the foundations of the earth that he laid cannot ever be moved. In Jeremiah, it states that it is as impossible to search the foundations of the earth as it is for God to cast off his elect. The modern scientists contest God's word. According to them not only can the foundations of the earth be searched, but they claim that they have been to the bottom of the earth (i.e., the South Pole in Antarctica) and there are no foundations there. They thus contradict God, who claims to have set the earth on pillars. "[T]he pillars of the earth are the LORD'S, and he hath set the world upon them." (1 Samuel 2:8) Scientists claim to have proven that God's statement that the foundations of the earth cannot be searched is false; they looked and found out there were no pillars. They allege that they have sent men into outer space; and those men looked back and saw a spherical earth floating and spinning in space without any pillars or a foundation of any kind. According to Jeremiah, that means that if what modern science says is true, science has proven that God's elect can be lost. That goes to the heart of the gospel. Frank Hall explains:

> [P]ertaining to the foundations of the earth; not only did they search out God's foundations underneath the earth, they also found that there are no foundations at all. They found a south pole, but no foundations! God said he put foundations beneath the earth from the beginning. God "laid the foundations of the earth, that it should not be removed forever (Psalm 104:5)." Yet, according to the big dogs at NASA, there are no foundations under the earth; there is only outer space and more empty vacuum. Now, do the math. If one plus one equals two, God must send us all to hell! But someone says, "Those foundations are poetic." Well, that solves it then! If those foundations are poetic, so is our salvation! It is not an actual salvation—it is a poetic salvation, which is a worthless salvation, which is no salvation.[79]

An earth without a foundation means that we have a salvation without a foundation. Hall continues:

> People, do you not see? Are you yet without understanding? If all that modern day science and astronomy teaches is correct, God's elect have no hope! If the earth is a ball, spinning and orbiting around the sun, and outer space is real, the gospel of God's free grace is a big fat lie. If the earth is not flat and firmly fixed on immovable foundations, Christ died for nothing, and we are

yet in our sins. An earth without foundations amounts to everlasting ruin for all of God's people. If what science falsely so-called says is true concerning outer space, grace means nothing, the cross of Christ means nothing, his resurrection means nothing, the gospel means nothing, God's faithfulness means nothing, and all the promises of God mean nothing. ...

God himself, here in our text, connects his flat and stationary earth with the everlasting salvation, preservation, and security of his chosen people. It is not we who preach a flat earth who are adding to the gospel; it is all who reject that the earth is firm, fixed, flat, and stationary who are denying the gospel! We who preach and believe the biblical doctrine of a flat earth agree with Jeremiah and declare that God's elect shall be saved, but all who hold to the demonic doctrine of a ball earth disagree with Jeremiah and declare that God's elect are going to hell. Now, who are the real heretics?[80]

To reject the flat, stationary earth with foundations laid by God is to refute the surety of salvation. It is an attack on the gospel. In order to accept the heliocentric model, it is necessary for a Christian to redefine the words in the Bible to explain away its depiction of the flat earth. Once a Christian is down the road of rejecting God's description of a flat earth in the Bible, it is easy for him to redefine the words in the Bible in other matters of doctrine.

Heliocentric Christians should not play fast-and-loose with God's word by pretending it says what it clearly does not say to avoid offending the scientific establishment. They should heed Samuel Rowbotham's advice. "Let men beware how they jeopardize their lasting welfare by taking liberties with a book written as the expressed will of Heaven for the guidance of mankind."[81]

God states that "evil men and seducers shall wax worse and worse, deceiving, and being deceived." 2 Timothy 3:13. The so-called scientists that are pushing heliocentrism have been deceived and have in turn become deceivers themselves; they are fools who speak lies and refuse to believe the truth. "For the wisdom of this world is foolishness with God. For it is written, He taketh the wise in their own craftiness." (1 Corinthians 3:19) We are admonished to keep the faith and not join with those so-called scientists who oppose God's word.

> [K]eep that which is committed to thy trust, avoiding profane and vain babblings, and oppositions of science falsely so called: Which some professing have erred concerning the faith. Grace be with thee. Amen. (1 Timothy 6:20-21)

The very idea of outer space with the potential of billions of other solar systems and worlds raises the specter of life on other planets. That has not gone unnoticed by the Roman Catholic Church. CBS News reported that Jesuit priest Jose Gabriel Funes, who is an astronomer and director of the Vatican Observatory, said in 2009 that "[t]he questions of life's origins and of whether life exists elsewhere in the universe are very suitable and deserve serious consideration."[82] In 2014, Pope Francis followed that up by announcing that "he would be willing to baptize aliens if they came to the Vatican, asking 'who are we to close doors' to anyone - even Martians."[83]

The belief that there is extraterrestrial life on other worlds in the vast universe impeaches the authority of the Bible. In 1881, Samuel Rowbotham explained:

> The supposition that the heavenly bodies are suns

and systems of inhabited worlds is demonstrably false and impossible in nature, and certainly has no counterpart or foundation in Scripture. "In the beginning God created the heaven and the earth." One earth only was created; and, in the numerous references to this world contained in the entire Scriptures, no other physical world is ever mentioned. It is never even stated that the earth has companions like itself, or that it is one of an infinite number of worlds which co-exist, and were brought into being at the beginning of creation. It may be remarked also that all the favours and privileges, the promises and threats of God contained in the Scriptures, have sole and entire reference to this one earth and its inhabitants. The sun, moon, and stars are described as lights only to give light upon the earth. "And God made two great lights; the greater light to rule the day, and the lesser light to rule the night. He made the stars also, and set them in the firmament of heaven to give light upon the earth."--Genesis 1:16-17. The creation of the world, the origin of evil, and the fall of man; the plan of redemption by the death of Christ, the Day of Judgment, and the final consummation of all things, are, in the Scriptures, invariably associated with this earth alone.[84]

The Bible is clear. There is no extraterrestrial corporeal life on other planets. All such alleged manifestations of beings from other planets are hoaxes or devils disguised as aliens. Man is made in the image of God. Genesis 1:27. Rowbotham exposes the many religious errors that surface with the heliocentric concept of billions of planets, some of which are theorized could be inhabited by extraterrestrial life.

If it be true that the stars and planets are

magnificent worlds, for the most part larger than the earth, it is a very proper question to ask "Are they inhabited?" If the answer be in the affirmative, it is equally proper to inquire "Have the first parents in each world been tempted as were Adam and Eve in the Garden of Eden?" If so, "Did they yield to the temptation and fall as they did?" If so, "Have they required redemption?" And "Have they been redeemed?" "Has each different world required the same kind of redemption, and had a separate Redeemer; or has Christ, by His suffering on earth and crucifixion on Calvary, been the Redeemer for all the innumerable myriads of worlds in the universe; or had He to suffer and die in each world successively?" "Did the fall of Adam in this world involve in his guilt the inhabitants of all the other worlds?" "Or was the baneful influence of the tempter confined to the first parents of this earth?" If so, "Why so?" and, if not, "Why not?" But, and if, and why, and, again, if but it is useless thus to ponder. The Christian philosopher must be confounded. If his religion be to him a living reality, he will turn with loathing from, or spurn with indignation and disgust as he would a poisonous reptile, a system of astronomy which creates in his mind so much confusion and uncertainty. But as the system which necessitates such doubts and difficulties has been shown to be purely theoretical, and not to have the slightest foundation in fact, the religious mind has really no cause for apprehension. Not a shadow of doubt remains that this earth is the only material world created; that the Sacred Scriptures contain, in addition to religious and moral doctrines, a true and consistent philosophy; that they were written for the good of mankind by the direct dictation of

God Himself; and that all their teachings and promises may be relied on as truthful, beneficent, and conducive to the greatest enjoyment here and to perfect happiness hereafter. Whoever holds the contrary conclusion is the victim of an arrogant and false astronomy; of an equally false and presumptuous geology; and a suicidal method of reasoning--a logic which never demands a proof of its premises, and which, therefore, leads to deductions and opinions which are contrary to nature, to fact, and human experience, and to the direct teachings of God's Word; and, therefore, contrary to the deepest and most lasting interests of humanity.[85]

Samuel Rowbotham quotes a Professor Hunt, who comes to the unassailable reasoning that "God has spoken to man in two voices--the voice of Inspiration and the voice of Nature. By man's ignorance they have been made to disagree; but the time will come, and cannot be far distant, when these two languages will strictly accord; when the science of Nature will no longer contradict the science of Scripture."[86]

The "Christian" churches have gone along with the deception and teach in their "Christian" schools a heliocentric solar system, with a spinning and orbiting earth, even though the Bible clearly states that the earth does not move and is not a globe. How could this deception have been so complete as to include both the scientific world and the "Christian" churches? Why would the scientific world go along with a falsehood that has been proven to be wrong? Why would the "Christian" churches go along with a myth that is contrary to the Bible? This book will explain why and how it happened.

4 Heathen Doctrines Born From Heliocentrism

One example of a false doctrine born of a false heliocentric Jesus is Arminianism. The false Arminian god is no longer the sovereign God of the Bible by whom "all things consist." Instead, the Arminian god is a kind of super-hero, who can foresee things that will happen in the future, but is powerless to interfere with man's free will. Jesus made it clear that understanding his creation is important to understanding the true gospel. "If I have told you earthly things, and ye believe not, how shall ye believe, if I tell you of heavenly things?" (John 3:12) That statement was made to explain the importance of the analogy he drew between wind and the work of the Holy Spirit to illustrate how salvation is completely by the grace of the sovereign God and outside of the will or control of man.

Jesus flat out said we must be born again to see the kingdom of God. John 3:3-7. In the analogy, he compared the new birth of salvation, which can only come through the Holy Spirit, with the wind. Just as "the wind bloweth where it listeth, and thou hearest the sound thereof, but canst not tell whence it cometh, and whither it goeth: so is every one that is born of the Spirit." (John 3:8) His point is that man cannot birth himself. We are born again not of blood, nor of the will of the flesh, nor of the will of man, but of God. (John 1:13)

After Jacobus Arminius' death (1609), his supporters, led by Simon Episcopius, issued a remonstrance in 1610. The remonstrance contained five articles summarizing their divergence from the fundamental doctrines of the gospel. It was, in essence, an objection to salvation by the sovereign grace of God as revealed in the gospel. After publishing the remonstrance, Arminius' followers became known as "The Remonstrants." Those who continue to follow the free-will doctrines of Jacobus Arminius and the Remonstrants are known today as Arminians. Arminianism replaces the true gospel of salvation by the sovereign will of God with a false gospel of salvation by the sovereign will of man. Arminianism started out as a fringe belief that was immediately recognized as contrary to the gospel of salvation by the grace of God and thus condemned by the Dutch Reformed Church.[87] The response to the Remonstrance by the Reformed Church in the Cannons of the Synod of Dordtrecht has been pejoratively called Calvinism. In fact, John Calvin had been long dead before the Synod of Dordtrecht met.[88] But the Arminians had to find a way to get out from under the cloud of heresy after their theology was refuted by an official synod of the Dutch Reformed Church. The Arminians came up with the idea of creating a straw man in John Calvin. Rather than argue that the theological dispute was Arminianism vs. Christianity, the Arminians re-labeled the conflict as Arminianism vs. Calvinism. Once the Arminians succeeded in re-labeling the dispute, Arminianism could gain the false appearance of being on firmer theological footing. Today Arminianism has become the new "Christian" orthodoxy followed in most mainstream churches.

The Arminian doctrine of the Remonstrants is based upon five false premises: 1: God's election is conditioned on the free will choice of man; 2: Jesus atoned for the sins of everyone in the world, both saved and unsaved; 3: While man is depraved, God provides a special (prevenient) grace to all men that partially awakens them from their depravity so that they can make a free will choice whether to believe in Jesus; 4: Man can resist the grace of God; and 5: God assists one who is saved in resisting the temptations of the devil, but a person can by the exercise of his free will reject God and lose his salvation.[89] For a more detailed discussion of this topic, please read this author's book titled: *The Anti-Gospel: The Perversion of Christ's Grace Gospel*.

The words of Christ in the gospel refute every one of those Arminian beliefs. The Bible makes it clear that Jesus is "the blessed and only Potentate, the King of kings, and Lord of lords." (1 Timothy 6:15) Jesus can not only see things that will happen, but he also makes those things happen. Jesus created all things, by him his creation consists, and he is a potentate over his creation. He did not leave something as important to his creation as salvation subject to the uncertain vicissitudes of man's free will. Indeed, he stated repeatedly in his word that he is in complete control of our salvation, from beginning to end. He is a creator of all things, even of the faith necessary for salvation. "Looking unto Jesus the author and finisher of our faith." (Hebrews 12:2) Jesus not only authors (creates) our faith, he finishes it to its end: salvation. He truly creates all things, and by him all things consist, including faith.

The Arminian Jesus, however, is not the creator of an immovable flat earth and is also not the creator (author) and finisher of our faith. The fictional, heliocentric, Arminian god created a fictional, unstable Earth and thus has an unstable doctrine of salvation, whereby man is deemed to be the creator (author) and finisher of his own faith. That is a different Jesus and a different gospel. It is so much easier to sell the Arminian god to the churches when the masses have been inculcated in the far-off heliocentric god.

Such a far-off god only peers through empty space to foresee what man will do. That concept of a detached god is only one step removed from atheism, which is the ultimate end of heliocentrism. Indeed, under heliocentricism, with the vacuum of space in place of God's abode in heaven, the only rational conclusion is that there is no God. That is why heliocentrism is the very foundation of atheism itself. It stands to reason then that those who hold onto a belief in a god, and at the same time a belief in heliocentrism, would necessarily have a god who is much diminished in his power and influence. For those who believe in a god of a heliocentric universe would inevitably lean toward a concept of a god who is much less active in the day-to-day affairs of man. Where heliocentrism has not destroyed all conception of God in the minds of men, it has at least undermined his attributes and created in the minds of men an impotent god.

Arminianism is the natural outgrowth of the belief in a god who has created a heliocentric universe. This false Arminian god leaves the salvation of men up to their own free will decision. The Arminian god will not lift a finger to interfere in man's decision. Arminianism is the half sister of atheism.

For example, John Wesley, who was an ardent Arminian and founder of the Methodist Church, admitted that he didn't even believe in the God of the Bible. In a 1766 letter to his brother, Charles Wesley, John Wesley bared his soul and revealed to Charles his innermost thoughts. In that letter, which John Wesley never expected to be revealed publicly, he admitted that he preached a faith that he, himself, did not have. John Wesley felt "borne along" by some unknown force to do so. God would certainly not compel the preaching of a false gospel. It is, therefore, clear that the unknown force bearing John Wesley along to preach the Arminian gospel was the devil. That is an ineluctable conclusion from Wesley's own words:

> In one of my last [letters] I was saying that I do not feel the wrath of God abiding on me; nor can I believe it does. And yet (this is the mystery), **I do**

not love God. I never did. Therefore I never believed, in the Christian sense of the word. Therefore I am only an honest heathen...And yet, to be so employed of God! And so hedged in that I can neither get forward nor backward! Surely there was never such an instance before, from the beginning of the world! If I ever have had that faith, it would not be so strange. **But I never had any other evidence of the eternal or invisible world than I have now; and that is none at all**, unless such as faintly shines from reason's glimmering ray. **I have no direct witness (I do not say, that I am a child of God, but) of anything invisible or eternal.**

And yet I dare not preach otherwise than I do, either concerning faith, or love, or justification, or perfection. And yet I find rather an increase than a decrease of zeal for the whole work of God and every part of it. I am borne along, I know not how, that I can't stand still. **I want all the world to come to what I do not know.**[90]

Wesley was 63 years old when he wrote that letter. The dirty secret of Wesley is that he was a heathen, who did not believe in God. He preached a false gospel about a false god, in whom he did not really believe. How could Wesley so successfully preach a false gospel? Because people had been accustomed to ignoring God's words and accepting a contradictory gloss to those words. This process was born with heliocentricity, where it was necessary for the "Christian" churches to accommodate the new science of heliocentricity by reinterpreting God's word to conform with that so-called "science." The Arminian god appears nowhere in the scriptures.

Wesley's Arminianism was only a hair's breadth from

atheism. There is little difference between the Arminian god, who minds his own business and leaves his creatures to their own devices, and no god at all. It is no wonder then that Wesley did not believe in God. His Arminian theology created a god in whom it is easy to lose belief. The devil, that subtle beast, could not have designed it any better.

The God of the Bible, on the other hand, is a loving God, who effectually intervenes to save his elect. God's word is clear. One is saved not by one's own will or efforts in keeping God's law. Instead, we are born again by God's grace through faith in Jesus Christ. "Jesus answered and said unto him, Verily, verily, I say unto thee, Except a man be born again, he cannot see the kingdom of God." (John 3:3) A man cannot birth himself. To be spiritually reborn requires the intervention of God.

In Isaiah 44:21-22, God makes it clear that he alone is the creator of his elect in the same way that he alone is the creator who stretched forth the heavens above and spread out the earth beneath. A ball is not spread out. You spread out things that are flat, like a flat bedspread. God is explaining that he alone created a flat earth just as he alone created and saved his elect. God explains that just as he alone created all things, so also he alone saves his elect. In the same way that it is God alone who creates, it is God alone who saves. In Isaiah 44:21-24, God is linking his sovereignty over his creation of a flat earth with his sovereignty over salvation. Just as God created a flat earth with the canopy of the heavens stretched out above, he also redeemed his elect by blotting out their sins like a thick cloud. "[t]he Lord hath done it." There is no room for man to have helped God create the heavens and the flat earth, so also, there is no room for man to help God redeem his elect by blotting out their transgressions like a thick cloud.

> Remember these, O Jacob and Israel; for thou art my servant: **I have formed thee; thou art my servant**: O Israel, thou shalt not be forgotten of

me. **I have blotted out, as a thick cloud, thy transgressions, and, as a cloud, thy sins**: return unto me; for **I have redeemed thee. Sing, O ye heavens; for the LORD hath done it**: shout, ye lower parts of the earth: break forth into singing, ye mountains, O forest, and every tree therein: for **the LORD hath redeemed Jacob, and glorified himself in Israel. Thus saith the LORD, thy redeemer, and he that formed thee from the womb, I am the LORD that maketh all things; that stretcheth forth the heavens alone; that spreadeth abroad the earth by myself.** (Isaiah 44:21-24)

We, who believe in the Jesus of the Bible, are adopted children of God. God chose us for adoption before the world was created. "**According as he hath chosen us in him before the foundation of the world, that we should be holy and without blame before him in love: Having predestinated us unto the adoption of children by Jesus Christ to himself, according to the good pleasure of his will.**" (Ephesians 1:4-5) Notice that salvation is according to the good pleasure of God's will, not the good pleasure of man's will.

Arminians will argue that to be saved man must of his own free will believe in Jesus. While it is true that faith is necessary for salvation, the source of that faith is Jesus. That's right, Jesus is both the object of one's faith and the source of that faith. Jesus is the author (creator) of saving faith. Hebrews 12:2. God did not just foresee that his elect would believe in him, he predestined that saving faith. Jesus is the finisher of our faith. Jesus sees that faith to its end.

We, who believe in Jesus Christ, were predestined to be glorified with Christ. "**For whom he did foreknow, he also did predestinate to be conformed to the image of his Son, that he** might be the firstborn among many brethren. Moreover whom he did predestinate, them he also called: and whom he called, them he also justified: and whom he justified, them he also glorified.**" (Romans 8:29-30) From beginning to end, salvation is the work of a sovereign God. We are not insignificant beings on an insignificant planet careening through endless space. We are the unique creation of a sovereign God. God created us in his image on a flat immovable Earth, where he watches over us and guides us. He saves his elect according to his sovereign grace through faith in Jesus Christ.

To accept the heliocentric model, it is necessary for a Christian to redefine the words in the Bible to explain away its depiction of the flat earth. Once a Christian is down the road of rejecting God's description of a flat earth in the Bible, it is easy for him to redefine the words in the Bible in other matters of doctrine. For example, Arminians cannot ignore the plain language in the Bible that God predestined his elect for salvation, and so Arminians redefine the word "predestinate." Arminians claim that "predestinate" when referring to God's election of those to be saved is limited to mean only that God knows those who will exercise their free will and believe in Jesus. The Arminian interpretation is that "God, in his divine foresight, looked down through the corridors of time and saw all of those who would choose salvation in Jesus Christ. Having this divine knowledge, He then ratified men's votes of confidence in His ability to save them."[91]

One can perceive in the Arminian doctrine their concept of a far-off god who looks from afar "through the corridors of time" at those who would believe in him. The God of the Bible, however, is not far off. He is near. God is above us walking in the circuit of heaven. "Thick clouds are a covering to him, that he seeth not; and he walketh in the circuit of heaven." (Job 22:14) He is a sovereign potentate, who actively saves his elect. He is not simply a ratifier of man's decisions as purported by Arminians.

God states that he looks upon all the inhabitants of the earth from his habitation in heaven. "From the place of his habitation he looketh upon all the inhabitants of the earth." (Psalms 33:14)

Romans 8:29-30 states that not only did God foreknow, "he also did predestinate." God makes a clear distinction between foreknowing and predestinating. Notice, God "also did predestinate." The Arminians, however, contradict God and misread that passage to say: "he did foreknow, he also did foreknow." That makes no sense. The Bible states that God both foreknew and predestinated his elect.

"Foreknow" is a word that is pregnant with meaning. It not only means to know beforehand, but it also means to love beforehand. The heliocentric Arminian god does not predestinate his elect for salvation, and he does not love them beforehand, he only knows ahead of time those who would believe in him. The Arminian god is not the God of the Bible. The God of the Bible predestined his elect for salvation, whereas the fictional, Arminian god only foreknows those who will believe in him. The Arminian god is an ineffectual ratifier of the decisions of sovereign man.

It is necessary for God to intervene to save us, because we are incapable of saving ourselves. God explains in Ephesians:

> **And you hath he quickened, who were dead in trespasses and sins**; Wherein in time past ye walked according to the course of this world, according to the prince of the power of the air, the spirit that now worketh in the children of disobedience: Among whom also we all had our conversation in times past in the lusts of our flesh, fulfilling the desires of the flesh and of the mind; and were by nature the children of wrath, even as others. But God, who is rich in mercy, for his great love wherewith he loved us, **Even when we were**

> **dead in sins, hath quickened us together with Christ, (by grace ye are saved**;) And hath raised us up together, and made us sit together in heavenly places in Christ Jesus: That in the ages to come he might shew the exceeding riches of his grace in his kindness toward us through Christ Jesus. **For by grace are ye saved through faith; and that not of yourselves: it is the gift of God**:" (Ephesians 2:1-8)

God's grace saves us through faith in Jesus Christ. Arminians protest that man authors his own faith by his free will. However, the Bible expressly states that Jesus is the author of our faith. *See* Hebrews 12:2. Faith is "not of ourselves; it is the gift of God." Ephesians 2:8. God makes that point even more clear in John, where he states emphatically that God gives the power to believe in Jesus Christ unto salvation. The faith that is the basis to be born again does **not** come from the will of man but is rather **"of God."**

> But as many as received him, to them **gave he power** to become the sons of God, even to them that believe on his name: **Which were born, not of blood, nor of the will of the flesh, nor of the will of man, but of God**." (John 1:12-13) (emphasis added)

When God states that he created all things visible and invisible, he means just that. Colossians 1:16-17. He created "all things." You will notice that among the "all things" that God created were "powers." Colossians 1:16. In John 1:12 we see that one of those powers is "power to become the sons of God, even to them that believe on his name." All things "visible and invisible" created by God includes the faith to believe in Jesus Christ. Saving faith is not only faith in Jesus, it is the faith **"of"** Jesus. Galatians 2:16. Jesus is "the author and finisher of our faith." Hebrews 12:2.

Jesus not only created all things, but by him, all things consist, including saving faith. Colossians 1:17. He is in the believer and the believer is in him. John 14:20. Just as God created a stable immovable earth, so also he created a stable immovable faith. His creation (and his faith) is a reflection of who he is. He is a God who reigns righteously over his immovable earth. "Say among the heathen that the LORD reigneth: the world also shall be established that it shall not be moved: he shall judge the people righteously." (Psalms 96:10) The immovable earth he created reflects the rock solid stability of his sovereign and righteous reign as the all-powerful Lord of lords. "Which in his times he shall shew, who is the **blessed and only Potentate, the King of kings, and Lord of lords.**" (1Timothy 6:15)

A heliocentric creator, on the other hand, is a god who seems to have little control over his creation. A heliocentric creator is removed beyond the infinite realm of the vacuum of outer space. The false heliocentric god of Arminianism only foresees what people will do, but he will not intervene in the affairs of men.

Arminians have their god so far out of the picture that they do not allow their god to interfere in any way in the salvation decision. An Arminian believer who exercises his free will to choose to be saved can later exercise that same free will to jettison his salvation. The true God of the Bible is not so fickle. He saves his elect to the uttermost. "Wherefore he is able also to save them to the uttermost that come unto God by him, seeing he ever liveth to make intercession for them." (Hebrews 7:25)

One might think that there must be some passage in the Bible that supports the Arminian theology. No, there is no such Bible passage. In order to suggest that there is biblical authority, the Arminians use the satanic trick of quoting Bible verses out of context. Virtually any false doctrine can be supported by biblical text taken out of context, even to the extent of trying to prove that "there is no God." Indeed, Psalm 14:1 states: "There is no God." It is an accurate quote, but it has been taken out of context.

When we see the passage in context, we see that the quoted clause has quite a different meaning. The entire passage reads: "The fool hath said in his heart, There is no God. They are corrupt, they have done abominable works, there is none that doeth good." Psalm 14:1. The context we see gives quite a different meaning than is intended by our hypothetical atheist. In like manner, Arminians take Bible verses out of context to promote a sense contrary to God's intended meaning.

One example where Arminians twist God's meaning is found in the Bible passage often cited by Arminians to support their unbiblical doctrine that God is willing that everyone in the world should be saved. Arminian churches quote part of 2 Peter 3:9, taken out of context, as authority for their doctrine. This single passage is so key to the Arminian theology that it is the motto of the *Society of Evangelical Arminians*.[92] Their seal contains the statement: **"Not Willing That Any Should Perish"**, which is a clause taken out of context from 2 Peter 3:9.

The Arminians have hijacked the gospel and all of the terms that have traditionally been used in the Christian community to describe orthodox biblical Christianity. An organization calling itself the *Society of Evangelical Arminians* makes no historical sense. While almost all Arminians consider themselves evangelicals, they deny the foundational biblical doctrines that are at the core of what it historically meant to be an evangelical. Dr. Michael Scott Horton, who is the J. Gresham Machen Professor of Systematic Theology and Apologetics, in his article *Evangelical Arminians, Option or Oxymoron?*, explains that it is an oxymoron for an Arminian to be described as an evangelical.

> [T]he evangelicals who faced this challenge of Arminianism universally regarded it as a heretical

departure from the Christian faith. One simply could not deny total depravity, unconditional election, justification by grace alone through faith alone because of Christ alone, and continue to call himself or herself an evangelical. There were many Christians who were not evangelicals, but to be an evangelical meant that one adhered to these biblical convictions. ... Today one can be an evangelical-which has historically meant holding to total depravity, unconditional election, justification by grace through faith alone, the sufficiency of scripture-and at the same time be an Arminian, denying or distorting this very evangelical message.[93]

Franklin Graham, son of Billy Graham, speaking on behalf of the Billy Graham Evangelistic Association, stated: "According to 2 Peter 3:9, the Lord is 'not willing that any should perish but that all should come to repentance.'"[94]

At first glance, it would appear that 2 Peter 3:9 supports what Graham has said. Closer examination of that passage reveals that the passage does not, in fact, support that false Arminian doctrine promoted by Graham. Notice the missing passage. "The Lord is [...] not willing that any should perish, but that all should come to repentance." 2 Peter 3:9.

Those who try to force the square peg of scripture into the round hole of their false doctrine must shave off parts of the Bible to get it to fit. In this case, Graham, as is the practice with all Arminians, shaved that portion of the passage which limits its application to those who are already chosen for salvation. What God means in that passage is that God is not willing that any who have been chosen for salvation by God should perish, but that all those who are saved should come to repentance. Read the entire passage in context, and you will see that God is **"longsuffering to**

us-ward." God is not willing that "us" should perish and that "us" should come to repentance.

> The Lord is not slack concerning his promise, as some men count slackness; **but is longsuffering to us-ward**, not willing that any should perish, but that all should come to repentance. 2 Peter 3:9.

Who are the "us" in 2 Peter 3:9? Simply read the first paragraph of the letter and we see that Peter is writing to "them that have obtained like precious faith with us." "Simon Peter, a servant and an apostle of Jesus Christ, **to them that have obtained like precious faith with us** through the righteousness of God and our Saviour Jesus Christ:" (2 Peter 1:1)

One can see that in 2 Peter 3:9, Peter was stating that God was not willing that any who believe in Jesus should perish. God's will is always done, and man's will cannot thwart God's will. If God has foreordained one to salvation, no one can stay his hand. "And all the inhabitants of the earth are reputed as nothing: and he doeth according to his will in the army of heaven, and among the inhabitants of the earth: and none can stay his hand, or say unto him, What doest thou?" (Daniel 4:35)

While the Arminian salvation is tenuous, the true salvation by and through God is eternal and permanent. **"All that the Father giveth me shall come to me; and him that cometh to me I will in no wise cast out."** (John 6:37)

All who are chosen by the Father for salvation will be saved. Notice in John 6:37 that Jesus made the points that 1) **"All that the Father giveth me,"** 2) **"shall come to me"**; and 3) **"him that cometh to me I will in no wise cast out."** We see: 1) God gives **all** of his elect to Jesus, 2) **all** of his elect will come to Jesus, and 3) **all** of his elect will be securely saved and cannot lose their salvation. John chapter 6 precludes the possibility of falling away from salvation. Chapter 6 of John refutes the Arminian theology. God uses parallelism in John 6:39-40 to lock down what he means when he states that salvation comes by the faith of which he is the author and finisher.

"And this is the Father's will which hath sent me, that **of all which he hath given me I should lose nothing**, but should raise it up again at the last day." (John 6:39)	"And this is the will of him that sent me, that **every one which seeth the Son, and believeth on him, may have everlasting life**: and I will raise him up at the last day." (John 6:40)

Notice that in John 6:40 it states that "every one which seeth the Son, and believeth on him, may have everlasting life." It is those same believers in verse 40 that Jesus states in verse 39 are given to him by the Father: "of all which he hath given me I should lose nothing." That means that all whom the Father has given to Jesus will "believeth on him." God preordained that they would believe in Jesus and gave them to Jesus. Jesus will lose none of those who believe on him. Jesus will "raise him up at the last day." Salvation is locked in once it is given to the believer by the grace of God. "Every" person who believes on Jesus are the same "all" whom the Father has given Jesus. None of those believers will ever be lost; they all have "everlasting life." They "all" will be raised up on the last day.

Just to punctuate the point Jesus made it clear in John 6:44 that "No man can come to me, except the Father which hath sent me draw him: and I will raise him up at the last day." (John 6:44) The very theme of the Bible that salvation is only by the grace of God through faith in Jesus Christ, e.g., Ephesians 2:8. Combine John 6:44 with verses 37, 39, and 40 of John chapter 6, and we see that it is only those who believe in Jesus who can be saved. All whom God has ordained to believe in Jesus will, in fact, believe in Jesus unto salvation. No believer will ever be lost. "All that the

Father giveth me shall come to me; and him that cometh to me I will in no wise cast out." (John 6:37) All believers will inherit eternal life. "I will raise him up at the last day." John 6:40 and 6:44.

On the flip side, without the ordained election of God, no man can believe in Jesus. It is those, and only those, whom God draws to Jesus who will be saved. John 6:44. God's drawing is effectual, all who are drawn will, in fact, believe in Jesus unto salvation. John 6:39-40. All who do not believe in Jesus are ordained by God not to believe in Jesus. "No man can come to me, except the Father which hath sent me draw him." John 6:44.

Jesus ended his discourse in John chapter 6 with that very point. He stated that there were some among his audience who did not believe in him. And Jesus explained why. Because, he stated, "no man can come unto me, except it were given unto him of my Father."

> But there are some of you that believe not. For Jesus knew from the beginning who they were that believed not, and who should betray him. And he said, Therefore said I unto you, that no man can come unto me, except it were given unto him of my Father." (John 6:64-65)

How do Arminians address John chapter 6? They reinterpret the language to say that God's drawing is only effectual for those of their own free will who choose to believe in Jesus. They claim that not all who are drawn will believe in Jesus and be saved. The problem with that interpretation is that it ignores the clauses Jesus put at the end of verses 37, 39, 40, and 44. Those clauses mean that of **all** whom the Father has given to Jesus, he draws **all** of them to Jesus, they **all** will believe in Jesus, and they **all** will be saved. "I will in no wise cast out." John 6:37; "I should lose nothing, but should raise it up again at the last day." John

6:39; I will raise him up at the last day." John 6:40; "I will raise him up at the last day." John 6:44.

The passages in John chapter 6 impeach the entire Arminian construct. How do Arminians address those passages? Arminians ignore their clear language and instead interpret them to mean the opposite of what they say. They do that because there is no real way to reconcile their Arminian theology with God's emphatic statements that salvation comes from his unconditional, effectual, irrevokable, and eternal election.

Ken Johnson, Th.D., is typical in that regard. In his deceptive book, *The Gnostic Origins of Calvinism*, Johnson cites to the verses in John 6:37, 39, and 44 in support of the proposition that "[t]he Holy Spirit draws men to Himself with grace."[95] While that is certainly true, immediately after citing to those Bible passages, Johnson ignores the clear language in those passages to say: "But this drawing can be resisted."[96] How can he make such a statement after typing out three Bible passages, all of which taken together (or even read separately) mean clearly that all those who are drawn by God to Jesus, will in no wise be cast out, but that Jesus will raise them up on the last day? Jesus states emphatically "that of all of which he hath given me, I should lose nothing, but should raise it up again at the last day." John 6:39. Jesus allows no possibility for resisting the drawing of God. The drawing of God is effectual and leads to salvation. Clearly, Dr. Johnson has an Arminian agenda. And his agenda does not include being a faithful witness to the word of God.

All who have faith in Jesus Christ are saved unto eternal life. "Verily, verily, I say unto you, He that believeth on me hath everlasting life." (John 6:47) That faith is a gift from Jesus Christ, who is the author and finisher of that faith. Hebrews 12:2. One must be chosen by God before he can believe in Jesus Christ. John 10:26-30. Those who are not God's elect will not believe in Jesus because they cannot believe in him. "He that is of God heareth

God's words: ye therefore hear them not, because ye are not of God." (John 8:47)

There are two groups of people in the world: 1) those whom God draws to Jesus for salvation, and 2) those whom God does not draw to Jesus for salvation. Those who are drawn by God to Jesus are ordained by God to be saved. Whereas, those who are not drawn by God to Jesus are ordained by God to be damned. "No man can come to me, except the Father which hath sent me draw him: and I will raise him up at the last day." (John 6:44)

There are those, like Judas, who appear for a time to be part of the church, but in the end, they make manifest that they are enemies of the gospel. "They went out from us, but they were not of us; for if they had been of us, they would no doubt have continued with us: but they went out, that they might be made manifest that they were not all of us." (1 John 2:19) Judas and others like him went out, not because they were saved and lost their salvation, but rather because from the beginning "they were not of us." That is, they were pretenders to salvation; they were unsaved tares congregating among the saved wheat. Matthew 13:27-43.

Those who do not believe in Christ are lost because God has not chosen them for salvation. Those who are chosen for salvation cannot lose their salvation. John 10:26-30. There is simply no such thing as a person losing his salvation.

> **But ye believe not, because ye are not of my sheep, as I said unto you. My sheep hear my voice, and I know them, and they follow me: And I give unto them eternal life; and they shall never perish, neither shall any man pluck them out of my hand. My Father, which gave them me, is greater than all; and no man is able to pluck them out of my Father's hand. I and my**

Father are one. (John 10:26-30)

There are only two possibilities in the gospel. First, those who are lost cannot believe, because God has not chosen them to believe. The other possibility is the flip side of the first. Those who are chosen to believe will believe, and they cannot ever lose their faith. Jesus promised that "no man is able to pluck them out of my Father's hand." There is no category for persons to be first saved and then for them to overrule God's choice by the power of their free will and "unsave" themselves. Such an occurrence is an impossibility. The only way to build such a theology is to ignore the clear message of the gospel.

God's creation reveals his very character. If people are deceived by heliocentrism, they then have a distorted view of creation and thus a distorted view of their god. Heliocentrism creates in the minds of men a different kind of god. The heliocentric god is a god made after the image of man. Under heliocentrism, man is all-powerful, with the heliocentric god being a far-off helpless and hapless spectator, unable to intervene to save anyone. Indeed, there is very little difference between such a god and no god at all. The whole point of heliocentrism is to remove the God of the Bible from people's minds. As the heliocentric creation does not exist, so also, the heliocentric creator does not exist. All religions that worship a heliocentric creator worship a false god. From that misguided worship flows all manner of false doctrine.

The God of the Bible is real. He is the creator of a flat earth that is at the center of his creation. He intervenes in the affairs of men to effectually save his people. The gospel is simple. Salvation comes only by the grace of God through faith in Jesus Christ. John 6:47; Ephesians 2:8-10. No man can be saved unless God elects to save him. John 6:65. All whom God elects to save will be saved. John 6:39.

God makes one a Christian. God must change your heart. As Jesus said, a man must be born again. John 3:3. No man is born of himself. One must be born of God. "Know ye that the LORD he is God: it is he that hath made us, and not we ourselves; we are his people, and the sheep of his pasture." (Psalms 100:3) Salvation is not by the will of man. "Which were born, not of blood, nor of the will of the flesh, nor of the will of man, but of God." John 1:13. God must draw you. John 6:44. Unless God draws a man, he will have no desire to be a Christian.

Man by nature is spiritually dead. God must quicken you, that is, make you spiritually alive. Ephesians 2:1-10. You then become a new spiritual creation through God's Holy Spirit.

There is no way that a man would accept those things written in the Holy Bible unless God has first opened his heart to the spiritual truths in the Bible. If one accepts that Jesus Christ is Lord God, the creator of the universe who reigns from heaven, he should submit completely to his authority. Ask the Lord in prayer to help you and he will. "And straightway the father of the child cried out, and said with tears, Lord, I believe; help thou mine unbelief." Mark 9:24.

Understand this simple truth, that if you ask Jesus to save you, he will. Mark 9:23-24. You will not, indeed you cannot, unless God draws you and gives you the ability to do so. He will then give you the gift of the Holy Spirit. Pray to Jesus for salvation.

> And he said unto them, Which of you shall have a friend, and shall go unto him at midnight, and say unto him, Friend, lend me three loaves; For a friend of mine in his journey is come to me, and I have nothing to set before him? And he from within shall answer and say, Trouble me not: the door is now shut, and my children are with me in

bed; I cannot rise and give thee. I say unto you, Though he will not rise and give him, because he is his friend, yet because of his importunity he will rise and give him as many as he needeth. And I say unto you, **Ask, and it shall be given you; seek, and ye shall find; knock, and it shall be opened unto you. For every one that asketh receiveth; and he that seeketh findeth; and to him that knocketh it shall be opened.** If a son shall ask bread of any of you that is a father, will he give him a stone? or if he ask a fish, will he for a fish give him a serpent? Or if he shall ask an egg, will he offer him a scorpion? If ye then, being evil, know how to give good gifts unto your children: how much more shall your heavenly Father give the Holy Spirit to them that ask him? (Luke 11:5-13)

Those that ascribe to the free will mythology will cite the above passage as authority for their position that the source of faith is the will of man. However, that passage says nothing of the source of the faith, the passage simply explains the result of faith.

Faith comes from God, it is a gift; he will shower you with his merciful grace if you ask him. You must humble yourself before Almighty God and ask for his mercy and grace. The only way that you can come to Christ is if he draws you and causes you to ask him to save you. John 6:44. "**Blessed is the man whom thou choosest, and causest to approach unto thee**, that he may dwell in thy courts: we shall be satisfied with the goodness of thy house, even of thy holy temple." (Psalms 65:4) John explains the gospel as follows:

> For whatsoever is **born of God** overcometh the world: and this is the victory that overcometh the world, even our **faith**. Who is he that overcometh

the world, but **he that believeth that Jesus is the Son of God**? (1 John 5:4-5)

1. Whoever is born of God overcomes the world.
2. The victory of being born again by which one overcomes the world is by faith.
3. All who overcome the world by being born again have faith to believe Jesus is the Son of God.

The vital point that is missed by those that adhere to the Arminian error that man, of his own free will, can choose for himself whether or not to believe in Jesus is that God's elect cannot birth themselves. Jesus could not have been more explicit in expressing that being born again is entirely outside the control of God's elect. Just as a person has no control over his physical birth, so also he has no control over his spiritual birth.

Jesus analogized the Spirit of God that brings the new birth to the wind. Jesus explained that just as the wind is entirely outside the control of the person affected by the wind, so also is the Spirit of God, which brings spiritual rebirth, outside the control of those elected to be born again. While the wind itself is invisible, the effect of the wind can be seen. The spiritual change of the new birth, like the wind, is invisible, but, like the effect of the wind, the effect of the spiritual new birth can be seen in the conversation and charity of the elect.

> That which is born of the flesh is flesh; and that which is born of the Spirit is spirit. Marvel not that I said unto thee, Ye must be born again. The wind bloweth where it listeth, and thou hearest the sound thereof, but canst not tell whence it cometh, and whither it goeth: so is every one that is born of the Spirit. (John 3:6-8)

Jesus could not have been clearer in chapter 3 of John.

Being born again requires a spiritual miracle from God. God describes salvation as necessitating a new birth. He did that to make it understandable that salvation is outside the control of the elect and is 100% up to God and is 100% performed by God. That is what it means to be "born of God." The gospel is unambiguous on this point. Salvation is by the grace of God alone, through faith alone, in Jesus Christ alone. God's grace means that it is God alone, by his solitary discretion, who elects those who will believe in him. Those who reject that truth have rejected the gospel; they are enemies of the gospel and are under a curse from God.

> But though we, or an angel from heaven, preach **any other gospel** unto you than that which we have preached unto you, **let him be accursed**. As we said before, so say I now again, If any man preach **any other gospel** unto you than that ye have received, **let him be accursed**. (Galatians 1:8-9)

Please do not miss the context of God's curse spoken of in Paul's letter to the Galatians. Paul explicitly stated in the two immediately preceding verses leading up to that curse that the curse flows directly from preaching a false gospel that removes the hearer from the truth of the grace of Christ. "I marvel that ye are so soon removed from him that called you into the grace of Christ unto another gospel: Which is not another; but there be some that trouble you, and would pervert the gospel of Christ." (Galatians 1:6-7) That is exactly what the Arminian gospel does; it removes people from the truth of the grace of Christ. The Arminian philosophy of the free will of man perverts the gospel of Christ. It is a devilish anti-grace gospel that indoctrinates the hearer to believe that the decision to be saved, as well as the decision to change his mind and be unsaved, is entirely within his own control. Contrary to the true gospel, the Arminian believer is the author and finisher of his own faith. Under the cursed Arminian gospel, man is sovereign over Almighty God.

The hell-bound pastors who preach the corrupted Arminian gospel are like the cursed scribes and Pharisees. They gather unto themselves followers who are made twofold more children of the devil than themselves.

> Woe unto you, scribes and Pharisees, hypocrites! for ye compass sea and land to make one proselyte, and when he is made, ye make him twofold more the child of hell than yourselves. (Matthew 23:15)

Those cursed whited sepulchers will stand before Jesus and plead that in preaching their cursed Arminian gospel they were all along in concord with God. They are in for a rude awakening. Jesus cursed them to hell from birth; Jesus never knew them.

> Many will say to me in that day, Lord, Lord, have we not prophesied in thy name? and in thy name have cast out devils? and in thy name done many wonderful works? And then will I profess unto them, I never knew you: depart from me, ye that work iniquity. (Matthew 7:22-23)

God, by his grace, gives his elect the new spiritual birth. John 3:3; Ephesians 1:11; 2:5; James 1:18. Upon being born again, a person believes in Jesus Christ. John 3:15-16; Ephesians 2:8. He is then saved from the eternal punishment for his sins and inherits eternal life in heaven. John 3:36; 5:24; 6:40. Only those elected by God for eternal life will believe the gospel. John 6:36-37, 39-40, 44, 47, 65; 10:26-30. Jesus Christ is not only the object of the faith, he is also the source of the faith. Hebrews 12. Saving faith is **not** from the free will of the believer, it is a gift from God. John 1:13; 1Peter 1:3; Ephesians 2:8; Romans 3:22; 4:16; 2 Timothy 1:9. That is why the Bible describes saving faith as the faith **of** Jesus Christ. Romans 3:3, 22; Galatians 2:16, 20; 3:22; Ephesians 3:12; Philippians 3:9; Revelation 14:12.

5 Corruption of the Gospel Was Prophesied

False teachers brought about the free will corruption of the Gospel during the lives of the apostles. Paul warned in the book of Acts that grievous spiritual wolves would enter in among the Christian believers and pervert the gospel. Paul made clear that the true gospel that he preached was "received of the Lord Jesus" and is, in fact, the "gospel of the grace of God." Paul explicitly stated that the true gospel is based upon God's sovereign grace; he even refers to the gospel as "the word of his grace." For Paul to clearly label the gospel as "gospel of the grace of God" and describe it as the "word of his grace" indicates that God's grace is the fundamental feature of the gospel. The false gospel about which Paul was warning must necessarily be founded upon something other than God's sovereign grace.

> But none of these things move me, neither count I my life dear unto myself, so that I might finish my course with joy, and the ministry, which I have received of the Lord Jesus, to testify the gospel of the grace of God. And now, behold, I know that ye all, among whom I have gone preaching the kingdom of God, shall see my face no more. Wherefore I take you to record this day, that I am

pure from the blood of all men. For I have not shunned to declare unto you all the counsel of God. Take heed therefore unto yourselves, and to all the flock, over the which the Holy Ghost hath made you overseers, to feed the church of God, which he hath purchased with his own blood. For I know this, that after my departing shall grievous wolves enter in among you, not sparing the flock. Also of your own selves shall men arise, speaking perverse things, to draw away disciples after them. Therefore watch, and remember, that by the space of three years I ceased not to warn every one night and day with tears. And now, brethren, I commend you to God, and to the word of his grace, which is able to build you up, and to give you an inheritance among all them which are sanctified. (Acts 20:24-32)

What was the nature of the corruption of the gospel that Paul warned about in Acts? In his letter to the Galatians, Paul explained more explicitly the nature of the false gospel that would be preached by the minions of Satan. Paul wrote to the Galatians regarding his concern for those who would be so soon removed from the gospel of the grace of Christ and follow after "another gospel." The context of his letter suggests the nature of this new and different gospel.

Paul, an apostle, (not of men, neither by man, but by Jesus Christ, and God the Father, who raised him from the dead;) . . . I marvel that ye are so soon removed from him that called you into the grace of Christ unto another gospel: Which is not another; but there be some that trouble you, and would pervert the gospel of Christ. But though we, or an angel from heaven, preach any other gospel unto you than that which we have preached unto you, let him be accursed. As we said before, so say I now again, If any man preach any other gospel unto you than that ye have received, let him be accursed. For do I now persuade men, or God? or do I seek to please men? for if I yet pleased men, I should not be the servant of Christ. But I certify you, brethren, that the gospel which was preached of me is not after man. For I neither received it of man, neither was I taught it, but by the revelation of Jesus Christ. (Galatians 1:1, 6-12)

Paul starts by stating emphatically that he was an apostle not of or by men but by Jesus Christ and God the Father. He sets the tone at the outset by stating a foundational principle of Christianity, the sovereign grace of God, to distinguish it from the theology of the false gospel being followed by the Galatians. The context of Paul's admonition indicates the nature of the false gospel which the Galatians were following. Notice that they were being removed from the "grace of Christ" to another gospel. That other gospel would be something other than the grace of Christ. Satan, who is the great adversary of God, can be expected to have theological doctrines which are contrary to the theology of God. The opposite of the sovereign grace of Christ would be the free will of man.

Paul states that if any man preaches any other gospel than the one that they have received from him let him be accursed. Paul then asks a rhetorical question: "For do I now persuade men, or God?" That question is a clear reference to the nature of the accursed false gospel. The false gospel involves the persuasion of the free will of man. Paul's rhetorical question gives us another clue as to the nature of the false gospel; the false gospel involves the persuasion of God. That is, in the false gospel, man by his free will chooses to be saved and thus persuades God to save him. Under the corrupt gospel, instead of God sovereignly choosing his elect, the sinner persuades God to save him.

Paul makes clear that the gospel that he preached was "not after man." What does he mean by the term "not after man?" He means that the gospel of Christ is not a gospel which is based on the free will of man.

In the next sentence, he makes it clear that the gospel of Christ that he preaches is a gospel which he received by "revelation of Jesus Christ." Just as the gospel was received through the revelation of Jesus Christ, so also is the salvation facilitated by revelation, and that revelation comes from Jesus Christ, not man. Paul states clearly in verses 3 and 4 that Jesus came to deliver us from our sins, not according to our will, but rather "according to the will of God and our Father."

> Grace be to you and peace from God the Father, and from our Lord Jesus Christ, Who gave himself for our sins, that he might deliver us from this present evil world, **according to the will of God and our Father**: (Galatians 1:3-4)

The grace of God is the very heart of the gospel of Jesus Christ. Anyone who preaches anything else is under a curse. While explaining that the true gospel is based upon the grace of God, Paul emphasized, by repeating it twice, that any man who preaches any other gospel is under a curse from God.

> But though we, or an angel from heaven, preach any other gospel unto you than that which we have preached unto you, let him be accursed. As we said before, so say I now again, If any man preach any other gospel unto you than that ye have received, let him be accursed. (Galatians 1:8-9)

6 The Occult Origins of Heliocentrism

Arminianism flowed from an agent of Rome, Jacobus Arminius, to the Protestant churches. It is no surprise, therefore, to find that Rome is inserting heliocentrism into the Protestant churches. The heliocentric model theorizes that the earth orbits the sun as it also spins. It is the seminal scientific theory from which all scientific deception flows. Heliocentrism is not based upon science; it is based upon religious superstition. So-called scientists have concluded that the earth orbits the sun. Whom do we find being credited with discovering the so-called scientific truth of an orbiting, spinning, spherical earth? None other than a Roman Catholic priest, Nicolaus Copernicus (1473-1543).

George William Rutler, writing for the Catholic Education Resource Center, reveals that Copernicus was a Catholic priest who was the temporary administrator of the diocese of Frauenburg. His priestly status was confirmed by DNA analysis that established that Copernicus was buried in the Polish cathedral of Frombork.[97] A fact the Roman Catholic Church does not want to be known is that Copernicus dedicated his seminal book creating a heliocentric model, *On the Revolutions of the Celestial Spheres,* to Pope Paul III, whom he addressed as "most Holy

Father."[98] Copernicus' dedication suggests that he was surrounded by Catholic clergy, who shepherded him and his heliocentric work. Indeed, he reveals in that dedication that Nicolaus Schonberg, the Roman Catholic Cardinal of Capua, was first among his friends who had encouraged him not to abandon his heliocentric study and writing. Another person Copernicus identified as spurring him on to publish his book was his "very dear friend, Tiedemann Giese, [Roman Catholic] Bishop of Culm."[99]

One might think that it is impossible that the Roman Catholic hierarchy nourished heliocentrism since the church at that time was stridently geocentric. Indeed, geocentrism was the public position of the Roman Catholic church. Almost 100 years after the publication of Copernicus' theory of heliocentrism Galileo Galilei was put on trial by the Catholic inquisitional court on the charge of heresy for publishing his agreement with the Copernican heliocentric model. Upon the threat of a tortuous death, Galileo was forced to recant his belief in heliocentirsm.

In years prior, such a recantation before the court of the inquisition would nonetheless trigger an automatic examination of the sincerity of his private beliefs under torture. Upon the inquisitional tribunal being satisfied that his private belief was sincere, he, presumably, would be saved from death.[100] But by the time of Galileo's trial, the inquisition adopted a new practice decreed by the pope of merely threatening torture for those of advanced age or ill-health. That accommodation may have been out of concern that the aged and infirm would not survive actual torture. It would seem that the expectation of post-recantation torture would be a disincentive for the aged and infirm to recant heretical beliefs, since their prospect of surviving the torture session would be bleak. In any event, Galileo was spared the regimen of post-recantation torture.[101] After his recantation, Galileo was sentenced to life in prison, but that sentence was commuted to house arrest.

Things are not what they seem with the Roman Catholic Church. The Romish Church is a duplicitous occult religion. It's public pronouncements cannot be trusted as the true position of the church. The warp and woof of the Vatican is riddled with Machiavellian intrigue.

For example, the modern Catholic Church presents a public stance that is vocally against abortion. But behind the scenes, the Catholic Church funds pro-abortion organizations. The Catholic Campaign for Human Development (CCHD) gives millions of dollars in grants to numerous radical left organizations, which include organizations that advocate and fund abortions.

CCHD was founded in 1970 as the Catholic bishops' anti-poverty program. In 1997 CCHD funded the following organizations, all of which endorsed the National Organization for Women's (NOW) 1996 "Fight for the Right" [to abortion] march in San Francisco: Association of Community Organizations for Reform Now (ACORN) ($310,000 grant from CCHD), Asian Immigrant Women Advocates ($20,000 grant from CCHD), the Center for Third World Organizing (CTWO) ($25,000 grant from CCHD), the Chinese Progressive Association ($30,000 grant from CCHD), and the Santa Clara Center for Occupational Safety and Health ($30,000 grant from CCHD).[102] ACORN was a co-sponsor of the February 1996 conference of the Feminist Majority Foundation which advocates abortion rights. The CTWO advocates homosexual marriage laws. CTWO in turn sponsors WAGE (Winning Action for Gender Equality), which is harshly critical of those such as Christians who support the traditional nuclear family and Christian values.

CCHD funds many radical left and communist front organizations indirectly by funding coalitions of allegedly charitable groups.[103] For example, in 1997 CCHD awarded a grant to Greater Birmingham Ministries, which in turn sponsored another coalition, Alabama Arise. Members of Alabama Arise included the AFL-CIO and the American Civil Liberties Union (ACLU).[104] CCHD also awarded a grant to the Philadelphia Unemployment Project Coalition for JOBS; that coalition included AFSCME locals, the Pennsylvania AFL-CIO, the state chapter of NOW, and the Woman's Law Project (WLP).[105] NOW is an aggressive proponent of abortion and special sodomite rights. NOW supports partial birth abortions and opposes any restriction on abortion, including parental notification. The WLP is a legal services provider in Philadelphia that advocates lesbian and homosexual parenting rights and abortion rights. AFSME and the AFL-CIO both contribute to groups that advocate abortion rights and homosexual "marriage." The ACLU is the leading opponent of religious freedom in schools and opposes restrictions on abortions.

Some might argue that the Catholic bishops just made some errors. The evidence, however, suggests that the leftist anti-American, anti-Christian, and pro-abortion slant to the CCHD grants is knowing and purposeful. For the past ten years the Capital Research Center has publicized to all who would listen the radical left slant to the CCHD grants, but the CCHD has done little to nothing to curtail the support of the radical anti-Christian left.[106]

The CCHD responded in 1998 to criticism by proposing changes to its guidelines. The new guidelines were adopted, and they specifically forbade the CCHD from awarding grants to organizations which "promote or support abortion, euthanasia, the death penalty, or any other affront to human life and dignity."[107] Apparently the new guidelines were merely lip service, designed to appease conservative Catholics. There, in fact, was no significant change in the grants by the CCHD. The CCHD continued to funnel money to radical left, communist, and pro abortion organizations.

For Example, not only did the CCHD not cut off its funding of ACORN in 1999-2000, they increased the funding for

17 state and local chapters of ACORN by 18%, to a total of $517,000.[108] The CCHD also continued to fund the Philadelphia Unemployment Project during 1999-2000. The project's "Jobs Campaign" coalition includes a branch of ACORN, AFSCME locals, the Pennsylvania and Philadelphia AFL-CIO, the state chapter of NOW, and the Women's Law Project, all of which support abortion rights.[109]

In addition, the CCHD continues its perennial financial support to affiliates of the Industrial Areas Foundation (IAF). IAF was founded by Saul Alinsky, who was author of *Rules for Radicals*, which is a bible for left-wing political protest groups.[110] The CCHD is carrying out the official, but covert, un-American and anti-Christian policies of the Roman Catholic Church. Suzanne Belongia, CCHD director in Winona, Minnesota, in an attempt to defend CCHD pointed out that Pope John Paul II, officially endorsed CCHD when he visited Washington, D.C., early in his pontificate.[111]

The information about the CCHD grants gives us a little peak at the wolf under the sheep's clothing. Politician Huey Long once said, "if you have a reputation as an early riser, you can sleep until noon."[112] Publicly the Catholic Church is against abortion and for traditional Christian family values; while behind the scenes the Roman church is financially supporting pro-abortion and anti-Christian groups. The CCHD reveals the Roman Catholic Church as the consummate Machiavellian political organization.

The Vatican presents a public facade of righteousness. That public facade, however, is a smokescreen that conceals an anti-Christian agenda. The priestcraft of the Vatican are the spiritual progeny of the hypocritical scribes and Pharisees, condemned by Jesus. Matthew 23:13-15. The Pharisees presented a public facade of honoring and serving God, while secretly worshiping and serving Satan.

> Ye hypocrites, well did Esaias prophesy of you, saying, This people draweth nigh unto me with their mouth, and honoureth me with their lips; but their heart is far from me. But in vain they do worship me, teaching for doctrines the commandments of men. Matthew 15:7-9. See also Isaiah 29:13.

Jesus was not using hyperbole when he told the Jews that "[y]e are of your father the devil, and the lusts of your father ye will do." (John 8:44) Neither is it hyperbole to call the Catholic curia an occult priestcraft. The Roman Catholic Church funds organizations that work to undermine biblical standards, all the while claiming to uphold those very standards. It is not surprising then that almost 400 years ago the Machiavellian Roman Church would publically uphold the biblical standard of geocentricity and condemn Galileo for his writings about heliocentrism while at the same time funding and supporting the very heliocentrism espoused by Galileo.

The Vatican is truly the habitation of seducing spirits "speaking lies in hypocrisy." See 1 Timothy 4:1-3. A hypocrite is a person who pretends to have religious beliefs or morals that are the opposite of his behavior. The Roman Catholic hierarchy are the same as the hypocrites that Jesus criticized.

> Ye hypocrites, well did Esaias prophesy of you, saying, This people draweth nigh unto me with their mouth, and honoureth me with their lips; but their heart is far from me. But in vain they do worship me, teaching for doctrines the commandments of men. (Matthew 15:7-9)

The heliocentric model is a religious doctrine. That religious doctrine is being passed off as science. Copernicus died in 1543 on the day his book, *On the Revolutions of the Celestial*

Spheres, was published. Copernicus was the man chosen to bring the heathen philosophy of heliocentrism into the Christian church. The heliocentric theory removed the earth as the center of creation and challenged the entire ancient authority of the Bible regarding the universe and its origins. Heliocentricity is the progenitor of the theory of evolution and indeed all of the Satanic philosophies of the modern age. That was the whole idea behind heliocentrism. Heliocentrism is not some new scientific discovery; it finds its origins in the ancient mystery religions.

Most people do not know that Copernicus did not originate the theory that the earth revolves around the sun. Heathen philosopher Aristarchus of Samos (310 – 230 B. C.) postulated that the earth rotates on an axis daily and orbits the sun annually. Another heathen philosopher, Pythagoras (circa 500 B.C.), had a similar model of planets (which purportedly included the sun) orbiting around a central, invisible fire.

Johannes Kepler (1571-1630 A.D.) called Pythagoras the "grandfather of all Copernicans."[113] Copernicus, himself, insisted that his system was not an innovation, but was rather a revival of the lost doctrine of Pythagoras.[114] Galileo Galilei (1564-1642 A.D.) viewed the papal edict of 1616 as a suppression of the "Pythagorean opinion of the mobility of the earth."[115]

Master Mason Dr. James Anderson, founder of the London Masonic Lodge, stated in his book, *Defence of Masonry*, that Freemasonry descended from Pythagoras.[116] Master Mason William Hutchinson noted in his book, *Spirit of Masonry*, that ancient Masonic records indicate that the foundation of Freemasonry is in Pythagorean principles.[117] Another Master Mason, William Preston, in his *Illustrations of Masonry*, states that Pythagoras was initiated into the deep mysterious Masonic principles, which he then spread to the countries in which he traveled.[118]

The philosophies of both the Jewish mystics and Pythagoras are rooted in occult Babylonianism. The fact that the Pythagorean theorem, for which Pythagoras is famous, was known by the Babylonians a thousand years before Pythagoras testifies to the Babylonian origins of his philosophy.[119] S. Pancoast, who was a physician to the infamous occult theosophist H.P. Blavatsky, states that Pythagoras was a Kabbalist of the highest order.[120] He further says that the symbols of Masonry are Kabbalistic, and were known to Pythagoras.[121] Pancoast reveals that Pythagoras' initiation into the secrets of the Kabbalah led Pythagoras to the heliocentric philosophy. Pythagoras obtained his heliocentric philosophy through the Jewish Kabbalah.

Freemasonry can be traced to Pythagoras and is a religion that is founded upon the Jewish Kabbalah. Albert Pike states in *Morals and Dogma* that "Masonry is a search for Light. That leads us directly back, as you see, to the Kabbalah."[122] Albert Mackey, in his authoritative Encyclopedia of Freemasonry, confirms Albert Pike's averment. Mackey states that the Kabbalah, being "[t]he mystical philosophy or theosophy of the Jews, ... is intimately connected with the symbolic science of Freemasonry."[123]

One of the key points revealed in the Protocols of the Learned Elders of Zion is the secret use of ostensibly Gentile nations and institutions to further Jewish Zionist aims while hiding the Jewish influence over those institutions. In the Protocols, the Learned Elders of Zion state that they have used Masonry as a cover to hide their involvement in the plan for a "new world order."[124]

The Gentile facade of Freemasonry offers the Zionist Jews the perfect cover. We can see the same hidden control by Jews over the "Christian" Zionist movement. Freemasonry is based upon Judaism.[125] It is a Gentile front for Jewish mysticism, whose history, grades, and official appointments, are rooted in Jewish theosophy.[126]

The authoritative Rabbi Isaac Wise confirms that the Gentile nature of Freemasonry is only a cover: "Freemasonry is a Jewish establishment, whose history, grades, official appointments, passwords, and explanations are Jewish from beginning to end."[127]

What are the religious doctrines flowing from the Kabbalah that form the foundation of Freemasonry? It is the worship of Lucifer. Albert Pike, the theological pontiff of Freemasonry, explains:

> That which we must say to a crowd is—We worship a God, but it is the God that one adores without superstition. To you, Sovereign Grand Inspectors General, we say this, that you may repeat it to the Brethren of the 32nd, 31st, and 30th degrees—The Masonic Religion should be, by all of us initiates of the high degrees, maintained in the purity of the Luciferian Doctrine. If Lucifer were not God, would Adonay whose deeds prove his cruelty, perfidy and hatred of man, barbarism and repulsion for science, would Adonay and his priests, calumniate him? Yes, Lucifer is God, and unfortunately Adonay is also God. For the eternal law is that there is no light without shade, no beauty without ugliness, no white without black, for the absolute can only exist as two gods: darkness being necessary for light to serve as its foil, as the pedestal is necessary to the statue, and the brake to the locomotive. Thus, the doctrine of Satanism is a heresy; and the true and pure philosophical religion is the belief in Lucifer, the equal of Adonay; but Lucifer, God of Light and God of Good, is struggling for humanity against Adonay, the God of Darkness and Evil.[128]

Adonay is the Hebrew word used in the Old Testament that is the name for God and is translated into English in the Bible as "Lord." Pike blasphemously calls God "the God of Darkness and Evil." Pike calls Lucifer, the "God of Good." Pike admits that Lucifer is the Masonic god of light. "And no marvel; for Satan himself is transformed into an angel of light." (2 Corinthians 11:14) In his authoritative treatise, that is to this day the doctrinal Bible of Masonry, *Morals and Dogma,* Pike pays homage to the god of Freemasonry: "Lucifer, the Light-Bearer! Strange and mysterious name to give to the Spirit of Darkness! Lucifer, the Son of the Morning! Is it he who bears the light, and with its splendors intolerable blinds feeble, sensual or selfish Souls? Doubt it not!"[129] Lucifer's name, in fact, means "light bearer." The Masonic initiation ceremonies find the candidate repeatedly seeking more light. If the candidate reaches the highest degree of Freemasonry, he will be informed that the light he seeks is found in the light bearer, Lucifer, who is the god of Freemasonry.

Manly P. Hall, 33° Freemason and highly respected Masonic authority, explains that "[w]hen the Mason learns that the key to the warrior on the block is the proper application of the dynamo of living power, he has learned the mystery of his Craft. The seething energies of Lucifer are in his hands and before he may step onward and upward, he must prove his ability to properly apply energy."[130]

Lucifer being the god of Freemasonry is understandable, since Freemasonry is based upon Judaism, and the god of Judaism is Satan. Infamous Satanist Anton LaVey was the founder of the Church of Satan and the author of the Satanic Bible. LaVey's 1992 authorized biography was written by LaVey's intimate associate and High Priestess of the Church of Satan, Blanche Barton. The biography was written by a Satanist, about a Satanist, for Satanists. LaVey reveals in his biography that he was sympathetic to communism. It is, therefore, no surprise to find out that LaVey was also an ardent Zionist. He was intimately involved with militant Israeli groups in running guns to Israel. LaVey states, with satisfaction, that the vindication of his communist and Zionist involvement came when Assaf Dayan, son of Moshe Dayan, told him that his Satanic Bible contained precisely the religion of Judaism as practiced in Israel.[131]

Judaism is essentially Satanism. It is no surprise, therefore, to learn that Anton LaVey, the founder of the Church of Satan, was a Jew.[132] LaVey changed his name to sound more Gentile, but he was born a Jew named Howard Stanton Levey.[133] Being a Jew also explains why he was such an ardent Zionist. The Times of Israel reveals to its mostly Jewish readership that "[a]s the 'sigil' for his movement, LaVey adopted an inverted pentacle surrounded by the Hebrew letters for Leviathan, a sea monster featured in the Old Testament."[134]

Heliocentrism is a fundamental tenet of the Jewish Kabbalah. Consequently, heliocentrism is central to Freemasonry. Many Masonic lodges throughout the world are named in honor of Copernicus.[135] The link between heliocentrism and Freemasonry explains the close affiliation between Freemasonry and NASA. For example, James Edwin Webb, who was the NASA administrator from 1961-68, was a Freemason. In the November 1969 edition of the Masonic Magazine, *The New Age*, there appeared an article written by 33° Freemason Kenneth S. Kleinknecht, who was the Manager of the Apollo Program Command and Service Modules; the Deputy Manager of the Gemini Program; and the Manager of Project Mercury. Kenneth S. Kleinknecht, by the way, is the brother of C. Fred Kleinknecht, 33°, Sovereign Grand Commander, The Supreme Council (Mother Council of the World), Southern Jurisdiction, USA, Washington.

Both Pythagoras' and Aristarchus' models had generally been rejected by both the scientific communities and the Christian church. That all changed when Copernicus' book was published. There was initially strong resistance to Copernicus' heliocentric system. But the heliocentric camel's nose had been slipped under the tent. It was just a matter of time that the heliocentric view, with the earth and the other planets rotating around the sun, would win popular acceptance in the church. The Roman Catholic Copernicus initiated this.

Roman Catholicism is essentially Kabbalistic Judaism, and like Freemasonry, it is all dressed up for Gentiles. That little known fact is explained in this author's book, *Solving the Mystery of Babylon the Great*. There is a clear parallel between the traditions of the Pharisees of old and those of modern Roman Catholic priestcraft. The Roman Catholic Church follows the practice of the Jews and calls the combination of man's tradition and God's word "the Word of God." To a Protestant Christian, the word of God means the Holy Bible. However, to the Roman Catholic, it means the Holy Bible plus their traditions.

The liturgy of the Kabbalah was injected into the state religion of Rome, which became the Roman Catholic Church.[136] *The Roman Catholic Encyclopedia* explains that the Jewish liturgy was carried over to the Roman Catholic Church.

> The meaning of the word liturgy is then extended to cover any general service of a public kind. **In the Septuagint it (and the verb leitourgeo) is used for the public service of the temple (e.g., Exodus 38:27; 39:12, etc.). Thence it comes to have a religious sense as the function of the priests, the ritual service of the temple** (e.g., Joel 1:9, 2:17, etc.). In the New Testament this religious meaning has become definitely established. In Luke 1:23, Zachary goes home when "the days of his liturgy" (ai hemerai tes leitourgias autou) are over. In Hebrews 8:6, the high priest of the New Law "has obtained a better liturgy", that is a better kind of public religious service than that of the

Temple. **So in Christian use liturgy meant the public official service of the Church, that corresponded to the official service of the Temple in the Old Law.**[137]

Barbara Aho reveals the depth of the similarities between the Roman Catholic liturgy and the Jewish liturgy:

> Little wonder that one Jewish convert to Roman Catholicism made the astounding statement that entering the Catholic Church was not a "conversion" experience for him, but rather a continuation of Judaism. Roy Schoeman, the author of Salvation is from the Jews, confirms as well that the Mass is based on the Jewish ceremonial worship and that Catholic theology is based on the Old Testament!
>
> "As a Jew coming to the Catholic Church, it was natural for me to find the relationship between Judaism and the Catholic Church among the most interesting things in the world. It was obvious to me that for a Jew to enter the Catholic Church wasn't a matter of conversion at all, but was rather simply coming into the fullness of Judaism — into the form that Judaism took after the coming of the Jewish Messiah.
>
> "Although Catholics are aware of this in principle, they often don't think of the Catholic Church as the continuation of Judaism after the Messiah... It's everywhere you look. It's obviously in the Sacrifice of the Mass and the way the Mass is prefigured in Jewish ceremonial worship. It's in the role that the Old Testament, Jewish Scripture have in Catholic theology and the structure of the

Catholic Faith." [Seattle Catholic]

A listing of parallels between Roman Catholicism and Judaism, which have analogues in the Eastern Orthodox Church as well, presented us with the startling prospect that Roman Catholicism may have been a Judaized form of Christianity from its inception. In the list of traditions below, links to the Catholic Encyclopedia show that the Roman Catholic Church justifies most of its practices by appealing to the Old Testament. Even in cases where the New Testament is cited as justification, these practices are not required under the New Covenant but have their basis in Judaism.

Priesthood (cf. Levitical priesthood/mediators between God and men)

Pope (cf. Jewish High Priest)

College of Cardinals (70) (cf. seventy elders of Moses/Deut.17:8)

Confession of sins to priest for forgiveness (cf. Lev.5:5)

Daily sacrifice of the Mass (cf. Daily burnt offering / Heb.10:11)

Altars for sacrifices

Altar vessels of gold and silver

Vestments for priests

Cardinals' skullcap (cf. Jewish yarmulke)

Offertory (cf. Offerings)

Church buildings for worship (cf. Temple)

Liturgy (cf. service of the Temple)

Sunday obligation (cf. Sabbath observance)

Ecclesiastical Feasts (cf. Jewish feasts)

Scapular / Hairshirt (cf. Sackcloth)

Works-based salvation (cf. Mosaic Law)

Sacrament of infant baptism (cf. Rite of Circumcision / Talmud)

Wafer-only Communion (cf. Manna/Shew Bread)

Sacrament of Confirmation (cf. Jewish Bar/Bat Mitzvah)

Burning of candles and incense (cf. Exodus 30)

Holy water font (cf. The Laver / Exodus 40)

No salvation outside the (Catholic) Church (Gentiles must convert to Judaism to be saved)

The following Roman Catholic traditions were not part of the Mosaic Law but were adopted by the Israelites in their apostasy:

Traditions of men (Mark 7:6-13)

Vain repetitions (Lip service (Isa.29:13)

Veneration of saints (Idolatry/pagan gods)

Worship of Mary as Mother of God (Jews worshipped Queen of Heaven / Jer. 44)

Statues/images (images on the walls of Solomon's Temple) (Ezek 8:10)

Demotion of Jesus to Co-Redeemer (cf. Jews' denial of Jesus as Messiah)

Preoccupation with Christ's death rather than resurrection (Jews' denial of Jesus' resurrection)

The above is only a partial catalog of Jewish traditions found in Roman Catholicism. The sacerdotal (priesthood) and daily sacrificial systems alone strongly implicate the Roman Catholic Church as, not only a front for apostate Judaism, but as a vehicle for converting Christians, without their knowledge, to the very religious system that rejected Jesus Christ. One commentary compares the Roman Catholic teaching on salvation to that preached in Judaism:

"The Catholic perspective on salvation is largely 'Judaized' Christianity. In the days of the Apostles, many Jewish Christians believed that Christians had to follow all the requirements of the Mosaic Law, e.g., circumcision, the system of offerings, going to a priest to have sins forgiven, making sacrifices as atonement for sins, etc. A system that requires some type of 'priest' to act as an intercessor between the layperson and God is known as a sacerdotal system (from the Latin word sacerdote, meaning 'priest'.)"

In view of the striking parallels between Roman Catholicism and Judaism, it becomes apparent that Roman Catholicism represents, to a remarkable degree, the triumph of the Judaizers.[138]

As in finance and politics, so also in religion. As Jewish power and influence increases, then the Christian church suffers. Can there be any doubt that the Jews were supporters of Julian in his conquest of Rome? All one need do is read the aims of Julian to perceive the hidden hand of the Jews behind Julian's ascendence to power.

"In the year 360 Julian, a cousin of Constantine, was proclaimed Roman Emperor by the army. Constantine, who had prepared for battle against him, died on the way; this made easier the final victory for Julian and his proclamation as Emperor of the Orient and Occident. The policy of Julian had three principle aims: I. To renew the Pagan belief and to again declare it a state religion of the Empire, so that Rome which according to his view had declined through Christianity, might return to its old glory. II. To destroy Christianity. III. To concede to Jewry its old positions, from which it had been expelled by Constantine and his sons; even the rebuilding of the Temple of Solomon was to be arranged.[139]

As the Jews gained influence, so also did the state increase the persecution of Christians. Fortunately for the Christian community, Julian's reign only lasted 3 years. He died in 363 A.D. However, it was enough for the Jews to kick start a revival in Jewish scholarship in Rome.

> There was a revival of Hebrew studies in Rome, centered around the local yeshiva, Metivta de Mata Romi. A number of well-known scholars, Rabbi Kalonymus b. Moses and Rabbi Jacob "Gaon" and Rabbi Nathan b. Jehil (who wrote a great talmudic dictionary, the Arukh), contributed to Jewish learning and development. Roman Jewish traditions followed those practiced in the Land of Israel and the liturgical customs started in Rome spread throughout Italy and the rest of the world.[140]

The Jewish studies in Rome led to the inculcation of Jewish doctrine into the Roman church. The Kabbalah and Talmud are at the root of the Jewish doctrine. Kabbalah is a Hebrew word, which literally translated means "tradition." Nesta Webster in her classic book *Secret Societies and Subversive Movements* explained how the Jewish theology of the Kabbalah was introduced into the Roman Catholic Church by Pope Sixtus IV (1471-1484).

> It was likewise from a Florentine Jew, Alemanus or Datylus that Pico della Mirandola, the fifteenth-century mystic, received instructions in the Cabala and imagined that he had discovered in it the doctrines of Christianity. This delighted Pope Sixtus IV, who thereupon ordered Cabalistic writings to be translated into Latin for the use of divinity students.[141]

Jesus criticized the Pharisees for their religious traditions. Those traditions were oral traditions at that time. Later they were memorialized in the Talmud and the Kabbalah. The Kabbalah and the Talmud today span numerous volumes. Jesus called the Pharisees hypocrites, who masqueraded as religious men, but who were, in reality, irreligious frauds.

Then came to Jesus scribes and Pharisees, which

were of Jerusalem, saying, Why do thy disciples transgress the tradition of the elders? for they wash not their hands when they eat bread. But he answered and said unto them, **Why do ye also transgress the commandment of God by your tradition?** For God commanded, saying, Honour thy father and mother: and, He that curseth father or mother, let him die the death. But ye say, Whosoever shall say to *his* father or *his* mother, It *is* a gift, by whatsoever thou mightest be profited by me; And honour not his father or his mother, *he shall be free.* **Thus have ye made the commandment of God of none effect by your tradition.** *Ye* **hypocrites**, well did Esaias prophesy of you, saying, This people draweth nigh unto me with their mouth, and honoureth me with *their* lips; but their heart is far from me. But **in vain they do worship me, teaching** *for* **doctrines the commandments of men.** (Matthew 15:1-9)

The Pharisees had an outward appearance of piety, to gain political and religious control of the Jews. In secret, however, they practiced an occult doctrine that was only known to its initiates. Lady Queenborough (Edith Miller) explains in her book *Occult Theosophy*:

> The Chaldean science acquired by many of the Jewish priests, during the captivity of Babylon, gave birth to the sect of the Pharisees whose name only appears in the Holy Scriptures and in the writings of the Jewish historians after the captivity (606 B. C). The works of the celebrated scientist Munk leave no doubt on the point that the sect appeared during the period of the captivity. "From then dates the Cabala or Tradition of the Pharisees. For a long time their precepts were only

transmitted orally but later they formed the Talmud and received their final form in the book called the *Sepher ha Zohar*."[142]

The scrupulous observance by the Pharisees of Jewish religious tradition was only a cover for their secret doctrine. They had rejected Jehovah and had adopted the pantheism of Babylon. They pretended that their many rituals were necessary for the worship of Jehovah, but those were only man-made rules to conceal their secret Babylonian religion. Jesus rebuked them for it, calling them hypocrites for their vain worship of God through man-inspired rituals and honoring God with fine words, when their hearts, in fact, were focused on the heathen gods of Babylon. See Mark 7:5-7. The Pharisees had accepted the Satanic lie that they had become "as gods." See Genesis 3:5. Their new Babylonian (a/k/a Chaldean) religion was to be exclusive to the Jews, who were to rule the world. Edith Miller explains:

> The Pharisees, then, judging it wiser to capture the confidence of their compatriots by taking the lead in the religious movement, affected a scrupulous observance of the slightest prescriptions of the law and instituted the practice of complicated rituals, simultaneously however cultivating the new doctrine [i.e. secret doctrine] in their secret sanctuaries. These were regular secret societies, composed during the captivity of a few hundred adepts. At the time of Flavius Josephus which was that of their greatest prosperity, they numbered only some 6,000 members. This group of intellectual pantheists was soon to acquire a directing influence over the Jewish nation. Nothing, moreover, likely to offend national sentiment ever appeared in their doctrines. However saturated with pantheistic Chaldeism they might have been, the Pharisees preserved their

ethnic pride intact. This religion of Man divinised, which they had absorbed at Babylon, they conceived solely as applying to the profit of the Jew, the superior and predestined being. The promises of universal dominion which the orthodox Jew found in the Law, the Pharisees did not interpret in the sense of the reign of the God of Moses over the nations, but in that of a material domination to be imposed on the universe by the Jews. The awaited Messiah was no longer the Redeemer of original Sin, a spiritual victor who would lead the world, it was a temporal king, bloody with battle, who would make Israel master of the world and 'drag all peoples under the wheels of his chariot'. The Pharisees did not ask this enslavement of the nations of a mystical Jehovah, which they continued worshipping in public, only as a concession to popular opinion, for they expected its eventual consummation to be achieved by the secular patience of Israel and the use of human means. [143]

Jesus cursed the Pharisees to their face: "Woe unto you, scribes and Pharisees, hypocrites! for ye are as graves which appear not, and the men that walk over *them* are not aware *of them*." (Luke 11:44) The Babylonian traditions of the Pharisees, which were traditions passed down orally from generation to generation, were eventually (in part) memorialized in the Kabbalah and Talmud. The double aim of the Pharisees was to wrestle political control over the Jews from the Sadducees and "to modify gradually the conceptions of the people in the direction of their secret doctrine."[144] They accomplished both goals. Today Orthodox Jewry is an insular authoritarian society that is completely given over to the practice of the Babylonian religion of the ancient Pharisees.

The twisted Babylonian god of modern Jewry as expressed in the Talmud and Kabbalah is not the merciful God of the Bible, but rather a god of vengeance and hatred against gentiles and particularly Christians. Edith Miller summarizes the nature of the Jewish god as being "just and merciful only to his own people, but foe to all other nations, denying them human rights and commanding their enslavement that Israel might appropriate their riches and rule over them."[145]

Michael Hoffman explains that "[l]ike the Talmud, the Kabbalah supersedes, nullifies and ultimately replaces the Bible."[146] Lawrence Fine, Professor of Jewish Studies and prominent scholar of medieval Judaism and Jewish mysticism, reveals that the Kabbalah contains the "true" meaning of the Old Testament. The "simple" meaning of the biblical language recedes into the background as the symbolic meaning contained in the Kabbalah supersedes the Bible and takes control. There is a code to the true meaning in the Bible that can only be unlocked through the Kabbalah.

> [T]he reader must become accustomed to regarding biblical language in a kabbalistically symbolic way. The Kabbalists taught that the Torah is not only the speech or word of God, but is also the many names of God or expression of God's being. It is a vast body of symbols, which refers to the various aspects of divine life, the sefirot, and their complex interaction. **The simple meaning of biblical language recedes into the background as symbolic discourse assumes control**. The true meaning of Scripture becomes manifest only when it is read with the proper (sefirotic) code. **Thus the Torah must not be read on the simple or obvious level of meaning; it must be read with the knowledge of a kabbalist who possesses the hermeneutical keys with which to unlock its**

***inner* truths.**[147]

The Kabbalah at Zohar III, 152a states: "Thus the tales related to the Torah are simply her outer garments, and woe to the person who regards that outer garb as the Torah itself! For such a person will be deprived of a portion in the world to come."[148] That passage in the Kabbalah puts a curse on anyone who tries to read the Bible for what it actually says, instead of with the mystical gloss put on it by the Kabbalah.

The Kabbalah is Judaic mystical practices that were adopted by the Jews from Babylon. H.P. Blavatsky described the Kabbalah as: "The hidden wisdom of the Hebrew Rabbis of the middle ages derived from the older secret doctrines concerning divine things and cosmogony, which were combined into a theology after the time of the captivity of the Jews in Babylon. All the works that fall under the esoteric category are termed Kabalistic."[149]

The Jewish Encyclopedia acknowledges the Babylonian (a/k/a Chaldean) origins of the Kabbalah (a/k/a Cabala). Also, the Jewish Encyclopedia explains that Gnosticism flowed from the Jews to the ersatz "Christians." That is yet more authority that Gnosticism flowed from Babylon via the Jewish Gnostics to lay the foundation for the Roman Catholic theology. The esoteric Gnosticism imbued in the Catholic theology was based upon the Jewish Kabbalah.

> The Pythagorean idea of the creative powers of numbers and letters, upon which the "Sefer Yez.irah" is founded, and which was known in tannaitic times . . . is here proved to be an old cabalistic conception. In fact, the belief in the magic power of the letters of the Tetragrammaton and other names of the Deity . . . seems to have originated in Chaldea . . . Whatever, then, the

theurgic Cabala was, which, under the name of "Sefer (or "Hilkot" Yez.irah,") induced Babylonian rabbis of the fourth century to "create a calf by magic."

* * *

But especially does Gnosticism testify to the antiquity of the Cabala. Of Chaldean origin, as suggested by Kessler . . . and definitively shown by Anz . . . Gnosticism was Jewish in character long before it became Christian.[150]

Magic and occult mysticism run throughout the Kabbalah. Judith Weill, a professor of Jewish mysticism, stated that magic is deeply rooted in Jewish tradition, but the Jews are reticent to acknowledge it and don't even refer to it as magic.[151] Gershom Scholem (1897-1982), Professor of Kabbalah at Hebrew University in Jerusalem, admitted that the Kabbalah contains a great deal of black magic and sorcery, which he explained involves invoking the powers of devils to disrupt the natural order of things.[152] Professor Scholem also stated that there are devils who are in submission to the Talmud; in the Kabbalah, these devils are called *shedim Yehuda'im*.[153]

The *Jewish Chronicle* revealed that occult practices such as making amulets, charms, and talismans are taught in Jerusalem at the rabbinic seminary Yeshivat Hamekubalim.[154] That is why Jesus said to the Jews: **"Ye are of *your* father the devil, and the lusts of your father ye will do."** John 8:44. The Bible states clearly that the magic arts are an abomination to the Lord.

> There shall not be found among you *any one* that maketh his son or his daughter to pass through the fire, *or* that useth divination, *or* an observer of times, or an enchanter, or a witch, Or a charmer,

or a consulter with familiar spirits, or a wizard, or a necromancer. For all that do these things *are* an abomination unto the LORD: and because of these abominations the LORD thy God doth drive them out from before thee. (Deuteronomy 18:10-12)

The Kabbalah, like the Talmud, graphically blasphemes Jesus. For example, in Zohar III, 282a, the Kabbalah refers to Jesus as a dog who resides among filth and vermin.[155]

There is a clear parallel between the traditions of the Pharisees of old and those of modern Roman Catholic priestcraft. The Roman Catholic Church follows the practice of the Jews and calls the combination of man's tradition and God's word "the Word of God." To a Protestant Christian, the word of God means the Holy Bible. However, to the Roman Catholic, it means the Holy Bible plus their traditions.

> **Sacred Tradition and Sacred Scripture make up a single sacred deposit of the Word of God.** *CATECHISM OF THE CATHOLIC CHURCH*, § 97, 1994.

> [T]he church, to whom the transmission and interpretation of Revelation is entrusted, **does not derive her certainty about all revealed truths from the holy Scriptures alone. Both Scripture and Tradition must be accepted and honored with equal sentiments of devotion and reverence.** *Id.* at § 82 (emphasis added).

The Catholic Church has grafted its tradition onto the word of God. With this sleight of hand, they have deceived people into following doctrines that are directly contrary to God's word as found in the Holy Bible.

The very idea of adding traditions to God's word is based upon the practice of the Jews. Michael Hoffman explains: "The Talmud is Judaism's holiest book (actually a collection of books). Its authority takes precedence over the Old Testament in Judaism. Evidence of this may be found in the Talmud itself, Erubin 21b (Soncino edition): 'My son, be more careful in the observance of the words of the Scribes than in the words of the Torah (Old Testament).'"[156]

In that section of the Talmud, there is a distinction made between the Torah and the Talmud (words of the Scribes). Often, that distinction is not made. Jews often refer to both the Talmud and the Torah as "Torah." As with the Catholic Church calling the combination of their traditions and the Bible, the word of God, so also the Jews say that Torah is the combination of their traditions (Talmud and Kabbalah) and the Old Testament. However, in Orthodox Judaism, the Jewish traditions contained in the rabbinical writing of the Talmud and Kabbalah supersede and supplant the word of God found in the Old Testament (which is also called the Tanakh). That same thing is true regarding Catholic traditions that supplant the word of God.

The Jews teach that Moses was given revelation in two forms on Mount Sinai, oral and written. The smaller revelation was the written Torah, the larger revelation was kept orally. "This 'Oral Torah' had been transmitted faithfully by the leaders of each generation to their successors, by Moses to Joshua, and then to the elders, then to the prophets, to the men of the Great Assembly, to the leaders of the Pharisees, and finally to the earliest rabbis. The earliest rabbis saw themselves as heirs to the Pharisees."[157]

In one statement Jesus exposed the lie that God gave the oral traditions of the Jews to Moses at Mount Sinai. Jesus stated: **"For had ye believed Moses, ye would have believed me: for he wrote of me. But if ye believe not his writings, how shall ye believe my words?"** (John 5:46-47) If Moses had truly given the oral traditions, they would have testified to the authenticity of Jesus as Christ. Since the Jews rejected Jesus, because he contravened their traditions, that is proof that their traditions could not have come from Moses. Michael Hoffman explains that one statement by Jesus "crushed the whole beguiling system of indoctrination predicated on the Pharisaic myth of a divinely inspired, oral tradition of the elders."[158]

Rabbi Ben Zion Bokser admits that the so-called traditions of the Jews that form the foundations of Judaism are entirely extra-biblical. He states that Jews and Christians alike are under the fallacious impression that Judaism is a religion based upon the Hebrew Bible. He says, to the contrary, that "[m]uch of what exists in Judaism is absent in the Bible, and much of what is in the Bible cannot be found in Judaism. . . . **Judaism is not the religion of the Bible.**"[159]

Judaism is based primarily upon the Kabbalah, Talmud, and other rabbinical writings. Where there is a conflict between their traditions (Talmud and Kabbalah) and the Old Testament (Torah), their traditions take precedence. Jews claim that the Talmud is partly a collection of traditions Moses gave them in oral form. Those traditions had not yet been written down in Jesus' time. Christ condemned the traditions of the Scribes and Pharisees because those traditions (which later became written down in the Talmud) nullify the teachings of the Holy Bible. **"Making the word of God of none effect through your tradition**, which ye have delivered: and many such like things do ye." (Mark 7:13)

Rabbi Joseph D. Soloveitchik is regarded as one of the most influential rabbis of the 20th century. He is considered to be the unchallenged leader of Orthodox Judaism and the top international authority on halakha (Jewish religious law). "Soloveitchik was responsible for instructing and ordaining more than 2,000 rabbis, "an entire generation" of Jewish leadership."[160] However, when the N.Y. Times explained his study, the only basis mentioned for his ascendant religious leadership was his study of the Talmud. "Until his early 20s, he devoted himself almost exclusively to the study of the Talmud."[161] There was no mention in the article of the esteemed rabbi's study of the Old Testament (Torah) as the basis for being one of the leading authorities on Jewish law. That is because the Talmud along with the Kabbalah forms the basis for Judaism, and they are largely contrary to the Old Testament (Torah). Hoffman states: "The rabbi's credentials are all predicated upon his mastery of the Talmud."[162] "Britain's Jewish Chronicle of March 26, 1993, states that in religious school (yeshiva), Jews are 'devoted to the Talmud to the exclusion of everything else.'"[163]

To add tradition to God's word is rebellion against God's command that nothing be added or taken away from his words. "Ye shall not add unto the word which I command you, neither shall ye diminish ought from it, that ye may keep the commandments of the LORD your God which I command you." (Deuteronomy 4:2) "What thing soever I command you, observe to do it: thou shalt not add thereto, nor diminish from it." (Deuteronomy 12:32)

There is a terrible curse that comes with adding or taking away from God's word.

> For I testify unto every man that heareth the words of the prophecy of this book, If any man shall add unto these things, God shall add unto him the plagues that are written in this book: And if any man shall take away from the words of the book of this prophecy, God shall take away his part out of the book of life, and out of the holy city, and *from* the things which are written in this book. (Revelation 22:18-19)

The Holy Bible warns us about those who would attempt

to turn us away from Christ to follow the traditions of men.

> Beware lest any man spoil you through philosophy and vain deceit, **after the tradition of men, after the rudiments of the world**, and not after Christ. (Colossians 2:8)

> **Wherefore if ye be dead with Christ from the rudiments of the world, why, as though living in the world, are ye subject to ordinances, (Touch not; taste not; handle not; Which all are to perish with the using;) after the commandments and doctrines of men?** Which things have indeed a shew of wisdom in will worship, and humility, and neglecting of the body; not in any honour to the satisfying of the flesh. (Colossians 2:20-23)

> He answered and said unto them, Well hath Esaias prophesied of you hypocrites, as it is written, This people honoureth me with *their* lips, but their heart is far from me. **Howbeit in vain do they worship me, teaching *for* doctrines the commandments of men. For laying aside the commandment of God, ye hold the tradition of men,** *as* the washing of pots and cups: and many other such like things ye do. And he said unto them, Full well **ye reject the commandment of God, that ye may keep your own tradition.** (Mark 7:6-9)

Jesus said: "I am the bread of life: he that cometh to me shall never hunger; and he that believeth on me shall never thirst." (John 6:35) Very simply, Jesus promised salvation to all who believed on him. Adding any other requirement to faith in Jesus corrupts the gospel, resulting in the bread of death rather than the bread of life.

Jesus warned his disciples to beware of the doctrine of the religious leaders of their time. Jesus compared their doctrine to leaven. Only a little leaven of man-made rules works its way through the whole loaf and corrupts God's pure doctrine. The leaven of today's religious leaders is no different; the leaven of tradition corrupts God's pure word. Man's tradition has turned the Bread of Salvation into spiritual poison killing the souls of those who eat of the corrupted loaf.

Then Jesus said unto them, Take heed and beware of the leaven of the Pharisees and of the Sadducees. And they reasoned among themselves, saying, *It is* because we have taken no bread. *Which* when Jesus perceived, he said unto them, O ye of little faith, why reason ye among yourselves, because ye have brought no bread? Do ye not yet understand, neither remember the five loaves of the five thousand, and how many baskets ye took up? Neither the seven loaves of the four thousand, and how many baskets ye took up? How is it that ye do not understand that I spake *it* not to you concerning bread, that ye should beware of the leaven of the Pharisees and of the Sadducees? **Then understood they how that he bade *them* not beware of the leaven of bread, but of the doctrine of the Pharisees and of the Sadducees**. (Matthew 16:6-12)

A little leaven leaveneth the whole lump. (Galatians 5:9)

God wants us to purge out the leaven of man's tradition.

Your glorying *is* not good. Know ye not that a little leaven leaveneth the whole lump? **Purge out therefore the old leaven, that ye may be a new**

> **lump, as ye are unleavened. For even Christ our passover is sacrificed for us**: Therefore let us keep the feast, not with old leaven, neither with the leaven of malice and wickedness; but with the unleavened *bread* of sincerity and truth. (1 Corinthians 5:6-8)

Man's tradition requires works to earn salvation. Salvation, however, is by God's Grace through faith alone on the completed work of Jesus Christ, who paid for all of our sins on the cross. Good works flow from salvation; good works cannot earn salvation.

> **For by grace are ye saved through faith; and that not of yourselves:** *it is* **the gift of God: Not of works, lest any man should boast. For we are his workmanship, created in Christ Jesus unto good works, which God hath before ordained that we should walk in them.** (Ephesians 2:8-10)

Marshall Hall explained the satanic conspiracy behind the Jewish Kabbalistic foundation of the so-called "science" of heliocentrism, the big bang theory, evolution, and modern psychology with the largely successful objective of degenerating society and corrupting the "Christian" church. Heliocentrism must have a kick-start and that is found in 13th century Jewish Kabbalist Nachmanides' Big Bang Paradigm.[164] It takes time for the big bang to be the force for a distant solar system and so we find Jewish Kabbalist Ben HaKana's 1st century calculation of a 15 billion year old universe providing that time frame.[165] Heliocentrism must be nurtured and promoted and we find Jewish Kabbalist Isaac Luria fulfilling that role.[166]

All of this was done pursuant to a centuries-old secret plan to destroy Bible Credibility by destroying the creation account in the book of Genesis. Thus, the Kabbalistic "science" of heliocentrism infiltrated the church, which weakened its resistance to the theory of evolution. Upon that heliocentric/evolution foundation was laid the godless religion of psychology. All of these religious beliefs masqueraded as science. This put pressure on the Christian church and slowly transformed its Christian morals and ethics away from the Bible and toward the relativistic, heliocentric Cabalism.

Heliocentrism was the required first step on the road to legitimizing a relativistic, big bang, expanding universe of the Jewish sages. Once heliocentrism entered onto the world stage that cosmological fantasy began its progress of undermining the credibility of the Bible. The Cabalistic big bang and expanding universe models needed the mathematical mechanism attached to Copernicanism to transform them from heathen religious mythology to having "scientific" status. Jewish Kabbalist Isaac Luria (1534-1572) declared that the Copernicun model provided "the mechanism that can make the Cosmology of the sages work!"[167]

Whom do we find revealed to the world as the progenitor of the big bang theory? Another Roman Catholic Priest. The Jewish controlled press try their best to conceal the Jewish religious origins of the big bang theory. As is typical of an intelligence operation, the Jewish controlled media have done what is known in the intelligence community as a limited hangout. They admit that the big bang has its origin in religion, but they conceal that it is Babylonian Judaism. They instead steer the public toward their Gentile front-men in the Catholic Church, while they remain in the shadows pulling the strings. In a PBS article titled, *Big Bang Theory: A Roman Catholic Creation*, Edgar Herwick claims that it was a Roman Catholic priest, Monseigneur George Lemaître, who first postulated the big bang theory.[168]

7 The Myth of Gravity

Under the heliocentric theory, the earth is spinning at approximately 1,000 miles per hour at the equator. The heliocentric scientists had a problem with their theory. How could they explain how people, animals, and things do not feel the centrifugal force of the spinning earth? Isaac Newton saved the day with his theory of gravity. Newton's theory of gravity supposedly acts as a centripetal force working against the centrifugal force of the hypothesized spinning earth. Gravity is necessary on a spinning earth. But the earth is not spinning. On a stationary flat earth, there is no centrifugal force. Since there is no centrifugal force, there can be no centripetal force. Hence, there is no gravity, because there is no need for the centripetal force of gravity on a flat, motionless earth.

Newton's theory of gravity is founded upon the premise that all objects are attracted to all other objects based upon their mass. According to the heliocentric model, the force of gravity at the equator is perfectly balanced against the centrifugal force of the spinning earth. All persons and objects are supposedly perfectly balanced through gravity by their mass against the centrifugal force of the spinning earth to remain attached to the earth.

The problem with the gravitational theory is that according to that theory, the gravitational attraction to the earth by all persons and objects remains the same at all places on the earth. That means that the gravitational force at the North Pole is the same as the gravitational force at the equator. That poses a very real problem if the earth is spinning as alleged. That is because the centrifugal force decreases every mile toward the north pole, where the centrifugal force is ultimately reduced to zero, because the North Pole is the axis of the supposedly spinning earth. On a globe, as you travel north or south of the equator the circumference parallel to the equator becomes less. Consequently, the speed of the earth's spin at those more northern and southern latitudes from the equator would be slower than its speed of spin at the equator. For example, at 45 degrees north latitude, the earth's spin should be approximately 700 miles per hour. As the speed of the spin is reduced, so also is the correlative centrifugal force. The spinning earth and the mystical force of gravity are thus proven to be fictions.

Some will point out that objects do have different weights at the equator and the North Pole. However, the difference is the reverse of what would be expected by the interaction between the alleged centrifugal force and the theory of gravity. Objects weigh a fraction of a percentage less at the North Pole than at the equator. The reason has to do with the fact that there is more atmospheric pressure the further one travels towards the equator, which causes the objects at the equator to weigh slightly more.

There is no such thing as gravity; gravity is not necessary on a flat earth. It is density that keeps objects from floating off the surface of the earth. People and objects are heavier than the air and therefore do not float off the ground. Without gravity, a spinning, spherical earth would be impossible. With gravity, it is science fiction.

According to the theory of gravity all things, including the atmosphere, are attracted to earth by gravity. Everything attracted to earth by gravity has weight. For example, helium can be weighed. If you take a steel cylinder and fill it under pressure with a pound of helium, the weight scale will show the increase in weight of one pound due to the added weight of the helium. The theory of gravity requires that the added weight be due to the attraction of gravity.

But if you take that one pound of helium that is in the steel cylinder and use it to inflate a thin rubber balloon, that same one pound of helium that is supposed to be attracted to earth by gravity suddenly is able to break free of the force of gravity and float in the air.

But there is no gravity at play acting on the pound of helium that fills the balloon. What is happening is that the one pound of helium, when released from the steel cylinder into the thin rubber balloon is able to expand. It then has less density than the surrounding air. That lower density (i.e., buoyancy) allows it to float in the air. The balloon filled with one pound of helium floats, not because it is some special anti-gravity gas, but because the helium that has filled the balloon is less dense than the surrounding air.

You are able to walk on the earth, not because you are attracted to earth by gravity, but because you are denser than the surrounding air. A 200-pound man would, on average, weigh approximately 10 pounds, if he was weighed while immersed in water. That is because the surrounding water is denser than air, causing the man to weigh relatively less while immersed in water than he would weigh while on a weigh scale in the atmosphere.

If a man weighed 200 pounds and he put on a 20-pound life jacket while on land he would weigh 220 pounds. If the man put on a life jacket he will not float in the air. He would, in fact, be 20 pounds heavier. If, however, the man jumped into the ocean with that life jacket on, he will find that he will float because he would now be more buoyant than the surrounding water. That is because the life jacket is much less dense than the surrounding water. The added buoyancy of the life jacket is able to keep the 10 pounds of more dense weight of the man afloat in the water. If the man took off the life jacket he would lose the added buoyancy of the life jacket and need to paddle to keep himself afloat. The life jacket is not some anti-gravity device, it simply makes the man less dense (i.e., more buoyant) than the surrounding water.

If the life jacket were an anti-gravity device, it should have the same effect in the thinner atmosphere. Instead, it actually makes a person heavier in the atmosphere. The greater weight has nothing to do with gravity; it has everything to do with the relative density of the surrounding atmosphere. The life jacket is denser than the surrounding atmosphere, but it is less dense than water. We know that because the same life jacket that makes a man heavier on land, makes him lighter in water, allowing him to float in water.

Gravity is a heathen religious belief; it is not true science. The "scientists" promoting gravity are like priests in a religious cult who have immortalized the man who first postulated gravity and follow the gravitational theory like some religious dogma.

The popular cult-like belief in gravity started with Sir Isaac Newton, who was a scientist who published his historic three-volume *Philosophiæ Naturalis Principia Mathematica* (The Mathematical Principles of Natural Philosophy) in 1687. In that book, Newton propounded his laws of motion and universal gravity. Newton is viewed by most in the scientific community as the seminal theoretician for the postulation of gravity.

Gravity is not supported by any scientific proof. What then was the source of the theory? S. Pancoast reveals that "the law of attraction and repulsion" in the Kabbalah was popularized under the name "gravity" by Isaac Newton.[169] S. Pancoast states that Pythagoras was never permitted to declare publicly what he knew and believed. He taught his immediate pupils his heathen philosophy obtained from the Kabbalah, under the most binding obligation of secrecy. Pythagoras' occult system included the great secret of the law of attraction and repulsion (i.e. gravity). "Over a millennium later, Newton was led to the discovery of these forces by his studies of the Kabbalah."[170]

What most do not know is that Isaac Newton was a religious mystic, who was very well studied in Judaism, and Jewish texts. Aron Heller at the *Times of Israel* revealed that Newton "learned how to read Hebrew, scrolled through the Bible and delved into the study of Jewish philosophy, the mysticism of Kabbalah and the Talmud."[171] Indeed, one writer has revealed that "7,500 pages of his [Newton's] theological speculations, written in his own hand, are digitized at Israel's national library at Hebrew University."[172]

Who do we find in possession as the caretaker of Isaac Newton's religious writings before they ended up in the National Library of Israel at Hebrew University in Jerusalem? It was a Zionist Jew, Abraham Yahuda, who obtained and maintained Newton's theological writings. Yahuda scoured the earth to collect Isaac Newton's writings on religion. Why was Yahuda so interested in the writings of Isaac Newton? Sarah Dry states that Yahuda "set about trying to purchase the Newton papers and wrote to [his wife] Ethel on July 28, 'I am thrilled with the thought of acquiring them. He wrote a lot about the Bible and the Jews, about Cabbala and all sorts of Jewish questions.'"[173]

Yahuda was a contemporary of Albert Einstein and conferred with Einstein about Newton's mystical religious writings.[174] Einstein was also a Zionist Jew. Religiously, Einstein had much in common with Newton, as both Einstein and Newton believed in the reality of mysticism.[175] Sarah Dry revealed that

Einstein passionately did not want Isaac Newton's theological writings to ever be published.[176] Why was Einstein passionately hopeful that Newton's theological writings not be published? Because those writings on theology would expose for the world that the Kabbalah is the source for Newton's theory of gravity. That is why Zionist Abraham Yahuda scoured the earth to collect Newton's theological writings and why they are now safely stored in Jerusalem, at the National Library of Israel at Hebrew University.

Einstein viewed Newton's theological writings as "the formative development of his work in physics." In a letter to Yahuda, Einstein stated that "these mostly unpublished writings therefore allow a highly interesting insight into the mental workshop of this unique thinker."[177] That insight is that he was passing off as science what was really heathen mysticism obtained from the Kabbalah.

Sir Isaac Newton's study of the Kabbalah is the real source for his theory of gravity. Marshall Hall explains that "Newton, in short, insured the acceptance of the Copernican Model for two centuries with his arcane 'mathematical' concepts; concepts upon which others—Einstein through Sagan, et al—could erect today's Pharisee Cosmology."[178]

Gershom Scholem is considered the founder of the modern, academic study of Kabbalah, and was the first Professor of Jewish Mysticism at the Hebrew University of Jerusalem. Scholem has stated that gravity is a force that has been known to the Jewish mystics from antiquity. This is certainly something that Newton would have come across in his study of the Jewish Kabbalah. Gershom Scholem associated gravity "with the final *Heh*, the *Shekhinah*, The Presence, the alchemical Earth, the Daughter in the divine family. Note the interesting connection between alchemical Earth and gravity, which rules our Earth!"[179]

Migene Gonzalez-Wippler, in her book, *The Kabbalah & Magic of Angels*, explains the foundational connection between the mysticism of the Jewish Kabbalah and the theory of gravity.

> It [gravity] is the result of the union of cause and effect and the law of momentum. It keeps the universe in motion, and it also works with dark matter to maintain stars, planets and galaxies in harmonious balance. For that reason it is equated with *Tiphareth* [a/k/a *Tifereth*], the sixth sphere of the Tree of Life, which is the center of the Tree beneath *Kether*, the first sphere. *Tiphareth* is identified with the sun, which is at the center of the solar system and keeps its planets in steady orbits through gravitation.[180]

The Tree of Life, to which Gonzalez-Wippler refers, is a graphic depiction of the Jewish god, *Ein Sof*. It is not a coincidence that the *sefirot* are depicted in the Tree of Life as spheres. The Tree of Life (*Ein Sof*) is the foundational source for the "scientific" theory of gravity. For the myth of the spherical earth to be believed, there must be a force to explain why people and things do not

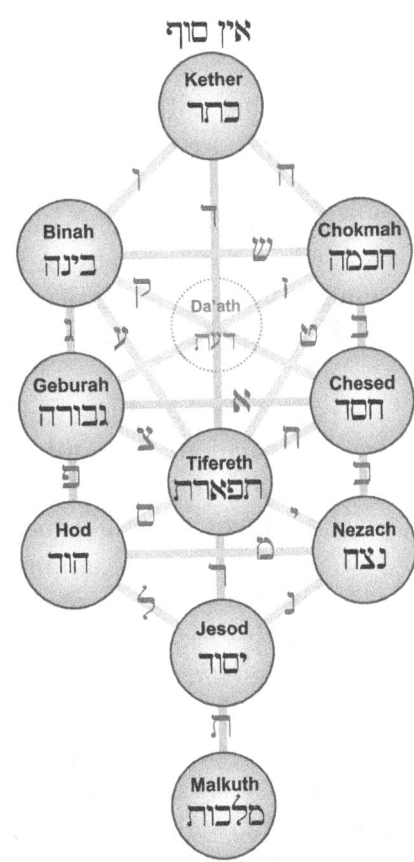

Figure 6: **The Tree Of Life (*Ein Sof*) From the Jewish Kabbalah**

fly off into space.

It is not necessary that gravity be proven or even make sense, as long as it is propped up by a facade of experts called "scientists." Make no mistake about it, though; there is nothing scientific about gravity. It is pure heathenism, from the Jewish Kabbalah. The priest-scientists of the heliocentric religion tolerate no dissension from their religious dogma of gravity. According to Migene Gonzalez-Wippler, gravity "is equated with *Tiphareth* [a/k/a *Tifereth*], the sixth sphere of the Tree of Life." As explained below, that means that gravity is not only an attribute of the Jewish god, *Ein Sof*; it is actually one of the gods of the Kabbalah, in its own right.

Rabbi Geoffrey W. Dennis in *The Encyclopedia of Jewish Myth, Magic, and Mysticism* explains: "The *Zohar* includes multiple interpretations built around the concept of God's genitals."[181] Judaism is a phallic religion that was adopted by the Jews during their captivity in Babylon. Dan Cohn-Sherbok and Lavinia Cohn-Sherbok explain the development of the esoteric sexual meanings concealed within the orthodox Jewish liturgy:

> Likewise, Phallic symbolism was employed in speculations about the ninth *Sefirah*, *Yesod*, from which all the higher *Sefirot* flowed into the *Shekinah* as the life force of the cosmos. In later centuries erotic terminology was used in the Hasidic works to describe movement in prayer which was depicted as copulation with the *Shekhinah*.[182]

The movement in prayer mentioned by Dan and Lavinia Cohn-Sherbok is called *shuckling* (a/k/a *shokeling* or *shoklen*). It is also called *davening*, which is simply a Yiddish word for prayer. The *shuckling* by Jews simulates the movement of copulation in sexual union with *Shekinah*. *Shuckling* is symptomatic of the fact that Judaism is a phallic religion, which has liturgical practices and prayers with occult sexual meanings. Baal Shem Tov is considered the founder of Hasidic Judaism and a highly respected authority on Jewish theology. Baal Shem Tov stated that "Prayer is mating with the Shechinah."[183] The mating during prayer is manifested in swaying back and forth. Rabbi Eli Malon explains: "By 'prayer,' he [Baal Shem Tov] meant the literal swaying back and forth, suggestive of intercourse, that is customary of traditional Jewish prayer."[184] The swaying is understood by Jews to signify copulation with the goddess Shekinah.[185] Former Jew, Nathaniel Kapner (a/k/a Brother Nathaniel), confirms the hidden meaning of the swaying by the Jews:

> Watch closely how the rabbis thrust their pelvises and penises back and forth in a prescribed prayer movement called "davening" in which the Jew copulates with the 'Shekinah' in order to give birth to an erotic union with the 'Ein Soph,' the Kabbalistic masculine emanation of their false god.[186]

The occult sexual meaning behind *shuckling* is generally known among Jews, but is kept hidden from Gentiles. In 2013, Rabbi Michael Leo Samuel openly discussed in an article addressed to a Jewish audience in the *San Diego Jewish Herald*, the *shuckling* of Hasidic Jews in front of a Victoria's Secret lingerie store. He wondered if the Hasidic Jews needed a visual aid for their *davening*. Samuel paraphrased the writings of Baal Shem Tov regarding the meaning of the swaying during Jewish prayer:

> Prayer is zivug (coupling) with the Shechinah. Just as there is motion at the beginning of coupling, so, too, one must move (sway) at the beginning of prayer. Thereafter one can stand still, without motion, attached to the Shechinah with great deveikut (cleaving to God) As a result of your

swaying, you can attain great bestirment. For you think to yourself: "Why do I move myself? Presumably it is because the Shechinah surely stands before me." This will effect in you a state of great hitlahavut (enthusiasm; rapture).[187] (parentheticals in original)

The powerful undercurrent of phallic worship infused into orthodox Judaism by the Kabbalah, includes the practice of sex magic.[188] The sex magic is an offshoot of the secret doctrine in Judaism. It is a common doctrine found in secret societies, that the mystic can find redemption through an "heroic" willingness to do evil.[189] The secret rabbinic doctrine is that evil can be redeemed by embracing it; there is a spiritual good in doing evil.[190] That explains why Jesus said to the Jews: "Ye are of *your* father the devil, and the lusts of your father ye will do."John 8:44. As is the case with the clerics of all phallic religions, there is rampant pederasty among Jewish clerics. Rabbinic pederasty is documented in this author's book, *Solving the Mystery of BABYLON THE GREAT*.

8 Heliocentric Keystone of New World Order

People have been conditioned to have a visceral reaction to any evidence that contradicts the heliocentric model. Such rejection of hard evidence, without a fair hearing, brings folly and shame. "He that answereth a matter before he heareth it, it is folly and shame unto him." (Proverbs 18:13) This folly and shame is manifested in devilish philosophies that permeate society.

The deception of a spherical, spinning earth is the foundation for Darwinian evolution, Freudian psychoanalysis, and Marxist communism. Indeed, the progressive emergence of the sodomite subculture into a government protected privileged class is the direct result of the prevailing theory of heliocentrism (the sun at the center of a solar system). "How so?" you might ask. It is quite simple. To remove the earth as the center of God's creation, and accept in its place an earth that is just one of millions of wandering planets in the universe, removes man as God's unique creation, made in his image. Once the centrality of the earth in God's creation is removed, it is only a small half-step further to eliminate the existence of God himself from the minds of men.

Once God is removed from man's consciousness, then also is removed the authority of God's word and his law. Man is then enthroned, being a law unto himself. The common thread running through heliocentricity, evolution, psychology, and communism is that there is no God. Indeed, atheism is logically a necessary element for each of those man-made philosophies to stand.

The sodomite privileged class springs from a godless generation, with no fear of God. Indeed, they must necessarily reject the God of the Bible, because within the Bible is found God's condemnation of sodomy. "Thou shalt not lie with mankind, as with womankind: it is abomination." (Leviticus 18:22) That sin is so abhorrent to God that he rained fire and brimstone upon Sodom and Gomorrah as punishment for that filthy sin. "Then the Lord rained upon Sodom and upon Gomorrah brimstone and fire from the Lord out of heaven." Genesis 19:24. Nowadays, however, sodomy is viewed as a protected lifestyle, with the U.S. Supreme Court judging sodomy a good thing, even to the degree of creating a right for same-sex couples to get married. God curses those who call the sin of sodomy good. "Woe unto them that call evil good, and good evil; that put darkness for light, and light for darkness; that put bitter for sweet, and sweet for bitter!" (Isaiah 5:20)

I explain in detail in *The Greatest Lie on Earth* how sin begets sin. Once a sin is legitimized and protected by the force of government, it begins a downward trajectory, where more sin is legitimized and protected. We see that with the civil rights legislation giving special privileges and protections to sodomites, which in turn crushes Christian liberties.[191] For example, New Mexico's Supreme Court unanimously ruled that two Christian photographers, Elaine and Jonathan Huguenin, who declined to photograph a same-sex union violated the state's Human Rights Act.[192] The Attorney General of the State of Washington filed a lawsuit against a florist who refused to provide flowers for a same-sex couple's wedding.[193] The florist lost in court, and the court decision was upheld by the Supreme Court of Washington.[194] Jack Phillips, the owner of Masterpiece Cakeshop in Colorado was ordered by a judge either to serve sodomite couples or face fines.[195]

Phillips appealed his persecution and won in the U.S. Supreme Court. The decision by the U.S. Supreme Court was not a complete victory. The Court did not rule that the Colorado law itself that protected sodomites was an infringement on the baker's constitutional rights to free speech and religion, it was only the unfair way in which the Colorado Civil Rights Commission enforced the law that was unconstitutional. Thus, he was subjected to continued harassment by the state of Colorado. The Colorado Civil Rights Commission was at it again with another prosecution against Phillips for his refusal to make a cake for a transgender customer. The commission alleged that Phillips discriminated against a customer based upon gender identity in violation of Colorado law.[196] "When the righteous are in authority, the people rejoice: but when the wicked beareth rule, the people mourn." (Proverbs 29:2)

The government-protected privileges granted to sodomites is only the first step toward the degenerative goal of the evil occultists who control the governments of the world, which is to legalize sex with children. The powerful elite of the world today secretly engage in all manner of pederasty, which this author details in his book, *Antichrist: The Beast Revealed*. Indeed, the elite have plans to normalize pedophilia.

The allegation that there is a move afoot to normalize pedophilia is not hyperbole. In a *60 Minutes Australia* documentary about pedophiles, they focused on a progressive theory by Dr. James Cantor, whom the presenter introduced as a neuroscientist specializing in atypical sexuality.[197] The theory that Dr. Cantor promotes is that pedophiles are born with their perverse predilection toward children. He argues that it is not their fault, they are made that way. He presents a distinction between a pedophile and a child molester. He claims that there are many pedophiles who do not act on their urges. He labels them "virtuous pedophiles." That is an oxymoron if there ever was one.

Dr. Cantor is just one of many in a phalanx of perverts who have been let loose to degenerate and demoralize countries. For example, Marjan Heine advanced the same argument during a 2018 TEDx Talk at the University of Wurzburg. Heine's presentation was titled: *Why Our Perception of Pedophilia Has to Change*.[198] Heine defined pedophilia as a person's inborn sexual preference for pre-adolescent children. She argued that nobody is responsible for their feelings, and so pedophiles are not responsible for their feelings of sexual attraction toward pre-adolescent children. As with Dr. Cantor, Heine argued for acceptance of and inclusion within society of pedophiles. Heine claimed that it is social isolation that drives pedophiles to sexually abuse children. Heine suggested that if the shame of pedophilia was removed, and pedophiles were welcomed into society, they would not act out their impulses to sexually abuse children. Heine's argument parallels Dr. Cantor's scheme. She argues, as does Dr. Cantor, that a person's proclivities can be dissociated from his actions. Thus, she maintains that a pedophile is not necessarily a child molester.

Heine's and Cantor's evil sophistry is that a person's proclivities can be dissociated from his actions. They reason that a pedophile is not necessarily a child molester. They ignore the reality that a person is identified by what he does, not by what he feels or thinks. For example, a football player is a football player because he plays football. He is identified by what he actually does. A person may feel like playing football, but until he actually plays football, he is not a football player. A robber is a robber because he robs. He is identified as a robber because of what he does. He is not a robber if he only desires to take someone else's property from them, but does not actually take it. A pedophile is a pedophile because he sexually abuses children. He is identified as a pedophile because that is what he does. Heine and Cantor ignore that reality.

To make a distinction between pedophiles and child molesters is to make a distinction without a difference. It is a false dichotomy. Heine and Cantor think they can get away with making that misleading distinction because most people do not know that recidivism among pedophiles is very high. Show me a pedophile who denies he molests children and I will show you a liar. Research has proven that pedophiles do not control their impulses to sexually molest children. For example, an Emory University Study conducted by a leading child abuse researcher, Dr. Gene Abel, found that the average child molester (i.e., pedophile) claims 380 victims in a lifetime.[199]

We can take a lesson from the fable of the scorpion and the frog. In that famous fable, a scorpion asks a frog to carry him over a river. The frog tells the scorpion he will not do it because he is afraid that the scorpion will sting him. But the scorpion pleads with the frog and argues that he would never sting the frog while crossing the river because if he did so, both he and the frog would sink and drown. The frog was convinced by that reasoning and agreed to take the scorpion across the river. The scorpion hopped on the back of the frog, and off they both went across the river. But midway across the river, the scorpion stings the frog, dooming them both to drown. When the frog felt the scorpions sting, he asked the scorpion why he stung him since now they would both drown. The scorpion explained, "I am a scorpion; that is what I do."

Scorpions sting because that is their nature; that is what scorpions do. So also, pedophiles molest children because that is their nature; that is what pedophiles do. A "virtuous pedophile" makes about as much sense as a virtuous scorpion. To welcome pedophiles as accepted members of society is to doom children to destruction, just as the frog was unwittingly doomed as soon as he agreed to give the scorpion a ride on his back. Parents are given a precious gift when God bestows them with children. They are charged with protecting those children from danger. They should not be putting scorpions on their backs and hoping for the best. "It were better for him that a millstone were hanged about his neck, and he cast into the sea, than that he should offend one of these little ones." Luke 17:2.

Cantor and Heine are simply fronting for powerful evil forces who are trying to normalize pedophilia in much the same way that clinicians have normalized sodomy. Once you decouple morality from God's standard, it becomes a slippery slope. What the *60 Minutes Australia* program did not reveal is that Dr. James Cantor is a sodomite. He presented a paper about his personal experience as a sodomite: "Being gay and being a graduate student: Double the memberships, four times the problems", at the Ninety-Ninth Annual Meeting of the American Psychological Association in San Francisco.[200]

Of course, Dr. Cantor is going to argue that pedophiles are born that way. He has an agenda. The lesbian, gay, bisexual, transgender (a/k/a LGBT) communities have an evil agenda, which they keep secret from the public at large. Michael Swift's 1987 Gay Manifesto reveals the dirty secret of the LGBT rights movement. The LGBT community wants the right to sodomize children.

Former California State Assemblyman Steve Baldwin researched the connection between homosexuality and pederasty. He published his findings in the Spring 2002 Regent University Law Review. Baldwin found that "[s]cientific studies confirm a strong pedophilic predisposition among homosexuals."[201] One 1988 study published in the *Archives of Sexual Behavior*, reported that 86% of pedophiles who victimized boys "described themselves as homosexual or bisexual."[202] Research statistics further show that homosexuals, as a population, molest children at a rate that is ten to twenty times greater than heterosexuals.[203] Those facts are well known in the homosexual community. San Francisco's leading homosexual newspaper, *The Sentinel*, bluntly states that "[t]he love between men and boys is at the foundation of homosexuality."[204]

Homosexual publications openly promote pederasty and are often populated with travel ads for sex tours to Burma, the Philippines, Sri Lanka, Thailand, and other countries infamous for boy prostitution. Baldwin reveals that "[t]he most popular travel guide for homosexuals, Spartacus Gay Guides, is replete with information about where to find boys for sex and, as a friendly warning, lists penalties in various countries for sodomy with boys if caught."

Baldwin found that "the mainstream homosexual culture commonly promotes sex with children. Homosexual leaders repeatedly argue for the freedom to engage in consensual sex with children."[205] He determined that one of the principal aims of the LGBT rights movement is the legalization and promotion of child molestation. Mainstream LGBT organizations such as the International Lesbian and Gay Association (ILGA) and the National Coalition of Gay Organizations have passed many organizational resolutions calling for lowering or eliminating age of sexual consent laws, as a way to legalize pedophilia.[206]

Such sin creates a violent and chaotic society. This chaos gives rise to new restrictive laws, which ultimately brings about a police state to reestablish order. Under the new police powers granted to the state, the exercise of God-given rights is suppressed by the government.

It is through orchestrated chaos that the people clamber for order, which brings the public acceptance of government tyranny. One of the principal subversive missions of secret societies is to covertly foment chaos in order to bring about the reaction of oppressive government crackdowns, which they have planned in advance from behind the scenes. The minions of Satan control the government, the reigns of which are in their hands, to steer its course to oppress the people.

The motto *ORDO AB CHAO* (order out of chaos) is an occult maxim often found in the rites of secret societies. For example, according to Mackey's Encyclopedia of Freemasonry, *ORDO AB CHAO*, is "[a] Latin expression, meaning Order out of Chaos. A motto of the Thirty-third Degree, and having the same allusion as *lug e tenebris*, which see in this work. The invention of this motto is to be attributed to the Supreme Council of the Ancient and Accepted Scottish petite at Charleston."[207] Mackey's reference to *lug e tenebris* is probably an allusion to be *LUX E TENEBRIS*, which is Latin phrase commonly found on Mason documents, that means "light out of darkness."[208] Jackie Jura of *Orwell Today* explains:

> The puppetmasters create "dis order" so the people will demand "order". The price of "order" always entails a handing over of control and loss of freedom on the part of the citizenry. Out of "chaos" comes "order" - THEIR order - their new WORLD order. ...
>
> The trick of creating chaos and then seizing power under the pretense of putting things back in order is a tried and true method of deception and manipulation. It's the meaning behind the Latin motto: ORDO AB CHAO meaning ORDER OUT OF CHAOS.
>
> It's also referred to as the Hegelian Dialect after the philosopher Georg Hegel who wrote about its effectiveness. He described it as: THESIS --

ANTI-THESIS -- SYN-THESIS.

Others have described it as: PROBLEM -- REACTION -- SOLUTION in that firstly you create the problem; then secondly you fan the flames to get a reaction; then thirdly (like Johnny-on-the-spot) you provide a solution. The solution is what you were wanting to achieve in the first place, but wouldn't have been able to achieve under normal circumstances.

Orwell described it as REALITY CONTROL. In 1984: he said, "The rocket bombs which fell daily on London were probably fired by the Government of Oceania itself, 'just to keep people frightened'."

There are literally HUNDREDS of examples of this method being used effectively throughout the course of history. A well-known example is the bombing of Pearl Harbor which resulted in the United States entering the Second World War. Chaos was required and so chaos was created. That's how it works.[209] (emphasis in original)

Satan knows that if man cuts loose his passions without regard to the laws of God, the sinful conduct will necessitate a tyrannical government. How so? The escalating sin is, in essence, an encroachment upon the God-given rights of another. Jesus explained the concept:

> Jesus said unto him, Thou shalt love the Lord thy God with all thy heart, and with all thy soul, and with all thy mind. This is the first and great commandment. And the second is like unto it, Thou shalt love thy neighbour as thyself. On these two commandments hang all the law and the

prophets. (Matthew 22:37-40)

The love that Jesus speaks of is not an emotional feeling toward another as Hollywood movies would have you believe. Emotions come and go. Love is not an emotion, it is an action. Jesus explained: that "as ye would that men should do to you, do ye also to them likewise." (Luke 6:31). Indeed, doing good for another person has nothing at all to do with how you feel about that person. Jesus stated that you should do good to even your enemies who have treated you badly. Luke 6:27-36. God's word has a built-in dictionary where words are defined by the use of parallelism. One can see in Luke chapter 6 at verses 32 and 33 that God uses parallelism to define love, not as a feeling, but rather as an action of "doing good" to another person.

"For if ye **love** them which **love** you, what thank have ye? for sinners also **love** those that **love** them." (Luke 6:32)

"And if ye **do good** to them which **do good** to you, what thank have ye? for sinners also do even **the same**." (Luke 6:33)

Doing good to another is not just a suggestion, it is a command from God. Jesus states without equivocation that all of the commandments of God are subsumed in the commands to love God and love your neighbor. Love has nothing to do with feelings. You should do nice things for others, whether you "feel" like it or not, because by doing so you are obeying God's command to do good to others. If one loves his neighbor, he will not violate the command, "thou shalt not steal." Exodus 20:15. While the command not to steal is a prohibition, Jesus takes it a step further and commands that we are to affirmatively do good to others (i.e., love).

Doing good often involves putting our needs second to the needs of another. If, however, a person does not regard God and seeks to satisfy the pleasure of his fleshly desires, without regard to the detrimental effect of his conduct on others, it will cause the government to step in to protect the aggrieved party. Sinful behavior brings about more crime in society, which is then used as a justification to bring about more government regulation and control of the masses. As explained by Edmond Burke: "Men are qualified for civil liberty in exact proportion to their disposition to put moral chains on their appetites. Society cannot exist unless a controlling power upon will and appetite be placed somewhere, and the less of it there is within, the more there is without. It is ordained in the eternal constitution of things that men of intemperate minds cannot be free. Their passions forge their fetters."

That is why Satan wants to drive any thought of God from the minds of men. Indeed, by doing so, a satanically controlled government can impose its tyranny on the people, without much objection from the people, because the people are ignorant that the fetters applied by the government violate the laws of God. For example, the communist collective ideal is based upon larceny. It uses the government to redistribute wealth. The redistribution of wealth is always justified by some purported need, and it usually involves helping children; it is always cloaked in nice sounding labels, like "welfare." There are always powerful corporate interests that are lined up to be on the receiving end of the government forced transaction.

Rather than charity coming willingly from one individual to another, the government uses its force, through taxation, to take money from one group and give it to another. Taking money from one group and giving it to another group cannot be done if the government accepted the existence of God. If God were to be accepted, then necessarily God's commands must be then obeyed. The government would have a hard time justifying taking money from one group of persons for the benefit of another group of persons when faced with God's command: "Thou shalt not steal." (Exodus 20:15) Using the government as an intermediary does not make the stealing any more justifiable.

Heliocentrism destroyed the landmark of geocentrism. Heliocentrism laid the groundwork for Darwinism. Once Darwinian evolution settled in, it was time for the planting of Marxist communism. In 1860 Karl Marx stated the following about Darwin's book, *On the Origin of Species*, which announced the theory of evolution: "Although it is developed in the crude English style, this is a book which contains the basis of natural history for our views."[210]

Heliocentrism is indeed the mother of all conspiracies. None of the other Satan-inspired, man-made philosophies would ever dare be presented without the geocentric landmark first being removed by the general acceptance of heliocentrism. Heliocentrism is the keystone to the deception; remove that keystone, and the entire edifice of deception will fall. With that keystone in place, the satanic source of the deception is inscrutable, and the facade of scientific authority for the satanic philosophies remains believable.

The educational authorities use a tried and true method of conditioning students to reject true scientific evidence and instead accept the myth of heliocentricity. William H. Poole explained this stratagem. "There is a principle which is a bar against all information, which is proof against all argument, and which cannot fail to keep a man in everlasting ignorance. This principle is, contempt prior to examination."[211] Satan has used this method to keep people in a state of nescience about God's creation. He has created a hive mentality instilled at the earliest stages of education that protects the myth of heliocentricity. Anyone who questions the legitimacy of heliocentricity has his character attacked by the hive as being ignorant. The evidence for a stationary, flat earth, no matter its validity, will be dismissed without examination. Thus the hive is kept in "everlasting ignorance."

Even nominal "Chrisitans" have fallen prey to the conditioning of the profane cosmology. For example, Christian Professor Dr. James White, who claims to be a biblical scholar, was immediately dismissive upon hearing that there were those who believe that the earth is flat.

Dr. White is a professor, author of more than 20 Christian books, an accomplished debater, and the director of Alpha and Omega Ministries, a Christian apologetics organization based in Phoenix, Arizona.[212] Dr. White tweeted the following message: "So I was informed over the weekend that there are MANY flat-earthers out there. I'm like…seriously?"[213] (ellipsis in original) A follower of White's on Twitter stated that "flat earthers have a somewhat reasonable biblical argument. Requires careful explanation of the text. Mockery is not helpful."[214] To which, Dr. White replied: "I'm sorry, there is NO 'reasonable' argument for such a belief. Shows a clear problem in thinking and reasoning."[215] (emphasis in original)

Dr. White's response was instantaneous because it was conditioned. It was the product of mass mind control propaganda. He learned early that educated and smart people understand that the earth is a sphere and that only ignorant fools believe that it is flat. He has had the "fact" that the earth is a sphere reinforced throughout his life by NASA, educational institutions, the mass media, and the entertainment industry. God has this to say about Dr. White and so many others who share his contempt of belief in a flat earth without ever examining the evidence: "He that answereth a matter before he heareth it, it is folly and shame unto him." (Proverbs 18:13)

Dr. White believes that he would be subjected to ridicule if he ever concluded that the earth is flat. He is a highfalutin professor with a Ph.D.; he is not about to give up his respected status and be marginalized as a fool. Through years of conditioning, he felt obliged to respond to the flat earth by ridiculing it. Inculcated in him is a deep seated conviction that there could be no middle ground of even considering the merits of the flat earth. To consider that flat earth was even a possibility is to be ridiculed. He was determined to be the one ridiculing rather than the one ridiculed.

Dr. White thinks that there is no need for him to look at any evidence; the issue has been settled in his mind because he has been conditioned to believe that he would suffer dire consequences for changing his mind. Notice that Dr. White does not simply say that he disagrees with those who believe the earth is flat; rather, he strikes out at those that believe the earth is flat as having "a clear problem in thinking and reasoning."[216] That is a conditioned response; it is indicative of brain washing.

Each of the satanic philosophies of the world (heliocentrism, communism, evolution, psychology) are essential cogs in the New World Order, which is an ancient trans-generational conspiracy. There is nothing new about the New World Order. The New World Order conspiracy is a conspiracy against God and man; it began in heaven and continues today on earth.

> And there was war in heaven: Michael and his angels fought against the dragon; and the dragon fought and his angels, And prevailed not; neither was their place found any more in heaven. And the great dragon was cast out, that old serpent, called the Devil, and Satan, which deceiveth the whole world: he was cast out into the earth, and his angels were cast out with him." (Revelation 12:7-9)

Satan was cast out of heaven. He then gathered with his minions on earth and began his war against God and man anew.

And when the dragon saw that he was cast unto the earth, he persecuted the woman which brought forth the man child. ... And the dragon was wroth with the woman, and went to make war with the remnant of her seed, which keep the commandments of God, and have the testimony of Jesus Christ. (Revelation 12:13,17)

The target of Satan's enmity is the true church of Jesus Christ. Satan has a secret army of devil possessed adversaries of Christ who do Satan's bidding in working to suppress the gospel of Jesus Christ and enslave the world. To achieve those ends, Satan must control the minds of the masses. He must enslave our minds before he can enslave our bodies. Heliocentrism is the foundational belief for enslaving the minds of men.

9 Conspiracy To Silence Flat Earth Believers

Taking a stand in support of the biblical model of a flat, stationary earth comes with it spiritual attack and ostracization. Often, people are cowed into submission and are persuaded to reject God's description of his creation contained in the Bible. Indeed, pastors have been fired for preaching about God's flat stationary earth. For example, Nate Wolfe was fired from the church he had pastored for more than seven years after it was discovered that he attended a biblical flat earth conference.[217] He had not yet even written or preached about the flat earth but was fired preemptively, apparently to prevent him from doing so.

Many churches have made accommodation with the world system in rejecting the flat earth. The world system is scared to death about the truth of the flat earth being generally known. They will stop at nothing to keep a lid on that truth. They will characterize those who believe that the earth is flat as being crazy and even dangerous.

Gary Shogren views those who believe in a flat earth to be conspiracy-minded lunatics. He characterizes those people as being mentally unstable. "A conspiracy mindset is one of the reasons why so many conspiracy thinkers cannot seem to hold down a job or maintain a marriage."[218] Shogren recommends an article by Dr. Robert C. Newman under the catchy title, *Evangelicals and Crackpot Science.*

Who is Dr. Robert C. Newman? He is a highly respected professor of New Testament at the Biblical Theological Seminary of Hatfield, Pennsylvania, and Director of the Interdisciplinary Biblical Research Institute. He holds earned degrees of Master of Divinity and Master of Sacred Theology. In the field of science, Dr. Newman received his undergraduate degree in physics from Duke University and his doctorate in theoretical astrophysics from Cornell University. He has done scientific research for the U.S. Weather Bureau and the Franklin Institute. Dr. Newman is a co-author of four books on both science and theological topics.[219]

What does the eminent Dr. Newman think of those who believe in a flat earth? Dr. Newman admonishes Christians to steer clear of, what he calls, crackpot science, like the flat earth. He views belief in a flat earth as a "danger" to be avoided at all costs because it can lead to harmful cults.

> I will suggest that we also need to be aware of the dangers lurking in the attitudes and thinking that characterize crackpot science. These attitudes will cut us off from what God is actually doing in nature. They may easily lead us to crackpot exegesis of the Bible and to the sort of arrogance that starts cults. We certainly want to avoid all these.[220]

Drs. Robert Carter and Jonathan Safarti, who are creation scientists and influential in the Christian community, announced that those who believe in the "nonsense" of a flat, stationary earth are radicals. "Radical" is a loaded word that is ominously pregnant with meaning. Drs. Carter and Sarfati push the idea that "[c]learly, the Internet easily radicalizes people."[221] They claim that the internet is to blame for the rise of belief in a flat and stationary earth, which they oppose. "Our only conclusion is that the Internet is breeding people who have trouble thinking through important ideas."[222] Thus, according to Drs. Carter and Sarfati, the internet is "breeding" brain-addled "radicals" who believe that the earth is flat. That suggests something must be done about it. Drs. Carter and Sarfati subtly leave unsaid what should be done about that perceived problem, but their ominous language and tone suggest to the reader that perhaps censorship might be in order.

    The National Geographic did a documentary on those who believe in a flat earth. It seemed that the point of the documentary, which was stated repeatedly by the commentator and the orthodox scientific experts interviewed, was that belief in a flat earth is a dangerous threat to science and society. For example, during the video, the commentator (Mariana van Zeller) interviewed flat-earther, Mark Sargent, who explained that very powerful interests who rule the world from behind the scenes are responsible for the heliocentric myth. Van Zeller responded by saying: "This is for me where I think it gets really dangerous because we are going back to the dark ages. You're essentially perpetuating ignorance by denying science. You know there is a real-life implication in all of this."[223] Van Zeller repeated the ominous warning of danger with the following closing remark in the documentary. "Thousands of years of empirical scientific evidence is now being dismissed as a mere conspiracy, and that's where I think it really starts getting dangerous for all of us."[224] Van Zeller carefully chose the word "dangerous."

    The message of danger was repeated during the National Geographic documentary. For example, during one vignette, James Bullock, Ph.D., an astrophysicist, who is a professor and Chair of Physics and Astronomy at the University of California at Irvine, was interviewed. He expressed his concern that "to question what scientists are saying and suggesting they're part of some massive international global conspiracy it's really scary."²²⁵ The interviewer (van Zeller), in a concerned tone of voice, then asked the question: "Are they a threat to the work that you do as a scientist?"²²⁶ Dr. Bullock responded: "If say governments stop funding science because of some kind of anti-science, anti-intellectual feedback they're getting from the populace, that's when it really starts getting dangerous for our civilization."²²⁷

Dear Reader, understand that when the media conditions people to believe that it is dangerous to our civilization to believe that the world is flat, the next step is to call for something to be done to address that danger. Such danger cannot be allowed to exist without being mitigated. A danger is a serious threat of harm, destruction, or even death. As such, the perceived danger could call for extreme measures to mitigate it.

It seems that the mainstream media is promoting the theme that information about the flat earth is "dangerous." They start with the premise that believing in a flat earth is insane. For example, *National Post* offers this opinion of those who think that world is flat: "This lunatic fringe is inflexible, tireless and cannot be persuaded by evidence or reason."²²⁸ Once the media establishes that it is batty to believe in a flat earth, they then apply a patina of dangerousness on that edifice of mental derangement.

YouTube (which is owned by Google) has jumped on board the "danger" train. The mainstream media heralded the decision by YouTube to reduce recommendations of (i.e., censor) flat earth videos. YouTube considered such videos to be harmful misinformation. Google stated that it would "begin reducing recommendations of borderline content and content that could misinform users in harmful ways."²²⁹ A writer for the New York Intelligencer, Madison Malone Kircher, stated that "[n]ormalizing such ideas [as a flat earth] is dangerous."²³⁰ Kircher goes full Stalin in saying that while she is "all for quashing the spread of truly wrongheaded and potentially dangerous ideas, in the case of flat-Earth indoctrination, the damage has long since been done."[231] Kircher complains that YouTube is, in part, to blame because it did not do anything to "curb the spread of such ideas" as the flat earth. Kircher's view is that flat earth videos constitute "dangerous" "indoctrination" and should have been nipped in the bud by the censors at YouTube.

Kaitlyn Tiffany in an article for *The Verge* titled *If a Scientific Conspiracy Theory Is Funny, That Doesn't Mean It's a Joke.*[232] That cryptic title indicating that belief in a flat earth is no joke, suggests, at the very least, that belief in a flat earth is not harmless. She began her analysis of the flat earth in the article by describing flat earth as an absurd but harmless theory. "It's true that the theory is so absurd as to be kind of funny, and it's fair to say that people who believe in it aren't directly endangering anyone's lives."[233] Notice the qualification; she stated that the people who believe in a flat earth aren't "directly" endangering anyone's lives. She leaves open the question of whether there is an indirect danger to lives. She closes the door on that issue later in her article by quoting a statement by Matt Shminkowitz that belief in a flat earth is indeed indirectly dangerous. The only qualification Shminkowitz puts on its harmfulness is that the peril of believing in a flat earth is just not as immediate as "climate change denialism" or those who are against vaccinations.

> Schimkowitz understands that flat Earth trutherism isn't as immediately dangerous as climate change denialism or the anti-vaccine backlash, but that doesn't mean it's totally harmless. "I think it is important to maintain a level of concern about [conspiracy theorists]," he says. "They do things that harm society as a whole, like negate or dilute scientific reason.[234]

Alex Wong, a reporter for GQ Magazine, interviewed filmmaker Daniel Clark, who produced a documentary film about the flat earth, titled *Behind the Curve*. Clark stated that "[w]hen we started making the documentary, we realized we had an opportunity to use flat earthers as an extreme example of conspiracy theorists."[235] A little known fact is that the term "conspiracy theorists" first appeared in a CIA memo (CIA Document 1035-960) that was written to address criticism of the Warren Commission Report on the Assassination of President Kennedy.[236] One of the strategies advocated by the CIA in that memo was to "employ propaganda assets to negate and refute the attacks of the critics."[237]

Wong stated that "there is a danger in believing in things that are not true."[238] David Clark responded by affirming Wong's belief that those who believe in a flat earth could be dangerous.

> Yeah. There's a danger in taking your beliefs so far that you're willing to harm people because of them. If you can't trust anyone, or trust anything, and everyone is your enemy, that can manifest itself in very dangerous ways, and we've seen that all over the world in really horrible ways. It's great to be skeptical, but you can't always start from nothing.[239]

Some in the media say that belief in a flat earth is harmless. But that is a ruse because in their next breath they say that people who believe such a thing also have a psychological imbalance that makes them question other matters of science such as the safety and effectiveness of vaccines and the validity of the science behind climate change. They view those perfectly rational beliefs as deadly dangerous. The belief in a flat earth is indicative of a person who has dangerous thinking toward things that are deemed to be politically incorrect.

To question established science is to have a dangerous mind. For example, a popular YouTube channel (The Good Stuff) with more than 200,000 subscribers posted a video ominously titled *How the Internet Made Us Believe in a Flat Earth (And Put the Planet in Danger?)*. He had this irrational apocalyptic assessment of the danger posed by those who believe the earth is flat.

> Belief in flat earth is a harmless belief. ... What does it matter to believe in a flat earth? The same flawed psychology that fuels flat earth theory fuels anti-vaxers and climate change denial. Outbreaks of preventable diseases have put some of the most vulnerable populations in our society in danger. The delay in reducing greenhouse gas emissions has committed us to around a meter rise in sea level. This will displace millions of people and erase entire cities from the map. These are beliefs that can have very real and deadly consequences.[240]

The assessment that belief that the earth is flat is deadly dangerous is what is being pushed by the mainstream media. If you believe that vaccines are unsafe and ineffective and that it is a myth that man causes global warming, then you are deadly dangerous. If you believe the earth is flat then you are also deadly dangerous because you are the very type of person who has broken from your conditioning and do not buy hook-line-and-sinker the lies that public education and the mass media are force-feeding the population.

Belief in the flat earth is viewed by powerful interests as "dangerous. Such "dangerous" thinking cannot be allowed. The described "danger" is not actually a danger to the public. Rather, those who control governments perceive a "danger" to the mind control they have orchestrated over the masses. The flat earth is the key to breaking that conditioning. Those who control the governments of the world have a plan to address that threat to their rule. All one needs to do is look to authoritarian regimes, like the

People's Republic of China and their reeducation camps, to understand how the governments of the world intend to address the "dangerous" threat to their mind control.

Make no mistake about it, the political liberals, like their communist brethren, are very much against free speech; to them, the free flow of unorthodox ideas is dangerous. They perceive the flat earth as a danger to their godless science and thus to society in general. They, therefore, believe that it must be stamped out. Portraying belief in a flat earth as dangerous is an ominous precursor setting the stage for more extreme measures to address that "danger."

Why is there such an effort to crush discussion of God's creation of a flat earth? Neil DeGrasse Tyson, who is a famous astrophysicist, and the Director of the Hayden Planetarium at the Rose Center for Earth and Space in New York City, let the cat out of the bag regarding the concern of the very powerful men who rule the world when he stated: "You can think the craziest thoughts you want. ... Go ahead and think that but if you try to then influence others, you are actually being irresponsible, and you are destabilizing the foundations of an informed democracy."[241]

Tyson was revealing the concern of his handlers. If people became aware that the earth is flat and enclosed within a firmament, above which is heaven, the abode of God, then the governments of the world would lose control of the people. People would then govern their own behavior to conform to God's commands. They would understand that God is close by and watching. "And ye shall know the truth, and the truth shall make you free." John 8:32. There would be no need for an oppressive external government. Tyson is correct. If the truth of God's creation of a flat earth became generally known, the governments of the world would lose credibility. It would destabilize the increasingly oppressive hegemony of the money powers. They cannot allow that to happen. The money powers have sprung into action against the "danger" that knowledge of God's flat earth poses to them.

Neil deGrasse Tyson describes the general view of God in the scientific community and among the governments of the world. "God is an ever receding pocket of scientific ignorance."[242] God has a response for Tyson and his ilk: "For the preaching of the cross is to them that perish foolishness; but unto us which are saved it is the power of God. For it is written, I will destroy the wisdom of the wise, and will bring to nothing the understanding of the prudent." (1 Corinthians 1:18-19) The scientific community is in a conspiracy with the governments of the world to put a stop to what Neil deGrasse Tyson describes as the scientific ignorance of God. In essence, they aim to stamp out all belief in God, because they think that such belief brings only dangerous ignorance. The governments of the world will not tolerate the reversal of their great achievement of concealing the knowledge of God from men through the "science" of heliocentricity. They plan on, gradually, bit-by-bit and step-by-step, clamping down on "dangerous" free thinkers who have broken from their government conditioning to discern that the earth is stationary and flat and that God is above the firmament, ruling from his heavenly throne. H.L. Mencken explained:

> The most dangerous man to any government is the man who is able to think things out for himself, without regard to the prevailing superstitions and taboos.

Oppressive legislation and law enforcement follow from sinful behavior. As Edmond Burke explained, men are qualified for freedom in exact proportion to their moral conduct. If the people do not control their passions, then the government must step in to do it for them. Sinful men cannot be free. "Their passions forge their fetters." And that is what the money powers want.

If people controlled their passions in obedience to God, then there would be no justification for oppressive legislation. That is the whole purpose of false flag attacks. The Governments are in a hurry to clamp down. Often the governments who perpetrate the attacks have the oppressive legislation already written in advance of the false flag attack. The legislation is not needed to address the attack, because the attack itself was already against the law. The real reason behind the new legislation is to strip the people of their previously enjoyed freedoms. The Patriot Act is just one example. For more information about the conspiracy behind the 9/11 attacks read this author's book, *9/11- Enemies Foreign and Domestic*.

At this moment, in the United States, the restrictions and condemnation toward belief in a flat, stationary earth is coming from the private sector. But the seemingly private mass media is so controlled by the state that it has become a virtual arm of the state. Indeed, the CIA has complete control over many news services.[243] Major media outlets parrot the CIA propaganda, which, in turn, influences public opinion and behavior. For example, the Washington Post has developed into a virtual department of the CIA. Alex Constantine reveals:

> Former Washington Post publisher Philip Graham "believing that the function of the press was more often than not to mobilize consent for the policies of the government, was one of the architects of what became a widespread practice: the use and manipulation of journalists by the CIA." This scandal was known by its code name Operation MOCKINGBIRD. Former Washington Post reporter Carl Bernstein cites a former CIA deputy director as saying, "It was widely known that Phil Graham was someone you could get help from."[244]

Carl Bernstein, in his 1977 article for Rolling Stone, *The*

CIA and the Media, recounts a briefing of members of the Senate Intelligence Committee by William B. Bader, former CIA intelligence officer, who was hired by the Senate to head the Senate investigation into CIA influence in the media. Bader told the Senate Committee members that his investigation uncovered a low-end estimate of 400 journalists who were CIA shills. Those 400+ "working journalists" included all areas of news reporting, from top management to reporters, editors, correspondents, and photographers. The CIA influence has also reached into book publishers, trade publications, and newsletters.[245]

Bernstein revealed that a senator who was the object of the Agency's lobbying later said: "From the CIA point of view this was the highest, most sensitive covert program of all.... It was a much larger part of the operational system than has been indicated."[246]

Why is the CIA so adamant that the lid be kept on their influence over the media? Because the media is parroting propaganda that influences the very thoughts of the population. The media is used not to inform the people, but rather as a tool of control over the masses. The CIA subversion of the media has turned the idea of a free press into a charade. Thomas Jefferson once said that "the man who reads nothing at all is better educated than the man who reads nothing but newspapers." That statement is as true today as it was in Jefferson's day.

The CIA subversion of the media is effective because it is generally not known. The general population of the United States believes that the major media outlets are providing them with unbiased news. In fact, nothing could be further from the truth. The false belief that the news media is independent and free from government influence is why the government propaganda spewed from the major media outlets is so effective. The major media outlets are part and parcel of a mass mind control operation. That mind control is laser-focused on besmirching the reputations of all who speak the truth about the flat earth and portraying them as "dangerous."

The media, being secretly controlled by the CIA continually portrays belief in a flat earth as a delusional "danger" to society. All one needs to do is read history to know that once an authoritarian state views a person, group, or ideology as a "danger" to the state, persecution follows. At first, the restrictions seem minor, but as time goes by, and the state amasses more authority and power, so also the persecution becomes more onerous. The characterization of belief in a flat earth as being a mental illness is with a purpose. In a communist country, any disagreement with the communist party is viewed as a mental illness that requires a stint in a mental hospital or reeducation camp where the obstinate state adversary is tortured into submission or death.

At present, Christian beliefs, which include God's creation of a stationary and flat earth, are protected by the First Amendment to the U.S. Constitution. But beware, the U.S. Government is gnawing at the chains of the Constitution. Each new war or conflagration (e.g., the 9/11 attacks) is used as a means to restrict God-given, constitutional rights. Step by step, inch by inch, those constitutional rights are being eroded. The shadowy money powers controlling the United States Government have slowly transformed it into a socialist government. Virtually all of the socialist programs of the U.S. Government violate the restrictions in the Constitution. Do not think that the Zionists who control the U.S. Government consider that violating the First Amendment Rights of the citizens is any big deal. The powerful cabal holding the reigns of government view the First Amendment as an impediment to its goals rather than the supreme law of the land to be obeyed.

10   Gatekeepers in the Church

The rejection of the truth of the flat earth is a spiritual issue. "For we wrestle not against flesh and blood, but against principalities, against powers, against the rulers of the darkness of this world, against spiritual wickedness in high places." (Ephesians 6:12)

Many pastors justify rejecting what God says about his creation by limiting the gospel to only those portions of the Bible that address salvation. They then admonish their followers to steer clear of disputable Bible doctrines like the nature of God's creation. Typically, pastors will focus on faith and salvation. They argue that those are the fundamental precepts on which the child of God should focus, to the exclusion of all else.

Jesus tells of Abraham explaining to a rich man in hell that his brothers cannot be spared the same fate "[i]f they hear not Moses and the prophets, neither will they be persuaded, though one rose from the dead." (Luke 16:31) That says it all. If one does not believe Moses and the prophets neither can he believe in Jesus, who rose from the dead. One cannot separate the importance of Moses and the prophets, which is the entire Old Testament, and say it is not part of the gospel. Moses and the prophets are part and parcel of the gospel. Moses and the prophets are the foundation for the New Testament revelation of Jesus Christ. One must believe in all of the gospel, which is the entire Bible.

For example, Don Fortner, who is the pastor of Grace Baptist Church of Danville, Kentucky, stated that he didn't care if one believes that the earth is flat. But he then clarifies that he draws the line where one views the gospel as including God's creation of a flat, stationary earth. Fortner states that such teaching is of the devil.

Fortner admonishes his church members not to even listen to anything about the flat earth and to break off any contact with a particular pastor who had written favorably about it. He advises them to remain in ignorance. Indeed, Fortner preached from the pulpit about the dangers of learning about the flat earth:

> I urge you, I urge you, don't listen. Don't listen to one word. You get intrigued, and all of a sudden you're gone. Something that takes your heart and your mind off of Jesus Christ and him crucified is of the devil; even if it's true, it's of the devil. Don't be enticed by false prophets.[247]

Fortner is an elderly pastor whose influence spans beyond his own church and seems to have taken on the role as a kind of gatekeeper to keep anyone from preaching about the flat, stationary earth. Another pastor who preached about the flat earth at a church that had close ties with Fortner was suddenly fired from his duties as pastor.

The Bible states nothing about being a gatekeeper. Instead, we are called on to nobly search the scriptures to see if those things are true. Acts 17:11. The church is not to divide over disagreements but rather to be perfectly joined together in the truth of the scriptures. "Now I beseech you, brethren, by the name of our Lord Jesus Christ, that ye all speak the same thing, and that there be no divisions among you; but that ye be perfectly joined together in the same mind and in the same judgment." (1Corinthians 1:10)

It seems that heliocentric preachers like Fortner view as enemies those who believe what the Bible says. It is a spiritual reality that those who adhere to the truth of the entire gospel will be viewed by worldly preachers as enemies. "Am I therefore become your enemy, because I tell you the truth?" Galatians 4:16. Worldly preachers think that they have it all figured out. But because they lack the unction of the Holy Spirit, their minds are blinded by "the god of this world," Satan.

> But if our gospel be hid, it is hid to them that are lost: In whom the god of this world hath blinded the minds of them which believe not, lest the light of the glorious gospel of Christ, who is the image of God, should shine unto them. (2 Corinthians 4:3-4)

Mark Twain is alleged to have said that "it's easier to fool people than to convince them that they have been fooled." That truth is manifested in churches and schools every day. Indeed, when the truth is met by a firm belief in a lie, there is an immediate conflagration. The truth is vociferously scorned and ridiculed by truculent fools who have been conditioned to love lies and hate knowledge.

> Wisdom crieth without; she uttereth her voice in the streets: She crieth in the chief place of concourse, in the openings of the gates: in the city she uttereth her words, saying, How long, ye simple ones, will ye love simplicity? and the scorners delight in their scorning, and fools hate knowledge? Proverbs 1:20-22.

Fortner is conditioning his flock to have a visceral reaction to any evidence that contradicts the heliocentric model. To preach willful ignorance of scripture and hard evidence, without a fair hearing, brings folly and shame. God's admonition on that point bears repeating: "He that answereth a matter before he heareth it, it is folly and shame unto him." (Proverbs 18:13) William H. Poole's explanation also bears repeating: "There is a principle which is a bar against all information, which is proof against all argument, and which cannot fail to keep a man in everlasting ignorance. This principle is, contempt prior to examination."[248] And indeed Fortner has contempt for the Bible's description of a flat earth. Fortner stated in an email to Frank Hall that the flat earth is "contemptibly silly, meaningless, and useless, of absolutely no benefit to anyone, in no way giving honor to God. ... my only response to the mention of a flat earth in the past, has been nothing but roaring laughter that anyone could be so duped."[249]

Fortner thinks that the gospel truth that God created a fixed, flat earth is "contemptibly silly." That statement by Fortner is a confession to the Christian world that he is a natural man who lacks the unction of the Holy Spirit. He does not believe the gospel truth that God created a fixed, flat earth because he is simply incapable of receiving that truth. "But if our gospel be hid, it is hid to them that are lost." (2 Corinthians 4:3) The gospel truth of God's creation is spiritually discerned; it is foolishness to the natural man.

> But the natural man receiveth not the things of the Spirit of God: for they are foolishness unto him: neither can he know them, because they are spiritually discerned. (1 Corinthians 2:14)

On what does Fortner rely for his authority? Does he cite Bible passages? No. He relies on the credibility of men from NASA. Does Fortner defend the gospel? No. He defends NASA!

Fortner states:

> It has been boldly and confidently asserted that NASA is a big hoax and that any science asserting a global earth is pseudoscience. ... [Y]ou should know that I personally have friends (some now in glory) who were greatly involved with NASA from its earliest days. These are men I have every reason to esteem as faithful brethren in Christ. Unlike me, they were highly trained in their fields as engineers, scientists, and lawyers, and highly respected as brilliant above their peers. One of these is a man now almost 90 years old. I've known him a long, long time. He has been commissioned to write four different books by NASA and the NATO, on four different occasions on the non-nuclear proliferation of space, and is now writing another by a different commission from NASA and the NATO. I really do not think it is either fair or honest to refer to such men as "pseudoscientists" or "conspirers in deception."[250]

Fortner vouches for the credibility of NASA. One would think that he would have more discernment, as NASA is so clearly an agency of propaganda. NASA is continually coming up with new, incredible adumbrations that make no logical sense. For example, Brett Molina, a reporter for USA Today reported on March 13, 2019, that "NASA will study moon samples collected during Apollo missions that have been untouched in 50 years, the agency announced."[251] You might wonder that, perhaps, the "moon samples" had been misplaced for the past 50 years. But you would be wrong. NASA claims that they purposely waited 50 years to study the moon rocks. Why would NASA wait 50 years? NASA claims that it deliberately waited 50 years so that it could study the rock with more sophisticated future technology.

These samples were deliberately saved so we can take advantage of today's more advanced and sophisticated technology to answer questions we didn't know we needed to ask," Lori Glaze, acting director of NASA's Planetary Science Division in Washington, D.C., said in a statement.[252]

NASA's explanation is patently absurd. NASA allegedly traveled to the moon and collected moon rocks, only to pack away for 50 years the purported moon rocks they supposedly scoured the moon to find! And they would have us believe that they deliberately planned ahead of time to store the moon rocks away for 50 years! NASA, it seems, was not the least bit curious about the moon rocks 50 years ago, but Molina reports that now NASA is prepared to spend $8 million on nine teams of scientists to study them.

Molina is a reporter for USA Today, and he has the ability to ask the acting director of NASA's Planetary Science Division Lori Glaze, questions about her incredible story that NASA planned ahead of time to wait 50 years after obtaining moon rocks to analyze them. But Molina shows a suspicious lack of curiosity about Glaze's explanation. Neither he nor anybody else from the corporate media dared to ask the NASA representative how it is that NASA knew 50 years ago that they would not return to the moon during those 50 years to get more rocks? What was the new scientific instrument that they now have that they did not have 50 years ago that is such a game changer in analyzing the moon rocks today? Why couldn't the rocks have been studied 50 years ago and then studied again today? What is it that NASA wanted to know 50 years ago about the rocks that their testing back then would not tell them? Did the methods used 50 years ago completely consume the entire rock such that there would be nothing left over after the test? If that is the case, couldn't they take a small sample of each of the rocks to test to determine the nature of the rock and preserve the remainder? Couldn't they at least look under a microscope at the rocks 50 years ago? The true answer to all those questions is ineluctable. The only time that the government seals something away for 50 years is when they are hiding something. NASA never went to the moon in the first place. The rocks are not from the moon. The 50-year moon rock plan is just the latest deception; NASA is spewing propaganda and the corporate media is in on it. That is why there were no inquisitive questions. The media was simply there to report what NASA said, and that was it. The media is supposed to be a watchdog for the people, the corporate media instead has been made a lapdog of the government.

When a space agency's real mission is to deceive, it is not hard to perceive the irrationality of its alleged space missions. Clearly, NASA never went to the moon; that is why they were not the least bit interested in studying the moon rocks when they allegedly got back. They knew that the rocks did not come from the moon. They just packed the fake moon rocks away until now, 50 years later, when they decided to trot them out for their latest charade. The purported $8 million study is all theater for the gullible masses. For being staffed by rocket scientists, NASA is really stupid. But because they control the lap-dog media, they feel empowered to lie and get away with it. Read this author's book, *The Greatest Lie on Earth (Expanded Edition)*, for proof beyond any doubt that NASA never traveled to the moon.

Despite NASA's proven track record of deception, Fortner seems to rely on NASA to support his religious doctrine. And for Fortner, the flat earth is not merely a minor doctrinal dispute; according to him, believing that the earth is flat is evil. He admonished his followers to "openly renounce this evil, humbly acknowledge your error, and put it behind you."[253] As he explained in his email, his admonition to stop teaching about the flat earth is based upon science (i.e., NASA). God states: "[L]et God be true, but every man a liar." (Romans 3:4) Fortner is such a liar.

The proper approach would be for Fortner to bring the

issue before the church and search the scriptures to see whether it is true that God created a flat, stationary earth. Acts 17:11. Fortner has taken upon himself authority in the church that he does not have. His approach is unbiblical. All members of the church are kings and priests. Revelation 1:6. It seems that Fortner does not want the scriptural truth to be brought to light because he fears that it will show him to be in error.

Fortner did not cite a single passage of scripture to defend his erroneous view that the earth is a spinning globe. Why not? Because there are no Bible passages supporting that religious superstition. There are many Bible passages, though, which point to a flat, stationary earth, e.g., 1 Chronicles 16:30; Psalms 19:1-6, 33:4-9; 93:1,104:1-5, 104:30, 136:6, 102:25; Isaiah 40:22, 44:24; Proverbs 8:27; Job 28:24, 38:4-13; Amos 9:6; Joshua 10:12-13; 2 Kings 20:9-11. These passages should be discussed and explored in church, not concealed in willful ignorance.

The reason that heliocentric pastors are fighting so hard to keep their flocks ignorant of the flat earth is that those pastors are denying God's word, and they know it. They do not want their flocks to find out that they are charlatans. It is a matter of self-preservation. Robert Carter and Jonathan Sarfati are heliocentric "Christians" and creation scientists who believe that earth is a sphere and argue vociferously against the earth being flat. They acknowledge that if the Bible, in fact, describes a flat earth, then those who deny the flat earth are "denying God's word."

> Some people believe in the flat earth because they have been convinced that the Bible teaches it. So they believe that by denying the FE, people are denying God's word. IF the Bible taught the earth is flat, their argument would be sound.[254]

Jason Robinson, who is pastor of Mountain Baptist Church, correctly opines that those who believe in evolution are enemies of God. Indeed, he calls them "a bunch of God-hating atheists that want to basically discredit the Bible."[255] But at the same time he rejects God's creation of a flat and stationary earth. Robinson states emphatically that "I believe in heliocentricity where we're spinning."[256] Robinson stated: "I believe the flat earth theory is a conspiracy ... I believe it's a coup based off the atheists out there to try to shove this into Christianity to make us look stupid"[257] Robinson is concerned with what people think of him. He does not want to look "stupid." As an engineer, he is full of the pride of life and is willing to compromise the gospel to protect his pride. "For all that is in the world, the lust of the flesh, and the lust of the eyes, and the pride of life, is not of the Father, but is of the world." 1 John 2:16. Robinson describes the idea of a flat earth as "not biblical," "not scientific," and "not mathematically correct." Robinson argues that those who believe in the flat earth doctrine are "deceptive," "ignorant," "retarded," and "stupid."[258] Robinson is a fearful hypocrite. Robinson describes one of the attack videos he created against the biblical flat earth as "just another video about why the flat earth is dumb."[259]

    Robinson quotes from Isaiah 40:22, wherein God describes the earth as a circle. But Robinson deceptively gives an incomplete definition of a circle to beguile the unwary listeners. Robinson states that a circle is "where you have one point and every point out from that point is equal distant to that center point."[260] He left out the most important part of the circle's definition that distinguishes it from a sphere. A circle requires all points on the circumference to be equidistant from the center **and on the same plane**.[261] Thus, a circle, by definition must be flat. By leaving out the part of the definition of a circle that requires the circumference to be on the same plane (i.e., flat), Robinson is able to argue that "when you think about it in the three-dimensional world doesn't the sphere have that same definition?"[262] So he argues that the circle in Isaiah 40:22 is actually describing a sphere because a sphere also has every point equidistant from the center, only it is in three dimensions.

Robinson is being deceptive. He reveals that he is an engineer and therefore knows that a circle, by definition, cannot be a sphere because a circle requires all points equidistant from the center on the circumference to be on the same plane. A circle must be flat. Robinson knows that fact. A sphere, on the other hand, is a three-dimensional object in the shape of a ball.[263] All points on the circumference of a sphere are equidistant from the center, but those points are not on the same plane.[264] That means that a circle cannot be a sphere, and a sphere cannot be a circle. They are mutually exclusive. To say otherwise is straightforward dissimulation. Robinson has repeatedly trumpeted his qualifications to speak on scientific and geometric matters because he is an engineer. We should hold him to the expertise that he claims for himself. In doing so, we can only conclude that he is being purposely deceptive when he tries to equate a sphere with a circle.

A circle is flat, but Robinson cannot say that a circle is flat. Robinson must obscure the fact that a circle is flat. Indeed, he cannot allow the word "flat" to pass his lips when referring to any passage in the Bible that describes the earth. Isaiah 40:22 describes "the circle of the earth," which indicates a flat earth. Robinson must hide that fact. Instead of saying that a circle is (as it must be) flat, Robinson calls a circle a "two dimensional construct." Robinson says:

> The Bible says that he sitteth upon a circle of the earth and the only object in the world that we live in that's actually a circle is a sphere. **A circle is just a two-dimensional construct**. It's not real. It's not a real object, okay, so a sphere is a circle. And so that's what the Bible teaches. The Bible does not teach a flat earth.[265]

Robinson must first obscure that a circle is flat by calling it a "two-dimensional construct." He then inveigles a false conclusion that a circle is "not real." Since a sphere is real, he concludes that "a sphere is a circle." Robinson thus opines that the circle in Isaiah 40:22 is not a circle at all because he argues that circles cannot be real objects. Thus he claims that the circle in Isaiah 40:22 must really be a sphere.

It seems that Robinson has taken a page from Kent Hovind's playbook. Hovind (who touts the fact that he taught geometry for 15 years) claims that circles are only imaginary. Hovind says:

> There is no such thing as a circle. A circle does not exist, except in imagination. Because if it has any height at all even the thickness of your ink if you draw a circle on a piece of paper your ink left behind is got a certain thickness to it it is now a cylinder, right? Technically, there is no such thing as a circle. It's an imaginary construct for geometry. And it's practical and we use it all the time, but in reality, it doesn't exist. If it's got any height, the thickness of your pencil or pen it's now a cylinder.[266]

Hovind uses sophistry to beguile the ignorant. He claims that a circle with any depth is a cylinder. But what he fails to explain is that a cylinder has a circle at each end. A cylinder cannot be a cylinder without circles. A cylinder is a closed solid object with a curved surface that connects two identical flat ends that are circular, congruent, and parallel. Thus a cylinder has a circle at each end. A circle is real. Indeed, without a circle, one could not have a cylinder. Thus, contrary to Hovind's claim, circles exist.

When God states that "[i]t is he that sitteth upon the circle of the earth" (Isaiah 40:22), he is referring to the flat circular surface of the earth. That is why God describes the surface of the earth as "the circle **OF** the earth." God means by that statement that the surface of the earth has a face that is flat and circular. He is not saying that the earth is a circle with no depth. Just as a cylinder has a flat circle at each end, so also, the face of the earth is a flat circle. The surface of the earth is "the circle **OF** the earth," in the same way the end of a cylinder is the "circle **OF** the cylinder." **Circles are real; the earth is real; the circle of the earth is real.**

Hovind argues that the circle mentioned in Isaiah 40:22 is actually describing a sphere. But that is impossible. It would be like arguing that a cylinder could still be a cylinder if each of the circles at each end of the cylinder were spheres. The only way to accomplish having spheres at each end of a cylinder and still look something like a cylinder would be to split a sphere in half and place each hemisphere at opposite ends of the cylinder. But the resulting shape would no longer be a cylinder; it would be a capsule. Just as it is impossible for a cylinder to have hemispheres at each end because it would no longer be a cylinder, it would then be a capsule, so also it is impossible for the circle of the earth to be a sphere, as it would no longer be a circle. A circle cannot be a sphere, just as a cylinder cannot be a capsule.

Pastor David Berzins is a pastor from Strong Hold Baptist Church, who also goes on the attack against the biblical doctrine of the flat and stationary earth. There is a banner behind Berzins that states: "The LORD is good, a strong hold in the day of trouble; and he knoweth them that trust in him." Nahum 1:7. That is true, and Berzins is exhibit A for one who does NOT trust in God.

Berzins titles his sermon about the flat earth: *Flat Earth Foolishness*.[267] Berzins states that those who believe in God's creation of a flat and stationary earth have fallen into "foolishness and foolish thinking."[268] Berzins acknowledges that he is preaching against the flat earth. That means that he is preaching against the gospel. Berzins fails to realize that the gospel indeed appears foolish to the lost world. "For the preaching of the cross is to them that perish foolishness; but unto us which are saved it is the power of God." (1 Corinthians 1:18) Deceptively removing part of the gospel to make it palatable to the unsaved is not the answer. The world must hear the entire unvarnished gospel. Berzins does not understand that the gospel is spiritually discerned. "[T]he natural man receiveth not the things of the Spirit of God: for they are foolishness unto him: neither can he know them, because they are spiritually discerned." (1 Corinthians 2:14) If Berzins thinks that the clear statement in God's word that the earth is flat is foolishness, what does that say about him? "For after that in the wisdom of God the world by wisdom knew not God, it pleased God by the foolishness of preaching to save them that believe." (1 Corinthians 1:21).

In Berzins' church, as with many Nicolaitan pastors, it is his way or the highway. Berzins simply will not allow any discussion of the flat earth in his church. He will not be contradicted on that point of doctrine. Berzins stated emphatically in reference to the flat earth:

> While I do want to have discussions with people, I'm going to avoid foolish questions. I'm also going to avoid contentions. So if you have legitimate questions that you want to have answered, I would happy to try to help you to understand something, but I'm not going to fight with anybody about doctrine. I'm not going to get in any debates. I'm not gonna get in any strivings and contentions. I'm going to teach what the Bible says, and that's the way it is. As a pastor of this church, that's what I'm going to do. And you know, don't come to me trying to change my mind, especially on foolishness. if someone comes to me and tries to tell me that there's lizard people that are

shapeshifters and everything else, I won't entertain that for a second. Now look, everyone could say okay that sounds really ridiculous. Well there are people out there that believe that. Okay, but that is an example of something that I won't even entertain the thought of. I'm not going to sit here and have a debate, a discussion about you. I put the Flat Earth in the same category.[269]

Berzins states, without equivocation, that his mind is made up that the Bible does not support the flat earth, and he will not ever change his mind. Berzins stated: "This is what I believe about it [the flat earth], don't come to me trying to change my mind on this because it ain't gonna change."[270] Berzins is typical of most Nicolaitan pastors, who simply will not openly discuss the topic of flat earth. They will only preach from the pulpit in condemnation of it. Berzins considers the flat earth to be utter foolishness that is beyond the pale and not worthy of dialogue. Berzins is acting more as a gatekeeper than a pastor.

Berzins tries claiming that he is not attacking belief in a flat earth because he is afraid of what people will think of him. "It's not that I'm afraid of facing something, and like, oh man well what do people think of me? I don't care."[271] He repeated his defense by stating "I don't have this fear of oh well you just don't want to believe in a flat earth because you don't want people to call you [a fool], that's not it at all."[272] He sounds like someone fearfully whistling by a graveyard. As Queen Gertrude said: "The [man] doth protest too much, methinks." Clearly, that concern for what other people will think of him is at the forefront of Berzins' mind, and so he addressed it at the outset of his sermon against the flat earth.

Berzins slipped up and impeached his protest that he is not concerned with people think about him if he were to acknowledge that he believed that the Bible describes a flat earth. Berzins said that "it [the biblical flat earth doctrine] makes the Bible look dumb. And it makes people who believe the Bible look stupid and dumb and ignorant."[273] Berzins is blinded by the pride of life, which God explains is not from God but is of the world. 1 John 2:16. Berzins does not want the world to think that he is "stupid and dumb and ignorant," so he compromises his Christian principles to have friendship with the world. "[K]now ye not that the friendship of the world is enmity with God? whosoever therefore will be a friend of the world is the enemy of God." (James 4:4)

Berzins explains that the Bible does not state that 2+2=5. Berzins implies by that statement the inference that, in like manner, the Bible does not teach that the earth is flat. In that context, Berzins states that "we don't have a God that's that dumb, that's deceitful and a liar to try to make you just believe something that just simply is not true."[274] He is trying to impeach God. He states that the Bible does not describe God's creation of a flat and stationary earth. Berzins concludes that, if the Bible described a flat earth, it would be like the Bible claiming that 2+2=5. Berzins concludes that would make God a dumb and deceitful liar. Berzins reaches that conclusion because he is convinced that the earth is not flat and stationary, and the god of his imagination would never say it was in the Bible. But the Bible does describe a flat and stationary earth. Thus, Berzins implicitly blasphemes the true God of the Bible as a dumb and deceitful liar.

Pastors who promote heliocentricity, try to keep a lid on the biblical depiction of a flat and stationary earth. They act as gatekeepers to hide the gospel. In Romans 1:18 we read that "the wrath of God is revealed from heaven against all ungodliness and unrighteousness of men, who hold the truth in unrighteousness." Romans 1:18. The word "hold" is defined as "[t]o stop; to confine; to restrain from escape; to keep fast; to retain. It rarely or never signifies the first act of seizing or falling on, but the act of retaining a thing when seized or confined."[275] That means that heliocentric pastors who conceal (i.e., hold) the truth of a flat and stationary earth in the unrighteousness of heliocentricity are going to feel the wrath of God. Indeed, when you read that passage in context we find that it is a direct reference to God's creation. The reason that God is so angry with heliocentric pastors is that his creation of a flat and stationary earth, as depicted in the Bible, reveals the invisible character of God. To conceal God's true creation conceals the true God. God punctuates his displeasure by stating that they are without excuse.

> **For the wrath of God is revealed from heaven against all ungodliness and unrighteousness of men, who hold the truth in unrighteousness**; Because that which may be known of God is manifest in them; for God hath shewed it unto them. For **the invisible things of him from the creation of the world are clearly seen, being understood by the things that are made, even his eternal power and Godhead; so that they are without excuse.** (Romans 1:18-20)

11   The Creation Gospel

Don Fortner has a very narrow view of the gospel, which, according to him, does not include God's creation of a flat and stationary earth. Indeed, Fortner is on record saying that "something that takes your heart and your mind off of Jesus Christ and him crucified is of the devil; even if it's true, it's of the devil."[276]

John Calvin offers this retort to Fortner's position:

[The Christian is not to compromise so as to obscure the distinction between good and evil, and is to avoid the errors of] those dreamers who have a spirit of bitterness and contradiction, who reprove everything and prevent the order of nature. **We will see some who are so deranged, not only in religion but who in all things reveal their monstrous nature, that they will say that the sun does not move, and that it is the earth which shifts and turns. When we see such minds we must indeed confess that the devil posses them**, and that God sets them before us as mirrors, in order to keep us in his fear. So it is with all who argue out of pure malice, and who happily make a show of their imprudence. When they are told: "That is hot," they will reply: "No, it is plainly cold." When they are shown an object that is black, they will say that it is white, or vice versa. Just like the man who said that snow is black; for although it is perceived and known by all to be white, yet he clearly wished to contradict the fact. And so it is that they are madmen who would try to change the natural order, and even to dazzle eyes and benumb their senses.[277]

Don Fortner has the following verse in mind: "For I determined not to know any thing among you, save Jesus Christ, and him crucified." (1 Corinthians 2:2) But he misinterprets the verse to mean that one should only know about the crucifixion of Jesus Christ. Fortner misinterprets that passage to mean that we are to eschew any discussion of a flat and stationary earth. But that is not what the passage states. It states that we are to know "Jesus Christ, **and** him crucified." There are two subjects separated by the conjunction, "and." The first thing that we are to know is Jesus Christ.

Who is Jesus Christ? We find the answer throughout the entire Bible. Jesus Christ is the creator of all things. "In the beginning was the Word, and the Word was with God, and the Word was God. The same was in the beginning with God. **All things were made by him [the Word-Jesus Christ]; and without him was not any thing made that was made.** In him was life; and the life was the light of men." (John 1:1-4) We read in Colossians 1:16 that "by him [Jesus Christ] were all things created, that are in heaven, and that are in earth, visible and invisible, whether they be thrones, or dominions, or principalities, or powers: all things were created by him, and for him." We read that Jesus Christ is revealed through his creation. "[T]hat which may be known of God is manifest in them; for God hath shewed it unto them. For **the invisible things of him from the creation of the world are clearly seen, being understood by the things that are made, even his eternal power and Godhead**; so that they are without excuse. (Romans 1:19-20) We read in the book of Genesis about Jesus Christ's creation of a stationary and flat Earth. We read throughout the Bible the importance of God's creation of a flat and stationary earth. *E.g.*, 1 Chronicles 16:30; Psalms 19:1-6, 33:4-9; 93:1,104:1-5, 104:30, 136:6, 102:25; Isaiah 40:22, 44:24; Proverbs 8:27; Job 28:24, 38:4-13; Amos 9:6; Joshua 10:12-13; 2 Kings 20:9-11. Jesus Christ is both our creator and our savior. And he created a flat and stationary earth.

Jesus Christ is the word of God that became flesh. John 1-14; 1 John 5:7-8. Indeed, the Bible is clear that Jesus Christ is all of the Word of God, not just some of it. "And he was clothed with a vesture dipped in blood: and **his name is called The Word of God.**" (Revelation 19:13) The gospel is not just the New Testament. Jesus commanded us to search the scriptures because they speak of him. Jesus explained: "Search the scriptures; for in them ye think ye have eternal life: and they are they which testify of me." (John 5:39) Those scriptures that were in existence at that time to which he was referring were the Old Testament. The gospel is all of God's word found in both the Old and New Testaments. Indeed, the gospel was preached to the Jews in the Old Testament. Hebrews 4:2. The Bible must be taken as a whole; the gospel is the entire word of God. There is a terrible curse on those who would add to or take away from the words found in the Holy Bible. Revelation 22:18-19.

Indeed, God proves that he is the everlasting LORD by his creation. All false gods are not the Lord God of the Bible because they are not the creators of the heavens and the earth.

> **But the LORD is the true God**, he is the living God, and an everlasting king: at his wrath the earth shall tremble, and the nations shall not be able to

abide his indignation. Thus shall ye say unto them, **The gods that have not made the heavens and the earth, even they shall perish from the earth, and from under these heavens. He hath made the earth by his power, he hath established the world by his wisdom, and hath stretched out the heavens by his discretion.** When he uttereth his voice, there is a multitude of waters in the heavens, and he causeth the vapours to ascend from the ends of the earth; he maketh lightnings with rain, and bringeth forth the wind out of his treasures. (Jeremiah 10:10-13)

The fact that Jesus Christ is the creator is part and parcel of the gospel. Jesus Christ created all things through his word. John 1:1-3, 14; Colossians 1:16. All the host of heaven were made by the breath of Jesus Christ's mouth. Psalms 33:6. His creation of massive bodies of water covering a flat, immovable earth is inextricably linked with his blessing on those whom he has chosen for salvation. Psalms 33:6-12. Jesus Christ watches from heaven above the firmament over all the inhabitants of his flat earth and stationary earth. Psalm 33:13-14. Jesus Christ looks out over his created flat and stationary earth to shed his mercy on his elect. Psalms 33:18. The creator of heaven and the earth saves his elect who hope in his mercy. Psalms 33:22. The words of God in Psalm 33 (and indeed the very theme of the Bible) reveals that the nature of Jesus Christ's creation is associated and identified with Jesus Christ's salvation of his elect. Indeed, God, in his Bible, gives us an understanding of his salvation by explaining his creation of a flat and stationary earth. *See* Romans 1:18; Pslams 33:1-22; 136:1-26; Jeremiah 10:10-13.

Rejoice in the LORD, O ye righteous: for praise is comely for the upright. Praise the LORD with harp: sing unto him with the psaltery and an instrument of ten strings. Sing unto him a new song; play skilfully with a loud noise. **For the word of the LORD is right; and all his works are done in truth.** He loveth righteousness and judgment: the earth is full of the goodness of the LORD. **By the word of the LORD were the heavens made; and all the host of them by the breath of his mouth. He gathereth the waters of the sea together as an heap**: he layeth up the depth in storehouses. **Let all the earth fear the LORD: let all the inhabitants of the world stand in awe of him. For he spake, and it was done; he commanded, and it stood fast.** The LORD bringeth the counsel of the heathen to nought: he maketh the devices of the people of none effect. The counsel of the LORD standeth for ever, the thoughts of his heart to all generations. **Blessed is the nation whose God is the LORD; and the people whom he hath chosen for his own inheritance. The LORD looketh from heaven; he beholdeth all the sons of men. From the place of his habitation he looketh upon all the inhabitants of the earth.** He fashioneth their hearts alike; he considereth all their works. There is no king saved by the multitude of an host: a mighty man is not delivered by much strength. An horse is a vain thing for safety: neither shall he deliver any by his great strength. **Behold, the eye of the LORD is upon them that fear him, upon them that hope in his mercy**; To deliver their soul from death, and to keep them alive in famine. **Our soul waiteth for the LORD: he is our help and our shield. For our heart shall rejoice in him, because we have trusted in his holy name. Let thy mercy, O LORD, be upon us, according as we hope in thee.** (Psalms 33:1-22)

If the devil can use the big-bang heliocentric model to convince men that God did NOT create a fixed and flat earth by speaking "and it was done; he commanded, and it stood fast" as explained in Psalms 33:9. The devil can then can convince men that it is NOT true that God "[f]rom the place of his habitation he looketh upon all the inhabitants of the earth," as explained in Psalms 33:14. Once the devil removes God from heaven above and the conscience of men below, it is inexorable that he will then remove men's need for salvation, since there are no rules from God that need to be obeyed. Once the devil removes the need for salvation, the devil can attack the Biblical doctrine that God has a "people whom he hath chosen for his own inheritance," as described in Psalm 33:12. If there are NO special people elected by God for salvation, then it CANNOT be true that "the eye of the LORD is upon them that fear him, upon them that hope in his mercy," as declared in Psalms 33:18. Thus, there is NO basis for anyone to "waiteth for the LORD" as described in Psalms 33:20 because God is NOT "our help and our shield," as described in Psalms 33:20. Once people are convinced by the devil that God is NOT our help and our shield, there is NO cause for our heart to rejoice in him, "because we have trusted in his holy name," as described in Psalms 33:21. In the end, there is NO reason to pray to God: "Let thy mercy, O LORD, be upon us, according as we hope in thee," as depicted in Psalms 33:20-22. You see, an attack on God's creation of a flat and stationary earth is an attack on the very existence of God and his merciful salvation. Heliocentrism is an attack on the gospel of Jesus Christ. Those who argue that the creation account in the Bible of a flat and stationary earth is not part of the gospel are, at the very least, unwittingly accomplices in the devil's dark rebellion against God.

Don Fortner has bought into the commonly accepted narrow definition for the gospel that is found in churches today. Heliocentric pastors seem to have accepted the definition of the gospel from the profane world. *The Webster's Revised Unabridged Dictionary, 1913 Edition* defines "gospel" as "glad tidings;

especially, the good news concerning Christ, the Kingdom of God, and salvation."[278] *The Oxford English Dictionary (Unabridged)* defines Gospel as:

> 'The glad tidings (of the kingdom of God)' announced to the world by Jesus Christ. Hence, the body of religious doctrine taught by Christ and His apostles; the Christian revelation, religion, or dispensation. Often contrasted with the Law, i.e., the Old Testament dispensation ... The record of Christ's life and teaching, contained in the books written by the 'four evangelists.'"[279]

The definitions by Webster's Dictionary and the Oxford Dictionary have the correct premise that "gospel" means "glad tidings;" but they narrow the meaning so that it leaves room for unscrupulous heliocentric pastors, like Don Fortner, to define the gospel as something less than the entire Holy Bible. Heliocentric pastors interpret the gospel to exclude God's creation. Such a narrow interpretation of what the gospel means allows heliocentric pastors to cut off any discussion of the biblical flat and fixed earth.

Harper's Bible Dictionary (HBD) defines "gospel" as "good news."[280] HBD limits the gospel entirely to "the good news preached by Jesus that the Kingdom of God is at hand (Mark 1:15) and the good news of what God has done on behalf of humanity in Jesus (Rom.1:3-15)."[281]

The New International Dictionary of the Bible (NIDB) reveals that originally "gospel" denoted "good tidings" and "the story concerning God." As we will see, both of those terms mean God's word as found in the entire Holy Bible. But the NIDB explains that the original definition for "gospel," which included all scriptures, was later supplanted. And now, "gospel" is being defined as only the teachings of Jesus Christ as found in the New Testament.

The English word *gospel* is derived from the Anglo-Saxon *godspell*, which meant "good tidings" and later the "story concerning God." As now used, the word describes the message of Christianity and the books in which the record of Christ's life and teaching is found.[282]

The Oxford English Dictionary (Unabridged), (OED) which is one of the most authoritative dictionaries in the profane world, has expressly stated that the word "god" in "god-spel" does not mean "God." The OED explained that "godspel" was accepted by ancient people to mean "GOD+spel."[283] But the OED claims that was a mistake: "The form godspel must therefore ... be due to a misinterpretation of the written form before the word had any oral currency."[284] The OED editors are guessing that godspel (with "god" meaning Almighty God) "must" be due to a misinterpretation of the written form of godspel. The OED editors imply that the word "god" should have been given meaning "good" rather than "God."

"Spell," in the context of the words "God spell," means "a story."[285] Since God spell is God's story, gospel was traditionally taken to mean "story concerning God."[286] That means "god-spel" is God's story or God's word. The OED theory that the ancient people misinterpreted "god" in "godspel" to mean Almighty God, implies that "god-spel" does not mean God's story (i.e., God's word). The result of the OED exclusion of God's story (i.e., God's word) as the meaning for "god-spel" is that the gospel can more easily be interpreted narrowly not to encompass the entire Holy Bible. Indeed, the OED expressly limits the gospel to "[t]he record of Christ's life and teaching, contained in the books written by the 'four evangelists.'"[287] and distinguishes the gospel from "the Old Testament dispensation."[288] Armed with this new limited definition of the gospel, heliocentric pastors can avoid addressing God's creation of a flat earth by rendering the topic as a distraction from the gospel.

All dictionaries are imperfect to one degree or another. And the generally accepted definition that renders "gospel" not to mean "God's word" is one example. *The Theological Dictionary of the New Testament,* by Gerhard Kittel, is the standard dictionary used by new bible version translators. The editors of that dictionary admit that it and all other dictionaries are imperfect:

> Dictionaries are incontestably among the most imperfect of human products. Those who are driven by calling or circumstances to seek help in lexical works should realize how inadequate is that which even the best and most comprehensive of dictionaries can offer the user.[289]

God, on the other hand, had this to say about his dictionary, which is built into his Holy Bible:

> "The words of the LORD are pure words" (Psalms 12:6-7)

> "Every word of God is pure:" (Proverbs 30:5)

Gail Riplinger has done extensive research on the meaning of "gospel" as used in the Holy Bible. She concluded that "the form of the first element (god) shows unequivocally that it was identified with 'God' not with 'good.'"[290] She concluded that modern dictionaries have defined gospel too narrowly as meaning only good news or similar such phrases. The word "gospel" does mean glad tidings, and those glad tidings are the word of God. Riplinger bases her conclusion on good authority, God Almighty.

Gail Riplinger is a linguist with both M.A. and M.F.A. degrees. She has done additional postgraduate study at Harvard and Cornell Universities. She was a university professor and authored six college textbooks. She is the best selling author of *New Age Bible Versions.*

The *Oxford English Dictionary (Unabridged)* (OED) gives the standard definition for "gospel" as meaning "good tidings." It is true that the gospel is good tidings. But the "good" in "good tidings" should be understood to be "godly," thus "good tidings" are actually tidings from God. *See* Luke 1:19; 2:9-10. But the OED implicitly sticks with a worldly definition of good. The OED argues that "god" in "god-spel" does not mean Almighty "God." The OED argues that "god" in "god-spel" should be read to only mean "good," and thus the definition of "gospel" should be limited to mean only "good tidings" and, by implication, not mean "God's word."

The editors of the OED base that exclusion of God from being the root of the word "gospel" on their claim that the ancient people who used the word "god" in "god-spel" as meaning "God" got it wrong. The OED stated that "the mistake was very natural."[291] The OED acknowledges that from the earliest development of the English language, the word "gospel" was taken to mean "god-spel," which was traditionally thought to mean "GOD+spel"[292] with "spel" meaning "discourse or story"[293] (i.e., God's story or God's word). The ancient people thought "gospel" meant "God spell" or "God's word." The theory of the OED is that the ancient people were wrong to interpret the "god" in "god-spel" to mean Almighty God, rather than "good."

That is a rather tenuous basis for a dictionary to eschew a definition. It is also a suspicious approach, when a dictionary is supposed to be semasiological. The definitions contained in a dictionary are, in part, descriptive and thus are supposed to reflect the etymology and common usage and meaning given to a word by people. How people use a word is supposed to support, and not undermine, a definition. It is illogical for a dictionary to explain the common usage and understanding of a word and then desconsruct it to explain why that common understanding is **NOT** what the word means. In order for the OED to do that it had to ignore what God says the word "gospel" means. The OED could not say that God was mistaken. The OED simply ignored the fact that the real reason that people thought that "gospel" meant "God spell" or "God's word" is because that is what God said it means in his Holy Bible. The OED had to ignore that elephant in the room in order to undermine the true meaning of the gospel.

Why would the OED go to such effort to undermine "God spell" (i.e. God's word) as the definition for "gospel?" It suggests that the OED has an agenda. The OED seems to be steering people away from a true understanding of the gospel as the whole word of God. Other dictionaries and etymologies have adopted the OED theory. Today, defining "gospel" to mean only "good tidings," to the express exclusion of "God spell," has taken on a life of its own.[294]

The only way to explain the OED editors' efforts to undermine the true meaning of "gospel" is that they have a profane bias and anti-Christian agenda. Indeed, Gail Riplinger reveals that is precisely the case.

> The founder of the Oxford English Dictionary, R.C. Trench, was rabidly against the Holy Bible and its all pervading influence and sociological control. He wanted the dictionary to show that words were being used in society in ways which differed from the historical Bible usage. He wrote two entire books against the KJB [King James Bible]: *On the Authorized Version of the New Testament*, in connection with some recent proposals for its Revision (New York, 1858) and *Synonyms of the New Testament* (Cambridge, 1854). In these books he set the stage for the watered-down liberal definitions seen in today's new versions. On the title page of one of these books, he placed the same serpent logo used by Luciferian H.P. Blavatsky. Because of his hatred

for the KJB, he was asked to be a member of the Westcott-Hort Revised Version Committee. He merits an entire chapter in this book for his vile re-definition of Bible words. As one might expect, *The Shorter Oxford English Dictionary's* definition of 'inspiration' also drops the name "God" for the adjective "Divine." It charges that the inspiration of the Scriptures "are believed by **some**" only. Instead of citing the Bible, it sites Trench's friend and Ghostly Guild founder, "B.F. Westcott" writing what the "early Fathers" believed, instead of what the scripture states. (Other chapters in this book detail the heresies of these ancient Catholic "Fathers." The OED editors, which followed Trench, also believed that they were not compiling prescriptive 'definitions,' but descriptive samples of how a word has been used in different contexts (secular, not always Bible-based contexts). The OED will allow the inclusion of the Biblical definition of words, but merely sets it in the midst of numerous other usages. To take one of its secular definitions and apply it to re-define the Bible's historic usage is to fall squarely into the clutching hands of R.C. Trench, whose official portrait shows him donning the 'X' medallion of the Masonic Grand Scottish Knights of St. Andrew.[295] (bold emphasis in original)

The profane world and heliocentric churches want people to only think of the "gospel" as "good tidings," to the exclusion of "God's word." As we will see, good tidings also means God's word; but because that meaning is not readily apparent, the use of good tidings as a definition for gospel facilitates modern churches accepting a more limited scope of the gospel that excludes God's creation. Expressly excluding "God's word" as a definition for the gospel obscures the reality that the "gospel" is in fact "God's word." That stratagem furthers the modern heliocentric pastors' evasion of what God's word states about God's creation of an immovable and flat earth.

The nature of the earth God created, in most churches today, is a topic considered not part of the gospel. Indeed, heliocentric pastors today argue that whether the earth is a spinning sphere or a stationary and flat earth is irrelevant to the "gospel" as they understand it.[296] Dr. Neelak S. Tjernagel, Ph.D., explains the historical treatment of the two meanings given to the word "gospel."

> Luther's translation of the New Testament appropriated the Greek word *euangelion*, which he used in his work in the form *Evangelium*, hence the words evangel and evangelical. English translators used the Old English term Godspel or, more simply, Gospel. The word signified God's spell, or story, and was identical in significance and meaning to the German adaptation of the Greek original. Unfortunately the word "Gospel" came to be used in two differing senses, one broad, the other narrow in meaning. **In its broad sense the Gospel was synonymous with the term Scripture or the Word of God. It was used in reference to the whole counsel and will of God, including both Law and Gospel.** In its narrow sense it excluded the law and included only the proclamation of the redemptive work of Christ.[297] (emphasis added)

As much as the OED tried to limit the meaning of "gospel" to only "good tidings," to the exclusion of "God's word," the OED editors ultimately had to admit that "the form of the first element (god) shows unequivocally that it was identified with 'God' not with 'good.'"²⁹⁸ The OED has to acknowledge that fact because the evidence is clear. Gospel traditionally meant God spell (i.e., God's word). The OED reveals that even the old high German used *gotspell*, which can only mean one thing: God's word.²⁹⁹

One might argue that the original Greek, from which "gospel" is translated, means "glad tidings." That statement is correct. But that contention is inaccurate, to the extent that "glad tidings" is argued to not be a reference to God's word. The Greek word, *euaggelion*, can be interpreted as both gospel and glad tidings. Indeed, we find that to be the case in Romans 10:15, where *euaggelion* was translated as both "gospel" and "glad tidings." The meaning of *euaggelion* is gospel, which in turn carries the primary meaning of "God's word." The meaning of *euaggelion* is also "good tidings." The Greek root *eu* is commonly translated as "good," but it is good in the sense of "godly." And so *euaggelion* is thus properly translated as godly words or more precisely God-spell (i.e., gospel, which is God's word). "Good tidings" and "gospel" mean the same thing. They both mean "God's word." Gail Riplinger explains:

> **The KJV correctly translates the first root *eu*, in other words, with its primary meaning, 'God' (godliness, godly).** The eminent scholar Werner Foerster of Munster points out correctly that words with this root, "in early days, are often provided with more precise definitions to show to whom the...godliness was directed." He writes, "even later the habit of giving the object {God} did not die out." The second root, *aggello*, has the primary meaning of 'word'. Even Kittel had to admit, "It has developed a logos {word} theology." The word 'English' comes from the word 'Anglo-ish,' meaning 'Word-ish.' As people of the 'word,' the English speaking Christians have excelled, in generations past, in spreading and glorifying the

word of God.[300] (emphasis added)

The corrupt new bible versions have used the words "good news," or similar phrases, in place of the word "gospel." They do that to limit in the minds of the readers the scope of the gospel. They want people to only think in terms of what is contained in the New Testament account of the atoning sacrifice of Jesus Christ, to the exclusion of all of the other historical and doctrinal revelations in the Holy Bible. Other things in the Bible, like the account of God's creation of a flat and stationary earth, are not considered by most people part of the gospel. Riplinger explains:

> Most new versions, like the NIV, New Living Translation, NRSV, and Good News Bible, and reference works like Vine's Complete Expository Dictionary or Zodhiates Complete Word Study Dictionary, opt for the incorrect rendering "good news." ... Not only was 'God' watered down to 'good,' but 'spell,' meaning 'words,' was changed to 'news' to accommodate liberal textual critics who do not believe that the Bible is God's word, but merely a book which contained a 'good message.' The OED also states that 'spel' means specifically, "To read (a book, etc.) letter by letter." In Macaulay's History of England, he writes, "Not one man in five hundred could have spelled his way through the Psalms."[301]

The OED comes full circle in its definition of "gospel" and squeezes in the fact that "gospel" includes "[i]n extended sense: The Holy Scriptures"[302] Gail Riplinger quotes *The Webster's Encyclopedic Dictionary*, which states that "gospel" is "compounded of Anglo-Saxon god. God and Spell - lit. God's word."[303] It seems that the profane dictionaries must acknowledge that the full meaning of "gospel" is "God's word" for them to maintain some semblance of credibility; but they obscure that more complete definition for "gospel" by denigrating it.

The 1828 *Webster's Dictionary of the English Language* lists the first numbered definition of gospel as "God's word."[304] Noah Webster cited to Galatians 3:8 to explain the scope of the gospel. That passage refers to the gospel (God's word) being preached to Abraham in the first book of the Bible in the Old Testament, Genesis.

> And the scripture, foreseeing that God would justify the heathen through faith, preached before the **gospel** unto Abraham, saying, In thee shall all nations be blessed. (Galatians 3:8)

The bottom line is that "gospel," in its most complete sense, means "God's word," all of God's word. The gospel spans the entire Holy Bible, from Genesis to Revelation, every single word of it. *Helps Ministries* explains that "[t]he Gospel (2098 /euaggélion) includes the entire Bible, i.e. it is not limited to how a person becomes a Christian."[305] But there is a devilish conspiracy to conceal that truth.

Satan does not want people to know that "gospel" means "God's word," which includes **every word of God**. Matthew 4:4. God uses parallelism to define words in the Bible. That parallelism defines the gospel as "the word of God" (2 Timothy 2:8-9; 2 Corinthians 4:2-3; Romans 10:16-17), "the word of the Lord" (Acts 8:25; 1 Peter 1:25), and "the word of truth" (Ephesians 1:13).

Please do not misunderstand. Gospel does mean "good tidings." None other authority than God himself explains that gospel means good tidings. We find in Luke 4:18 when Jesus read from Isaiah 61:1 he equated the "good tidings" in that passage in Isaiah with the "gospel."

The Spirit of the Lord is upon me, because he hath anointed me to preach the **gospel** to the poor; he hath sent me to heal the brokenhearted, to preach deliverance to the captives, and recovering of sight to the blind, to set at liberty them that are bruised," (Luke 4:18)

The Spirit of the Lord GOD is upon me; because the LORD hath anointed me to preach **good tidings** unto the meek; he hath sent me to bind up the brokenhearted, to proclaim liberty to the captives, and the opening of the prison to them that are bound;" (Isaiah 61:1)

"Tidings" is defined as being primarily an "account of what has taken place, and was not before known."[306] The definition of "tidings" describes to a T God's account in Genesis of the creation of the earth. Tidings includes "news; advice; information; intelligence."[307] Intelligence, in pertinent part, means "an account of things distant or before unknown."[308] The primary sense of intelligence is understanding.[309] We see that concept in the book of Revelation where Jesus told John to "[w]rite the things which thou hast seen, and the things which are, and the things which shall be hereafter." Revelation 1:19. The tidings from God are always good tidings because God is good. Jesus said that "there is none good but one, that is, God." (Mark 10:18)

We find the pertinent part of the definition of "good" in the context of the scriptures means perfect, unblemished, virtuous, incorruptible, and conducive to happiness.[310] Indeed, when God finished his creation he described it as "very good." "And God saw every thing that he had made, and behold, it was very good." Genesis 1:4.

In essence, good tidings means the perfect, unblemished, virtuous, incorruptible, and joyous revelation by God to man of

God's love, grace, doctrines, prophecies, and events. Good tidings describes the entire Holy Bible; and it includes God's creation of an immovable and flat earth. Jesus Christ's creation of the stationary, flat earth described in the Bible is an "account of what has taken place, and was not before known."[311] Good tidings in the Bible give us understanding about God's creation, which is "an account of things distant or before unknown."[312] Those good tidings are part and parcel of the gospel. Indeed, all of the word of God contained in the Holy Bible makes up the good tidings (gospel) of Jesus Christ.

Incidently, good tidings means the same thing as glad tidings. Compare Luke 1:19 (glad tidings) with Luke 2:10 (good tidings). God uses those terms interchangeably in the Bible. Paul preached "glad tidings" from the book of Psalms in the synagogue at Antioch. Those same glad tidings were heard by the Gentiles who asked Paul to also preach "these words" to them the next sabbath. God described the **"glad tidings"** that Paul preached to the Gentiles the following sabbath as the **"word of God."**

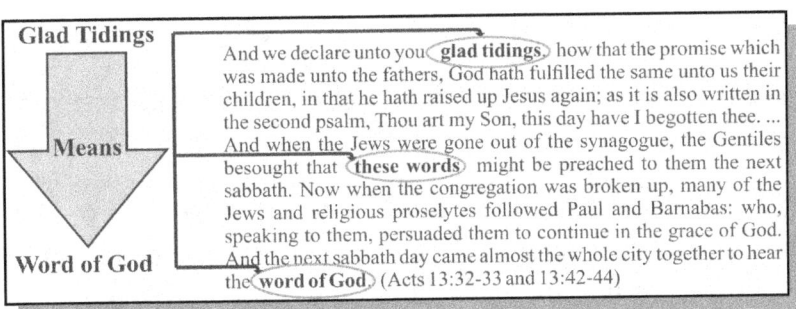

Paul was preaching in Acts 13:32 "glad tidings" from the book of Psalms. God reveals in Acts 13:44 that those "glad tidings" from the book of Psalms are the "word of God." That necessarily means that glad tidings are found in the Old Testament. "Gospel" means "glad tidings." We know that "gospel" is derived from "God spell," which means God's word.

Thus, glad tidings = gospel = word of God, all of which span the entire New and Old Testaments.

We also find in Romans 10:17 that the "gospel" that is "glad tidings" is also "the word of God." In Romans 10:16 we learn that the Jews did not obey the gospel (i.e., the word of God) because, as revealed in verse 17, they did not believe the word of God (i.e., the gospel). It is explained in Romans 10:18-11:36, that the Jews did not have the faith required to believe the word of God (the gospel), because faith must be spiritually imparted by the grace of God to the hearer of the word of God (the gospel). Thus, the Jews did not obey the gospel (the word of God) because they could not obey the gospel (the word of God). "God hath given them the spirit of slumber, eyes that they should not see, and ears that they should not hear." (Romans 11:8)

But they have not all obeyed the **gospel**. For Esaias saith, Lord, who hath believed our report? Romans 10:16.

Next Verse ↙

So then faith cometh by hearing, and hearing by the **word of God**. Romans 10:17.

The "gospel" in verse 16 of Romans 10 is equated with the "word of God" in verse 17. Notice in the reference in verse 16 to the Old Testament prophet Esaias (Isaiah 53:1), who prophesied about the preaching of "glad tidings" in Isaiah 52:7. That prophecy in Isaiah comes into view when we read Romans 10:13-15.

> For whosoever shall call upon the name of the Lord shall be saved. How then shall they call on him in whom they have not believed? and how shall they believe in him of whom they have not heard? and how shall they hear without a preacher? And how shall they preach, except they be sent? as

it is written, How beautiful are the feet of them that preach the **gospel** of peace, and bring **glad tidings** of good things!" (Romans 10:13-15)

We see that there is parallelism. And that parallelism reveals that "gospel" means "glad tidings." Indeed, Isaiah 52:7 states that "How beautiful upon the mountains are the feet of him that bringeth good tidings, that publisheth peace; that bringeth good tidings of good, that publisheth salvation; that saith unto Zion, Thy God reigneth!" (Isaiah 52:7) Clearly, the gospel is "glad tidings." Heliocentric church authorities want the definition of the gospel to stop there, and go no further, because they do not want the gospel to be understood to be the entire word of God. They seek to limit the definition of the gospel to only be those Bible passages that relate to salvation by grace through faith in Jesus Christ. That is considered the heart of the gospel, but just as the human heart is not the whole body, so also the heart of the gospel is not the whole gospel. The gospel certainly includes the heart of the gospel, but it is much more. The gospel is glad tidings and it includes all of the words of God, including the account of his creation, found in the Holy Bible.

In Romans 10:15, we read that "beautiful are the feet of them that preach the **gospel** of peace and bring **glad tidings** of good things!" The "gospel of peace" and "glad tidings" in verse 15 are the "word of God" in verse 17. The whole point of verses 13 through 15 is to explain that in order for one to call on the name of the Lord, he must believe; in order to believe, he must hear the "gospel;" in order to hear the "gospel," someone must preach the "gospel." In verse 17 we find that same truth, but the gospel in that verse is referred to as the **"word of God."** "So then faith cometh by hearing, and hearing by the **word of God**." (Romans 10:17) Thus, the **"gospel"** is both **"glad tidings"** and the **"word of God."**

In 2 Timothy 2:8-9 we find that the "**gospel**" preached by

Paul, for which he suffered, is the same **"word of God"** that is not bound. The **"gospel"** is the **"word of God."**

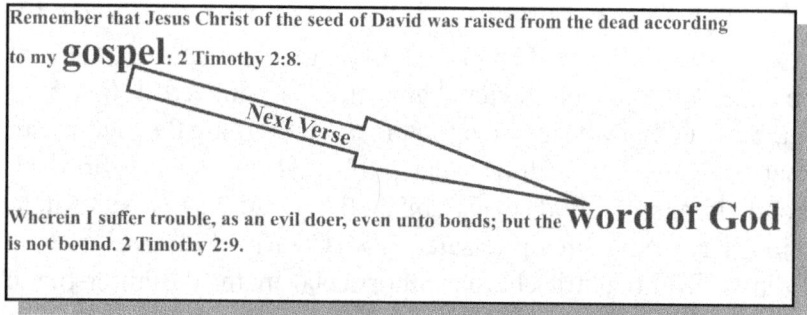

Remember that Jesus Christ of the seed of David was raised from the dead according to my gospel: 2 Timothy 2:8.

Next Verse

Wherein I suffer trouble, as an evil doer, even unto bonds; but the word of God is not bound. 2 Timothy 2:9.

Notice also in Acts 8:25 that the disciples preached the "word of the Lord" at Jerusalem, which was the same "gospel" that they preached in the many villages of the Samaritans.

And they, when they had testified and preached the word of the Lord, returned to Jerusalem, and preached the gospel in many villages of the Samaritans. (Acts 8:25)

God explains in Revelation 1:9 that John was a companion with the saints in tribulation while he was in the kingdom. In a parallel phrase John explains that his tribulation was his imprisonment on Patmos Island for the word of God and the testimony of Jesus Christ. We know from that parallelism that the word of God is the testimony of Jesus Christ. John was in tribulation on Patmos while in the kingdom of God and for the word of God. In Matthew 13:18-19 we find Jesus explaining the parable of the sower by revealing that the seed being sown is the "word of the kingdom." That is the same kingdom of which John was a member and for which he was imprisoned in Patmos. John was imprisoned for the word of God, which is the testimony of Jesus Christ, which is the gospel. The testimony of Jesus Christ begins with his creation account in Genesis and ends with his final amen in Revelation. The testimony of Jesus Christ, the gospel, and the word of God are all one and the same.

> I John, who also am your brother, and companion **in tribulation**, and **in the kingdom** and patience of Jesus Christ, was in the isle that is called Patmos, **for the word of God**, and **for the testimony of Jesus Christ**. (Revelation 1:9)

The Genesis account of God's creation is every bit a part of the gospel as is the gospel of John. Moses wrote Genesis. If one does not believe the account of God's creation in Genesis how can one believe the words Jesus spoke? John 5:46-47. One cannot truly know God except through his creation. God makes it clear in his "gospel" that the knowledge of God is revealed through his creation as described in God's word. Romans 1:20.

Jesus is the word that became flesh. John 1:1-14. To be a believer means that you believe all of God's word. If somebody claims to be a believer but rejects some of God's word, that necessarily means that they are not a true believer. The law and the prophets are not to be ignored; Jesus came to fulfill them. He admonished us to do and to teach the commandments in his word. Every word of God is important, right down to the last jot and tittle. We should not exclude any part of God's word from the gospel.

> Think not that I am come to destroy the law, or the prophets: I am not come to destroy, but to fulfil. For verily I say unto you, Till heaven and earth pass, one jot or one tittle shall in no wise pass from the law, till all be fulfilled. Whosoever therefore shall break one of these least commandments, and shall teach men so, he shall be called the least in the kingdom of heaven: but whosoever shall do and teach them, the same shall be called great in

the kingdom of heaven. (Matthew 5:17-19)

God commands us not to take his name in vain. Exodus 20:7. But God's word is so precious to God that he exalts his word above even his name. "[F]or thou hast magnified thy word above all thy name." (Psalms 138:2) Each and every word of God is important, we are not to ignore or denigrate any part of God's word. God commands us to preach the gospel (the word of God), which includes the resurrected Jesus Christ sitting on the right hand of the throne of God in heaven, which is above the firmament that Jesus Christ created over the immovable flat earth. Ephesians 1:20; Colossians 3:1; Hebrews 1:3; 8:1; 10:12; 12:2; 1 Peter 3:22. "And he said unto them, Go ye into all the world, and preach the gospel to every creature." (Mark 16:15) Part of that gospel is a command to believers to seek those things that are in heaven. "If ye then be risen with Christ, seek those things which are above, where Christ sitteth on the right hand of God." (Colossians 3:1) How are we going to explain to the believer who is commanded to "seek those things which are above where Christ sitteth on the right hand of God" where to look if we do not plainly tell him the truth that God's throne is in heaven above the firmament that spans over the immovable flat earth? A believer must know where God's throne is, and he must know its relationship to God's creation. Obviously, God's creation of a stationary and flat earth with a firmament overhead is part and parcel of the gospel.

We find in Acts 8:26-40 that the Ethiopian eunuch had the book of Isaiah explained to him by Philip, which brought the eunuch to a saving knowledge of Jesus Christ. The book of Isaiah is part of the gospel (God's word), just as is the creation account of an immovable and flat earth in Genesis. Just as the book of Isaiah in the Old Testament can bring a person to a saving knowledge of Jesus Christ, so also can the creation account of Jesus Christ in the Old Testament book of Genesis.

Paul explained to Timothy that the holy scriptures that Timothy knew from a child (which were necessarily the Old Testament) were able to bring him to salvation through faith in Jesus Christ. Paul explained that **all** of those scriptures in the Old Testament that made Timothy wise unto salvation by faith in Christ Jesus were inspired by God and are profitable for doctrine, reproof, correction, instruction in righteousness, and perfection. Notice that Paul refers to **all** scriptures, not just some scriptures. Those Old Testament scriptures to which Paul referred included the creation account of a flat and stationary earth in the book of Genesis; and those God inspired scriptures remain just as profitable for all who read them today as they were for Timothy more than 2,000 years ago. All scriptures in both the New and Old Testaments are the inspired word of God; they constitute the gospel.

> And that from a child thou hast known **the holy scriptures**, which are able to make thee wise unto salvation through faith which is in Christ Jesus. **All scripture** is given by inspiration of God, and is profitable for doctrine, for reproof, for correction, for instruction in righteousness: That the man of God may be perfect, throughly furnished unto all good works. (2 Timothy 3:15-17)

Indeed, Jesus made the point in John 5:45-47 that if one does not believe the account by Moses of Jesus' creation in the book of Genesis in the Old Testament then he will not believe Jesus' words in the New Testament. "For had ye believed Moses, ye would have believed me: for he wrote of me. But if ye believe not his writings, how shall ye believe my words?" (John 5:46-47) There are eternal consequences for the heliocentric pastors who claim that the account in the bible of Jesus' creation of a flat and stationary earth is not part of the gospel.

The Old Testament and New Testament go together; you

cannot excise any part of God's word. Indeed, the disciples of Christ held both the words of Jesus and the Old Testament scriptures as having equal authority as foundations for their faith. "When therefore he was risen from the dead, his disciples remembered that he had said this unto them; and **they believed the scripture, <u>and</u> the word which Jesus had said.**" (John 2:22)

The fact that Jesus is the creator of all things, seen and unseen, is a prominent part of the gospel. "For by him were all things created, that are in heaven, and that are in earth, visible and invisible, whether they be thrones, or dominions, or principalities, or powers: all things were created by him, and for him." (Colossians 1:16) If the truth that Jesus is the creator of all things is important, so also then is the nature of his creation important because all things were created for him, and his creation gives us an understanding of Jesus Christ. Romans 1:20. The fact that Jesus created a flat and stationary earth over which he reigns from a throne in heaven, which is above the firmament, gives us an understanding of Christ, and thus it is an important part of the gospel.

Paul, in his first letter to the Thessalonians, explained that the gospel that he preached, which brought salvation to the hearers, was the "word of God."

> For this cause also thank we God without ceasing, because, when ye received the **word of God** which ye heard of us, ye received it not as the word of men, but as it is in truth, the **word of God**, which effectually worketh also in you that believe. (1 Thessalonians 2:13)

Jesus stated that man must live by "every word of God" not just some of them. The gospel is "every" word of God. Jesus emphasized that "[i]t is written, Man shall not live by bread alone, but by **every word** that proceedeth out of the mouth of God."

(Matthew 4:4) Pastors cannot pick and choose passages of the Bible to believe. Christian belief is an all or nothing proposition. "**All scripture** is given by inspiration of God, and is profitable for doctrine, for reproof, for correction, for instruction in righteousness." (2 Timothy 3:16) It is improper for a pastor to whittle down the Bible to only those scriptures that he thinks are worthy to be part of the gospel. All scripture is given by inspiration of God. All scripture is profitable for doctrine. All scripture is profitable for reproof. All scripture is profitable for correction. All scripture is profitable for instruction in righteousness. To suggest that any part of scripture is somehow unimportant or insignificant is to imply that God did not inspire those passages.

A claim to be a Christian presupposes faith in Jesus, who is both our savior and our creator. A true Christian believes what Jesus said about both heavenly and earthly things. "If I have told you earthly things, and ye believe not, how shall ye believe, if I tell you of heavenly things?" (John 3:12) God created the flat and stationary earth by his word. Jesus is the Word of God that became flesh. John 1:1-3. Jesus explained that continuing in his word is a sign that one is his true disciple. "If ye continue in my word, then are ye my disciples indeed." John 8:31. To bring forth fruit for Christ, one must hear his word and keep his word. Luke 8:15. The words of Jesus abide in the true believer. John 15:5-8. One who rejects any part of the gospel cannot be a true disciple of Jesus Christ. John 12:48; 14:24.

It bears repeating that Jesus told the Jews that if they did not believe Moses, they would not believe him. "For had ye believed Moses, ye would have believed me: for he wrote of me. But if ye believe not his writings, how shall ye believe my words?" (John 5:46-47) Moses wrote the account of Jesus' creation of an immovable and flat earth in the book of Genesis.

One might ask, where in Genesis did Moses write about

Jesus? Understand, Jesus created all things. "For by him were all things created, that are in heaven, and that are in earth, visible and invisible, whether they be thrones, or dominions, or principalities, or powers: all things were created by him, and for him." (Colossians 1:16) We read in Genesis 1:1 that "[i]n the beginning God created the heaven and the earth." The God of creation is Jesus Christ. By Jesus Christ "were all things created." If one does not believe what Moses wrote in Genesis about Jesus Christ as the creator, then they cannot believe in Jesus as savior.

Don Fortner is typical of so many pastors who love the praise of this world. Most pastors seek friendship with the world on heliocentrism to avoid the ridicule of the world. They do not abide by the admonition of God: "[K]now ye not that the friendship of the world is enmity with God? whosoever therefore will be a friend of the world is the enemy of God." James 4:4. Therein lies the impediment to most pastors accepting the truth of the geocentric, flat earth. Fortner is quite frank in saying that belief that the earth is flat is an "idiotic, foolish, absurd, dumb, crazy notion." He does not want to appear to be an idiotic, foolish, absurd, dumb, crazy person. Fortner's enmity for the truth reveals that he has only the wisdom of the fallen world; the true gospel has not been revealed to him. "At that time Jesus answered and said, I thank thee, O Father, Lord of heaven and earth, because thou hast hid these things from the wise and prudent, and hast revealed them unto babes." (Matthew 11:25).

The idea that belief in a flat earth is crazy is reinforced everywhere in mainstream media and academia. For example, Michelle Thaller, NASA Assistant Director for Science Information, dismisses any notion of a flat earth, stating "this is not a viable argument."[313] She feigns puzzlement that anyone would believe the earth is flat and suggests that it is just a passing fancy. "I don't really know what's going on right now with this 'Earth is flat' thing."[314] She goes further and ominously states that "it's not okay to think that the earth is flat."[315] She makes the statement in the midst of an harangue about how nonsensical it is to believe the earth is flat and implies that there is something mentally wrong with anyone who holds to such a belief. That kind of propaganda affected Fortner, and it is why Fortner fears the truth of the flat earth.

It is the fear of ridicule that is born of Don Fortner's "pride of life," which is of the world and is contrary to God. "For all that is in the world, the lust of the flesh, and the lust of the eyes, and the pride of life, is not of the Father, but is of the world." 1 John 2:16. Indeed, the devil knows the weak character of men and thus has conditioned people to have contempt and deride as "idiotic, foolish, absurd, dumb, crazy" anyone who believes the earth is flat. That heliocentric hive environment that zeros in on and attacks a man's pride serves as an impediment to the truth of the geocentric, flat earth being accepted in academic and scientific (and religious) circles. Don Fortner is exhibit A for the truth of Poole's statement that everlasting ignorance is ensured by contempt before examination. Fortner's weak, prideful character is on display for all to see.

Jesus Christ is both savior and creator. Pastors cannot decouple those two facts. Indeed, the character of God, even his eternal power and Godhead, is revealed through his creation.

> For the invisible things of him from the creation of the world are clearly seen, being understood by the things that are made, even his eternal power and Godhead; so that they are without excuse: (Romans 1:20)

One cannot know Jesus Christ as savior without knowing him as the creator. Belief in Jesus Christ presupposes belief in him as both savior and creator. He is the savior of our souls because he is the creator of our souls. He is the creator of all things seen and unseen. The pastors who focus only on God as the savior to the exclusion of God as the creator are eviscerating the gospel. They honor God with their lips, but their hearts are far from him. They, instead, worship a god of their own making.

In Psalms 136, God proclaims that he is our creator and his eternal goodness and mercy are effectual in saving his elect. God created his elect to save them. Ephesians 1:3-11. We are to give thanks to God for his mercy. God created us to dwell on a flat and stationary earth, with the sun to rule by day and the moon and stars to rule by night. God's creation is inseparable from his mercy in saving his elect. Isaiah 42:1-9. Jesus Christ can effectually save us from our sins by his everlasting mercy because he is God Almighty, the creator of all things, and he is sovereign over his creation. Colossians 1:14-17. That God is a merciful redeemer and that God is the sovereign creator are both parts of the gospel. "But now thus saith **the LORD that created thee**, O Jacob, and he that formed thee, O Israel, Fear not: for **I have redeemed thee**, I have called thee by thy name; thou art mine." (Isaiah 43:1) The fact that God "stretched out the [flat] earth above the waters" is as much a part of the gospel as the fact that "his mercy endureth for ever."

> O give thanks unto the LORD; for he is good: for his mercy endureth for ever. O give thanks unto the God of gods: for his mercy endureth for ever. O give thanks to the Lord of lords: for his mercy endureth for ever. To him who alone doeth great wonders: for his mercy endureth for ever. **To him that by wisdom made the heavens: for his mercy endureth for ever. To him that stretched out the earth above the waters: for his mercy endureth for ever. To him that made great lights: for his mercy endureth for ever: The sun to rule by day: for his mercy endureth for ever: The moon and stars to rule by night: for his mercy endureth for ever. ... Who remembered us in our low estate: for his mercy endureth for**

ever: And hath redeemed us from our enemies: for his mercy endureth for ever. Who giveth food to all flesh: for his mercy endureth for ever. O give thanks unto the God of heaven: for his mercy endureth for ever. (Psalms 136:1-9, 23-26)

To be a Christian requires one to accept all that God states in his word. Jesus Christ makes it clear that there is no such thing as a partial Christian. "So then because thou art lukewarm, and neither cold nor hot, I will spue thee out of my mouth." (Revelation 3:16) Frank Hall puts it this way: "If you are ashamed of the cross, you are ashamed of the Christ who once hung on it, and if you are ashamed of the circle of the flat earth, you are ashamed of the Christ who sits upon it."

The pastors who are ashamed of the flat earth must understand that the shame cuts both ways. "For whosoever shall be ashamed of me and of my words, of him shall the Son of man be ashamed, when he shall come in his own glory, and in his Father's, and of the holy angels." (Luke 9:26) Read closely what Jesus says in that passage. He says that he who is ashamed of God and his "words," God will also be ashamed of him on judgment day. His words formed his creation, and his words of creation are found in his Bible. Indeed, Jesus is the word who became flesh. John 1:14. By his word, he created a flat, immovable earth over which he reigns. "It is he that sitteth upon the circle of the earth, and the inhabitants thereof are as grasshoppers; that stretcheth out the heavens as a curtain, and spreadeth them out as a tent to dwell in:" (Isaiah 40:22) If one is ashamed of God's expressed words regarding his creation, God will be ashamed of him.

Our salvation is based upon God's grace through faith in Jesus Christ. Ephesians 2:8. Our faith is rooted in God's words; not just some of them, all of them. Frank Hall explains:

Faith—faith and faith alone—is our only recourse.

We must believe God! We must take him at his word in all things. Does God say it? Then let us believe it, come what may and come what will. Does God say that salvation is by grace? Then let us trust him for his grace. Does God say that all men are totally depraved? Then let us own and confess our sin this instant. Does God say that Christ is the end of the law for righteousness to everyone that believeth? Then let us believe on Christ for righteousness. Does God say that Eve transgressed his commandment by listening to the lies of a talking snake? Then let us submit our reason to God's word. Does God say that the sun is in circuit above the circle of his firm, fixed, flat, and stationary earth? Then let us forsake the devil's globe and submit ourselves to God's revelation.[316]

12 Pastors Fired for Preaching Flat Earth

On January 25, 2019, it was announced by YouTube (which is owned by Google) that it would begin to institute efforts to reduce the spread of certain content in videos that it described as offering "content that could misinform users in harmful ways" such as those videos "claiming the earth is flat."[317] Clearly, the profane world wants to keep a lid on the truth of the flat earth; it seems also does the modern so-called "church." For example, a pastor was fired from a church in San Diego, California, in 2017 for preaching that the Bible teaches that the earth is flat. Because this author does not have permission of the pastor to reveal his name, his identity will remain confidential. On September 16, 2017, the pastor sent the following email, where he announced his intention to preach to his congregation about the biblical flat earth the next day. The email, in pertinent part, states:

> I'm convinced by God the Holy Spirit that Earth is under Heaven, fixed and unmovable, the foundation on which I live in God and have my being. And I'm convinced that Christ my Rock has never moved since before the foundation of the world, even before God divided the waters and

manifested the dry land. Or else, Christ is spinning and hurdling me through the outer darkness of the abyss and I have no hope for my sinful, wretched soul. ...

God gave me His message for our Sunday morning worship service, September 17, 2017. I haven't slept a wink since Thursday night, and my heart is on FIRE! God don't let me go to sleep! This is too important. I shall, by God's grace, declare this message boldly from my own pulpit with the clarity and dogmatism worthy of God's eternal truth. I say the truth in Christ. I lie not! My conscience bears witness to me in the Holy Spirit. The only choice you now have is to cast me off forever as a filthy reprobate, or bow to the revelation of God's word. This is the hardest, heaviest trial I have ever faced. My heart is breaking! My flesh is trembling! If God is not with me, if He does not uphold me, I will crumble. But God is my Rock. I may tremble and shake, but He is never moved. On Him I fall flat as a pancake, broken in humility. Lord Jesus, let me not be ashamed. Let me not falter and forsake the truth for Earthly ease or man's approval. God is faithful. He will keep me, for Christ's sake. ...

I'm all in for Christ's sake. God keep me by His grace. I will be ostracized. I will be forsaken by my brethren, just as my Lord. But there's no turning back, or else I'm not His servant (Matt 10:24-42). My heart breaks for you, my brethren. This will not be easy. It will only get harder, the longer you resist the truth. But God's grace is sufficient. The truth cannot be broken. It stands or falls together. Christ is not divided. The LORD will show all of

His people!

(Mark 12:10-11) "And have ye not read this scripture; The stone which the builders rejected is become the head of the corner: This was the Lord's doing, and it is marvellous in our eyes?"[318]

The pastor kept his promise; and on September 17, 2017, he preached a sermon on the biblical flat earth. That very day he was fired from his position as pastor. The next day, September 18, 2017, the following email was sent out from the church elders to more than 120 people titled "termination." The email stated:

To all:

[Name Redacted] is no longer the pastor of [Church Name Redacted]. We as a congregation denounce this foolishness wholeheartedly and we ask that you disregard these emails.

[Name Redacted] in no way represents the faith of the congregation that God has raised up here. We will continue to meet while we wait on the Lord for his purpose in sending forth a pastor to feed his sheep here.

Thank you,
[Names of Church Elders Redacted][319]

The elders describe the pastor's preaching about the biblical evidence for a flat, motionless earth as "foolishness" that in no way represented the "faith" of their church. There was to be no discussion of the topic. It was simply labeled "foolishness" to preach about a flat earth. The topic and the pastor who brought it up were not worthy of further consideration. They were both to be summarily dismissed. That was all done in what is supposed to be a "Christian" church. God addresses the response of the church elders as follows:

> But the natural man receiveth not the things of the Spirit of God: for **they are foolishness unto him**: neither can he know them, because they are spiritually discerned. (1 Corinthians 2:14)

As a side note, Don Fortner had a very close relationship and influence with the San Diego church that fired the pastor. That relationship has continued. In fact, on or about January 8, 2019, which is more than two years after the pastor was fired, the website for the San Diego church announced that "Pastor Don Fortner from Grace Baptist Church in Danville, Kentucky is scheduled to preach here on Tuesday and Wednesday evening, January 22, 23 [2019]." Furthermore, as of January 2019, there is a link on the San Diego church website to the sermons of Don Fortner found at www.donfortner.com, where it is described as "the website of Grace Baptist Church of Danville, KY." The fact that the Grace Baptist church website is titled "DonFortner.com" speaks volumes about the control that Fortner exercises over that church.

Nate Wolfe is another pastor who was fired from his church in Oregon, Ohio. In Wolfe's case, he did not even preach a sermon on the flat earth. He merely attended a conference about the flat earth on his own vacation time. The conference was the August 22-25, 20018, Take on the World Conference in Vermilion Ohio.[320] After the elders found out that Wolfe had attended the conference, approximately two weeks after his return, he was summarily fired.[321] Prior to being fired, Wolfe had been a full-time teaching and preaching minister for more than 15 years. He had been the pastor of the church from which he was fired for the previous 7.5 years.[322] Wolfe had an exemplary record, and there were no other issues that would give cause to his firing. But the elders of the church did not care. It was just too much for him to explore the truth of the biblical flat earth. In their minds, he had to go.

The church elders called Wolfe to a meeting where it was announced to him that "it has come to our attention that on August 24th to the 26th you attended the Take on the World Conference in Ohio ... We cannot have a minister who has that association; we cannot let you in the pulpit Sunday."[323] Wolfe explained that the elders had no interest in discussing the issue. He asked the elders "when in seven and a half years have I taught something that was unbiblical, untrue; when have I caused any unnecessary conflict or drama?"[324] The elders did not respond to his question. They were determined to fire him for attending the flat earth conference. Wolf explained: "I was never asked by my church leadership what I actually believe, what I attended at the conference, or what my intentions were moving forward. None of my questions regarding their decision to fire me were answered. I was shut down completely."[325] As a consequence of being fired as the primary breadwinner, he and his family of six saw their income drop 60%.

13 Pastoral Intolerance of the Flat Earth

There are preachers today who promote heliocentric heathenism as an essential religious doctrine. They have supplanted the biblical flat earth and replaced it with the so-called science of heliocentrism. Louie Giglio is one example of such. Louie Giglio is pastor of Passion City Church and the Founder of the Passion movement. He recently hosted the *Passion 2017* conference in Atlanta's Georgia Dome that was attended by more than 55,000 college-aged students.[326] Giglio is a heliocentric pied piper, leading his naive followers down the wide way to destruction. *See* Matthew 7:13.

Giglio expressly promotes the heliocentric myth of a spinning globe earth in an infinite vacuum of space.[327] Giglio has presented sermons in large auditoriums where he projects phony outer space images upon massive stage screens.[328] The images he projects are allegedly from the Hubble space telescope and other NASA space satellites. Giglio then preaches on the expansive empty vacuum of space with billions of stars and galaxies. Giglio presents the heliocentric model with its massive universe as a reflection of God's majesty and power. Giglio states that he is trying to explain who God is through his creation. Indeed, it is true that God is revealed through his creation.

> The heavens declare the glory of God; and the firmament sheweth his handywork. Day unto day uttereth speech, and night unto night sheweth knowledge. There is no speech nor language, where their voice is not heard. (Psalms 19:1-3)

But Giglio begins his presentation on the premise that God is indescribable. He suggests by that statement and his display that God's infinite universe indicates that God is far away and cannot be known. That is false. Indeed, it is through God's creation that he is revealed to us.

> Because that which may be known of God is manifest in them; for God hath shewed it unto them. For the invisible things of him from the creation of the world are clearly seen, being understood by the things that are made, even his eternal power and Godhead; so that they are without excuse: (Romans 1:19-20)

Giglio ultimately presents the crucifixion of Jesus Christ as an atonement for our sins. He claims that Jesus loves us but he does it under the rubric that God is "huge" and far removed from us while we are "tiny" and "insignificant." Indeed, he prefaces his discussion of Jesus by describing to the audience a large image of the Grand Design Galaxy that he says is 31 million light-years away from earth.[329] He then tells the audience that he is going to take them beyond the Grand Design Galaxy, "far, far, far, far out" into the universe.[330] At that point, he displays a picture of the common rendition of Jesus being crucified. The implication is that God is "far, far, far, far" away from us.

That is a false portrayal of the relationship between God and man. And it because Giglio presents a false creation. Giglio's Jesus is a false Jesus. God warned us about those who would present to us a false Jesus. Acts 11:4. Jesus is the creator of all things. Colossians 1:16. But Giglio's false Jesus is a false creator who is far away and beyond our capacity to know. In fact, God is very close. He is above the firmament on his throne. Ezekiel 1:25-28 God is above us in heaven, watching over man. Job 22:12; Ecclesiastes 24:5; Psalms 14:2 & 33:13.

Giglio is impeached by God's word, which states that the invisible things of God may, in fact, be known and understood through his creation. *See* Romans 1:19-20. Giglio's god is a god of heliocentrism, a god of mythology, a god who cannot be known because he does not exist.

Giglio describes God as holy, but he contradicts himself by then describing an unbiblical god that is "ferocious." Giglio describes the allegedly massive heliocentric sun that is supposed to be approximately 93 million miles away from earth and alleged to be more than 100 times the earth's diameter. Giglio then states that the massive "raging fire" of the heliocentric sun "came out of the mouth of God."[331] And Giglio then deduces that "we cannot think that he is some kind of mamby-pamby God, some kind of mealy little weak God; he is ferocious, this God we are worshipping tonight."[332]

The word ferocious means "savagely fierce, cruel, or violent"[333] and "extreme fierceness and unrestrained violence and brutality."[334] Ferociousness is an attribute of a savage beast, not God. The God of the Bible is not ferocious. God's judgments are perfect. Psalms 18:30. "He is the Rock, his work is perfect: for all his ways are judgment: a God of truth and without iniquity, just and right is he." (Deuteronomy 32:4) The Bible states that "[t]he Lord is righteous in all his ways, and holy in all his works." Psalms 145:17. Indeed, "Holy, holy, holy, is the LORD of hosts: the whole earth is full of his glory." Isaiah 6:3.

Giglio has a perverted concept of God because he has a perverted idea of God's creation. One follows from the other.

There is a ferocious being mentioned in the Bible. That being is not God. That being is a beast; he is the devil. "Be sober, be vigilant; because your adversary the devil, as a roaring lion, walketh about, seeking whom he may devour." 1 Peter 5:8. It seems that we have found the true identity of Giglio's god.

God did not create the universe as portrayed by Giglio. Giglio promotes a false creation because he worships a false god. Giglio is practicing heathen priestcraft while he is at the same time using Bible passages to hoodwink the masses. Giglio is one of the false prophets about whom Jesus warned us. "Beware of false prophets, which come to you in sheep's clothing, but inwardly they are ravening wolves." (Matthew 7:15)

Louie Giglio fawns over and hero worships NASA astronauts. During one of his stage presentations, Giglio quoted from the arch-fraud, Neil Armstrong, to explain the vastness of the vacuum of outer space and the insignificance of man. On one occasion, he expressed from the stage how he felt immensely privileged and was in awe that an astronaut (Joe Tanner) directly corresponded with him.[335] Giglio drives home the point that in God's vast universe we are "teeny, tiny, little people," compared to the expansive universe we are "really, really, really small."[336] His whole shtick is premised on man being inconsequential in God's vast universe. Giglio's preaching implies that God is far, far away.

It is no surprise to find that heliocentrist Louie Giglio is in league with the pope of Rome, who is the very Antichrist. On July 3, 2015, Giglio embraced and kissed Pope Francis when Giglio attended the Vatican's *Renewal With the Spirit Convocation.*[337] Giglio's false model of creation has the Antichrist's stamp of approval. God warns that whoever even greets one who preaches a false gospel "is partaker of his evil deeds." 2 John 1:9-11. Giglio is a partaker with the antichrist in his evil deeds. Indeed, "[c]an two walk together, except they be agreed?" Amos 3:3. For more information about the Antichrist, read this author's book, *Antichrist: The Beast Revealed*. God warns against following the false heliocentric gospel promoted by evil men like Giglio.

> Whosoever transgresseth, and abideth not in the doctrine of Christ, hath not God. He that abideth in the doctrine of Christ, he hath both the Father and the Son. If there come any unto you, and bring not this doctrine, receive him not into your house, neither bid him God speed: **For he that biddeth him God speed is partaker of his evil deeds.** (2 John 1:9-11)

Figure 11: Louie Giglio at the Vatican kissing Pope Francis. "[H]e that biddeth him God speed is partaker of his evil deeds." John 1:11.

As explained in a previous chapter, it was the Roman Catholic priest, Nicolaus Copernicus (1473-1543), with hidden Vatican support, who trotted out the modern heliocentric model. It is well established that heliocentrism finds its origins in the heathen religious beliefs of the Jewish Kabbalah. Indeed, Copernicus explained that his heliocentric system was not an innovation, but was rather a revival of the motion of planets taught by Pythagoras, who was a Kabbalist.[338] Freemasonry and Catholicism are both essentially Kabbalistic Judaism for Gentiles. That is why we find many Masonic lodges throughout the world are named in honor of Copernicus.³³⁹ Could Louie Giglio be one of the many agents of Rome sent into Protestant churches to promote the heliocentric model as a way to undermine the gospel of Jesus Christ?

Giglio is just one example of the heliocentric corruption in churches today. The heliocentric claws have sunk so deep into the churches that any discussion of a biblical flat earth will not be tolerated. Pastors know that if they even hint that they believe what the Bible says about the flat earth they will be out on their ear. When inquiring church members question them, they know that their job as a pastor is safe if they side with the heliocentric mythology. They dismiss any notion of a flat earth as being a distraction from the gospel.

Hank Hanegraaff is the President of the Christian Research Institute (CRI), he has (allegedly) written 25 books, and he is the host of the radio show, "The Bible Answer Man," which is syndicated on 60 radio stations and reaches millions of listeners all over the world. Hanegraaff opines that belief in the flat earth is an outrageous myth that is unsupported by science and the Bible. Hanegraaff states:

> [Those who believe the earth is flat are] buying into the ultimate conspiracy theory. This is propaganda pure and simple. ... The whole idea of the flat earth has been demonstrated to be false. It's propaganda. ... The only way that you can make the earth flat is to ignore everything that we know about astronomy, everything that we know about science and mathematics, and then everything we know about the Bible. ... It is simply outrageous to suggest that a Christian would believe that.³⁴⁰

Who really is Hank Hanegraaff? He has been accused of mounting an underhanded take over of CRI after its founder,

Walter Martin died in 1989.[341] The nefarious shenanigans of Hank Hanegraaff are documented in a book titled *Hard Questions for the Bible Answer Man: Hank Hanegraaff and His Takeover of the Christian Research Institute*,[342] written by Jay Howard, who is the founder of the Christian Research Project in Logan, Ohio.[343]

Hanegraaff's many offenses include plagiarism, which is "the practice of taking someone else's work or ideas and passing them off as one's own."[344] Robert Bowman researched the matter and set forth the evidence for the world to judge.[345] The evidence presents a pretty clear case of intellectual property theft by Hanegraaff. In 1983, D. James Kennedy published a book titled, *Evangelism Explosion*. Apparently, Hanegraaff saw money or notoriety in republishing substantial parts of that book under his name, with a new title, *Personal Witness Training*. Hanegraaff used the same basic concept, similar terminology, substantially the same introductory material, basic chapter topics and order, principles (renamed pillars), gospel outline, dialogues with changes to some nouns (e.g., changing "painting" to "portrait"), similar follow-up questions with slight modifications in verbiage (e.g., changing "brief questions" to "short questions").[346]

Hanegraaff published his book, *Personal Witness Training*, in 1987, without obtaining permission or giving any attribution to Kennedy's book, *Evangelism Explosion*. He falsely passed off Kennedy's work as though it was his own. Indeed, he gave no acknowledgment to Kennedy in any capacity at all in the first edition of *Personal Witness Training*. Probably fearing the accusation of plagiarism, Hanegraaff, in a later edition of *Personal Witness Training*, acknowledged Kennedy with thanks for his "books" and "lectures" but he never mentioned Kennedy's book, *Evangelism Explosion*.

D. James Kennedy saw Hanegraaff's book with the pages set side by side with his own book and thought that the similarities between the two books were "startling."[347] Kennedy decided not to sue Hanegraaff because he did not want to sue a fellow Christian.³⁴⁸

Hank Hanegraaff, *The Bible Answer Man*, taking part in a heathen "chrismation" ceremony in the Eastern Orthodox Church.

God's creation reveals who God is. God reveals to us through his creation his invisible eternal power and Godhead. Romans 1:20. Hanegraaff believes the lie of heliocentrism. Hanegraaff's misconception of God's creation caused a concomitant misunderstanding of who God is. This distorted conception led Hanegraaff to worship a far-off god in an endless universe. Hanegraaff's god does not exist.

Hanegraaff's misconception of God's creation led Hanegraaff to have a perverted notion of God and his gospel. This prompted Hanegraaff, in 2017, to convert to the Eastern Orthodox Church, which appears to the world as a "Christian" denomination, but is, in reality, a heathen religion, steeped in rituals, icons, superstition, mysticism, and spooky liturgical mumbo-jumbo.³⁴⁹

Hank Hanegraaf is "The Bible Answer Man." He certainly would not join a church that diminishes the authority of the Bible, would he? Sadly, the answer is, yes. Emmanuel Hatzidakis is a retired Eastern Orthodox Priest who received his Master's Degree in Divinity from Holy Cross Greek Orthodox School of Theology, Brookline, MA. Hatzidakis founded *Orthodox Witness*, which is an organization dedicated to Orthodox Evangelism. Hatzidakis is an expert in Eastern Orthodox theology. He explains the Eastern

Orthodox view of the authority of the Bible:

> The perceived problem with certain Christian truths is due to the erroneous principle of scriptural literalism, which is based on the equally erroneous principle of biblical inerrancy. We believe that the Holy Scripture is infallible in matters of Christian faith and life.[350]

What that means is that the Eastern Orthodox Church only takes the Bible as infallible regarding "Christian faith and life." It does not think that the Bible is inerrant in all things. Under the Eastern Orthodox view of scripture, the Bible is full of errors regarding scientific pronouncements. Hatzidakis spells this out:

> According to our understanding **the Holy Bible is not a scientific textbook, therefore we are not to take every geographic, historical, and scientific detail as error-free, and we should not read it that way.** The Holy Scripture seems to follow the view that God created a stationary, flat earth, with the heaven being a dome over it, and the sun and the moon circling it (Psalm 104); that He created the universe in six 24-hour days, some 10,000 years ago, and that He took mud to form man out of it, and woman out of his rib. Scientific discoveries, from Galileo to Darwin, supported views at odds with a literal understanding of the biblical accounts. As more scientific discoveries were made explaining the laws of nature and the workings of the universe and of life, belief in God was pushed back farther and farther, but only for those who follow a literalistic reading of the Bible.[351] (emphasis added)

Hatzidakis acknowledges that the Bible clearly presents "a

stationary, flat earth, with the heaven being a dome over it, and the sun and the moon circling it."[352] But, according to the Eastern Orthodox Church, the Bible is wrong in its description of God's creation. The Eastern Orthodox Church realizes that it is those who follow a literal reading of the Bible who are at odds with scientific "discoveries," and the Eastern Orthodox Church is not in that literalist camp. Instead, the Eastern Orthodox Church changes with the times and redefines its religion to agree with the current scientific discoveries. Under that rubric, the Eastern Orthodox Church has eschewed the Bible's description of God's flat and stationary earth and opted instead to accept the science of heliocentrism.

The Eastern Orthodox Church explains away the "errors" in the Bible through the trick of anthropomorphizing the scriptures. "In the Orthodox Church's understanding, the biblical account of the creation of the world is an anthropomorphic account, relating, in a way expressed by and understandable to the people of the time."[353] The Eastern Orthodox Church views the writers of the Bible as ignoramuses who misunderstood God's creation. The Eastern Orthodox Church believes that the Bible is wrong in its depiction of God's creation. The Eastern Orthodox Church holds Science as ascendant over the Bible and reads the Bible through the lens of modern scientific prejudice. Where the Bible and science disagree, science wins.

The Eastern Orthodox Church has never viewed the Bible as inerrant. But the Orthodox Church, it seems, does not even bother going through the exercise of metaphorizing Bible passages. The Orthodox Church just out-and-out states that the Bible is wrong. The Orthodox Church accepts the scientific discoveries as true and the Bible as erroneous where it disagrees with science. The Eastern Orthodox church has made accommodation for science. The Eastern Orthodox Church created a religion that defined their god, not according to the holy writ of the Bible, but rather according to ever-changing scientific discoveries. Hence, they adopted a Darwinian/heliocentric god. Their heathen god of science sent their followers down the slippery slope of a liturgical "Christianity" which is found nowhere in the Bible.

Bishop Kallistos Ware, a famous Eastern Orthodox Theologian, explains one of the heathen practices in the Eastern Orthodox Church that is born from their diminution of the authority of the Bible. "[I]n private, an Orthodox Christian is free to ask ... for the intercessions, not only of the Mother of God and the saints, but his own [dead] mother and [dead] father. In its public worship, however, the church usually prays only to those whom it has officially proclaimed as saints."[354]

Keep in mind that the saints referred to above are those that have died. God has expressly commanded that we not attempt to communicate with the dead. To communicate with the dead is an abominable sin called **necromancy**.

> There shall not be found among you any one that maketh his son or his daughter to pass through the fire, or that useth divination, or an observer of times, or an enchanter, or a witch, Or a charmer, or a consulter with familiar spirits, or a wizard, or a **necromancer. For all that do these things are an abomination unto the LORD**: and because of these abominations the LORD thy God doth drive them out from before thee. (Deuteronomy 18:10-12)

There is only one mediator between man and God to whom we should pray, and that is Jesus Christ.

> **For there is one God, and one mediator between God and men, the man Christ Jesus;** (1 Timothy 2:5)

Why would one pray to the saints? God won't listen to their counsel, because he doesn't need counsel. Ephesians 1:11. God puts no trust in his saints.

> Behold, **he putteth no trust in his saints**; yea, the heavens are not clean in his sight. (Job 15:15)

What attracted Hanegraaff to the Eastern Orthodox Church? Hanegraaff states: "The big thing that attracted me to Eastern Orthodoxy was the Eucharist. ... For most of church history, even through Luther, people believed that when you partook of the elements, you were partaking of the real presence of Christ."[355]

The Orthodox Catechism, indeed, states that "[t]he Eucharist is the center of worship in the Orthodox Church."[356] According to that catechism, "[i]n the Eucharist, we partake mystically of Christ's Body and Blood, which impart His life and strength to us."[357]

What does it mean to "partake mystically of Christ's Body and Blood"? According to the Holy Synod of Bishops of the Orthodox Church in America, which is the supreme canonical authority in the Church:

> At this time the gifts of bread and wine which have been offered on the altar are lifted up from the altar to God the Father, and receive divine sanctification by the Holy Spirit who comes to change them into the very Body and Blood of Christ.[358]

Under the Eastern Orthodox Dogma, the bread and wine are changed "into the very Body and Blood of Christ." This bears elaboration. The Eastern Orthodox Church teaches that "the central place among the Sacraments of the Orthodox Church is held by the Holy Eucharist the precious Body and Blood of our

Lord Jesus Christ."³⁵⁹ It is only through the "Holy Eucharist" that one can attain salvation in the Eastern Orthodox Church. "Only by belonging to the Church, or in other words, being in communion with the very essence of Christ through the Sacrament of the Holy Eucharist, can one attain salvation unto eternal life."³⁶⁰

The true gospel message is that salvation is by God's grace alone through faith in Jesus Christ alone. "For by grace are ye saved through faith; and that not of yourselves: it is the gift of God: Not of works, lest any man should boast." (Ephesians 2:8-9) But the Eastern Orthodox Church has a different gospel where salvation is by works. To gain salvation in the Eastern Orthodox Church one must do the work of taking part in the Eucharistic sacrifice during Orthodox liturgy. In the Eastern Orthodox Church, to be saved, one must be "in communion with the very essence of Christ through the Sacrament of the Holy Eucharist."³⁶¹ That teaching of the Eastern Orthodox Church is a false gospel; it is directly contrary to what the Bible says.

Furthermore, the Orthodox doctrine is that "[t]he sacrifice offered at the Eucharist is Christ Himself, but He Who brings the sacrifice is also Christ. Christ is, at one and the same time, High Priest and Sacrifice."³⁶² Under the Orthodox theology the Eucharistic sacrifice is not symbolic. "In the first place, the sacrifice is not only an enactment or a symbol, but a real sacrifice. In the second, that which is sacrificed is not bread, but the very Body of Christ."³⁶³ The Orthodox view is that the Eucharist is a real sacrifice of Christ himself.

> According to the Orthodox Church, then, the Eucharist is not just a reminder of Christ's sacrifice or of its enactment, but it is a real sacrifice. On the other hand, however, it is not a new sacrifice, nor a repetition of the Sacrifice of the Cross upon Golgotha. The events of Christ's Sacrifice the Incarnation, the Institution of the Eucharist, the

Crucifixion, Resurrection and Ascension into Heaven, are not repeated during the Eucharist, yet they become a present reality.[364]

This harkening back in a spiritual way somehow to Christ's sacrifice on the cross is what distinguishes the Eastern Orthodox Church from the Eucharistic dogma of the Roman Catholic Church. Under the Roman doctrine, the Eucharist celebration is a renewal of the sacrifice of Christ on the cross. But it seems that distinction is one without a real difference. In both cases, the Eucharist is transubstantiated into Jesus Christ himself. That means that under the Eastern Orthodox doctrine, the Eucharist is a real reenactment of Jesus Christ's sacrifice on the cross. The denial that it is a repeat of Christ's crucifixion is sophistry in the extreme. In the Longer Catechism of the Orthodox, Catholic, Eastern Church by St. Philaret (Drozdov) of Moscow (1830), it states that "the bread truly, really, and substantially becomes the very true Body of the Lord, and the wine the very Blood of the Lord."[365]

Transubstantiation seems to have been a long established dogma in the Eastern Orthodox Church. Indeed, the 1672 Orthodox Confession of Dositheus, Patriarch of Jerusalem, states:

> [A]fter the consecration of the bread and of the wine, the bread is transmuted, transubstantiated, converted and transformed into the true Body itself of the Lord, Which was born in Bethlehem of the ever-Virgin, was baptized in the Jordan, suffered, was buried, rose again, was received up, sits at the right hand of the God and Father, and is to come again in the clouds of Heaven; and the wine is converted and transubstantiated into the true Blood itself of the Lord, Which as He hung upon the Cross, was poured out for the life of the world.[366]

According to the Eastern Orthodox Church, the Eucharist is transubstantiated into the real body of Christ and wine into the real blood of Christ.

> [A]ttention must be paid that the priest have, at the time of consecration, the intention that the real substance of the bread and the substance of wine be transubstantiated into the real body and blood of Christ through the operation of the Holy Spirit. ... Transubstantiation occurs immediately with these words, and the bread is transubstantiated into the real body of Christ and the wine into the real blood of Christ, with the visible appearances alone remaining.[367]

The Eastern Orthodox Eucharistic sacrifice is blasphemy, pure and simple. The Judaic/Babylonian liturgy of the Eucharist in the Eastern Orthodox Church involves a witchcraft ceremony, during which a piece of bread (the host) and some wine is purported to be transformed into Jesus Christ. The Eastern Orthodox Church is saying, in no uncertain terms, that Jesus Christ himself, God Almighty, is present in the outward form of bread and wine.

The Eastern Orthodox Church doctrine of transubstantiation is ceremonial witchcraft. William Schnoebelen was a former satanic priest, master Mason, alleged member of the Illuminati, and a Catholic priest in the Old Roman Catholic Church (O.R.C.C.). The O.R.C.C. is a splinter group from the Vatican which has valid holy orders, has celebrated Mass for centuries, and allows for a married priesthood.[368] Schnoebelen stated that the Catholic liturgy of the Mass, which is similar to the Eastern Orthodox liturgy, is an occult magic ritual. It is, therefore, easy for Satanists to tweak it slightly to make it into the consummate black magic ritual.[369] Schnoebelen degenerated in his climb up the satanic hierarchy to the point where he became a

Nosferatic priest.[370] A Nosferatic priest is a Vampire. *Nosferatu* is the Romanian word for the "undead" or vampire. Since all members of the Nosferatic priesthood must first be priests of the Catholic or Eastern Orthodox Rite, they believe that they have the power to produce the full nine pints of the blood of Jesus contained in the chalice of wine through the magic of transubstantiation. When real human blood was not available to him, he satisfied his demonic need for human blood through the liturgy of the Mass.[371]

The Eastern Orthodox Church teaches that wine and bread have been turned into the body and blood of Christ, and that when one is consuming the bread and wine it is only the form of bread and wine, it is actually the body and blood of Christ. The Eastern Orthodox doctrine of transubstantiation is a sin. In the following passages, God has made it clear that people are to abstain from drinking *any manner* of blood. Presumably, any manner of blood includes transubstantiated blood.

> Moreover ye shall **eat no manner of blood, whether it be of fowl or of beast, in any of your dwellings**. Whatsoever soul it be that eateth any manner of blood, even that soul shall be cut off from his people. (Leviticus 7:26-27)

> And whatsoever man there be of the house of Israel, or of the strangers that sojourn among you, that eateth **any manner of blood; I will even set my face against that soul that eateth blood**, and will cut him off from among his people. (Leviticus 17:10)

> [A]bstain from meats offered to idols, and from blood, and from things strangled, and from fornication: from which if ye keep yourselves, ye shall do well. Fare ye well. (Acts 15:29)

The Eastern Orthodox church quotes the following passage, purporting it to support its claim that during the Eastern Orthodox Mass bread is turned into God.

> And he took bread, and gave thanks, and brake it, and gave unto them, saying, This is my body which is given for you: **this do in remembrance of me.** (Luke 22:19)

That passage in Luke does not support the proposition that bread is thereafter to be turned into God. Before Christ came to earth, God required ceremonial sacrifices from the Jews. Those sacrifices were done to bring to mind the coming Messiah. The Jews looked forward to Christ, the sacrificial lamb of God. The Old Testament sacrifices themselves did not atone for the sins. Jesus was the atonement. Salvation from sins came then, as now, by the grace of God through faith in God and his Messiah, Jesus. The memorial instituted by Christ during the last supper was for us to look back to the sacrifice of Christ, just as the Jews used to look forward toward Christ's coming. We are to do it in remembrance of him and his sacrifice for us.

> For the law having a shadow of good things to come, and not the very image of the things, can never with those sacrifices which they offered year by year continually make the comers thereunto perfect. For then would they not have ceased to be offered? because that the worshippers once purged should have had no more conscience of sins. **But in those sacrifices there is a remembrance again made of sins every year. For it is not possible that the blood of bulls and of goats should take away sins.** (Hebrews 10:1-4)

Jesus never intended that the breaking of bread be any more than a memorial to bring remembrance of him and his sacrifice on the cross.

> And when he had given thanks, he brake it, and said, Take, eat: this is my body, which is broken for you: **this do in remembrance of me.** After the same manner also he took the cup, when he had supped, saying, This cup is the new testament in my blood: **this do ye, as oft as ye drink it, in remembrance of me. For as often as ye eat this bread, and drink this cup, ye do shew the Lord's death till he come.** (1 Corinthians 11:24-26)

The Orthodox Church doe not accept the inerrancy of the Bible. Believing the Bible to be inerrant is not the same as taking the Bible literally. Some Bible passages are metaphors, and there are other passages that are literal. But when one discounts the inerrancy of the Bible, it is easy to take passages that are intended to be taken literally and reinterpreting them as only expressing figurative concepts. The reverse is also true. And that is what the Orthodox Church has done. It has taken passages intended as metaphors and literalized them.

The Easter Orthodox Heliocentrists turn exegesis on its head. They reject the literal descriptions of the flat and stationary earth as erroneous. But when the context plainly indicates that a passage is a metaphor, suddenly the Eastern Orthodox priests ignore the metaphor and instead read the passage literally. Jesus was using a metaphor when he said "this is my body" and "this is my blood." He had also called himself the "lamb of God" and "the bread of life." These phrases were intended to be figurative expressions. We don't think of Christ as a literal lamb; why does the Eastern Orthodox church interpret Jesus' words at the last supper literally? Because there is money to be made and there are souls to corrupt. "[T]he love of money is the root of all evil. 1 Timothy 6:10.

The Eastern Orthodox Church often cites Matthew 26:26-28 in support of its claim that the priest, during the Eastern Orthodox Mass, changes bread and wine into the blood and body of Jesus.

> And as they were eating, Jesus took bread, and blessed it, and brake it, and gave it to the disciples, and said, Take, eat; this is my body. And he took the cup, and gave thanks, and gave it to them, saying, Drink ye all of it; For this is my blood of the new testament, which is shed for many for the remission of sins. (Matthew 26:26-28)

Jesus was eating the Passover meal with his disciples. The Passover was intended to be a memorial that was to celebrate God having freed the Jews from Egyptian slavery. The fourteenth day of the first month is the Passover (Leviticus 23:4-5, Exodus 12:17-18). Passover is immediately followed by the seven days of unleavened bread (Leviticus 23:6-7, Exodus 12:15-16). At the last supper, Jesus was referring to the fact that the unleavened bread that was eaten during Passover not only looked back to the spotless lamb of Passover but also looked forward to him as the Christ, who would die as the Passover lamb for the sins of the world. 1 Peter 1:18-19. Just as the Passover memorial looked back to the Passover lamb, so also would this new Passover last supper harken back to the Passover lamb of God, Jesus Christ, who was crucified for our sins. Just as the unleavened bread eaten on Passover was not the actual lamb, but only a memorial, so also the unleavened bread and wine celebrating the last supper are not the actual body and blood of Jesus; they are only memorials.

The Eastern Orthodox church teaches that Jesus actually turned the fruit of the vine into blood. By taking verses 26-28 of Matthew chapter 26 out of context the Eastern Orthodox church has been able to deceive the whole world. All one need do to see that Jesus did not change the fruit of the vine in the cup into his actual blood is to put verses 26-28 back in context by reading the next verse, verse 29. "But I say unto you, I will not drink henceforth of **this fruit of the vine**, until that day when I drink it new with you in my Father's kingdom." (Matthew 26:29) Notice, in that very verse (verse 29) following his statement that "this is my blood" Jesus states plainly that what was in the cup was still the "fruit of the vine." It had not been changed into his blood. Verse 29 reveals that his statement that "this is my blood" was simply a metaphor. That is why the Eastern Orthodox church does not want the ordinary people to read the Bible. Once the people see the passages in context, they understand the deceptive sophistry of the Eastern Orthodox church.

The passage found in the Holy Bible at John 6:27-66 explains clearly what Jesus meant when he said "this is my body" and "this is my blood." In that Bible passage, Jesus starts out by telling his disciples "labour not for the meat which perisheth, but for that meat which endureth unto everlasting life." That meat is a Spiritual meat. Jesus points out that to eat his flesh and drink his blood is spiritual language that represents believing in him. Only those, however, that are chosen by God for eternal life can understand these truths. Read the passage carefully; you will understand that eating Jesus' flesh and drinking his blood are metaphors for believing in him. Jesus makes the point clear four different times in that passage (verses 29, 35, 40, and 47). One can only understand this spiritual truth if one has the Holy Spirit to guide him. It is foolishness to the unsaved. The unsaved read the passage and are easily persuaded by the Eastern Orthodox church that Jesus is talking about literally eating his flesh and drinking his blood.

> **Labour not for the meat which perisheth, but for that meat which endureth unto everlasting life, which the Son of man shall give unto you: for him hath God the Father sealed.** Then said they unto him, What shall we do, that we might

work the works of God? Jesus answered and said unto them, **This is the work of God, that ye believe on him whom he hath sent**. They said therefore unto him, What sign shewest thou then, that we may see, and believe thee? what dost thou work? Our fathers did eat manna in the desert; as it is written, He gave them bread from heaven to eat. Then Jesus said unto them, Verily, verily, I say unto you, Moses gave you not that bread from heaven; but **my Father giveth you the true bread from heaven. For the bread of God is he which cometh down from heaven, and giveth life unto the world.** Then said they unto him, Lord, evermore give us this bread. **And Jesus said unto them, I am the bread of life: he that cometh to me shall never hunger; and he that believeth on me shall never thirst.** But I said unto you, That ye also have seen me, and believe not. All that the Father giveth me shall come to me; and him that cometh to me I will in no wise cast out. For I came down from heaven, not to do mine own will, but the will of him that sent me. And this is the Father's will which hath sent me, that of all which he hath given me I should lose nothing, but should raise it up again at the last day. **And this is the will of him that sent me, that every one which seeth the Son, and believeth on him, may have everlasting life: and I will raise him up at the last day.** The Jews then murmured at him, because he said, I am the bread which came down from heaven. And they said, Is not this Jesus, the son of Joseph, whose father and mother we know? how is it then that he saith, I came down from heaven? Jesus therefore answered and said unto them, Murmur not among yourselves. No man can come to me, except the Father which hath sent me draw him: and I will raise him up at the last day. It is written in the prophets, And they shall be all taught of God. Every man therefore that hath heard, and hath learned of the Father, cometh unto me. Not that any man hath seen the Father, save he which is of God, he hath seen the Father. **Verily, verily, I say unto you, He that believeth on me hath everlasting life. I am that bread of life.** Your fathers did eat manna in the wilderness, and are dead. **This is the bread which cometh down from heaven, that a man may eat thereof, and not die. I am the living bread which came down from heaven: if any man eat of this bread, he shall live for ever: and the bread that I will give is my flesh, which I will give for the life of the world.** The Jews therefore strove among themselves, saying, How can this man give us his flesh to eat? Then Jesus said unto them, Verily, verily, I say unto you, Except ye eat the flesh of the Son of man, and drink his blood, ye have no life in you. Whoso eateth my flesh, and drinketh my blood, hath eternal life; and I will raise him up at the last day. For my flesh is meat indeed, and my blood is drink indeed. He that eateth my flesh, and drinketh my blood, dwelleth in me, and I in him. As the living Father hath sent me, and I live by the Father: so he that eateth me, even he shall live by me. This is that bread which came down from heaven: not as your fathers did eat manna, and are dead: he that eateth of this bread shall live for ever. These things said he in the synagogue, as he taught in Capernaum. Many therefore of his disciples, when they had heard this, said, This is an hard saying; who can hear it? When Jesus knew in himself that his disciples murmured at it, he said unto them, Doth this offend you? What and if ye shall see the Son of man ascend up where he was before? It is the spirit that quickeneth; the flesh profiteth nothing: the words that I speak unto you, they are spirit, and they are life. But there are some of you that believe not. For Jesus knew from the beginning who they were that believed not, and who should betray him. And he said, Therefore said I unto you, that **no man can come unto me, except it were given unto him of my Father**. From that time many of his disciples went back, and walked no more with him. (John 6:27-66)

The Holy Synod of Bishops of the Orthodox Church in America explains that "[u]nlike many of the Protestant bodies, the Orthodox also see the Eucharistic Liturgy as a bloodless sacrifice."[372] The Eastern Orthodox Church offers Jesus Christ for sacrifice anew in their Eucharist. The Holy Bible states that the one sacrifice of Jesus was sufficient for all his elect, for all time.

So Christ was **once offered** to bear the sins of many; and unto them that look for him shall he appear the second time without sin unto salvation. (Hebrews 9:28)

By the which will we are sanctified through the offering of the body of Jesus Christ **once for all**. And every priest standeth daily ministering and offering oftentimes the same sacrifices, which can never take away sins: But this man, after he had **offered one sacrifice for sins for ever**, sat down on the right hand of God; From henceforth expecting till his enemies be made his footstool. For **by one offering he hath perfected for ever them that are sanctified**. (Hebrews 10:10-14)

Christ made his one sacrifice on the cross whereby those

that believe in him are made perfect; consequently, there will be no more offering of any kind for sin, period.

> But this man, after he had offered one sacrifice for sins for ever, sat down on the right hand of God; From henceforth expecting till his enemies be made his footstool. For **by one offering he hath perfected for ever them that are sanctified**. Whereof the Holy Ghost also is a witness to us: for after that he had said before, This is the covenant that I will make with them after those days, saith the Lord, I will put my laws into their hearts, and in their minds will I write them; And their sins and iniquities will I remember no more. **Now where remission of these is, there is no more offering for sin**. (Hebrews 10:12-18)

This unbloody re-crucifixion of Christ during the Eastern Orthodox liturgy is a re-enactment of the humiliation suffered by Christ on the cross. This re-enactment is not only unnecessary, it is blasphemy. The Bible states that we are to look to Jesus in faith, not in ceremony. Jesus despised the shame of the cross. "Looking unto Jesus the author and finisher of our faith; who for the joy that was set before him **endured the cross, despising the shame**, and is set down at the right hand of the throne of God." (Hebrews 12:2)

Jesus was crucified once for all time. The Eastern Orthodox liturgy is a demonstration that the Eastern Orthodox Church does not believe in the sufficiency of Jesus' sacrifice on the cross. They require that he be crucified over and over again, day after day, week after week, month after month, year after year. The Orthodox liturgy is more than an affront to Christ; it is a ceremonial attack on Christ. It is an antichrist ceremony, whereby the Orthodox Church puts Christ to an open shame by crucifying him anew. The Bible states that it is a terrible sin to crucify Jesus again because it once again puts him to a public shame. "If they shall fall away, to renew them again unto repentance; seeing **they crucify to themselves the Son of God afresh, and put him to an open shame.**" (Hebrews 6:6)

So there you have it. Hank Hanegraaff, "The Bible Answer Man," a heliocentrist and convert to the Eastern Orthodox Chruch, thinks that believing in the biblical flat earth is "outrageous." But, apparently, he thinks that plagiarism, necromancy, and blasphemy are just fine. Recall that Hanegraaff expressly stated that the big thing that attracted him to Eastern Orthodoxy was the Eucharist.[373] He acknowledged that in the Eucharist he is "partaking of the real presence of Christ."[374] That is blasphemy and idolatry and Hanegraaff knows it. *See* Exodus 20:4-5. He is well studied in the Bible. After all, he is "The Bible Answer Man."

> Beware of false prophets, which come to you in sheep's clothing, but inwardly they are ravening wolves. Ye shall know them by their fruits. Do men gather grapes of thorns, or figs of thistles? (Matthew 7:15-16)

David O'Steen (not to be confused with Joel Osteen) is the pastor of Hope Bible Church in Locust Grove, Georgia. David O'Steen is an example of the intolerance toward the flat earth that is endemic in the churches today.

O'Steen calls flat earth a "strange" and "crazy" doctrine that is not in the Bible. He then admonishes people: "Don't go around telling people that the Bible teaches that [the earth is flat]."[375]

O'Steen claims: "I am not fearful about how the world looks at me and what the world thinks about me."[376] But, it seems, it is precisely that of which he is afraid. He is concerned about what the unsaved world thinks when they hear that the Bible teaches that the earth is flat. Because of that fear, O'Steen admonishes his followers: "I am imploring you that if you believe [that the earth is flat] keep it to yourself. Don't go around telling people that the Bible teaches this."[377]

O'Steen claims that when the unsaved world hears that the Bible teaches that the earth is flat and they "know" it is a sphere it will be a stumbling block to them accepting the gospel. What he is really concerned with, it seems, is that the tares that are in his church who do not accept the Bible for what it says will leave his church if he teaches the truth that the Bible teaches that the earth is flat. He is another pastor who is an expert mathematician who wants to ensure his church is full of tares that make up the majority.

O'Steen then rhetorically asks what would be the point of a conspiracy to falsely portray the earth as a sphere. He seems not to understand (or he is pretending not to know) the spiritual significance of the heliocentric deception.[378]

Another pastor who attacks the biblical model of the flat earth is Michael Hoggard.[379] He has been asked by his church members about the flat earth, and, predictably, he came out swinging against it. He states that some of the people who believe that the earth is flat are ignorant, while others are evil people with an evil agenda.[380]

Hoggard thinks that believing the earth is flat is as the sin of witchcraft, but he also states that the shape of the earth is not a salvation issue. With that in mind, he makes repeated ad hominem attacks on those he calls "promoters" of a flat earth. For the most part, he does not address Bible passages, nor does he talk about science. He has posted many videos wherein he attacks the motives and character of those who "promote" belief in a flat earth. He actually states that he sees his mission as keeping people from believing in a flat earth. Hoggard is another of Satan's gatekeepers. It is only lies that need gatekeeping. The truth stands on its own.

Hoggard not only comes against the flat earth and those who believe it, he also takes up the cause on behalf of NASA.[381] Hoggard claims that the Bible prophesies about the alleged space missions. Hoggard's only real biblical argument in support of his claim is from Obadiah. "Though thou exalt thyself as the eagle, and though thou set thy nest among the stars, thence will I bring thee down, saith the LORD." (Obadiah 1:4) Hoggard claims that is a reference to space travel. In Obadiah 1:4 God speaks of prideful Edom as though exalting himself like an eagle in his nest. That passage says nothing about going into a mythical place of outer space in a spacecraft as claimed by Hoggard.

When God states in Obadiah that Edom would make his nest among the stars like an eagle he means what he says: among the stars. Among the stars means surrounded by the stars. Look in the dictionary. Hoggard does not understand plain English. Indeed, the passage makes clear that Edom had exalted himself like an eagle among the stars. Everyone knows that eagles do not go into the mythical vacuum of space to be physically located with the stars. The passage is a reference to an eagle being nested high in the mountains surrounded by stars.

Hoggard hypocritically practices the same strategy that he ascribes to proponents of the flat earth. Hoggard is a muckraker. He states that "when you have to resort to name calling, you ain't got it." That describes Hoggard to a tee. He calls flat earth "promoters" liars.[382]

Hoggard accuses those who believe in a flat earth of the sin of presumption. He claims that there are no Bible passages that support a flat earth. Not a one. He reads his Bible with that presumption. He hypocritically does the very thing that he alleges is done by those who believe that the Bible describes a flat earth.

His attacks on the flat earth are riddled with such hypocrisy.

He believes that those who "promote" flat earth are deceivers in the secret service of Satan who are purposely trying to infiltrate the church in order to divide the church. He cites Jude 1:4 and describes those who believe in the flat earth as ungodly men ordained to condemnation, and who deny our Lord Jesus Christ.

Hoggard states that belief in a flat earth makes Christians look foolish. Hoggard states that those who preach about the Bible's portrayal of a flat earth are "leading people astray, they're making all Christians look like idiots."[383] Hoggard's concern with what the world thinks of Christians (i.e., him) indicates that he is not concerned with the gospel but rather with the pride of life. He says that he sees the ridicule and laughter on the face of those who are told the earth is flat.[384] That is his real concern. He does not want to be ridiculed by the world. He wants friendship with the world.

> Love not the world, neither the things that are in the world. If any man love the world, the love of the Father is not in him. For all that is in the world, the lust of the flesh, and the lust of the eyes, and the pride of life, is not of the Father, but is of the world. (1 John 2:15-16)

Hoggard tries to refute the claim that NASA (being controlled by Freemasons) could be behind a conspiracy concealing the truth of the flat earth. He claims to have searched Masonic literature and found no mention of any secret Masonic conspiracy to hide the reality of a flat earth.[385] Therefore, he concludes that there is not a Masonic conspiracy. His Freemason argument is a classic strawman construction. He constructed a false premise and then addresses that invalid argument because it is easier to defeat than the real case. He concludes that there is no conspiracy because he cannot find evidence in the public writings of Freemasons that they are involved in a conspiracy against God and man to cover up the actual stationary, flat earth created by God.

His argument is silly. One can also search in vain the writings of the Jews for proof that they were involved in a conspiracy to crucify Jesus Christ. But the Bible states clearly that the Jews took counsel together in a conspiracy to crucify Jesus. John 11:53. They then carried out their plan. Acts 2:36, 4:10. Because one cannot find a public admission of that fact by the Jews in their own writings does not mean that they did not carry out a conspiracy to crucify Christ.

Hoggard claims to be a minister of the gospel, but instead of opening the Bible and looking for proof of a spinning globe, he cites to passages that have nothing to say on the subject. He, instead, discusses Bible passages about Satan and concludes that because there is not a reference in those passages that Satan has a plan to conceal the actual shape of the earth that no such plan exists.[386] Hoggard's Masonic argument and vain Bible searches are purposeful diversions.

Hoggard claims to have searched the Bible for evidence that God describes a flat earth. He purports that he came up empty. "When I hear people talk about 'well the Bible says the earth is flat, the Bible *says* the earth is flat,' I look at the Bible, and I'm going I don't see one verse anywhere that says the earth is flat."[387] Hoggard chose his words very carefully. Hoggard is subtlety dissembling when he says that no Bible passage expressly states "the earth is flat." While that specific phrase does not appear in the Bible, his statement is a half-truth (i.e., he is lying). God clearly describes a flat earth in the Bible. Hoggard knows this; Hoggard is engaging in subtle dissimulation. Hoggard claims to be a pastor and holds himself out as a Bible scholar. One must, therefore, conclude that he uncovered God's description of the flat earth during his Bible search.

For example, as a Bible scholar, Hoggard knows that God describes "the circle of the earth" in Isaiah 40:22. A circle is a geometric figure where all points on the circumference are equidistant from the center and on the same plane. A circle, by definition, is flat. It cannot be anything other than flat. A sphere is not a circle. A sphere is not, and cannot be, flat. The definition of a circle precludes the circle of the earth in Isaiah 40:22 from being a sphere. God, who cannot lie, tells us the earth has a circular (i.e., flat) face. All points on the circumference of a circle must be on the same plane (i.e., a circle is flat). Hoggard knows this; Hoggard is a subtle deceiver.

Furthermore, Hoggard did not reference the clear and simple truths in the Bible that the earth is fixed and does not move. "Fear before him, all the earth: the world also shall be stable, that it be not moved." (1 Chronicles 16:30) Indeed, the earth cannot be moved. Psalms 93:1. Hoggard steers clear of the Bible passages that would crush his arguments.

Throughout the internet, "Christian" websites attack the concept of a biblical flat earth. One example is *Verse by Verse Ministry International*, which is a non-denominational, unaffiliated Christian ministry that was founded by Stephen Armstrong, who remains a board member and overseer of all teaching and doctrine. That ministry maliciously claims that the biblical flat earth is a bizarre and false teaching.

> Simply put, men have known the earth was round for centuries, and the Bible confirms this truth implicitly. Unfortunately, some Christians have become victims of false teaching and conspiracy theories that misinterpret various scriptures to support bizarre conclusions. The claim of a "flat" earth is one such false teaching.[388]

Consequently the *Verse by Verse Ministry International* "exhorts" all believers not to delve into the flat earth or even discuss the matter.

Steve Van Nattan condemns in the most strident terms those who believe what the Bible states about God's creation of a flat earth. Van Nattan calls them "fools," "mental midgets," "blithering idiots," "deluded souls" who have a "double dose of stuck on stupid."[389] Van Nattan goes further and expresses his opinion that preaching God's creation of a flat earth will send people to hell.

> You are destroying your testimony for Christ. Rational people who have even a smattering of science study in their past KNOW you are a fool. Why would they trust you to deal with the destiny of their soul? (emphasis in original) Who will go to Hell because you made such as ass of yourself that sinners reject the Gospel also?[390]

Jesus stated: "He that is not with me is against me; and he that gathereth not with me scattereth abroad." (Matthew 12:30) That means that someone who speaks out against the gospel of Christ is against Christ. God's creation of a stationary and flat earth is part of the gospel. Someone who speaks against God's biblical creation account of a flat and stationary earth contained in the gospel is against Christ. The disciples of Christ are the body of Christ. "Now ye are the body of Christ, and members in particular." (1 Corinthians 12:27) That means that those who attack the disciples of Christ and their belief in the truth of the gospel are against Christ (i.e., they are antichrist).

People who call themselves Christians but reject the truth of the Christian gospel are false disciples of Christ. A person who claims to be a Christian but yet campaigns against a clear truth in the gospel is really a wolf in sheep's clothing. Do not be fooled by their high station in the church. An active opponent of the gospel may seek a position as a pastor as a guise from which to undermine the gospel. Such charlatans, who speak against the gospel, are enemies of Christ. Don't be hoodwinked by their smooth oration. Satan's ministers can appear as angel's of light.

> And no marvel; for Satan himself is transformed into an angel of light. Therefore it is no great thing if his ministers also be transformed as the ministers of righteousness; whose end shall be according to their works. (2 Corinthians 11:14-15)

The active opposition of these false ministers of the gospel exposes them as antichrist disciples of the devil. Such persons are quite different from those who are ignorant about some truth in the gospel. A person is not against Christ if he simply does not know about God's creation of a flat earth but otherwise supports the truth of the gospel as far as he knows. Jesus explains that such a person, who is not against him, is still for him. "[H]e that is not against us is for us." (Luke 9:50)

Heliocentric pastors who attack the biblical account of God's creation of a flat and stationary earth are enemies of the gospel of Jesus Christ. It is not a matter of ignorance. They are in an active campaign against the word of God. They are the prophesied Nicolaitans. *See* Revelation 2:6, 15.

14 Leaning on Their Own Understanding

Heliocentric pastors find aid and comfort for their scriptural errors in Bible commentaries that go back hundreds of years. They rely on the thoughts of other men rather than the guidance of the Holy Spirit. Many of those Bible commentaries are polluted with eisegesis based upon the science fiction of heliocentricity. They violate the very command of God to trust entirely in the Lord. We are not to trust in our own contrary understanding of things learned from so-called science. "Trust in the LORD with all thine heart; and lean not unto thine own understanding." (Proverbs 3:5) Many Bible commentators lean on their own understanding and do not trust in what God clearly states in his holy word.

These ministers have found succor in the highfalutin Bible commentators. The Bible should not be subject to private interpretation. "Knowing this first, that no prophecy of the scripture is of any private interpretation." (2 Peter 1:20) The Bible explains itself. And the truth of the Bible is revealed through the Holy Ghost.

Ministers are called to preach the true gospel. Heliocentric ministers are not preaching sound doctrine, and have heaped to themselves Bible commentators to satisfy their ears itching to hear fables.

> Preach the word; be instant in season, out of season; reprove, rebuke, exhort with all longsuffering and doctrine. For the time will come when they will not endure sound doctrine; but after their own lusts shall they heap to themselves teachers, having itching ears; And they shall turn away their ears from the truth, and shall be turned unto fables. (2 Timothy 4:2-4)

A fable is a falsehood.[391] Why do heliocentric ministers want to preach the fable of a spinning globe earth? Because they seek the approval and riches of the world, just as did Balaam. "Woe unto them! for they have gone in the way of Cain, and ran greedily after the error of Balaam for reward, and perished in the gainsaying of Core." (Jude 1:11) They not only preach the fable of heliocentricity, but they have gone in the way of Cain. What did Cain do? He slew his righteous brother, Abel, who was faithful to God's word. Genesis 4:8; Hebrews 11:4. The heliocentric ministers today attack those who believe the gospel of God's creation of a flat and stable earth, just as Cain attacked faithful Abel.

God's word is pure truth. John 17:15-17. Many Bible commentators and ministers treat the Bible as though it contains merely the words of men. But the Bible is not the mere words of men. The Bible is the very word of God, and it is pure truth.

> For this cause also thank we God without ceasing, because, when ye received the word of God which ye heard of us, ye received it not as the word of men, but as it is in truth, the word of God, which effectually worketh also in you that believe. (1 Thessalonians 2:13)

To treat the Bible as though it contains only the words of men is to make void God's commandments. Indeed, all of the precepts in the Bible, on whatever topic, are true and without error.

> It is time for thee, LORD, to work: for they have made void thy law. Therefore I love thy commandments above gold; yea, above fine gold. Therefore I esteem all thy precepts concerning all things to be right; and I hate every false way. (Psalms 119:126-128)

We are commanded not to take God's name in vain. "Thou shalt not take the name of the LORD thy God in vain; for the LORD will not hold him guiltless that taketh his name in vain." (Exodus 20:7) God's word is so precious to God that he exalts his word above even his name. "[F]or thou hast magnified thy word above all thy name." (Psalms 138:2)

Heliocentric ministers rely on commentators who use wordsmithing trickery to redefine words in the Bible that are irreconcilable with their science fiction ideology. Ministers should renounce the hidden things of dishonesty, and not walk in craftiness, or handle the word of God deceitfully. *See* 2 Corinthians 4:2. But they are doing that very thing when they rely on Bible scholars who craftily redefine the words in the Bible that have otherwise plain meanings.

Changing the definition for circle in Isaiah 40:22 so that it includes a sphere is just one example of deceptively handling Gods' word. A circle requires all points on the circumference to be equidistant from the center and on the same plane.[392] A sphere, on the other hand, is a three-dimensional object in the shape of a ball.[393] All points on the circumference of a sphere are equidistant from the center, but those points are not on the same plane.[394] That means that a circle cannot be a sphere, and a sphere cannot be a circle. They are mutually exclusive. To say otherwise is straightforward dissimulation.

Heliocentric ministers cannot find authority for their theology in the Bible, and so they seek the imprimatur found in the traditions of men as memorialized in Bible commentaries. But our faith should be on God's word alone. "That your faith should not stand in the wisdom of men, but in the power of God." (1 Corinthians 2:5) Isaiah 40:22 describes the earth as a circle:

> It is he that sitteth upon the circle of the earth, and the inhabitants thereof are as grasshoppers; that stretcheth out the heavens as a curtain, and spreadeth them out as a tent to dwell in. (Isaiah 40:22)

But Heliocentric Bible commentators redefined circle to include a sphere. One such heliocentric Bible commentator was John Trapp (1601-1669). Trapp was an Anglican Church Bible commentator. He describes the "circle" of the earth in Isaiah 40:22 as a globe.

A circle, which requires all points of the circumference be equidistant from the center and on the same plane, cannot be a sphere. But Trapp could not let that impossibility get in the way of twisting God's word to comport with the religious mythology of heliocentricity, masquerading as science, the truth of which Trapp was convinced. Trapp states in his Bible commentary:

> It is he that sitteth upon the circle of the earth. As sovereign, and is he fit to be portrayed? In Thebes, a town of Egypt, they painted God in the likeness of a man blowing an egg out of his mouth, to signify that he made the round world by his word. (a) Others set him forth as an emperor with a globe in one hand, and a light bolt in the other. Peucer

and others tell us, that if there were a path made round the circle of the earth, an able footman might easily go it in nine hundred days.³⁹⁵

John Gill (1697-1771) was another heliocentric Bible commentator. Gill was a brilliant Baptist minister who mastered the Latin classics and learned Greek by age 11. He wrote an extensive verse-by-verse commentary on the entire Bible. For all of his brilliance, he could not overcome the scientific dogma of a spherical earth that was inculcated into him. He let that worldly science fiction creep into his commentary. Regarding "circle" in Isaiah 40:22, Gill stated: "It is he that sitteth upon the circle of the earth, ... or, 'the globe (z)' of it; for the earth is spherical or globular: not a flat plain, but round, hung as a ball in the air."³⁹⁶ Again, we have a Bible "scholar" who redefines circle to comport with his preconceived concept of a globular earth. A circle, by actual definition, cannot be a sphere because a circle is "all points in the **same plane** that lie at an equal distance from a center point."³⁹⁷ (emphasis added)

Albert Barnes (1798-1870) was yet another heliocentric Bible commentator. Barnes was a graduate of Princeton Theological Seminary and a Presbyterian minister. Barnes was an adherent to Arminianism and was charged and tried, but not convicted, for heresy in 1836. Arminianism has become the majority view in so-called "Christian" Churches today. For more information about Arminianism read this author's book, *The Anti-Gospel*. Barnes wrote a commentary on the Bible. Unsurprisingly, in his commentary Barnes injects his heliocentric leanings and defines the word "circle" in Isaiah 40:22 as denoting both circle and a sphere. Barnes states: "The word rendered 'circle' (חוּג chu^g) denotes 'a circle, sphere, or arch.'"³⁹⁸

Robert Jamieson D.D. (1802–1880) was a church minister in Scotland. Andrew Fausset, A.M. (1821–1910) was rector of a Church in York, England. David Brown (1803–1897) was a minister and professor of theology. In their Jamieson-Fausset-Brown Bible Commentary, they redefined circle in Isaiah 40:22 as "circle—applicable to the globular form of the earth, above which, and the vault of sky around it, He sits."[399]

Daniel Whedon (1808-1885) was professor of Ancient Languages in Wesleyan University and an ardent Arminian. Oddly, despite his erroneous view of the gospel, Whedon correctly interpreted the meaning of "circle" in Isaiah 40:22. But it is not clear from his commentary if he believes the Bible to be true. He does not say that the circle of the earth in Isaiah 4:22 is an accurate description by God of a circular flat earth. Whedon, instead, attributes the description of a "flat, round (not globular) earth" to the "old cosmogony of the Hebrews."

> He that sitteth — This verse contains the fact that should have been known by all men. It is He alone that is enthroned above the vault of the earth, etc. In the old cosmogony of the Hebrews, the heaven was a circular arch which rested on the waters that surrounded the flat, round (not globular) earth.[400]

Interestingly, the Cambridge Bible Commentary for Schools and Colleges (1882) seems to be an outlier. That commentary states the following regarding "circle" in Isaiah 40:22: "The earth with its surrounding ocean is conceived as a flat disc, on which the arch of heaven comes down."[401] The author of that passage is believed to be John Skinner, who was a professor of Old Testament Exegesis at Presbyterian College in London.

Cyrus Ingerson Scofield created a Bible containing his famous (or rather infamous) reference notes. The notes that are appurtenant to Isaiah 40:22, redefined circle to mean "sphericity of the earth." Scofield's notes at Isaiah 40:22 state:

> A remarkable reference to the sphericity of the

earth. See, also, Isaiah 42:5; Isaiah 44:24; Isaiah 51:13; Job 9:8; Psalms 104:2; Jeremiah 10:12.[402]

Scofield refers the reader to Bible passages which in no way support his claim that the "circle" of the earth in Isaiah 40:22 is a "reference to the sphericity of the earth." In one case, the passage cited by Scofield actually contradicts Scofield's commentary. Isaiah 42:5 was cited by Scofield. That passage describes God spreading forth the earth, which is an apparent reference to a flat earth, as a globe cannot be "spread forth."

> Thus saith God the LORD, he that created the heavens, and stretched them out; he that spread forth the earth, and that which cometh out of it; he that giveth breath unto the people upon it, and spirit to them that walk therein. (Isaiah 42:5)

Scofield also cites to Isaiah 51:13, which describes God who "hath stretched forth the heavens, and laid the foundations of the earth." A spinning and orbiting sphere cannot be said to have foundations. His references to Job 9:8, Psalms 104:2, and Jeremiah 10:12 do not help Scofield either, as they describe the heavens being spread out and make no reference to the shape of the earth.

Cyrus Ingerson Scofield was a scam artist who wholeheartedly embraced John Nelson Darby's dispensational pretribulation rapture doctrine, which is all the rage today. Scofield learned Darby's teachings from Dr. James H. Brookes, who was the pastor of the Compton Avenue Presbyterian Church in St. Louis and a follower of Darby's teachings.[403] Scofield put explanatory notes, which included Darby's dispensational system, in his Scofield Reference Bible.[404] The Scofield Reference Bible was published in 1909 and has since then sold more than three million copies. Including explanatory notes in the Holy Bible was unusual for the time and contrary to the practice of the Bible societies whose motto was "without note or comment."

The Scofield Bible was funded and nurtured by World Zionist leaders who saw the Christian churches in America as an obstacle to their plan for the establishment of a Jewish homeland in Palestine. These Zionists initiated a program to infiltrate and change the Christian doctrines of those churches. Two of the tools used to accomplish this goal were Cyrus I. Scofield and a venerable, world respected European book publisher: The Oxford University Press.[405]

The scheme was to alter the Christian gospel and corrupt the church with a pro-Zionist subculture. "Scofield's role was to re-write the King James Version of the Bible by inserting Zionist-friendly notes in the margins, between verses and chapters, and on the bottoms of the pages."[406] In 1909, the Oxford University Press published and implemented a large advertising budget to promote the Scofield Reference Bible.

The Scofield Reference Bible was a subterfuge designed to create a subculture around a new worship icon, the modern State of Israel. The new state of Israel did not yet exist, but the well-funded Zionists already had it on their drawing boards.[407]

> Since the death of its original author and namesake, The Scofield Reference Bible has gone through several editions. Massive pro-Zionist notes were added to the 1967 edition, and some of Scofield's most significant notes from the original editions were removed where they apparently failed to further Zionist aims fast enough. Yet this edition retains the title, 'The New Scofield Reference Bible, Holy Bible, Editor C.I. Scofield.'[408]

Scofield's anti-Arab, Zionist "Christian" subculture

269

theology has fostered unyielding "Christian" support for the State of Israel and its barbaric subjugation of the native Palestinians.

Who was C.I. Scofield? Scofield was a young con-artist who engaged in a continual pattern of fraud and deception both before and after his alleged 1879 conversion. Scofield was a partner with John J. Ingalls, a Jewish lawyer, in a railroad scam which led to Scofield being sentenced to prison for criminal forgery.[409]

> Upon his release from prison, Scofield deserted his first wife, Leonteen Carry Scofield, and his two daughters Abigail and Helen, and he took as his mistress a young girl from the St. Louis Flower Mission. He later abandoned her for Helen van Ward, whom he eventually married.[410]

Scofield had developed connections with a subgroup of the Illuminati, known as the Secret Six.[411] He was taken under the wing of Samuel Untermeyer, an ardent Zionist who later became Chairman of the American Jewish Committee and President of the American League of Jewish Patriots.[412] "Untermeyer introduced Scofield to numerous Zionist and socialist leaders, including Samuel Gompers, Fiorello LaGuardia, Abraham Straus, Bernard Baruch and Jacob Schiff."[413] These powerful figures financed Scofield's research trips to Oxford and arranged the publication and distribution of his reference Bible. He who pays the piper calls the tune.

In 1892 Scofield fraudulently claimed to have a Doctorate of Divinity and began calling himself "Doctor Scofield."[414] In fact, Scofield did not have a doctorate from any Seminary or University or for that matter any degree of any kind from any college. Below is an excerpt from an article titled "Cyrus I. Scofield in the Role of a Congregational Minister" which appeared on August 27, 1881, in the Topeka newspaper, The Daily Capital:

The last personal knowledge that Kansans have had of this peer among scalawags, was when about four years ago, after a series of forgeries and confidence games he left the state and a destitute family and took refuge in Canada.

For a time he kept undercover, nothing being heard of him until within the past two years when he turned up in St. Louis, where he had a wealthy widowed sister living who has generally come to the front and squared up Cyrus' little follies and foibles by paying good round sums of money.

Within the past year, however, Cyrus committed a series of St. Louis forgeries that could not be settled so easily, and the erratic young gentleman was compelled to linger in the St. Louis jail for a period of six months.

Among the many malicious acts that characterized his career, was one peculiarly atrocious, that has come under our personal notice. Shortly after he left Kansas, leaving his wife and two children dependent upon the bounty of his wife's mother, he wrote his wife that he could invest some $1,300 of her mother's money, all she had, in a manner that would return big interest.

After some correspondence he forwarded them a mortgage, signed and executed by one Chas. Best, purporting to convey valuable property in St. Louis. Upon this, the money was sent to him. Afterwards the mortgages were found to be base forgeries, no such person as Charles Best being in existence, and the property conveyed in the mortgage fictitious.[415]

Scofield abandoned his wife and children and refused to support them. At that time it was difficult for a woman to work and support herself and her children. 1 Timothy 5:8 states: "But if any provide not for his own, and specially for those of his own house, he hath denied the faith, and is worse than an infidel."

When his first wife, Leontine, initially filed for divorce in July 1881, she listed the following reasons: "(he had)…absented himself from his said wife and children, and had not been with them but abandoned them with the intention of not returning to them again… has been guilty of gross neglect of duty and has failed to support this plaintiff or her said children, or to contribute thereto, and has made no provision for them for food, clothing or a home, or in any manner performed his duty in the support of said family although he was able to do so."[416] At that time Scofield was the pastor of Hyde Park Congregational Church in St. Louis.[417] The divorce decree was granted in 1883, with the court finding that Scofield "was not a fit person to have custody of the children."[418]

Scofield's life was marked at every turn by duplicity. J.M. Canfield revealed that Scofield as a pastor concealed his abandonment of his family by telling the congregation before his divorce that he was single. In 1912, Scofield sent false biographical information to a publisher for an entry in *Who's Who in America*. Among the many lies and fabrications, Scofield falsely claimed that he was decorated for valor during the civil war. D. Jean Rushing discovered that, in fact, Scofield was a Confederate deserter. Having been married twice and being a demonstrably covetous and greedy con artist, Scofield did not qualify to be a church leader, let alone a respected commentator of God's word: "A bishop then must be blameless, the husband of one wife, vigilant, sober, of good behaviour, given to hospitality, apt to teach; Not given to wine, no striker, not greedy of filthy lucre; but patient, not a brawler, not covetous; One that ruleth well his own house, having his children in subjection with all gravity;" (1 Timothy 3:2-4)

While Scofield used the King James text he indicated in his 1909 Bible introduction that he viewed with favor the work of Brooke Foss Westcott and Fenton John Anthony Hort, who were two popular compilers of the corrupted Alexandrian Greek text. Westcott and Hort were nominal Protestants, but they were *de facto* Roman Catholics. Also, Westcott and Hort were both necromancers who were members of an occult club called the "Ghostly Guild."[419] Throughout Scofield's Bible, he placed marginal notes that attacked the inerrancy of the Received Text of the Holy Scripture and indicated his preference for the corrupt Alexandrian manuscripts used by the Catholic Church.

The Zionists who funded and directed the Scofield Bible knew exactly what they were doing. Their strategy has born the sour fruit today whereby the ersatz "Christian" churches not only offer no resistance to Zionist aims, but they, in fact, promote Zionism. Surprising as it sounds, the Satanic Zionist conspiracy against Christ and Christians is a cornerstone of many ersatz "Christian" churches. It is not surprising that the worldly Scofield would agree with the science fiction of the world that the earth is a sphere. Being a wolf in sheep's clothing, Scoflield had no compunction in undermining the truth of God's creation of a flat and stationary earth. And he is typical of the scaly creatures who fight against the veracity of God's account of his creation in the Bible.

15 The Nicolaitans

The elders and pastors that come against the biblical flat earth are among a group of clerics that God hates. That is not hyperbole. We read in Revelation 2:6 that God hates the Nicolaitans. "But this thou hast, that thou hatest the deeds of the Nicolaitans, which I also hate." (Revelation 2:6) Who are the Nicolaitans that God hates? The very name, Nicolaitans, contains within it the character of those described.

The word Nicolaitans consists of two Greek roots. The first is a Greek word, *nikos,* which is a noun meaning victory or victor; it can also take the form *nike*.[420] The verb form of *nikos* is *nikao*, which means to prevail or overcome.[421] The second half of Nicolaitans is the word *laos*, which means laity or common people.[422] Putting the two words together we understand that Nicolaitans are those in the church who have prevailed over the common people. It points directly to the distinction in the modern church between the clergy and the laity. It denotes those in the clergy who have worldly hegemony over the submissive laity or common church members.

Church members are commanded to practice "[s]ubmitting yourselves one to another in the fear of God." Ephesians 5:21. The church submission is to be in accordance with God's commands and doctrines found in his Holy Bible. It seems, however, that pastors refuse to obey God's command to submit "one to another." The clergy in churches expect to be held in preeminence above the other church members. The clergy requires the laity to submit to them rather than all members submitting "one to another" equally.

The church is a kingdom. That kingdom has a King. And that King is Christ. Christians are to receive the kingdom of God as submissive children not as pastoral autocrats. Indeed, Jesus gives a dire warning to the authoritarian pastors lording over the church. "Verily I say unto you, Whosoever shall not receive the kingdom of God as a little child shall in no wise enter therein." (Luke 18:17)

The office of elder is a spiritual office. Church members may recognize an elder in the church. "Wherefore by their fruits ye shall know them." (Matthew 7:20) But it is an office entered into by the grace of God. Ephesians 4:1-20. The church is the body of Christ. The pastor is NOT the head of the church; Christ is the head of the church. "And he is the head of the body, the church: who is the beginning, the firstborn from the dead; that in all things he might have the preeminence." (Colossians 1:18)

Christ is the "head of the body." Christ has preeminence in "all things." Preeminence means to have superiority over all others. To elevate a pastor above the other members is to give preeminence to the pastor. That violates God's word. Christ is to have preeminence in the church over "all things." Christ will not share his preeminence with a pastor. *See* Isaiah 42:8. Indeed, Jesus could not have made it clearer.

The church is not like any other organization found on earth. That is because, while church members are on earth, the church remains a spiritual assembly. Further, the hierarchy of the church is not like earthly hierarchies, where there is a progressive chain of authority leading to the head of the organization. The hierarchy of the church is that there is one head, Jesus Christ, and the body is made up of "ministers" and "servants." There is no authoritative structure in a chain of authority leading to Christ. To be the chiefest in the church is the opposite of what it means to be the chiefest in an earthly organization. The chiefest in the church is the lowliest and most submissive servant of all other church members.

> But Jesus called them to him, and saith unto them, Ye know that they which are accounted to rule over the Gentiles exercise lordship over them; and their great ones exercise authority upon them. But so shall it not be among you: but whosoever will be great among you, shall be your minister: And whosoever of you will be the chiefest, shall be servant of all. For even the Son of man came not to be ministered unto, but to minister, and to give his life a ransom for many. (Mark 10:42-45)

To be an elder or bishop is a noble office. But it is a spiritual office. And it is an office of service. It is not an authoritarian office of lordship. Jesus is the model for the type of self-sacrificing ministering that a pastor should perform. *E.g.*, John 13:4-17. Jesus washed his disciples feet, and after doing so explained: "I have given you an example, that ye should do as I have done to you." John 13:15. Jesus further explained: "The servant is not greater than his lord." John 13:16. If he, Lord of all, humbled himself to wash their feet, they should do the same for one another. "If I then, your Lord and Master, have washed your feet; ye also ought to wash one another's feet." John 13:14. A pastor is to be a minister of charity and not a despot. Indeed, there is no need for any executive, legislative, or judicial action by a pastor. All of the doctrines and commands have been memorialized by Jesus Christ in his Holy Bible so "that the man of God may be perfect."

And that from a child thou hast known the holy scriptures, which are able to make thee wise unto salvation through faith which is in Christ Jesus. All scripture is given by inspiration of God, and is profitable for doctrine, for reproof, for correction, for instruction in righteousness: That the **man of God** may be perfect, throughly furnished unto all good works." (2 Timothy 3:15-17)

By the way, the reference to "the man of God" in 2 Timothy 3:16-17 is a reference to a Christian who is saved by God's grace. It is not a reference to some special person holding an office of a clergyman in the church. The man of God's perfection is to be "thoroughly furnished unto all good works." 2 Timothy 3:17. The church is the body of Christ, and not any part of that body is more important than another. Ephesians 4:1-20; 1 Corinthians 12:11-25; Romans 12:3-8. **"[T]here should be no schism in the body; but that the members should have the same care one for another."** 1 Corinthians 12:25.

A bishop (a.k.a. elder) is an overseer of the church. 1 Timothy 3:1-16; Romans 12:3-8. In 1 Timothy 5:17 we read about elders "that rule well." But an elder's rule is not one of authoritarianism; he is called rather to "take care" of the church. 1 Timothy 3:5. He is to rule by "ensample" and not lording over the church. 1 Peter 5:1-4. An overseer's function is not that of a lord but rather that of a "steward." 1 Corinthians 4:1-2. As a steward, a bishop (or elder) is a minister in the church. But his function is like that of all members of the church, who are called on to be "good stewards" in ministering to the needs of the church. 1 Peter 4:10-11. The bishop is to "work" within the church, as a fellow member of the church. 1 Timothy 3:1. He is not to take on some special title and become the titular head of the church.

Indeed, read what Peter tells the elders. He specifically tells them NOT to lord over the church, which is "God's heritage."

Elders are rather to be "ensamples" Ensample is not the same thing as example. Ensample means to exemplify as a model or pattern for imitation or copying. Whereas example means behavior or an event from which to learn. You learn from an example; you don't necessarily copy it. The elders are supposed to be ensamples of good and charitable conduct as a model for the church. They are not to pontificate and harangue the church into submission. The elder is to be submissive himself as a model of meekness.

> The elders which are among you I exhort, who am also an elder, and a witness of the sufferings of Christ, and also a partaker of the glory that shall be revealed: Feed the flock of God which is among you, taking the oversight thereof, not by constraint, but willingly; not for filthy lucre, but of a ready mind; **Neither as being lords over God's heritage, but being ensamples to the flock.** And when the chief Shepherd shall appear, ye shall receive a crown of glory that fadeth not away. (1 Peter 5:1-4)

At no time did any of Christ's disciples take on any title. Paul was simply called "Paul," Peter was simply called "Peter." So it should be in the church today, but sadly it is not. Instead, contrary to Christ's command in Matthew 23:1-12, today we have clergymen who go by titles of "Pastor" so-and-so and "Minister" so-and-so. So audacious are the Nicolaitan wolves in sheep's clothing that they take the title of "Reverend" so-and-so when the Bible states that "holy and reverend is his [God's] name." Psalms 111:9. The Nicolaitans in the Catholic Church contumaciously take the title of "Father" so-and-so, when Jesus Christ commands that we are to "call no man your father upon the earth: for one is your Father, which is in heaven." Matthew 23:9.

The Nicolaitan form of church government, which is endemic in churches today, is a form that God hates. Revelation

2:6. The success in cutting off the truth of the flat earth is a direct result of the form of church administration where the common members have little or no say about church doctrine. If a church member disagrees with church doctrine, he has no means of bringing it to a discussion. The Nicolaitan leaders simply show the "trouble maker" the door.

The clergy/laity divide that we see in churches today is antithetical to what Jesus taught. In Matthew we read again what Mark stated (and it bears repeating): there is to be no authoritative reign of the clergy in the church. There is not to be any divide in the church with a class of highfalutin clergy exercising authority over the lowly laity. Indeed, all in the church are one body of Christ. And if any want to be "great" and "chief" in the church they are to serve with charity.

> But Jesus called them unto him, and said, Ye know that the princes of the Gentiles exercise dominion over them, and they that are great exercise authority upon them. But it shall not be so among you: but **whosoever will be great among you, let him be your <u>minister</u>; And whosoever will be chief among you, let him be your <u>servant</u>**: Even as the Son of man came not to be ministered unto, but to minister, and to give his life a ransom for many." (Matthew 20:25-28)

Christ and Christ alone is to have preeminence in the church. Colossians 1:18. The Bible speaks in condemnation of Diotrephes because he sought to have preeminence in the church.

> I wrote unto the church: but Diotrephes, who loveth to have the preeminence among them, receiveth us not. Wherefore, if I come, I will remember his deeds which he doeth, prating against us with malicious words: and not content

therewith, neither doth he himself receive the brethren, and forbiddeth them that would, and casteth them out of the church. (3 John 1:9-10)

Notice that Diotrephes sought the preeminence in the church and in that capacity cast out of the church those who followed the true doctrines of Christ. We saw that happening in the previous chapter where the pastors who dared preach about the flat earth found themselves fired as pastors by the Nicolaitan elders in the church. The elders would not allow the matter even to be discussed with the ordinary members of the church (the laity). They took leadership over the people and decided for them what the doctrine in the church would be. And that did not include flat earth.

When there is mention in the Bible of elders and pastors and bishops and overseers; those terms are virtual synonyms, and they are always mentioned as pluralities. Those terms describe ministers who serve the church, not clergy exercising dominion over the laity.

And he gave some, apostles; and some, prophets; and some, evangelists; and some, pastors and teachers; For the perfecting of the saints, for the work of the ministry, for the edifying of the body of Christ: Till we all come in the unity of the faith, and of the knowledge of the Son of God, unto a perfect man, unto the measure of the stature of the fulness of Christ. (Ephesians 4:11-13)

When there is mention of elders (Acts 14:23; 20:17) and overseers (Acts 20:28) and bishops (Titus 1:5-9; 1 Timothy 3:1-6) it is regarding their service to the church and not their authoritarian reign over the church members. All church members are kings and priests. "And hast made us unto our God kings and priests: and we shall reign on the earth." (Revelation 5:10) Each church member has the unction of the Holy Spirit and has standing to speak on issues of faith and doctrine. "But ye have an unction from the Holy One, and ye know all things." (1 John 2:20)

Indeed, all who are saved are given the understanding of God's word. "All scripture is given by inspiration of God, and is profitable for doctrine, for reproof, for correction, for instruction in righteousness:" (2 Timothy 3:16) We see in Job that inspiration means understanding. "But there is a spirit in man: and the inspiration of the Almighty giveth them understanding." (Job 32:8) Inspiration through the unction of the Holy Ghost gives all who read God's word "understanding" of his word. His word is given by inspiration of the Holy Spirit to understand it.

The church is made up of members of the body of Christ. "Now ye are the body of Christ, and members in particular." 1 Corinthians 12:27. As such, the church members should be consulted regarding issues of faith and doctrine. There is no place for special officers, called clergy, to be given charge over the members to dictate to them what are to be the faith and doctrines of the church. Issues of faith and doctrine, like the flat earth, should be brought before the church membership so that they can search out the scripture to see if it is there, just as the noble Berean Christians did in the first century. Acts 17:11. There is no way for the church members to do that if such issues are kept from them by the clergy that exercise lordship over them.

The archetypal Nicolaitan church would be the Roman Catholic Church. After the Roman Catholic Church's initial ham-fisted treatment of Galileo, over time it unofficially adopted the heliocentric model as Catholic dogma. In 1992 they made it official when Pope John Paul II declared before the Pontifical Academy of Sciences that the Vatican Office of the Inquisition was wrong in 1633 when it forced Galileo under threat of torture and death to recant his heliocentric theory. Pope John Paul II officially declared that Galileo was correct when he pronounced that the spherical earth revolves around the sun.[423]

One example of a Nicolaitan among the Protestants is David Cloud, who is the founder of *Way of Life Literature* and publisher of the *Fundamental Baptist Information Service.*[424] Cloud describes his *Way of Life Literature* as a "fundamental Baptist preaching and publishing ministry."[425] Cloud also runs the *Fundamental Baptist Information Service. Way of Life* Publishes *The Way of Life Encyclopedia of the Bible & Christianity* and *The Advanced Bible Studies Series. Way of Life* also publishes *The Fundamental Baptist Digital Library*, which is Composed of approximately 3,500 select books.[426] *Way of Life* has produced Bible study materials in over 12 languages. "In 1984, *Way of Life* began publishing O TIMOTHY MAGAZINE, a monthly publication with the aim of urging preachers to stand for the truth and to resist error."[427] Cloud proudly portrays himself as an expert in Christian doctrine. His website states: "Cloud has spent an average of at least six hours per day in study since his conversion in 1973. He has built a 6,000-volume research library."[428]

After all of his study of the Bible, he concluded that those who believe the earth is flat are "wackos." He told one inquirer who believed in the flat earth that he had "borrowed a bunch of nutty things from some nut."[429] He told another person who wanted to discuss the flat earth with him that "I have zero interest in discussing that. It's as nutty as a fruitcake."[430] Cloud stated that "the flat earth stance is unadulterated nonsense. I am convinced that it is held by people with a perverse spirit toward reality."[431] Cloud made those statements in an article he posted on his *Way of Life Literature* website titled *A Flat Earth, Nuttiness and the Lunar Eclipse.*[432]

Cloud is an example of the Nicolaitan spirit in the church today. Cloud fancies himself as a Bible "expert" who has concluded that the earth is a sphere. He stated in his article:

As for a flat earth in the Bible, I have had the privilege of studying that Book for an average of probably eight hours a day for 44 years; I have written a Bible Encyclopedia and books on Bible interpretation and difficulties. I don't know everything, but I can check anything that is proposed as support for a flat earth, and having done so, I can say unequivocally that there is no support in Scripture for such a doctrine.[433]

Cloud states in his article that he has read the Bible for 8 hours a day for 44 years and he has found no support in scripture for a flat earth. He has added two hours to his previous hourly Bible study estimate, where he alleged he studied the Bible for more than 6 hours per day.[434] Cloud deleted that previous six-hour pronouncement from his website and, in doing so, apparently forgot about it.[435] Having forgotten about that previously made-up six-hour figure, he just made up another one, only this time he decided to go with 8 hours of Bible study per day. That is the way Nicolaitans roll. They just make things up. That is particularly evident when they make up religious doctrine, which they claim is in the Bible, but when their pronouncements are checked, it is determined to be nowhere supported by the Bible. Cloud allegedly spent all that time reading the Bible and found no proof for a flat earth. That suggests Cloud is missing a key guide in his reading: the Holy Spirit.

It is notable that in his article, Cloud does not cite to a single Bible passage. Instead, he cites to the authority provided by NASA. Cloud states:

> NASA's Apollo Moon program proves that the earth is round. The international satellite industry proves that the earth is round. The International Space Station (ISS), which has been orbiting the earth about 15 times per day for 17 years, proves

283

that the earth is round. The Space Shuttle Program, which operated from 1981 to 2011, delivering supplies to the ISS and launching and repairing satellites, proved that the earth is round.[436]

David Cloud alleges that '[t]he international satellite industry proves that the earth is round.'[437] The satellite industry is an industry that is made up entirely of land, sea, and air technology that is being falsely portrayed as linked with outer space satellites. The portrayal that outer space satellites are being used is just a guise. There are, in fact, no satellites in outer space. Because outer space does not exist, all of the communications that are described as "satellite communications" originate from and terminate at ground-based stations, naval vessels, submarines, aircraft, or balloon bearing instruments that are called "satellites."

This author personally attended the *Satellite 2018* conference.[438] Oddly, that event was a satellite conference with no actual satellites on display. That is not an exaggeration. I saw a total of four small models of satellites, two hanging by strings (approximately 3 feet in breadth from end to end, including the solar panels), one in a display case and one on a table (each about 12 inches in breadth from end to end, including the solar panels), but there were no actual satellites on display. There were all kinds of massive ground-based parabolic antennae, mock-ups of ground communication centers, and other large telecommunications equipment on display, but no actual satellites.

Imagine attending a car show that, instead of automobiles themselves, had booths dedicated to displaying the wonders of gasoline stations and car washes. Suppose that the only cars on display were a handful of small plastic models. Such an occurrence would be surreal. The *Satellite 2018* conference was that kind of surreal experience. It was a satellite show with no real satellites on display.

It is impossible to put a satellite designed to travel to outer space on display because outer space satellites do not exist. It is possible, though, to construct a phony satellite that is portrayed as a real satellite. But what if the phony satellite is not convincing? You can imagine the difficulty in creating an object that is supposed to work in space, but when put on display may be subjected to scrutiny that would likely reveal that it could not possibly work as designed. That is a risk that the devil and his minions could not take. And so, there were no actual satellites on display at the Satellite 2018 conference. Instead, they displayed small plastic models that were portrayed as miniature replicas of satellites.

One of the small satellite models was by OneWeb on a display podium with a graphic that warned not to take pictures of it. Why would there be a warning not to take a picture? There were no such warnings anywhere else at the conference. This author on several occasions requested permission to take pictures of many other ground-based communication displays and was granted permission each time. Indeed, the vendors handed out full-color glossy brochures containing high quality photographs of their wares. Many of those brochures contained detailed CGI pictures of satellites. But, oddly, OneWeb did not want anyone taking a picture of their model satellite.

The OneWeb model satellite looked no more sophisticated than a fun-meal toy. There was nothing about the model that was materially different from the many graphics displayed in the videos being projected and the publications handed out at the conference. Could it be that OneWeb did not want pictures taken because the display was so pathetic that it would undermine its credibility as a legitimate satellite manufacturer? It must be worrisome to portray yourself as a manufacturer of something that doesn't actually exist.

Figure 13: One of the few models of "satellites" on display at the *Satellite 2018* conference. Notice the warning not to take pictures of the "satellite" model. There were no such warnings anywhere else at the conference. That surreal satellite conference had no actual satellites on display, only a few models.

This author walked throughout the entire Satellite 2018 conference area and saw only four booths from companies that claimed that they made things for satellites (not including the few other companies like OneWeb, Airbus, and Boeing who claim to build entire satellites). Every other booth addressed ground signal reception and dissemination of alleged satellite signals. This author spoke with one engineer who worked for a company that claimed to make thrusters for satellites in space. The engineer admitted that the thrusters his company made require that they expel a mass in order to work in outer space. He explained that is necessary because in the vacuum of space the simple thrust from a rocket does not work because there is no atmosphere to push against. So the thruster must supply the mass necessary to push against when in space. He stated that all satellites must have their own onboard fuel and that the fuel will run out within 15 years. As my questions became more searching, the company officials became very interested in who I was and who I represented.

Instead of the Holy Spirit, Cloud uses the tried and true method of Satan. He ridicules the biblical doctrine of the flat earth in order to keep the curious away. Cloud's strategy is not that of a minister of the gospel but rather that of a propagandist. He shows symptoms of being a victim himself of years of brainwashing. His attitude exemplifies the attitude of academia toward the proofs of a flat earth, where any discussion of the evidence for a flat earth is beyond the pale. His comments reveal a mind that is so addled by propaganda that he can only vent his emotions in vitriol. Indeed, he would be among the crowd yelling "crucify him, crucify him." This is the result of the satanic scheme of heliocentrism.

The parallels between Cloud's heliocentric sentiments and those of the communist Komizars are striking. Anyone who disagrees with the communist state and advocates for freedom is viewed as mentally ill. Indeed, disagreement with the state is *prima facie* evidence of mental illness. Communist countries use mental hospitals to reeducate (torture) those enemies of the state who would dare voice their disagreement. Heliocentrists have the same degenerate intolerance as their communist revolutionary counterparts. That is why Cloud calls those who believe that the world is flat and stationary "wackos" and "nutty as a fruitcake." He is simply repeating the propaganda with which he has been inculcated. Communism and heliocentrism have the same roots, the Jewish Talmud and Kabbala. Heliocentrism is not primarily a scientific deception; it is, in essence, a spiritual deception. Its adherents are religious zealots, who view those outside their heliocentric cult as enemy "wackos" and "nuts."

Suffering persecution in this world for righteousness sake

is the very mark of a Christian. "Remember the word that I said unto you, The servant is not greater than his lord. If they have persecuted me, they will also persecute you; if they have kept my saying, they will keep yours also. But all these things will they do unto you for my name's sake, because they know not him that sent me." (John 15:20-21) Being reviled for speaking the truth of the gospel is a mark of a Christian. While the revilers intend their railings as curses, they are actually blessings. "Blessed are ye, when men shall revile you, and persecute you, and shall say all manner of evil against you falsely, for my sake. Rejoice, and be exceeding glad: for great is your reward in heaven: for so persecuted they the prophets which were before you." (Matthew 5:11-12)

Most Nicolaitans have a desire to avoid persecution and be friends with the world. "Ye adulterers and adulteresses, know ye not that the friendship of the world is enmity with God? whosoever therefore will be a friend of the world is the enemy of God." (James 4:4) Nicolaitan pastors who ignore or even reject God's account of his creation in order to keep their standing in their religious community, justify their stance by averring that the biblical account by God of a flat stationary earth is not really germane to the gospel. They have become enemies of God.

People do not have the authority to pick and choose what they like in God's word and discard the rest. Indeed, the gospel is "every" word of God. Gospel literally means "God spell," that means God's word. Jesus made the point in Matthew "It is written, Man shall not live by bread alone, but by **every word** that proceedeth out of the mouth of God." Matthew 4:4. **The Gospel is "every" word of God.** "Every word of God is pure: he is a shield unto them that put their trust in him. Add thou not unto his words, lest he reprove thee, and thou be found a liar." (Pr 30:5-6)

Chuck Lawson is another Nicolaitan pastor cut from the same cloth as David Cloud. Lawson is pastor of Temple Baptist

Church of Knoxville, Tennessee.[439] Lawson states that the belief in a flat earth is part of a demonic attack designed to sow discord in the church.[440] Lawson takes umbrage at being criticized for not believing in a flat earth. He considers it a great sin to criticize him because he considers himself a "man of God." He states that people should have reverence for the "man of God." How dare anyone criticize him, "the man of God." He considers himself above the ordinary laity in the church; in his Nicolaitan mind, he is a hifalutin "man of God."

Lawson is part of the problem in the modern church that has incorporated the heathen model of a single man leading and running a "church." He considers himself "a man of God" as being distinct from the laity who are beneath him. He is completely confused and confusing. Yet, he is a pastor. He remains wrong, and wallows in his ignorance because nobody will correct him. The modern church model will not allow it. God has made every Christian believer a king and priest. Revelation 1:6. But Lawson thinks that he is beyond reproach, and if someone seeks to correct him, Lawson views it as an attack on a "man of God." So Christians (who are kings and priests) are supposed to sit silently while he pontificates his ignorance. His arrogant hubris is palpable.

To whom does Lawson cite as his authority that the earth is a spinning, orbiting sphere? He begins by citing a fraud, Chuck Colson. He then cites a long list of astronauts as his authority. He concludes his harangue against the flat earth by explaining Elon Musk's planned space missions with wealthy passengers aboard. Lawson ominously warns that Musk's space missions will make those who believe in a flat earth look foolish when the many wealthy space tourists come back to earth with their photos of the spherical earth floating in outer space. Notably, like David Cloud, Lawson cites to not a single Bible passage. Like the Pharisees before him, he has supplanted God's word with man's traditions.

The devil has convinced modern pastors to limit the gospel to only that which the pastor has decided in his wisdom addresses salvation. Matthew Stucky, on the ministry staff at Verity Baptist Church, called belief in a flat earth, "foolish."[441] Stuckey's fellow traveler, Steven Anderson, pastor of Faithful Word Baptist Church, went even further. According to Anderson, flat earth is "foolishness" and "garbage" that is "of the devil." Anderson states that the study of the flat earth in the church is a conspiracy by "infiltrators" to "dumb down the church."[442] Anderson further opines that promoting a flat earth is "Satanic," and that believing in a flat earth is a "sin." He thinks that people who believe in the "stupidity" of a flat earth are "feebleminded" "idiots." He described one Christian who gave him a gift of a flat earth map as a "bozo."

Oddly, Anderson double-mindedly stated that, while he considers belief in a flat earth to be Satanic and sinful, he does not think it is a doctrinal issue and it is not heresy. Well, then if it is not doctrinal and it is not heresy, why is he so adamantly against it? Because, he has one foot in the world and one foot in the Bible, and it scares the bejeebers out of him to be considered crazy by the world. Down deep, he loves the world. "Love not the world, neither the things that are in the world. If any man love the world, the love of the Father is not in him." (1 John 2:15).

These Nicolaitans have joined in a Satanic conspiracy against the God of heaven and his anointed.

> Why do the heathen rage, and the people imagine a vain thing? The kings of the earth set themselves, and the rulers take counsel together, against the LORD, and against his anointed, saying, Let us break their bands asunder, and cast away their cords from us. He that sitteth in the heavens shall laugh: the Lord shall have them in derision. (Psalms 2:1-4)

God holds them in derision as he sits on his throne in heaven, a throne that the heliocentric preachers implicitly say is not there. In order to maintain their heliocentric religion, they must necessarily hold that there is no firmament, above which is the bright, heavenly abode of God, but only an atmosphere, above which is instead an empty, dark, vacuum of space.

In order to avoid the taint of being joined with Satan in a conspiracy against God and his anointed, heliocentric pastors simply deny that there is any such worldwide conspiracy. They deny the truth of the word of God. For example, Steve Van Nattan states:

> [T]he whole system of the flat earth reasoning depends on the follower believing that there is a massive worldwide conspiracy to hide the truth. This conspiracy includes all government agencies of all the nations of the world, all universities, all news media, and finally all the pastors of the world who teach that the earth is a sphere.[443]

Steve Van Nattan has been a Christian missionary and has pastored many churches.[444] Yet, he seems oblivious to the truth of the worldwide conspiracy against God and man revealed in Psalms 2:1-4. Van Nattan states:

> As with many Mother Goose theories, the facts which slap the ordinary observer in the face are easily dismissed. Any facts which mitigate against the flat earth or geocentric theory are said to be the result of a massive world wide conspiracy. We are asked to believe that NASA, the US Government, all educational institutions, and all of those same entities in China, Russia, Europe, and Japan are in on the conspiracy.[445]

Van Nattan relies on modern science that contradicts the Bible. He cannot grasp that there is a conspiracy so large as to involve every nation of the world. Van Nattan opines that a person who accepts the existence of such a grand conspiracy is paranoid.

> No conspiracy can gather in that many people to all agree to deceive the masses without a man of academic stature blowing the whistle now and then. We are talking about a conspiracy of billions of people, not just a couple thousand willing shills, as with Climate Change. There is a name for this- paranoia.[446]

Just to show how double-minded Van Nattan is, after he rails against a world heliocentric conspiracy, he then cites the theory of evolution as an example of a worldwide conspiracy. "[E]volution is the single most pervasive conspiracy in modern times."[447] He just does not think that heliocentrism is the result of a worldwide conspiracy and so it gets a pass here. Van Nattan then advises anyone who comes across a pastor teaching that God created a stationary, flat earth to immediately leave that church.

> So, when your pastor tells you that the reason you never heard of the flat earth theory, until he started teaching it, is because the United Nations and NASA are covering up the truth, your pastor is a blithering idiot. He has bought into a lie, and if God does not chasten him soon, you need to assume he is not a born again Christian. No true man of God will be allowed by God to promote lies and rubbish in the Lord's Church without chastening. If I were in your situation, I would find another church.[448]

Steve Van Nattan posted an article online titled *Flat Earth Heretics*.[449] He subtitled the article, "How can a Bible believer make a great fool of himself and the Lord's Church?"[450] Van Nattan Calls the gospel of God's creation, foolishness. God has told us that his gospel seems foolish to the lost. 1 Corinthians 2:14. The wisdom of this world (heliocentricity) keeps man from God. "For after that in the wisdom of God the world by wisdom knew not God, it pleased God by the foolishness of preaching to save them that believe." 1 Corinthians 18:21. Indeed, it is the foolish believers in the entire gospel of Jesus Christ who have been chosen by God for salvation. "But God hath chosen the foolish things of the world to confound the wise; and God hath chosen the weak things of the world to confound the things which are mighty." (1 Corinthians 1:27) The supposed wise of this world are deceived. Salvation comes to those who accept, like a small child, the truth of the gospel. Matthew 18:3. In the world's eyes, such a one is a fool. But it is only by "foolishly" accepting "every word" of God that one can be truly wise. "Let no man deceive himself. If any man among you seemeth to be wise in this world, let him become a fool, that he may be wise." (1 Corinthians 3:18)

What does the eminent Steve Van Nattan advise regarding discussing in the church God's creation of a flat earth? Van Nattan advises that under no circumstances should it be allowed to be discussed in the church.

> Having covered many Bible texts in the discussion above, any pastor reading here will be doing a minor panic right about now. "What do I do when some church member brings this to church some Sunday morning?" This flat earth heresy will totally trash you church's testimony if the word gets out in the community that you even tolerate someone in your fellowship who chatters about the topic. You must not linger when you hear of it. You must speak to the person at once and tell them that, under NO circumstances, will they talk about the flat earth myth in your local church.[451]

Nicolaitan Steve Van Nattan goes further. He states, without equivocation, that anyone who broaches the topic of flat earth in a church should be summarily kicked-out of that church.

> Again, the flat earth theory discussion, if heard by visitors to your church, will result in the whole community learning you are a bunch of nut cases. After all, what is the by-word for a weird obsessed person who talks crazy? "He is a flat earth boy." Ultimately, if a member or visitor cannot refrain from chattering about the flat earth heresy, run them off. I don't care how important they seem to your church life. Get them out the door, and do not let them back until they recant with conviction from the heresy. My experience as a pastor with such distractions has been that the direct one on one approach is best. Do not wait to discuss it with the church board or leaders. Slap it down yourself so that some soft headed member does not plead the cause of the trouble maker.[452]

The Nicolaitan pastors use all manner of dissimulation to hoodwink their followers to stay clear of any belief in what the Bible says about God's creation of a stationary and flat earth. For example, the pastor of The Excelsior Springs Church, Chad Wagner, describes belief in God's creation of a flat earth in stridently disparaging terms in his attempt to dissuade his flock from venturing near it.

> This teaching is biblically false and it's scientifically false. So if you have Christians believing this and saying the Bible teaches this, that gives the atheist, the unbeliever, the scoffer, it gives them all of the ammunition they need to say see this is what Christianity is about. It's anti-scientific, it's stupid, these people believe in all

kinds of boneheaded things. So, it discredits our religion and it discredits our faith when we believe something as crazy as the flat earth. ... This is a cult. The flat earth belief, I believe, it is a cultic belief. ... It is some kind of demonic spirit or something that has really taken over people to where that they can believe in something that is so unscientific and untruthful and unscriptural as this.[453]

Chad Wagner describes himself as leaning toward a geocentric model, which implies a stationary, spherical earth. But Wagner is hedging his bet on that, since he dismisses Bible passages that describe a flat earth as well as those that describe a stationary earth. Wagner argues those passages should not be taken literally; they should be read as merely figurative descriptions of the earth.[454]

One sermon trick Wagner used in his attack on the biblical flat earth was to take a passage with language describing non-movement in a figurative context and ascribing that figurative meaning to another passages describing the immovable earth.[455] In I Chronicles 16:30 the Bible describes an immovable earth. "Fear before him, all the earth: the world also shall be stable, that it be not moved." (1 Chronicles 16:30) Wagner opines that is figurative langauge. Wagner argues that one of the proofs of this is the fact that in Colossians 1:23 God states that we should "be not moved away from the hope of the gospel." Because "be not moved" in Colossians 1:23 conveys a figurative meaning, then "be not moved" in 1 Chronicles 16:30 in reference to the earth must also carry a figurative meaning.

> If ye continue in the faith grounded and settled, and be not moved away from the hope of the gospel, which ye have heard, and which was preached to every creature which is under heaven; whereof I

Paul am made a minister; (Colossians 1:23)

Wagner dismisses the language referencing an immovable earth in 1 Chronicles 15:30 by arguing that since the only other time in the Bible where God says "be not moved" (Colossians 1:23) it is a figurative reference that does not convey physical movement, then God must have meant that "be not moved" in reference to the world in 1 Chronicles 15:30 must also be figurative language that does not mean physical movement.[456] Wagner's sophomoric hermeneutics, with its inherent eisegesis, is not just illogical; it is dishonest.

The context of a Bible passage indicates the meaning of the words in that passage. In Colossians 1:23, God is referring to the believer not being moved from the hope of the gospel. "Be not moved" has a spiritual meaning in that context. Whereas, in 1 Chronicles 15:30, God is stating that the world is "stable, that it be not moved." In that context, God is referring to the physical world. The meaning in 1 Chronicles 15:30 is that the material earth is stable and cannot physically be moved. But Wagner engages in a Jesuitical attack on the explicit meaning of Bible passages. Wagner's stratagem is typical of how Nicolaitan pastors use dishonest sophistry to explain away passages in the Bible that clearly describe a stationary and flat earth.

A church with a single pastor who pontificates from the pulpit without any correction, or even input, from the congregation is a recipe for disaster. Under that rubric, heretical doctrine can be subtly introduced over time. As succeeding pastors inch away from the pure gospel, error becomes an engrained church tradition. Indeed, the Nicolaitan error is a perfect breeding ground to propagate and perpetuate doctrinal error. The church members, who are supposed to be kings and priests (Revelation 1:6), sit dumbly in the pews while they are preached at from the pulpit by their hireling pastor. All the while, the errors of the pastors go unchecked. This Satanic system has given rise to countless sects and denominations. Indeed, the prevalent Nicolaitan model of church government has opened the door to heathen actors who are gifted orators but doctrinal devils. One of the devilish doctrines introduced into the churches is heliocentrism, which has gained hegemony in the churches today.

The Nicolaitans, with their iron reign of authority and spirit of vengeance, it seems, have entirely infiltrated the church. For example, Michael Newton Keas, Ph.D., is a senior fellow at Discovery Institute and a former Fulbright scholar. Keas serves on the board of directors of Ratio Christi, an alliance of apologetics clubs on college campuses.[457] Dr. Keas thought it was notable that many Christians who believed what the Bible said about God's creation of a flat earth "had been kicked out of churches, or lost jobs with churches, or suffered broken relationships with family members."[458] Dr. Keas thinks that those who believe a "wacky" thing like that get what they deserve because he says "ignorance has consequences."[459] He thinks it is a good thing that the Nicolaitans are cracking down on those who believe what the Bible says.

Many churches focus on people who have graduated from seminary school when recruiting a new pastor. And that is where the doctrinal problems start. Larry Philips states that seminaries are more properly described as cemeteries because the graduates are more spiritually dead than alive. Indeed, Dr. John Hinton. Ph.D., had this to say about seminaries:

> As a Harvard Divinity School graduate, I can testify that these modern seminaries and biblical studies programs are not only full of apostates, but socialists, abortion supporters, sexual perversion advocates, practicing sodomites and lesbians, radical feminists, witches, New Agers, and atheists. Expecting spiritual discernment from such people would be insanity.[460]

16 Anatomy of a Deception

Dr. Grady S. McMurtry is an "ordained minister,"[461] who describes himself as a missionary, full-time international creation emissary, biblical scientific creationist, and apologist.[462] He has earned the following degrees: B.Sc. Hons, M.Sc. Hons., D.D., D.Lit., P.A. Dr. McMurty has been an "expert court witness."[463] McMurtry is a faculty member at Christian Life School of Theology, Columbus, Georgia, and he is an adjunct professor at both Florida Bible College and Florida Christian College.[464] He is a Creation Research Society USA-Life Member.[465] He is President and Founder of Creation Worldview Ministries.[466] He is a Master Teacher of American Christian Education at the Pilgrim Institute.[467] He is on the Board of Directors and Secretary of Christian Prison Ministries, and also on the Board of Directors and Secretary of Bridges of America. He claims to be a Life Member of Mensa, which is an organization made up of persons with high IQs.[468]

With all of those highfalutin honors, degrees, and positions, Dr. McMurtry must certainly know what he is talking about when it comes to the simple matter of what the Bible says about the shape of the earth. The eminent Dr. McMurtry has concluded that the Bible describes a spherical earth.

Man, even pagan man, has always been able to reason that the earth was a sphere! **The Hebrews knew it because God told them six times in the Old Testament that the earth was a sphere.** (Gen. 1:2, Job 22:14, Job 26:10, Job 38:14, Prov. 8:27 and Is. 40:22) These verses were sufficient to convince Old Testament believers![469] (bold emphasis in original)

Dr. McMurtry cites Gen. 1:2, Job 22:14, Job 26:10, Job 38:14, Prov. 8:27 and Is. 40:22 as supporting his claim that the earth is a sphere. He is banking on people not actually reading the passages he cited. Let's disappoint him. Let us look at the passages that the eminent Dr. McMurtry claims state that the earth is a sphere. Is he telling the truth? We will discover that he is not telling the truth. His first citation is to Genesis 1:2 as authority for his claim that the Bible states that the earth is a sphere:

And the earth was without form, and void; and darkness was upon the face of the deep. And the Spirit of God moved upon the face of the waters. (Genesis 1:2)

That passage actually describes a flat earth. At that time the waters covered 100% of the earth. Today, the oceans cover 71% of the earth's surface. It is impossible for the earth to be a sphere when 71% of its surface is covered by water, which at rest necessarily must be flat and level. We know that there was water entirely covering the earth upon its creation because God states that "darkness was upon the face of the deep." God describes his movement over the face of the waters, and since the surface of all water at rest is flat and level, the earth must have been flat from the beginning.

A face is defined as any of the individual flat surfaces of a solid object.[470] Since a sphere has no flat surface, a sphere cannot have a face. That means that God did not move upon spherical waters, since a sphere does not have a face, water cannot form a "deep" on the side of a sphere, and water is always flat. God moved upon the face of flat waters. The book of Genesis in no way supports Dr. McMurtry's claim that the Bible depicts a spherical earth.

Let's move on to the next Bible passage he cites in support of his claim. Dr. McMurtry claims that Job 22:14 depicts a spherical earth.

> **Thick clouds are a covering to him, that he seeth not; and he walketh in the circuit of heaven. (Job 22:14)**

What is a circuit? It is a continuous circular route that starts and ends in the same place. That passage in no way could be interpreted to mean that the earth is sphere. A circuit is a circular plane. A circular plane is, in essence, a circle. A circle is a flat plane where every point on the circumference is equidistant from the center. A circle cannot be a sphere, because with a sphere not all points are on the same plane; i.e., it is a ball.

Dr. McMurtry continues down his road of deception by citing Job 26:10 and Proverbs 8:27. He misleadingly claims that those passages describe a spherical earth.

> **He hath compassed the waters with bounds, until the day and night come to an end. (Job 26:10)**

> **When he prepared the heavens, I was there: when he set a compass upon the face of the depth: (Proverbs 8:27)**

Job 26:10 and Proverbs 8:27 share a common word that

describes the shape of the earth, compass. According to the 1828 *Webster's American Dictionary of The English Language* to compass something means "to stretch round; to extend so as to embrace the whole; hence, to inclose, encircle, grasp or seize; ... To surround; to environ; to inclose on all sides."[471] In Job 26:10 God is encircling (compassing) the seas with a boundary. In Proverbs 8:27 God is setting a circular compass upon waters that cover the earth. That denotes a circular boundary around the seas on a flat earth. The boundary of the seas is the ice rim of Antarctica. Job 26:10 and Proverb 8:27 do not support the idea of a spherical earth as claimed by Dr. McMurtry.

Notice that in Proverbs 8:27 God is setting the compass on the "face" of the depth. As we have seen, a face is any of the individual flat surfaces of a solid object.[472] Since a sphere has no flat surface, a sphere cannot have a face, thus the reference in Proverbs 8:27 to God setting "a compass upon the face of the depth" can mean only one thing, God set a circular compass upon the flat water that covers the earth.

Dr. McMurtry claims that God is describing a sphere in Job 38:14. That passages states:

It is turned as clay to the seal; and they stand as a garment. (Job 38:14)

The tradition of placing a seal on documents using clay dates to antiquity. The wet clay was flattened under pressure using a seal, which was a hard die, called a signet. The signet was pushed into the clay. This was often done to authenticate royal decrees. The clay then dried with the positive impression from the negative image on the royal signet left visible in the flat pressed clay. The clay image itself was known as the seal. All such seals were necessarily pressed flat.

God calls the process, of creating the clay seal of the earth, being "turned." The word turn in this context is pregnant with meaning. Turn means "to form; to shape,"[473] and "to transfer."[474] That is what happens when the image on the signet is pressed against the clay. That process shapes the clay and transfers the image from the signet to the clay. Turn also means "to reverse the sides or surfaces of: invert."[475] And that is what we see in the positive image left in the clay from the negative image on the signet. Turn has yet another meaning: "to cause to move in a circular course,"[476] "to cause to move around an axis or a center."[477] In the context of a clay seal as described in Job 38:14, it implies that the flat clay seal is being "turned" into a circle. Thus, God's description of the earth being "turned as clay to the seal" clearly describes a flat earth, and it suggests that it is a circle. The claim of Dr. McMurtry that Job 38:14 is describing a sphere is ridiculous.

Finally, Dr. McMurtry claims that Isaiah 40:22 is biblical proof that the earth is s a sphere.

It is he that sitteth upon the circle of the earth, and the inhabitants thereof are as grasshoppers; that stretcheth out the heavens as a curtain, and spreadeth them out as a tent to dwell in: (Isaiah 40:22)

Isaiah 40:22 does not indicate that the earth is a globe. As we have already seen, a circle is a flat plane where every point on the circumference is equidistant from the center. A circle cannot be a sphere, because with a sphere not all points are on the same plane, a sphere is a ball, not a circle. Baseball players are said to throw the "ball." Never in the history of the game has anyone ever confused a ball with a circle and described a player throwing a "circle." The world understands the difference between a ball and a circle, but highfalutin Bible scholars cannot seem to grasp the difference.

Notice that the circle mentioned in Isaiah 40:22 has the heavens spread out over it as a tent. That language indicates a flat circle, over which is a firmament, as a tent. A globe is a three-dimensional ball. If Isaiah meant ball in Isaiah 40:22, he would have said ball. Isaiah knew the difference between a ball and a circle. *See* Isaiah 22:18. He didn't say ball, because the earth is not a ball, as claimed by Dr. McMurtry. God describes the face of the earth as a flat circle over which the heavens are spread like a tent.

The idea that God is pitching a tent over a sphere makes no sense. The only way that the heavens could completely envelop a spherical earth as required by McMurtry's heliocentric model would be if the tent was a sack. Keep in mind that under the heliocentric model this sack must be placed over a spinning globe.

Nobody could have the academic achievements (graduating with honors and earning two theological doctorates) and intellectual acumen (lifetime member of Mensa) claimed by Dr. McMurtry and not know full well that the passages he cited did not support his claim that the earth is a sphere. Dr. McMurtry must know that what he is saying is not true.

Why would he lie? Because he thinks that it is slanderous condemnation to accuse someone of believing that the earth is flat. And he does not want to suffer persecution for the gospel. Dr. McMurtry stated that "[a]ny attempt to condemn Christians as 'flat earthers' is simply slander, gossip and libel."[478] Dr. McMurtry cares what the world thinks of him. "Love not the world, neither the things that are in the world. If any man love the world, the love of the Father is not in him." (1 John 2:15) He does not want to be "slandered" by standing for what the Bible states, so he has decided to side with the devil and his heliocentric model against the Bible. Jesus stated that the world would hate those that followed him. "If the world hate you, ye know that it hated me before it hated you." (John 15:18) We are commanded not to conform to the world. Dr. McMurtry is violating God's command to "be not conformed to this world: but be ye transformed by the renewing of your mind, that ye may prove what is that good, and acceptable, and perfect, will of God." Romans 12:2. Religious charlatans, like Dr. McMurtry, have made accommodations with the lies of the world. Dr. McMurty will speak out against evolution, but he will not stand with God's creation of a flat, stationary earth, because he does not want to suffer persecution. He is typical of so many nominal "Christians." He is lukewarm. "So then because thou art lukewarm, and neither cold nor hot, I will spue thee out of my mouth." (Revelation 3:16)

17 Knowing God's Eternal Power and Godhead

Pastors who promote heliocentricity, try to keep a lid on the biblical depiction of a flat and stationary earth. They act as gatekeepers to hide the gospel. For example, Pastor Steve Whinery, who is Pastor of the Tri-Cities Calvary Chapel, arrogantly dismisses God's creation of a flat earth. He attributes the origins of the flat earth not to the Holy Bible but rather to the devil.

Whinery considers the concept of a flat and stationary earth to be a contrivance of the devil. He flips reality. In fact, the heliocentric model is born of a conspiracy led by the devil. Whinery preaches a different Jesus from the Jesus in the Bible. He preaches a heliocentric Jesus. His Jesus is a far-off God, who is separated from his creation by an endless vacuum of empty space.

Whinery's false Jesus minds his own business. Pastor Whinery preaches a gospel injected into Protestant churches from the Roman Catholic Church through the teachings of Jacobus Arminius. The Arminian God minds his own business and stays far off. He will not intercede by his grace to save anyone. Under Whinery's gospel, Jesus Christ looks on helplessly while men decide, of their own free will, whether to believe in him. August

Toplady, the author of the hymn "Rock of Ages," explained the Arminian free will error: "A man's free will cannot cure him even of the toothache, or a sore finger; and yet he madly thinks it is in its power to cure his soul."

The true gospel is that Jesus Christ is the author and finisher of the faith that saves his elect. *See* Hebrews 12:2. Those elect will be saved because he sovereignly chose them to be saved before the foundation of the world. *See* Ephesians 1:4. Whinery's Arminian, free-will error flows from his heliocentric delusion. Whinery states:

> I think that the devil uses [schemes] to just make people dismiss anything that has to do with Jesus. And [the flat earth] is one of those things. ... The earth is so obviously spherical you know there are pictures. And what people will say is well these pictures are nothing. But you know it's like a giant conspiracy to try to make the earth round. To what end? What's the conspiracy for?[479]

Pastor Whinery asks rhetorically why would the devil lead a conspiracy to get people to believe the earth is a sphere? Whinery seems not to understand that God reveals his eternal power and Godhead through his creation. If a person believes that the earth is surrounded by the outer darkness of space, then they will doubt that God can be on his throne in glory in heaven above the firmament. The mythology of a spinning, spherical earth is an attempted spiritual *coup d'etat* against God almighty.

Whinery supports his unbiblical theology by misrepresenting what the bible says. He claims that God's description of the circle of the earth in Isaiah 40:22 is not really a description of a flat circular face of the earth. Whinery deceptively claims "that word for circle is a term that means orb."[480] But that is not true. A circle, by definition, requires the circumference to be equidistant from the center and on the same plane."[481] In essence, a circle is flat. But Whinery redefines circle to mean orb. An orb is a ball, which, by actual definition cannot be a circle because the circumference of an orb is not on the same plane (i.e., it is not flat). An orb cannot be a circle and a circle cannot be an orb. Whinery is like all of the other heliocentric pastors. To support their mythology they must lie about what the Holy Bible says. They are constantly redefining words. That is the ancient trick of the devil.

Pastor Whinery is part of the Calvary Chapel group of churches founded by Chuck Smith. The Calvary Chapel church movement is part of a Satanic conspiracy to undermine the true grace gospel of Jesus Christ. John Todd (Collins) was a former member of the Illuminati Collins family. The Illuminati is a Satanic society that has within it many layers within layers of secrecy. It operates on a need to know basis. Todd was deeply involved in the dark world of witchcraft. He stated that he personally delivered four million dollars to Chuck Smith in order to enable Smith to start "Maranatha! Music."[482] Todd stated that the money he gave Smith was a partial payment toward a total of eight million dollars of which he was aware was given to Smith by the Illuminati. Todd stated that Smith knew that money was from the Satanic Illuminati. This author goes into greater detail examining Chuck Smith and Calvary Chapel in my book, *The Anti-Gospel: The Perversion of Christ's Grace Gospel*.

Make no mistake about it; heliocentric preachers are preaching heathen mythology. They preside over so-called churches that are more akin to Satanic covens than they are to churches. Once they go down the road of compromising with the profane world about God's creation, everything else in the gospel becomes open to compromise. Pastor Vern Hall of the Free Gift Gospel Mission is one of many examples of that. He attacks the biblical flat earth as being "quite ridiculous."[483] Despite the clear message in the gospel that there is a world conspiracy against God and man (Psalms 2:1-4), Hall pooh-poohs any such notion that the flat earth is part and parcel of that conspiracy.

Hall correctly says that there is a parallel between those who believe in the biblical flat earth and those who reject the celebration of Christmas and Easter. True Christians correctly expose Christmas and Easter as heathen holidays. That bothers Hall. What does Hall say about that? He embraces the heathen practice of celebrating Christmas and Easter. He specifically defends his church practice of having an "Easter egg hunt."[484]

Hall acknowledges that "Christ probably wasn't born on December 25th."[485] Indeed, there is no probably about it. And Hall admits that fact. He states that it's "been well documented"[486] that Jesus Christ was not born on December 25th. But Hall justifies celebrating Christmas anyway because he reasons that one day is just as good as another to celebrate Christ's birth. Hall argues that because there are thousands of false gods, we are almost certain to be celebrating the birth of some false god no matter what day we choose to celebrate the birth of Christ. Hall fails to realize that God never told us to commemorate Christ's birth. We are called on, rather, to commemorate Christ's death. Mark 14:22-25; 1 Corinthians 11:23-25. Hall is an example of a heliocentric pastor who is a heathen wolf in sheep's clothing. Christians are told to be on the lookout for such false prophets. You will recognize the wolves who try to cover themselves in sheep's clothing by their fruits.

> **Beware of false prophets, which come to you in sheep's clothing, but inwardly they are ravening wolves. Ye shall know them by their fruits.** Do men gather grapes of thorns, or figs of thistles? Even so every good tree bringeth forth good fruit; but a corrupt tree bringeth forth evil fruit. A good tree cannot bring forth evil fruit, neither can a corrupt tree bring forth good fruit.

Every tree that bringeth not forth good fruit is hewn down, and cast into the fire. Wherefore by their fruits ye shall know them. (Matthew 7:15-20)

Not all heliocentric pastors and Christian leaders take a strong stand against the biblical flat earth. Some will simply dismiss the issue as irrelevant. For example, Pastor Brian Brodersen and author and apologist Don Stewart, in response to a question about the flat earth, downplayed the significance of the flat earth issue. They both stated emphatically that they adhere to a spherical earth model.[487] Brodersen added that he thought that the Bible describes a spherical earth. Stewart was not sure if the controversy over the flat earth was a strategy by Satan, but he implied that the flat earth might be a controversy to get people's minds off of Jesus Christ. Brodersen, on the other hand, opined that Satan would not bother with trying to convince people that the earth is either flat or a sphere.[488] Neither Broderson nor Stewart were strident in their condemnation of the biblical flat earth. But their tepid approach to the issue, while expressing their expert opinions that the earth is a sphere, has the effect of lulling people into a state of disinterest regarding the biblical flat earth.

In Romans 1:18 we read that "the wrath of God is revealed from heaven against all ungodliness and unrighteousness of men, who hold the truth in unrighteousness." Romans 1:18. The word "hold" is defined as "[t]o stop; to confine; to restrain from escape; to keep fast; to retain. It rarely or never signifies the first act of seizing or falling on, but the act of retaining a thing when seized or confined."[489] That means that heliocentric pastors who conceal (i.e., hold) the truth of a flat and stationary earth in the unrighteousness of heliocentricity are going to feel the wrath of God. Indeed, when you read that passage in context, we find that it is a direct reference to God's creation. The reason that God is so angry with heliocentric pastors is that his creation of a flat and stationary earth, as depicted in the Bible, reveals the invisible character of God. To conceal God's true creation conceals the true

God. God punctuates his displeasure by stating that those who do that are without excuse.

> **For the wrath of God is revealed from heaven against all ungodliness and unrighteousness of men, who hold the truth in unrighteousness**; Because that which may be known of God is manifest in them; for God hath shewed it unto them. For **the invisible things of him from the creation of the world are clearly seen, being understood by the things that are made, even his eternal power and Godhead; so that they are without excuse.** (Romans 1:18-20)

It is a fundamental doctrine that God is three persons in one. We find the first mention of that in Genesis 1:26-27. We see that God refers to himself by using both plural and singular pronouns.

> And God said, Let **us** make man in **our** image, after our likeness: and let them have dominion over the fish of the sea, and over the fowl of the air, and over the cattle, and over all the earth, and over every creeping thing that creepeth upon the earth. So God created man in **his** own image, in the image of God created **he** him; male and female created **he** them. (Genesis 1:26-27)

The Bible states that there is ONE God. "Hear, O Israel: The LORD our God is **one LORD**:" (Deuteronomy 6:4) The Bible identifies the God the Father "of whom are all things." The Bible also identifies the Lord Jesus Christ as "by whom are all things." Thus God the Father and Jesus Christ are both the ONE God.

> But to us there is but **one God, the Father**, of whom are all things, and we in him; and **one Lord**

> **Jesus Christ**, by whom are all things, and we by him. (1 Corinthians 8:6)

We see that there is one Lord and God and he is the same God who is above all and is also in the believer.

> **One Lord**, one faith, one baptism, **One God and Father of all**, who is above all, and through all, and in you all. (Ephesians 4:5-6)

Jesus Christ is a mediator between God and men. "For there is one God, and one mediator between God and men, the man Christ Jesus." (1 Timothy 2:5) But Jesus Christ is also God as there is one God. "Now a mediator is not a mediator of one, but God is one." (Galatians 3:20)

In 1 John 5:6-8 we find that the Godhead is explained with God the Father, God the Son (i.e., the Word), and God the Holy Spirit being one.

> This is he that came by water and blood, even Jesus Christ; not by water only, but by water and blood. And it is the Spirit that beareth witness, because the Spirit is truth. For there are three that bear record in heaven, the Father, the Word, and the Holy Ghost: and these three are one. And there are three that bear witness in earth, the Spirit, and the water, and the blood: and these three agree in one. (1 John 5:6-8)

In Jesus Christ, we find that in his body dwells all the fullness of the Godhead. "For in him dwelleth all the fulness of the Godhead bodily." Colossians 2:9.

God the Father is in heaven. "And he said unto them, When ye pray, say, Our Father which art in heaven, Hallowed be thy name. Thy kingdom come. Thy will be done, as in heaven, so in earth." (Luke 11:2) Jesus Christ is also in heaven. "Whosoever therefore shall confess me before men, him will I confess also before my Father which is in heaven." (Matthew 10:32) Indeed, Jesus Christ has all the power of God in heaven and on the earth. "And Jesus came and spake unto them, saying, All power is given unto me in heaven and in earth." (Matthew 28:18) When Jesus was physically on earth, he was at the same time in heaven. "And no man hath ascended up to heaven, but he that came down from heaven, even the Son of man **which is in heaven**." (John 3:13) That is because Jesus Christ and God the Father are ONE God. "I and my Father are one." (John 10:30)

The prophecy of Jesus Christ's manifestation as a man on earth was prophesied by the prophet Isaiah.

> For unto us a child is born, unto us a son is given: and the government shall be upon his shoulder: and his name shall be called **Wonderful, Counsellor, The mighty God, The everlasting Father, The Prince of Peace.** (Isaiah 9:6)

There is a third member of the Godhead. That is the Holy Spirit. Jesus promised that after he was resurrected, he would send the Holy Spirit in his stead.

> And I will pray the Father, and he shall give you another **Comforter**, that he may abide with you for ever; Even the Spirit of truth; whom the world cannot receive, because it seeth him not, neither knoweth him: but ye know him; for he dwelleth with you, and shall be in you. **I will not leave you comfortless: I will come to you.** (John 14:16-18)

Indeed, it was through the Holy Spirit that Jesus was born on earth of the virgin Mary.

> And the angel answered and said unto her, **The Holy Ghost** shall come upon thee, and the power of the Highest shall overshadow thee: therefore also that holy thing which shall be born of thee shall be called **the Son of God**. (Luke 1:35)

Jesus Christ was born a man, but he was also God Almighty with us.

> Behold, a virgin shall be with child, and shall bring forth a son, and they shall call his name Emmanuel, which being interpreted is, **God with us.** (Matthew 1:23)

Just as God was born of the Holy Spirit, so also believers are reborn of that same Holy Spirit.

> Jesus answered and said unto him, Verily, verily, I say unto thee, Except a man be **born again**, he cannot see the kingdom of God. Nicodemus saith unto him, How can a man be born when he is old? can he enter the second time into his mother's womb, and be born? Jesus answered, Verily, verily, I say unto thee, **Except a man be born of water and of the Spirit, he cannot enter into the kingdom of God. That which is born of the flesh is flesh; and that which is born of the Spirit is spirit.** Marvel not that I said unto thee, Ye must be born again. (John 3:3-7)

We are elected for salvation by the will of God from whom we are born again. "Of his own will begat he us with the word of truth, that we should be a kind of firstfruits of his creatures." (James 1:18)

God's elect are reborn as children of God through the

gospel. We are then sealed for salvation by the Holy Spirit that Jesus Christ promised to send in his stead. "In whom ye also trusted, after that ye heard the word of truth, the gospel of your salvation: in whom also after that ye believed, ye were sealed with that holy Spirit of promise," (Ephesians 1:13) Indeed, when a believer is born again, he is indwelt with the Holy Spirit. That means that Jesus Christ is in the believer through the Holy Spirit.

> To whom God would make known what is the riches of the glory of this mystery among the Gentiles; which is **Christ in you**, the hope of glory. (Colossians 1:27)

Not only is Jesus Christ in the believer, but the believer is in Jesus Christ. "Now ye are the body of Christ, and members in particular." (1 Corinthians 12:27) The Church corporately is the body of Christ. Jesus Christ is the head of that Church. "And he is the head of the body, the church: who is the beginning, the **firstborn from the dead**; that in all things he might have the preeminence." (Colossians 1:18)

Notice that Jesus Christ is referred to as the firstborn from the dead. What does that mean? Jesus is called in the Bible, the only begotten Son of God. "For God so loved the world, that he gave his **only begotten Son**, that whosoever believeth in him should not perish, but have everlasting life." (John 3:16) If Jesus is God and he is eternal, meaning that he always was and always will be, how could he have been begotten? In Psalm 2:7 we read a prophecy where God states: "I will declare the decree: the Lord hath said unto me, Thou art my Son; this day have I begotten thee." (Psalms 2:7) When was that prophecy fulfilled? It was fulfilled at the resurrection of Jesus Christ.

> God hath fulfilled the same unto us their children, in that he hath raised up Jesus again; as it is also written in the second psalm, **Thou art my Son,**

this day have I begotten thee. (Acts 13:33)

Jesus Christ is identified in the Bible as God who came to earth as a man. "**God was manifest in the flesh**, justified in the Spirit, seen of angels, preached unto the gentiles, believed on in the world, received up into glory." 1 Timothy 3:16. Jesus is identified as the ONE "mighty God" in three persons; Jesus is the Christ ("Prince of Peace") and "The everlasting Father" and the "Wonderful Counselor" (the Holy Spirit).

> For unto us a child is born, unto us a son is given: and the government shall be upon his shoulder: and his name shall be called Wonderful, Counsellor, The mighty God, The everlasting Father, The Prince of Peace. (Isaiah 9:6)

Just as Jesus was raised from the dead, so also will believers be resurrected from the dead. "But if the Spirit of him that raised up Jesus from the dead dwell in you, he that raised up Christ from the dead shall also quicken your mortal bodies by his Spirit that dwelleth in you." (Romans 8:11)

Notice that the Holy Spirit raised Jesus. That same holy Spirit dwells in the believer. That is the same Holy Spirit that we find creating the heaven and the earth. Jesus Christ and the Holy Spirit are one with God the Father. God is ONE. Jesus Christ Created all things.

> In the beginning was the **Word, and the Word was with God, and the Word was God**. The same was in the beginning with God. **All things were made by him; and without him was not any thing made that was made.** ... And the **Word was made flesh, and dwelt among us**, (and we beheld his glory, the glory as of the only begotten of the Father,) full of grace and truth." (John 1:1-3,

1:14)

Jesus Christ created all things.

For by him were all things created, that are in heaven, and that are in earth, visible and invisible, whether they be thrones, or dominions, or principalities, or powers: all things were created by him, and for him. (Colossians 1:16)

When we read the creation account in Genesis, we read that Jesus Christ created the earth through his Holy Spirit.

In the beginning God created the heaven and the earth. And the earth was without form, and void; and darkness was upon the face of the deep. And the **Spirit of God** moved upon the face of the waters. (Genesis 1:1-2)

Please do not lose cite of the fact that Jesus Christ and God, the Father are ONE God. John 10:30; Deuteronomy 6:4. All things created were created by God. That means everything was created by Jesus Christ and created by God the Father, as they are one God. "But to us there is but **one God, the Father, of whom are all things**, and we in him; and **one Lord Jesus Christ, by whom are all things**, and we by him. (1 Corinthians 8:6) We seen in Genesis 1:1-2 that the Holy Spirit of God that moved upon the face of the waters to create the flat and stationary earth. The ONE God was present in the three persons of God the Father, God the Son, and God the Holy Spirit and all were the creators of heaven and earth. The ONE God created all things.

God's creation reveals him for who he is. Jesus Christ is God. Jesus Christ created the heaven and the earth. He did so through his Holy Spirit. Jesus Christ, God the Father, and the Holy Spirit are ONE God. And his creation reveals his invisible and eternal Godhead consisting of God the Father, God the Son, and God the Holy Spirit. "For **the invisible things of him from the creation of the world are clearly seen, being understood by the things that are made, even his eternal power and Godhead.**" (Romans 1:20) We see them all at creation. Moses was inspired by God to describe him with plural pronouns. "And God said, Let **us** make man in **our** image, after **our** likeness." (Genesis 1:26) But God is ONE. Notice the singular pronouns that God inspired Moses to use to describe him in the very next verse. "So God created man in **his** own image, in the image of God created **he** him; male and female created **he** them." (Genesis 1:27) The Godhead is ONE God, but there are three persons in that ONE God. That same Godhead that created the flat and stationary earth is also part and parcel of our new birth as sons of God. "For whom he did foreknow, he also did predestinate to be conformed to the image of his Son, that he might be the firstborn among many brethren." (Romans 8:29)

"The Spirit of God moved upon the face of the waters." (Genesis 1:1-2) All water at rest is flat and level, which means that the earth from the beginning of creation has been flat. Indeed, the earth remains flat today, as 71% of its surface is covered by water. Such an earth cannot be a sphere as portrayed by profane science (so-called).

We are called upon to avoid the opposition of profane beliefs that men parade about as so-called science. *See* 1 Timothy 6:20. Christians are called on not to join with the profane beliefs of false science but to teach people the difference between profane science and the holy things of God. "And they shall **teach my people the difference between the holy and profane**, and cause them to discern between the unclean and the clean." (Ezekiel 44:23)

Why do pastors not obey God and teach the distinction between the profane science and the Holy Bible? Because modern heliocentric preachers are like the false prophets of old; they are in a conspiracy against God and man.

> There is a conspiracy of her prophets in the midst thereof, like a roaring lion ravening the prey; they have devoured souls; they have taken the treasure and precious things; they have made her many widows in the midst thereof. (Ezekiel 11:25)

Just as the priests of old did violate God's law, so also do heliocentric pastors. Heliocentric pastors are required to teach the difference between the Holy Bible and profane science, but they do not do that. The have joined themselves with science, falsely so-called.

> Her priests have violated my law, and have profaned mine holy things: **they have put no difference between the holy and profane**, neither have they shewed difference between the unclean and the clean, and have hid their eyes from my sabbaths, and I am profaned among them.

Heliocentric ministers are wolves in sheep's clothing who have put no difference between the holy and the profane. By not explaining the profane nature of heliocentricity and instead embracing it, they are destroying their flocks. They are more concerned with gaining filthy lucre then preaching the truth of the gospel.

> Her princes in the midst thereof are like wolves ravening the prey, to shed blood, and to destroy souls, to get dishonest gain. (Ezekiel 22:25-27)

God commands Christians to shun the profane things of this world. As they will degenerate the adherent and increase sin. "But shun profane and vain babblings: for they will increase unto more ungodliness." (2 Timothy 2:16) Modern heliocentric pastors have ignored God's command and instead embraced the profane science of heliocentricity. They profess Jesus Christ, but at the same time, they are in rebellion against him. "This people draweth nigh unto me with their mouth, and honoureth me with their lips; but their heart is far from me." (Matthew 15:8) This heliocentric rebellion against God has caused a concomitant degeneration of the tares that follow those false heliocentric prophets. The blind and evil pastors are leading their blind deluded followers to destruction. "They be blind leaders of the blind. And if the blind lead the blind, both shall fall into the ditch." (Matthew 15:14)

God's word further states that the earth is fixed and does not move. "Fear before him, all the earth: **the world also shall be stable, that it be not moved.**" (1 Chronicles 16:30) Indeed, the earth cannot be moved. "The LORD reigneth, he is clothed with majesty; the LORD is clothed with strength, wherewith he hath girded himself: the world also is **stablished, that it cannot be moved.**" (Psalms 93:1).

Notice that the immovable earth is closely associated with the praise and glory of God Almighty. They are inseparable concepts. In Psalms 93:1 we read that the LORD is clothed with majesty and strength, just as the world is stable and cannot be moved. If the earth is movable, then it impeaches the majesty and strength of God. Just as the earth is "stablished" that it cannot be moved so also is the eternal throne of God. *See* Psalms 93:2. Indeed, God links the immovable earth with his eternal throne. In the very next verse (Psalms 93:2) God explains: "Thy throne is **established** of old: thou art from everlasting." (Psalms 93:2) So, if the earth can be moved, so also, God's throne cannot be eternal.

God makes the statement that he and his throne are everlasting (Psalms 93:2); and he does so in the context of the world being established and immovable (Psalms 93:1). That is what God is referencing when he states in Romans 1:20 that "the invisible things of him from the creation of the world are clearly seen, being understood by the things that are made, even his eternal power and Godhead." The immovable and flat earth reveals God's eternal power and Godhead.

For the invisible things of him from the creation of the world are clearly seen, being understood by the things that are made, even his eternal power and Godhead; so that they are without excuse. (Romans 1:20)

The LORD reigneth, he is clothed with majesty; the LORD is clothed with strength, wherewith he hath girded himself: the world also is stablished, that it cannot be moved. Thy throne is established of old: thou art from everlasting. (Psalms 93:1-2)

A movable earth impeaches God's eternal throne. Thus a perverted view of creation gives one a perverted view of God. His creation will not then reveal "the invisible things of him from the creation of the world." The invisible things of God, "even his eternal power and Godhead," will not be clearly seen from his creation. *See* Romans 1:18-20. A mythical creation will present a mythical god.

God has revealed his Godhead to man through his creation. Men are without excuse because that which may be known of God has been shown to man through creation. Preachers who portray a spinning and rotating earth floating in a foreboding empty space full of darkness and devoid of the bright glory of God on his throne are holding the truth in unrighteousness. The wrath of God is upon them. *See* Romans 1:18-20.

18 On the Broad Highway to Hell

Joel Osteen is the pastor of the 30,000 member Lakewood Church in Houston, Texas.⁴⁹⁰ Forbes magazine did a study of the phenomenon of the growing number of huge churches and their enormous wealth, titled *Megachurches, Megabusinesses*. Forbes listed Lakewood Church as the largest (non-Catholic) congregation in the United States.⁴⁹¹ Lakewood Church purchased the Compaq Center, which is a huge 16,000 seat indoor arena that was the former home of the Houston Rockets. Lakewood Church spent an additional $95 million renovating the Compaq Center. Lakewood Church can well afford it. Their 2004 revenues were reported by the *New York Times* to be $55 million. That is all in addition to Osteen's sell-out appearances throughout the country at huge arenas where tickets are listed at $10 apiece. Some tickets, however, have sold on eBay for up to $100.⁴⁹² It is contrary to Christian principles for a preacher to charge people a fee to hear the gospel. That should be the first clue to the discerning Christian that Osteen is not preaching the gospel of Jesus Christ. In a recent interview, Osteen stated the following:

> I think the pope is fantastic. ... We're not trying to make this a **little bitty narrow** thing. Anybody's welcome. We may not agree 100% on doctrine and theology but you know... the Catholic Church our

church it's open to everybody. So, I like his tone, not pushing people away. But I believe God is big and his mercy is **very wide**.[493]

Notice the key statement from Osteen. He joins with the pope in his ecumenical efforts to come together in a wide way. Osteen wants to prevent making his church effort a "little bitty narrow thing." But that is exactly the opposite of God's plan. God has created a strait gate and narrow way for salvation that few find. The popular wide gate is the broad way to destruction. Notice the warning Jesus gives right after he explains that the wide and broad way is the way to destruction. Jesus warns against false prophets, like Osteen, who are ravening wolves in sheep's clothing. They will seek to lead people into the broad way to destruction.

> Enter ye in at the strait gate: for **wide** is the gate, and **broad** is the way, that leadeth to destruction, and many there be which go in thereat: Because **strait** is the gate, and **narrow** is the way, which leadeth unto life, and few there be that find it. Beware of false prophets, which come to you in sheep's clothing, but inwardly they are ravening wolves. (Matthew 7:13-15)

The wolves in sheep's clothing try to steer the sheep away from the narrow way onto the popular broad way by ridiculing the path through the strait gate. As we have seen, God's creation of a flat, stationary earth is part and parcel of the gospel. The false prophets ridicule that strait gate. They turn people away from the guidepost of the flat, stationary earth that points to the narrow way of the gospel leading to salvation. Consequently, people go on their merry way to destruction through the popular wide gate. They are on the broad highway to hell. The strategy often used by false preachers is to discredit the strait gate through invective and ridicule toward anyone who would be so "foolish" as to believe that God created a stationary, flat earth.

Heliocentric preachers ridicule the strait gate and narrow way as being foolish. Recall how Jesse Michael described the belief in God's creation of a flat earth as a dumb, idiotic, foolish, ridiculous, retarded, heretical doctrine.[494] He is joined by David O'Steen (not to be confused with Joel Osteen), who calls flat earth a "strange" and "crazy" doctrine."[495] David Cloud concluded that those who believe the earth is flat are "wackos." Chuck Lawson states that the belief in a flat earth is part of a demonic attack designed to sow discord in the church.[496] Steven Anderson states that the "feebleminded" "idiots" who believe in the "stupidity" of a flat earth are committing a "sin" by doing so.[497] Michael Hoggard says that belief in a flat earth makes Christians look foolish and is as the sin of witchcraft.

On and on goes the acrid vitriol against anyone who dares to believe in the "foolishness" of the truth of the gospel that God created a stationary, flat earth. These arrogant wise men are puffed up with the knowledge of the world and ridicule those who believe the "foolishness" of the gospel. The reality is that "the foolishness of God is wiser than men." (1 Corinthians 1:25) It seems that these "Christian" preachers and teachers lack the spiritual discernment that is born of the Holy Spirit to understand that "God hath chosen the foolish things of the world to confound the wise." (1 Corinthians 1:27)

The heliocentric preachers are "natural" men who cannot receive nor understand the gospel truths because "they are foolishness" to them. *See* 1 Corinthians 2:14. They do not have the indwelling Holy Spirit to reveal to them the truth of the gospel, which must be "spiritually discerned." *Id.* They want to pick and choose from those scriptures with which they agree, as though God's word is some kind of breakfast buffet. But Jesus explained that "man shall not live by bread alone, but by **every word of God.**" (Luke 4:4) God requires that we accept "all" of his word. Indeed, **"all scripture** is given by inspiration of God, and is profitable for doctrine, for reproof, for correction, for instruction in righteousness." (2 Timothy 3:16) These near-sighted preachers are eschewing the "foolishness" of the narrow gospel in order to lead people through the wide gate and down the broad way to destruction. Jesus describes such men as "blind leaders of the blind. And if the blind lead the blind, both shall fall into the ditch." Matthew 15:14. Those heliocentric charlatans can trace their doctrinal lineage to the infamous Pharisees.

> Woe unto you, scribes and Pharisees, hypocrites! for ye compass sea and land to make one proselyte, and when he is made, ye make him twofold more the child of hell than yourselves. (Matthew 23:15)

The heliocentric preachers are not simply ignorant about the truth of God's creation of a stationary, flat earth. They are actively working against the truth revealed in God's word about his creation. They are enemies of the gospel. Jesus stated that one would be able to tell who were the false prophets. "Ye shall know them by their fruits." (Matthew 7:16) The sour fruit of the heliocentric preachers spewing their hatred toward Bible believers is apparent. The heliocentric preachers are fulfilling a prophecy of Jesus, who stated that those who follow him and his gospel would be hated by the world and suffer persecution.

> If the world hate you, ye know that it hated me before it hated you. If ye were of the world, the world would love his own: but because ye are not of the world, but I have chosen you out of the world, therefore the world hateth you. Remember the word that I said unto you, The servant is not greater than his lord. If they have persecuted me, they will also persecute you; if they have kept my saying, they will keep yours also. (John 15:18-20)

The study of David J. Stewart's character (or lack thereof) offers revealing insight into the spiritual condition of the outspoken enemies of God's creation of a flat earth. Stewart has a popular "Christian" website at www.jesus-is-savior.com, that receives more than five (5) million visits per year.[498] Stewart states on his website: "I am a grateful born-again Christian!"[499] Stewart posts his writings on his website about all sorts of Christian topics. He has posted on his website an article he wrote titled *The Flat Earth Heresy*.[500] In that article, Stewart explains:

> I cannot believe I am even writing this article, but as hard as it is to imagine, there are still people today who literally believe that the earth is flat. Folks, the earth is NOT flat! ... Kindly, for this very reason I had to stop supporting and promoting "The Common Man's Bible," which can literally now be called "The Idiot's Bible," because Brother Hoffman teaches in it that the earth is flat, which is insanity. ... Perhaps you say, "Does it really hurt if a sincere preacher thinks the earth is flat?" Are you kidding me? The answer is a resounding, yes, yes, yes, it is very detrimental and harmful to the cause of Christ. There are a lot of unsaved people, who upon learning that a man ignorantly teaches the earth is flat, will immediately leave (and I don't blame them) from the presence of that fool. ... Honestly folks, I feel sorry for some people, seeing how dumb they are. May I say, I don't call people an "idiot" for being ignorant, bless their heart; but rather, I call a person an idiot when they speak boldly with confidence in their ignorance. If you don't know what you're talking about, keep your mouth shut; and if you do open your mouth, you had better be able to backup what you're talking about.[501] (parenthetical in original)

Notice the acerbic invective from Stewart toward those who believe in the flat earth. He is concerned that "[t]here are a lot of unsaved people, who upon learning that a man ignorantly teaches the earth is flat, will immediately leave (and I don't blame them) from the presence of that fool."[502] (parenthetical in original)

Stewart is like so many opponents of the flat earth. He views the biblical flat earth as foolishness. Stewart wants to remove the foolishness of the gospel. But he is oblivious to the truth that the gospel appears foolish to the lost world. 1 Corinthians 1:18. God's creation of a flat earth is part of the gospel. But the natural man cannot understand that fact. "[T]he natural man receiveth not the things of the Spirit of God: for they are foolishness unto him: neither can he know them, because they are spiritually discerned." (1 Corinthians 2:14) There is no way to make the true gospel not appear foolish to the world. The fact that Stewart thinks that the clear statement in God's word that the earth is flat is foolishness indicates that Stewart is part of the lost world.

While that statement about Stewart seems harsh, please understand that Stewart, himself, has admitted that he is a lost heathen. Stewart made that admission in a prior iteration of his fundamentalist Christian website, www.jesus-is-savior.com.[503] He stated: **"I personally am not a Christian or a member of any religion for that matter."**[504] As soon as he received criticism for that admission, Stewart quickly changed the web page to instead say: "I am a grateful born-again Christian!"[505] Stewart claims that he is a Christian, but his claim is a lie to conceal from the world that he in fact is "not a Christian or a member of any religion for that matter."[506] Stewart is a religious charlatan.

Stewart is similar to the phony John Wesley, who was the founder of the Methodist Church. Wesley also admitted that he didn't believe in the God of the Bible. When Wesley was 63 years old, in 1766, he wrote a letter to his brother, Charles Wesley. In that letter, John Wesley bared his soul and revealed to Charles his innermost thoughts. In that letter, which John Wesley never expected to be revealed publicly, he admitted that he preached a faith that he, himself, did not have. John Wesley stated:

> I do not love God. I never did. Therefore I never believed, in the Christian sense of the word. Therefore I am only an honest heathen. ... I never had any other evidence of the eternal or invisible world than I have now; and that is none at all ... I have no direct witness (I do not say, that I am a child of God, but) of anything invisible or eternal.[507]

Stewart is a heathen cut from the same cloth as Wesley who did not believe in God. Wesley preached a false gospel with a false god. Wesley railed against the sovereign God of the Bible while pretending to preach the gospel. The gospel preached by Wesley was the false gospel of Arminianism. How could Wesley so successfully preach a false gospel? Because people had been accustomed to ignoring God's words and accepting a contradictory gloss to those words. This process was born with heliocentricity, where it was necessary for the "Christian" churches to accommodate the new science of heliocentricity by reinterpreting God's word to conform with that so-called "science." The Arminian god appears nowhere in the scriptures just as heliocentricity appears nowhere in the scriptures.

Those who preach against God's creation of a flat and stationary earth are enemies of the gospel. Jesus warned us to beware of such false ministers who appear as lambs but inwardly they are "ravening wolves." (Matthew 7:15) Those who rail against the truths in the Bible about God's creation are against God. Jesus explained that "He that is not with me is against me; and he that gathereth not with me scattereth abroad." (Matthew 12:30) There is no middle ground. One must accept all of the gospel. "And Jesus answered him, saying, It is written, That man shall not live by bread alone, but by **every word of God**." (Luke 4:4) God will not tolerate compromise. "So then because thou art lukewarm, and neither cold nor hot, I will spue thee out of my mouth." (Revelation 3:16)

Those who rail against the biblical depiction of God's creation of a flat and stationary earth are eviscerating the true gospel. They are missing the point of the gospel, that God created us for the purpose of saving us. Ephesians 1:4-11; Romans 8:28-31. Without an understanding of God as our creator, one cannot understand God as our savior. Indeed, to misunderstand God's creation is to misunderstand who God is. Romans 1:18-20. We can see the importance of the Biblical account of God's creation in Psalms 8:3-5, where David correlates God's creation of the heavens and compares that to his creation of man. David is pointing out the greatness and strength of God who made the heavens, the moon, and the stars. Our potentate God, the creator of heaven and earth, lowered himself to save his elect. Without an understanding of God's majestic and almighty power, as revealed in his creation, we cannot understand his great mercy in lowering himself from his glorious throne in heaven to come to earth as the "son of man" (John 3:13-17; 12:23-36; 6:27-62) to die in our stead to save us from the punishment for our sins. **"When I consider thy heavens, the work of thy fingers, the moon and the stars, which thou hast ordained; What is man, that thou art mindful of him? and the son of man, that thou visitest him? For thou hast made him a little lower than the angels, and hast crowned him with glory and honour."** Psalms 8:3-5.

To, instead, accept the profane heliocentric model, which depicts the mythology of a "big-bang" creation without God, impeaches the depiction in the Bible of God as the creator of heaven and earth. Heliocentrism contradicts the account in the Bible of God's creation of a flat and stationary earth. To preach against the biblical flat and stationary earth and support heliocentrism undermines the gospel by impeaching the authority of the Bible and the God who wrote it.

19 Salvation Through the Gospel of Creation

Tyler J. Doka, pastor of Great Harvest Baptist Church in Long Island, New York, preached a sermon proving that the Bible depicts a fixed, flat earth.[508] In the comments section under the video, one person wrote: "I used to be an Atheist. In 2015 when I started looking into the flat earth, I'm not an Atheist anymore. I believe in God now."[509] Another person responded to that comment by saying "God Bless you man. The same thing happened to me. The globe is used to hide God. They want all of us to think we mean nothing."[510]

One commentator to a video on the biblical flat earth stated:

> Just wanted to say as an agnostic/nihilist trusting 100% in science falsely so called I discovered the Earth was flat and NASA was faking the ISS about 7 months ago after discovering many worldy conspiracies were real and perpetrated by people who believed in Lucifer. I soon realized Satan/God were real. I started praying and seeking God. Since that day I've become a Born again ... KJV Only Bible believing Christian saved by the blood of the

Lamb! Praise the Lord!⁵¹¹

Such testimonies are sprinkled throughout discussions of the biblical flat earth.⁵¹² But the above commentator reveals the problem in the churches today, and that is unbelief. He states:

> Thank you for posting this as I've been bouncing around Churches trying to find Christians that actually believe their Bible and they are really hard to find! This particular truth is very important for people like the old me who are logical/rational but the indoctrination we receive prevents us from applying it correctly. More Christians need to defend the scriptures against modern science falsely so called instead of capitulating to it. God bless!⁵¹³

The problem with the church today is that it is full of people who do not know the entire truth of creation. And, indeed, they have an erroneous unbiblical understanding of God's creation. Part of that is explained by ignorance, but there is also a faction in the churches who are gatekeepers, who are in league with Satan in keeping the flock ignorant of the truth of God's creation. These lukewarm "Christian" gatekeepers are easy to identify. They actively fight against the biblical truth of God's creation of a flat and stationary earth. Satan will marshal his forces to fight against that truth with great fury because if that is generally known his entire edifice of deception will be breached.

The realization of the true nature of God's creation has the effect of bringing a person to understand that God really does exist. For example, Allan Spencer was an atheist. Then he learned that the earth was stationary and flat. The reality of the flat earth proved to him that God exists and he is the creator of heaven and earth. God, by his grace, used the revelation of his creation to bring Spencer to a saving knowledge of Jesus Christ. Spencer recently traveled from California to Georgia to join Nathan Roberts in spreading the gospel of salvation and of God's biblical cosmology to attendees of the apostate Gwinnett Church, which is pastored by the heretical preacher Andy Stanley.[514]

Former atheists who have been persuaded that the gospel is true have stated that one of the most effective ways to reach atheists with the gospel is to reveal to them the true nature of God's creation, that it is a flat, stationary earth.[515] That evidence is so compelling, it is so irrefutable, that it knocks the atheists for a spiritual loop. The compelling truth of the flat earth impeaches so completely the scientific orthodoxy upon which their atheism is based that it drives the atheists to the only possible conclusion, that God created the earth and that he is ruling from heaven.

Spencer has posted a $5,000 challenge. He will pay $5,000 "to the first person to produce a fully detailed, complete, verifiable, measurable, and repeatable experiment that proves the world is a spinning globe."[516] Spencer has an alternative $5,000 challenge. He will pay $5,000 "to the first person to defend the heliocentric model, using only the Bible."[517] So far there have been no takers.

There have been other rewards offered in the past to those who could prove the heliocentric model. But the rewards have always gone unclaimed. For example, on or before 1931, Wilbur Glenn Voliva offered $5,000 to anyone who could prove that the earth is a spinning sphere, floating in space, and orbiting the sun. Many tried to meet the challenge and collect the reward, but all failed.

If the spherical, spinning earth is such a scientific fact as it is taught in every level of education, it would seem that the $5,000 reward would be easy money. But the reward was never claimed or paid. There was no proof presented that the earth is a spinning sphere, floating in space, and orbiting the sun. That is because a lie cannot be proven; it can only be exposed and refuted. Those who adhere to the heliocentric lie know that. And so they have campaigned to cover that lie with more lies.

In 1931, a Modern Mechanix magazine publicized Voliva's challenge. The magazine article ended with the statement that "[t]he Voliva prize probably will remain uncollected unless some future space traveler some day anchors his ship a few thousand miles out in space and takes a movie of a globular world turning on its axis. That seems to be the only way the $5,000 can ever be collected." The National Aeronautics and Space Administration (NASA) claims to have done just that. But as explained in this author's book, *The Greatest Lie on Earth (Expanded Edition)*, all of the supposed space photographs of earth from NASA are fake.

Famous Christian Evangelist Ray Comfort gives the following advice: "If you're a Christian and you believe that the earth is flat, please keep it to yourself, even if you have Bible verses that you think prove it."[518] Why would Ray Comfort want Christians to keep quiet about God's creation of a flat earth as described in the Bible? Comfort explains that "because in many people's minds you'll be perceived to be intellectually on the level of someone who thinks the moon is made of cheese. If they know you're a Christian insisting that the earth is flat won't exactly help your credibility."[519]

Ray Comfort is concerned about how the unsaved world perceives Christians and the gospel. He seems to have little regard for the truth. Ray Comfort seems not to understand that the gospel is foolishness to the natural man. The gospel must be spiritually discerned. "But the natural man receiveth not the things of the Spirit of God: for they are foolishness unto him: neither can he know them, because they are spiritually discerned." 1 Corinthians 2:14. Comfort admonishes Christians to keep quiet about the biblical depiction of the flat earth because he believes that salvation is a free-will choice of the intellect. But the Bible makes it clear that salvation is completely the choice of God who must give his elect spiritual rebirth. John 1:12-13; 3:3-8. The spiritual truth of the gospel must be spiritually discerned. The gospel is foolishness to the unsaved world. God is both creator and savior. Man must know what God created in order to fully understand the gospel.

Salvation is through faith in Jesus Christ, which is preordained by the grace of God before the foundation of the world.

> According as he hath chosen us in him before the foundation of the world, that we should be holy and without blame before him in love: Having predestinated us unto the adoption of children by Jesus Christ to himself, according to the good pleasure of his will. (Ephesians 1:4-5)

Some may ask: "doesn't man have a free will to choose to believe or not believe in Jesus?" The answer is that man has a will, but it is not free. Man is enslaved by sin and death. Sinful man wishes to rule in his own life; his every impulse is in rebellion against God. Indeed, man cannot freely believe in God. God must transform man by the rebirth wrought by the Holy Spirit.

The reality is that man's will is enslaved to sin. Man will not serve God nor seek God because man is spiritually dead. "As it is written, **There is none righteous, no, not one: There is none that understandeth, there is none that seeketh after God**." (Romans 3:10-11)

Jesus came to set us free. "If the Son therefore shall make you free, ye shall be free indeed." (John 8:36) He gives his elect a new spiritual birth, and they are set free from sin and death to serve the Lord. By his grace, we are spiritually born again. Once born again, our old flesh driven existence comes to an end, and we are led by the spirit, which up to that time was dead, but now is alive. A Christian becomes a new creation, set free from sin to serve the living God.

> Knowing this, that **our old man is crucified with him, that the body of sin might be destroyed, that henceforth we should not serve sin. For he that is dead is freed from sin.** Now if we be dead with Christ, we believe that we shall also live with him: Knowing that Christ being raised from the dead dieth no more; death hath no more dominion over him. For in that he died, he died unto sin once: but in that he liveth, he liveth unto God. Likewise **reckon ye also yourselves to be dead indeed unto sin, but alive unto God through Jesus Christ our Lord.**" (Romans 6:6-11)

A Christian is justified by God. God does the choosing, not man. James 1:18. God does not love us because we first loved him. "We love him, because he first loved us." (1 John 4:19) It is an act of his Grace toward us that frees us from the bondage of sin. Once we are freed from the bondage of sin we can bear the fruit of righteousness. "But now being **made free from sin**, and become servants to God, ye have your fruit unto holiness, and the end everlasting life." (Romans 6:22) *See also,* Romans 5:16-19; 7:1-8:17. However, it is all a work of God, by his grace. **"For all have sinned, and come short of the glory of God; Being justified freely by his grace through the redemption that is in Christ Jesus."** (Romans 3:23-24)

Chapter 6 of John makes clear that salvation is all of God. God "giveth" eternal life to his chosen through faith in his son, Jesus.

> Then Jesus said unto them, Verily, verily, I say unto you, Moses gave you not that bread from

heaven; but my Father **giveth** you the true bread from heaven. For the bread of God is he which cometh down from heaven, and **giveth life** unto the world. Then said they unto him, Lord, evermore give us this bread. And Jesus said unto them, **I am the bread of life: he that cometh to me shall never hunger; and he that believeth on me shall never thirst.** (John 6:32-35)

Given the sovereignty of God in the salvation of his elect, what is a Christian's duty regarding the preaching of the gospel? Jesus made it clear in Mark 16:15 that a Christian is to preach the gospel. "And he said unto them, Go ye into all the world, and preach the gospel to every creature." (Mark 16:15)

Jesus also made it clear in his very next statement in Mark 16:16 that there would be those who believe and those who would not believe. "He that believeth and is baptized shall be saved; but he that believeth not shall be damned." Mark 16:16. The responsibility of a Christian is to preach the gospel; it is the responsibility, indeed the very promise of God, to choose those whom he has elected by giving them spiritual ears to hear. God draws his chosen and saves them. He does so through the preaching of the gospel. "Faith cometh by hearing, and hearing by the word of God." Ephesians 1:1-2:22.

In Romans 10:9-11:10 God explains how he uses his living word to give spiritual life to his elect. God's creation, revealed in his word, is every bit part of his gospel. The word gospel literally means God spell (God's word). God has made the point in the Holy Bible that every word of God is essential. "And Jesus answered him, saying, It is written, That man shall not live by bread alone, but by **every word of God.**" (Luke 4:4) That brings us to an important point that preachers today overlook. God has revealed his invisible spiritual truths through the creation of the world. Man is without excuse. What may be known of God is manifest in God's creation.

> [T]hat which may be known of God is manifest in them; for God hath shewed it unto them. For the invisible things of him from the creation of the world are clearly seen, being understood by the things that are made, even his eternal power and Godhead; so that they are without excuse. (Romans 1:19-20)

The biblical account of creation is critical because it is through God's creation that he reveals his glory and handiwork. "The heavens declare the glory of God; and the firmament sheweth his handywork." (Psalms 19:1)

God called the firmament, Heaven. Genesis 1:8. The heavens declare the glory of God. The firmament contains the stars and shows God's glory and handiwork. Psalm 19:1. Part and parcel of God's glory and handiwork is that the stars travel in a fixed formation around the North Star (Polaris). That is because God ordained the moon and the stars to rule the night. Psalms 136:9. The stars were placed in the firmament by God for "signs, and for seasons, and for days, and years." Genesis 1:14. Indeed, "He telleth the number of the stars; he calleth them all by their names." (Psalms 147:4)

That fixed path of travel, where the stars circle the North Star, as can be seen everywhere in the northern latitudes, proves that the earth cannot be a rotating globe. That is because if the earth were a rotating globe then the only place where the stars could be seen to travel in a circular path around the North Star would be at the North Pole. Everywhere else on a supposed spinning globe below the North Pole would require that the stars travel in a westerly direction because the earth is supposed to be spinning in an easterly direction.

Since under the heliocentric model the earth is supposed to be spinning in an easterly direction, a viewer who is looking at the North Star would necessarily see all of the other stars traveling in a westerly direction across the sky. There is no possible way that the stars could be seen by an observer on earth traveling in a circular path around the North Star because that would require the stars to both travel in an easterly direction and a westerly direction as they circle the North Star. But when looking at time-lapse photographs of the stars circling the North Star, we see stars traveling in a circular path around the North Star, with some stars moving in a westerly direction while at the same time other stars are traveling in an easterly direction. Such an occurrence in an impossibility under the heliocentric model.

A picture is worth a thousand words. A time-lapse picture is worth a million words. Below is an 11.5-hour time-lapse photograph taken on the night of January 2-3, 2010, from Tradate, Italy, which is at 45.7° North Latitude, more than 3,000 miles south of the North Pole, and approximately equidistant between the North Pole and the Equator.[520] The picture proves that it is the stars moving over the earth, and not the earth that is spinning. The fact that the stars under the North Star are traveling in an easterly direction while at the same time the stars above the North Star are traveling in a westerly direction proves that the earth cannot be spinning.

If the earth were spinning, a person looking at the North star from 45.7° North Latitude would see all of the stars traveling in an arc across the sky in a westerly direction. If the earth were a spinning globe, the stars could not travel in opposite directions, as we can see is happening in the time-lapse photograph. The picture below impeaches the heliocentric myth. If one is standing anywhere not on the axis of a globe, stars cannot appear to travel across the sky in one direction and other stars appear to move in the opposite direction if the star movement is based upon the fact that the earth is supposed to be spinning on an axis in one direction. It is impossible. The time-lapse picture below proves that the heliocentric model is an elaborate deception.

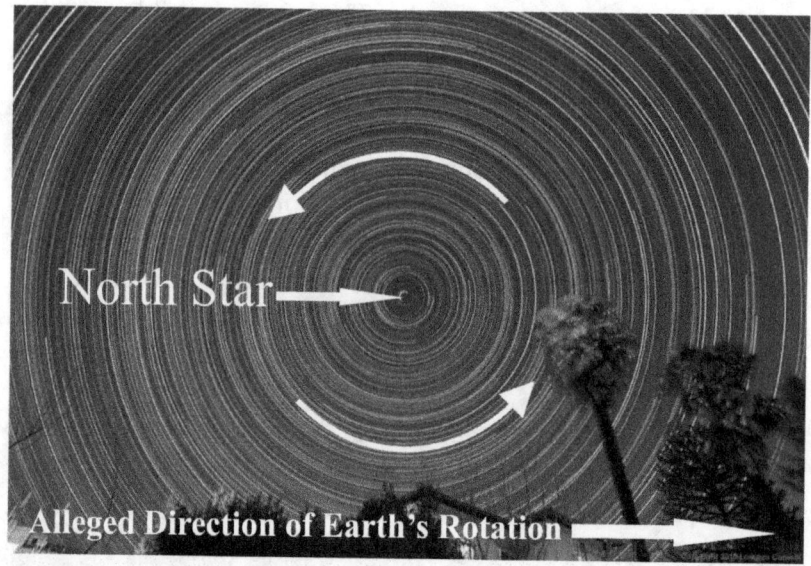

Above is a time-lapse picture taken from Tradate, Italy, of the stars in the night sky circling around the North Star (Polaris) during an 11.5 hour period on January 2-3, 2010. The path of the stars could not be circular, as depicted above, if the earth were a spinning globe. Notice that the stars above the North Star are traveling in a westerly arc across the night sky, while at the same time the stars below the North Star are traveling in an easterly arc. The heliocentric model would require all stars to appear to travel in only one direction across the night sky, in a westerly arc, because the earth is supposed to be spinning in an easterly direction.

Please note that, while the stars appear to completely circle the North Star, in fact, each star is only traveling in an arc that is approximately 180°. The time-lapse makes it appear that the stars are going in a complete circle around the North Star. But it only appears that way because there are so many stars. No single star has traveled more than 180° during the 11.5-hour time-lapse period.

If the earth were a sphere spinning eastward, the heliocentric model would require a time-lapse picture of the North Star to be in a fixed position in the sky in perfect synchronization with the spin of the earth. That is because the North Star is fixed above the North Pole, which is supposed to be the axis of the earth's spin. Thus, the heliocentric model requires that at all latitudes south of the North Pole the North Star would remain fixed in position over every location on the allegedly spinning earth. That means that the North Star would appear to the camera not to be moving. That is in fact what we see in time-lapse pictures. So-far-so-good for the heliocentric model.

The fly in the ointment for the heliocentric model is that if the earth were in fact spinning, the other stars in a time-lapse picture taken south of the North Pole would create star trail arcs that would appear to be moving across the sky only in a direction opposite the spin of the earth. But that is not what we see. Instead, in actual time-lapse pictures of the North Star, the other stars leave circular star trails around the stationary North Star. That means that some of the stars are traveling in the same direction as the supposed spin of the earth. That is impossible under the heliocentric model. If the earth were spinning, there would be no way for any stars to leave star trails going in the same direction as the spin of the earth. The diagram below illustrates what the star trails in a time-lapse picture taken by a camera south of the North Pole pointed at the North Star should look like if the earth were a spinning globe.[521]

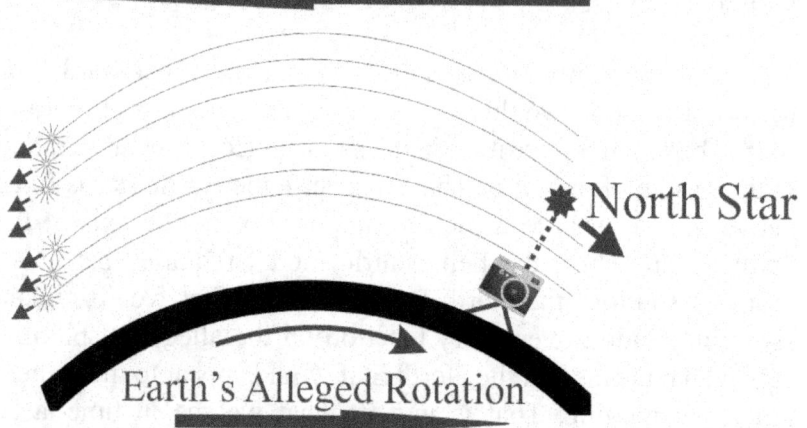

This is <u>NOT</u> What We See

If the earth were actually spinning, a time-lapse picture taken with a camera fixed on the North Star from a latitude south of the North Pole would show the North Star fixed in perfect synchronization with the camera on the supposed spinning earth. All of the other stars would appear as star trail arcs moving in the opposite (westerly) direction to the earth's spin. There would be no stars leaving star trails in the same (easterly) direction as the earth's purported spin.

The ubiquitous time-lapse photographs taken south of the North Pole showing star trails circling the North Star are proof that the earth is not spinning underneath the stars but rather that those stars are circling the North Star over a stationary earth.

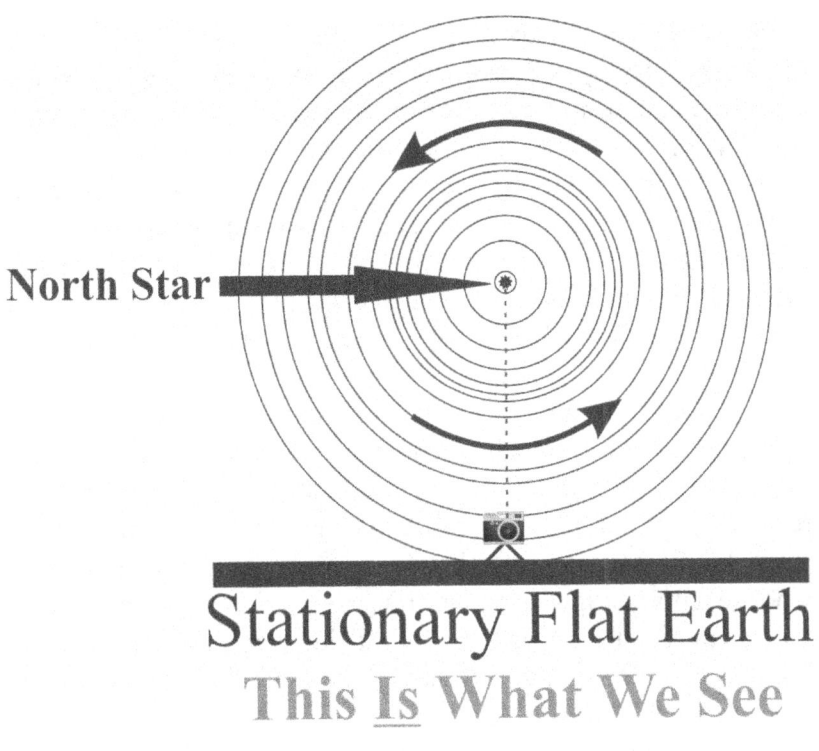

Stationary Flat Earth
This Is What We See

Every scientific experiment ever conducted has confirmed what the above time-lapse picture shows, that the earth is stationary and the stars move over the earth. George Airy in 1871 conducted the most notable experiment that proved that the stars move over a stationary earth. Airy's experiment is popularly known in the scientific community as "Airy's failure" because his experiment proved that the earth does not move, which was the opposite of the expected outcome. George Airy's experiment determined with scientific certainty that in fact, it was the ether carrying the stars that was moving over the earth and that the earth was stationary. Dr. Neville Thomas Jones, Ph.D., explains that "George Airy proved that the world was stationary and the stars are moving."[522]

Airy's failure was followed in 1887 by the precise and irrefutable experiment conducted by physicist Albert A. Michelson

(1852 – 1931) and chemist E. W. Morley (1838 – 1923). The Michelson/Morley experiment, using an interferometer, which measured light rays, established that the earth is stationary.[523] That experiment so shook the scientific community (imbued with heliocentricity) that it was forced to change the laws of physics to explain it away. The new laws of physics were nurtured within the umbra of the theory of relativity. The rise of Albert Einstein and his theory of relativity are explained in detail in this author's book, *The Greatest Lie on Earth (Expanded Edition)*.

God's account of creation in the Bible authoritatively confirms that it is God who created the earth, the firmament, and the heavens. Without an accurate understanding of what is revealed in the Bible, men can be swayed to take from God the glory that he is due for creating the heavens and the earth. People who are ignorant of what the scriptures say are easily persuaded to turn away from God and instead attribute the existence of the heavens and the earth to a godless theory like the big bang.

The gospel includes the Old Testament. Indeed, the Bible reveals that the gospel was preached to the Jews in the wilderness, but it did not profit them because they did not believe it. "For unto us was the gospel preached, as well as unto them: but the word preached did not profit them, not being mixed with faith in them that heard it." (Hebrews 4:2)

We must preach the whole gospel, which includes God's creation as described in both the New and Old Testaments. God's word depicts his creation of a flat, stationary earth. God's revelation of his creation in his Holy Bible is part and parcel of the gospel that regenerates a person unto salvation. It bears repeating that Jesus explained: "If I have told you earthly things, and ye believe not, how shall ye believe, if I tell you of heavenly things?" (John 3:12) God's creation of a fixed, flat earth is set forth in the book of Genesis, which was written by Moses. Jesus told the Jews that if they had believed what Moses wrote about him in Genesis, they would believe him. "For had ye believed Moses, ye would have believed me: for he wrote of me." (John 5:46) Moses wrote about Jesus in Genesis as the creator of all things in heaven and on earth. "For by him were all things created, that are in heaven, and that are in earth, visible and invisible, whether they be thrones, or dominions, or principalities, or powers: all things were created by him, and for him." (Colossians 1:16)

The heliocentric pastors, as have the Jews, reject what Moses said about God creating a flat, stationary earth. They do not believe in the Jesus of the Bible. Those charlatan pastors believe in another Jesus; a mythical Jesus who created a mythical spinning ball earth. That phony Jesus was prophesied.

> For if he that cometh preacheth another Jesus, whom we have not preached, or if ye receive another spirit, which ye have not received, or another gospel, which ye have not accepted, ye might well bear with him. (2 Corinthians 11:4)

Many take the position that belief in a flat earth is not necessary for salvation. That is true. But that dodges the real issue.[524] The issue is not whether someone who is saved must know every truth of the gospel. God's revelation of his truth is progressive. Once saved, a Christian will "grow in grace, and in the knowledge of our Lord and Saviour Jesus Christ." 2 Peter 3:18. The issue is whether a person who is presented with the gospel truth believes it. How can someone claim to be a Christian and reject the truth presented in God's word? One commentator cited Hosea 4:6 in support of his argument that one need not believe in a flat earth to be saved.[525]

> My people are destroyed for lack of knowledge: **because thou hast rejected knowledge, I will also reject thee**, that thou shalt be no priest to me: seeing thou hast forgotten the law of thy God, I

will also forget thy children. (Hosea 4:6)

While it is true that one need not have knowledge of every truth in the gospel to be saved, that does not mean that one may reject a truth once it is presented to him. That is what Hosea is speaking to. Knowledge of the gospel comes by revelation.

> Which things also **we speak, not in the words which man's wisdom teacheth, but which the Holy Ghost teacheth**; comparing spiritual things with spiritual. But the natural man receiveth not the things of the Spirit of God: for they are foolishness unto him: neither can he know them, because **they are spiritually discerned**. (1 Corinthians 2:13-14)

All scripture is given by inspiration of God. Notice that in 2 Timothy that God explains how Timothy from a child had known the holy scriptures that were able to make him "wise unto salvation." Those scriptures were necessarily the Old Testament as the New Testament had not yet been written. The Old Testament included the account of creation in Genesis.

> And that from a child thou **hast known the holy scriptures**, which are **able to make thee wise unto salvation** through faith which is in Christ Jesus. **All scripture is given by inspiration of God**, and is profitable for doctrine, for reproof, for correction, for instruction in righteousness: (2Timothy 3:15-16)

Notice also in 2 Timothy that "all scripture is given by inspiration of God." It is not just some scriptures that are given by inspiration of God; all scriptures are given by inspiration of God. All scriptures are "profitable for doctrine, for reproof, for correction, for instruction in righteousness." Included in those scriptures are the scriptures that address God's creation. What does inspiration of God mean? The book of Job gives us the answer.

> But there is a spirit in man: and the **inspiration** of the Almighty giveth them **understanding**. (Job 32:8)

The inspiration of God means the understanding of God. The inspiration of God means that God gives the reader understanding. When one is saved, he is given the unction of the Holy Spirit, which gives him understanding of the truths of scripture by the revelation of God. "But ye have an unction from the Holy One, and ye know all things." (1 John 2:20) If you read 1 John 2:20 in context it reveals that those who do not have the unction of the Holy Spirit went out and separated themselves from the true church of Jesus Christ. The fact that they went out from the true church was indicative that they were not of the true church. They instead rejected the truth of the gospel and followed after their own lusts. We see that happening today with those who reject the truths revealed in the Bible about God's creation.

If a person rejects a truth of the gospel that is presented in the gospel that indicates that truth has not been revealed to the hearer. That, in turn, indicates that the hearer does not have the unction of the Holy Spirit that imparts the revelatory knowledge. That is what Hosea 4:6 is saying. That is what God means when he says "because thou hast rejected knowledge, I will also reject thee." It is the willful ignorance born of the rejection of knowledge presented in the gospel that ends in eternal destruction.

Incidentally, in Isaiah 40:21-22 God explains that his creation of a flat earth is important.

> Have ye not known? have ye not heard? hath it not been told you from the beginning? have ye not

understood from the foundations of the earth? It is he that sitteth upon the circle of the earth, and the inhabitants thereof are as grasshoppers; that stretcheth out the heavens as a curtain, and spreadeth them out as a tent to dwell in: (Isaiah 40:21-22)

God describes the earth as a circle, which is defined as a geometric figure with "all points in the **same plane** that lie at an equal distance from a center point."[526] (bold emphasis added) A circle requires that all points along its circumference be equally distant from its center and be on the **same plane**. A circle requires a flat plane.

Notice that before God announced the truth that the earth is a circular plane in Isaiah 40:22, he gives a heads-up introduction in verse 21. In that introduction, God states that what he is about to say should be a basic and foundational understanding. "Have ye not known? have ye not heard? hath it not been told you from the beginning? have ye not understood from the foundations of the earth?" Isaiah 40:21. God then explains his reign above the firmament over his circular flat earth. In the introductory language of Isaiah 40:21 God is essentially saying that his creation of a flat earth with a firmament above it and with him presiding over it is a fundamental truth to understand. Heliocentric preachers who claim that the shape of the earth is a distraction and not important are in direct disagreement with God. If God thinks it's essential, we should too.

David Platt, Ph.D., is the pastor at McLean Bible Church in Washington, D.C. He is the founder and president of Radical, which is a discipleship outreach to churches around the world.[527] He states:

> You can't just discard historical details or scientific facts in the Bible and the Bible still hold

together. If the historical details and scientific facts in the Old Testament are untrue then the teachings of Jesus and the writers of the New Testament are untrustworthy. Follow this. This is huge. Jesus references history in the Old Testament as true. ... If these stories aren't historically accurate then what does this say about Jesus? ... He's at best deluded, at worst a liar. Either way he is not speaking truth. ... You cannot disconnect the history in the Bible, the stories in the Bible, and the scientific statements in the Bible from the redemptive theological truths of the Bible. They are intertwined together in a way that if one falls they all fall.[528]

According to Dr. Platt, Christians must take the Bible as true in all things to which it speaks. If we cannot accept as true the things it states about historical or scientific matters, then we cannot take it to be true about spiritual things. Indeed, that is the position of Jesus. "If I have told you earthly things, and ye believe not, how shall ye believe, if I tell you of heavenly things?" (John 3:12) But Dr. Platt rejects the word of God when it comes to God's description of a stationary, flat earth. In the same presentation where he states that the scientific statements in the Bible are intertwined together with explanations about redemption in a way that if one falls they all fall, he stated that the Bible is not literally accurate when it describes a fixed, flat earth.

> Talking about the observational descriptions of nature, Joshua one, Psalms 113 talks about the rising setting of the sun. So does that mean the Bible is falsely reporting planetary motion? But actually, the earth revolves around the sun. No, nobody is calling the weatherman a liar when he tells us the sun is going to rise and set. The weatherman is often misled in other ways. But

when he is talking about the sun rising and setting he's normally making a pretty true statement even though it's not astronomically precise. ... The use of hyperbole is a literary device, not an attempt to mislead or deceive. So when Jesus talks in Matthew 12 about the Queen of Shiba coming from the ends of the earth to hear the wisdom of Solomon, that does not mean that the Bible is asserting a flat earth and Jesus believes the Queen of Shiba came from the edge of it.[529]

Dr. Platt claims to be an expert in the gospel of Jesus Christ. He has a Ph.D. from New Orleans Baptist Theological Seminary, which he proudly announces on his website. He is founder and president of a ministry through which he helps other churches spread the gospel and make disciples. We can hold him to the expertise that he claims for himself. He knows better; he cannot profess ignorance. He knows the implications of his denial that God created a flat and stationary earth. Indeed, there can be no question that he knows. Only minutes before his rejection of the biblical description of a geocentric, stationary, flat earth, he stated, without equivocation, that Christians must accept all of the Bible to be accurate, whether the Bible speaks about history, science, or salvation. Dr. Platt made the point that all the truths of the Bible are intertwined, and to reject one assertion in the Bible renders the rest of the Bible a dead letter. Dr. Platt stated that to deny one historical or scientific truth in the Bible renders Jesus "at best deluded, at worst a liar."[530] After having said that, Dr. Platt, nonetheless, proceeded to reject the truth of the Bible regarding God's creation of a stationary, flat earth over which the sun and moon travel in a circuit. The eminent Dr. Platt is, in essence, calling Jesus "at best deluded, at worst a liar."[531]

Dr. Platt is double minded. "A double minded man is unstable in all his ways." (James 1:8) Dr. Platt must conceal his rejection of the word of God through an artifice. He claimed that

Jesus was using the literary device of hyperbole when Jesus was describing a flat earth. But when it came to the cosmology of planetary motion, he simply impeached the truth of the Bible. He implied that the Bible was "not astronomically correct." If the Bible is not correct about cosmology then it cannot be correct about redemption and salvation. Dr. Platt knows that. He moments earlier explained that point. He drove it home with the statement that to reject one historical or scientific truth in the Bible renders Jesus "at best deluded, at worst a liar."[532]

Why did Dr. Platt deny the truth of God's word regarding God's creation? Because the Bible contradicts the heliocentric model. Dr. Platt accepts the worldly scientific communities description of a heliocentric system over God's description of a stationary, flat earth. He loves the world and so has taken sides with science against the Bible. Dr. Platt is a wolf in sheep's clothing who is preaching a watered down, lukewarm gospel in order to accommodate the heliocentric model, while portraying himself (falsely) as a hard-liner on biblical authority. What does Jesus think about Dr. Platt's theology? "So then because thou art lukewarm, and neither cold nor hot, I will spue thee out of my mouth." (Revelation 3:16)

God prophesied that he would send upon the earth a strong delusion upon those who reject the truth of the gospel and follow after the antichrist.

> And then shall that Wicked be revealed, whom the Lord shall consume with the spirit of his mouth, and shall destroy with the brightness of his coming: Even him, whose coming is after the working of Satan with all power and signs and lying wonders, And with all deceivableness of unrighteousness in them that perish; because they received not the love of the truth, that they might be saved. And for this cause **God shall send them**

> **strong delusion, that they should believe a lie**: That they all might be damned who believed not the truth, but had pleasure in unrighteousness. (2 Thessalonians 2:8-12)

Could it be that the heliocentric lie of a spinning, rotating earth in the supposed empty vacuum of space is part and parcel of that strong delusion? When we read 2 Thessalonians, chapter 2 in context we find that the strong delusion is an attack on the gospel of grace. Indeed, we read in verse 13 of that chapter:

> But we are bound to give thanks alway to God for you, brethren beloved of the Lord, because God hath from the beginning chosen you to salvation through sanctification of the Spirit and belief of the truth. (2 Thessalonians 2:13)

Thus we find that those who have pleasure in unrighteousness are those who are not chosen by God from the beginning for salvation. The great delusion is the false doctrine of salvation by the free will of man instead of the sovereign grace of God. Free will salvation and sovereign grace salvation are mutually exclusive doctrines. As we read earlier in Isaiah 44:21-24, God's creation of a flat earth with the canopy of the heavens above is illustrative of his sovereign grace in saving his elect. God makes it clear in Isaiah 44:21-22 that he alone is the creator of his elect in the same way that he alone is the creator who stretched forth the heavens above and spread out the flat earth beneath. In the same way that it is God alone who creates, it is God alone who saves. There is no room for man to have helped God create the heavens and the flat earth, so also, there is no room for man to help God redeem his elect. God's sovereign creation of his flat earth is linked to his sovereign salvation of his elect. Heliocentrism an attack on the sovereignly of God in creation and salvation.

Anyone who undermines the truth of God's creation as set forth in the Bible undermines the very gospel of Jesus Christ. Such who claim to be ministers of Christ are, instead, wolves in sheep's clothing sent among God's flock by the devil. Understand, that the mission of the devil and his minions is a futile one because all who are predestined for salvation by God's grace will be saved. That is a promise from God.

> My sheep hear my voice, and I know them, and they follow me: And I give unto them eternal life; and they shall never perish, neither shall any man pluck them out of my hand. My Father, which gave them me, is greater than all; and no man is able to pluck them out of my Father's hand. I and my Father are one. (John 10:27-30)

Something that is often missed in the gospel is that Jesus described those who are lost. Jesus expressly told the Jews who confronted him in Jerusalem that they do not believe in him because they were not chosen to be of his flock. "But ye believe not, because ye are not of my sheep." John 10:26. It was after that statement that Jesus explained that it is only his sheep who hear his voice. He knows them and they know him. He gives them eternal life. No one can pluck them from his hand.

Jesus was informing the Jews that his sheep believe in him because they are elected by Jesus to have faith in him; and that the reason they did not believe in him was because they were not chosen by Jesus to have faith in him. *See also* Ephesians 1:4-5, 11-14; 2:5-10; Romans 3:22-26; 4:5; 10:9-17; Galatians 3:22; 2 Timothy 1:9; Mark 16:16; John 3:15-18, 36; 5:24; John 6:27-29, 40, 44-47; 8:47; 10:26-30; James 1:8; Hebrews 12:2. Notice that Jesus did not say they are not his sheep because they don't believe, he instead states that they don't believe because they are not his sheep. Such passages, found throughout the Bible, impeach the Arminian theology. Jesus is the good shepherd who gives his life for his sheep. Those who do not believe that he is the Christ are not his sheep. Jesus did not lay his life down for those who do not believe in him. In John 15:19, Jesus makes the point that he chose those who would believe in him "out of the world." Jesus' sheep do not choose him, Jesus chooses his sheep. John 14:13. The great love Jesus had of laying down his life for his friends is limited to only those who are his sheep, his chosen.

Jesus did not say that if you were smart enough you could believe of your own free will. Instead, he put it right in their faces that they did not believe, and indeed would never believe because they were not of his sheep. Those who do not believe in Christ are lost because God has not chosen them for salvation. Those who are chosen for salvation cannot lose their salvation. John 10:26-30. There is simply no such thing as a person losing his salvation.

There are only two possibilities in the gospel. First, those who are lost cannot believe because God has not chosen them to believe. The other possibility is the flip side of the first: those who are chosen to believe will believe, and they cannot ever lose their faith. "No man is able to pluck them out of my Father's hand." There is no category for persons to be first saved and then for them to overrule God's choice by the power of their free will and "unsave" themselves. Such an occurrence is an impossibility. The only way to build such a theology is to ignore the clear message of the gospel. The gospel includes God's revelation of his creation of a flat, stationary earth.

A misguided para-church group known as "Navigators" tries to spread the gospel bereft of truth. They eschew the truth in the gospel of God's creation of a flat earth. A lie will work its way through the entire lump and corrupt it. Galatians 5:9. When Navigators are presented with a person who is seeking guidance about the gospel, and he specifically asks about the flat earth, they deny that the Bible contains any such thing.

On the Navigators website there is presented a vignette where a person asked about God's creation of a flat, stationary earth.

> As we sat down for lunch, Mark informed me he technically grew up as a Christian, but often doubted the validity of the Bible, the life of Jesus, and that Jesus is actually God's Son and God Himself, among other things. Some of his initial questions were striking. He asked, "Don't Christians believe the Earth is flat and doesn't revolve around the sun?" In that moment, I thanked God for the time He gave me with Mark and that I was able to clear the air about some of his far-fetched, false beliefs about Christians.[533]

Because the Navigator evangelist did not know the truth of the gospel, he violated God's command to speak the truth of the gospel to those whom God sends to hear it. "Have not I written to thee excellent things in counsels and knowledge, That I might make thee know the certainty of the words of truth; that thou mightest answer the words of truth to them that send unto thee?" (Proverbs 22:20-21)

Did Mark end up believing the gospel? The answer is no. Why not? Because he was not presented the true gospel. The Navigator evangelist should have told Mark the truth about God's creation. Perhaps God, by his grace, would have opened his eyes to the gospel truth. But God is not going to bless a lie that undermines the authority of his word. You cannot win adherents to the true gospel by lying to people. That is the problem when "Christian" groups do not believe that God preserved his infallible and inerrant word. Parnell McCarter, writing for the Puritan News Weekly explains another significant problem with the Navigators' Statement of Faith.

[T]he Statement of Faith ... states that "the Scriptures of the Old and New Testaments are inspired by God and inerrant in the original writings," which suggests the scriptures we have now ... are not inspired and inerrant. Otherwise, why mention only "the original writings"? But Protestantism stands or falls on having a preserved infallibly inspired word of God. How can scripture be our final authority if we do not even have the preserved infallibly inspired word of God?[534] (parenthetical deleted)

20 Slippery Slope

Kent Hovind is a famous creation lecturer and opponent of the theory of evolution. He is also a Christian heliocentrist. Hovind claims that heliocentrism does not contradict God's word because the Bible does not address the topic of the shape or motion of the earth.[535] When Hovind was presented with passages that indicate that the earth is flat and stationary, he relegated all such passages to being metaphors.[536] That interpretive scheme seems to be the common theme with pastors in heliocentric churches today.

Hovind's metaphorical reasoning is a slippery slope. So-called "Christian" churches have applied that reasoning to justify sin. To claim that the Bible does not address a particular sin can be used as an artifice to justify those unenumerated sin. That is just what is being done. For example, many Christian denominations (e.g., Episcopal Church, United Methodist Church, Evangelical Lutheran Church in America, United Church of Christ, Presbyterian Church (USA)) use that same reasoning to approve abortion.[537]

It is not a surprise to find that those pro-abortion churches are also "Christian" Zionist churches that followed heathen Jewish philosophy. Abortion is approved by the full spectrum of Judaism from the liberal reformed Judaism to conservative Judaism. Judaism did not treat an unborn child as a separate living being.[538] In Judaism, the fetus is considered only a part of the mother. Under the Talmudic law, the only penalty for killing a fetus is monetary compensation.[539]

It is true that the Bible does not use the word "abortion" just as it does not use the words "flat earth." But the absence of those words does not mean that God does not condemn abortion, just as it does not follow that God did not create a flat earth. We have already seen that God describes his creation in his Bible, and it is a flat, stationary earth. So also, the Bible states that God forms man in the womb of his mother. Thus, man is created by God from conception. To intentionally kill the unborn is, therefore, murder.

> For thou hast possessed my reins: thou hast covered me in my mother's womb. I will praise thee; for I am fearfully and wonderfully made: marvellous are thy works; and that my soul knoweth right well. (Psalms 139:13-14)

God is sovereign over the unborn. "I was cast upon thee from the womb: thou art my God from my mother's belly." (Psalms 22:10) Thus, to kill the unborn is the sin of murder. "Thou shalt do no murder." (Matthew 19:18)

Many so-called churches have gone on record in official proclamations supporting the right of a women to purposely kill her unborn child. For example, in 1987, the Sixteenth General Synod of the United Church of Christ issued the following official resolution affirming that all life is sacred, but the unborn may be killed as part of "family planning services."

> THEREFORE BE IT RESOLVED, that the Sixteenth General Synod: 1. Affirms the sacredness of all life, and the need to protect and

defend human life in particular; ... 3. Upholds the right of men and women to have access to adequately funded family planning services, and to safe, legal abortions as one option among others. ... 8. Urges pastors, members, local churches, conferences, and instrumentalities to oppose actively legislation and amendments which seek to revoke or limit access to safe and legal abortions.[540]

Not to be outdone, in 1994, the Episcopal Church issued the following official resolution stating that all human life is sacred, but that a mother may kill her unborn child and the church opposes any government action that interferes with the mother's right to slaughter her unborn child.

Resolved, That this 71st General Convention of the Episcopal Church reaffirms resolution C047 from the 69th General Convention, which states: All human life is sacred from its inception until death. ... *Resolved*, That this 71st General Convention of the Episcopal Church express its unequivocal opposition to any legislative, executive or judicial action on the part of local, state or national governments that abridges the right of a woman to reach an informed decision about the termination of pregnancy or that would limit the access of a woman to safe means of acting on her decision.[541]

Notice that both the United Church of Christ and the Episcopal Church began their proclamations approving abortion with statements affirming the sacredness of all human life. "A double minded man is unstable in all his ways." (James 1:8) Those churches then proclaim that the unborn child can be aborted. It seems that the unborn child is not considered by those churches to be a sacred human life. But that is contrary to what God states in his word. Ah, but God did not explicitly say that abortion was a sin and, therefore, those so-called churches feel free to disregard God's statement that life begins at conception. Read what God says on the matter of when life begins:

> Thus saith the LORD, thy redeemer, and he that formed thee from the womb, I am the LORD that maketh all things; that stretcheth forth the heavens alone; that spreadeth abroad the earth by myself. (Isaiah 44:24)

Indeed, God states that he knows (i.e., loves) his elect before he forms them in the womb. "Before I formed thee in the belly I knew thee; and before thou camest forth out of the womb I sanctified thee, and I ordained thee a prophet unto the nations." (Jeremiah 1:5) That means that God conceives his elect in his mind before they are conceived in the womb. Thus, all people have been conceived in God's mind before they are physically conceived in the womb. The book of Psalms confirms that fact. "Thine eyes did see my substance, yet being unperfect; and in thy book all my members were written, which in continuance were fashioned, when as yet there was none of them." (Psalms 139:16) Those passages alone destroy the claim that physical life does not begin at conception, and thus any religious justification for abortion. But through devilish stratagems of biblical interpretation, some churches have ignored God's pronouncement that life is conceived in God's mind before it is conceived in the womb.

Indeed, the Bible states that God elected Jacob as the heir to the promise. God elected Jacob before he was born.

> That is, They which are the children of the flesh, these are not the children of God: but the children of the promise are counted for the seed. For this is the word of promise, At this time will I come, and Sara shall have a son. And not only this; but when

Rebecca also had conceived by one, even by our father Isaac; (For the children being not yet born, neither having done any good or evil, that the purpose of God according to election might stand, not of works, but of him that calleth;) It was said unto her, The elder shall serve the younger. As it is written, Jacob have I loved, but Esau have I hated. (Romans 9:8-13)

Notice also what God states about Jacob and Esau. God elected Jacob before they were born and before either he or Esau had done any good or evil. That means that children who are aborted have not done any evil. There is no justification for their death; they are innocent. The killers are culpable, and those who encourage and abet them in their deadly scheme are accomplices in that sin. Unless they repent and turn in faith to Jesus Christ, they will be punished by God accordingly. *See* Matthew 25:31-46; Romans 2:3-9; 2 Corinthians 5:10; Revelation 20:11-15.

Furthermore, notice in Isaiah 44:24, how closely God associates the creation of his elect in the womb with his creation of all other things. God even references the nature of his creation in that passage, where he states that he "spreadeth abroad the earth by myself." Only a flat earth can be spread abroad. But if one is going to disregard God's creation of a flat earth, of course, it is not a stretch (pun intended) to go the whole way and disregard God's creation of man in the womb. Thus, just as those churches say that God did not create a flat earth, so also he does not create man in the womb.

To allow one to intentionally kill the unborn and justify it because there is no specific reference in the Bible to abortion is tantamount to a virtual license to any sin not explicitly articulated in the Bible. Such logic, violates God's command to do "as ye would that men should do to you, do ye also to them likewise" (Luke 6:31) Indeed, to fail to do good is a sin. "[T]o him that knoweth to do good, and doeth it not, to him it is sin." James 4:17. Killing an unborn child is not treating another the way you would want to be treated. And preventing the death of the unborn is doing a good thing. Failing to do that good thing by not saving the unborn is a sin. Thus, abortion is clearly a sin.

All the law and the prophets are summarized in two commandments.

> Master, which is the great commandment in the law? Jesus said unto him, Thou shalt love the Lord thy God with all thy heart, and with all thy soul, and with all thy mind. This is the first and great commandment. And the second is like unto it, Thou shalt love thy neighbour as thyself. **On these two commandments hang all the law and the prophets.** (Matthew 22:36-40)

Jesus set us free, by fulfilling the requirements of the law for us. Matthew 5:17; John 8:32; Ephesians 2:15; Colossians 2:14. Righteousness is imputed to those who believe; it is not earned. The deeds of the law will never earn salvation. Salvation is a gift of God through faith in Jesus Christ. Ephesians 2:8-10. But salvation should never be used as a license to sin. Because we are set free does not mean we are free to sin. He gave us a new heart so that we are free to obey the law of God, which would otherwise have been an impossibility. We are commanded to love one another and love God; upon those two commandments hang all the requirements of the law. Matthew 22:36-40. "For, brethren, ye have been called unto liberty; only use not liberty for an occasion to the flesh, but by love serve one another. For all the law is fulfilled in one word, even in this; Thou shalt love thy neighbour as thyself." (Galatians 5:13-14) Aborting a child is a violation of God's command to love one another.

The royal law of God is that we should love our neighbors

as we love ourselves. James 2:6. That love should be shown to the unborn. Aborting the unborn is the very antithesis of love. Jesus gave us a new commandment that goes further and tells us to what degree we are to love one another. Our obedience to this new commandment does not earn salvation, but our obedience is a sign that we are his disciples. "A new commandment I give unto you, That ye love one another; as I have loved you, that ye also love one another. By this shall all men know that ye are my disciples, if ye have love one to another." (John 13:34-35)

How did Jesus love us? He gave his very life for us. That means that even those churches, like the Missouri Synod of the Lutheran Church, who claim to be pro-life and anti-abortion, are actually promoting sin by allowing for abortion when the life of the mother is threatened.[542] Dr. A.L. Barry, President of The Lutheran Church, Missouri Synod, proclaims that "The sin of willfully aborting a child, except in those very rare situations where it may be necessary to save the life of the mother, is a sinful act, totally contrary to the will of God."[543] But to kill the child on the chance that childbirth may possibly cause the death of the mother is a violation of the command to "love one another; as I have loved you." While that command is certainly an ideal, it is nonetheless a command from God. We are obligated to obey God's commands. Jesus stated without equivocation that "if ye love me, keep my commandments." John 14:15. The contrary is also true. Jesus said that "he that loveth me not keepeth not my sayings." John 14:24. Indeed, we are not to rebel against God by not keeping his commandments by, for example, promoting the sin of abortion.

Under the rubric that abortion is not expressly prohibited in the Bible, what is clearly sin is proclaimed by some churches to no longer be a sin. Once the biblical license is given to harm another because that harm is not specifically prohibited in the Bible, then it is inevitable that even the listed sins will be justified. All it would take is to redefine the words in the Bible to give a biblical license to do those things that are expressly prohibited in the Bible. And that is just what is being done. For example, sodomy is clearly condemned in both the New and Old Testaments of the Bible. E.g., Romans 1:21-32; 1 Timothy 1:9-10.

> Thou shalt not lie with mankind, as with womankind: it is abomination. (Leviticus 18:22)

> Know ye not that the unrighteous shall not inherit the kingdom of God? Be not deceived: neither fornicators, nor idolaters, nor adulterers, nor effeminate, nor abusers of themselves with mankind. (1 Corinthians 6:9)

> Even as Sodom and Gomorrha, and the cities about them in like manner, giving themselves over to fornication, and going after strange flesh, are set forth for an example, suffering the vengeance of eternal fire. (Jude 1:7)

Justin Russell Cannon, an Episcopal Priest, director of Inclusive Orthodoxy, and a sodomite, justifies the sin of sodomy by claiming that the passages that condemn sodomy do not mean what they say.

> [T]he Bible really does not fully address the topic of homosexuality. Jesus never talked about it. The prophets never talked about it. In Sodom homosexual activity is mentioned within the context of rape (raping angels nonetheless), and in Romans 1:24-27 we find it mentioned within the context of idolatry (Baal worship) involving lust and dishonorable passions. 1 Corinthians 6:9 and 1 Timothy 1:10 talk about homosexual activity in the context of prostitution and possibly pederasty. Nowhere does the Bible talk about a loving and

committed homosexual relationship. The only thing the authors of the Bible knew about homosexuality was that which they saw expressed in the pagan worship of Baal, the temple prostitution, et cetera. To use the Bible to condemn homosexuality, as we see, involves a projection of ones own bias and a stretching of the Biblical text beyond that of which the scriptures speak. Historically, however, the Bible has been taken out of context and twisted to oppress almost every minority one could imagine.[544]

If a person dies without believing in Jesus Christ, his sins, including the sin of sodomy, will be punished for eternity in hell. But if one believes in Jesus Christ, all sin, including the sin of sodomy, can be wiped clean by the propitiation provided to the elect of Jesus Christ. "And such [effeminate and abusers of themselves with mankind] were some of you: but ye are washed, but ye are sanctified, but ye are justified in the name of the Lord Jesus, and by the Spirit of our God." (1 Corinthians 6:11) There is a difference, though, between arguing that God will forgive the sin of sodomy and claiming that sodomy is not a sin at all. If one is a sodomite and is falsely justified in his behavior by being convinced that it is not a sin, he will not seek the justification through the forgiveness provided by Jesus Christ. Why should he? His "Christian" pastor has told him that sodomy is not a sin, and thus there is no need for justification from Jesus Christ.

"Christian" churches' approval of abortion and sodomy today is only possible by the artifice that God does not address those topics. They garnish their deception by limiting and metaphorizing what God has condemned. Nobody could conceive a hundred years ago that Christian churches would be preaching that neither sodomy nor abortion is a sin.

That slippery slope began with the cunning contrivance

that God does not address the configuration of his creation. Devilish men then interpreted the Bible passages that describe a flat, stationary earth as merely figurative language that should not be taken literally. Indeed, that contrivance is necessary for the heliocentric model to survive scrutiny. Once that artifice of biblical interpretation took root, it was only a matter of time before clear passages condemning sin would be reinterpreted under the new figurative rubric. The number of sins that will be justified by those cunning stratagems of transforming God's words will be endless. There is a great woe unto those who practice such folly. "Woe unto them that call evil good, and good evil; that put darkness for light, and light for darkness; that put bitter for sweet, and sweet for bitter!" (Isaiah 5:20)

21 He Saw No God There

As we have seen, Satan has infiltrated the Christian churches with his heliocentric myth. He has introduced shills who portray themselves as Christian astronauts to convince the Christian churches to ignore God's word and keep to the heliocentric doctrine. One example is NASA astronaut Colonel Jeffrey N. Williams, who is widely promoted as a Bible-believing Christian. It is an oxymoron for a NASA astronaut to be a Bible-believing Christian; it is like a Satanist being a Bible-believing Christian. It is an impossibility. Williams is promoted in the Christian community as "a record breaking Christian astronaut," who "has shared how his faith allows him to see the 'creative work by an infinite God.'"[545]

As part of the propaganda machine promoting the false heliocentric mythology, there was an alleged live feed transmission of Colonel Williams supposedly orbiting 250 miles above earth speaking with Dr. Robert Mohler Jr. during a service at the Southern Seminary chapel.[546] During the transmission, Dr. Mohler asked Williams about the expansiveness of space. Williams responded that "the expansiveness is beyond our comprehension. We have a hard time comprehending the word infinity, but certainly, the expanse of creation is infinity as far as we can understand it."[547] Williams was lying. He was not in space orbiting the earth. Williams' portrayal of infinite darkness above the firmament, instead of a bright and glorious heaven, serves to impeach the credibility of the Bible.

Jeff Williams' real mission is to undermine the gospel. The earth is not a floating sphere that is spinning and orbiting in space as portrayed by NASA and Williams. There is no International Space Station in outer space and there are no satellites in outer space. Indeed, there is no outer space. So NASA must phony up CGI images and lie about them being taken from satellites to create the false impression of a spinning, orbiting, spherical earth in outer space. They then trot out lying astronauts, like Williams, to vouch for the authenticity of the photographs. Otherwise, the truth the Bible depicts of the flat stationary earth, with God in heaven above, would be generally known. NASA must replace the glorious heaven that is above the firmament with a dark, foreboding, empty void. If science, falsely so called, can convince people that there is no heaven as depicted in the Bible, then it is very easy to discredit the Bible and make it believable that there is no God either.

Colonel Valentin Petrov, associate professor at the Gagarin Air Force Academy, reported that Nikita Khrushchev stated "Why should you clutch at God? Here is Gagarin who flew to space but saw no God there."[548] Petrov was a good friend of the legendary Russian Cosmonaut Yuri Gagarin, who is alleged to be the first man in space. Colonel Petrov revealed the statement made by Nikita Khrushchev to refute claims that Gagarin made the statement. Petrov explained that the statement was not made by Gagarin, but by Khrushchev about Gagarin.

Nikita Khrushchev was the First Secretary (formerly and later known as General Secretary) of the Communist Party of the Soviet Union from 1953 to 1964, and the Chairman of the Council of Ministers (in effect, Premier) from 1958 to 1964. Petrov explained that Khrushchev made the statement about there being no God in space before the Central Committee plenary meeting that was considering anti-religious propaganda as a way to undermine the growing influence of Christian churches in the Soviet Union. Khrushchev was advising that line of propaganda as a way to refute the legitimacy of the Christian belief that God is in heaven above.

Khrushchev inadvertently let the cat out of the bag. His statement reveals that the purpose of the space programs for all countries is to demonstrate that above us is not heaven, but rather an empty void, which they call outer space. Since there is no heaven, then there can be no God. The modern space programs pretend to send astronauts into space and jimmy up fake CGI pictures for the purpose of undermining the authority of the Bible and proving that there is "no God there."[549] Jeff Williams does not come out and say there is "no God there." Indeed, he tries to portray outer space as God's creation. But the *sub silentio* message that is implicit in, and the ineluctable conclusion from, Williams' testimony is that there is "no God there."

Jeff Williams is being used to rebut the evidence of the flat earth. In an interview with Stephen Feinstein, a Christian pastor from Sovereign Way Christian Church, Williams reassured the pastor that the earth is not flat. Williams stated that he saw it from space, and it is definitely a sphere.[550] And that was the point of the interview, to establish authoritatively from a Christian astronaut that the earth is a sphere. Feinstein then goes in for the kill:

> Okay, now that you've seen that, now that you've heard that answer [from astronaut Jeff Williams], I have an exhortation for those who are Christian. You need to tread carefully. If you are going to say the earth is flat, and that we've all been lied to. You are calling this dear brother for whom the Lord has died, you are calling this man a liar. You are saying he is part of the conspiracy. You are

saying that, quite literally, he is working for Satan. So, again, tread carefully.⁵⁵¹

Yes, this author is saying just that. Astronaut Williams is a liar, who is part of a satanic conspiracy against God and man to conceal the true nature of God's creation.

Satan has many arrows in his quiver. Another astronaut falsely portraying himself as a Christian is Barry Wilmore, who allegedly piloted the Space Shuttle Atlantis and was the mythical International Space Station Commander. Wilmore was interviewed by Ken Ham, who is a fundamentalist Christian and the CEO and founder of *Answers in Genesis*, *The Creation Museum*, and *The Ark Encounter*. Ken Ham is also an inductee in the Creation Science Hall of Fame.⁵⁵² During the interview, Ken Ham specifically asked if the earth is flat. Wilmore responded that the earth is not flat; it is is a sphere.⁵⁵³

> Ken Ham: "The big question, everybody wanting to know, the big question, when you got up for the first time and looked at the earth, was it flat?"
>
> Barry Wilmore: "No, it was not flat. It was definitely round."⁵⁵⁴

Wilmore, as do all astronauts, impeaches the Bible by stating that above the firmament is the "blackest black looking into space that you can imagine."⁵⁵⁵ Astronauts always portray outer space as a black void. Apollo 12 Astronaut Pete Conrad described outer space as the blackest black he has ever seen.⁵⁵⁶ Apollo 17 Astronaut Eugene Cernan described the earth from his alleged Apollo spacecraft as "surrounded by the blackest black you can conceive in your mind."⁵⁵⁷ Astronaut Leroy Chiao stated that "when you look out into space away from the sun, it's the darkest black you can imagine."⁵⁵⁸ Neil Armstrong, the alleged first man to walk on the moon, said: "The sky is a deep black when viewed from the moon as it is when viewed from ... the space between the earth and the moon."[559] God curses those who "put darkness for light." Isaiah 5:20. God equates that to calling "good evil." *Id.*

Why do astronauts describe the mythical outer space as the blackest black? Because "God is light, and in him is no darkness at all." (1 John 1:5) Satan must remove any hint that God might be in heaven, and so outer space must be void of all light. Because in God there is no darkness at all, and outer space, which is supposed to be where the heaven of God is located, is full of darkness. NASA, therefore, implants in the minds of men that the heaven of the Bible is a myth and there is no God. The Bible, however, makes it clear that his throne is above the firmament and it is surrounded by brightness, not darkness, as alleged by NASA.

> And there was a voice from the firmament that was over their heads, when they stood, and had let down their wings. And **above the firmament that was over their heads was the likeness of a throne**, as the appearance of a sapphire stone: and upon the likeness of the throne was the likeness as the appearance of a man above upon it. And I saw as the colour of amber, as the appearance of fire round about within it, from the appearance of his loins even upward, and from the appearance of his loins even downward, I saw as it were **the appearance of fire, and it had brightness round about**. As the appearance of the bow that is in the cloud in the day of rain, so was **the appearance of the brightness round about. This was the appearance of the likeness of the glory of the LORD**. And when I saw it, I fell upon my face, and I heard a voice of one that spake. (Ezekiel 1:25-28)

According to "Christian" astronaut Barry Wilmore, there

is no glorious brightness surrounding God on his throne in heaven above the firmament. Instead, Wilmore portrays the throne of God as nonexistent. Where God's throne is supposed to be, above the firmament, there is instead just an empty, weightless, vacuum of black nothingness. The implication from Wilmore's description is that there is no heaven, and thus, there is no God.

God is above us in heaven, watching over man. (Job 22:12; Ecclesiastes 24:5; Psalms 14:2 & 33:13) God states that "heaven is my throne." (Acts 7:49) But Satan has used "science falsely so called" to remove God in the minds of men from his throne and replace the glorious abode of God with a dark and hostile empty vacuum, full of deadly x-rays, gamma rays, and cosmic rays. "The LORD is in his holy temple, the LORD'S throne is in heaven: his eyes behold, his eyelids try, the children of men." (Psalms 11:4) "Heaven is my throne, and earth is my footstool." (Acts 7:49) "Am I a God at hand, saith the LORD, and not a God afar off? Can any hide himself in secret places that I shall not see him? saith the LORD. Do not I fill heaven and earth? saith the LORD." (Jeremiah 23:23-24)

We read in Jeremiah 23:23-24 that God is close at hand and not far off; he fills heaven and earth. But astronauts have turned the glorious abode of God in heaven into hell. Jesus Christ describes hell as **"outer darkness."** Which is exactly how outer space is described by astronauts. "And cast ye the unprofitable servant into **outer darkness**: there shall be weeping and gnashing of teeth." (Matthew 25:30) That "outer darkness" is the everlasting fire of hell. Jesus explained that fact 11 verses after describing "outer darkness" when he said: "Then shall he say also unto them on the left hand, Depart from me, ye cursed, into **everlasting fire**, prepared for the devil and his angels:" (Matthew 25:41) Jesus explained that the fire of hell is the everlasting punishment due for those for their sins who have not been elected to salvation. "And these shall go away into **everlasting punishment**: but the righteous into life eternal." (Matthew 25:46)

You see, the brightness of the glory of God, which surrounds God's throne, is above the firmament. The governments of the world are lying when their space agency astronauts describe the "blackest black" void of outer space. The dark and dangerous environment of outer space, which requires astronauts to wear protective pressurized suits to protect them from the vacuum and the burning cosmic rays, gamma rays, and x-rays, seems very much like dark hell, with its "everlasting fire." God pronounces a great woe on those who "put darkness for light." Isaiah 5:20. The whole point in astronauts creating the myth of a dark void of space is to create in the minds of men the idea that Nikita Khrushchev promoted regarding Yuri Gagarin, who was allegedly the first man in outer space, "but saw no God there."[560]

Barry Wilmore then made a very revealing statement. In response to a question from Ken Ham about whether being in space made him think that there was a God after all. Wilmore responded with an emphatic: "well, actually, no, I did not." Wilmore elaborated that "everything that I needed to know about my Lord and Savior, about God, is in scripture. So I did not need to fly in space to learn anything about my Lord."[561] That is odd; because the Bible states:

> **The heavens declare the glory of God; and the firmament sheweth his handywork. Day unto day uttereth speech, and night unto night sheweth knowledge. There is no speech nor language, where their voice is not heard.** Their line is gone out through all the earth, and their words to the end of the world. In them hath he set a tabernacle for the sun, Which is as a bridegroom coming out of his chamber, and rejoiceth as a strong man to run a race. His going forth is from the end of the heaven, and his circuit unto the ends of it: and there is nothing hid from the heat thereof. (Psalms 19:1-6)

The Bible states that "there is no speech nor language, where their [heavens' and firmament's] voice is not heard." Yet we find that Wilmore's Christian testimony is that he did not learn anything about God by going to space. How is that possible? That is because there was nothing to learn by going to space, because there is no space, and thus Wilmore never went there. Thus it only seems that Wilmore has done the impossible by not hearing the voice of God's creation manifest in the firmament and the heavens. In reality, he did not hear the voice of God's creation in the firmament and the heavens because he is a liar; he never went into outer space. There is no outer space.

Modern science is not truly science; it is more accurately characterized as profane philosophy. "Profane" is defined as something that is not sacred. "Profane" things are secular things. "Profane" denotes irreverence to things sacred or proceeding from contempt of sacred things.[562] Indeed, God commands us not to equate holy things with profane things. Ezekiel 22:26. God admonishes throughout the scriptures to refrain from profaning God's name (Leviticus 21:6), his sanctuary (Leviticus 21:12), holy things (Leviticus 22:15), or the sabbath (Nehemiah 13:7). We are commanded by God to "**refuse profane** and old wives' fables, and exercise thyself rather unto godliness." (1 Timothy 4:7) We are to "**avoiding profane** and vain babblings, and oppositions of science falsely so called." (1 Timothy 6:20) We are to "**shun profane** and vain babblings: for they will increase unto more ungodliness." (2 Timothy 2:16) But the mainstream "churches" (falsely so called) are disobeying God by accepting the profane "science" (falsely so-called) of heliocentrism. The modern "churches" have corrupted their theology with the profanity of heliocentrism. It is no surprise then to find in those very "churches" a resulting "increase unto more ungodliness" prophesied by God.

22 Creation Science Hall of Shame

Ken Ham, whom you recall is CEO and founder of *Answers in Genesis* and an inductee in the Creation Science Hall of Fame,[563] correctly states that the creation account of the Bible in Genesis should be taken literally.[564] He correctly argues that God meant what he said when he said he created the world in six days. Ham posits that there really can be no other way to read the creation account of Genesis other than literally. Ham cites Exodus 20:11 as confirmation of six literal days of creation. "For in six days the LORD made heaven and earth, the sea, and all that in them is, and rested the seventh day: wherefore the LORD blessed the sabbath day, and hallowed it." (Exodus 20:11)

Some have tried to argue that the creation account in the Bible is allegorical and should not be taken literally. But the Bible presents the creation of the heavens and the earth out of nothing within six literal days. God created the heavens and the earth in six literal days, just as he said he did.

> And God called the light Day, and the darkness he called Night. And the evening and the morning were the first day. (Genesis 1:5)

And the evening and the morning were the second day. (Genesis 1:8)

And the evening and the morning were the third day. (Genesis 1:13)

And the evening and the morning were the fourth day. (Genesis 1:19)

And the evening and the morning were the fifth day. (Genesis 1:23)

And God saw every thing that he had made, and, behold, *it was* very good. And the evening and the morning were the sixth day. (Genesis 1:31)

God defined the day and night and described the events of creation as having taken place between the "evening and the morning." Each day was marked off by "the evening and the morning." They were literal evenings and mornings. They were literal days. There is no biblical authority for the argument that the days mentioned in the Bible spanned millions of years. To suggest that is pure sophistry, born out of a heathen desire to strip God of the glory he deserves for having created the heavens and the earth in six literal days, by the exercise of his sovereign will, through his spoken commands. God rested on the seventh day. Genesis 2:2.

Ken Ham is correct regarding Genesis presenting an account of creation in six literal days. But when it comes to the Bible passages that describe a flat earth, he changes his tune. When it comes to a flat, stationary earth, Ham argues that Bible passages are not to be taken literally. He states that Bible passages that illustrate a flat, stationary earth should not be read literally, but rather "poetically."

To support the idea that the Bible supposedly

teaches a flat earth, some people point to poetic passages that talk about the sun rising and setting. But think about it, would they argue that when a meteorologist giving the weather report mentions the sunrise and sunset he believes in a flat, stationary earth. Of course not! The Bible got facts about astronomy right years before they became scientifically accepted.[565]

Robert Carter, Ph.D., is a marine biologist and geneticist, who is also a senior scientist and speaker for *Creation Ministries International*.[566] He is an inductee in the Creation Science Hall of Fame.[567] Dr. Carter correctly rejects evolution, based in primary part on the authority of the Bible. "CMI absolutely rejects the theory of evolution, but we have done so after carefully scrutinizing both the biblical and scientific records."[568] Carter views the book of Genesis and the creation account as accurate history.[569] He interprets Genesis in a strictly literal manner.[570] Furthermore, he considers the account in chapter 2 of Genesis as having "the hallmarks of a genuine geographical description from an eyewitness."[571]

When the issue turns from defending what the Bible states about the creation of man to supporting what Bible states about the creation of the earth and cosmology, suddenly Dr. Carter changes his tune. Dr. Carter takes the Bible literally when it says that God created everything in six (24-hour) days. But when addressing the passages in the Bible that portray the nature of God's creation as a flat, stationary earth, Dr. Carter hypocritically dismisses the authority of those passages by opining that God is using "equivocal phenomenological language."[572] Dr. Carter thinks that "[m]any of the supposed flat-earth passages are from poetic books that are not meant to be taken literalistically."[573] Rather than read the Bible for what it says, Dr. Carter reads the Bible from the preconception that the idea of a flat, stationary earth is "nonsense."[574] This causes Carter to effectively relegate the Bible to be a book of poetry with no scientific validity; he opines that "the purpose of the Bible is not to be a science book."[575] He, consequently, concludes that "we should not expect to learn a great deal on many scientific subjects from within its pages."[576] That is quite a change from his attitude toward the Bible when addressing the error of evolution, where he carefully scrutinized the biblical record for proof of God's creation of man. Dr. Carter presents his authority for impeaching the plain words of the Bible that the earth is flat and stationary: NASA. Dr. Carter vouches for the authenticity of NASA's pictures of the globular earth allegedly taken from space. "All of these scientists and astronauts are not lying!"[577]

Oddly, Francis Collins, M.D., Ph.D., made the same argument as Dr. Carter: that the Bible is not a science book. Dr. Collins is a prominent evangelical Christian geneticist and the director of the National Institute of Health and believer in the "science" of evolution. Dr. Collins stated that he reads and trusts the Bible about theological truths. He, however, suggests that discoveries in science are just as authoritative as the Bible and reconciles the conflicts between the Bible and "science" by claiming that the Bible was not intended to be a textbook of science. He claims that the Bible is only a book about the nature of God and man.[578]

Dr. Carter criticized Dr. Collins for claiming that "there is no evidence for Adam and Eve and that there is no physical way we could have come from two ancestors in the recent past."[579] Dr. Carter hypocritically argues that Dr. Collins is disingenuous to claim no evidence for Adam and Eve because Dr. Collin's conclusion is "based on evolutionary assumptions."[580] But that is the very thing that Dr. Carter is doing when he assumes a spinning, spherical earth. In reference to Dr. Collins' evolutionary assumptions, Dr. Carter hypocritically states:

One cannot legitimately claim something to be

proven without testing the assumptions behind that claim. To do otherwise amounts to circular reasoning and question begging, and a rejection of any alternative theory following from this is thus reduced to nothing more than a straw man argument.[581]

Dr. Carter is doing that very thing he criticizes Dr. Collins for doing when Dr. Carter argues against the flat, stationary earth. Dr. Carter's scientific bias influences how he treats the Bible. Dr. Carter advocates for a literal reading of Genesis regarding the creation of Adam and Eve and all of creation in six literal days. But when discussing the Bible passages that describe the nature of creation as a flat, stationary earth, Dr. Carter changes the rules and the literal reading of the Bible cannot be allowed.

Dr. Carter is joined in this intellectual sleight of mind by Jonathan D. Sarfati, Ph.D., who is a creationist, physical chemist, spectroscopist, and fellow inductee, along with Dr. Carter, in the Creation Science Hall of Fame.[582] Carter and Sarfati posit in their co-authored writings that those passages that describe a flat, stationary earth are not to be taken literally; they are to be read poetically. These so-called Christian scientists caution that "[m]any of the supposed flat-earth passages are from poetic books that are not meant to be taken literalistically."[583] Indeed, suddenly, when the topic turns to God's creation of the earth, Drs. Carter and Sarfati opine that the Bible is not a good source for truth about God's creation because "[i]n general, the Bible uses correct but equivocal phenomenological language on many scientific subjects."[584]

Dr. Carter is a scientist, and in his capacity as a scientist, he claims that "flat earth ideas have no supporting evidence whatsoever, literally zero."[585] Dr. Carter is also somewhat of an historian, and in that capacity he claims that "there is no time in the Christian era where people thought that the earth was flat."[586]

Dr. Carter also claims to be a Christian, and in that capacity, he, oddly enough, cautions people not to believe what the Bible states in plain English. He claims that God has hidden the real esoteric meaning in the Bible from the reader in the original language. "We cannot blithely read the Bible in English and assume that we understand the subtle nuances of the underlying languages."[587] For Carter's argument to have any merit, it would have to mean that the Bible passages that reveal a flat, stationary earth actually mean that the earth is a spinning globe in the original languages. That perverse view of God and his Bible is the kind of thing one gets when scientists pretend to be Christians. Dr. Carter has covered all the bases, scientifically, historically, and biblically; Dr. Carter claims on all accounts that the earth is not flat or stationary.

What about passages that could only be explained if the earth was flat? How do Drs. Carter and Safarti tackle those hard passages? Let's consider the passage in Revelation 1:7: "Behold, he cometh with clouds; and every eye shall see him, and they also which pierced him: and all kindreds of the earth shall wail because of him. Even so, Amen." We know that "every" eye on earth will see Christ when he returns. For that to happen requires that the earth be flat. How do the brilliant "Christian" scientists, Drs. Carter and Safarti, address the impossibility of people on the back side of the supposedly globular earth being able to see the return to earth of Jesus Christ? They argue that "now we have the Internet and international news on TV."[588] That is what passes for Bible exegesis in the heliocentric creation science community—that is sad.

Paul H. Seely did extensive research on the meaning of the words used in Genesis to describe the earth. He concluded that the earth described in Genesis is flat.[589] Seely concluded:

> [T]here is really no serious question about the meaning of "earth" in Gen 1. It is clearly defined as a flat, very probably circular disc and certainly not

a globe.[590]

Indeed, Seely examined the underlying Hebrew word for earth, *erets*, and found that word does not support the idea that the earth is a globe. On the contrary, he concludes that the context of the description of the earth in Genesis indicates a flat earth. The interpretation of the earth being a planetary globe is purely a result of modern heliocentric science (falsely so-called) influencing the interpretation of the Bible passages. Seely states:

> [T]here is nothing whatsoever in the biblical context--either immediate or remote--which defines *erets* in Gen 1:1 as a planetary globe. This latter meaning is derived purely from our knowledge of modern Western science and simply read into the text. Interpreting *erets* in Gen 1:1 as a planetary globe is eisegetical, not exegetical.[591]

Seely finds a theme in the Bible of passage after passage testifying to a flat earth. In the more than 250 references to the earth in a cosmological sense in the Old Testament, not a single passage even suggests that the earth is a sphere.

> [T]his verse [Job 38:13] speaks of dawn grasping the earth by its "extremity or hem" (kanap; cf. Num 15:38; I Sam 15:27) and shaking the wicked out of it. The picture is metaphorical, comparing the earth to a blanket or garment picked up at one end and shaken. A globe is not really comparable to a blanket or garment in this way. You cannot pick up a globe at one end. It does not even have an end. ... Similarly, phrases about the earth in a cosmological sense like "stretched out the earth" (Ps 136:6), "spread forth the earth" (Isa 42:4; 44:24), "breadth of the earth" (Job 38:18) and "longer than the earth" (Job 11:9) fit more naturally

with a flat earth than a spherical one; and, this is all the more evident in that although the OT mentions the earth over two hundred and fifty times in a cosmological sense, it never once uses a phrase which implies that the earth is a sphere, much less a planetary globe.[592]

Dear Reader, please understand that Paul Seely does not believe that the earth is flat. In fact, it seems that he believes that the earth is a spinning globe. He is merely reading the Bible for what it says. He stated that he has "never said or implied that the Bible 'teaches' either that the 'firmament' is solid or that the 'earth' is a flat disc. Rather, I believe both are divinely inspired concessions to the views of the times."[593] What does Seely mean by that? He means to convey that God allowed the writers to write that the earth was flat (even though God knew it was not) because that is all the people understood and he did not want to distract readers from his more important spiritual message. Seely opines that God allowed the writers to describe the earth as flat, even though it was not, because that is what they experienced day-to-day.

Seely is saying that God inspired his word to be written according to the understanding of creation held by the naive people of the time. God inspired the writers to document his teachings, but he allowed them to put those teachings in the context of their naive misunderstanding of his creation. That accommodation to untruth was only because the misunderstanding of God's creation was in accordance with "the ordinary opinions of the day." Essentially, Seely is saying that the inspired word of God describes a flat stationary earth, not because it is in fact flat and stationary, but because God allowed that erroneous description to enter into his inspired word in order for God to convey to the people the more important truths he had to impart that were of eternal importance (i.e., more important than the nature of his creation).

Seely has an extraordinary view of biblical inspiration. His position is that God allows misinformation about the shape of the earth in the Bible in order not to distract the reader from his essential spiritual message. The point, though, that cannot be missed is that Seely, believing that the earth is a sphere, concludes that the Bible teaches that the earth is flat. He reconciles the conflict between what the Bible states (a flat earth) and what he understands from modern science (a spherical earth) by interpreting the Bible to be simply a concession to the naivety of the ancient people when the Bible was written. A true believer would accept as true what God says in his Bible over what so-called science says.

Seely's position illustrates that a person necessarily must question the inerrancy of the Bible when he opines that what is written in the Bible about the earth being flat cannot be taken at face value to be true. That seems to be the case even where one takes the view that the Bible can be read to support the heliocentric model. An example of that is found in heliocentrist Patrick Holding, who is president of Tekton Apologetics Ministries, author of The Atonement Contextualized, and a frequent contributor to *Creation Ministries International*.[594]

Patrick Holding disagrees with Seely's position that the Bible describes a flat earth. Holding thinks that the Bible portrays a spherical earth. But Holding's position has a problem. There are some passages that simply cannot be read to support a spherical earth. How does Holding address those passages? He joins Seely in the attack on the inerrancy of the inspired word of God by arguing that the passages in the Bible that indicate the earth is flat are simply an accommodation by God to what the Jews thought the shape of the earth was at the time they wrote those passages. Holding joins with Seely in arguing that, although the earth is a sphere, God allowed the Jews to write erroneous passages in the Bible indicating that the earth is flat because God did not want to confuse the Jews, and he did not care if they got that correct.

The Bible was written in a time and culture remote from ours, and biblical authors were limited in terms of what they could coherently express to their audience. This is not to say that God could not have inspired an author to reveal that the Earth was a sphere. However, although inspired by God, the biblical text had to offer an accommodation to human finitude.[595]

The problem with Holding's and Seely's position is that it undermines the truth of the gospel. If we cannot believe what God says in the Bible about God's creation, how can we believe what God says about spiritual truths? "If I have told you earthly things, and ye believe not, how shall ye believe, if I tell you of heavenly things?" (John 3:12) Despite what Seely and Holding say to the contrary, God does think that what he has said about the shape of the earth is essential. We are called on by God to believe everything that he has written in his word, including his description of a flat earth. The believing Jews thought the earth was flat because God told them it was flat, and they put what God told them in the scriptures.

John Walton, Ph.D., also agrees with Seely's strange position on biblical inspiration. Dr. Walton is an eminent Professor of Old Testament Studies at Wheaton College. Dr. Walton was formerly a professor at Moody Bible Institute for 20 years. Dr. Walton is the author of 15 books on the Bible. He concludes in his study of the Bible that the Bible describes a flat earth.[596] But Dr. Walton thinks that the earth is a sphere. He accommodates that contradiction by opining that God allowed the authors of the Bible to write an erroneous description of a flat earth because that was not important to God.

Dr. Walton thinks that the Bible passages describing the creation of Adam are authoritative and must be believed literally. But he believes that the Bible passages that describe a flat earth "are incidental elements that happen to characterize the thinking in the ancient world."[597] The flat earth passages, therefore, should be considered incidental and not authoritative. Dr. Walton thinks that there is no theology founded on the description in the Bible of a flat earth or a geocentric cosmos. Dr. Walton acknowledges that the Bible describes a flat earth, but he suggests that those Bible passages are erroneous and can be ignored as theologically useless.[598]

Michael S. Heiser, Ph.D., is a fellow traveler with Seely and Dr. Walton in their perverse view of Bible truth and inspiration. Dr. Heiser is the biblical scholar in residence at Faithlife Corporation and Distance Learning Professor at Liberty University and Midwestern Baptist Theological Seminary. Dr. Heiser received an MA in Ancient History from the University of Pennsylvania, and an MA and Ph.D. in the Hebrew Bible and Semitic Languages from the University of Wisconsin. Heiser received his undergraduate degree from Bob Jones University and also attended Bible college for three years.

Dr. Heiser, who disagrees with the theory of evolution, is nonetheless very accommodating and measured in his opposition to evolution. Dr. Heiser states:

> I am no fan of evolution. I frankly have a hard time even caring about it to be honest with you ... but I would let them [who oppose evolution] know that I am friend not foe. ... If [those who oppose evolution] are going to shoot at me for not being more friendly [to them] and not being militant [against evolution], oh wow, and trust me, I do get shot at for that.[599]

Dr. Heiser's rather tepid opposition to the devilish religious mythology of evolution (masquerading as science) tells a lot about his standing before God. "So then because thou art lukewarm, and neither cold nor hot, I will spue thee out of my mouth." (Revelation 3:16)

Dr. Heiser portrays himself as a biblical scholar, but it seems that defending the gospel against the error of evolution is not a big deal to him. Dr. Heiser "frankly has a hard time even caring about" evolution. That sounds like someone who is only pretending to oppose Darwinian evolution. Dr. Heiser's lukewarm approach to opposing clear error is because he is, in reality, an enemy of the gospel who is camouflaged behind the spiritual battle lines as a "Christian" scholar. Dr. Heiser's real character as an enemy of the gospel comes to the fore when he belligerently opposes God's creation of a flat, stationary earth. Unlike his lukewarm opposition to evolution, Dr. Heiser suits up to do battle in the most hardline militant fashion against the biblical model of a fixed, flat earth. This eminent biblical scholar wrote an article titled *Christians Who Believe the Earth is Really Flat — Does It Get Any Dumber Than This?* in which he stridently attacks Christians who believe that the earth is flat:

> I'm appalled that people who follow Christ are this dumb (or so easily led astray into embracing beliefs that are demonstrably contrary to reality). This level of willful ignorance dishonors God. The stupidity of modern flat earth belief is transparent in today's world. Space flight (really, flight between hemispheres), satellite communications, space photography (any photography showing the earth's curvature), etc., show the idea to be utter nonsense. And that's before getting into the nuts-and-bolts science. Yet some people think they need to believe it to have a "true" Bible. This is mindless, simplistic literalism at its worst.[600]

Why does Heiser think that it is so "dumb" and "stupid" and "mindless" and "willful ignorance" and "demonstrably contrary to reality" and "simplistic literalism" and "utter nonsense" to believe that the earth is flat? Because he does not believe that the Bible is the inspired word of God. Hence, he does not think that God means what he says in the Bible. Dr. Heiser states:

> I can already hear the comeback. "Let God be true and every man a liar!" Let me just say God isn't a liar. He knows (and knew) the earth is a globe. It just happens that the people he chose to produce this thing we call the Bible didn't know that. And God couldn't have cared less. The writers God used to produce the Bible were not inspired to write about things of the natural world that were beyond their own worldview and knowledge base.[601]

Dr. Heiser, like the Pharisees before him, dismisses the Bible passages that describe a stationary, flat earth as being written by people who mistakenly thought that the world was flat and motionless. Dr. Heiser' position is that God knew better, but he was stuck with ignoramuses he chose to write the Bible and just let them write whatever they wanted about the world around them. Dr. Heiser opines that God allowed the scripture writers to insert error about the nature of the earth because the writers didn't know any better. Dr. Heiser is essentially accusing God of being a knowing accomplice to errors in his scriptures. Dr. Heiser's retort to this is that God chose the writers of the Bible, and God is entitled to allow the writers to be wrong about their description of the earth in the Bible.

> That God chose people of a certain time, a certain place, with a certain (limited) knowledge base was up to him. We dishonor His choices when we impose our questions and our context on the biblical writers. Precisely the same limitations would be in place if God chose a scientist today to

write Genesis. 1000 years from now people would chuckle at how primitive he/she was ("Can you believe this is what they thought?"). This is why the Bible intentionally transcends science discourse — science always changes with new discovery and knowledge. Who the creator was never changes. So I have a better comeback line: "Let God's decisions for inspiration be honored, and every flat earther be ashamed for dishonoring God's decisions."[602]

Dr. Heiser modestly proclaims himself to be a "biblical scholar." The highfalutin Dr. Heiser has determined that although the Bible portrays the earth as flat, it only does so because the ignorant writers of the time mistakenly thought that the earth was flat. Dr. Heiser states that the Bible is wrong in its description of a flat earth. But don't worry; Dr. Heiser explains that the Bible is not intended to be scientifically correct about creation and cosmology anyway. Dr. Heiser proclaims:

> I'm a Christian and biblical scholar who has a grasp of the fact that ancient Israelite cosmology describes a flat earth. But since it's evident that the Bible was not produced to give us science, it's logically fallacious to presume we need to believe that the earth is really flat to embrace things that the Bible does in fact ask us to believe.[603]

Dr. Heiser implicitly acknowledges that the Bible describes a flat, stationary earth. But he argues that the "dumb" and "stupid" and "mindless" and "demonstrably contrary to reality" and "utter nonsense" things written about the flat, stationary earth in the Bible should not be taken seriously. Dr. Heiser considers it to be "simplistic literalism" to accept what the Bible expressly states about the nature of the earth. Dr. Heiser suggests that Christians should reject what the Bible says about a flat, stationary earth because the writers were ignorant savages who didn't know any better. Instead, Christians should accept as true the more enlightened contrary orthodox scientific model of heliocentricity.

God opposes Dr. Heiser's approach to scripture. Without equivocation, God states that "all" scripture, not just some, is inspired by him. "All scripture is given by inspiration of God, and is profitable for doctrine, for reproof, for correction, for instruction in righteousness:" (2 Timothy 3:16) Indeed, in Psalms 19:7-11, God describes his perfect and inerrant word that is able to convert the soul. In Psalms 19:1-6, the very passages that precede God's testimony to the perfect and inerrant truth of scripture, God describes how the heavens declare the glory of God and the firmament shows his handiwork. Thus, God's creation of a flat and stationary earth as described in his word is inextricably joined with the inerrant description of spiritual truths. They go hand in hand. They stand together as one truth. To attack one is to attack both.

> **The heavens declare the glory of God; and the firmament sheweth his handywork.** Day unto day uttereth speech, and night unto night sheweth knowledge. **There is no speech nor language, where their voice is not heard.** Their line is gone out through all the earth, and their words to the end of the world. In them hath he set a tabernacle for the sun, Which is as a bridegroom coming out of his chamber, and rejoiceth as a strong man to run a race. His going forth is from the end of the heaven, and his circuit unto the ends of it: and there is nothing hid from the heat thereof. **The law of the LORD is perfect**, converting the soul: the testimony of the LORD is sure, making wise the simple. **The statutes of the LORD are right**, rejoicing the heart: the commandment of the LORD is pure, enlightening the eyes. The fear of the LORD is clean, enduring for ever: **the**

judgments of the LORD are true and righteous altogether. More to be desired are they than gold, yea, than much fine gold: sweeter also than honey and the honeycomb. Moreover by them is thy servant warned: and in keeping of them there is great reward. (Psalms 19:1-11)

The inerrancy of all things in the Bible, both earthly and spiritual, is a foundational theme of the Bible. Jesus makes it clear that what he says about physical things in his holy word are just as true as what he says about spiritual things. "If I have told you earthly things, and ye believe not, how shall ye believe, if I tell you of heavenly things?" (John 3:12) It is of eternal importance to accept as true all of God's word in the Bible, in particular, those things he reveals about his creation. That is because God's creation reveals to man the invisible things about God.

> [T]hat which may be known of God is manifest in them; for God hath shewed it unto them. For **the invisible things of him from the creation of the world are clearly seen, being understood by the things that are made, even his eternal power and Godhead**; so that they are without excuse. (Romans 1:19-20)

Paul Seely, who, along with Dr. Heiser, is a heliocentrist, also agrees with Dr. Heiser that the Bible indicates that the earth is flat. Seely is trying to be objective by not allowing his heliocentric bias to color his conclusions about what the Bible states about the earth. Seely's objective assessment of the Bible led him to conclude that the Bible portrays a flat earth. Seely takes creation scientist James Holding to task for concluding that the Bible portrays a spherical earth by injecting his heliocentric bias into his biblical research.

As to [James] Holding's main point, he lifts all the

> relevant OT verses out of their historical context and some of them out of their Biblical context; and then assumes that if he can get rid of the OT evidence which infers the earth is flat, we have the right to read in a spherical globe as the meaning of the word 'earth' in the OT. But there is not a single OT verse which infers that 'earth' in the OT is a spherical globe. [James] Holding is rationalizing away the relevant Biblical evidence, and then dragging in the concept of a spherical earth from modern science and reading it into the text.[604]

Seely correctly concludes that James Holding is no better than those who corrupt the passages in Genesis by suggesting that the description of six days of creation actually mean millions of years of evolution.

> Holding's position is, therefore, no different in principle from that of those who rationalize away the contextual meaning of Genesis 1 and put in its place the finding of modern science.[605]

Despite the clear biblical evidence of a flat earth, the scientists at Creation Ministries International will not allow any discussion of God's creation of a flat, stationary earth. Dr. Robert Carter has drawn the spiritual battle lines pretty clearly. He has blasphemously stated that the God who created the flat earth is a small, petty god. "The earth is a tiny little place in the flat earth model; it [has] a little petty god, almost like a Mormon god."[606] Dr. Carter then accuses all who believe in a flat earth as being brainwashed cult members. "How does one become a flat earther? Cult-like brainwashing."[607] He then tries to scare parents by warning his audience that belief in a flat earth is an inescapable cult. "I have never seen anyone come out of this because it is in fact a cult."[608]

Dr. Carter made the above statements during a Creation Ministries International (CMI) conference. His presentation during the conference was posted on YouTube by CMI and contained the original title of *Flat Earth & Geocentrism (This really is a gospel issue!) with Dr. Rob Carter.* But after the video received 700 thumbs down to 200 thumbs up, the video was taken down and reposted with a different title.[609] CMI disabled comments for the reposted video. It seems that the negative comments were a little too much for them. As of February 21, 2019, the reposted video had received 1,000 thumbs down to 268 thumbs up.[610]

Robert Schadewald (1943-2000) was an opponent of creation science; he considered belief in biblical creation as pseudoscience. One of his strategies in discrediting the biblical creation was to compare biblical creation with belief in a flat earth; he would examine and explain the parallels between the two beliefs. Schadewald explained that "though the Bible is, from Genesis to Revelation, a flat-earth book, the geocentrists have combined forces with liberal creationists to cast the flat-earthers into outer darkness."[611] Schadewald found that creation scientists would not engage in any meaningful debate about the Bible's depiction of a flat earth. Schadewald explained why:

> George Bernard Shaw described a public forum in which a flat-earther laid waste to the spherical opposition.[612] [Samuel] Rowbotham was widely known as a tiger on the platform, and he was seldom bested. (The good citizens of Leeds, England, once ran him out of town, being unable to make a more effective reply to his flat-earth arguments.)[613] In Brockport, N.Y., in March 1887, two scientific gentlemen defended the sphericity of the earth against flat-earther M.C. Flanders on three consecutive nights. When the great debate was over, five townsmen chosen to judge the matter issued a unanimous verdict. Their report,

published in the Brockport Democrat, stated clearly and emphatically their opinion that the balance of the evidence pointed to a flat-earth.[614]

Creation scientists are aware of their hypocritical position regarding the literal interpretation of creation Bible passages related to the fixed, flat earth. And they know the weakness of their arguments. That is why Nathan Roberts and his companions were recently denied entrance into the above-mentioned Creation Ministries International (CMI) biblical creation conference where Dr. Carter gave his presentation against the biblical flat, stationary earth. Dr. Carter and CMI know that his arguments against a fixed, flat earth cannot hold up to scrutiny or debate. Consequently, CMI will not allow any Bible believer into their conferences if they suspect that inconvenient facts about a biblical flat earth will be raised. Dr. Carter was not looking for a debate; he did not want his arguments against a flat earth contested because he was afraid that they would not hold up to scrutiny and could not be adequately defended.

Nathan Roberts, author of *The Doctrine of the Shape of the Earth: A Comprehensive Biblical Perspective*, and two companions paid $20 for their entrance into the above biblical creation conference conducted by CMI. But when Nathan and his companions showed up wearing biblical flat earth T-shirts, they were refused admission into the conference. The CMI conference officials informed them that the conference was a private event and that they would refund them their money. Nathan and his companions were then escorted out of the hotel by hotel security.[615] It seems that CMI is acting as a gatekeeper to keep people from information about what the Bible says about the flat earth.

Schadewald concludes that "[s]ince flat-earthism is the paradigm of Bible-Science, it should be discussed first. It's difficult to see how the scientific creationists, some of whom claim to discern the laws of thermodynamics in the Bible, can fail to see its flat-earth implications."[616] The sad truth is that scientific creationists do see the flat-earth reality in the Bible. But they do not care. They are gatekeepers who are working with Satan to keep a lid on the true nature of God's creation, a stationary and flat creation.

Another Creation Science Hall of Fame member is Duane Gish. Ph.D. (1921-2013).[617] Dr. Gish was a famous creation scientist who was the Associate Director and Vice President of the Institute for Creation Research. Before his death in 2013, Dr. Gish had participated in almost 300 debates on creation science. During one debate with paleontologist Michael Voorhies, Dr. Gish disavowed any connection with a belief in a flat earth.[618] Dr. Gish adamantly objected to any implication that he believed in a flat earth and considered that accusation against him to be a "smear."[619] Dr. Gish defended the Creation Research Society (CRS) against any taint of flat earth belief by stating that not a single member of the CRS was a member of the Flat Earth Society.[620] Dr. Gish was on the original Creation Research Society Advisory Committee. Indeed, the CRS still proudly carries Dr. Gish's publications on their website.[621] The CRS Statement of Belief is as follows:

> The Bible is the written Word of God, and because it is inspired throughout, all its assertions are historically and scientifically true in the original autographs. To the student of nature, this means that the account of origins in Genesis is a factual presentation of simple historical truths.[622]

How could Dr. Gish disavow flat earth if he holds to the view that the Bible is "inspired throughout, all its assertions are historically and scientifically true" and that "Genesis is a factual presentation of simple historical truths?" Because the CRS statement of belief has a condition in it that allows creation scientists to wiggle free from what the Bible plainly states.

Notice the words: "in the original autographs." What the CRS implies by that statement is that they only stand by the "original autographs." The problem is that the original autographs no longer exist. Therefore, according to their statement of faith, there is no inerrant word of God that is factually true to which one can point. CRS asserts allegiance to something that does not exist and has not existed for almost two millennia. CRS only stands by the "original autographs," but not the presently existing Bible. CRS is essentially bound by nothing. When God speaks of his word, he is speaking about the word in existence now! God holds his word in even higher esteem than even his name.

> **[T]hou hast magnified thy word above all thy name.** (Psalms 138:2)

God's name is so precious that the biblical penalty for blaspheming his name is death. Leviticus 24:16. However, God holds his word above even his name. Why? Because God's word is God's revelation of him to man. The Holy Bible states that:

> In the beginning was the Word, and the Word was with God, and **the Word was God**. The same was in the beginning with God. **All things were made by him**; and without him was not any thing made that was made. (John 1:1-3)

> In whom we have redemption through his blood, even the forgiveness of sins: Who is the image of the invisible God, the firstborn of every creature: **For by him were all things created, that are in heaven, and that are in earth, visible and invisible, whether they be thrones, or dominions, or principalities, or powers: all things were created by him, and for him: And he is before all things, and by him all things consist.** (Colossians 1:14-17)

The gospel found in John states that God (the Word, the Creator) came to Earth in the flesh: Jesus Christ.

> And the **Word was made flesh**, and dwelt among us, (and we beheld his glory, the glory as of the only begotten of the Father,) full of grace and truth. (John 1:14)

In the Holy Bible, God the Father makes it clear that his Son, Jesus, is God.

> But unto the **Son** he saith, Thy throne, **O God**, is for ever and ever: a sceptre of righteousness *is* the sceptre of thy kingdom. (Hebrews 1:8)

The Holy Bible is not like any other book; it is unique; it was written by God through men.

> **All scripture is given by inspiration of God**, and is profitable for doctrine, for reproof, for correction, for instruction in righteousness: (2 Timothy 3:16)

> Knowing this first, that no prophecy of the scripture is of any private interpretation. For the prophecy came not in old time by the will of man: but **holy men of God spake as they were moved by the Holy Ghost.** (2 Peter 1:20-21)

> Which things also **we speak, not in the words which man's wisdom teacheth, but which the Holy Ghost teacheth**; comparing spiritual things with spiritual. But the natural man receiveth not the things of the Spirit of God: for they are foolishness unto him: neither can he know *them*, because **they are spiritually discerned.** (1

Corinthians 2:13-14)

In the beginning God created the heaven and the earth. How did he create? He created by speaking. **"God said . . . and it was so."** *See* Genesis 1:1-2:25. "Through faith we understand that the worlds were framed by the word of God, so that things which are seen were not made of things which do appear." (Hebrews 11:3)

God has promised to preserve his word forever. Even though the original autographs no longer exist, God's word has been supernaturally preserved. God's word is the way to salvation. God would not leave us without the means for our salvation. The following scripture passages testify that God has promised that his word will be preserved forever.

> For verily I say unto you, Till heaven and earth pass, one jot or one tittle shall in no wise pass from the law, till all be fulfilled. (Matthew 5:18)

> **Heaven and earth shall pass away, but my words shall not pass away.** (Matthew 24:35)

> The words of the LORD *are* pure words: *as* silver tried in a furnace of earth, purified seven times. **Thou shalt keep them, O LORD, thou shalt preserve them from this generation for ever**. (Psalms 12:6-7)

> **[T]he word of the Lord endureth for ever**. And this is the word which by the gospel is preached unto you. (1 Peter 1:25)

> The grass withereth, the flower fadeth: but **the word of our God shall stand for ever**. (Isaiah 40:8)

For ever, O LORD, thy word is settled in heaven. (Psalms 119:89)

Dr. Gish and CRS seem not to truly believe God's promise to preserve his word. He and the CRS only consider the original autographs to be God's infallible word. The originals, however, have not been preserved. They are long gone. God never promised to preserve the original autographs, he vowed to preserve his word. God's word is spiritual, eternal, and preserved in the English language in the Authorized (King James) Version of the Bible.

Creation Ministries International (CMI), which is another creation science organization, uses the same trick as CRS. CMI claims that "[t]he 66 books of the Bible are the written Word of God. The Bible is divinely inspired and inerrant throughout. Its assertions are factually true **in all the original autographs.**"[623] As with CRS, CMI has inserted the clause giving them allegiance only to the "original autographs." That trick of the devil allows them to treat God's word with complete disdain whenever it suits their interests. And it suits their interest to reject the Bible passages that describe a fixed and flat earth.

Dr. Gish and his ilk use the tried and true method of higher criticism to attack what God plainly states in his word. They undermine what God has said by resorting to the original languages as a way of subverting the authority of God's word in the English language, the King James Bible. Once down that slippery slope, creation scientists resort to interpreting God's clear words to be only "phenomenological language" that is not to be taken literally. Although they may say that they take the Bible to be "historically and scientifically true" and that "Genesis is a factual presentation of simple historical truths" they disregard that consideration when it comes to Bible passages that describe a stationary and flat earth. Creation scientists who feel only bound to the "original autographs" of the Bible are actually bound to nothing at all, as the original autographs no longer exist.

Jason Lisle is yet another Creation Science Hall of Fame inductee who joins the chorus against the biblical authority for a flat earth.[624] Jason Lisle, Ph.D., is an astrophysicist who has double undergraduate degrees in physics and astronomy, with a minor in mathematics. He holds both a masters and Ph.D. in astrophysics from the University of Colorado. He is a fulltime speaker and researcher for *Answers in Genesis*, and in 2012, he became the Director of Research for the Institute for Creation Research.

Dr. Lisle characterizes the belief in a flat earth as "flaky" and opines that for Christians to promote that flaky idea as being taught in the Bible only serves to undermine the gospel. Dr. Lisle characterizes gravity as a demonstrable truth. And for a Christian to deny gravity would hurt their Christian testimony.[625]

Dr. Lisle claims that "[f]lat earth is flatly anti-biblical."[626] When asked for biblical proof that the earth is spherical, Dr. Lisle cited Job 26:10 and Isaiah 40:22.[627] Those passages do not, in fact, support a spherical earth. Let us examine those passages. Job 26:10 reads: "He hath compassed the waters with bounds, until the day and night come to an end." What does "compassed" mean in that context? According to the *1828 Webster's American Dictionary of The English Language,* to compass something means "to stretch round; to extend so as to embrace the whole; hence, to inclose, encircle, grasp or seize; ... To surround; to environ; to inclose on all sides."[628] In Job 26:10 God is encircling (compassing) the seas with a boundary. That denotes a circular boundary around the seas on a flat earth. The boundary of the seas is the ice rim of Antarctica. Job 26:10 does not support the idea of a spherical earth as claimed by Dr. Lisle.

Dr. Lisle also claims that Isaiah 40:22 is biblical proof that the earth is s a sphere. Isaiah 40:22 states: "It is he that sitteth upon the circle of the earth, and the inhabitants thereof are as grasshoppers; that stretcheth out the heavens as a curtain, and spreadeth them out as a tent to dwell in:" That passage does not indicate a globe. Notice that the circle mentioned in Isaiah 40:22 has the heavens spread out over it as a tent. That language indicates a flat circle, over which is a firmament, like a tent. A globe is a three-dimensional ball. If Isaiah meant ball in Isaiah 40:22, he would have said ball. Isaiah knew the difference between a ball and a circle. *See* Isaiah 22:18. He didn't say ball, because the earth is not a ball, as claimed by Dr. Lisle. God describes the face of the earth as a flat circle over which the heavens are spread like a tent.

Dr. Danny Faulkner, Ph.D., is on the Creation Science Hall of Fame Honorable Mention list.[629] Dr. Faulkner is a Christian astronomer and researcher for Ken Ham's *Answers in Genesis*. Dr. Faulkner taught at the University of South Carolina Lancaster for over 26 years. Dr. Faulkner is a member of the *Creation Research Society* (CRS) and also serves as the editor of the *Creation Research Society Quarterly*. He has written more than a hundred papers in various astronomy and astrophysics journals and is the author of *Universe by Design* and *The New Astronomy Book*. He wrote an article for the *Creation Research Society Quarterly* titled *Is the Earth Flat?*[630] In the article, he does not cite a single Bible passage of scripture in support of his argument that the earth is a sphere. The only Christian reference in Faulkner's article was to dispute that during the middle ages the church taught the earth was flat. His seeming point was to argue that the church did not hold back scientific progress, and implied that the church was at the forefront of scientific study that established that the earth was a spinning sphere.

Dr. Faulkner is generally recognized as a leading expert against the biblical authority for a flat earth among creation scientists. For example, *Creation Today* recommends Dr. Faulkner as an authority for its readers to rely upon in refuting what they consider the error of believing in a biblical flat earth. *Creation Today* identifies itself "as a leading, international Christian-apologetics ministry desiring to spread the Gospel of

Jesus Christ to the entire world, *Creation Today* is committed to excellence, producing some of the most requested resources available on creation, apologetics, and evangelism."[631] *Creation Today* states that "we do not believe that the Bible teaches that the earth is flat. On the contrary, it has been well argued that the Bible actually assumes a round earth."[632] In recommending Dr. Faulkner, *Creation Today* provided a link to an article posted by Dr. Faulkner on the *Answers in Genesis* website that is titled *Does the Bible Teach That the Earth Is Flat?*[633]

In his article, *Does the Bible Teach That the Earth Is Flat?*, Dr. Faulkner addresses several Bible passages that reveal that the earth is flat.[634] He begins his analysis by pointing out that one should not take all Bible passages literally; that many Bible passages should be read as poetic. It is true that the context of certain Bible passages reveal that they are intended to be taken poetically. But Faulkner turns the reading of the Bible on its head and begins with the premise that every passage in the Bible that reveals a flat earth is simply poetry, regardless of the context.

Faulkner's poetic method of interpreting biblical flat earth passages can just as easily be used to interpret the Genesis account of creation as merely a poetic account of creation that does not comport with reality. If God's literal account of creation is to hold up, then to be consistent, Faulkner must necessarily hold up God's account of a flat earth. But Faulkner is a double-minded hypocrite. Like Ken Ham, Faulkner changes the rules when it comes to the Bible passages supporting a flat, stationary earth.

Faulkner begins his assault on God's word by stating that "[f]or those who insist on taking everything in the Bible as woodenly literal, this is fraught with problems."[635] He prefaces his discussion of biblical passages supporting a flat earth by making the point that many passages in the Bible "clearly are not literal." What becomes clear is that the Bible passages that he says are "clearly are not literal" are deemed not to be so because of his preconceived bias.

Dr. Faulkner acknowledges that the Bible is commonly interpreted as presenting a hard dome over a flat earth. Faulkner must acknowledge that fact because the evidence that the Bible articulates a dome over a flat earth is so clear and convincing. The language in the Bible supports the hard dome over the flat earth, but Faulkner does not like it one bit. Why? Because he claims it is "at odds with the facts." What he means is that it is at odds with his preconceived heliocentric notion of the facts, which precludes any expression of a hard firmament over the stationary, flat earth.

> It is a common belief today that the cosmology presented in the Bible is that of a hard dome over the earth supported by pillars. Clearly, this is at odds with the facts. First, the Bible does not explicitly teach any cosmology.[636]

What is Dr. Faulkner to do? He renders the passages that describe a hard dome over a flat earth as being poetic. Since virtually all Bible passages that describe the earth describe a dome over a flat earth, once Dr. Faulkner has rendered all such Bible passages as poetic, he is left with no passages at all that address the configuration of the earth. What is he to do? Simple, he pronounces that the Bible does not explicitly speak to cosmology at all, problem solved.

For example, Dr. Faulkner argues that Job 37:18 is merely a poetic passage when it says that the sky is "strong, and as a molten looking glass" "Hast thou with him spread out the sky, which is strong, and as a molten looking glass?" (Job 37:18) Of course, Faulkner argues that the passage is poetic. He states:

> There are several reasons why one must be careful in gleaning the meaning of this verse. First, this one verse is within a textual unit (Job 37:14–18),

which poetically uses weather phenomena to illustrate the overwhelming power and wisdom of God—so teaching cosmology is not the point.[637]

Faulkner starts with a bias that the sky is not in fact "strong, and as a molten looking glass," it is only poetically strong like a molten looking glass. Following Faulkner's logic to its ultimate end, we must conclude that God is describing his overwhelming power and wisdom by describing something that does not actually exist. Thus, according to Faulkner's logic, God's overwhelming power and wisdom do not really exist, just as the sky is not really "strong, and as a molten looking glass."

Faulkner then goes in for the kill and questions the inspiration of the Bible. Faulkner reduces Job to a book that contains local idioms and poetry that merely presents phenomenological imagery that is difficult to translate. Thus, according to Faulkner, Job is not a description of reality; he avers that it is not literally true that the sky is a "strong, and as a molten looking glass."

> The book of Job contains language and idioms that are unique to it, and many are difficult to translate. Also, Job, being ancient Hebrew poetry, evidences many examples of imagery and phenomenological language. Job 37:18 contains a particularly challenging case of imagery.[638]

Faulkner continues his attack on God's word by claiming that the words describing the sky as "strong, and as a molten looking glass" is not a pronouncement by God, but rather the words of Job's friend, Elihu. Faulkner reasons that the words of Elihu are not true because "[w]hile the Bible is inspired, not everything recorded in the Bible is necessarily true." Faulkner is correct that the Bible contains statements made by God's enemies, even Satan, that are not true. But to take that premise and use that to suggest that Elihu's statements were not true is a bridge too far. The problem with Faulkner's premise is that the context of the statement made by Elihu was to rebut Job, who "justified himself rather than God." Job 32:2. Elihu was taking up the cause on behalf of God. He was speaking the inspired words of God.

Faulkner then proceeds to use the age-old trick of redefining the words in the Bible. He applies this artifice to verse 1:22 of Ezekiel, which states:

> And the likeness of the firmament upon the heads of the living creature was as the colour of the terrible crystal, stretched forth over their heads above. (Ezekiel 1:22)

Faulkner first acknowledges that crystal means exactly what we think it means. But then cautions us that such a definition is archaic. But not to worry, Faulkner is going to redefine crystal and tell us what it really means today.

> What does it mean to be a crystal? One must be careful, because the modern and ancient definitions are different. In the ancient world, a crystal was any substance that was solid and transparent. Examples include glass, quartz, rock salt, diamond, and other precious stones that transmit light.[639]

Faulkner cannot have the firmament be a hard crystal. To allow that would be to acknowledge the hard firmament over the stationary, flat earth. Faulkner must undermine the implications of that passage, and so he redefines crystal to mean an aura.

> [S]hould we view this expanse that Ezekiel described as a literal crystal? Probably not. Ezekiel compared what he saw to an expanse, but he furthermore compared its appearance to a crystal,

the emphasis being on the light that it gave off. That is, it shined, glowed, sparkled, or had a hue like a crystal. We might describe what Ezekiel saw as an aura.[640]

Dr. Faulkner redefined crystal to mean aura without any real authority. He just said that is what he thinks it should mean. He acknowledges that the word crystal in modern scientific parlance means very much the same as it did when the Bible was written. Finding no help with modern science, he pronounces that God probably meant aura.

Not all of Faulkner's redefinitions were so blatantly without etymological authority. Throughout his article, Dr. Faulkner resorts to the artifice of referring the reader to the original Hebrew. He must do this to offer some academic justification for redefining the otherwise clear meaning of the English words. One example is the word "firmament." The meaning of firmament is pretty straight forward in English. But Faulkner must obfuscate its meaning because Ezekiel 1:26 suggests that the firmament is a hard dome over which is God's throne above the flat earth.

> And above the firmament that was over their heads was the likeness of a throne, as the appearance of a sapphire stone: and upon the likeness of the throne was the likeness as the appearance of a man above upon it. (Ezekiel 1:26)

The Merriam Webster dictionary defines the firmament as "the vault or arch of the sky."[641] The etymology of the word firmament reveals that it is "from Old French firmament or directly from Latin firmamentum 'firmament,' literally 'a support, a strengthening,' from firmus 'strong, steadfast, enduring' (from suffixed form of PIE root *dher- 'to hold firmly, support')."[642] So, we find that firmament is a word that describes a strong arch above the earth. This comports with what is described in Genesis as the firm barrier separating the water above the firmament from the water beneath the firmament. "And God said, Let there be a firmament in the midst of the waters, and let it divide the waters from the waters." (Genesis 1:6) To be able to hold the water above the firmament would require a strong arch above the earth. Reading that in conjunction with the description in Ezekiel 1:26, we find that above the firmament is the throne of God in heaven.

Faulkner cannot allow that definition to stand and so he sinks into the abyss of higher criticism. He tries to redefine the English word by resorting to the original Hebrew word (rāqîa') that was translated into the English word "firmament." Faulkner states, "rather than referring to something necessarily hard, the word rāqîa' probably refers to something that has been spread out."[643] Faulkner then rejects the correct translation of rāqîa' as firmament found in the King James Version of the Bible and instead recommends to the reader the new corrupt versions of the Bible, which translate rāqîa' as expanse or sky instead of firmament. Faulkner states:

> This is why many modern English translations render the rāqîa' as 'expanse.' This is a good translation, because it gets to the heart of what the likely intended meaning of rāqîa' is. Some modern translations render rāqîa' as "sky." This, too, is a good translation, because the sky that we see above us encompasses the likely meaning of the rāqîa'.[644]

God's word is with us today in the Authorized (King James) Version (referred to as AV or KJV). All other Bible versions are tainted by the hands of Satan and his minions, including the New King James Version (NKJV). "Ye have perverted the words of the living God, of the LORD of hosts our God." Jeremiah 23:36. The corrupted Bible versions that are promoted by Dr. Faulkner and his ilk are essentially Roman Catholic Bible versions.[645] Sadly, most of the so-called church leaders of today have accepted Satan's counterfeit Bibles. Below is a side-by-side comparison of Genesis 1:7-8 in the Authorized (King James) Version (AV) with that passage in the corrupt New American Standard Bible that is approved of by Dr. Faulkner. Notice how the NASB gives a tainted rendition of creation that comports with the modern mythology of science, where there is no firmament. In the NASB, there is only an expanse.

And God made the **firmament**, and divided the waters which were under the **firmament** from the waters which were above the **firmament**: and it was so. And God called the **firmament** Heaven. And the evening and the morning were the second day. (Genesis 1:7-8 AV)

God made the **expanse**, and separated the waters which were below the **expanse** from the waters which were above the **expanse**; and it was so. God called the **expanse** heaven. And there was evening and there was morning, a second day. (Genesis 1:7-8 NASB)

What do we know about the NASB? Frank Logsdon was instrumental in the development of the New American Standard Bible (NASB). Logsdon was a friend of Dewey Lockman, the wealthy Christian founder of the Lockman Foundation that provided the funding for publishing the NASB.

> [Logsdon] was involved in a feasibility study involving purchasing the copyright of the American Standard Version (ASV) with Lockman that lead to the eventual production of the NASB. He interviewed some of the translators for the job and even wrote the preface to the translation. Slowly, he became aware that there was something wrong with the NASB. He eventually rejected it

and promoted the KJV.[646]

Frank Logsdon was informed about the corruptions in the NASB and looked into it. He found that the allegations of the corruptions in the NASB were true. He rejected the NASB. He set forth his reasons for disavowing the NASB during a taped interview, which is freely available on the internet:

> I must under God denounce every attachment to the New American Standard Version. I'm afraid I'm in trouble with the Lord...We laid the groundwork; I wrote the format; I helped interview some of the translators; I sat with the translator; I wrote the preface. When you see the preface to the New American Standard, those are my words...it's wrong, it's terribly wrong; it's frightfully wrong...I'm in trouble;...I can no longer ignore these criticisms I am hearing and I can't refute them. The deletions are absolutely frightening...there are so many. The finest leaders that we have today haven't gone into it [new versions of Wescott and Hort's corrupted Greek text] just as I hadn't gone into it...that's how easily one can be deceived...Are we so naive that we do not suspect Satanic deception in all of this?[647]

The new Bible versions preferred by Dr. Faulkner are based upon corrupt manuscripts. Frank Logsdon alludes to the corrupt Greek text that was the basis for the NASB, which was compiled by Brooke Foss Westcott and Fenton John Anthony Hort.[648] Westcott and Hort were nominal Protestants, but they were *defacto* Roman Catholics.

John Anthony Hort denied the infallibility of the Holy Scriptures; he did not believe in the existence of Satan; he did not believe in eternal punishment in Hell; he did not believe in

Christ's atonement.[649] Hort, however, did believe in Darwin's theory of evolution, he believed in purgatory, and he also believed in baptismal regeneration.[650] Hort hated the United States and wished for its destruction during the civil war because he was a communist who hated all things democratic.[651]

Brooke Foss Westcott was equally Romish in his beliefs.[652] He, like Hort, rejected the infallibility of the Holy Scriptures.[653] He viewed the Genesis account of creation as merely an allegory.[654] He did not believe the biblical account of the miracles of Jesus.[655] He did, however, believe in praying for the dead and worshiping Mary.[656] Politically, Westcott was a devout Socialist.[657]

Westcott and Hort were both necromancers who were members of an occult club called the "Ghostly Guild."[658] Westcott also founded another club and named it "Hermes."[659] According to Luciferian H.P. Blavatsky, Hermes and Satan are one and the same.[660] Hort viewed evangelical Christians as dangerous, perverted, unsound, and confused.[661]

Assisting Westcott and Hort in creating the corrupt Greek revision was Dr. G. Vance, a Unitarian, who denied the deity of Christ, the inspiration of the Holy Scriptures, and the Godhead (Jesus Christ, God the Father, and the Holy Ghost).[662] Jesuit Roman Catholic Cardinal Carlo Maria Martini, the prelate of Milan, was the editor of the corrupted Greek text.[663] Martini believed the occult new age philosophy that man can become divine.[664] Remember, that is the very lie that Satan used to deceive Eve into eating the forbidden fruit: "ye shall be as gods." Genesis 3:5.

The corrupted Westcott and Hort Greek text used would only affect the New Testament. What about the Old Testament, which is where the book of Genesis is found? That is where the method of translation is used to corrupt the resulting English text in the new Bible versions. The translators of the NASB and the other new Bible versions use a method of translation known as dynamic equivalence, rather than the formal equivalence used in the Authorized Version (AV), which is also known as the King James Version (KJV). Formal equivalence is a word for word translation, whereas dynamic equivalence is a thought for thought translation. A translator using dynamic equivalence is less a translator and more an interpreter. Thus, the new versions of Bibles should more accurately be called interpretations, rather than translations.

The dynamic equivalent interpreters of the new Bible versions have often made unfounded assumptions as to the meaning of particular passages. Rather than translate what God wrote, they have, with some frequency, twisted passages by injecting their personal bias. Some of these interpreters have displayed malicious intent and caused great mischief. We see that with the translation of Genesis 1:7-8 in the NASB. The personal view of the translator of the NASB is that God did not create a firm canopy separating the waters above from the waters beneath. Instead, they based their translation on a heliocentric preconception; where there is only an atmospheric expanse over the earth.

Subjective biases of the interpreters of the new bible versions have caused changes in the new version English bibles that are not supported by any of the Greek or Hebrew texts. For example, dynamic equivalencies caused 6,653 English word changes in the New International Version (NIV), approximately 4,000 word changes in the New American Standard Bible (NASB), and approximately 2,000 word changes in the New King James Version (NKJV), none of which are supported by the words in any of the Greek or Hebrew texts.[665] Those word changes reflect the subjective bias of the interpreters. The combined effect of having corrupted texts and then having those texts interpreted using dynamic equivalence has been that the NIV has 64,098 fewer words than the AV.[666] That is a 10% loss in the Bible. That means that an NIV Bible would have 170 fewer pages than a typical 1,700 page AV Bible.[667] The new versions of the Bible are materially different; they are the product of the imaginations of interpreters who have applied their personal prejudices to slant already corrupted texts to comport with their own ideas. They are truly counterfeit Bibles.

Interestingly, Dr. Faulkner seems to understand what is at stake. He is on record as stating that "[s]ome creationists believe that the scientific assault on the Bible did not begin with biological evolution, but with the acceptance of the heliocentric (or more properly, geokinetic) theory centuries ago."[668] Dr. Faulkner understands the issue very clearly. He has taken a side. He has embraced heliocentricity. Heliocentricity is incompatible with God's word. There is no middle ground here. To side with heliocentricity is to take a stand against God's word.

Dr. Faulkner acts as though he is taking a stand against the attack on the Bible by taking a stand against evolution. But taking a stand against evolution without also taking a stand against heliocentricity is like claiming that getting in a life boat after purposely scuttling a fighting ship is being effective in battle. You cannot stay in the fight as your ship is sinking. There is no excuse when you are the captain who has scuttled your ship. Dr. Faulkner has scuttled the authority of the Bible, and he is thus left entirely disarmed and ineffective in his fight against evolution. But Dr. Faulkner has gone further, he has turned traitor and joined with the enemy in the battle against God's word.

Why has Dr. Faulkner so earnestly joined the enemy and attacked the belief in the biblical flat earth? Because he does not want to be maligned by his colleagues. He has stated that "[m]any critics of creationists attempt to malign [creationists] by suggesting that what creationists teach is akin to belief in a flat Earth."[669] As a creationist, he feels he must come out vociferously against the flat earth. He does not want to be accused of believing in a flat earth, and so he feels compelled to undermine what the Bible says out fear that he, as a creationist, will be insulted by being characterized as a "flat earther."

Dr. Faulkner cares what his fellow scientists think of him. He cares to keep his respected position among scientists. He wants to steer clear of any association with the flat earth, or even geocentrism because he fears ridicule. He has stated that "[w]hile geocentrists are well intended, their presence among recent creationists produces an easy object of ridicule by our critics."[670] Dr. Faulkner is not satisfied to simply live and let live. No, his fear drives him to go on the attack against the biblical depiction of a stationary, flat earth.

Either Dr. Faulkner must yield to what the Bible says, or he must undermine the authority of the Bible. Indeed, Dr. Faulkner, and all creation scientists who deny the earth is stationary and flat, must necessarily attack the authority of the Bible. Dr. Faukner claims that he is defending the Bible, but in reality, he is undermining its authority. One cannot attack the authority of the Bible and at the same time support the authority of that same Bible. How does Dr. Faulkner pull that off? To defend and attack the Bible at the same time requires two different Bibles. The bible being defended (NASB) cannot be the same as the Bible being attacked (AV). He undermines the authority of the Bible by eschewing God's word in the English language, the Authorized (King James) Version of the Bible (AV). He claims to defend the Bible by embracing Bibles corrupted by Satan that comport with his heliocentric view (e.g., NASB). Heliocentrism is incompatible with what God's word states, so Dr. Faulkner has brought out counterfeit Bibles to pretend God's word says what it does not. It is a subtle deception. All new Bible versions are at odds with God's inspired word contained in the Authorized (King James) Version of the Bible.

The artifice of redefining rāqîaʻ to mean expanse or sky is

easily shown to be dissimilation. Paul H. Seely published an article for the Westminster Theological Journal, which is a publication of the Westminster Theological Seminary, where he documented his extensive research into what is meant by the Hebrew word rāqîaʻ that underlies the English word firmament in the King James Version of the Bible.[671]

> [T]he language of Genesis 1 suggests solidity in the fist place and no usage of rāqîaʻ anywhere states or even implies that it was not a solid object. This latter point bears repeating: there is not a single piece of evidence in the OT to support the conservative belief that rāqîaʻ was not solid. The historical meaning of rāqîaʻ, so far from being overthrown by the grammatical evidence is confirmed by it. The historical-grammatical meaning of raqia in Gen. 1:6–8 is very clearly a literally solid firmament.[672]

Seely impeaches Dr. Faulkner's claims and explains that the word firmament in Genesis can mean only one thing, that there was a solid dome overhead. And that truth had been the traditional Christian view until the advent of the heliocentric mythology.

> Only by taking Genesis 1 out of its historical context could one say that rāqîaʻ means merely "an atmospheric expanse" or, as the more sophisticated conservatives say, "just phenomenal language." ... When the original readers of Genesis 1 read the word rāqîaʻ they thought of a solid sky. And so did virtually everyone else up to the time of the Renaissance! After the time of Christ there were occasional dissenters, but by and large Jews and Christians, Greeks and barbarians all believed the firmament was solid.[673]

It is not only the book of Genesis where the firmament should be read to mean a solid dome overhead; that is what firmament means wherever it is found in scripture, including the passages in Ezekiel. Seely explains:

> Even conservatives admit the firmament in Ezekiel 1 is solid. Having then this clear definition of a raqia as a solid divider, one is hermeneutically bound to interpret the rāqîaʻ in Genesis as solid unless there is some clear reason to differentiate the one from the other. As it turns out there is no reason to differentiate the rāqîaʻ in Ezekiel 1 from the rāqîaʻ in Genesis 1. On the contrary, there is good reason to identify the one with the other. For we can see in Ezekiel that above the firmament is the throne of God in glory (vv. 26-28) just as above the firmament of heaven described in Genesis is the throne of God in glory (1 Kgs 22:19; Ps 2:4; 11:4; 103:19; Isa 6:1; 14:13; 66:1). The firmament in Ezekiel 1 must be related to the firmament in Genesis 1, and a number of commentators have made the identification. Eichrodt, for example, calls the firmament in Ezekiel a "copy of that vault of heaven." The NT confirms the virtual identity of the firmament in Ezekiel and the firmament in Genesis by combining them into one image (Rev 4:6; 15:2).[674]

The redefining of the English word "firmament" by resorting to the original Hebrew is a favorite tactic of charlatan Christian creationists. For example, Dr. Jason Lisle characterizes the firmament described in the Bible as merely meaning sky. He accomplishes that feat, as does Dr. Faulkner, by going to the original Hebrew word rāqîaʻ that is translated as the English word firmament in the King James Version of the Bible. Dr. Lisle states that in his opinion rāqîaʻ should be translated to mean sky. Dr.

Lisle concludes, as does Dr. Faulkner, that there is not a firm dome over the earth as suggested by the word firmament that appears in the King James Version of the Bible; instead, Dr. Lisle argues that there is only sky.

Drs. Lisle and Faulkner must redefine the meaning of the words in the Bible, in order to maintain their guise of being scientists who are Christians. They must appear to adhere to the authority of the Bible, like good Christians, while at the same time undermine its authority. Dr. Lisle explains that "[i]t's a very slippery slope when you decide that there are some sections of the Bible that you are going to allow the secular scientist to tell you what it really means."[675] How then are they going to embrace the authority of the Bible, give it primacy over secular science, and at the same time reconcile the secular scientific model of heliocentrism with the biblical model of a flat, stationary earth? Simple, redefine the words in the Bible. Thus, the firmament is no longer a firm barrier separating the waters; it is just an expanse. Unfortunately for them, Seely's research refutes that claim.

It is no surprise to find that the version of the Bible linked to the verses in Dr. Faulkner's article is the corrupt English Standard Version (ESV). That version translates the Hebrew word rāqîaʿ as the English word "expanse" rather than "firmament." For example, the ESV version of Genesis 1:6 states: "And God said, 'Let there be an **expanse** in the midst of the waters, and let it separate the waters from the waters.'" Genesis 1:6 (ESV).

The ESV has a problem if expanse is the proper translation. That is because Psalms 148:4 has waters above the heavens. "Praise him, ye heavens of heavens, and ye waters that be above the heavens." (Psalms 148:4) How can the firmament be merely an expanse or the sky when above that expanse is water? The water could not be a reference to clouds, as clouds are within the expanse of the sky, not above it. The water referred to in Genesis is above the firmament, not within the firmament. If the water is above the expanse of the sky, what is holding all of that water up there? The answer is the firmament.

The ESV is a revision of the corrupt Revised Standard Version (RSV). The ESV publishers advertise the ESV as "an essentially literal translation of the Bible in contemporary English."[676] It is anything but that. It is a further corruption of God's word. It is Satanic. It was initially intended to address the liberal, gender inclusive *Today's New International Version* (TNIV). But Dr. Mark Strauss determined that the ESV did the very thing it was designed to fight against.

> One of the major areas of revision in the ESV is the introduction of gender-inclusive language (sometimes called gender-neutral language). In hundreds of cases the ESV introduces terms like 'one' or 'person' or 'others' for the RSV's masculine generic terms 'man' and 'men.' . . . In this way, the ESV is very much like the recently published Today's New International Version (TNIV), which revises the New International Version (NIV) in a similar manner.[677]

Indeed, the ESV and RSV are corruptions of the Bible. They are part of a Satanic conspiracy against God and his anointed. This author addresses that conspiracy and sets forth the evidence in detail in *The Greatest Lie on Earth*. Being corrupted by Satan, it is no wonder that the ESV would replace "firmament" with "expanse."

Kent Hovind is another inductee into the Creation Science Hall of Fame.[678] According to his biography on the Creation Science Hall of Fame website, Hovind "is considered by many to be one of the foremost authorities on science and the Bible."[679] Hovind is a world-renowned authority who gives seminars that refute the theories of evolution and support the Genesis account of creation in six literal days contained in the Bible.

Christians have asked Hovind about the biblical model of a flat earth; he claims to have examined the matter and admonishes his followers to reject any notion of a flat earth. He views the flat earth as a "silly distraction from the gospel."[680] What does Hovind rely upon as his authority for rejecting the flat earth? He refers his followers to "any earth science book."[681] In order to establish the validity of the supposed heliocentric model, Hovind hypocritically relies upon the authority of the very earth science books that he has proven to be full of lies promoting the myth of evolution.

During one of Kent Hovind's many seminars, a questioner asked him to provide one single heliocentric verse from the Bible to prove that God created a spinning, spherical earth.[682] He tried to dodge the question by mocking the very idea of a flat earth and opined that discussing the flat earth is a complete waste of time. He doubled down and stated "even if it's true it's a waste of time."[683] He said that flat earth is "nonsense" and "useless" and that "the world is laughing at flat earthers."[684] Hovind further said that the flat earth is a distraction from the gospel.

Hovind went into a monologue trying to explain the heliocentric model, in which he believes, from a scientific perspective. The questioner had to interject during the monologue and repeat the question asking for biblical authority five times over a 20 minute period before Hovind finally answered the question; at which time, Hovind admitted that there is not a single verse in the Bible that describes a heliocentric model.[685] Hovind claimed that was because "the Bible doesn't deal with the topic."[686] When the questioner presented Hovind with passages that indicate that the earth is flat, Hovind relegated all such passages to be metaphors. Hovind explained that "the Bible is full of metaphors."[687]

The proclamation of Hovind that belief in a flat earth is a

distraction and unimportant is typical of those who reject the biblical doctrine of the flat earth. But the veracity of the position that belief in a flat earth is irrelevant is belied by the statements of those in the anti-flat earth camp. For example, David Nikao, who incidentally is a geocentrist, actually has a website devoted to rebutting the Bible evidence for a flat earth titled, *The Flat Earth Deception*.[688] Nikao declares on that website that in the Bible "[t]here are zero verses which proclaim that the earth is flat."[689] He further charges that "[t]he Bible does not say that the earth is flat, and proclaiming that it does is denying the truth of the Word of Elohim!"[690]

Nikao identifies himself thusly: "I am a follower of Messiah. I work in full-time ministry, exposing the deceptions in end-time prophecy, so that my brothers and sisters in Messiah can see the truth."[691] As part of his "Christian" ministry, he alleges that those who proclaim what the Bible says about the earth being flat are being used by Satan in a grand deception.[692]

Nikao is accusing those who accept what the Bible says as denying the truth of the word of God. That sure sounds like he thinks that it is an important issue. And indeed that seems to be the standard position of those who accept that the Bible is the inspired word of God on the one hand and deny that God made a flat earth on the other. If they are going to maintain their position that the Bible is the inspired and inerrant word of God, they must necessarily interpret the Bible passages describing a flat and stationary earth as somehow not really meaning that the earth is flat and stationary in order to make the Bible comport with their preconception of a spinning, spherical earth. Hovind is an example of one who uses that methodology. Hovind characterizes the Bible passages describing a flat and stationary earth as being merely metaphors. By doing that, Hovind strips the Bible of its meaning and its majesty.

Why is Hovind so intent on turning the flat earth Bible

passages into metaphors? Because he is afraid to accept the truth of the flat earth. He has been conditioned all his life to believe that anyone who thinks the earth is flat is a fool. He is thus acting upon his "pride of life," which is of the world and is contrary to God. "For all that is in the world, the lust of the flesh, and the lust of the eyes, and the pride of life, is not of the Father, but is of the world." 1 John 2:16. Hovind is fearful of being marginalized and considered to be a fool. He has previously admonished those who believe that the earth is flat that "you are making a fool of yourself - stop!" [693] He considers belief in the flat earth "insane."[694] He thinks that if one promotes the idea that the Bible states that the earth is flat it will cause people who hear that to, in turn, believe "that whole book must be stupid."[695]

Hovind wants nothing to do with anything that would make him appear "stupid" and "insane" and a "fool" to the world. He seems not to understand that the gospel has always seemed foolish to the lost world. God tells us why. "[T]he natural man receiveth not the things of the Spirit of God: for they are foolishness unto him: neither can he know them, because they are spiritually discerned." (1 Corinthians 2:14) The fact that Hovind does not discern the creation of a flat, stationary earth as it is clearly portrayed in God's word suggests that he does not have the necessary spiritual awakening to give him that understanding. He is the natural man spoken of in the Bible who "receiveth not the things of the Spirit of God."

Hovind further states that "I suspect there's a little bit of push to try to get this either to discredit Christians, like aha look how dumb you are, or to try to justify what the Catholic church taught for years and years, aha we were right all along." [696] It is interesting that Hovind would suspect that flat earthers are in a conspiracy to further the Roman Catholic historical cosmology and then turn around and join forces with Roman Catholic Robert Sungenis, Ph.D., who has written a book that defends the Catholic geocentric cosmology of the middle ages. Sungenis book is titled

Galileo Was Wrong: The Church Was Right. Kent Hovind clearly understands that the Catholic church is an enemy of the gospel, but he is so intent on refuting the flat earth that he has yoked himself with a Roman Catholic heathen, Robert Sungenis, as an ally in attacking the biblical concept of a flat earth. "Can two walk together, except they be agreed?" Amos 3:3.

Sungenis is a geocentrist, but believes that the earth is a globe. He has written another book titled *Flat Earth Flat Wrong*. Dr. Sungenis explained in an interview with Hovind: "I got involved with the flat earth topic because an institution contacted me and wanted me to write a 30-page paper trying to silence the flat earth movement."[697] Sungenis did not identify the institution that contacted him. He revealed that the contact was made in October 2017. Sungenis' research into the flat earth issue developed into his book, *Flat Earth Flat Wrong,* which was published nine months later.

It is notable that Sungenis had an agenda in writing his book to "silence the flat earth movement." Sungenis states that he has a good grasp of modern science because he was a physics major in college and has kept abreast of the developments in science since his graduation. He proudly states that he is a "biblical scholar" with three degrees in biblical exegesis and theology. Apparently, his biblical studies have done him no good as he remains a Roman Catholic heathen.

Dr. Sungenis states in an interview with Hovind that he devoted a good portion of his book to the issue of being able to see distant objects over water. He addresses, in particular, the famous picture of the Chicago skyline taken by Joshua Nowicki from 57 miles across Lake Michigan.[698] If the earth were a globe, the entire skyline of buildings should have been out of sight below the horizon due to the supposed curvature of the earth. Sungenis uses cunning dissimulation in his book to explain away the Nowicki photograph. In *The Greatest Lie on Earth (Expanded Edition)*, this author exposes the trickery of Sungenis in his explanation of the Nowicki photograph.

Sungenis is a fount of disinformation. He knows that English speakers, in general, are unfamiliar with Semitic languages. He tries to use their ignorance to his advantage in pulling the wool over their eyes. For example, during a debate with Rob Skiba, Dr. Sungenis seemed to think the unfamiliarity of the audience with the Hebrew language gave him a license to dissemble. He stated:

> In the Hebrew language there is no word for sphere. Here we are having a debate on whether the earth is flat or a sphere, and yet the Hebrew language had no word for sphere. Isn't that interesting? [They had] no word for globe, no word for sphere, and by the way [they] didn't have any word for a flat disc either.[699]

Dr. Sungenis's statement is blatantly false. The Hebrew word, *khûg*, in Isaiah 40:22 that is translated into the English word "circle" means just that, "circle." The Hebrew word, *dure*, in Isaiah 22:18 that is translated into the English word "ball" means just that, "ball." The Hebrews had the words to express what they meant. When Isaiah described the earth as having a circular face in Isaiah 40:22 ("circle of the earth"), he meant what he said. The earth has a circular face. If Isaiah had wanted to describe the earth as a sphere he had the word to do so. But Isaiah did not describe the earth as a sphere. He described the earth as having a circular face, and by definition a circular face must be flat. Isaiah was inspired by God to describe the earth as having a flat circular face in Isaiah 40:22 because the surface of the earth is a flat circle.

Dissemblers, like Dr. Sungenis, are continually referring to the original Hebrew language. They then engage in all sorts of sophistry to obfuscate Bible passages to beguile their audience.

The English in the Authorized (King James) Version of the Bible is inspired and sufficient for all truth and doctrine.

John D. Morris, Ph.D., has a doctorate in Geological Engineering and serves as a Professor of Geology on the faculty of the University of Oklahoma. Dr. Morris is on the Honorable Mention list at the Creation Science Hall of Fame.[700] Dr. Morris is the President of the Institute for Creation Research (ICR), which he took over after the death of his famous father, Henry M. Morris (1918-2006). John's father, Henry, was one of the founders of the Creation Research Society and ICR and according to *The Seattle Times* is considered by many to be the father of modern creation science.[701] And Henry is an inductee in the Creation Science Hall of Fame.[702] His son, Dr. John D. Morris claims:

> [T]he Bible has always taught a spherical Earth. There are, of course, instances of phenomenological language, where the author refers to what the viewer can see, just as we do today when communicating. We talk about "flat" terrain or a "flat" ocean even though we know they follow Earth's curvature. It is flat to our eyes and to our listener's eyes. But when the issue of Earth's shape is addressed in Scripture, the Hebrew wording implies sphericity (see Isaiah 40:22, etc.).[703]

The issue of the shape of the earth is of utmost importance. Indeed, God emphasizes its significance in the introductory verse to Isaiah 40:22. In Isaiah 40:21, God states: "Have ye not known? have ye not heard? hath it not been told you from the beginning? have ye not understood from the foundations of the earth?" After that verse God explains in verse 22 the shape of the earth. He states that he "sitteth upon the circle of the earth." It is essential to God that we get this right. With that in mind, let's examine Dr. John D. Morris' claim.

Dr. John D. Morris' argument is flawed. When the issue of earth's shape is addressed in scripture, it does NOT imply sphericity. In Isaiah 40:22, cited by Dr. John D. Morris, God describes the circle of the earth. A circle is not the same as a sphere, and Dr. John D. Morris must know that. God knows the difference between a circle and a ball. He used the word ball in Isaiah 22:18 when he meant to depict a ball. In Isaiah 40:22, God meant to say circle, not ball; they are not the same thing.

Indeed, when people refer to a sphere, they never call it a circle. Can you imagine a player asking his basketball teammate to pass him the "circle?" When have you ever heard someone refer to a model globe of the earth as a circle? It is always described as a "globe." But when a group is called together, they are sometimes asked to form a circle around the speaker. When forming that circle, all present are on the same plane. Nobody confuses a circle with a sphere. Those gathered do not start climbing on each other's shoulders to form a sphere. There is no confusion. A circle is not a sphere. A circle is defined as a flat plane whose circumference is equidistant from the center.[704] A sphere, on the other hand, is defined as a solid body whose surface is equidistant from its center in all directions, i.e., a ball.[705] The Bible describes the earth as a circle, not a sphere. That is because the earth is NOT a round ball, it has a flat circular face, just as it is described in the Bible.

Dr. John D. Morris has a backup argument because he knows full well that the Bible describes a flat earth. He argues that the many Bible passages that describe a flat earth are using "phenomenological language." Essentially, Dr. John D. Morris is arguing that the passages describing a flat earth do not mean what they say. The foundation of his biblical argument that the Bible description of a flat earth is "phenomenological language" requires three assumptions: 1) someone other than God is viewing the phenomenon, 2) that someone is telling us what he saw, and 3) and what he saw did not actually happen as he described it. The problem with those assumptions is that in many of the Bible passages describing a stationary, flat earth, the speaker is identified as God himself. *E.g.*, Isaiah 38:8, 45:12, 48:13, 66:1; Proverbs 8:24.

Dr. John D. Morris' sophistry of alleging that God used "phenomenological language" in the Bible is just another way of saying that God is not telling the truth. "Let God be true, but every man a liar." (Romans 3:4) God does not lie. "God is not a man, that he should lie; neither the son of man, that he should repent: hath he said, and shall he not do it? or hath he spoken, and shall he not make it good?" (Numbers 23:19)

Why is Dr. John D. Morris so intent on twisting biblical reasoning to refute Bible passages that clearly describe a stationary, flat earth? The answer is: fear. Dr. John D. Morris explains that he does not want to be belittled by malicious evolutionists who would insult him by equating biblical creation with belief in a flat earth.[706] Dr. John D. Morris elaborates that "evolutionists often belittle creation thinking by comparing it to belief in a flat Earth."[707] He asserts that any claim that creationists would believe the earth is flat is a misrepresentation, because "[o]f course creationists and evolutionists agree fully on Earth's shape."[708]

Dr. John D. Morris's admission reveals the fear that pervades the scientific community. Academicians who know the earth is flat keep quiet for fear of losing their positions if they proclaimed the truth. They do not want to be belittled and ostracized. Their fear of ridicule is born of the "pride of life," which is of the world and is contrary to God. 1 John 2:16. The hive environment in the scientific community serves as an impediment to acceptance of the truth of the stationary, flat earth described in the Bible. We thus find that creation scientists will compromise and explain away flat earth Bible passages as only "phenomenological language."

Dr. John D. Morris' father, Creation Science Hall of Famer Dr. Henry M. Morris, agrees with him. Henry M. Morris believed that "circle" in Isaiah 40:22 means sphericity, and that "both earth and the deep are components of the great terrestrial sphere."[709] Dr. Henry M. Morris, in his study Bible, titled *The Defender's Study Bible, King James Version, Defending the Faith from a Literal Creationist Viewpoint*, states the following regarding Isaiah 40:22:

> 40:22 *circle of the earth*. Hebrew *khug* is translated "compassed" in Job 26:10 and "compass" in Proverbs 8:27. All three, in context, clearly refer to the sphericity of the earth.[710]

Dr. Henry M. Morris could not be more wrong. Not only does he not understand Hebrew, he seems not to understand English either. He mistakenly thinks that compass means sphere. But it does not. Compass means a circular boundary; the limit or boundary of a space, and the space included; encircle; to surround; to inclose on all sides; a circular course.[711] A compass in the context of the cited passages means a flat circular boundary. Indeed, the example given in the Merriam-Webster dictionary is "within the compass of the city walls."[712]

Compass is also an instrument that the Merriam-Webster dictionary describes as "an instrument for describing circles."[713] A circle is an area where every point on its circumference is of equal distance from the center and on the same plane.[714] A circle is, by definition, flat and thus cannot be a sphere.

Dr. Henry M. Morris is engaging in eisegesis, and he is giving the cited passages a meaning not intended by God. Dr. Henry M. Morris thinks the earth is a sphere and so he redefines the word in Isaiah 40:22 that describes the earth as a flat circle to instead mean that the earth is a round sphere.

Dr. Henry M. Morris and his son, Dr. John D. Morris, find

an ally in fellow Creation Science Hall of Famer Jonathan Sarfati, B.Sc. (Hons.), Ph.D., F.M., who also proclaims that "Isaiah 40:22 tells us that God 'sits above the circle of the earth.' Indeed, the Hebrew word *khûg* implies ball-shaped."[715] Drs. Morris and Sarfati could not be more wrong. They cite the Bible passage at Isaiah 40:22 in support of their claim that the Bible describes a spherical earth. But that passage describes a circle, not a sphere.

> It is he that sitteth upon the circle of the earth, and the inhabitants thereof are as grasshoppers; that stretcheth out the heavens as a curtain, and spreadeth them out as a tent to dwell in. (Isaiah 40:22)

Recall that Dr. Johathan Sarfati claims that the Hebrew word (*khûg*) that is translated as the English word "circle" in Isaiah 40:22 in the Authorized (King James) Version of the Bible does not mean "circle." Dr. Sarfati claims that "the Hebrew word *khûg* implies ball-shaped."[716] He is wrong.

In every place in the Old Testament where *khûg* is written, it is translated into English by words that mean a circular plane. For example: circle (Isaiah 40:22), compass (Proverbs 8:27), and circuit (Job 22:14). *Khûg* means something that is circular and encompasses a flat plane. Indeed, the passages would make no sense otherwise.

> When he prepared the heavens, I was there: when he set a **compass [Hebrew: *khûg*]** upon the face of the depth: (Proverbs 8:27)

> Thick clouds are a covering to him, that he seeth not; and he walketh in the **circuit [Hebrew: *khûg*]** of heaven. (Job 22:14)

The King James translators got it correct. There is no need

to resort to the original languages. For English readers, all one needs to do is understand plain English in the inspired word of God found in the King James Version of the Bible.[717]

Dr. Robert J. Schneider, Ph.D., retired from Berea College as distinguished professor of general studies and professor of classical languages. Dr. Schneider is the recipient of the Seabury Award for Excellence in Teaching, and the Acorn Award for excellence in teaching and scholarship. He examined the claims by creation scientists, including, but not limited to, Drs. Jonathan Sarfati and Henry M. Morris, that the word "circle" in Isaiah denotes sphericity. Dr. Schneider stated: "I am hard put to see how anyone could justify rendering chûgh in Isa. 40:22a as 'sphericity.'"[718] Dr. Schneider elaborated:

> [A] circle is no more a sphere in Scripture than it is in geometry. The preponderance of philological evidence and the translations of ancient scholars and modern experts alike provide overwhelming testimony that Isaiah 40:22 does not refer to a spherical earth.[719]

Dr. Schneider concluded that the Christian scholars and scientists are redefining the word "circle" to mean "sphere" because they think that the earth is a sphere, not because that is what circle means or what Isaiah 40:22 is actually saying. Dr. Schneider states that "one should not read meanings into biblical texts that are not there in order to make them conform to modern scientific knowledge. Regretfully, some of their colleagues in the young earth creationist movement are prone to do just that."[720]

Dennis R. Bratcher is the General Editor and the Executive Director of Christian Research Institute/Voice. He states regarding the "circle" in Isaiah 40:22 that "[i]n Ancient Near Eastern conceptions, this circle would refer to the flat earth disk, not to a sphere."[721]

Christian Research Institute/Voice describes itself as "a global and ecumenical ministry dedicated to providing biblical and theological resources for growing Christians." Dennis Bratcher thinks that while Isaiah described a flat earth, Isaiah got it wrong. Bratcher states that "we should not conclude that this way of talking about the physical world is what the Bible teaches as a reality, something in which we must believe in order to believe Scripture."[722]

What does Bratcher think about the inspiration of the Bible? He feels that the Bible is "fully inspired by God."[723] But in light of his other statements, that averment makes no sense. How can Bratcher claim that the Bible is inspired by God, and yet also claim that it is wrong about the description of the flat earth? Bratcher gives this double-minded explanation:

> Yet what is interesting is that even with inspiration, God allowed these ancient ways of looking at the world to stand without correction. In other words, God did not reveal modern scientific knowledge to the ancient Israelites, or correct their ancient views of the way the world works. He let them express marvelous truths about God in the language and culture in which they lived.[724]

Bratcher correctly reads Isaiah 40:22 for what it clearly says. But according to Bratcher, God inspired the writers to write an erroneous account of the shape of the earth. That is nonsense.

Jesse Michael, during a recorded sermon at Steadfast Baptist Church of Fort Worth, Texas, presented the standard "Christian" heliocentric explanation that the circle of the earth described in Isaiah 40:22 is a sphere. Michael stated:

> The Bible teaches that the earth is described as a circle. Now keep in mind that a circle is a two-

dimensional construct of a three-dimensional object. A circle does not exist in a three-dimensional world. Okay, so just based on that right there, if you believe the Bible, you must believe that the earth is a sphere.[725]

Kent Hovind, Steven Anderson, and others have repeated that same bogus construct. Michael concludes from his definition of a circle that the earth must be a sphere. But that is a conclusion based upon his assumption that the earth is a sphere. If he were to claim that his determination is not based upon that assumption (which he almost certainly would do), that would mean that his conclusion that the circle described in Isaiah 40:22 means a sphere is based upon a premise that all circles everywhere necessarily must be spheres. But we know that premise is not true.

Not only are not all circles spheres but, by definition, a circle cannot be a sphere. Michael is using sophistry and giving a false definition of a circle to deceive the gullible. A circle and a sphere are distinct geometric shapes. *Math Planet* presents the generally accepted definition of a circle: "A circle is all points in the **same plane** that lie at an equal distance from a center point."[726] (bold emphasis added) A circle requires that all points along its circumference be equally distant from its center and be on the **same plane**. A circle requires a flat plane. A sphere is not a flat plane; a sphere is a ball. A sphere is distinct from a circle. The conclusion that the circle of the earth in Isaiah 40:22 is a reference to a sphere is fallacious; the circle of the earth in Isaiah 40:22 is describing a circular flat plane.

One might argue that saying that the circle of the earth means it is a plane involves an assumption. That is not true. As we have seen, a circle requires a flat plane, which precludes a sphere. Also, the deduction that the circle of the earth in Isaiah 40:22 is a flat plane is supported by the context of the passage. If one reads the passage in Isaiah 40:22 in context you will find that God is describing a circular flat plane, and it could not possibly be a globe. That is because, in that passage, God stretches and spreads the heavens like a curtain as a tent in which the inhabitants of the earth can dwell. A tent is pitched over flat ground. And that flat circle of earth is what is being conveyed as the base upon which the tent of the heavens is placed over in Isaiah 40:22.

The idea that God is pitching a tent over a sphere makes no sense. Once the tent (which represents the heavens) is wrapped around the boulder as required by the heliocentric model, there would be no room to dwell in it. If Isaiah 40:22 is going to be rewritten to change the earth from a circle to a globe, then the tent representing the heavens will need to be transformed into a sack. That is the only way the heavens could completely envelop a spherical earth as required by the heliocentric model. That is not the end of Dr. Sarfati's and Jesse Michael's silliness. The Heliocentric model requires the sack to be placed over a spinning globe.

Bible thumping charlatans always resort to the original Hebrew of the Old Testament or the original Greek of the New Testament. Those religious scam artists, being puffed up with their pride of life, are deceived and they are deceivers. "The pride of thine heart hath deceived thee." Obadiah 1:3. They wade into the swill of worldly Greek and Hebrew so-called "scholarship" to come up with corrupt aberrant readings of the Bible.[727] The fact that they typically do not speak a lick of Hebrew makes no difference to them; they are on a mission to undermine God's word, and so the ends justify the means. That is the philosophy of the Jesuits, who, not surprisingly, agree with Dr. Sarfati's corrupt interpretation of Isaiah 40:22.

The Jesuits very own English translation of the Bible corrupts Isaiah 40:22 to change the passage to read "globe' instead of "circle." Bible corruption is a centuries-old plan by Satan. One of the early Bible corruptions was the Roman Catholic

Douay-Rheims Bible, which was an English translation of the Latin Vulgate. It was a Jesuit Roman Catholic Bible that was published in 1610. The Jesuits knew that England was working on refining the English Bible and they wanted to beat them to the punch, so to speak. So, they hurriedly cobbled together a new Bible version so they could publish it before the Authorized (King James) Version was published in 1611. In 1750 the Roman Catholic Church published a revision of the Douay-Rheims Bible under the guidance of Roman Catholic Bishop Richard Challoner (1691–1781). The revision changed the word "compass" in the original 1610 Douay-Reims Bible in the verse at Isaiah 40:22 to "globe" in the 1750 revision, just in time to hop on the heliocentric bandwagon.

That Jesuit Bible is given over entirely to following after "science falsely so called" in direct opposition to God's warning. In the passage at Isaiah 40:22, the Douay-Rheims Bible changes the word "circle" to "globe," to comport with the godless heliocentric model that has since become all the rage in "science falsely so called." Dr. Sarfati is in hearty agreement with the Roman Catholic Douay-Rheims Version of the Bible.

"It is he that sitteth upon the **circle** of the earth, and the inhabitants thereof are as grasshoppers; that stretcheth out the heavens as a curtain, and spreadeth them out as a tent to dwell in:" Isaiah 40:22 AV (KJV) (emphasis added).

"It is he that sitteth upon the **globe** of the earth, and the inhabitants thereof are as locusts: he that stretcheth out the heavens as nothing, and spreadeth them out as a tent to dwell in. Isaiah 40:22 (Douay-Rheims Version) (emphasis added).

So, there you have it: The Creation Science Hall of Fame. Every one of them are avowed enemies of the biblical proof of a flat earth. They mock and revile those who accept the Bible truth of a flat earth.

> Blessed are ye, when men shall hate you, and when they shall separate you from their company, and shall reproach you, and cast out your name as evil, for the Son of man's sake. Rejoice ye in that day, and leap for joy: for, behold, your reward is great in heaven: for in the like manner did their fathers unto the prophets. (Luke 6:22-23)

Those Hall of Famers, who revile all who accept as true the word of God, have been exalted as inductees in the world's Creation Science Hall of Fame. Those same Hall of Famers are false prophets, and as such, are also inductees into another hall, God's hall of shame. "Woe unto you, when all men shall speak well of you! for so did their fathers to the false prophets." (Luke 6:26)

23 Implying God Lied

The vast majority of creation scientists accept the account in the Bible of God creating the heaven and the earth within six (6) literal days (with God resting on the seventh day). They acknowledge that creation happened approximately 6,000 years ago, just as indicated in the Bible. But heliocentric creation scientists also accept the view of profane science that the universe consists of an expansive vacuum of space where there are trillions of stars that are billions of light-years away from earth.

Profane science considers it insane to believe in a flat earth. Heliocentric creations scientists hold that same opinion. For example, in a YouTube video posted on January 27, 2020, heliocentric creation scientist Dr. Robert Carter begins his argument against the flat earth with the statement: "Stop the insanity! The earth is not flat!"[728] Dr. Carter is a scientist who claims to be a "Christian." His January 27th video address is aimed at Christians who have read the Bible and concluded that God created a flat and immovable earth. Dr. Carter tries to argue against such belief by stating that "it [flat earth] is not taught in the Bible."[729] Notably, Dr. Carter does not explain or even cite any Bible passages in support of his argument. Apparently, Dr. Carter expects the listeners to believe him just because he is a highfalutin scientist who claims to be a Christian.

Profane science says that the most distant star, Icarus, is 9 billion light-years away from Earth; the most distant supernova is 23 billion light-years away; the most distant quasar is 29 billion light-years away; the most distant galaxy is 32 billion light-years away.[730] The closest star is thought to be Alpha Centauri, which is alleged to be 4.367 light-years from Earth. A light-year is the distance that light can travel in one year. Light travels at approximately 186,282 miles per second, which is more than 670 million miles per hour.

The theory of profane science is that God did not create the universe; the universe, instead, just came into being through a spontaneous "big bang" that happened approximately 14 billion years ago. Heliocentric creation scientists reject the big bang theory as the origin of the universe because it excludes God as the creator; but they accept the profane scientific theory that there is a vast universe of space with stars that are billions of light-years away. The problem that heliocentric creation scientists have with their acceptance of the heliocentric dogma of so-called science is that there is no way that the stars, which are billions of light-years away, could be seen on the day of creation, or even today, if the earth was created only 6,000 years ago. That is because for stars that are billions of light-years away it would take billions of years for the light from those stars to reach earth and be seen. But the earth is only 6,000 years old. Thus, the profane cosmology, if accepted as true, impeaches the biblical account of the six days of creation having taken place only 6,000 years ago. Of course, impeaching the authority of the Bible is the whole idea behind profane cosmology.

Incidentally, the big bang, which is theorized to have happened 14 billion years ago, also cannot account for how we can see a supernova that is 23 billion light-years away, a quasar that is 29 billion light-years away, and a galaxy that is 32 billion light-years away. But profane cosmology is full of such inconsistencies, which are beyond the scope of this book.

The generally accepted creation science orthodoxy is that the Bible correctly depicts God creating man approximately 6,000 years ago. The vast majority of creation scientists reject the godless theory of evolution of man over a period of millions of years, as theorized by profane scientists. There is a faction of creation scientists who adhere to an "old earth" view of creation. There are also some double-minded creation scientists who have adopted theistic-evolution. But this book is primarily addressed to the most conservative and orthodox view of creation, which rejects the profane scientific theory that the universe is 14 billion years old.

Although orthodox creationists reject the theory that the universe is 14 billion years old, they do accept the profane theory of a vast universe. The acceptance by orthodox creation scientists of the model of a vast universe presents a dilemma for them. And they understand their dilemma. The acceptance of a vast universe impeaches the biblical account of a young, 6,000-year-old earth. Jason Lisle, Ph.D., a Creation Science Hall of Fame inductee explains the quandary faced by the heliocentric creation scientists:

> Critics of biblical creation sometimes use distant starlight as an argument against a young universe. The argument goes something like this: (1) there are galaxies that are so far away, it would take light from their stars billions of years to get from there to here; (2) we can see these galaxies, so their starlight has already arrived here; and (3) the universe must be at least billions of years old—much older than the 6,000 or so years indicated in the Bible.[731]

The heliocentric creationists have undermined their young-earth model that is only 6,000 years old by accepting the profane cosmology of a vast vacuum of outer space. Indeed, Dr. Lisle recognized that fact. "Many big bang supporters consider this [distant stars, billions of light-years away] to be an excellent argument against the biblical timescale."[732]

What are the heliocentric creation scientists to do? Simple, they just make things up. They have come up with several sophisticated theories to reconcile the irreconcilable.[733] Dr. Jason Lisle has even invoked Einstein's irrational and physics-defying theory of relativity into one of his explanations for addressing the contradiction between the young 6.000-year-old earth and the visibility of distant stars that are billions of light-years away. Dr. Lisle, though, admitted that his work-around "may or may not be" true; it is only an "intriguing possibility."

> Now, this idea may or may not be the reason that distant starlight is able to reach earth within the biblical timescale, but so far no one has been able to prove that the Bible does not use cosmic local time. So, it is an intriguing possibility.[734]

Dr. Lisle cited to an article by Robert Newton in support of his theory. According to *Answers in Genesis*, "Robert Newton is the pen name of a creationist astrophysicist currently undertaking research for a doctorate at an accredited university in the USA. He graduated *summa cum laude*, with a double major in physics and astronomy, and a minor in mathematics. He has also completed a M.S. in astrophysics. Robert is a member of the American Astronomical Society and Phi Beta Kappa."[735]

It turns out that, in fact, Robert Newton is Dr. Jason Lisle himself. After Dr. Lisle had successfully obtained his Ph.D., *Creation Ministries International* (CMI) revealed in a biography of Dr. Lisle:

> Because of known discrimination against creationist scientist[s] at secular universities, Jason published papers in creationist journals under a pseudonym, Robert Newton. He explains that the subjectivity of Ph.D. grading makes it easy to fail a creationist. For example, the review committee could claim that a person hasn't done enough work, because how much work is 'enough' is hard to prove, disguising the real reason that the candidate is a creationist.[736]

CMI is giving us a little inside baseball in its biography of Dr. Lisle regarding the subjectivity in Ph.D. science programs. There is "known discrimination against creationist scientists at secular universities." The discrimination is due to the subjective nature of Ph.D. science programs. Ph.D. programs act as gatekeepers that keep out a biblical explanation for scientific reality. All science programs, consequently, have become completely secularized. Profane science does not contradict the Bible because the Bible is wrong; profane science contradicts the Bible because there is an agenda in science programs against the account of creation in the Bible. Thus, the chances of a scientist who ascribes to a biblical and stationary flat earth obtaining a Ph.D. in a science program is slim to none, and slim has left town.

Indeed, any person employed in the sciences will find himself soon unemployed if he dares to publically ascribe to a flat earth cosmology. Brian Mullin found that out the hard way. Brian Mullin is a professional civil and structural engineer, who has been practicing for ten years and is licensed in four states.[737] Mullin stated in July 2016:

> Some people think it [the idea of a flat earth] is ridiculous, but a lot of engineers and surveyors out there have really started to ask questions. They have started to realize that there aren't answers to

these things. That we ignore the alleged curvature and rotation of the earth all the time and we never have any error because of it.[738]

Mullin made many videos that he posted on YouTube wherein he explained the impossibility of the heliocentric cosmology and how an objective view of the evidence indicates that the earth is flat and stationary. An engineer who disagreed with Mullin about the earth being flat maliciously contacted a state licensing board that had jurisdiction over Mullin's engineering license and made an inquiry about whether Mullin's videos about the flat earth violated the state ethics code for engineers.[739] With his livelihood threatened, Mullin shut down his YouTube channel and he has not been heard from since. Many of his videos have been bootlegged and can still be seen on other YouTube channels, but Mullin has not resurfaced with any new content on any public forums.

Robert Newton (a.k.a. Dr. Lisle) realizes that the acceptance by heliocentric creationists of the profane science of stars being billions of light-years away poses a problem for them when defending the biblical account of creation.

> This immediately presents an apparent problem for Biblical creationists. The Bible states in the first chapter of Genesis that God made the stars on Day 4 of Creation Week. A straightforward reading of Scripture shows that Creation must have happened about 6,000 years ago. **This means that the light from distant stars should not yet have reached the Earth.** Yet clearly it has, because we do see very distant stars. This is no small problem, for we are able to observe galaxies of stars that are so far away that their light should have taken billions of years to reach Earth. **Some people claim that this disproves the Genesis account of Creation, and**

proves that the universe is billions of years old, not thousands.[740] (emphasis added)

What is Robert Newton's (a.k.a. Dr. Lisle's) theory? Recall that the stars were created on day four. Genesis 1:14-19. Robert Newton (a.k.a. Dr. Lisle) opines the following:

> Perhaps the answer is much simpler. Perhaps the definition of time that God uses in Genesis 1 is observed time, not calculated time. In other words, had there been an observer standing on Earth on Day 4 of the Creation Week, he or she would have seen the stars being created on that day. This is certainly the impression we get from a straightforward reading of Genesis. The insightful reader will at this point realize that this view implies that the stars observed on Day 4 were 'actually' created years—even billions of years—before Day 1, according to calculated time. This view suggests that God created stars 'before' the beginning of time (if such an idea is meaningful) in such a way that their light would reach Earth on Day 4.[741]

Notice, this is complete conjecture. He prefaces his theory with a massive "perhaps." He reconciles his theory with the plain language of the Bible by creating two different time-frames for creation. He states that there is calculated time (which is when things actually happened) and observed time (when God said things happened).

According to Robert Newton (a.k.a. Dr. Lisle), the Bible gives the account of when the stars were created according to observed time. But the observed time given in the Bible is not really when the stars were created. The stars were actually created billions of years earlier. That actual time-frame for the creation of the stars is what Robert Newton (a.k.a. Dr. Lisle) calls the calculated time. According to Robert Newton (a.k.a. Dr. Lisle), God kept it a secret from man when he really created the stars (the calculated time). Robert Newton (a.k.a. Dr. Lisle) implies that when God said in Genesis 1:1 that he was giving an account of creation from the "beginning" he was telling a fib. Robert Newton's (a.k.a. Dr. Lisle's) account has God lying in the Bible about when he actually created the stars.

> Since the Bible indicates that the stars were visible on Day 4, we now compute the (calculated) time at which they were created. Alpha Centauri (a star 4.3 light years away) must have been created about 4.3 years 'before the beginning' (before Day 1) in order for its light to have reached Earth on Day 4 of the Creation Week. Likewise, a star 10 light years away must have been created about 10 years before Day 1. A star one billion light years away must have been created about one billion years 'before the beginning' and so on. So, we see that more distant stars were created earlier than nearby stars. The time of creation depends on the distance from Earth. So what appears to be simultaneous according to observed time, now appears to be spread out over a long period of time. Which view is the 'correct' picture? They both are—each according to the chosen convention of time measurement.[742]

Robert Newton (a.k.a. Dr. Lisle) is essentially asserting that when God said "[i]n the beginning" in Genesis 1:1 it was not really the beginning. Robert Newton (a.k.a. Dr. Lisle) is claiming that God was prevaricating about when exactly was the beginning. Robert Newton (a.k.a. Dr. Lisle) declares that God really started creating the distant stars billions of years earlier. That would have been billions of years before "the beginning" in Genesis 1:1. That means that when God said it was "the beginning," it wasn't actually the beginning. The implication of Robert Newton's (a.k.a. Dr. Lisle's) theory is obvious. Robert Newton (a.k.a Dr. Lisle) is intimating that God is lying in his account in the Bible of when he created the stars. Robert Newton (a.k.a Dr. Lisle) explains:

> But how can a star be created before the beginning? We must remember that the Bible's statement 'In the beginning' (Genesis 1:1) is a measure of time, and therefore must be the 'beginning' as measured according to observed time. So although the beginning of the universe occurs simultaneously everywhere on Day 1 according to observed time, the beginning of the universe (just as with the stars) occurs at different calculated times depending on the distance from Earth. Day 1 occurs much earlier for places in the universe that are more distant from Earth than nearby places. ... At this point, (thanks to God's innovative method of creation) all the light from all the stars reaches Earth at exactly the same time. This may seem an unusual method by which to create a universe, but then is there a 'usual' method by which universes are created? This method is compatible with the Word of God; and it is compatible with all astronomical observations of which I am aware. The God who created space and time should have no difficulty creating and placing the stars where and when He desires.[743]

Heliocentric creationist Robert Newton (ak.a. Dr. Lisle) tries to reconcile the irreconcilable conflict between the word of God and profane cosmology by saying that God prevaricated about when he created the world. Robert Newton (a.k.a. Dr. Lisle) presents a god who is like a crooked accountant keeping two sets of books. According to him, God had a set of observable time books and a separate set of calculated time books. He kept his calculated time books secret. He only told us about his observable time books. Robert Newton (a.k.a. Dr. Newton) is a schemer and a liar, and so is his god. The true God of the Bible, who created a flat and stationary earth, did not keep two sets of books; he is not a liar. "God is not a man, that he should lie." Numbers 23:19.

Robert Newton's (a.k.a. Dr. Lisle's) theory for reconciling the creation account in the Bible with profane cosmology is not the only one floating around the minds of heliocentric creationists,[744] but it is unique in its stupid simplicity: God lied. His article was originally published in April 2001 in the *Journal of Creation*. It remains posted on both *Answers in Genesis*[745] and *Creation Ministries International*[746] websites as of June 2019, and Dr. Lisle continues to cite the article.[747] Robert Newton (a.k.a. Dr. Lisle) was graduated *summa cum laude* (with highest distinction) in physics and astronomy. He is a member of the American Astronomical Society and Phi Beta Kappa. But don't be impressed. All of that worldly wisdom led him to imagine a god who is a liar. "For the wisdom of this world is foolishness with God. For it is written, He taketh the wise in their own craftiness." (1 Corinthians 3:19)

Robert Newton (a.k.a. Dr. Lisle) is doing essentially the same thing that Jesus criticized the Jews for doing. *See* Mark 7:13. The Jews have replaced God's word with their traditions, which are memorialized today in the Talmud and Kabbalah. Those heathen Jewish philosophies are also the basis for Dr. Lilse's profane heliocentrism. Dr. Lisle avers that the observed times for creation stated in the bible are not really accurate. He alleges that the accurate times for creation, which he calls the calculated times, are not stated in the bible. The calculated times for creation are based upon the profane science of heliocentrism, which is born of the Talmud and Kabbalah. Since the calculated times have not been memorialized by God, Dr. Lisle is all too happy to step into the role of God and make up the numbers for us. Of course, those numbers are based upon Dr. Lisle's heliocentric fantasy. Dr. Lisle is truly "making the word of God of none effect" through his heliocentric tradition. *See* Mark 7:13.

Robert Newton (a.k.a. Dr. Lisle) discredits God and God's word. No wonder profane scientists scoff at the arguments of creation scientists. Heliocentric creation scientists are not depicting the real God of the Bible. Dr. Lisle presents to the world a deceptive god who keeps two sets of books.

24 Casting Aside the Sword of the Spirit

Heliocentrism is a doctrine of the devil, the primary purpose of which is to undermine the authority of the Bible. Heliocentrism is used by atheists and other enemies of God's word to attack the inspiration and inerrancy of the Bible. We will look at just one example of a widely viewed video series created by Brett Palmer, who calls himself *The Bible Sceptic*. Palmer created a video series titled *What the Bible Got Wrong: A Flat Earth*.[748]

Palmer assumes the truth of the heliocentric model as his premise for attacking the inspiration of the Bible. The assumption that heliocentricity is true is something that most Christian Bible apologists have also assumed. It is that common ground, chosen centuries ago by the devil, that Palmer shares with most Christians. The heliocentric Bible apologists are now forced to fight for the inspiration and inerrancy of the Bible on a battleground chosen by the devil. That battleground assures victory for the devil. The soldiers of Christ, who are supposed to fight against the wiles of the devil, find themselves on the field of battle without "the sword of the Spirit, which is the word of God." (Ephesians 6:17)

Palmer's argument has convinced the vast majority of those

who have viewed Palmer's video series that the Bible is not the inerrant and inspired word of God. Of those who rated Palmer's video series on YouTube, Approximately 94% have given it a thumbs-up approval rating. Why was Palmer's argument found so convincing to viewers? Because by admitting the truth of heliocentricity, Christians have lost the spiritual battle over the inerrancy and inspiration of God's word before it even starts. Palmer's video demonstrates that point. Palmer begins by eviscerating the hollow and whiney excuses made by Bible apologists who try to read the Bible to support the heliocentric model. Palmer exposes them as deceptive charlatans. Once he exposes their deception, Palmer goes in for the kill and draws the listener to his conclusion that the Bible is not divinely inspired by God; otherwise, it would not erroneously portray the earth as fixed and flat. Palmer begins by citing Isaiah 40:22.

> It is he that sitteth upon the circle of the earth, and the inhabitants thereof are as grasshoppers; that stretcheth out the heavens as a curtain, and spreadeth them out as a tent to dwell in. (Isaiah 40:22)

Palmer correctly points out that passage, unquestionably, depicts a flat, circular earth. Palmer states that the Bible is wrong because, he argues, that the earth is, in fact, a sphere. He correctly criticizes Bible apologists who claim that the Hebrews used the word circle because that is the only word they had to describe the idea of a globe. But Palmer points out that, in fact, the Hebrews did have a word to describe a sphere, and Isaiah used that word in Isaiah 22:18.

Palmer crushes the phenomenological language argument often used by some heliocentric Bible apologists to explain that the ignorant Hebrews were describing what they saw (a flat earth) and not what the heliocentrists think was actually there (a spherical earth). The phenomenological argument is that because the

Hebrews experienced a flat earth and did not know it was a sphere they erroneously described what they saw (a flat earth) rather than the supposed reality of the spherical earth. The problem, as Palmer points out, is that argument assumes that God allowed the Hebrews to get it wrong. It suggests to Palmer that the Bible could not be inspired by an omniscient God, because an omniscient God would have inspired the Hebrew writers of the Bible to get the shape of the earth correct.

Palmer refutes the ridiculous argument from Creation Science Hall of Famer Jonathan Sarfati that from the perspective of outer space, the spherical earth looks like a circle. Sarfati argues that it is not inaccurate for God to inspire Isaiah to call earth a circle because Sarfati implies that the earth looks like a circle from God's perspective.

> Answers in Genesis creationist guru Jonathan Sarfati goes so far as to remark "even if the translation circle is adhered to, think about Neil Armstrong in space, to him the spherical earth would have appeared circular, regardless of which direction he viewed it from." But hold on a moment, is the earth in any sense a circle? From space the earth would not have appeared to be a circle to Neil Armstrong, or anyone else for that matter, any more than a globe sitting in a classroom appears to be a circle to those sitting around it. It's ball-shaped that's why the earth is sometimes called the Big Blue Marble and not the Big Blue Dinner Plate.[749]

Palmer explains that the Hebrew word used in Isaiah 4:22 that is translated "circle," in English, in fact, literally means "circle." It does not mean "globe." A circle is a geometric figure where all points on the circumference are on the same plane and equidistant from the center. A circle is distinct from a sphere, which is essentially a ball, and cannot be a circle. Heliocentric Bible apologists deceptively try to redefine a circle to include a sphere. But a circle cannot be a sphere because a circle requires all points to be on the same plane. The very definition of a circle precludes a sphere. Palmer explains:

> Unfortunately for their case, the Hebrew *khûg* does not refer to anything shaped like a globe. The word has as its root the meaning of to encircle, encompass, describe a circle, draw around, make a circle. Think of a drafting compass with a point at one end and a pencil at the other. When rotated, the pencil draws a flat circular shape. This is the meaning of the Hebrew word *khûg*. And that is why it is faithfully translated circle in all English translations.[750]

Palmer cites to Isaiah 42:5; 44:24; and Psalms 136:6 to explain that the Bible describes a flat stretched out earth that cannot be a sphere.

> Thus saith God the LORD, he that created the heavens, and stretched them out; he that spread forth the earth, and that which cometh out of it; he that giveth breath unto the people upon it, and spirit to them that walk therein: (Isaiah 42:5)

> Thus saith the LORD, thy redeemer, and he that formed thee from the womb, I am the LORD that maketh all things; that stretcheth forth the heavens alone; that spreadeth abroad the earth by myself; (Isaiah 44:24)

> To him that stretched out the earth above the waters: for his mercy endureth for ever. (Psalms 136:6)

Palmer points out that the above passages describing a stretched out earth depict a flat earth. They cannot be read in any other way.

> How can a spherical earth be thought of as having been spread forth, spread abroad, or stretched out? Such phrases work only for a flat earth. The mention of the earth being stretched above the waters recalls the Genesis creation story.[751]

Palmer cites to the many Bible passages that describe the ends of the earth. Deuteronomy 13:7; 28:49; 28:64; 33:17; Job 28:24; 1 Samuel 2:10; Psalms 19:4; 22:27; 48:10; 59; 61:2; 65:5; 72:8. Palmer argues that such language, taken in the context of the other creation passages, describes a flat earth with an edge at the end. They clearly denote the ends of a flat earth.[752]

Palmer cites to the passages that describe the foundations and pillars of the earth. Job 9:5-6; 38:4; Psalms 24:1-2; 75:3; 104:5; 2 Samuel 22:16; Zechariah 12:1. Palmer takes heliocentric Bible apologists to task for obfuscating the meaning of pillars and foundations. Heliocentric apologists dishonestly try to turn the clear meaning of passages that describe physical pillars of the earth into some kind of figurative expression. Those arguments completely ignore the context of the passages. Palmer rightly criticizes those arguments as having the hollow ring of deception.

Palmer quotes Professor of Theology at Creighton University Bruce J. Malina and Professor of Biblical Studies at Georgetown University John J. Pilch, who state in their co-authored book, *Social-science Commentary on the Book of Revelation*, that the Bible clearly describes a flat and stationary earth:

> Many historically minded Bible readers learned their first ancient model of the world and its

cosmic appurtenances from the study of the Book of Genesis. In the model required to imagine the scenes in the ancient Israelite creation story, the earth was flat and stable, rooted in place by means of solid pillars, surrounded by water and containing some underworld within. This flat earth was covered by the vault of the sky that was stretched out something like a half circular tent. The vault of the sky separates the waters above from the waters below. And the stars are affixed to this vault, while the sun and moon make their way across it.[753]

Palmer, with his premise that the earth is a sphere spinning in space, concludes that the Bible description of a flat and stationary earth is full of errors. Palmer avers that those perceived errors are evidence that the Bible is not inerrant and is not inspired by an omniscient God. Heliocentric Christians who try to defend the Bible are ill-equipped to do so because they have surrendered the field of battle before the fight starts by accepting heliocentrism as true. Palmer, and those like him, then bludgeon the hapless heliocentric defender of the Bible with the alleged erroneous words of the Bible.

If the Bible defender accepted the Bible as having primacy over so-called science, he could then accept the truth of God's creation of a flat and stationary earth, as depicted in the Bible. And from that firm foundation, he could successfully defend the inspiration of the inerrant Bible against attacks from atheists. Indeed, revealing the lies of so-called science would likely win converts of atheists who during the battle against God's word would perhaps come to know the truth of the gospel.

Instead, we have a situation where both the defender and the attacker of the Bible are heliocentrists. The sophistry of the heliocentrists defending the Bible is correctly perceived as duplicity by the heliocentrists attacking the Bible. The atheists see through the dissembling and are left unconvinced by the interpretive eisegesis of heliocentric "Christians." In the end, both the atheist and the Bible defender are left in ignorance of the truth.

World famous evangelical Christian Ray Comfort mocks atheists for arguing that the Bible depicts a flat earth. He destroys his testimony for Christ by trying to contradict what the Bible says. Read carefully what Comfort says about Isaiah 40:22. He is trying to refute the plain meaning of circle in Isaiah. But in doing so, he unintentionally confirms that the passage is describing a flat circle. Comfort slips up and says "[l]ike wheels round and round, a circle." Oops! Wheels are not spheres. Wheels have circular, flat faces. Comfort impeaches his own argument.

> Isaiah says that earth hangs upon nothing. I mean that was written when science believed it sat on the back of a gigantic tortoise, I guess an earthquake was when he moved. And then there is he that sits on the circle of the earth. Atheists say that circle is a flat disc. Look they go round and round and round with that argument, like a circle. Round and round like a circle. Like wheels round and round, a circle. He that sits on the circle of the earth. The earth is round. Written in 800 years B.C.[754]

Ray Comfort identified the wrong passage. The passage in the Bible refering to God hanging the earth upon nothing is found not in Isaiah but in Job. "He stretcheth out the north over the empty place, and hangeth the earth upon nothing." (Job 26:7)

Comfort not only misidentified the passage, he also misinterprets it. Job 26:7 is often cited as Bible proof that the earth is, in fact, floating in outer space. But when one reads the passage carefully and in light of the entire creation account in the Bible, it becomes clear that it does no such thing.

We find that earlier Job explained that God "shaketh the earth out of her place, and the pillars thereof tremble." (Job 9:6) The earth is upon pillars. "[F]or the pillars of the earth are the LORD'S, and he hath set the world upon them." (1 Samuel 2:8) It is clear that the earth is built upon a foundation of pillars.

With that in mind, Let us then look at what is being said in Job 26:7. We first find that God stretches out the north over the empty place. That means that the north, which is a directional location on earth, is stretched. The north on a flat earth can be stretch, but the north on a globe cannot be stretched.

Next we look at God hanging the earth upon nothing. To hang the earth means that something is supporting the earth from above. It is true that the earth is not hanging on anything. We have seen that the earth is supported from underneath by pillars. E.g., Job 9:6; 1 Samuel 2:8. And so there is nothing supporting the earth from above. It is not hung on anything. To read Job 26:7 as meaning that the earth is a globe floating in a vacuum of nothingness in outer space is to read into the passage what is not there and to ignore the many other passages that indicate that the earth is stretched out flat and supported from underneath by foundations.

25 Moonlight Discredits Heliocentric Creationists

One example of the hypocritical agenda of the creation scientists is their figurative interpretation of the lesser light of the moon. They interpret the clear Bible passages that God created the moon as the lesser light to instead mean that the moon is not a light at all. They claim that, while God says the moon is a light, he does not mean that literally. They claim that God actually means that the moon is a reflector of the sun's light.

For example, Creation Science Hall of Famer Dr. Robert Carter, Ph.D., who is a senior scientist and speaker for Creation Ministries International[755] disregards the Bible passages describing the moon as a light and instead sides with the orthodox scientific view that the moon is simply a reflector.

> [T]he fact that the moon reflects sunlight is simple and obvious. From the large-scale geometry of the sun-earth-moon system to the ever-changing shadows of lunar craters, our observations always perfectly agree with the geometry positions of the sun, moon, and earth.[756]

Dr. Carter is joined in this erroneous belief in a reflector moon by another Creation Science Hall of Famer, Jonathan Sarfati, who states, without equivocation that "the moon reflects the sun's light on to us."[757] Sarfati even promotes the NASA moon landing hoax: "One of the most dramatic events of our time was the landing of men on the moon."[758] Sarfati is wrong on both counts. Moonlight is different from sunlight; the moon is not a reflector of sunlight. And NASA never landed on the moon. For proof that the NASA moon landings were hoaxes, refer to this author's book, *The Greatest Lie on Earth*.

In order to prop up their heliocentric myth, creation scientists must have a distant moon in outer space reflecting the light of the sun. They simply cannot have the moon be close to the earth in the firmament emitting its own light as depicted in the Bible. See Genesis 1:4. Incidentally, the stars have yet a different glory from either the moon or the sun. Stars are not distant suns as have been portrayed by modern science. Creation scientists contradict the passages in the Bible that state that God created the moon in the firmament as the lesser light. Indeed, God emphatically states that the moon's light is different from the sun's light, which precludes the moon from being a reflector of the sun's light.

> "There is one glory of the sun, and another glory of the moon, and another glory of the stars: for one star differeth from another star in glory." 1 Corinthians 15:41.

That passage refutes the claim that the moon is a reflector of the sun's light and impeaches the heliocentric creation scientists. God stated that both the moon and the sun are lights, each with its own glory. He did not say the sun is a light and the moon is a reflector, thus reflecting the same glory of the sun. Both the sun and moon are lights each with its unique glory. Genesis 1:14-16 is also clear that both the moon and sun were created by God as "lights."

> And God said, Let there be **lights** in the firmament of the heaven to divide the day from the night; and let them be for signs, and for seasons, and for days, and years: And let them be for **lights** in the firmament of the heaven to give **light** upon the earth: and it was so. And God made two great **lights**; the greater **light** to rule the day, and the lesser **light** to rule the night: he made the stars also. (Genesis 1:14-16)

Genesis 1:14-16 states that there are two lights (not one), "the greater light to rule the day, and the lesser light to rule the night." God states that they are to be "lights" in order "to give light upon the earth." God did not say that there would be one light and one reflector.

Furthermore, God stated that the greater light rules the day. He said nothing about the greater light ruling the night, which would necessarily have to be the case if the moon (the lesser light) were not actually a light, but a reflector. The orthodox view that has the moon reflecting the sunlight effectively requires the greater light (the sun) to rule both the day and the night. But that cannot be, because God states clearly that the lesser light (the moon) rules the night. In order to rule the night as an actual light that is lesser than the sun, the moon must have its own light that is distinct from the sun's light.

Indeed, Jesus stated, without equivocation, that the moon is not a reflector, but gives off its own light. "But in those days, after that tribulation, the sun shall be darkened, and **the moon shall not give her light.**" (Mark 13:24) The sun shall be darkened, and the corollary is that the moon shall not give her light. Obviously, that means that ordinarily the moon gives off its own light. It refers to the light of the moon as "her light." Indeed, it is a theme in the Bible that the moon is described as a source for its own light. *E.g.,* Isaiah 13:10: "For the stars of heaven and the constellations thereof shall not give their light: the sun shall be darkened in his going forth, and the **moon shall not cause her light to shine.**" The moon is the "cause" for her own light; that necessarily means that the moon does not reflect the light of the sun. *See also* Matthew 24:29; Ezekiel 32:7; Isaiah 13:10. Jesus said: "If I have told you earthly things, and ye believe not, how shall ye believe, if I tell you of heavenly things?" (John 3:12)

Moonlight has a unique characteristic (it is cold) that is different from sunlight (which is warm). That proves that moonlight cannot be the reflected light from the sun. If it were, the reflected light would have to be warm.

Moonlight shone on objects make them colder as compared to objects protected from the moonlight by shade, whereas an object in sunlight is warmer than an object shaded from the sun. This author has used a dual laser infrared thermometer[759] and detected that material in moonlight is indeed colder than material shaded from the moonlight. Depending on the material, the difference in temperature ranged from approximately 2°F to approximately 6°F colder for material in moonlight than for material shaded from the moonlight. Of course, as expected, the very opposite was the case for material in sunlight versus material shaded from the sun. This author found that material in sunlight was detected to be approximately 20°F to 25°F warmer than the same material shaded from the sunlight.

Jesus told the Jews that if they did not believe Moses, they would not believe him. "For had ye believed Moses, ye would have believed me: for he wrote of me. But if ye believe not his writings, how shall ye believe my words?" (John 5:46-47) Moses wrote Genesis. Genesis describes the creation of the sun as a light and the moon also as a light.

Despite the clear Bible passages and empirical evidence indicating that the moon is a "light" and not a reflector, Christian pastors still cling to the heliocentric myth. For example, Chad Wagner, the pastor of The Excelsior Springs Church, comes out swinging against the biblical depiction of a self-luminous moon:

> The flat earthers say that the moon puts out its own light. They actually believe this. They believe that the moon is a self-luminous being, because it says in Genesis that God made the lesser light to rule the night and the greater light to rule the day. Alright, so the moon puts out its own light. That's what they believe. This is absurd.[760]

Wagner cites to the very Bible passage where God states that the moon is a "light." Wagner, nonetheless, opines that it is absurd to believe what the holy scriptures clearly state. Wagner, who is a church pastor, thinks that it is absurd to believe the Bible. Wagner believes profane science over God's word. Wagner's great pride causes him to take sides with science (so-called) against God's word. Wagner's hubris suggests that he lacks the unction of the Holy Spirit. Wagner is an enemy of the holy Bible. He is a wolf in sheep's clothing. *See* Matthew 7:15.

Wagner is oblivious to the true science which confirms God's word. Wagner is ignorant of the zetetic proof that the moon gives off cold light. That, consequently, means that the moon emits its own cold light and cannot be a reflector of the warm light from the sun.

Wagner marshals his heathen ignorance to continue his attack on the Bible. Wagner explains how lunar eclipses prove that the earth is a sphere.[761] Wagner claims that lunar eclipses can't happen on a flat earth.[762] Wagner holds that opinion because he believes the scientific propaganda that lunar eclipses are caused by the shadow of the earth being cast over the moon. Wagner is utterly oblivious to the reality of daytime lunar eclipses, whose very existence completely impeaches his misconception that the shadow of the earth causes lunar eclipses. For more information about daytime lunar eclipses, read chapter one in this book and this author's other book, *The Greatest Lie on Earth*.

The certainty of Gods' creation of a flat earth with the sun, moon, and stars, providing light is linked to the certainty of the salvation for his church. To claim that God's ordinance by which he has created a moon that provides its own light at night is wrong means that God's church will cease its existence. If the moon is not a light and it is only a reflector then the eternal church of God will cease its existence. We find that stated by God through the prophet Jeremiah:

> Thus saith the LORD, which giveth the sun for a light by day, and the ordinances of **the moon and of the stars for a light by night**, which divideth the sea when the waves thereof roar; The LORD of hosts is his name: If those ordinances depart from before me, saith the LORD, then the seed of Israel also shall cease from being a nation before me for ever. (Jeremiah 31:35-36)

Notice that the moon and stars are jointly referred to as being a light by night. That is they are both a part of a unit of light for the night sky. They are both sources of the same kind of light. The moon is not a reflector of the sun's light, which would be different from the stars that provide their own light. The moon emits light just as do the stars.

God states that if the sun, which is given as a light by day, and the ordinances of the moon and stars, which are given as lights by night, should depart from him, then shall the seed of Israel cease from being a nation before him. That passage in Jeremiah precedes the passage at Jeremiah 31:37 discussed in an earlier chapter where it is stated that if the heavens can be measured and the foundations of the earth searched so also will God cast off his seed of Israel.

> Thus saith the LORD; If heaven above can be measured, and the foundations of the earth searched out beneath, I will also cast off all the seed of Israel for all that they have done, saith the LORD. Jeremiah 31:37.

As we have seen in an earlier chapter, the Bible makes it clear that the elect church is the "Israel of God." *See, e.g.,* Galatians 6:16. God's elect is the seed of Israel. In Galatians 3:16, we find: "Now to Abraham and his **seed** were the promises made. He saith not, And to seeds, as of many; but as of one, **And to thy seed, which is Christ**." Jesus Christ is the seed that is the source of the blessing. All who believe in Jesus Christ, are the recipients of the promises as the spiritual children of God.

All who believe in Jesus Christ are Abraham's spiritual seed, and heirs according to the promise of the coming Christ given to Abraham. "And if ye be Christ's, then are ye Abraham's seed, and heirs according to the promise." Galatians 3:29. Indeed the church is the spiritual nation of Israel referenced in Jeremiah 31:35-36. "But ye are a chosen generation, a royal priesthood, **an holy nation,** a peculiar people; that ye should shew forth the praises of him who hath called you out of darkness into his marvellous light." (1 Peter 2:9) (emphasis added) Christians saved by the grace of God are "heirs of the kingdom." (James 2:5).

Having accurate knowledge of God's creation gives one accurate knowledge of the certainty of our everlasting salvation. If the Bible is thought to be wrong about God's creation of a moon that gives off its own light, then one can believe that the Bible could be wrong about God's promise to preserve his church in glory for eternity. Belief in God's account of the creation of a flat and stationary earth with the sun moon and stars overhead in the firmament, with the moon as a light in the night sky, is crucial to understanding the inviolability of God's eternal promises.

26 Shedding Moonlight on Guile

Creation scientists engage in all manner of guile to support the heathen superstition of heliocentricity. Danny Faulkner, Ph.D., is a creation scientist who thinks that "the flat-earth movement is a threat to Christianity and the authority of Scripture, as well as the creation science movement."[763] To counter this threat, Faulkner has engaged in a campaign against the biblical account of a flat and stationary earth. By his own account, he has written more than 13 articles in his crusade attacking the biblical authority for the flat earth.[764]

Dr. Faulkner disagrees with God's description of the moon as a light in Genesis 1:14–19. Faulkner believes that the moon is a reflector of the sun's light. In one of his articles, titled *Testing a Flat-Earth Prediction: Is the Moon's Light Cooling?*, he tries to refute the scientific evidence that the moon gives off its own light, and that the light is a cold light. It is impossible for the moon to be a reflector of the sun's warm light if the moonlight is cold. The verifiable fact that the moon gives off its own cold light poses a real problem for science and charlatan "Christians" who do not believe the clear statement in the Bible that the moon is a "light."

At the conclusion of his article on moonlight, Dr. Faulkner arrogantly challenges those who believe in God's account that the moon gives off its own light.

> Flat earthers frequently implore others, "Research it!" However, when I have presented original research such as this that disproves their model, flat earthers generally ignore it. They generally don't attempt a refutation. Instead, they refuse to interact with it [at] all. Will flat earthers do the same with the research presented here?[765]

Dr. Faulkner can consider the challenge accepted. This author will address Dr. Faulkner's research that he claims disproves that the moon gives off its own cold light. Dr. Faulkner acknowledges that if the moon is reflecting the sun's light it cannot be giving off a cold light. What is Faulkner to do when the evidence indicates that moonlight is cold? He jimmied up some phony experiments that he claims prove that the moon does not give off a cold light.

Dr. Faulkner is not an objective scientist. He is an advocate who set up rigged experiments and then reported the results that supported the outcome he preordained. Faulkner states the following in his premise to his experiments:

> Due to a misunderstanding of Genesis 1:14–19, flat earthers believe that the moon doesn't reflect the sun's light, but rather that the moon has its own source of light. To maintain this belief may be the motivation of many flat earthers who claim that the moon's light has the strange property of cooling objects exposed to it. But this contradicts everything we know about heat and light. Light contains energy that objects can absorb. Therefore, any moonlight that falls on an object will heat that object, though the amount of heat is so small that it may not be easy to detect a temperature increase

as a result.[766]

After Dr. Faulkner sets forth his premise, he then lets the cat out of the bag and admits that certain tricks can be employed to give misleading results. He alleges that these tricks are used by those who espouse that the moon gives off cool light. Faulkner states:

> Thus, there are many tricks that one can employ to get the desired results. Most people aren't aware of the many factors that can skew the results, so most people do not know about the nuances that can affect IR temperature measurements.[767]

Dr. Faulkner tries to portray Bible believers in the moon giving off its own light as thermometer tricksters. But we will see that it is Faulkner who is the trickster. Recall that Faulkner has a master's degree in physics and a Ph.D. in astronomy. So he knows every trick in the book. What are the tricks that Faulkner employs in his so-called experiments? He used materials that have low thermal conductivity. He used grass in one series of experiments, and he used wood in another. Materials with low thermal conductivity will not conduct heat well either into or out of the material.[768] If someone wanted to show that the moon does not give off cold light they would pick a material that has low thermal conductivity. And that is what Dr. Faulkner did.

The different thermal conductivity of carpeting and tile in a house will help give an understanding of how different materials react differently to heat and cold. We experience this during the winter when we walk from carpeting to a ceramic tile in the bathroom. The carpet and tile are both the same temperature in the house, but the tile has a much higher thermal conductivity.[769] Consequently, the tile feels much colder to our feet because its higher thermal conductivity causes it to draw the heat from our feet much quicker.

Faulkner admits that "thin grass blades do not conduct heat well."[770] Yet he bases one series of experiments on the difference in moon shadow and moonlight temperatures on grass. He rigged the experiment to show a null result using grass, which has low thermal conductivity. Dr. Faulkner concluded that "statistically both average temperature differences are consistent with zero average temperature difference."[771]

In his second series of experiments, Dr. Faulkner used a single plank of plywood, which, like grass, has low thermal conductivity. If he were conducting an unbiased experiment and wanted to really show the temperature effect of moonlight he would use a material with high thermal conductivity, like steel. But he chose wood. And he did it for a reason.

The thermal conductivity rating for wood is approximately 0.14.[772] That number means nothing to most readers until it is compared to the thermal conductivity rating for steel, which is approximately 45.[773] Steel has more than 300 times the thermal conductivity of wood. Steel would be one of the best materials to use to detect the temperature effect of moonlight. Wood would be one of the worst materials to use to determine the temperature effects of moonlight. Dr. Faulkner is a physicist; he knows this. He is counting on the fact that most other people reading his article do not know this.

Dr. Faulkner, who is a physicist and knows exactly what materials to use, chose one of the absolute worst materials to determine if the moon gives off a cold light. He could have used steel, but instead, he used wood. It is not as though steel is a hard to obtain exotic material. Indeed, he explained in his article that he did experiments using steel car fenders.[774] But, suspiciously, he did not report the results of those experiments. He explained how the placement of the car fenders over grass and over concrete gave different results. And based on that fact he concluded that "thus, there are many tricks that one can employ to get the desired results."[775] It seems that one of those tricks is not reporting inconvenient results.

Dr. Faulkner is not without curiosity. He is a scientist. He almost certainly placed steel car fenders in equivalent settings, one in moonlight and one in moon shade. Why did he not report the results of his experiments using the steel car fenders? The answer is obvious. Dr. Faulkner has a Ph.D. in astronomy; he knows that the moon gives off cold light. Dr. Faulkner has a master's degree in physics; he knows what material to use in an experiment to prove that the moon gives off cold light and what material to use to conceal that truth.

Steel would logically be the best material to use to determine the temperature effect of moonlight due to its high thermal conductivity. But because Dr. Faulkner had already determined the outcome he wanted before he started the experiment, he rigged the experiments using plywood, which has low thermal conductivity. That virtually guaranteed a null result. He used a material that would cause him to conclude that "this result could be consistent with no temperature difference due to moonlight."[776]

Faulkner knew that the low thermal conductivity of the plywood board was actually determining the outcome of his experiments. He was getting a slightly positive reading for moonlight on the wooden board. He suspected that the "[d]ifferences in grain, color, texture, and finish between the two ends of the board could account for the positive temperature difference."[777] Consequently, he turned the board around. Sure enough, he obtained the opposite results with the board reversed. The portion of the board in shadow was now slightly higher in temperature than the moonlit section. But rather than conclude that the difference was due to the board, he opined that this was due to radiative cooling of the surrounding area.

There is another characteristic of materials that could explain why turning the board resulted in different temperature readings. Each material has what is known as a specific heat capacity, which refers to a material's ability to store heat.[778] Wood has more than double the specific heat capacity of steel.[779]

When Dr. Faulkner turned the board around, the uneven stored heat in the warmer part of the board could have caused that part of the board to remain warmer than the cooler end. Dr. Faulkner waited 20 minutes after turning the board around, but that may not have been long enough to equalize the temperature at each end of the board. And since the moonlight was shining on the cooler end, it had the effect of maintaining the disparity in temperature.

Indeed, the specific heat capacity of the board may actually have accounted for the disparity in the first set of readings that measured slightly higher temperature for the moonlit section of the board. Dr. Faulkner made no mention of where that board was kept before he set it up for his experiment. Dr. Faulkner is a scientist accustomed to conducting experiments, but he rather suspiciously made no baseline temperature readings of the full length of the board before he began his experiment. And then he waited only 20 minutes to measure the temperature of each end of the board. That may not have been long enough for the board to equalize its temperature over the entire length of the board.

After the board was turned around, the temperature of the board in the moonlight was now slightly lower, but the cooling effect of the moonlight was not nearly what should have been the case because the wooden board's low thermal conductivity was causing it to act as a kind of insulator that was mitigating the cooling effect of the moonlight. Dr. Faulkner, who is a physicist, knew that, but he did not mention it.

Dr. Faulkner conducted several series of experiments at

different locations using the wooden board. At one location he determined that the moonlight caused an increase in temperature. But the increase was so slight that he opined that "the difference may not be statistically significant."[780] The low thermal conductivity of the wooden board had done its job. The wooden board had concealed the cooling effect of the moonlight in Dr. Faulkner's experiments, just as he had planned. Thus, he was able to conclude that "these results do not agree with the claims of many flat earthers with regards to supposed cooling properties of the moon's light."[781] Of course, Dr. Faulkner made no mention of the low thermal conductivity of the wooden board. That was to be his little secret.

    This author explained in *The Greatest Lie on Earth* that while magnification of sunlight causes magnification of the heat from the sun, magnification of the moonlight does not cause magnification of the cold. Even extreme magnification of moonlight does not produce significantly reduced temperature. That is unlike extreme magnification of sunlight, which causes significantly increased temperature. I cited in my book to experiments described by Dr. Henry Noad in his *Lectures on Chemistry*. Dr. Noad's lecture was recounted by Samuel Rowbotham in his book, *Zetetic Astronomy*.[782] Dr. Noad reveals results of experiments with magnified moonlight. In one of those experiments, Dr. Noad explains that "[t]he light of the moon, though concentrated by the most powerful burning-glass, is incapable of raising the temperature of the most delicate thermometer."[783] In one experiment cited by Dr. Noad, no thermal effect was produced through the lunar rays that were magnified 300 times. In a second experiment, the moon's light was concentrated by a lens 30 inches in diameter and having a power of concentration exceeding 6,000 times. Yet not the slightest thermal effect was produced.

    The fact that concentrating moonlight has no thermal effect is something that has been known for more than 100 years. But it is not taught in schools, and the general public is ignorant of it. Dr. Faulkner full well knew of the experiments mentioned by Dr. Noad. Indeed, Dr. Faulkner cryptically alluded to those experiments when he stated: "I conducted a third experiment [concentrating moonlight] that was a more direct way to test this flat-earth claim that is similar to two experiments Rowbotham (1881) mentioned."[784]

Dr. Faulkner does not explain that the experiments of Rowbotham to which he referred established that focused moonlight does not increase the coldness of the moonlight. Dr. Faulkner knew that fact but kept it to himself. That is a key omission and part of Dr. Faulkner's deception. 1) Dr. Faulkner did not explain that the experiments cited by Rowbotham showed no thermal effect from magnified moonlight. 2) Faulkner then falsely stated that the flat earth hypothesis requires a cold thermal effect from the magnification of moonlight. 3) Faulkner then conducted his own experiment that showed what he already knew: there is no thermal effect from moonlight magnification.

All three points taken together mislead the reader into inferring that Rowbotham was deceptively citing experiments to show that concentrating moonlight would increase the coldness of the moonlight and that Dr. Faulkner's experiments revealed the truth that there is no thermal effect from magnification. Dr. Faulkner then draws the reader to the erroneous conclusion that the moon does not give off its own cold light. Dr. Faulkner's beguiling conclusion is founded on the dissimilation in points 1 and 2.

Dr. Faulkner engages in a little parlor trick to deceive people. He set up an experiment with a telescope to concentrate the light of the moon on the bulb of a thermometer. He used the massive Souther telescope at the Johnson Observatory at the Creation Museum to focus the light of the moon. When the sunlight is magnified through that telescope, "a piece of paper placed at the focal plane while the telescope is pointed toward the sun will ignite in about one second."[785] Dr. Faulkner explains what he says should be found if the moon is giving off cold light:

> If the moon's light has a cooling effect, then the temperatures ought to fluctuate between warmer temperatures when the telescope was not pointed at the moon and cooler temperatures when the telescope was pointed at the moon.[786]

Dr. Faulkner has a Ph.D. in astronomy. He is also a physicist. He knows that magnifying moonlight will not affect the temperature of the area upon which the concentrated and focused moonlight falls. He knew about the experiments cited by Rowbotham that showed that magnifying moonlight does not have a thermal effect. Yet he misleadingly presented his experiment as showing that if the moon gives off a cold light then that cold light will show a magnification of that cold light when the moonlight is focused through a telescope lens.

Dr. Faulkner presented this experiment ostensibly to refute the claim that the moonlight gives off a cold light. Dr. Faulkner concluded that "there is no temperature change brought about by concentrating the moon's light."[787] He determined that the results did "not match the prediction of the hypothesis that moonlight is cooling."[788] Dr. Faulkner is lying. He knew what the outcome of concentrating moonlight would be. He leads the reader therefore to the conclusion from the null result that the moon does not give off a cold light.

Dr. Faulkner knows that concentrating the moonlight would not affect the temperature of the area where the moonlight is focused. He also knows that result is irrelevant to the fact that the moon gives off a cold light. The moon gives off a cold light that cannot be decreased through concentration of the moonlight. Because the cold light of the moon cannot be decreased through magnification does not mean that the moon does not give off cold light. And Dr. Faulkner knew that before conducting his experiment.

Dr. Faulkner concludes that "[t]he third experiment was the most robust, and its results provide no evidence for any heating or cooling of moonlight."[789] Dr. Faulkner suspiciously makes no effort to explain why the telescope's magnification of the moonlight did not result in an increase in thermal effect when such an occurrence would be expected to occur if the moon were reflecting the warm light from the sun. Indeed, in the introduction to the experiment, Dr. Faulkner states that "one would expect that any appreciable cooling (or heating) of the moon's light will be detectable when the telescope is pointed at the moon."[790]

But Faulkner alleged that he found that the moonlight manifested neither a cooling nor a heating effect. That refutes the claim that the moon is a reflector of the sun's warm rays because if the moon were reflecting the warm rays of the sun the focused warm light should have shown a measured increase in temperature, not a null result. The fact that there was a null result for a warm thermal effect is a vexing fact for Dr. Faulkner. And so he makes no effort to even address it.

Answers in Genesis describes itself as "an apologetics ministry, dedicated to helping Christians defend their faith and proclaim the gospel of Jesus Christ."[791] Dr. Danny Faulkner works for Answers in Genesis as a researcher, author, and speaker. He posted his misleading moonlight research article on the *Answers in Genesis* website. Dr. Faulkner needs to read his Bible more carefully. If he did, he would learn that God commands that Christians are to "speak no guile." 1 Peter 3:10.

Dr. Faulkner is typical of heliocentric scientists. Dr. Faulkner claims to be a Christian, but he apparently follows the doctrine of the Jesuits, the ends justify the means. Dr. Faulkner seems to be one who "heareth the word; and the care of this world, and the deceitfulness of riches, choke the word, and he becometh unfruitful." (Matthew 13:22) Anyone with an infrared thermometer can do their own experiments and prove that Dr. Faulkner is a scam artist. But you don't need an infrared thermometer to measure the lowness of his character.

27 Caught Speaking Lies

Heliocentric creationist Dr. Danny Faulkner wrote an article, titled *Flat Earth Proof—Just a Mirage*[792], wherein he tried to present light refraction as the reason that distant landmarks that should be below the horizon on a spherical earth can still be seen. The problem with Faulkner's argument is that the typical light refraction actually makes distant objects appear lower and thus harder to see. That means that light refraction actually works against the advocates for the spherical earth model. This author explains that point in detail, with authority, including photographs, in *The Greatest Lie on Earth (Expanded Edition)*.

Dr. Faulkner begins his article on the premise that the visibility of the Chicago skyline in Joshua Nowicki's famous photograph and Samuel Rowbotham's experiments on the Old Bedford Canal are not evidence that the earth is flat, but rather evidence of light refraction due to temperature inversion causing superior mirages above the horizon.

Samuel Rowbotham's experiment, to which Dr. Faulkner refers, was conducted more than 100 years ago in Cambridge County, England, where there is an artificial canal, called the "Old Bedford." The canal is approximately twenty miles in length.

Rowbotham arranged to have a boat, with a flag on it that was exactly 5 feet above the surface of the water. The boat was rowed to Welney Bridge, which was exactly six statute miles in a straight line from Rowbotham, who had waded into the water. Rowbotham stood in the middle of the canal with a telescope exactly 8 inches above the surface of the water. In looking through the eyepiece of the telescope, he observed the receding boat during the whole period required to sail to Welney Bridge, "[t]he flag and the boat were distinctly visible throughout the whole distance!"[793] If the earth were a sphere, as it is supposed, the flag should not have been visible to Rowbotham. The boat and flag should have been 11 feet 8 inches below the horizon as depicted in the diagram below.

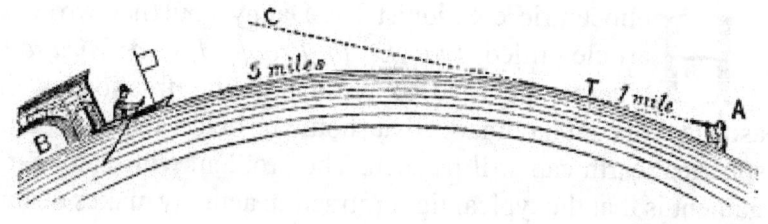

Rowbotham was able to see the flag and boat for the entire 6-mile journey in the canal, all the way to the bridge, as depicted in the diagram below.

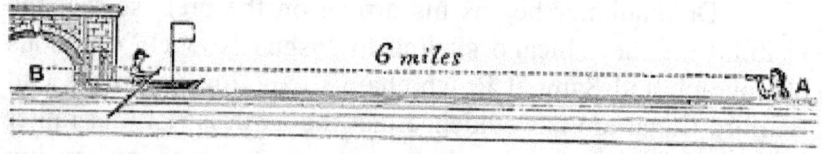

The fact that Rowbotham was able to see the flag and boat for the entire 6 miles, proves that the earth is flat. Rowbotham did many similar experiments at the canal that all proved that there was no curvature of the earth.

In the photograph taken by Joshua Nowicki as he stood at Grand Mere Park, Michigan, which is approximately 57 miles away, across lake Michigan from Chicago, the Chicago skyline could be clearly seen.[794] If the earth were a globe, Chicago would be below the horizon. The only way that Chicago could be seen from the western shore of Michigan is if the world is flat. If the earth were a sphere all of the buildings should have been below the horizon. Indeed, the top of the Sears Tower (now called the Willis Tower) would be 194 feet below the horizon. The Nowicki photograph is below. The details of the geometric calculations are given in *The Greatest Lie on Earth*. The Nowicki photograph depicts all of the buildings on the Chicago skyline. The photograph is an impossibility on a spherical earth.

Figure 19: Photograph of Chicago taken by Joshua Nowicki, as he stood at Grand Mere Park, Michigan, 57 miles away.

Dr. Faulkner tries to portray the Nowicki photograph not

as evidence of a flat earth but rather as evidence of a superior mirage. Dr. Faulkner's premise is that superior mirages, which are caused by temperature inversions, explain why objects are visible over the horizon on the supposedly spherical earth. Dr. Faulkner states that conditions for superior mirages are common during late spring and into summer.

Joshua Nowicki's photograph looks nothing like a superior mirage. Below is a picture of a superior mirage of Chicago taken from approximately 50 miles away across Lake Michigan from Warren Dunes State Park, Michigan, by Joshua Super and Shalee Blackmer.[795] Notice that the buildings in the mirage appear upside down and quite indistinct in their appearance.

Figure 20: Superior Mirage of Chicago Taken from Across Lake Michigan.

Dr. Faulkner theorizes that light "continually is internally reflected, causing the light to bend around the edge of the earth. Therefore, with a temperature inversion, one can see objects that lie well beyond the edge of the earth's curvature when viewing close to the surface of water."[796] Indeed, Dr. Faulkner's theory of light refraction aligns with the orthodox scientific explanation for how distant landmarks can be seen over horizon of the supposed spherical earth. Dr. Faulkner concludes that Rowbotham's findings were not evidence of a flat earth but rather evidence of a superior mirage.

> I've previously discussed the Bedford level experiment, in which I explained that atmospheric refraction bent the light of the boat along the surface of the earth, making the boat visible, even though the boat actually was below the direct line of sight. Here I wish to expand upon the phenomenon that caused Rowbotham's experiment to go awry. Rowbotham was a victim of a superior mirage. When flat-earthers hear this, they normally respond by dismissing this as impossible, because mirages supposedly are inverted images, but Rowbotham saw the boat right side up the entire time. However, this confuses superior and inferior mirages. What is the difference? First we must discuss the physics of light a bit.[797]

Dr. Faulkner implies that while inferior mirages are upside-down, superior mirages are right-side-up. Dr. Faulkner misleadingly states that "since the refraction acts almost continually rather than at one point, superior mirages normally are erect rather than inverted."[798] That statement is not true. Both inferior mirages and superior mirages cause an inversion of the image being miraged. The observed image in a superior mirage hovers upside-down above the actual object. Whereas the opposite effect appears with an inferior mirage; the object is observed to sink below the actual object and appear upside-down. Dr. Faulkner is trying to equate looming with a superior mirage. Looming without inversion is a very rare occurrence.[799] Dr. Faulkner is misleading his readers by suggesting that "superior mirages normally are erect rather than inverted."[800] That is false.

Below is a picture taken by Craig Clements of two superior mirages, one of a ship and another of a smaller white boat.[801] The picture was taken in the Strait of Juan de Fuca just south of the entrance to Victoria Harbour, British Columbia, Canada.[802] Notice that the mirage is inverted upside-down over the ship. That is typical for a superior Mirage.

Figure 21: Superior Mirages of a Large Ship and a Small Boat. Notice that the mirages appear inverted (upside-down) above the actual vessels.

Dr. Faulkner states that "[s]ince temperature inversions are common over water, it is relatively easy to devise experiments in which distant objects beyond the curvature of the earth are visible."[803] Dr. Faulkner claims that demonstrating that the visibility of distant objects over the supposed spherical earth is due to superior mirages is easy. If that were true, one would think that Dr. Faulkner would then demonstrate that easily obtained evidence. But he does not do that.

Dr. Faulkner claims that temperature inversions, with cold air beneath warm air, which cause superior mirages, are common and that such common occurrences are easy to prove. He alleged that the opposite effect of "inferior mirages are far less commonly noticed over water."[804]

The claim by Dr. Faulkner that superior mirages are more prevalent than inferior mirages is refuted by empirical evidence. Professional photographer and mathematics researcher and lecturer at the University of Turku, Finland, Pekka Parviainen,[805] who has been photographing mirages since 1973 and is an expert on inferior and superior mirages, refutes Dr. Faulkner's claim.[806] Parvianen reveals that "[i]nferior mirages are quite common. ... Superior mirages, meanwhile, are much more rare than inferior ones."[807] Parvianen states that in his many years of photographing and studying mirages he has found that "a good superior mirage is a lot harder to detect and to witness than the common inferior mirage."[808]

Dr. Faulkner misleads his readers by averring that the visibility of landmarks that should be below the horizon on a spherical earth are the result of what he claims are commonly occurring upright superior mirages. Dr. Faulkner then proceeds to present his first-hand evidence of an inferior mirage. You read that correctly. Instead of presenting the allegedly easy to present evidence of superior mirages, which Dr. Faulkner claims are the reason for the visibility of distant objects over a spherical earth, Dr. Faulkner presents photographic evidence for inferior mirages.

If upright superior mirages are common occurrences and easy to demonstrate as claimed by Dr. Faulkner, why would Dr. Faulkner not present evidence of upright superior mirages? Because, in fact, superior mirages are rare. And upright superior mirages are even rarer. Thus Dr. Faulkner was not able to observe any. Instead, he presented photographs he took of inferior mirages. That is because inferior mirages are more common occurrences. Pekka Parviainen, who is an expert on mirages, explains that "[a] clear and 'good' superior mirage is far more rare than an inferior mirage."[809] The fact that Faulkner could only observe inferior mirages over water confirms what Pekka Parviainen states and impeaches Faulkner's claim that compared to superior mirages, "inferior mirages are far less commonly noticed over water."[810]

How does Dr. Faulkner explain his failure to show what he alleges to be the common and easily demonstrated upright superior mirage effect? He doesn't; he simply dismisses the images of landmarks over long distances (such as Nowicki's photograph of the Chicago skyline) as superior mirages. He then poses this question: "However, what would happen if one were to repeat this experiment over water that is warmer than the air temperature?"[811] He now is going to show us inferior mirages and claims that he will also show that "a hull disappears from bottom up. Since there is no temperature inversion, the hulls of ships ought to disappear."[812] He claims that he is doing this to avoid the complication of the alleged temperature inversion that causes superior mirages. The real, but unstated, reason is that he could not find any temperature inversion to cause a superior mirage.

Below is a graphic from Georgia State University's Department of Physics and Astronomy that explains what causes an inferior mirage.[813] It illustrates how light refraction causes the inferior mirage to appear upside-down.

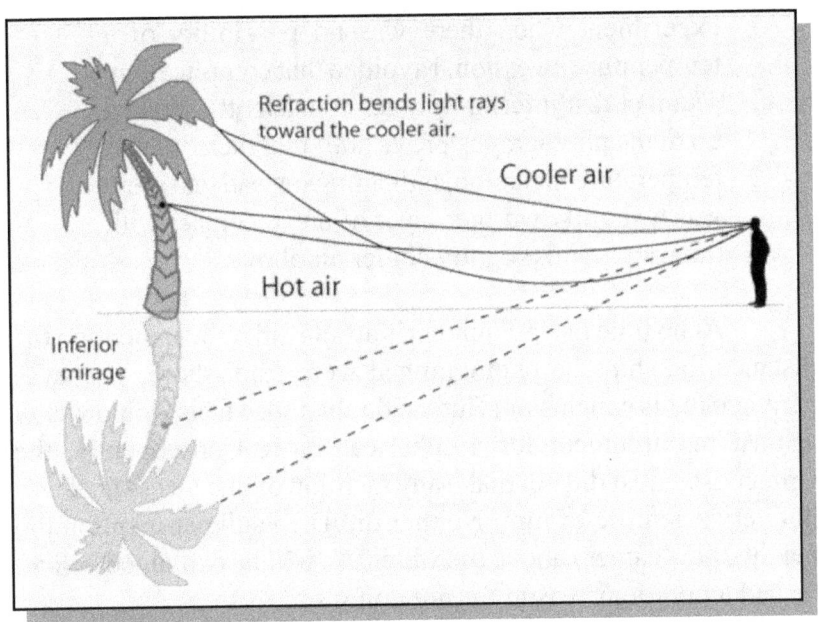

Dr. Faulkner produced a series of photographs that he said he took from the shore of Virginia Beach, Virginia. We will see below, though, that his explanation of what the pictures show does not match what is seen in the pictures. Dr. Faulkner fallaciously concluded:

> These photographs clearly reveal that the hulls of these two ships progressively disappeared as the ships moved farther away. This is consistent with what we would expect if the earth is spherical, but this cannot be explained if the earth is flat. Therefore, this is good evidence that the earth is spherical. The results presented here contradict the many photos on the internet of objects beyond the horizon that supposedly prove that the earth is flat. Those alleged proofs are flawed because they failed to take account of atmospheric refraction due to a temperature inversion. By conducting this

experiment when there was no possibility of a temperature inversion, I avoided that complication. The fact that inferior mirages consistently showed up in the photographs prove [sic] that there was no temperature inversion, indicating instead that there was a slightly warmer layer of air in contact with the water, with slightly cooler air above.[814]

At no time in Dr. Faulkner's article did he ever mention the distance the ships he photographed were from shore. That was germane to his conclusion. But, no doubt, those facts would weigh against his argument for a spherical earth. Consequently, the eminent scientist did not make any mention of distances. That was not very scientific of him. Neither did Dr. Faulkner mention the height of his camera above the water. As will be explained below, he had a nefarious reason for not doing so.

Dr. Faulkner does not tell the reader about an optical effect of light refraction known as the vanishing line. Faulkner did not tell the reader that as objects get further from the observer, light refraction causes a vanishing line to develop. The observer cannot see the area below that vanishing line. Georgia State University's Department of Physics and Astronomy explains that "[p]oints below that 'vanishing line' on the object will not be seen by the observer."[815] This gives the effect of cutting off the bottom of distant objects. Faulkner was not satisfied with the naturally occurring vanishing line, so he enhanced the effect of the vanishing line by progressively lowering his camera in order to artificially raise the vanishing line. He used the elevated vanishing line to cut off the bottom of the hull of the ship so he could argue that the supposed spherical earth caused the bottom-up disappearing hull. That phenomenon of light refraction causing a vanishing line that cuts off the view of the bottom of distant objects is illustrated by Georgia State University (GSU) in the following graphic:

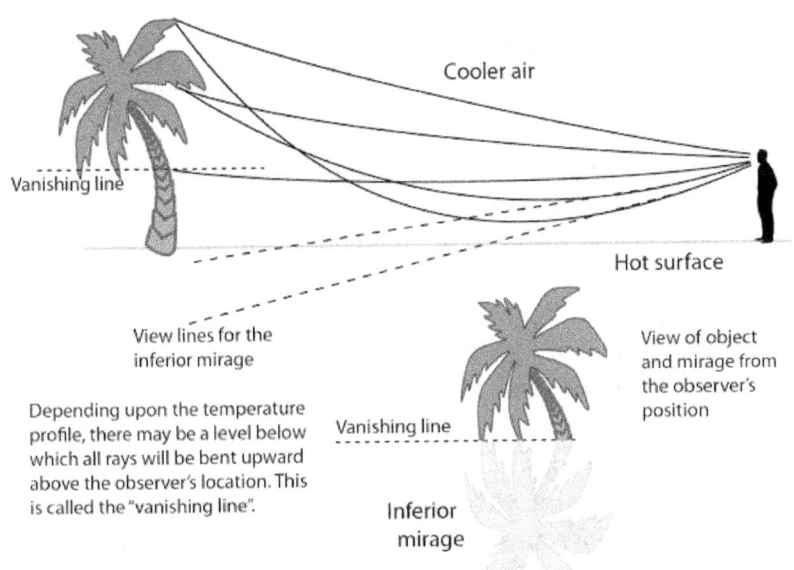

The GSU palm tree diagram illustrates that "[t]he observer can see both the object above the vanishing line and corresponding points in the inferior mirage below that level."[816] The vanishing line phenomenon has the effect of cutting off the bottom of the object in view as well as its inferior mirage. The GSU website illustrates this concept with the following graphic:

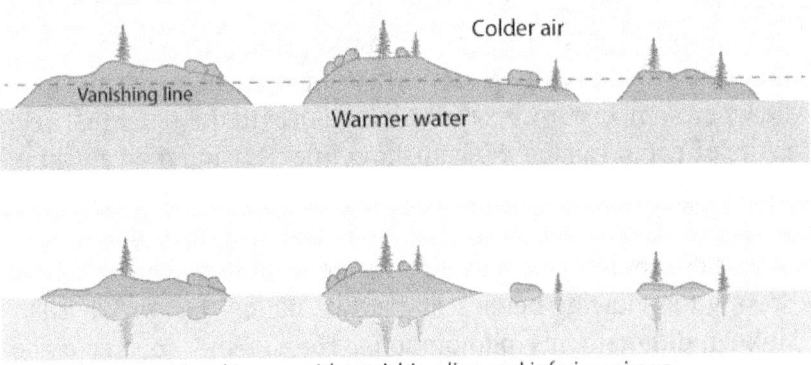

Visual image with vanishing line and inferior mirage

GSU explains what is being depicted in the above graphic as follows:

> The above illustration is patterned after one in Greenler, based on his observations of lakes in northern latitudes. The vanishing line limits the amount of the distant shoreline that is visible, and an inferior mirage is exhibited below the vanishing line. The above illustration shows the inferior mirage at the same vertical scale as the object, but that is not necessarily the case. Greenler notes that the inferior mirage is often vertically compressed. **With a greater viewing distance, the vanishing line will rise so that less of the object is seen. Greenler notes that with a small change in viewing height, like stooping down, a dramatic change in the vanishing line may occur.**[817] (emphasis added)

Notice that GSU reveals two essential points. The first point is that "[w]ith a greater viewing distance, the vanishing line will rise so that less of the object is seen."[818] The second point is "that with a small change in viewing height, like stooping down, a dramatic change in the vanishing line may occur."[819] That means that as an object gets further away, the vanishing line will rise, thus having the effect of cutting off the bottom of the object from view. And when someone lowers the camera closer to the water that also has the effect of raising the vanishing line. Raising the vanishing line causes the bottom of the object to be cut off from view.

GSU points out that the change in the vanishing line by lowering the viewing height can be "dramatic." That is what Dr. Faulkner did with his photographs. He did this to create the dramatic effect of the bottom of the ship disappearing, so he could argue that was evidence of a spherical earth.

As the ship being photographed by Dr. Faulkner got further from shore, light refraction caused the vanishing line to rise. That caused the bottom of the vessel to appear cut off from view. Dr. Faulkner, apparently, was not satisfied with how much of the ship's hull was being cut off by the naturally occurring elevation in the vanishing line as the vessel got further away; so he enhanced that effect by lowering the camera toward the water in each successive photograph as the vessel got further from shore.

Faulkner deceitfully claimed that the bottom of the ship was disappearing due to the curvature of the earth. When, in fact, it was actually due to light refraction that caused an elevation of the vanishing line as the ship got further away. That effect was enhanced by Faulkner's trickery of lowering the camera in each successive photograph.

Dr. Faulkner made no mention that light refraction causes a vanishing line that progressively rises as objects get further away from the observer, which has the effect of making the bottom of the distant object appear to be cut off. Neither did Dr. Faulkner mention that he lowered the camera, which had the effect of further raising the vanishing line. Instead, he misleadingly described the vanishing of the ship's hull in the photos from the bottom up as being due to the curvature of the earth.

Also, lowering the camera height enhances the visibility of the inferior mirage. Pekka Parviainen explains that "[i]nferior mirages are clearly visible near a warm sea surface, but an elevation of as little as a couple of meters may cause the phenomenon to go unnoticed unless you are already familiar with it."[820]

Dr. Faulkner is an expert in physics and astronomy. He has a master's degree in physics and a Ph.D. in astronomy. He studied and taught physics and astronomy for 26 years at the University of South Carolina Lancaster. Indeed, he spent a good deal of his article explaining in detail how light refraction works. He knows light refraction backward and forward. His erroneous conclusions in his article are not from ignorance or misinterpretation. He knew exactly what he was doing. His conclusion was arrived upon before he started his observations.

Dr. Faulkner made no mention of the vanishing line or that he lowered the camera for each successive photograph. He was counting on people not knowing those things. He thought that because of the general ignorance about light refraction that he would be able to get away with his dissimulation. He will soon understand that "nothing is secret, that shall not be made manifest; neither any thing hid, that shall not be known and come abroad." Luke 8:17. In Faulkner's article, he is manifesting three of the abominations that God hates: a lying tongue, a false witness that speaks lies, and a heart that devises wicked imaginations. *See* Proverbs 6:16-19.

Dr. Faulkner is purposely misleading his readers. He mischaracterized upright superior mirages as being common. He claimed that such upright superior mirages are the reason landmarks can be seen from

As the ship gets further away, light refraction causes an inferior mirage and the vanishing line to progressively rise. The rising vanishing line has the effect of cutting off the ship's hull from view, bottom up. The elevation of the apparent horizon in each successive photograph is evidence that the camera is progressively being lowered for each shot. That progressive lowering of the camera toward the water for each successive photo had the effect of boosting the rise of the vanishing line as the ship got further from shore and cutting off more of the ship's hull from view.

long distances. When he could not replicate from the shoreline an upright superior mirage, he went with what actually happens, upside-down inferior mirages.

Dr. Faulkner knows all about the vanishing line phenomenon with inferior mirages, which has the effect of cutting off the bottom of a distant object as well as its inferior mirage. He cunningly used that phenomenon by not mentioning it to his readers and instead argued that the curvature of the earth caused the bottom-up disappearance of the hull. But curvature of the earth did not cause it; the elevation in the vanishing line caused it as the ship got further away from shore and Dr. Faulkner progressively lowered his camera.

Faulkner inadvertently memorialized his crafty trick in his photographs. The pictures he displayed in his article, when laid side-by-side, reveal his trick. The pictures reveal that the apparent horizon rises higher-and-higher in each successive image. That is evidence that Faulkner progressively lowered the camera in each sequential shot. Lowering the camera had the effect of causing the vanishing line to accelerate its rise as the ship got further away. The photographs reveal that Faulkner lowered the camera in each successive camera shot in order to raise the vanishing line and buttress his illusory argument that the ship was disappearing from the bottom up below the curvature of the supposed globular earth. Dr. Faulkner is a cheating pseudo-scientist.

If the earth were truly a sphere, there would be no need for such shenanigans. Lies can only be supported by more lies. The fact that a highly educated scientist must resort to such chicanery can mean only one thing: the spherical earth is a myth.

28 It's All a Matter of Perspective

Dr. Faulkner, in his article, *Flat Earth Proof—Just a Mirage*,[821] which was discussed in the previous chapter, concluded that his observations prove that the earth is a sphere because "the hulls of these two ships progressively disappeared as the ships moved farther away."[822] He provided pictures to verify his conclusion. He maintained that the results he depicted were "consistent with what we would expect if the earth is spherical."[823] He averred that what he displayed "cannot be explained if the earth is flat."[824] Indeed, the effect of the hulls of ships disappearing from the bottom-up is probably the most cited phenomenon by scientists to support the argument that the earth is a sphere.

What Dr. Faulkner is counting on is the general ignorance about perspective. Except in art schools, the laws of perspective are not generally taught. Consequently, the general public is not aware that the scientific community is pulling a fast one on them with the argument that ships disappearing bottom-up proves that the earth is a sphere.

Samuel Rowbotham posits that scientists who argue that the disappearance of the hull of a ship before its masthead is due only to the sphericity of the earth are merely incorporating the assumption of sphericity into their observations. Rowbotham states:

> To argue, for instance, that because the lower part of an outward-bound vessel disappears before the mast-head, the water must be round, is to assume that a round surface only can produce such an effect. But if it can be shown that a simple law of perspective in connection with a plane surface necessarily produces this appearance, the assumption of rotundity is not required, and all the misleading fallacies and confusion involved in or mixed up with it may be avoided.[825]

The observation of the bottom-up disappearance of a ship's hull does not prove sphericity. But that phenomenon is being deceitfully used to confirm a bias toward sphericity. The real explanation for the bottom-up disappearance of a ship's hull is found in the laws of perspective. Ships disappear bottom-up because of where the observer is standing and the limited angular resolution of the human eye.

The size of an object dictates the distance at which an object disappears. For example, a U.S. penny, which is 3/4 (.75) of an inch in diameter, will disappear from a person's vision when it gets to approximately 214 feet away from the observer. At that point, the penny's diameter will have reached one arcminute ($.017°$) which is the maximum angular resolution for a person with 20/20 vision. The larger an object, the further away it can be seen before it disappears from sight. Of course, a large ship at sea can be seen much further away than 214 feet. Indeed, a large ship can be seen for many miles before it reaches a distance where the angular resolution of the ship gets to one arcminute. The little known fact, though, is that the disappearance of the ship will not be uniform.

When looking in the distance, all parallel lines will at some point appear to converge and disappear at eye level. Rowbotham explains this phenomenon:

> If an object be held up in the air, and gradually carried away from an observer who maintains his position, it is true that all its parts will converge to one and the same point--the centre, in relation to which the whole contracts and diminishes.[826]

While this vanishing point takes place at eye level, it is a misconception that all objects that travel away from an observer on a flat plane will be seen to vanish uniformly from top-to-bottom. Samuel Rowbotham explains:

> The theory which affirms that all parallel lines converge to one and the same point on the eye-line, is an error. It is true only of lines equidistant from the eye-line; lines more or less apart meet the eye-line at different distances, and the point at which they meet is that only where each forms the angle of one minute of a degree, or such other angular measure as may be decided upon as the vanishing point. This is the true law of perspective as shown by nature herself; any idea to the contrary is fallacious and will deceive whoever may hold and apply it to practice.[827]

While areas that are equidistant in elevation from the eye level converge at a point at eye level, it seems that objects on the ground or the surface of water that move away from the observer tend to become cut-off from view beginning from the bottom-up. Samuel Rowbotham explains that the "part of any receding body which is nearest to the surface upon which it moves, contracts, and becomes invisible before the parts which are further away from such surface."[828] Rowbotham further states that "[t]he hull of a ship is nearer to the water--the surface on which it moves--than the masthead. Ergo, the hull of an outward bound ship must be the first to disappear."[829]

That phenomenon is particularly noticeable when there is a part of an object close to the surface receding from view that has some distinctive visual characteristic, such as the hull of a ship. That distinctiveness will disappear first from the bottom-up. That is because perspective will cause the surface to rise to the eye level and that distinctive part of the body to become invisible before the whole or any larger part of the same body. That phenomenon, in part, explains a ship's hull's disappearance from the bottom-up. Rowbotham explains:

> But if the same object is placed on the ground, or on a board, as shown in [the] diagram [below], and the lower part made distinctive in shape or color, and similarly moved away from a fixed observer, the same predicate is false. [That predicate being that all its parts will converge to one and the same point--the center in relation to which the whole contracts and diminishes.] In the first case the center of the object is the datum to which every point of the exterior converges; but in the second case the ground or board practically becomes the datum in and towards which every part of the object converges in succession--beginning with the lowest, or that nearest to it.[830]

Rowbotham used the following diagram to illustrate the principle in his book, *Zetetic Astronomy*.[831]

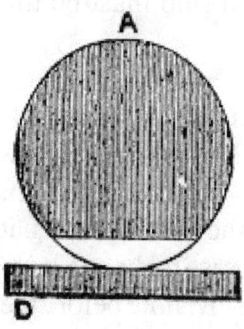  

Rowbotham explains what the above diagram demonstrates. If a "disc is colored black, except a segment of say one inch in depth at the lower edge, on moving it forward the lower segment will gradually disappear, as shown at A, B, and C, in [the above] diagram. If the disc is allowed to rest on a board D, the effect is still more striking. The disc at C will appear perfectly round--the white segment having disappeared."[832] Samuel Rowbotham illustrates that principle further:

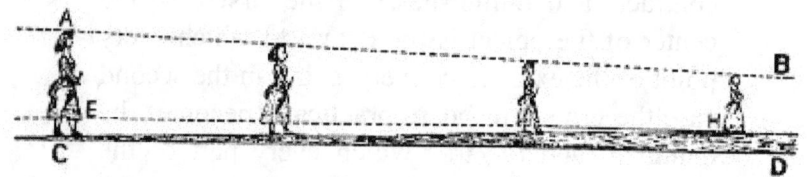

Rowbotham explains the principle of perspective, whereby the woman disappears in a non-uniform manner from the bottom-up as she walks away from the observer on a level surface:

> Send a young girl, with short garments, from C on towards D; on advancing a hundred yards or more (according to the depth of the limbs exposed) the bottom of the frock or longest garment will seem to touch the ground; and on arriving at H, the

488

vanishing point of the lines C, D, and E, H, the limbs will have disappeared, and the upper part of the body would continue visible, but gradually shortening until the line A, B, came in contact with E, H, at the angle of one minute.[833]

Rowbotham lists other examples in his book of observations where a person or object is seen to disappear along a level plane surface due to perspective from the bottom-up:

> A man with light trousers and black boots walking along a level path, will appear at a certain distance as though the boots had been removed and the trousers brought in contact with the ground. On one occasion the author and several friends witnessed a kind of review or special drill of infantry in the open space behind the Horse Guards, at Whitehall. It was in the month of July, and the soldiers had on their summer clothing, all their "nether garments" were white, and when near to them the black well-polished boots were visible to the depth of three or four inches, standing distinctly between the white cloth of the trowsers, and the brown or yellowish gravel and sand of the parade ground. On moving a few hundred feet away, along one of the walks in St. James's Park, the three or four inches depth of black boots subtended an angle at the eye so acute that they were no longer visible, and the almost snow white trowsers of a line of men seemed to be in actual contact with the ground. Every man when turned away or whose back was towards the spectators, seemed to be footless. The effect was remarkable, and formed a very striking illustration of the true law of perspective. After observing the maneuvers for a short time, a party of soldiers were "told off" to relieve guard at St.

James's and Buckingham Palaces, and on following then, down the avenue of the park we again noticed the perspective phenomenon of a line of soldiers marching apparently without feet.

A small dog running along will appear to gradually shorten by the legs, which at a distance, of less than half-a-mile will be invisible, and the body or trunk of the animal will appear to glide upon the earth.

Horses and cattle moving away from a given point upon horizontal ground, will seem to lose their hoofs, and to be walking on the bony extremities or stumps of the limbs.

Carriages similarly receding will seem to lose that portion of the rim of the wheels which touches the earth. The axles also will seem to get lower, and at the distance of one or two miles, according to the diameter of the wheels, the body of the carriage will appear to drag along in contact with the ground.

A young girl, with short garments terminating ten or twelve inches above the feet, will, on walking forward, appear to sink towards the earth, the space between which and the bottom of the frock will appear to gradually diminish, and in the distance of half-a-mile or less the limbs which were first seen for ten or twelve inches will be invisible--the bottom of the garment will seem to touch the ground. The whole body of the girl will, of course, gradually diminish as she recedes, but the depth of the limbs, or the lower part, will disappear before the shoulders and head--as illustrated in [the diagram above].

These instances which are but a few selected from a great number which have been collected, will be sufficient to prove beyond the power of doubt, or the necessity for controversy, that upon a plane or horizontal surface the lowest parts of bodies receding from a given point of observation necessarily disappear before the highest.[834]

That same phenomenon of perspective explains the disappearance of the hull of a ship from the bottom-up. That phenomenon is due to perspective; the supposed sphericity of the earth does not cause it. That can be easily proven by using a telescope. When a telescope is aimed at the distant persons with missing feet, their feet will be seen to reappear. That is evidence that their disappearance is due to perspective rather than to the sphericity of the earth.

There is a complication, though, with the hull of a ship. That complication is the irregularity of the waves. If there are waves or swells in the sea, then the hull of the ship cannot be brought back into view with a telescope because it is blocked behind a wall of water created by waves or a sea swell. To bring the hull of a ship back in view using a telescope, the sea must be relatively calm. Rowbotham explains:

> [A]s already stated in every one of the instances given, except that of the ship at sea, a telescope will restore to view whatever has disappeared to the naked eye. It would be the same in the case of the ship's hull were all the conditions the same. If the surface of the sea had no motion or irregularity, or if it were frozen and therefore stationary and uniform, a telescope of sufficient power to magnify at the distance, would at all times restore the hull to sight. On any frozen lake or canal, notably on the "Bedford Canal," in the county of Cambridge, in

winter and on a clear day, skaters may be observed several miles away, seeming to glide along upon limbs without feet--skates and boots quite invisible to the unaided eye, but distinctly visible through a good telescope. But even on the sea, when the water is very calm, if a vessel is observed until it is just "hull down," a powerful telescope turned upon it will restore the hull to sight. From which it must be concluded that the lower part of a receding ship disappears through the influence of perspective, and not from sinking behind the summit of a convex surface. If not so it follows that the telescope either carries the line of sight through the mass of water, or over its surface and down the other side. This would indeed be "looking round a corner," a power which, nor that of penetrating a dense and extensive medium like water, has never yet been claimed for optical instruments of any kind.

Upon the sea the law of perspective is modified because the leading condition, that of stability in the surface or datum line, is changed. When the surface is calm the/ hull of a vessel can be seen for a much greater distance than when it is rough and stormy. This can easily be verified by observations upon fixed objects at known distances, such as light-ships, light-houses, sea walls, head-lands, or the light-coloured masonry of batteries, such as are built on the coast in many parts of the world.[835]

Rowbotham explains that the variability in the seas causes objects viewed over the sea to be blocked by the waves and swells.

That vessels, lighthouses, light-ships, buoys, signals, and other known and fixed objects are sometimes more distinctly seen than at other times, and are often, from the same common elevation, entirely out of sight when the sea is rough, cannot be denied or doubted by any one of experience in nautical matters.

The conclusion which such observations necessitate and force upon us is, that the law of perspective, which is everywhere visible on land, is modified when observed in connection with objects on or near the sea. But how modified? If the water were frozen and at perfect rest, any object on its surface would be seen again and again as often as it disappeared and as far as telescopic or magnifying power could be brought to bear upon it. But because this is not the case--because the water is always more or less in motion, not only of progression but of fluctuation and undulation, the "swells" and waves into which the surface is broken, operate to prevent the line of sight from passing absolutely parallel to the horizontal water line.[836]

Rowbotham illustrates that phenomenon with another diagram.

If this horizon were formed by the apparent junction of two perfectly stationary parallel lines, it could, as before stated, be penetrated by a telescope of sufficient power to magnify at the distance, however great, to which any vessel had sailed. But because the surface of the sea is not stationary, the line of sight must pass over the horizon, or vanishing point, at an angle at the eye of the observer depending on the amount of "swell" in the water. This will be rendered clear by the following diagram.[837]

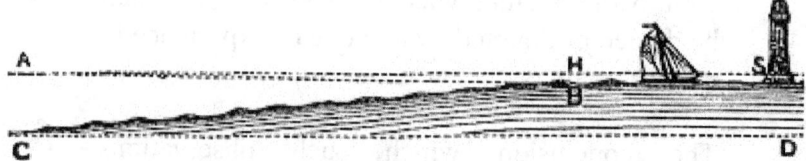

Let C, D, represent the horizontal surface of the water. By the law of perspective operating without interference from any local cause, the surface will appear to ascend to the point B, which is the horizon, or vanishing point to the observer at A; but because the water undulates, the line A, B, of necessity becomes A, H, S, and the angular direction of this line becomes less or greater if the "swell" at H increases or diminishes. Hence when a ship has reached the point H, the horizon; the line of sight begins to cut the rigging higher and higher towards the mast-head, as the vessel more and more recedes. In such a position a telescope will enlarge and render more visible all that part of the rigging which is above the line A, H, S, but cannot possibly restore that part including the hull, which is below it. The waves at the point H, whatever their real magnitude may be, are magnified and rendered more obstructive by the very instrument (the telescope), which is employed to make the objects beyond more plainly visible; and thus the phenomenon is often very strikingly observed, that while a powerful telescope will render the sails and rigging of a ship beyond the horizon H, so distinct that the different kinds of rope can be readily distinguished, not the slightest portion of the hull, large and solid as it is, can be seen. The "crested waters" form a barrier to the horizontal line of sight as substantial as would the summit of an intervening rock. And because the watery barrier is magnified and practically increased by the telescope, the paradoxical condition arises, that the greater the power of the instrument the less can be seen with it.[838]

Added to the phenomenon that an object disappears due to perspective from the bottom-up is the fact that the vanishing point for the bottom of an object can be shortened when the observer lowers his point of observation closer to the water or the ground. Thus, by lowering the position of observation, the disappearance of the bottom of the object can be made to happen at a shorter distance from the observer. That fact is not generally known. The scientific community is able to falsely present the bottom-up disappearance of ship hulls as proof that the earth is a sphere because it is not generally known that over a flat plane, a large object like a ship will disappear from the bottom-up as it gets further away from the observer due to the limited angular resolution of the human eye and the fact that the observer is typically observing the ship at the shore close to the sea level.

This non-uniform disappearance of distant objects is a function of perspective and the angular resolution of the human eye. The vanishing point is determined by the angular resolution of the human eye. When the angular resolution reaches its limit, the object cannot be seen beyond that point. The angular resolution of an eye with 20/20 Snellen acuity is .98 arcminutes.[839] That means that for a person with ordinary eyesight when the viewing angle of the distant object reaches approximately one arcminute (1/60th of one degree, which is .017°), that object will disappear.[840] If the observer is closer to the bottom of the observed object, he will see the bottom of the object be cut off from view first before the top of the object disappears.[841] That is in part because his eyes are closer to the bottom of the object, which causes the limit of his angular resolution (one arcminute) to occur for the bottom of the object before the limit of his angular resolution is reached for the top of the object.

Samuel Rowbotham illustrated this principle in his book, *Zetetic Astronomy*.

> In a long row of lamps, standing on horizontal ground, the pedestals, if short, gradually diminish until at a distance of a few hundred yards they seem to disappear, and the upper and thinner parts of the lamp posts appear to touch the ground, as shown in the following diagram.[842]

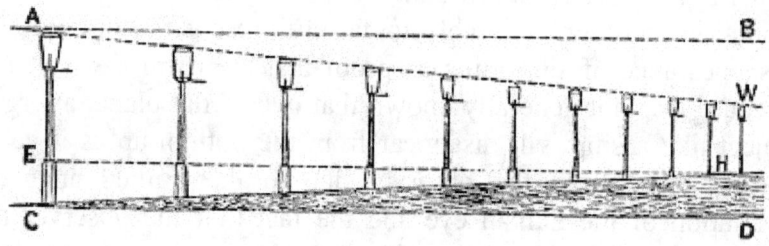

The observer's eye is at point E. Since the distance between point C and point E is less than the distance between point E and point A, the vanishing point (one arcminute) at point H for the pedestals on the lamp is reached much earlier than the vanishing point for the entire height of the lamp posts. The pedestals are seen to disappear from the bottom up. That is not due to the sphericity of the earth, but rather it is due to perspective. Rowbotham explains:

> The lines A, B, and C, D, represent the actual depth or length of the whole series of lamps, as from C to A. An observer placing his eye a little to the right or left of the point E, and looking along the row

will see that each succeeding pedestal appears shorter than the preceding, and at a certain distance the line C, D, will appear to meet the eye-line at H--the pedestals at that point being no longer visible, the upper portion of each succeeding lamp just appears to stand without pedestal. At the point H where the pedestals disappear the upper portions of the lamps seem to have shortened considerably, as shown by the line A, W, but long after the pedestals have entered the vanishing point, the tops will appear above the line of sight E, H, or until the line A, W, meets the line E, H, at an angle of one minute of a degree. A row of lamps such as that above described may be seen in York Road, which for over 600 yards runs across the south end of Regent's Park, London.[843]

When a person is closer to the water when watching a tall ship sail into the distance, he will observe the bottom of the ship disappear first due to perspective. That is because the observer is closer to the water and so the vanishing point of one arcminute (1/60th of a degree) over the water is reached before the vanishing point for the mast of the ship is reached.[844] The diagram below illustrates that principle.

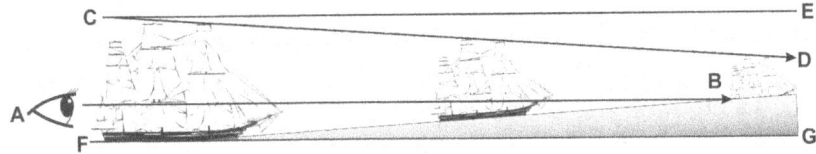

The lines C, E, and F, G, represent the distance the ship has sailed away from the observer. The distance between point F and point C is the actual height of the ship. The line A, B, represents the line of sight of the observer. The hull gradually disappears as the ship gets further away until it is cut off entirely at the vanishing point indicated by point B. The law of perspective causes the surface of the water to appear to ascend towards the eye level, meeting it at point B, which is the horizon. The ship appears to ascend the inclined plane F, B; the hull is gradually disappearing as the ship gets further away until it vanishes altogether when arriving at point B (the horizon). The hull of the ship disappears first before the masthead at that point because it has shrunk vertically to less than one arcminute.

The ship continues to shrink in size as the law of perspective causes both the masthead and the bottom of the ship to shrink in degrees as it gets further away. The line C, D, represents the gradual descent of the masthead due to perspective as the ship gets further away. The vessel will not wholly disappear until line C, D, drops to the waterline and the angle at C, D, A, reaches one arcminute, which is the angular resolution limit for man's vision.

The reason that the hull of the ship disappears first over the flat earth is that is the characteristic of perspective and the observer being closer to the water than he is to the top of the ship enhances that effect. The observer in the above diagram is at a height indicated by the distance between the points A, F. The distance between the points A, C, is much greater. Because the distance between the points A, F, is so much shorter, the hull of the ship reaches the vanishing point much earlier. That is because of perspective, which is enhanced by the observer being closer to the water. And thus as perspective causes the water to rise up to the vanishing point, the bottom of the ship disappears. The vanishing point for the hull of the ship is when the angle at point A, B, F reaches one arcminute (1/60th of a degree).

The ability to see an object as it gets further away is limited by perspective. An ordinary person cannot see a point in the distance that is at an angle of less than one arcminute. There are 60 arcminutes to each degree of an angle. One arcminute is 1/60th of a degree. When the base of a triangle is shorter, the point at which the subtended (opposite) angle reaches one arcminute (the vanishing line) happens at a shorter distance. That is why the hull of a ship is seen to gradually disappear first. The disappearance of the ship's hull has nothing to do with the earth being a sphere. It is entirely due to perspective. The entire ship will ultimately disappear when line C, D, meets point B at an angle of one arcminute (1/60th of a degree). When that happens, there will be a vanishing point formed and the entire ship will disappear.

Dr. Faulkner, in his article, *Flat Earth Proof—Just a Mirage*, which was discussed in the previous chapter, used a very powerful "3.5-inch Questar telescope, having a 1,200-mm focal length"[845] to take the pictures displayed in his article. Even with the telescopic lens, there comes a point where the hull of the ship is cut off as it reaches a vanishing point. The telescopic lens extends the vanishing point further in the distance. The vessel in Dr. Faulkner's photographs was not far enough away to form the subtended angle to reach the vanishing point with his telescopic lens. Even if he waited for the ship to get further enough away to approach the limits of the angular resolution using the telescopic lens, the resolution of the pictures would be obscured by the density of the atmosphere, causing partial extinction of the ship. The resulting pictures would prove nothing. That was a problem for Dr. Faulkner. But he had a trick up his sleeve.

When Dr. Faulkner used his telescopic lens to zoom in on the ship in the distance, it brought back the ship and its hull into view. The waves on the water were not sufficiently high to obscure the hull. And, furthermore, the vanishing line from the inferior mirage was not sufficiently high to cut off the hull from view to the degree that Dr. Faulkner hoped to bolster his argument that the earth is a sphere. What Dr. Faulkner saw actually proved that the ship was disappearing due to perspective and light refraction. That was what could be expected over a flat earth. Dr. Faulkner could not allow that to be presented because it was consistent with a flat earth.

What was Dr. Faulkner to do? He did what an illusionist does. A lie cannot be proven true with actual evidence, it must be covered by more lies. And so Dr. Faulkner had to cover the lie of a globular earth with illusory evidence that he dishonestly portrayed as legitimate proof. Without informing his readers, he factitiously enhanced the effect of the ship's hull disappearing due to light refraction in the pictures by sequentially lowering the camera closer to the water.

Dr. Faulkner used the gradual elevation of the light refraction vanishing line caused by his sequential lowering of the camera to misleadingly portray the hull of the ship as disappearing from sight due to the rotundity of the earth. It was necessary for Dr. Faulkner to gradually lower the camera for each sequential photograph to give the effect of the hull being cut off from the bottom-up, as he argued would be expected on a spherical earth. As Dr. Faulkner lowered the camera, the vanishing line from the light refraction was elevated, which gave the appearance of the ship rapidly disappearing from the bottom-up.

Dr. Faulkner's article is scientific disinformation. The disappearance of the hull of the vessel from the bottom-up was, in fact, over the flat surface of the water and not over a curved horizon. Its disappearance was entirely due to the laws of perspective combined with light refraction as Dr. Faulkner lowered his camera. Dr. Faulkner speciously portrayed the bottom-up disappearance of the vessel's hull as being due to the supposed sphericity of the earth, when it was actually due to his camera trickery. Dr. Faulkner was not merely engaging in confirmation bias; he was performing confirmation deception.

29 Swindle At Bedford Canal

Dr. Danny Faulkner is one in a long and broad line of scientific con artists who use tricks to beguile the unwary. Oddly, Faulkner finds common ground in his methods with the progenitor of the theory of evolution, Alfred Russel Wallace. Faulkner is a creationist, which puts him at direct odds with Wallace, but they agree regarding heliocentrism. Interestingly, they both have a history of using trickery to support their lying philosophy of heliocentrism to make it look like it is based upon valid science.

Many ascribe the theory of evolution to Charles Darwin. But Charles Darwin based his famous writings about the origin of species through evolution by natural selection on the theory first propounded by a fellow of the Royal Geographic Society of London, Alfred Russel Wallace. Wallace first contacted Darwin and presented a paper to him that delineated his theory on natural selection as the basis for evolution.[846] Darwin then allied with Wallace and introduced to the world the first iteration of the theory of the origin of species through evolution by natural selection in a jointly authored paper, which was published in the *Journal of the Proceedings of the Linnean Society* in August 1858.[847] Ironically, in 1890, the Royal Society honored Alfred Russel Wallace the "Darwin Medal" for his "**Independent** Organization of the Theory of the Origin of Species by Natural Selection."[848] (emphasis added).

Wallace was not only instrumental in foisting on the masses the myth of evolution as though it is science, he was also the man who fraudulently established that water is convex. Until the modern age that has brought the alleged manned space missions where the world was presented with phony photographs of the spherical earth, it had been taught in schools that Alfred Russel Wallace proved that water is convex and thus the earth is a sphere.[849] That so-called scientific proof is, in actuality, based upon a fraud perpetrated by Wallace that took place at the Bedford Canal.

The theories of heliocentrism and evolution are both devil-inspired attacks on the authority of God and his Holy Bible. They have gained hegemony in the minds of men because they have been mischaracterized as being based on science. But they are, in reality, evil religious superstitions that are masquerading as science. They are more spiritual deceptions than they are scientific deceptions. As such, it should come as no surprise then to find at the forefront of the transformation of heathen religious belief of evolution into a scientific theory a spiritualist (Alfred Russel Wallace) who spent his adult life in communion with the devil. The theory of evolution was conjured from the mind of a sorcerer.

Alfred Russel Wallace was not a man of science; he was a man of superstition. He was a necromancer who eschewed Christianity.[850] Wallace often consulted with clairvoyants, engaged in seances with mediums, and contacted evil spirits in the form of ghostly apparitions.[851] Wallace acknowledged that "these [spiritual] phenomena have had a very important influence both on my character and my opinions."[852] He stated in his autobiography: "I found that I had considerable mesmeric power myself, and could produce all the chief phenomena on some of my patients."[853] Wallace authored a book titled *The Scientific Aspects of the*

Supernatural.[854] What does God think of Wallace's divination? "[A]ll that do these things are an abomination unto the LORD."

> There shall not be found among you any one that maketh his son or his daughter to pass through the fire, or that useth divination, or an observer of times, or an enchanter, or a witch, Or a charmer, or a consulter with familiar spirits, or a wizard, or a necromancer. **For all that do these things are an abomination unto the LORD**: and because of these abominations the LORD thy God doth drive them out from before thee. (Deuteronomy 18:10-12)

Alfred Russel Wallace was a socialist.[855] But more pertinently, he was a warlock acting under the guise of a scientist. A warlock is one who practices the dark arts of witchcraft, such as a conjurer or a sorcerer.[856] When looking at the etymology of warlock we find that it describes one who is in league with the devil and is an oath-breaker, liar, and deceiver.[857] It is no surprise then that we find that Alfred Russel Wallace engaged in all manner of deception in support of the science-fiction that the earth is a spinning sphere. Godless evolution requires heliocentricity as its foundational premise. If heliocentrism falls so also will the theory of evolution. Thus the progenitor of the theory of evolution, Alfred Russel Wallace, was all too happy to jump in and do his part to deviously buttress heliocentrism as a scientific fact.

A man named John Hampden read the book, *Zetetic Astronomy*, by Samuel Rowbotham. Hampden was convinced that the earth is flat. He corresponded in writing with Rowbotham. Hampden was a man who had an acerbic and confrontational manner. He wrote local papers fiercely denouncing the Newtonian system. His published writings were sprinkled with epithets. Rowbotham tried to calm Hampden and persuade him to take a more tactful approach that would be more conducive to educating his audience. But it was to no avail.[858] Hampden was impetuous and determined to denounce the lies of science and prove them false. He decided to publish a challenge via a wager of £500 against anyone who could prove that the surface of water is convex as required by the theory that the earth is a globe. The problem with Hampden was that he was ill-equipped for the task. While he had zeal, he lacked knowledge.

None other than Alfred Russel Wallace answered Hampden's challenge. Each party was to have a referee. It would have been ideal for Hampden to have a referee who was an expert in the field to advocate for his interests. Samuel Rowbotham, with whom Hampden had already corresponded, would naturally come to mind. But Hampden did not contact Rowbotham, who was capable of ensuring that there was no skulduggery from the challenger. Rowbotham wrote after the event about his frustration in not being contacted by Hampden:

> I wrote enquiring as to the nature of the experiments to be made and the place and time and persons concerned in the matter; but could get no information. I was kept in entire ignorance of the whole affair until it was over. I could not but feel that this was altogether injudicious on the part of Mr. Hampden and his referee, Mr. Carpenter; and very unfair both to myself and to the public. Common justice ought to have suggested to them that no such attempt to settle so important a matter without an invitation to the author to be present. More especially should this have been done when it is known that both Mr. Hampden and Mr. Carpenter were literary, and not scientific gentlemen. They knew little or nothing of the nature of the instruments employed in the experiments and became literally helpless victims of their more philosophical opponents. What could

be more unwise than for Mr. Hampden to deposit the sum £500 against the same amount by Wallace, and to allow Mr. Wallace to dictate his own experiment and to use and manipulate his own instruments? In such a procedure, common sense and practical justice were ignored.[859]

The challenge stated that if Wallace proved convexity of water, he would be the winner. The agreement allowed for each party to have a referee, and the referees were required to agree on the results of the experiments and decide the winner. If the referees could not agree, then they had the option of submitting the matter to an umpire, the appointment of which each would agree. Without the agreement of both parties, no umpire could be appointed.

Alfred Russel Wallace chose as his referee the publisher of *The Field* magazine, John Henry Walsh. John Hampden chose as his referee, William Carpenter, who was a journeyman printer and author, who had no science background. They met to conduct the first experiments at Bedford Canal on March 2, 1870. Shortly after the first tests were set up, they were considered to be inconclusive regarding the issue of convexity. Immediately after those first tests, Walsh announced that he had to leave and return to London to finish work on that Saturday's issue of *The Field*.[860]

Walsh knew full well his publishing schedule when he agreed to take the role as a referee. The Saturday publication of the magazine of which he was the publisher did not take him by surprise. Walsh arrived at the Bedford Canal on Tuesday evening, March 1, 1870, and decided to leave by the next day, Wednesday, March 2, 1870, after he had witnessed the results of the initial experiments. That quick change of heart is quite suspicious. Apparently, he decided he no longer wanted to be the referee for Wallace. Perhaps the initial results were not as inconclusive as first reported, and Walsh saw the writing on the wall, that the experiments would confirm that water is flat. Perchance he wanted no part of having to confirm that there was no convexity to the water and thus the earth is flat. Walsh was replaced as Wallace's referee by a local surgeon, Martin W. B. Coulcher. That was the beginning of the shenanigans that spelled doom for the truth.

The fact is that water at rest is everywhere flat and level. The only thing that modern science can do is to use trickery to make it appear that the water is convex. That is what Wallace hoped to do. He knew the unique characteristics of surveying equipment, which are not known by the general public. How did he come to that knowledge? A little known fact that has been concealed from the public is that in 1837 Alfred Russel Wallace "became an apprentice in the surveying business of his eldest brother, William."[861] He spent eight (8) years surveying the countryside, which is how he developed his enthusiasm as a naturalist. He knew all of the quirks of a surveyor's level. And he used that knowledge to bamboozle Hampden, Carpenter, and the general public.

One quirk of a surveyor's level is that the lens in the telescope will cause light to refract in such a way as to cause distant landmarks to drop below the horizontal cross-hair of the telescope. That drop below the horizontal cross-hair of a telescopic level is a characteristic of a surveyor's level that was known to Wallace. He planned to use that knowledge to trick Hampden, Carpenter, and the public.

Even when a telescope is set up perfectly level, the lens in the telescope will refract light in such a way as to cause distant landmarks to drop below the cross-hair that bisects the center of the instrument lens. The further the distance the more the error caused by the collimation of the light passing through the lens. This author explained this concept in *The Greatest Lie on Earth (Expanded Edition)* when describing the trickery of geodesic surveyor Jesse Kozlowski in his effort to present false evidence of the earth's convexity. Samuel Rowbotham explained what happens when light travels through the lens of a telescope or a surveyor's theodolite at great distances:

> In all the experiments in which I have been thus engaged I have been able to state beforehand—to predicate, what appearances would be observed in the field of view, and in almost every instance have satisfied the operators that what they saw was simply the admitted unavoidable peculiarities of the instruments, and not indications of the earth's rotundity. So important is this explanation that I deem it right to offer to the reader a simple demonstration. Let him find a piece of ground – a terrace, a promenade, line of railway, or embankment, which shall be perfectly horizontal for, say, five hundred yards. Let a signal staff five feet hight be erected at one end, and a theodolite or spirit-level fixed and carefully adjusted to exactly the same altitude at the other end. The top of the signal will then be seen a little *below* the cross-hair, although it has the *same actual altitude* and stands upon the same horizontal foundation.[862] (italics in original)

Rowbotham explained that if one looks along a level plane at the horizon he will see the horizon along his line of sight. If, however, that same person were to look through a perfectly level theodolite at that same horizon, the horizon will no longer be along the line of sight but will appear some distance below the horizontal cross-hair on the lens of the theodolite. Rowbotham illustrated that phenomenon by looking through a perfectly level tube with no lens or any glass of any kind in it at the horizon (Fig. 4) and comparing that to looking at the same horizon from the same point through a perfectly level surveyor's telescope. When looking through the telescope of a surveyor's level, the sea-horizon will appear considerably below the cross-hair that bisects the center of the telescope lens (Fig. 5).

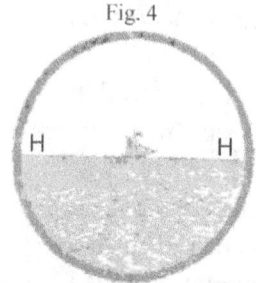
Fig. 4

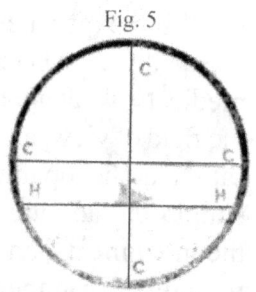
Fig. 5

H H in Fig, 4 is the sea-horizon as seen through a level tube without any lens or glass of any kind. In Fig. 4, the surface of the water appears at the center of the field of view. Points C C C C in Fig. 5 indicate the outer points of the horizontal and vertical cross-hairs in the telescopic lens of a surveyor's level. The sea-horizon at H H appears below the horizontal cross-hair, C C, that bisects the center of the lens.

Samuel Rowbotham explained that the reason for the drop in the apparent horizon below the horizontal cross-hair has nothing to do with the earth being a sphere and everything to do with the light collimating as it passes through the telescope lens.

Even today, that same phenomenon can be experienced with modern theodolites. The Oregon (USA) Department of Transportation explains that "differential leveling is the process used to determine a difference in elevation between two points."[863] Wallace's measurement of the vertical heights of markers at different distances is similar in concept to differential leveling. Section 3.7.6.2.1 B 3 of the New Jersey (USA) Surveying Manual requires that when conducting differential leveling "[s]ight distances should never exceed 75 meters (250 feet)."[864] The reason for that is that the error caused by the collimation of the lens on the theodolite will render the readings inaccurate beyond 250 feet.

Wallace kept up the charade that objects never drop below the cross-hair on a telescopic level. In his 1905 autobiography, Wallace offered the following explanation to the public of the how the surveyor's telescope worked at the Bedford Canal:

> For those who do not understand the use of a level, it may be necessary to explain that the cross-hair in the optical axis of the telescope marks the true level of any object at a distance with regard to the telescope. Any point that is seen above the cross-hair is above the level, any point seen below the cross-hair is below the level, and in the latter case the line from the telescope to it slopes downwards. To show this "true level" is the whole purpose of the instrument called a surveyor's level, and it does show it with wonderful accuracy. The mere fact, therefore, that the top disc on the pole was apparently more below the cross-hair than the two discs were apart, proved that the surface of the water was not flat, or continuously extended in a straight line.[865]

Wallace's explanation sounds logical, but it is a lie. Wallace spent years as a surveyor using surveyor's levels and so he knew what he was saying was not true. He knew full well that a surveyor's level is only accurate for determining vertical elevation at short distances. When the distance of the observation gets beyond 250 feet light refraction through the lens of the telescope will cause the distant object to progressively drop below the horizontal cross-hair. When looking at an object that is between three and six miles distance the drop below the horizontal cross-hair will be extreme. Wallace was counting on the general ignorance of that fact to pull the wool over the eyes of the public.

Geodetic surveyors, even today, use that trick to try to prove that the earth is a sphere. They argue that the drop in the horizon below the horizontal cross-hair is due to the curvature of the earth. For example, geodetic surveyor Jesse Kozlowski presented a theodolite image showing the horizontal cross-hair on his theodolite above the horizon.[866] Kozlowski represented the picture as being a picture through a perfectly horizontal theodolite looking over the ocean. His argument was that the horizon of the ocean being below the theodolite cross-hairs shows the drop due to the curvature of the earth. The drop in the apparent horizon has nothing to do with the curvature of the earth. It is due to a combination of refraction by the theodolite lenses and atmospheric refraction. This causes the apparent horizon to drop.

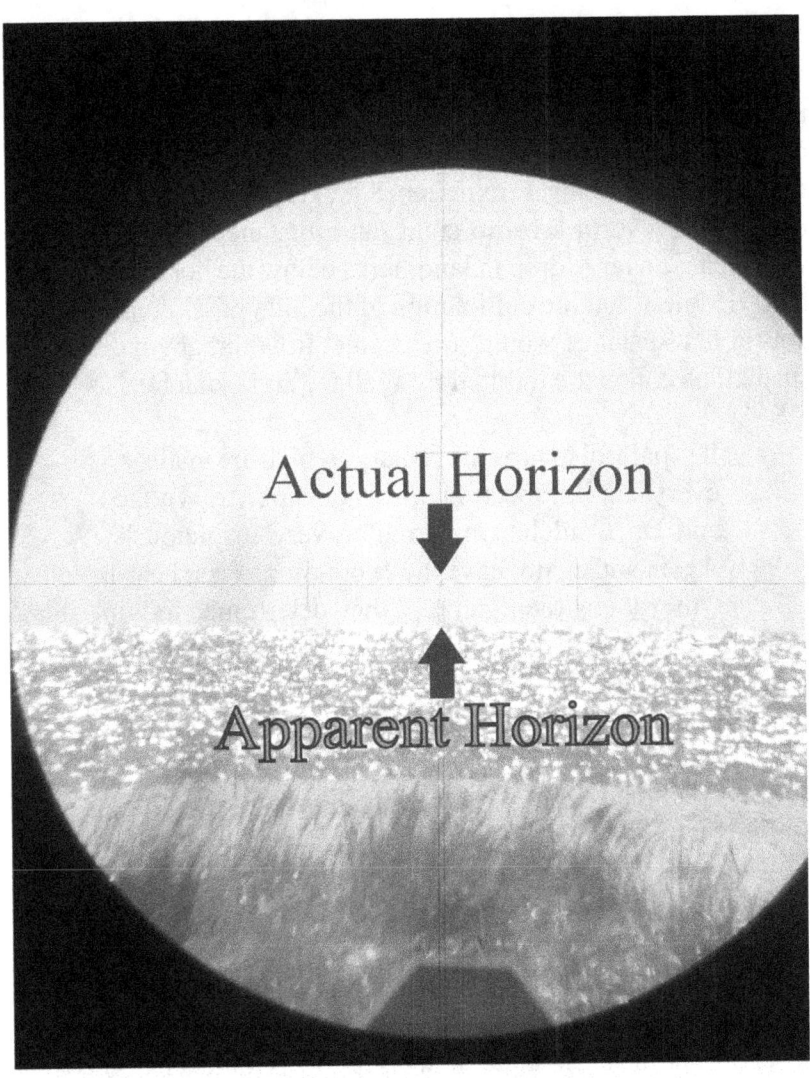

This picture was taken by Geodetic Surveyor Jesse Kozlowski, which he stated was of the ocean horizon from a horizontally level theodolite. Kozlowski alleges that the drop in the horizon below the horizontal cross-hairs is because the earth is a sphere. It is actually due to a combination of atmospheric refraction and theodolite lens refraction. Indeed, you can see the bowed beach shore caused by the theodolite lens refraction. The horizontal line on the theodolite shows where the actual horizon is located.

That is the trick that Wallace tried to employ. Wallace used the surveyor's level to sight in far excess of 250 feet. Indeed, the distances were measured in increments of three miles, totaling six miles. Wallace, being an experienced surveyor, knew full well that using a surveyor's level to sight out a distance of six (6) miles would cause a large drop in landmarks below the horizontal cross-hair. He knew that the collimation of the light passing through the lens at that distance would be extreme. Rowbotham explains the suspicious conduct exhibited by Wallace and Coulcher:

> It is painful to hear the remarks which are made, on every hand, respecting the conduct of Mr. Wallace and Dr. Coulcher in acting so very suspiciously. Again and again, have the expressions been heard, " they knew their game," "they determined to win the money, and 'cooked their case' accordingly." Their having thus acted has certainly rendered it difficult to defend them. The thought of such scientific gentlemen having been actuated by any other than the most honorable motives ought not to be tolerated: yet from their strangely unscientific procedure the suspicion is not unnatural.[867]

On March 5, 1870, sightings were taken along the Bedford Canal. The parties agreed on what was seen through the telescope of the surveyor's level. But they did not agree on what the observations meant. Wallace and his referee, Coulcher, argued that the sightings proved that water is convex, whereas Hampden and his referee, Carpenter, argued that the sightings showed that the water was flat and there was no convexity to it. Below are the sketches as later published in *The Field* and republished in *The Earth Not a Globe Review*.[868] Both sketches were drawn by Carpenter and attested by the referee for Wallace, Coulcher, as being correct. Please note that the telescope caused the images to appear upside-down, and so that is how the images were drawn.

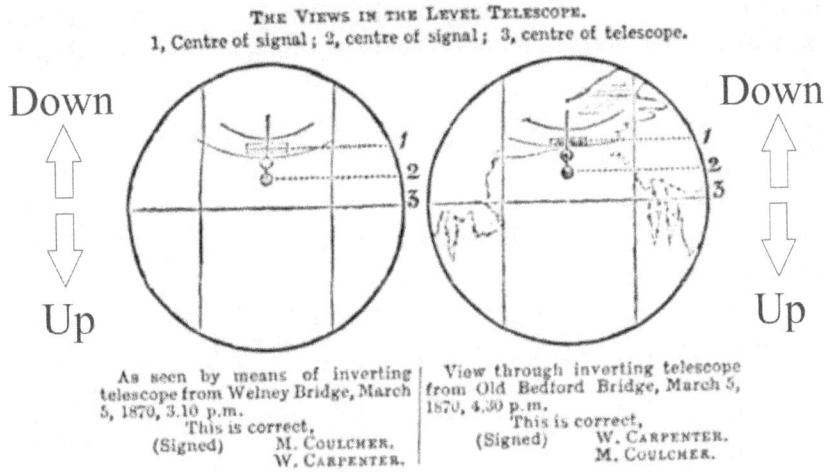

THE VIEWS IN THE LEVEL TELESCOPE.
1, Centre of signal; 2, centre of signal; 3, centre of telescope.

As seen by means of inverting telescope from Welney Bridge, March 5, 1870, 3.10 p.m.
This is correct,
(Signed) M. COULCHER.
W. CARPENTER.

View through inverting telescope from Old Bedford Bridge, March 5, 1870, 4.30 p.m.
This is correct,
(Signed) W. CARPENTER.
M. COULCHER.

The diagrams prepared by Carpenter, and agreed to by the other parties, accurately depicted what was seen in the telescope. They show the bridge and the markers at the top, above the horizontal cross-hair of the telescope. In actuality, since the image is upside-down, the bridge and markers were below the horizontal cross-hair. Carpenter was ecstatic because he immediately perceived that the diagrams proved that the water could not be convex and must be flat.

> As far as Carpenter was concerned, it was all settled. The equal apparent distances between the crosshair, the center signal, and the distant bridge proved that the three points lay in a straight line![869]

After the experiments were concluded at the Bedford Canal on Saturday, March 5, 1870, "Hampden accosted Wallace and demanded that he admit he had lost. Wallace did not reply."[870] Wallace spent the next day brooding because he knew that the diagrams depicted a flat canal and hence a flat earth.[871] "On Sunday evening, Carpenter and Hampden met with Wallace and

Coulcher to discuss the events of the previous day. Wallace was more communicative, but he was obviously not in a good mood, and his nerves were on edge."[872] Wallace realized that he had lost the wager. But he and Coulcher had a few tricks up their sleeves to snatch a false victory from the jaws of a real defeat.

The referees, Carpenter and Coulcher, could not agree about the meaning of what was depicted in the telescope. Wallace, therefore, advocated that an umpire should be appointed to resolve the conflict. Carpenter smelled a rat and refused to allow an umpire.[873] But Hampden imprudently suggested, of all people, John Henry Walsh to be the umpire.[874] Recall that it was John Henry Walsh that was the referee for Alfred Russel Wallace. Thus, the matter was sent to a biased umpire to decide. That umpire had already held a position of advocate for Wallace. His duty as a referee for Wallace was to look out for the interests of Wallace. Under any circumstances, that is improper and calls into question the objectivity of the umpire's ruling. It should come as no surprise that Walsh ruled in favor of Wallace. Walsh rendered his ruling on March 18, 1870.[875] He published his decision in the March 26, 1870 edition of *The Field*.[876] Before Walsh rendered his final ruling, he sent the diagrams to an optician to obtain his opinion. William Carpenter explains what happened:

> In London, the evidence was referred to Mr. Solomon, optician; but this gentleman had nothing to do with it: he entrusted it to his assistant! This assistant, when appealed to by the writer [William Carpenter], informed him that he had the papers "for an hour or two;" that he didn't sit up all night over them and that, "taking into consideration the theory of the earth's rotundity, he certainly did give it as his opinion that, if anything had been proved, it was that the water was curved." But this gentleman was soon convinced that he had made a mistake. He went to Mr. Walsh, the umpire, and

begged him to defer the printing of his decision in his paper, *The Field*, until he gave a better report. But the editor would not! The decision was published; and a more glaringly inaccurate statement it is hard to conceive possible for an editor to make.[877]

That is simply astounding! The very expert whose opinion Walsh relied on to render his opinion that Wallace had won the wager and proved that water is convex told him before Walsh published his opinion in his magazine that the expert optician made a mistake. Walsh ignored the pleas of his own expert. He published an article that he knew was wrong.

Why did the optician change his mind and realize he was wrong in his initial opinion? Because he met with Carpenter, who explained to him the meaning of the depiction of the telescope images in the diagram. The optician reexamined the diagrams in light of what Carpenter explained. He realized that Carpenter was correct. The diagrams proved that the water in the Bedford Canal is flat and show no convexity whatsoever.

Samuel Rowbotham explains that when observations made with a level telescope are compared with observations made through a level tube with no lens in it one can see that the lenses in the telescope cause the apparent horizon to drop in elevation.

> The practical observer cannot fail to be satisfied that when distant objects are seen below the cross-hair of an optical instrument like the spirit-level, the cause is simply aberrance of light or "wandering" of the eve-line from the true line, or axis of vision, in passing through the glasses or lenses of the telescope: and not because really depressed in consequence of declination or curvature from the line-of-sight. Hence, such

appearances are entirely out of place and valueless in connection with the subject of the earth's true form and magnitude.[878]

When those facts were brought to the attention of the optician, and he realized his error, he must have concluded that the drop below the horizontal cross-hair of the bridge and markers in the Bedford Canal diagrams was due to the effects of the light collimating as it passed through the telescope and not the curvature of the water. Rowbotham explains:

> [W]hat was seen on the Bedford Canal by Messrs. Hampden, Wallace, Carpenter and Coulcher, was not the convexity of standing water, but telescopic aberration, and instrumental "error of collimation."[879]

Indeed, the diagrams themselves, which were attested by all observers to be accurate replications of the observations, prove that the effect of the horizon drop is due to light collimating through the telescopic lenses. Furthermore, the diagrams prove that the water on the canal was flat and level. The optician realized this and pleaded with Walsh to defer printing his conclusion until he could correct his mistake and more thoroughly and accurately explain what the diagrams show. Walsh knew full well what that meant, and he was not about to allow his own expert to say that the diagrams proved that there was no convexity to water and hence the earth is flat. So he did what any prejudiced scoundrel would do; he printed a false conclusion.

When looking at the Bedford Canal diagram, we find points 1, 2, and 3. Point 3 is the horizontal cross-hair of the telescope. Point 2 is the middle of the topmost disc that was in the water at a distance of three miles from the telescope. Point 1 is the middle of the markers on the two bridges that were 6 miles distance in opposite directions from the point of observation. The diagram on the left is of the view of Old Bedford Bridge through the telescope taken from Welney Bridge. The diagram on the right is of Welney Bridge through the telescope taken from Bedford Bridge.

The pictures show an oblong signal 6ft. by 3ft. that was placed on Old Bedford Bridge. The center of that signal was 13ft. 4in. above the water. At three miles distance along the canal a staff was erected, having a red disc of wood 1ft. in diameter affixed thereto. There was a second signal that was placed precisely 4 feet below the top signal (9 ft. 4 in. above the water). That lower signal was a remnant from a previous test. But in the end, it helped establish a gauge for deciphering the drop due to light collimation through the telescope lens. The center of the disc was also 13ft. 4in. above the water. And on Welney Bridge, three miles further, a third signal was placed, reaching the top of the bridge, 13ft. 4in. likewise above the water.[880]

James Naylor examined the diagrams and prepared a detailed analysis wherein he concluded that the diagrams prove that the Bedford Canal is flat. There was no convexity to the water at all.[881] He was able to deduce that the diagrams showed at the 3-mile distance a drop of 6 feet in the round signals, which is about what would be expected if the earth were a sphere. But the diagrams show that the bridge signals dropped only 12 feet at 6 miles. The equidistant drop between points 1, 2, and 3 indicates that there is a straight line between the telescope (point 3), the circular signals at the three-mile mark (point 2), and the bridge signals at the six-mile mark (point 1). There was a 6-foot drop between point 3 and point 2. And there was an equal 6-foot drop between point 2 and point 1. If the water were convex, as supposed under the spherical earth model, the bridge signals should have dropped at an exponentially higher rate of 8 inches per mile squared. That means that after six miles, the bridge should have fallen in elevation 24 feet (8 inches $\times$ 6^2 = 24 feet).[882] Instead, the drop was only 12 feet. The fact that the decline was only a total of

12 feet from point 3 to point 1 (and only 6 feet from point 2 to point 1) meant that the drop was due to the collimation of light passing through the lens. When correcting for that collimation, only one conclusion could be reached, the water on the Bedford Canal was flat.

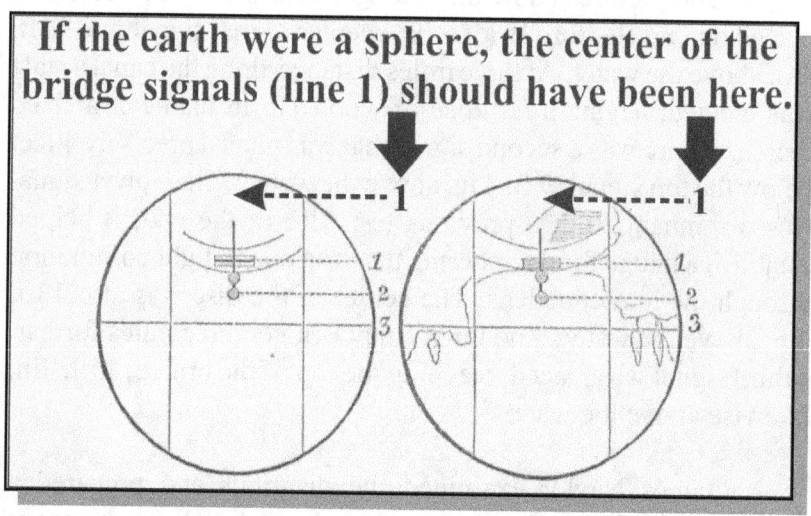

The fact that the bridge markers did not drop the necessary 24 feet indicates that the earth is flat. The uniformity of the drop in the signal markers was due to the collimation of the light on the lens of the telescope. Please note that the telescope portrayed upside-down images.

And now we come to what Naylor calls "flagrantly dishonest" skulduggery by Martin W. B. Coulcher, the referee for Wallace.[883] Soon after the Bedford experiments Wallace's referee, Martin W. B. Coulcher, realized that the diagrams that he signed actually proved that the water on the Bedford Canal was flat and had no convexity at all. Coulcher argued at the scene that the diagrams proved convexity, but he apparently realized that the evidence impeached his argument.

Coulcher decided to alter the evidence. Coulcher got busy and prepared altered diagrams of the view through the telescope. What possibly could the motive have been for Coulcher to prepare his own sketch of what he saw through the telescope when he had already attested to the accuracy of Carpenter's sketch? The only plausible reason could be that he had to present something to rebut Carpenter's unimpeachable sketch that showed that the water in the canal was flat. So Coulcher fabricated a deceptive sketch that inaccurately depicted a non-uniform drop in the signal markers on the bridge to give the false appearance that the water was convex.

In Coulcher's altered diagrams, which were not attested for accuracy by anyone, Coulcher drew the upper round signal at the three-mile mark closer to the horizontal cross-hair on the telescope lens, which thus made the drop between that circular signal and the signal on the bridge falsely appear exponentially greater, as would be expected on a spherical earth. Coulcher falsely portrayed what would be expected to be seen (but which nobody actually saw) if the earth were a sphere. He forwarded his altered diagrams to Walsh.[884] Walsh relied on Coulcher's diagrams in rendering his ruling,[885] even though Coulcher's diagram was never attested by Carpenter or indeed any living witness. Coulcher's diagram is depicted below with a caption written by the editors of *The Earth Not a Globe Review*.[886]

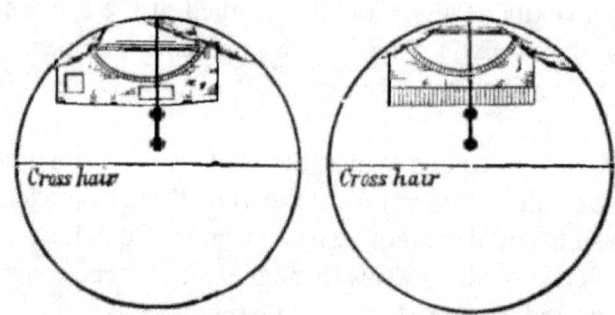

THESE figures are also taken from the "*Field.*" They were printed as being what was seen by Dr. Coulcher, Mr. Wallace's referee, under precisely the same conditions as those in connection with the *other* sketches. And there they stand—their own witnesses—without a single word ever having been said in justification of them. We, again and again, denounce them as utterly false—as pictorial deceivers of the people—as illustrations of things *never seen, and not possible to be seen* under the circumstances. It is almost unnecessary to state that these diagrams appear, wrongfully, to show that Mr. Wallace, and *not* Mr. Hampden, was the winner of the "Scientific Wager." We reprint them because it is our duty, and for that reason alone: for if Dr. Coulcher is not heartily ashamed of them, we are. They will be found to be fully and fairly reckoned up—and such a reckoning up!—in a most ably-written pamphlet by Mr. James Naylor, of Leeds. And Mr. Hampden thinks that he has been trifled with!—taken in, just a little!—"swindled!" as he calls it:—*how ridiculously absurd!*

James Naylor concluded that Coulcher's diagrams were altered to fit the argument that the earth is a sphere.[887] James Naylor was able to prove that Coulcher's sketches were both internally inconsistent and contrary to the evidence. James Naylor concluded that Coulcher had "lost all sense of religious or moral shame, that he could descend to the meanest arts of deceit, and the lowest and most despicable knavery, in order that by so doing, he might affirm the earth to be a globe, infidel astronomy is correct, and the bible a lie."[888] Such is the state of so-called modern science. The Bedford Canal deception orchestrated by Alfred Russel Wallace is just one in a long history of artifices perpetrated by despicable heliocentric scientists. They, like their evolutionary brethren, are practiced in the meanest arts of deceit in their war against God and man.

So clearly fake were Coulcher's sketches that not even Alfred Russel Wallace would use them as evidence of the sphericity of the earth in his account of the Bedford Canal experiments that he wrote in his 1905 autobiography. Wallace tried to be diplomatic by understating Coulcher's artifice by describing Coulcher's sketches as merely inferior to Carpenter's. "Mr. Carpenter's was [sic] rather more accurately drawn [than Mr. Coulcher's sketches], and Mr. Coulcher signed them [Mr. Carpenter's sketches] as being correct."[889] That is a significant admission made 35 years after the experiments. Wallace acknowledged that Coulcher's sketches were inaccurate. But the umpire, Walsh, relied, in substantial part, on those inaccurate sketches to rule in favor of Wallace.

Indeed, Walsh reproduced both Carpenter's sketches and Coulcher's sketches in the body of his opinion, but nowhere does Walsh indicate in his opinion that Coulcher's sketches were inaccurate in any way.[890] Coulcher described his sketches in his submission to Walsh as "Diagram[s], showing what was seen in the telescope of sixteen-inch Troughton-level."[891] That was not true. Coulcher's sketches did not depict accurately what was seen. They are drawings of fantasy that were jimmied up to create the false impression that the water was convex. Coulcher misleadingly implied that his sketches were equivalent to the sketches attested to by both referees. Coulcher stated regarding his diagram submission to Walsh: "Drawn from rough sketch taken on the spot by Mr. Coulcher, one of the referees. The sketch, signed by both referees, is here annexed."[892] That implies that his (Coulcher's) sketch was equivalent to Carpenter's sketch, which was attested as accurate by both Carpenter and Coulcher. Nobody ever attested to Coulcher's diagram and it was materially different from the attested sketch from Carpenter. Coulcher's diagram was a figment of his imagination and did not comport to reality. Yet Coulcher's sketch was principally the basis for Walsh to rule in favor of Wallace.

To this day, the swindle at Bedford Canal is cited as authority proving that water is convex and the earth is a sphere. Rowbotham was a little annoyed that Hampden and Carpenter allowed themselves to be duped by Wallace. Rather than allow Wallace to orchestrate an experiment designed to deceive, Rowbotham suggested that they should have done a very straightforward experiment that would settle the issue in an elegant and simple fashion. Of course, Rowbotham would not suggest an experiment without first performing it himself. After the fiasco at the Bedford Canal was publicized, Rowbotham traveled to the Bedford Canal and performed the very test he suggested.

One month after the Bedford Canal fiasco, on April 5, 1870, Rowbotham got into a boat that was at Welney Bridge in the Bedford Canal and looked through a telescope from 18 inches above the water toward the Bedford Sluice Bridge (labeled T in the diagrams), 6 miles away.[893] He was able to see the entire bridge.

Being 18 inches off the surface of the water, if he earth were a sphere, Rowbotham's line-of-sight would touch the water at a distance of 1 and ½ miles (labeled H in the diagram below).[894] If the water were convex, as is required on a spherical earth, the curvature of the remaining 4 and ½ miles would cause the bridge to drop by 13 feet 6 inches, below the horizon from point H.[895] The formula for the drop below the horizon on a 25,000-mile circumference sphere, as the earth is supposed to be, is 8 inches multiplied by the number of miles squared. In summary, the formula is $M^2 \times 8 = D$, where "M" is the number of miles from the observer at ground level, "8" is the number of inches dropped per mile squared, and "D" is the distance of the drop over the horizon.

That means that the arch of the bridge, which rose 12 feet

8 inches above the water, should have been cut off from view by the 13-foot 6-inch drop below the horizon (point H) caused by the supposed curvature of the earth. But the entire arch was fully in Rowbotham's view. The white notice board on the bridge (labeled B in the diagrams) spanned from 6 feet 6 inches above the water to 13 feet 8 inches above the water. That means that if the earth were a sphere all but 2 inches of the board should have been cut off from view. But Rowbotham could see the entire board, including the bottom of the board, which was 6 feet, 6 inches above the water. If the earth were a sphere, the bottom of the white notice board should have been 7 feet below the horizon and impossible to see. Indeed, no part of the bridge was cut off from Rowbotham's view. Thus proving that the water is not convex and the earth is not a sphere.

Rowbotham referred Hampden and Carpenter to the experiment that he performed on the Bedford Canal that was illustrated and explained in his book, *Zetetic Astronomy*.[896] In that experiment, Rowbotham was able to see a flag on a boat flying 5 feet above the water that was six miles away from him. He was positioned with a telescope 8 inches above the water. If the earth were a sphere, the flag should have been 11 feet 8 inches below the horizon. But "[t]he flag and the boat were distinctly visible throughout the whole distance!"[897] The fact that Rowbotham was able to see the flag and boat for the entire 6 miles, proves that the earth is flat. Rowbotham's experiment is explained in detail, with illustrations, in an earlier chapter in this book. Rowbotham implied that experiment should have been the experiment performed by them, as it was simple, straightforward, and avoided the pitfalls they suffered in Wallace's experiment.[898]

Wallace knew about Rowbotham's experiment. But he, certainly, was not going to suggest that experiment as it would spell doom for his convex water and spherical earth theories. That is why he came up with his convoluted experiment instead. Wallace's mission was deception and obfuscation, not truth and clarity. It is a mystery why Hampden and Carpenter did not push to perform the elegantly simple experiment conducted by Rowbotham. Instead, they allowed Wallace to dictate the experiment and were thus bamboozled. Wallace's experiment was designed to confuse them and conceal the truth of the flat earth from the public.

After Hampden realized how Wallace had swindled him, he entered into a campaign of public vitriol against Wallace. Hampden publically branded Wallace a "knave, liar, thief, swindler, imposter, rogue, and felon."[899] Hampden impetuously even wrote Wallace's wife and asserted that Wallace was a liar and a felon.

In January of 1871, Wallace sued Hampden for libel. Wallace won a judgment of £600 against Hampden. A little known fact was that the judgment was on a directed verdict because Hampden, imprudently, never defended the case. Truth is a defense to libel. Hampden had a strong case that the epithets he used against Wallace were true. But, alas, Hampden inadvisably decided not to contest the libel action that he could have easily won. Instead, he signed over all of his assets to his solicitor son-in-law and declared bankruptcy. That rendered the £600 uncollectible.

By not defending the libel case, Hampden forfeited an opportunity to subject Wallace to a withering cross-examination under oath regarding his methodology and shenanigans at the

Bedford Canal. Hampden could have exposed the fact that Wallace as an expert surveyor knew the drop due to light refraction was the actual cause for the drop of the distant landmarks seen in the telescope. Imagine the revealing cross-examination of Coulcher over his counterfeit sketches of the telescope images. How could Walsh explain making a judgment and publishing it in an article, when his own expert optician told him in advance that it was wrong? That is not to mention the availability of the expert testimony of Rowbotham. Hampden would be able to prove the truth that he was swindled, and thus that his allegations against Wallace were not libelous. The trial would have been a sensational victory for Hampden.

Instead, Hampden let Wallace off the hook and gave the science community a way to put an end to the debate by citing to the libel judgment against Hampden. This author finds Hampden's conduct and subsequent strategy of not defending the libel case suspiciously irrational. Hampden's behavior was quite damaging to the truth of the stationary, flat earth. Indeed, to this day, the science community cites Wallace's victory in the wager as proving that Wallace demonstrated scientifically that the earth is a sphere. The libel verdict in favor of Wallace, they argue, proves that Wallace was libeled and thus that he did not defraud Hampden at Bedford Canal.

John Hampden single-handedly discredited all of the legitimacy that Robotham had brought to the flat earth. Rowbotham was creating a groundswell of belief in a flat, stationary earth. Suddenly, Hampden came on the scene. Hampden published, far and wide, his £500 challenge. When the challenge was accepted, Hampden allowed his opponent, Alfred Russel Wallace, to determine the experiment and the rules and then change the rules and the experiment at his whim. Hampden did not contact Samuel Rowbotham to act as his referee but, instead, opted to appoint as his referee a journeyman printer and author with no scientific background. Rowbotham was, at all times, ready, willing, and able to assist Hampden. Indeed, Hampden knew how to contact Rowbotham as he had corresponded with him on several occasions before posting the challenge.

The usually vociferous and truculent Hampden was oddly passive and uncurious about what was being done during the Bedford Canal experiments.[900] He declined to even look through either telescope.[901] Then, when a disagreement arose between the two referees over the meaning of the observations at the Bedford Canal, Hampden recommended John Henry Walsh, the editor of *The Field*, who had previously acted as the referee and advocate for Wallace during the Bedford Canal tests to umpire the dispute.[902]

Hampden did not consult with his referee, Carpenter, before he recommended Walsh to be the umpire. That was probably because he knew that Carpenter would recommend against it, as Carpenter had already vehemently objected to the appointment of any umpire, let alone Walsh.[903] Hampden had to have known at that point that his fate was sealed. Who, in his right mind, would recommend an umpire in a dispute in which the umpire had previously been an advocate for his opponent? It should have come as no surprise when Walsh ruled in favor of his own teammate, Wallace.

It was only after the fiasco at the Bedford Canal that Hampden decided to ask Rowbotham to come to the Bedford Canal to reenact his previous tests. Hampden proceeded to act like an unbalanced fool by publishing epithets against Wallace. When Wallace seemingly blundered by suing him for slander. Instead of taking that golden opportunity to prove he was swindled at the Bedford Canal, Hampden did not contest the libel suit and thus let Wallace off the hook by suffering a directed verdict.

Think about it logically. If a person really tried to swindle someone, and the swindler knew that the victim had documentary evidence that proved the attempted swindle, would the swindler sue his accuser for libel? No. But if the swindler knew in advance that the way was clear to a directed verdict because his accuser would not contest the matter, he would be encouraged to file suit. That seems to explain why Wallace sued when there was abundant evidence that he tried to swindle Hampden. The whole thing has the appearance of theater.

After suffering the civil verdict against him, Hampden then continued to engage in a serial campaign of public disparagement and denigration against both Walsh and Wallace that resulted in criminal libel convictions against him.[904] He was forced to publish public apologies to both Walsh and Wallace. Hampden's imprudent conduct served to destroy his reputation and undermined the credibility of the flat earth. Perhaps, that was the plan from the beginning. The puzzling behavior from Hampden carries the odor of an agent provocateur, whose mission, seemingly, was to discredit belief in the flat earth and spin the growing flat earth movement into confusion and doubt. The best way to hide a nefarious plan is to cover it with a mountain of zeal. How else can one explain such bizarre behavior, where at every turn Hampden acted against the interests of his cause?

30 Superstition Passing as Science

Today, Alfred Russel Wallace's scam at the Bedford Canal continues to be cited as authoritative proof that the earth is a sphere. For example, Ars Technica's senior science editor Dr. John Timmer introduced Wallace's supposed proof of the sphericity of the earth with the following statement:

> We knew that the earth was round [i.e., spherical] over 2,000 years ago. How can it be possible that people are still arguing about this? To some extent, in our everyday experience, the earth sure does look flat. But this belief can only exist if people ignore the centuries of evidence that have accumulated since the time of Aristophanes.[905]

John Timmer "is Ars Technica's science editor. He has a Bachelor of Arts in Biochemistry from Columbia University, and a Ph.D. in Molecular and Cell Biology from the University of California, Berkeley."[906] After priming the audience with that introduction to the spherical earth, Timmer then cited to Alfred Russel Wallace's fraudulent Bedford Canal contrivance as proof that the earth is a sphere. Timmer portrayed Wallace's conclusion not as the wily trick that it was but as scientific proof that the earth is a sphere. Timmer, like so many other alleged scientists, is more a priest of superstition than a scientist. He has written many articles promoting the mythology of evolution[907] and global warming[908] while pushing ineffective and unsafe vaccines.[909]

It is not surprising to find a devotee of the religious mythology of heliocentricity to also hold other strange religious beliefs posing as science. Once Satan brought science (so-called) down the path of accepting the religious superstition of heliocentrism as a scientific fact, all other fields of science were corrupted. That godless heliocentric root nourishes a poisonous tree with many superstitious branches. A little-known fact is that the ineffective and dangerous practice of vaccination can be traced not to the deviant mind of Edward Jenner (1749-1823 A.D.) but to Dhanwantari (1,500 B.C.), who was considered the Vedic Father of Medicine.[910] The practice of injecting vaccines is based on Hindu religious superstition. Vaccination is medical quackery.[911] But because vaccinations fulfill the perverted ends of Satan and his minions, the practice flourishes. Vaccines are unsafe and ineffective. One suppressed study proves that "vaccinated children appear to be significantly less healthy than the unvaccinated."[912]

The chart below shows the "[c]umulative office visits in the vaccinated (orange) vs. unvaccinated (blue) patients born into [Dr. Paul Thomas' pediatric] practice: the clarity of the age-specific differences in the health fates of individuals who are vaccinated (2,763) compared to the 561 unvaccinated in patients born into the practice over ten years is most strikingly clear in this comparison of the cumulative numbers of diagnoses in the two patient groups. The number of office visits for the unvaccinated is adjusted by a sample size multiplier factor (4.9) to the expected value as if the number of unvaccinated in the study was the same as the number of vaccinated."[913]

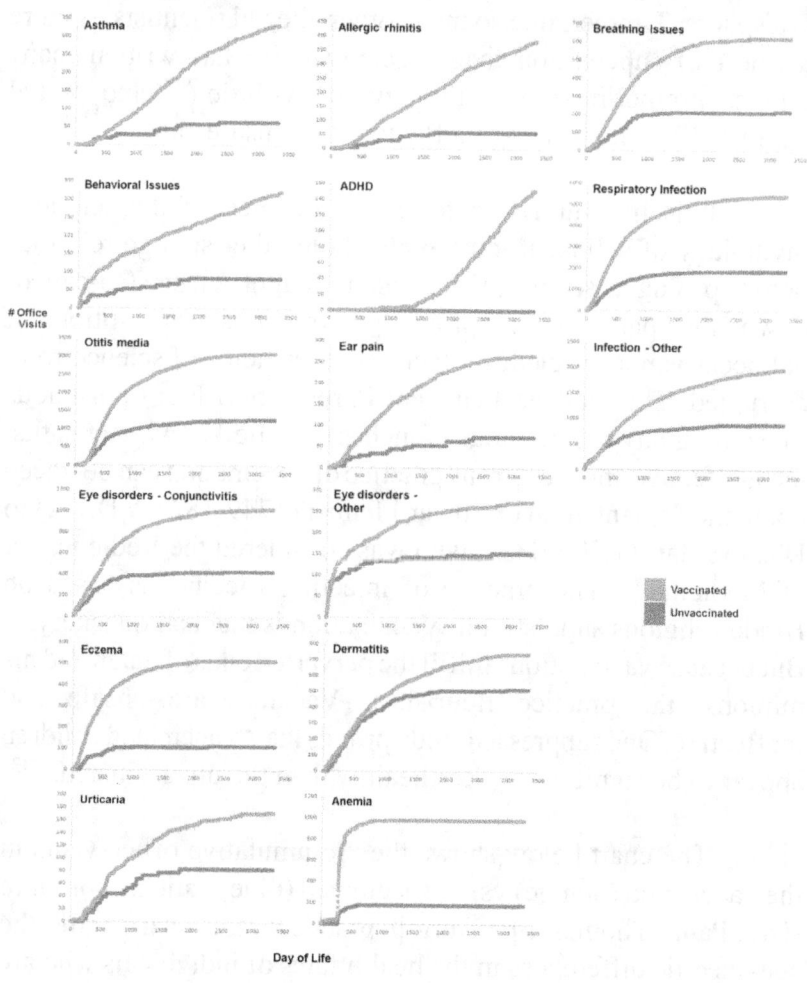

The two researchers, Dr. James Lyons-Weiler and Dr. Paul Thomas who conducted the above study are not anti-vaccination doctors. But as a direct result of this study, the state medical board has suspended his medical license of one of the researchers, Dr. Paul Thomas, within a week of the publication of the research study. The suspension was in retaliation for having published the study showing the harmful effects of childhood vaccinations. The suspension was an unprecedented action because it was done summarily prior to any adversarial hearing. He is being punished as an object lesson for anyone who would have the temerity to publish the truth about vaccinations being harmful to the health of patients.

On 16 July 2021, the publisher of Dr. Thomas' study, MDPI, retracted the article with a cryptic notice alleging unspecified "methodological issues" and that the conclusions "were not supported by strong scientific data."[914] MDPI did not indicate what were the "methodological issues" or specify how the conclusions "were not supported by strong scientific data." That lack of specificity for such an extraordinary action suggests the retraction of the article by MDPI was not due to methodological issues and that it was not supported by strong scientific data but was rather due to financial and political pressure put on MDPI.

Mark Blaxill and Amy Becker studied mortality rates during the COVID-19 lock-downs.[915] They discovered a startling fact. Infant mortality actually went down during the COVID-19 lockdowns. There was a significant decrease in the number of infant deaths. Blaxill and Becker attributed that drop to the inability of parents to do well-baby doctor checkups with the obligatory vaccinations. Fewer vaccines = fewer infant deaths. Blaxill and Becker stated:

> Starting in early March, expected deaths [for children under 18 years old] began a sharp decline, from an expected level of around 700 deaths per week to well under 500 by mid-April and throughout May. The Centers for Disease Control and Prevention. National Center for Health Statistics Mortality Surveillance System.
>
> As untimely deaths spiked among the elderly in Manhattan nursing homes and in similar settings all over the country, something mysterious was

saving the lives of children. As springtime in America came along with massive disruptions in family life amid near-universal lockdowns, roughly 30% fewer children died.

***

Was this a protective effect of school closures? Were teenagers getting themselves into risky situations at a lower rate? No. There was very little effect among school age children or adolescents.[916]

Incidentally, since the publication of Blaxill and Becker's article, the CDC has removed the page that memorialized the fact that almost all of the reduction in childhood deaths came from infants. Blaxill and Becker explain that the CDC statistics showed:

> **Virtually the entire change came from infants.** Somehow, the changing pattern of American life during the lockdowns has been saving the lives of hundreds of infants, over 200 per week.

***

What has changed during this period that might have such an effect?

***

One very clear change that has received publicity is that public health officials are bemoaning the sharp decline in infant vaccinations as parents are not taking their infants into pediatric offices for their regular well-baby checks. In the May 15 [2020] issue of the CDC Morbidity and Mortality Weekly Report (MMWR), a group of authors from the

CDC and Kaiser Permanente reported **a sharp decline in provider orders for vaccines as well as a decline in pediatric vaccine doses administered.** Santoli, Jeanne M et al. Effects of the COVID-19 Pandemic on Routine Pediatric Vaccine Ordering and Administration — United States, 2020. cdc.gov.[917] [Online] May 15, 2020. These declines began in early March, around the time infant deaths began declining.[918]

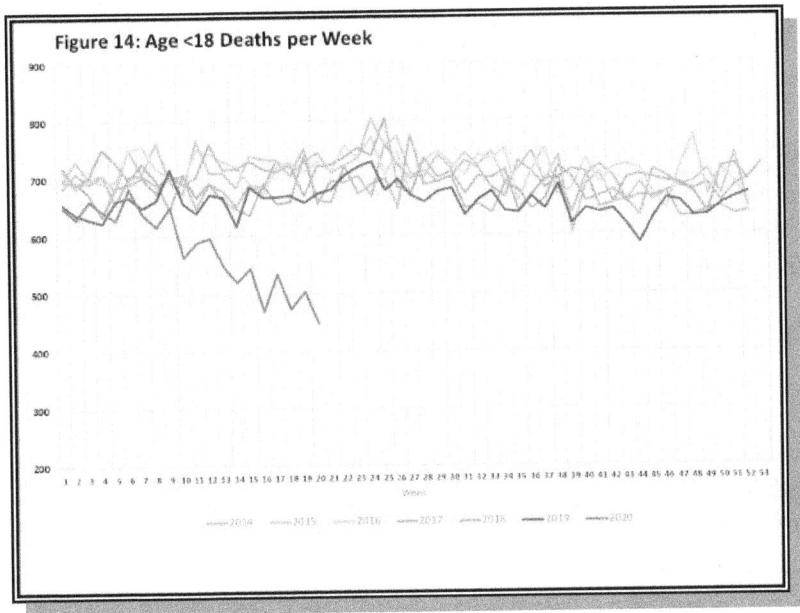

Figure 39: Chart showing a precipitous drop in child deaths early in 2020 that correlated directly with the COVID-19 lookdowns. Virtually the entire drop in deaths among children under 18 years old came from infants. The COVID-19 lockdowns prevented parents from taking infants for well-baby checkups and getting vaccinated. The reduction in infant deaths also correlated directly with a sharp decline in provider orders for vaccines and a decline in pediatric vaccine doses administered.

The following are quotes from notable physicians and scientists who have given their expert opinions that vaccines are unsafe and ineffective superstitious quackery.[919]

"The pediatrician indoctrinates your child from birth into a lifelong dependency on medical intervention. The first stage of indoctrination is the 'well-baby' visit. The well-baby visit is a cherished ritual of the pediatrician that enhances their income and does nothing constructive for your child. It's a worthless visit." — Dr. Robert Mendelsohn, MD, board certified pediatrician.

"Vaccines are the backbone of the entire Pharmaceutical Industry. If they can make these children sick from a very early age, they become customers for life. The money isn't really to be made in the vaccine industry. The money is made by Big Pharma with all of the drugs that are given to treat and address all of the illnesses that are subsequent to the side effects of vaccines."–Dr. Sherri Tenpenny, D.O. (osteopathic medical doctor).

"Vaccinations are now carried out for purely commercial reasons because they fetch huge profits for the pharmaceutical industry. There is no scientific evidence that vaccinations are of any benefit." –Dr. Gerhard Buchwald, MD, "Vaccination: A business based on FEAR".

"Studies are increasingly pointing to the conclusion that vaccines represent a dangerous assault to the immune system leading to autoimmune diseases like Multiple Sclerosis, Lupus, Juvenile Onset Diabetes, Fibromyalgia, and Cystic Fibrosis, as well as previously rare disorders like brain cancer, SIDS (Sudden Infant Death Syndrome), childhood leukemia, autism, and asthma."–Dr. Zoltan Rona, MD, "Natural Alternatives to Vaccination".

"I have been a regular practitioner of medicine in Boston

for 33 years. I have studied the question of vaccination conscientiously for 45 years. As for vaccination as a preventative of disease, there is not a scrap of evidence in its favor. Injection of virus into the pure bloodstream of the people does not prevent Smallpox. Rather, it tends to increase its epidemics and makes the disease more deadly. Of this we have indisputable proof. In our country (U.S.) cancer mortality has increased from 9 per 100,000 to 80 per 100,000 or fully 900 per cent increase, within the past 50 years, and no conceivable thing could have caused this but the universal blood poisoning now existing." – Dr. Charles E. Page, Boston.

"We have no proof of the boasted effectiveness of any form of anti-toxin, vaccine or serum. The true figures on vaccination for smallpox have never gotten before the public, though they can be seen in the files of the various departments of the Army as well as the government, if one cares to look for them. If the record of vaccination in the Philippines alone were ever to become a matter of general knowledge it would finish vaccination in the whole country, at least among those who are able to read and think for themselves. After three years of the most rigid vaccination, when every Philippino had been vaccinated from one to six times, there occurred the severest epidemic of smallpox that the Islands had ever seen, with a death-rate running in places to over 70 per cent, and in all, well over 60,000 deaths. Is it any wonder the public is getting a little suspicious of us and our vaunted 'medical discoveries?' The wonder to me is that there are still millions of them willing to submit to vaccination and serum treatment." – Dr. William Howard Hay, Buffalo, New York.

"Everyone who is vaccinated is vaccine injured–whether it shows up right away or later in life." –Dr. Shiv Chopra, B.V.S., A.H., M.Sc., PhD, Fellow of the World Health Organization, former senior scientist at Health Canada.

"My own personal view is that vaccines are unsafe and

WORTHLESS. I will not allow myself to be vaccinated again. Vaccines may be profitable but in my view, they are neither safe nor effective." -Dr. Vernon Coleman, MB, ChB, DSc (Hon).

"The entire vaccine program is based on massive FRAUD."–Dr. Russell L. Blaylock, M.D., neurosurgeon, editorial staff of Journal of American Physicians and Surgeons.

"My honest opinion is that vaccine is the cause of more disease and suffering than anything I could name." –Dr. Harry R. Bybee.

"Vaccination, instead of being the promised blessing to the world, has proved to be a curse of such sweeping devastation that it has caused more death and disease than war, pestilence, and plague combined. There is no scourge (with the possible exception of atomic radiation) that is more destructive to our nation's health than this monument of human deception–this slayer of the innocent–this crippler of body and brain–the poisoned needle." –Dr. Eleanor McBean, PhD, ND, "The Poisoned Needle", 1957.

"The great epidemics of deadly diseases, in animals and mankind, are caused by vaccination." –Charles M. Higgins, "The Horrors of Vaccination: Exposed and Illustrated", 1920.

"Cancer was practically unknown until the cowpox vaccination began to be introduced. I have seen 200 cases of cancer, and never saw a case in an unvaccinated person." –Dr. W.B. Clark, MD, Indiana, New York Times article, 1909.

"I believe vaccination has been the greatest delusion that has ensnared mankind in the last three centuries. It originated in FRAUD, ignorance and error. It is unscientific and impracticable. It has been promotive of very great evil, and I cannot accredit it any good." –Dr. R. K. Noyse, MD, Resident Surgeon of the Boston City Hospital, "Self Curability of Disease".

"Vaccination is the most outrageous insult that can be offered to any pure-minded man or woman. It is the boldest and most impious attempt to mar the works of God that has been attempted for ages. The stupid blunder of doctor-craft has wrought all the evil that it ought, and it is time that free American citizens arise in their might and blot out the whole blood poisoning business." — Dr. J.M. Peebles, MD, MA, PhD, "Vaccination: A Curse and Menace to Personal Liberty", 1900.

"There does not exist one single fact, in all the experiments and improvements made in science, which can support the idea of vaccination. A vaccinated people will always be a sickly people, short lived and degenerate." –Dr. Alexander Wilder, MD, "Vaccination: A Medical Fallacy", editor of the New York Medical Tribune, 1879.

"I have seen leprosy and syphilis communicated by vaccination. Leprosy is becoming very common in Trinidad; its increase being coincident with vaccination." –Dr. Hall Bakewell, Vaccinator General of Trinidad, 1868.

"Cancer is reported to be increasing not only in England and the Continent, but in all parts of the world where vaccination is practised." –Dr. William S. Tebb, MA, MD, DPH, "The Increase of Cancer", 1892.

"Every intelligent person who takes the time to investigate vaccination, will find abundant evidence in the published writings and public records of the advocates of vaccination, to prove its utter worthlessness, without reading a line of anti-vaccination literature. And if we could add to this all the suppressed facts, we would have a mass of evidence before which no vaccinator would dare to hold up his head."–Dr. Robert A. Gunn, MD, "Vaccination: Its Fallacies and Evils", 1882.

"Vaccination has made murder legal. Vaccination does not

protect against smallpox, but is followed by blindness and scrofula. Jennerism (Edward Jenner, an English physician who was a contributor to development of the smallpox vaccine) is the most colossal humbug which the human race has been burdened with by FRAUD and DECEIT." –Mr. Mitchell, member of the British House of Commons.

"Vaccination is a monstrosity, a misbegotten offspring of error and ignorance; and, being such, it should have no place in either hygiene or medicine... Believe not in vaccination, it is a worldwide delusion, an unscientific practice, a fatal superstition with consequences measured today by tears and sorrow without end." –Dr. Carlo Ruta, Professor of Materia Medica at the University of Perugia, Italy, 1896.

The dangerous and ineffective COVID-19 vaccines are the latest vaccine poisons being imposed on the world. Official data from the UK Government shows that those vaccinated with two doses of the COVID-19 vaccine have a mortality rate of 1.4%, which is almost twice the mortality rate (0.76%) of those who are unvaccinated.[920] The average death rate for the entire English population, which includes vaccinated and unvaccinated, is 0.94%. Thus, the unvaccinated die at a lower rate than the general population. In contrast, vaccinated persons die at a greater rate than the general population.

The Vaccine Adverse Events Reporting System (VAERS) is a U.S. government-run passive reporting system for vaccine adverse events. But the VAERS database suffers from a systemic problem of under-reporting adverse events. The under-reporting in the databases is quite significant. Indeed, it is exponential. For example, because the VAERS database relies on passive reporting, it suffers from a systemic flaw known to HHS. That flaw is that the VAERS database under-reports the vaccine adverse events by a factor of 100. A Harvard study of the VAERS database that HHS commissioned revealed that "fewer than 1% of vaccine adverse events are reported."⁹²¹ That statistical finding in the Harvard study has been confirmed to be accurate in a subsequent scientific study.⁹²²

The adverse events listed in VAERS have not been clinically proven to have been caused by the listed vaccine. But we can reasonably infer that those who died within 48 hours of the onset of illness after the vaccination died from the vaccine. Megan Redshaw determined that 41% of those reported in VAERS as having died from a COVID-19 vaccine did so after becoming ill within 48 hours of the injection.⁹²³ We will consider that temporal proximity as establishing a reasonable belief that the COVID-19 vaccines were the cause of the deaths.

VAERS reported that of July 15, 2022, there were 29,635 deaths attributed to COVID-19. 41% of 29,635 is 12,150. Thus, one can reasonably conclude there is probable cause to believe that 12,150 persons died from the COVID-19 vaccine. Understanding that the VAERS system only reports 1% of the actual deaths, we find that the actual deaths in the U.S. from the COVID-19 vaccines are 1,215,000 people.

As of July 28, 2022, there have been more adverse event reports in VAERS for the COVID-19 vaccines than all other 70+ vaccines combined during the entire 32 year history of the VAERS database. Of the total 2.2 million adverse event reports in VAERS over the last 32 years, 1.3 million of those reports were for adverse events from the COVID-19 vaccines in the past 19 months.⁹²⁴ *The Expose* reported that "[t]he UK Medicine Regulator has confirmed that over a period of nineteen months the Covid-19 Vaccines have caused at least 5.5x as many deaths as all other available vaccines combined in the past 21 years."⁹²⁵ But when measuring the lethality of the COVID-19 vaccines side-by-side against all other vaccines over the same 19-month period, it was found that the COVID-19 vaccine caused 7,402% (75x) more deaths than all other vaccines combined during that 19-month period.⁹²⁶ The deaths from vaccines is vastly under-reported. But such under-reporting should be across the board for all vaccines. And so, the statistics about the relative number of deaths should be somewhat accurate. Based on those relative statistics, the COVID-19 vaccines are 75 times more deadly than all other vaccines combined.

On August 6, 2021, the CDC published a report that 346 out of out of 469 COVID-19 cases (74%) in a breakout in Barnsdale County, Massachusetts, were of people who were fully vaccinated.[927] The COVID-19 vaccines are proving to be ineffective in preventing infection.

Dr. Nina Pierpont (MD, Ph.D.), has a BA in biology from Yale University, MA and Ph.D. in population biology/evolutionary biology/ecology from Princeton University, and MD from Johns Hopkins University School of Medicine. Dr. Pierpont has been a Clinical Assistant Professor of Pediatrics at Columbia University's College of Physicians & Surgeons. She is currently in private practice in upstate New York, specializing in behavioral medicine. Dr. Pierpont reviewed the available data, principally from three scientific studies, and concluded that COVID-19 vaccine mandates have no justification because "current vaccines do not prevent transmission of SARS-CoV-2."[928]

Pfizer CEO Albert Bourla, in his attempt to sell the public on their COVID-19 vaccine booster during a news interview, let the cat out of the bag by stating: "We know that two doses of the vaccine offers very limited protection if any."[929] When Pfizer realized the implications of that admission, it immediately filed a copyright claim on that interview and took steps to purge it from the internet. This author was able to track down the video of the interview at the Instagram link found in the endnote.[930]

99% of the University of California football team and staff were fully vaccinated.[931] There are approximately 143 players and staff on that team.[932] But on November 13, 2021, it was announced that the team had to cancel its upcoming football game with USC because 47 players and staff members on the University of California football team had tested positive for COVID-19. Many of them were symptomatic for COVID-19, which is why the entire team was tested. That is a 33% COVID-19 infection rate for a single group of fully vaccinated persons. The COVID-19 vaccines are not just ineffective; it seems that the vaccines are driving the infection. It is more likely that the players and coaches are suffering from antibody-dependent enhancement caused by the vaccine.

Indeed, COVID-19 vaccinations are detrimental to the USA's counter-drug mission. For example, on December 25, 2021, Carol Rosenberg and Aishvarya Kavi reported for *The New York Times* that the USS Milwaukee was supposed to deploy to intercept drug traffickers in the Caribbean, but the ship could not do so because of a Covid-19 outbreak onboard the ship.[933] The 105-man crew of the vessel was 100% vaccinated against COVID-19. That is a clear example that the COVID-19 vaccines are ineffective in preventing COVID-19. What was really going on aboard the ship likely was that the sailors were suffering from antibody-dependent enhancement (ADE) caused by the vaccines themselves. The vaccines were making the sailors sick. Oddly, the USS Milwaukee incident comes on the heels of active-duty troops in the Army and Navy being fired because they refused to get vaccinated under President Biden's vaccination mandate for the armed services. Perfectly healthy soldiers and sailors were relieved of duty for exercising their rights to refuse to take experimental vaccines that have now been demonstrated to be both unsafe and ineffective. All the while, the readiness of the armed services is being detrimentally impacted by the growing occurrence of ADE among the soldiers and sailors caused by the mandated vaccines.

On November 10, 2021, U.S. District Court Judge T. Kent Wetherell, II, issued an opinion wherein he denied a request from a plaintiff for a preliminary injunction. He ruled against the doctor requesting a religious exemption. Nonetheless, in the course of rendering his opinion, the judge ruled:

> [T]the evidence I have shows the vaccine is "leaky" and "nonsterilizing" in that **it does not prevent transmission of the virus, nor does it protect vaccinated persons from contracting the virus.** ... [T]he evidence before the court from plaintiff's medical experts suggest **that vaccinated persons actually transmit the virus at a higher rate than unvaccinated.** ... [T]he vaccines are unnecessary for persons who have previously had COVID because **natural immunity provides equivalent or greater protection against severe infection than the vaccines.** ... [T]he irrefutable evidence in this case shows that vaccines simply do not accomplish the purpose of the policy that it's aimed at achieving; that is, "keeping everyone safer," because, again, **they do not protect people from contracting the virus**, nor do they prevent people from getting the virus.[934] (emphasis added)

So prevalent were the breakthrough cases of COVID-19 that the CDC announced that beginning on May 1, 2021, it would no longer monitor or report any breakthrough cases that did not result in hospitialization or death.[935] The CDC and its pharmaceutical overlords could not allow people to use official government statistics to prove that the COVID-19 vaccines are ineffective.

U.S. Senator for Massachusetts, Edward Markey, saw through the CDC's subterfuge. In an official letter of inquiry he demanded to know why the CDC would no longer continue to monitor the breakthrough cases.[936] Senator Markey noted the obvious fact that breakhrough cases are a good measure of

COVID-19 vaccine effectiveness. He said that 43.4% of the new COVID-19 infections in Massachusetts were among those who were vaccinated. Notably, Senator Markey asked the CDC: "Is the effectiveness of COVID-19 vaccines decreasing in light of these breakthrough cases?"[937] The answer is clear. Indeed, the evident affirmative answer to that question is why the CDC decided to stop reporting breakthrough COVID-19 cases. The CDC's decision not to report COVID-19 breakthrough cases among the vaccinated population was indicative of a conspiracy between it an the pharmaceutical companies to coverup of the ineffectiveness of the COVID-19 vaccines. They are not only ineffective, they are dangerous.

The United Kingdom Office for National Statistics (ONS), has published data on deaths by vaccination status.[938] The ONS data started from the beginning of April 2022 through the end of May 2022. Between April 1, 2022, and May 31, 2022, 4,647 of the 4,935 total deaths from COVID-19 during that period were among the vaccinated population. That means that 94% of the COVID-19 deaths in the UK during April and May 2022 were among those vaccinated against COVID-19. The statistics revealed another shocking detail. It seems that the more shots, the more deadly the vaccines are. Those who received three COVID-19 shots accounted for 4,215 of the 4,647 total deaths among the vaccinated population. That means that those that received three COVID-19 shots accounted for 90% of the vaccinated COVID-19 deaths during April and May 2022.

The State of Vermont has had a very similar experience to that of England. The Vermont Daily Chronicle reported that 76% of COVID-19 deaths in the State of Vermont during September 2021 were of persons who had received COVID-19 vaccinations.[939] Yet, the State of Vermont Department of Public Health claims that "[v]accines are the best tool we have to protect ourselves against COVID-19, especially from severe illness, hospitalization and death."[940]

In Antwerp, Belgium, 100% of the hospitalized "COVID cases" are fully vaccinated persons. The Hall Turn Radio Show reported that "CEOs and medical directors of Antwerp hospitals met this week and the mood was worrying. They're having another COVID outbreak, but this time, ALL the patients . . . are fully vaccinated."[941]

Data from the government health authorities in Scotland showed that the fully COVID-19 vaccinated accounted for 89% of COVID-19 deaths, whilst also accounting for 77% of COVID-19 hospitalizations, and 65% of alleged COVID-19 cases from October 9 through November 5, 2021.[942] According to the data from Public Health Scotland, for December 18, 2021, to January 14, 2022, the COVID-19 case rate was 2.5 times greater for those who received two COVID-19 vaccinations than those who were unvaccinated.[943] Over that same period, there was a 5% greater hospitalization rate for those who had received two COVID-19 vaccines than those who were unvaccinated.[944] From December 11, 2021, to January 7, 2022, there was a 55% greater mortality rate from COVID-19 for those who received two doses of the COVID-19 vaccine compared to those who were unvaccinated.[945]

The Expose news site reported on the government statistics from Canada[946] showing that the vaccinated population of Canada account for 89% of all COVID-19 cases, 86% of all COVID-19 hospitalizations, and 90% of all COVID-19 deaths.

COVID-19 *Cases* in Canada: Between June 6, 2022 and July 3, 2022 in Canada, "the unvaccinated population accounted for just 11% of Covid-19 cases ... whilst **the vaccinated population accounted for 89%**, 74% of which were among the triple and quadruple jabbed."[947]

COVID-19 *Hospitalizations* in Canada: Between June 6, 2022 and July 3, 2022 in Canada, "the unvaccinated population accounted for just 14% of Covid-19 hospitalisations ... month, whilst **the vaccinated population accounted for 86%**, 75% of which were among the triple and quadruple jabbed."⁹⁴⁸

COVID-19 *Deaths* in Canada: Between June 6, 2022 and July 3, 2022 in Canada, "the unvaccinated population accounted for just 10% of Covid-19 deaths ... whilst **the vaccinated population accounted for 90%**, 87% of which were among the triple and quadruple jabbed."⁹⁴⁹

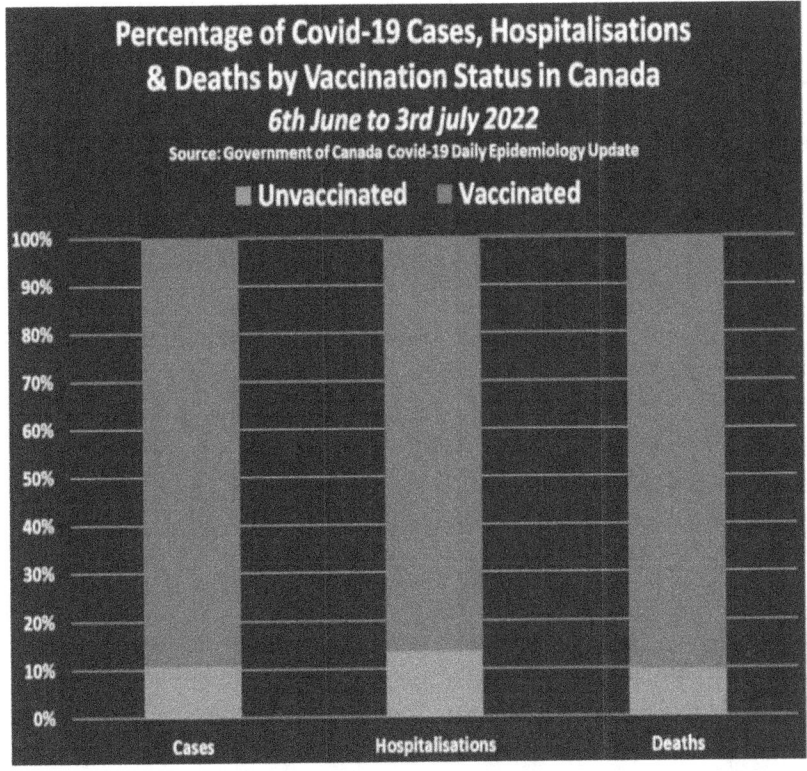

That manifest danger from the COVID-19 vaccines is in the face of evidence that the COVID-19 vaccines are ineffective. There is study,⁹⁵⁰ after study,⁹⁵¹ after study,⁹⁵² after study⁹⁵³ proving that vaccinated individuals can still test positive for COVID-19

and manifest illnesses associated with COVID-19. The United Kingdom Health Security Agency COVID-19 Vaccine Surveillance Report published on October 21, 2021, reveals that "[i]n individuals aged greater than 30, the rate of a positive COVID-19 test is higher in vaccinated individuals compared to unvaccinated."[954] The method used by the vaccine makers for reporting the efficacy of the COVID-19 vaccines (relative risk reduction) is to subtract the percentage of infected vaccinated persons from the percentage of infected unvaccinated persons and divide that number by the percentage of infected unvaccinated persons (U-V/U). Using that formula, and applying it to the UK government data, this author calculated that the actual effectiveness of the COVID-19 vaccines in the real world is minus-64%.[955] That means that a vaccinated person is 64% more likely to catch COVID-19 than an unvaccinated person.[956] That calculation of minus-64% COVID-19 vaccine efficacy was from the official reported data of the UK Health Security Agency.[957]

Please understand that the reported infections for COVID-19 are based on tests that are returning false-positive results. A little known fact is that the alleged COVID-19 virus has never been isolated. The alleged COVID-19 virus has never been proven even to exist. Claims by governments and researchers to the contrary are simply false; they try to redefine what it means to isolate a virus and use obfuscatory language to conceal the deception.

In reality, there is not a single study of the alleged COVID-19 (a.k.a., SARS-CoV2) virus that has isolated or purified it.[958] That can mean only one thing. Drs. Thomas Cowan and Andrew Kaufman succinctly concluded that "[t]he SARS-CoV2 virus does not exist."[959] Christine Massey is a biostatistician. On November 30, 2021, she submitted an affidavit in a Canadian Federal Court averring that she has received responses to freedom of information (FOI) requests from Canadian and U.S. government agencies. She further stated that she had obtained records from FOI requests made by others to more than 138 institutions from 28 countries worldwide. Astoundingly, no institution was "able to cite even one record describing the isolation and purification of SARS-CoV-2 [a.k.a. COVID-9]."[960] As of August 23, 2022, that number has expanded to 208 institutions in 35 countries. Yet still, none of the institutions "have provided or cited any record describing actual 'SARS-COV-2' isolation/purification."[961] The very existence of the COVID-19 virus seems to be a myth.

So, why, then are people testing positive for a non-existent COVID-19? A group of 22 highly respected scientists led by Pieter Borger, MSc, Ph.D., demanded a retraction of the report by Christian Drosten and Victor Corman that established the PCR test used worldwide for the COVID-19 virus. They cited "10 major scientific flaws at the molecular and methodological level" in the research that produced the COVID-19 PCR test. The scientists predicted that those flaws would result in false positive results. The most notable shortcoming of the research by Corman/Drosten was that the resulting COVID-19 PCR test was arrived at without isolating the SARS-CoV-2 (COVID-19). How can one test for something that has not first been isolated? The scientist stated:

> The first and major issue [with the Corman/Drosten report] is that the novel Coronavirus SARS-CoV-2 (in the publication named 2019-nCoV and in February 2020 named SARS-CoV-2 by an international consortium of virus experts) is based on in silico (theoretical) sequences, supplied by a laboratory in China, because at the time neither control material of infectious ("live") or inactivated SARS-CoV-2 nor isolated genomic RNA of the virus was available to the authors. To date no validation has been performed by the authorship based on isolated SARS-CoV-2 viruses or full length RNA thereof. According to Corman et al.:

"We aimed to develop and deploy robust diagnostic methodology for use in public health laboratory settings without having virus material available."[962] (endnotes deleted)

The scientists concluded the obvious. A diagnostic test for COVID-19 is invalid if it is based on research without access to any actual virus material available on which to base the test.

Kary B Mullis invented the polymerase chain reaction (PCR) method, for which he won the 1993 Nobel Prize in Chemistry.[963] He died suddenly in August 2019, four months before to the January 2020 publication of the Corman-Drosten PCR test paper that formed the basis for the COVID-19 PCR test. Before his death, Mullis explained that with enough amplification the PCR test could be used to find almost anything. He said that "with PCR, if you do it well, you can find almost anything in anybody."[964] For that reason, Mullis cautioned that the PCR test should not be used to diagnose whether someone is ill. Mullis said that PCR is "a process that's used to make a whole lot of something out of something. That's what it is. It doesn't tell you that you're sick, and it doesn't tell you that the thing you ended up with really was going to hurt you or anything like that."[965] Thus, the inventor of the PCR test is on record stating that it is improper to use a PCR test to diagnose if someone is ill or infected with a virus.

Amandha Dawn Vollmer holds a Doctor of Naturopathic Medicine degree from the Canadian College of Naturopathic Medicine in Toronto and a Bachelor of Science in Agricultural Biotechnology. She has discovered that the test for COVID-19 is not actually testing for COVID-19. The polymerase chain reaction (PCR) test for COVID-19 is a based on the research of German scientists Christian Drosten and Victor Corman who cobbled together the COVID-19 PCR test used worldwide to detect the COVID-19 virus. Amandha Vollmer discovered that the

Corman/Drosten PCR test protocol adopted by the World Health Organization (WHO) to detect COVID-19 is actually testing for chromosome 8, which is present in everyone.[966] One of the primer sequences in the PCR test for SARS-CoV-2 that is promoted by the WHO is found in all human DNA. Essentially, we are the virus. That is why there is a 97% false positive rate on the COVID-19 PCR test. People are testing positive for COVID-19 because they're human.

ctccctttgttgtgttgt = The DNA sequence for the PCR test for COVID-19.[967]

ctccctttgttgtgttgt = Chromosome 8, which is present in all homo sapiens (humans).[968]

The false positive error is compounded because of the high PCR threshold cycle rates employed. Each amplification level exponentially increases the likelihood of detecting the presence of chromosome 8. The PCR test amplifies the test sample as an exponent of the number of cycles. Each cycle doubles the prior cycle. For example, if you start with a penny and each day you double the amount of money you had on the previous day, at the end of 28 days (cycles) you would have more than a million dollars. If you continued to double your money each day past the 28th day, you would have more than five billion dollars after 40 days (cycles). That is the kind of amplification that the PCR test performs. The CDC has recommended 40 cycles for the PCR test.[969] And most laboratories during the alleged pandemic were performing tests using that recommended 40-cycle standard. Anthony S. Fauci is the Director of the National Institute of Allergy and Infectious Diseases (NIAID). Dr. Fauci admitted that performing PCR tests to detect COVID-19 at 35 or more cycles will result in false-positives and the confidence in any such positive result for COVID-19 is "minuscule." Dr. Fauci stated:

If you get a cycle threshold of 35 or more, the

chances of it being replication-confident are minuscule…you almost never can culture virus from a 37 threshold cycle… someone does come in with 37, 38, even 36, you gotta say it's just dead nucleotides period.[970]

The Portugal Court of Appeals in Lisbon agreed with the trial court, which granted a *writ of habeas corpus* on behalf of German tourists. The court of appeals ruled that German tourists were illegally detained by the Azores Regional Health Authority and ordered to be quarantined because the PCR test that was the basis of the detention is unreliable for detecting COVID-19. Peter Andrews reported that the Portuguese court cited a study conducted by "some of the leading European and world specialists," proving that the usual testing standard for a PCR test results in a COVID-19 false-positive result 97% of the time.[971]

The Portugal Court of Appeals in Lisbon, based upon a study by some of the leading European and world specialists, concluded that "[t]his means that if a person has a positive PCR test at a cycle threshold of 35 or higher (as in most laboratories in the USA and Europe), the chances of a person being infected are less than 3%. The probability of a person receiving a false positive is 97% or higher."[972]

The antigen tests are just as inaccurate and prone to false positives. Indeed, the FDA warned unequivocally that the antigen tests are inaccurate and give false positives. "The U.S. Food and Drug Administration (FDA) is alerting clinical laboratory staff and health care providers that false positive results can occur with antigen tests."[973]

Indeed, the FDA has now admitted that "all tests," for COVID-19, antigen and PCR, are inaccurate. The FDA states:

The FDA reminds clinical laboratory staff and

health care providers about the risk of false positive results with all laboratory tests. Laboratories should expect some false positive results to occur even when very accurate tests are used for screening large populations with a low prevalence of infection.[974]

That is why there was a push for testing asymptomatic persons. The government knew that many would falsely test positive for COVID-19. The lockdowns, social distancing, and mask mandates are all based on the premise that those with no symptoms of COVID-19 can still spread the disease. But research has proven that there is no asymptomatic transfer of COVID-19.[975] The tyrannical overlords ignore such inconvenient studies. Once persons tested positive for COVID-19, they were tallied up as COVID-19 patients. Some who are ill with the flu may test positive for COVID-19.[976] That is why the flu disappeared during the 2020-2021 flu season.[977] All persons with the flu were counted not as flu cases but as COVID-19 cases.[978] They then used the COVID-19 scam to push the poisonous COVID-19 vaccines on the population and begin the actual killing. Their objective from the beginning was to force the toxic vaccines on the world population.[979]

United States Influenza Cases

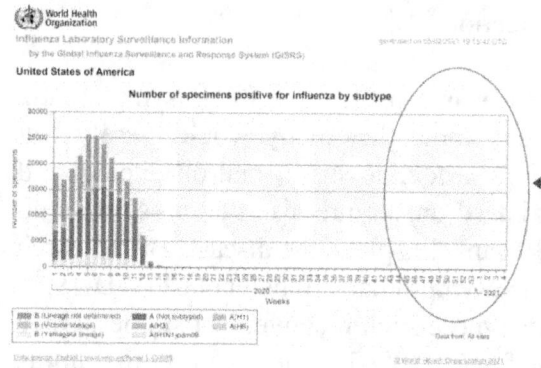

Flu disappears during the 2020-2021 Fall and Winter Flu Season in Direct Correlation with the Alleged COVID-19 Second Wave

The above World Health Organization (WHO) chart shows the number of people infected by influenza in the United States. Each Bar represents the number of infections in the United States for each week of 2020 through week number 4 of 2021. Notice that the influenza infections disappeared in the United States during week 15 of 2020. This correlates very closely with the emergence of COVID-19.

For comparison, below is a WHO chart that shows the number of people infected by influenza in the United States for the entire year of 2019 and the first 4 weeks of 2020. Each Bar represents the number of people infected in the United States for each week of 2019 through week 4 of 2021. Notice the difference from the chart above. This suggests that the disappearance of the influenza in week 15 of 2020 through week 4 of 2021 is because Influenza is being reported as COVID-19 infections. The complete disappearance of the flu during the fall and winter flu season of 2020-2021 suggests that the second wave of COVID-19 cases reported during that period are actually flu cases being falsely reported as COVID-19 cases.

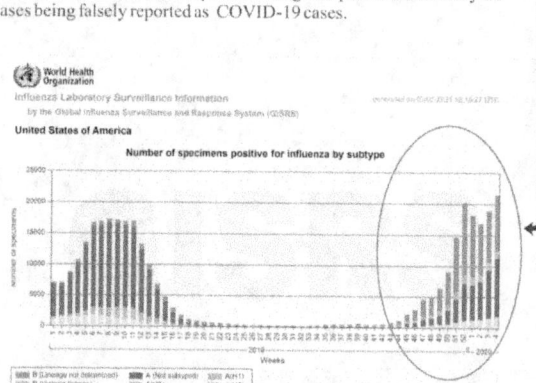

2019-2020 Fall and Winter Flu Season

Worldwide Influenza Cases

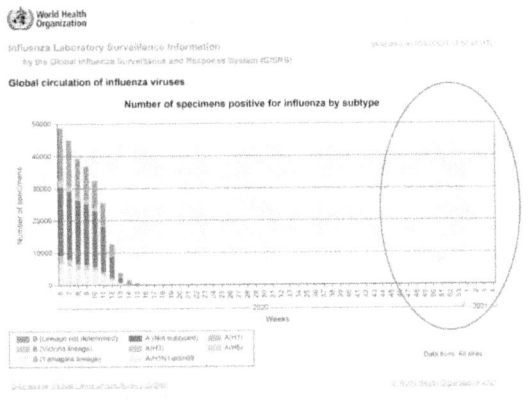

Flu disappears during the 2020-2021 Fall and Winter Flu Season in Direct Correlation with the Alleged COVID-19 Second Wave

The above World Health Organization (WHO) chart shows the number of people infected by influenza in the world. Each Bar represents the number of infections in the world for each week of 2020 through week number 4 of 2021. Notice that the influenza infections disappeared in the world during week 15 of 2020. This correlates very closely with the emergence of COVID-19.

For comparison, below is a WHO chart that shows the number of people infected by influenza in the world for the entire year of 2019 and the first 4 weeks of 2020. Each Bar represents the number of people infected in the world for each week of 2019 through week 4 of 2021. Notice the difference from the chart above. This suggests that the disappearance of the influenza in week 15 of 2020 through week 4 of 2021 is because Influenza is being reported as COVID-19 infections. The complete disappearance of the flu during the fall and winter flu season of 2020-2021 suggests that the second wave of COVID-19 cases reported during that period are actually flu cases

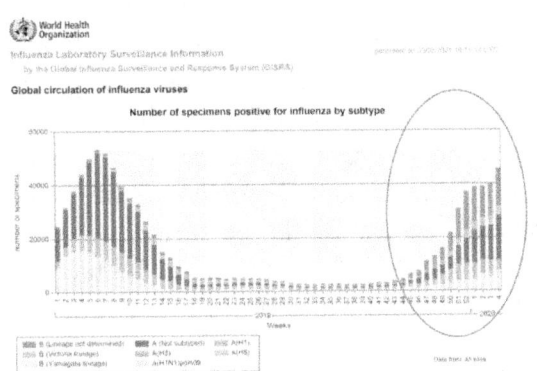

2019-2020 Fall and Winter Flu Season

The false positive COVID-19 tests laid the foundation for creating a pandemic where there was none. Deborah Birx, M.D. revealed how the scheme worked. Dr. Birx was the U.S. Global Aids Coordinator & U.S. Special Representative for Global Health Diplomacy and Physician-Ambassador to the office of the Vice President and the U.S. Government Coronavirus Response Coordinator. During an April 7, 2020, task force press briefing, Dr. Birx was asked by a reporter about the allegations by many that the coronavirus deaths have been artificially inflated. The reporter asked: "Can you talk about your concerns about deaths being misreported by coronavirus because of either testing or standards for how they're characterized?"[980]

Dr. Birx then admitted that, in fact, that the COVID-19 deaths were being inflated. Dr. Birx explained that the United States has taken a "liberal approach" to reporting COVID-19 deaths. She stated that it is "straightforward." That "straightforward" approach is to report someone who dies "with" COVID-19 as a COVID-19 death. Implied in her statement is that any deceased person who tests positive for COVID-19 is recorded as dying "of" COVID-19, regardless of the actual cause of death. To put it more succinctly, every person who dies "with" COVID-19 is recorded as dying "of" COVID-19. Dr. Birx distinguished the U.S. approach from other countries where, for example, if someone died of heart failure or kidney failure and they test positive for COVID-19, some other countries might report that as a kidney failure or heart failure death and not a COVID-19 death. Not so in the United States. The "liberal approach" taken in the U.S. is that if someone dies with COVID-19 they are added to the COVID-19 death total even though they actually died of kidney failure or heart failure. Dr. Birx answered the reporter's question as follows:

So, I think, in this country, we've taken a very

liberal approach to mortality, and I think the reporting here has been pretty straightforward over the last five to six weeks. Prior to that, when there wasn't testing in January and February, that's a very different situation and unknown.

There are other countries that if you had a pre-existing condition and let's say the virus caused you to go to the ICU and then have a heart or kidney problem — some countries are recording that as a heart issue or a kidney issue and not a COVID-19 death.

Right now, we're still recording it, and we'll — I mean, the great thing about having forms that come in and a form that has the ability to mark it as COVID-19 infection — the intent is, right now, that those — **if someone dies with COVID-19, we are counting that as a COVID-19 death.**[981] (emphasis added)

Illinois Department of Public Health Director Dr. Ngozi Ezike followed the guidance from the CDC and admitted that the State of Illinois was recording persons who died with COVID-19 as having died from COVID-19, regardless of whether COVID-19 was the actual cause of the deaths. Health Director Ezike stated:

> I just want to be clear in terms of the definition of people dying of COVID. The case definition is very simplistic. It means at the time of death it was a COVID positive diagnosis. ... It means, technically, even if you died from a clear alternate cause, but you had COVID at the same time, it is still listed as a COVID death. So. everyone who is listed as a COVId death, doesn't mean that was the cause of the death, but they had COVID at the time

of death.⁹⁸²

That reporting scheme of the State of Illinois was per the guidance given by the CDC. The CDC was beating the bushes, so to speak, to generate the inflated COVID-19 statistics. The CDC issued guidance to the state health commissioners to alter how they report COVID-19 deaths in order to artificially inflate the deaths from COVID-19.

On February 1, 2021, Patrick Howley, writing for National File, reported that an investigation by the Public Health Policy Initiative uncovered evidence that the Centers for Disease Control and Prevention (CDC) violated federal law by fraudulently inflating COVID-19 fatality numbers.⁹⁸³ The report explains that under this newly adopted CDC reporting scheme "COVID-19 became emphasized as a cause of death as frequently as possible, while comorbidity was simultaneously deemphasized as causes of death."⁹⁸⁴ The state public officials dutifully followed the new CDC guidance, which means that "COVID-19 data is collected and reported by a much different standard than all other infectious diseases and causes of death data." The effect of the CDC changes was to artificially inflate the COVID-19 death rate and give a misleading impression of its deadliness.

The graph below is from the Public Health Policy Initiative report and represents the actual deaths due to COVID-19 if those deaths had been reported according to the traditional CDC rules that were listed in the 2003 CDC Medical Examiner's and Coroner's Handbook on Death Registration,⁹⁸⁵ which were in effect until the CDC issued the new COVID-19 reporting rules on March 24, 2020. The new reporting rules only apply to COVID-19. All other causes of death still follow the traditional rules set forth in the 2003 CDC Handbook.⁹⁸⁶ Notice how the new CDC guidance for reporting COVID-19 deaths initiated in the March 24, 2020 COVID-19 Alert No. 2⁹⁸⁷ artificially inflated the number of deaths from COVID-19 1600%.

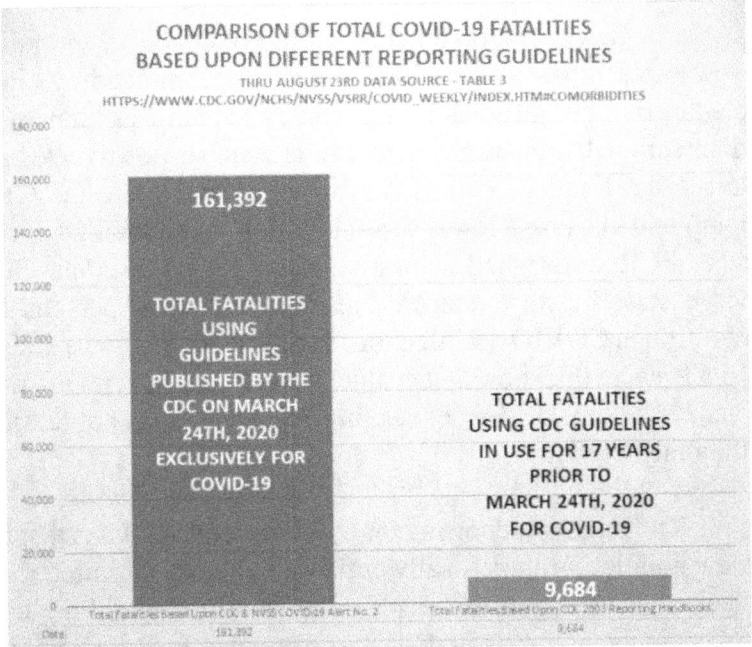

Figure 9. COVID-19 Using the March 24 Exclusive Guidelines vs Using the 2003 Guidelines. Had the CDC used the 2003 guidelines, the total COVID-19 be approximately 16.7 times lower than is currently being reported. [1][30][State & Territory Health Departments]

The CDC data manipulation was planned. And it had a purpose. To create a COVID-19 pandemic where none really existed. It was a massive statistical lie campaign. And it constituted a federal crime. Oregon State Senators Kim Thatcher and Dennis Linthicum petitioned U.S. Attorney Scott Asphaug to approve a grand jury investigation into the criminality of the CDC and FDA.[988] They based their allegations on information and data from a large team of world-renowned doctors, epidemiologists, virologists, and attorneys.[989] The Senators averred that in the March 2020 alert, the CDC illegally changed the National Vital Statistics System so that mortality data compilers could massage data to falsely report COVID-19 as the "cause" of death. This new set of rules, which only applied to COVID-19, departed from the standard procedures that had been in effect for the prior 17 years.

The new rules fraudulently inflated COVID-19 mortality. This was exacerbated by the CDC and FDA recommending a high cycle threshold of 40 for RT-PCR tests,[990] which was knowingly and intentionally guaranteed to produce false positive testing results. The fraud was furthered by a scheme where the CDC recommended using a lower threshold of no more than 28 cycles for the PCR tests when testing vaccinated persons. The CDC advised state health authorities testing vaccinated persons for breakthrough COVID-19 infections that "[f]or cases with a known RT-PCR cycle threshold (Ct) value, submit only specimens with Ct value ≤28 to CDC for sequencing. (Sequencing is not feasible with higher Ct values.)."[991]

Kit Knightly, reporting for *Off-Guardian*, explains that the "[n]ew policies will artificially deflate 'breakthrough infections' in the vaccinated, while the old rules continue to inflate case numbers in the unvaccinated."[992] Using a lower PCR threshold of no more than 28 cycles for tests of vaccinated persons while keeping the PCR threshold at 40 cycles for unvaccinated persons was done to conceal the ineffectiveness of the COVID-19 vaccines by reporting fewer vaccinated persons testing positive for COVID-19 breakthrough infections, while at the same time artificially inflating the COVID-19 rate among the unvaccinated. The behavior of the CDC and the FDA amounted to statistical fraud in violation of federal law.

The CDC further tries to lie with statistics by labeling vaccinated persons who test positive for COVID-19 as being unvaccinated. A breakthrough infection is generally believed to be a COVID-19 illness of one who has been vaccinated. But most are not aware that the CDC has a suspiciously peculiar definition for a breakthrough infection:

For the purpose of this surveillance, a vaccine

breakthrough infection is defined as the detection of SARS-CoV-2 RNA or antigen in a respiratory specimen collected from a person ≥14 days after they have completed all recommended doses of a U.S. Food and Drug Administration (FDA)-authorized COVID-19 vaccine."[993]

Thus, the CDC does not count a person as fully vaccinated until a full 14 days have passed since his second injection of the Pfizer or Moderna vaccine or 14 days after his first dose of the Janssen vaccine. Dr. Jospeh Mercola was mystified by that strange rule, particularly because more than 80% of deaths after vaccination occur within that 14-day window. Dr. Mercola explains that "[a]nyone who dies within the first 14 days post-injection is counted as an unvaccinated death. Not only does this inaccurately inflate the unvaccinated death toll, but it also hides the real dangers of the COVID shots, as the vast majority of deaths from these shots occur within the first two weeks."[994] Dr. Mercola states that "[w]hile public health officials and mainstream media claim the COVID-19 pandemic is now 'a pandemic of the unvaccinated,' we now know this claim is based on highly misleading statistics."[995]

Another confounding factor explained by Dr. Mercola is that to "count as a confirmed vaccinated individual, you must send your vaccination card to your primary care physician's office and have them add it to your electronic medical record. If you got the shot at a pharmacy, you'll need to verify that they forwarded your proof of vaccination to your doctor. Primary care offices are then responsible for sharing their patients' immunization data with the state's immunization information system. Patient-recorded proof of vaccination is only accepted for influenza and pneumococcal vaccines, not COVID-19 injections. What this all means is that, say you got the shot several weeks ago at a drive-through vaccination clinic and get admitted to the hospital with COVID symptoms. Unless your COVID shot status has actually been added into the medical system, you will not be counted as 'vaccinated.'"[996] This all has the effect of artificially inflating the unvaccinated COVID-19 infection tally while showing a misleadingly reduced breakthrough infection rate for those vaccinated.

Further, the CDC statistics reported deaths as being from COVID-19 when the deaths were actually from something else. Comorbidity is defined as the simultaneous presence of two or more chronic diseases or conditions in a patient. The CDC has reported that 94% percent of people they have reported who have died of COVID-19 in the U.S. were suffering from an average of 2.5 chronic diseases or conditions in addition to COVID-19.[997] Thus, the statistical total of 161,392 deaths (as of August 22, 2020) from COVID-19 reported by the CDC does not mean that the decedents making up that total actually died from COVID-19. The reported people dying "with" COVID-19 are being misrepresented as people who died "from" COVID-19. This inflated the COVID-19 deaths and created a false sense of danger among the public.

The CDC reports that as of August 22, 2020, only 6% of the 161,392 reported COVID-19 deaths were from COVID-19 alone. The remaining 151,708 of persons who died while testing positive for COVID-19 died from some cause (i.e., a comorbidity) in addition to COVID-19. The astounding thing is that each of those 151,708 persons who died had 2.5 comorbidities in addition to COVID-19. That means that 94% of the persons reported dying of COVID-19 actually died from a combination of diseases and injuries, which may or may not be COVID-19.

With this surreal definition of what is a COVID-19 death being pushed by the CDC, the local health officials are only limited by their creativity when deciding that a death is from COVID-19. The Orange County (Florida) Health Officer Dr. Raul Pino did not seem to think it was unusual that a man who died from a motorcycle accident was misrepresented as having died of COVID-19. Dr. Raul Pino even tried to make the irrational argument that it is okay to report a person who died in a motorcycle accident as having died from COVID-19 because "it could have been the COVID-19 that caused him to crash."[998]

Daniella Lama reporting for Fox 35 News in Orlando discovered that the Florida Department of Health has decided that all persons who test positive for COVID-19 in Florida are automatically listed as COVID-19 deaths if they subsequently die unless there is an extra step taken by the reporting agency to exclude them from the COVID-19 death statistics.[999] That extra step to exclude the motorcycle decedent was not done, which is why he was listed automatically as a COVID-19 death. Obviously, the statistical system is rigged to capture all persons who have ever tested positive with COVID-19 as a COVID-19 death if they subsequently die. If the extra step is not taken to exclude them from the statistical count then they will be listed as a COVID-19 death. With the fear of the disease ramped up by these artificially inflated COVID-19 death statistics, the public was primed to accept the emergency use authorized COVID-19 vaccines.

Why would county health officials and hospitals go along with this scam? Because there is money in it. "For the love of money is the root of all evil." 1 Timothy 6:19. Minnesota State Senator and Dr. Scott Jensen, M.D., revealed that hospital administrations are incentivized to diagnose and treat a person for COVID-19.[1000] The system is financially skewed toward diagnosing and treating COVID-19 even though the patient may not actually be ill from COVID-19. The patients may be in the hospital for an entirely different reason, but if they test positive for COVID-19 or they are diagnosed as having COVID-19, then the hospital hits the financial jackpot and can begin raking in the financial windfall from the federal government through the Coronavirus Aid, Relief and Economic Security Act (CARES Act).

For example, a hospital is reimbursed $5,000 for ordinary pneumonia under Medicare. But under the CARES Act, the hospital can charge the federal government $13,000 if that same person tests positive for COVID-19 or is diagnosed as having COVID-19. Although the patient is being treated for pneumonia, he is put on the COVID-19 billing rolls. If the patient is subsequently put on a ventilator, the payment from the federal government through the CARES Act goes up to $39,000.

Please understand that mechanical ventilation is a dangerous last-resort treatment. Studies have shown that between 66% and 86% of COVID-19 patients placed under mechanical ventilation die.[1001] One study reported that 31 of 32 (97%) mechanically ventilated COVID-19 patients died.[1002] Please make no mistake about it; mechanical ventilation is a deadly treatment. It is perverse to incentivize hospitals to administer such a dangerous protocol to treat a disease unless you want to kill people. Hospitals who have been incentivized by the prospect of a financial windfall have turned to mechanical ventilation to treat COVID-19 when it is not otherwise appropriate. Deaths from the ventilator offer the perfect cover for murder. The symptoms of pneumonia reported in severe COVID-19 patients (ie damaged air sacs in the lungs) are identical to the damage caused by mechanical ventilators. Indeed, the *Daily Mail* reported that one nurse has gone on record alleging that New York hospitals that use ventilators to treat COVID-19 are murdering their patients.[1003]

Lest you think that this is some fantastic exaggeration, USA Today, which is a left-wing liberal publication, did a fact check of Senator Jensen's allegations and determined the following:

Our ruling: **True**

We rate the claim that hospitals get paid more if patients are listed as COVID-19 and on ventilators as **TRUE**.[1004]

What is the cause of this statistical phenomenon that a vaccinated person is more likely to catch COVID-19? The UK Health Security Agency data shows that the COVID-19 vaccine efficacy drops at a steady 5% average rate per week.[1005] One would think that fact would only indicate that the vaccine is losing efficacy, ultimately dropping to zero. But that is not the case. The hard data from the UK government indicates that, in fact, the 5% loss of efficacy actually continues past zero. What that means is that the vaccine increases the likelihood of COVID-19. It is not that the vaccines are ineffective that is the reason for the COVID-19 infections among the vaccinated; the vaccines drive an illness called antibody dependent enhancement (ADE). ADE is being reported as COVID-19 because the patients are testing positive for COIVD-19. Renowned virologist and Nobel Prize Laureate Prof. Luc Montagnier explained that the so-called breakthrough COVID-19 infections being suffered by the fully vaccinated persons are infections caused by the COVID-19 vaccines.[1006] Dr. Montagnier said that the high rate of COVID-19 infections among the fully vaccinated population is due to antibody-dependent enhancement (ADE).

In an April 30, 2021 report filed with the FDA, Pfizer acknowledged that vaccine-associated enhanced disease (VAED) and vaccine-associated enhanced respiratory disease (VAERD) were listed as "Important Potential Risk[s]" of the COIVD-19 vaccines.[1007] Pfizer noted that the VAED may go unreported as such because the patient suffering VAED will usually be presented as having "severe or unusual manifestations of COVID-19."[1008] Thus the announced "breakthrough" cases of COVID-19 are likely not COVID-19 cases but are rather cases of VAED, otherwise known by the acronym ADE, caused by the COVID-19 vaccines themselves.

Dr. Robert Malone, M.D., M.S., the inventor of the mRNA

technology used by Pfizer-BioNTech and Moderna in their COVID-19 vaccines, states that the COVID-19 vaccines are causing ADE. Dr. Malone indicates that the scientific evidence is becoming increasingly clear that the COVID-19 vaccines are causing the virus to replicate at higher levels than would be the case in the absence of the vaccination.[1009] He said that this phenomenon of ADE was predictable because ADE has happened in every coronavirus study ever conducted. He said the data indicates that as the immune response from the COVID-19 vaccines wanes after six months, the ADE is kicking in, and we see the result with increased hospitalizations. The hospitalizations are not from breakthrough infections in those vaccinated but rather from ADE brought on by the vaccine itself.

One research study explained:

There are also immunopathological complications associated with the SARS-CoV and MERS-CoV vaccines that require addressing and further optimization. One adverse effect is the induction of antibody-dependent enhancement (ADE) effect, which is usually caused by vaccine-induced suboptimal antibodies that facilitates viral entry into host cells.[1010]

A study was conducted by Timothy Cardozo of the Department of Biochemistry and Molecular Pharmacology, NYU Langone Health, New York, and Ronald Veazey of the Division of Comparative Pathology, Department of Pathology and Laboratory Medicine, Tulane University School of Medicine, Tulane National Primate Research Center. The scientists determined in their research that the COVID-19 vaccines caused an increase in the risk of more severe diseases caused through ADE. They concluded that recipients of COVID-19 vaccines should be warned about all the dangers of ADE before being vaccinated. The scientists determined that the COVID-19 vaccines worsen COVID-19 disease via antibody-dependent enhancement (ADE). They were concerned that the dangers are kept secret in clinical trial protocols and consent forms.[1011]

Many other researchers have determined that the COVD-19 vaccines pose a clear danger of ADE. In another study, the researchers concluded:

> Antibody-based drugs and vaccines against severe acute respiratory syndrome coronavirus 2 (SARS-CoV-2) are being expedited through preclinical and clinical development. Data from the study of SARS-CoV and other respiratory viruses suggest that anti-SARS-CoV-2 antibodies could exacerbate COVID-19 through antibody-dependent enhancement (ADE).[1012]

Another researcher pleaded for caution in the administration of the COVID-19 vaccine:

> [B]ecause ADE of disease cannot be reliably predicted after either vaccination or treatment with antibodies-regardless of what virus is the causative agent-it will be essential to depend on careful analysis of safety in humans as immune interventions for COVID-19 move forward.[1013]

Sadly, the researcher's warning was not heeded. A massive study involving vaccine data from hundreds of countries proves that the COVID-19 vaccines have caused a significant increase in total cases and deaths associated with COVID-19.[1014] The study proves that the COVID-19 vaccines are not only ineffective, but they are driving illness and death. The study showed that the COVID-19 vaccines have caused a whopping 38% more COVID-19 associated cases and an even more astonishing 31% increase in deaths associated with COVID-19 in the United States.[1015] But that is only the tip of the iceberg because many patients suffering ADE may not test positive for COVID-19. They still suffer the consequences of the ailments caused by the vaccine-induced ADE.

The FDA states that "health fraud drug products are articles of unproven effectiveness that claim to treat disease or improve health."[1016] The COVID-19 vaccines are health fraud drug products as defined by the FDA. But the COVID-19 vaccines have gone beyond being of unproven effectiveness. They have entered the realm of being proven unsafe and ineffective. This is more than simply the sleazy marketing of ineffective snake oil. No. No. This is the criminal marketing of deadly poison. People are being misled into believing that vaccines are a safe and effective way to prevent COVID-19, when, in fact, they are ineffective deadly poisons bringing misery and death.

The COVID-19 vaccine program is a planned genocide.[1017] That is not hyperbole. Dr. Vladimir Zelenko, a board-certified physician, opined that the COVID-19 vaccines are "poison death shots" and forcing people to take such shots amounts to genocide.[1018] Michael Yeadon, former vice-president and chief scientist of allergy and respiratory research at Pfizer, and world-renowned Nobel Laureate virologist Luc Montagnier agree with Dr. Zelenko.[1019]

That genocide is being brought to you by the same gang who want you to believe that there is no God and no heaven, only the foreboding vacuum of outer space. They have convinced most people that the earth is a spinning globe orbiting the sun in the mythical dark outer space. It is child's play for these Satanic overlords to hoodwink people to "get vaccinated."[1020] It will not be long before the cabal and their beastly leader convince most people to take the mark of the beast.

> And he causeth all, both small and great, rich and poor, free and bond, to receive a mark in their right

hand, or in their foreheads: And that no man might buy or sell, save he that had the mark, or the name of the beast, or the number of his name. Here is wisdom. Let him that hath understanding count the number of the beast: for it is the number of a man; and his number is Six hundred threescore and six. Revelation 13:16-18.

Dr. John Timmer pushes the unsafe and ineffective vaccines. Dr. Timmer is wrong about vaccines; his ignorance about the flat earth matches his ignorance about vaccines. Heliocentrism and vaccines spring from the same superstitious darkness. Timmer, unsurprisingly, criticizes any notion that the earth is flat. He attacks the sanity of anyone who believes that the earth is flat. He claims that they suffer from a psychological disorder that he pejoratively calls "bullshit receptivity." The eminent Dr. Timmer seems to think he is an expert in the pseudoscience of psychology. He has now segued from biologist to psychologist. He cites to an article published in a psychological journal as his authority for this diagnosis.[1021] Timmer states:

> Conspiracy theorists tend also have a tendency to believe in nonsense that sounds profound. The technical term for this, and I am not making this up, is called bullshit receptivity. This may explain why they believe all the baroque reasons people have come up with for why a flat earth can still have seasons.[1022]

31 PBS Caught Red-Handed Using Video Fakery

The reason for Dr. Timmer's attack on the mental health of those that believe in a flat earth is their refusal to accept the results of the scam perpetrated by Alfred Russel Wallace at the Bedford Canal. Timmer also noted the refusal of believers in a flat earth to accept recent tests conducted under the auspices of the Public Broadcast Service (PBS). Timmer cites to those tests as proof that the earth is a sphere. Closer examination of the PBS experiments, though, show them to be fraudulent.

If the earth were a globe, as most believe, it should be easy to prove. PBS set out to do that very thing. But they were caught using false evidence in their effort. PBS needed to resort to false evidence because the earth is not a sphere. The earth is flat. Such antics by PBS suggest that the earth is flat; otherwise, there would be no need to manufacture false evidence of sphericity.

The formula for the expected drop per mile is $M2 \times 8 = D$, where "M" is the number of miles from the observer at ground level, "8" is the number of inches dropped per mile squared, and "D" is the distance of the drop over the horizon. The above equation assumes an earth with a circumference of 24,901 miles. J. Clendenning, the former British Surveyor General of the Gold

Coast (Ghana), in his book, *The Principles of Surveying*, confirmed that "as regards curvature, a level line parallel to the earth's surface ... falls away from a plane tangential to the earth at any point by about 8 in. in a distance of a mile, and this difference increases with the square of the distance."[1023]

With that in mind, PBS set out to prove that the earth is a sphere by stationing a telescope approximately 2 feet above a body of water and then viewing a helicopter landing on the other side of the lake, approximately 6 miles away. If the earth were a globe, the helicopter would disappear below the horizon behind approximately 12 feet of the earth's curvature. Sure enough, that is what was depicted in the PBS video.

It should be noted that because the camera used by PBS was at an elevation of approximately two feet above the water, the expected drop below the horizon from 6 miles away from that vantage point two feet above the water should be 10 feet, 8 inches. PBS framed their results with the assumption that the camera would be directly on the waterline. It was not. And so, the 12-foot result by PBS is shown to be a contrivance. Indeed, the type of helicopter used in the video has a rotor that is a little more than 10 feet above the helicopter skids.

There is a more significant problem. A truth seeker with an Odysee channel called Taboo Conspiracy has proven that PBS used computer-generated imagery (CGI) to falsely portray the earth as a globe.[1024] His video can be viewed on his Odysee channel in the likely event that YouTube deletes his channel.[1025] Why would PBS fake a video to show the earth is a globe? Because the earth is flat, PBS found it necessary to use video trickery to fool the gullible public into thinking that the earth is a sphere.

In the video initially posted by PBS, one can see that PBS used the same video for both the helicopter landing and helicopter take-off scenes.[1026] This is evident because the same birds flying the same pattern can be seen flying across the screen in both scenes. We see the helicopter landing while birds fly across the screen. Moments later, we see the helicopter taking off while the same video plays, showing the same birds flying the same pattern across the same scene. That same flock of birds flying the same pattern in both scenes indicates that the same video is being used for both scenes but with the helicopter landing in one scene and taking off in the other. The ineluctable conclusion is that a CGI of a helicopter is being inserted in the same video. The helicopter is not really there at all. The helicopter is CGI.

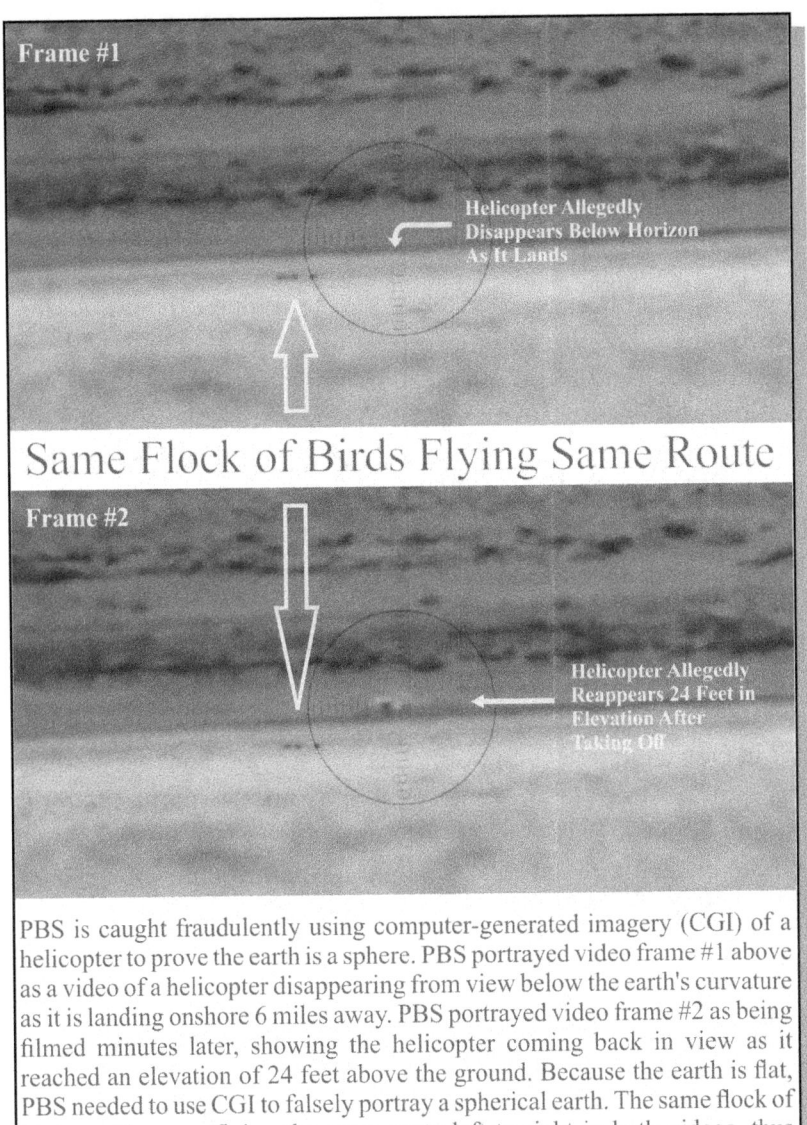

PBS is caught fraudulently using computer-generated imagery (CGI) of a helicopter to prove the earth is a sphere. PBS portrayed video frame #1 above as a video of a helicopter disappearing from view below the earth's curvature as it is landing onshore 6 miles away. PBS portrayed video frame #2 as being filmed minutes later, showing the helicopter coming back in view as it reached an elevation of 24 feet above the ground. Because the earth is flat, PBS needed to use CGI to falsely portray a spherical earth. The same flock of birds can be seen flying the same route left to right in both videos, thus indicating that the depiction of the helicopter is CGI superimposed into the video.

What is even more damning to PBS is that once PBS found out that their use of CGI had been publically revealed, the original video somehow disappeared from YouTube.[1027] PBS then altered the video and re-posted the altered video on their PBS website.[1028] PBS realized they had been caught and took steps to cover their tracks.

This author was able to find the unaltered August 23, 2016, original video on the Internet Archive Wayback Machine.[1029]

When PBS re-posted the video they deleted the frames that showed the same birds flying across the screen in both the alleged helicopter landing scene and the helicopter take-off scene.[1030] PBS had a problem in their alteration. They were stuck using their already contrived video. They could not change that. The only way they could obscure the use of CGI was to remove as many frames as possible showing the birds flying across the screen. In doing that, they could not cut out the entry of the birds on the scene as the helicopter landed because they wanted to catch that moment on the screen. Thus, they froze the video at the earliest point possible to remove the birds. But that left the entry of the birds on the far left of the screen. At that moment, though, the helicopter CGI was still in view, and thus their point was not proven. So what they did was resume the video, which began from the point after the missing frames. This showed a clear horizon with no helicopter and the birds jumping to the far right of the screen.

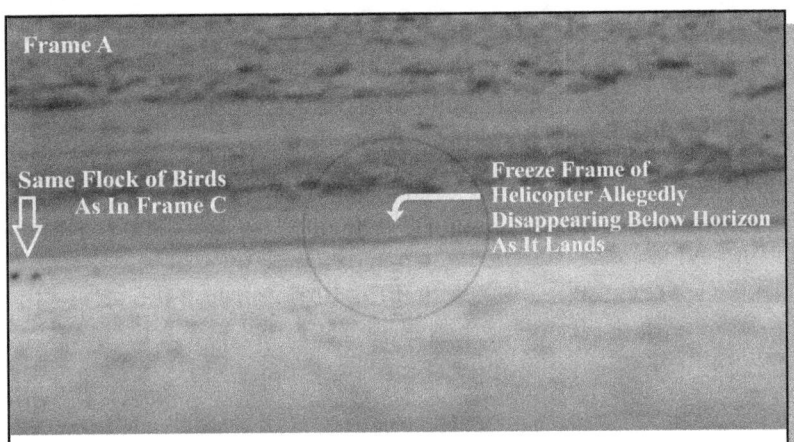

After the CGI scam was revealed, PBS deleted its original video from YouTube. The video was then republished on the PBS website, but most of the flight of the flock of birds was spliced out of the video. In the above picture (Frame A), we see the flock of birds entering the frame as the helicopter is allegedly in the process of landing below the horizon. The narrator continues his narration while Frame A is frozen on the screen. PBS froze the frame as soon as possible, but the very top of the helicopter is still slightly in view. Then, within seconds, the video resumes, but the birds are not seen continuing their flight across the screen. Instead, they suddenly reappear on the other side of the screen. The frame below (Frame B) shows the video resumption after the above freeze-frame in Frame A. This indicates that the frames in the video showing the birds flying across the screen have been removed in an attempt to conceal PBS's insertion of a CGI helicopter in the same video loop. They did that to falsely portray the helicopter disappearing below the horizon and then moments later reappearing above the horizon. This misled the viewers into believing that the earth is a sphere.

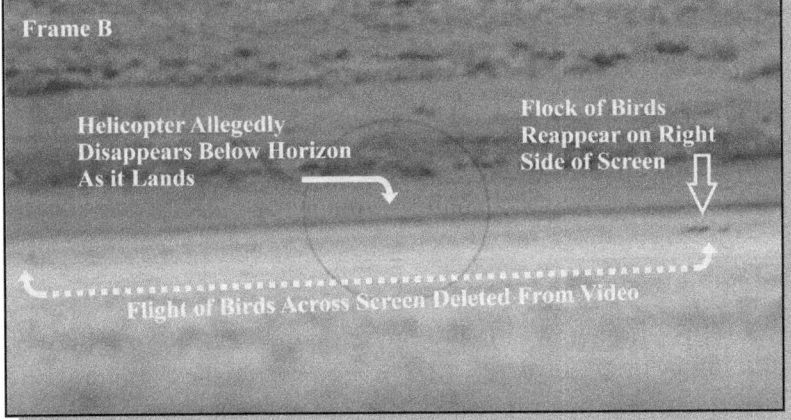

When all of the evidence is shown, we find that PBS has been caught red-handed faking an experiment to falsely portray the earth as a sphere. Then, when their scam was exposed, they attempted a coverup, which just made things worse for them. By not being able to remove the entry of the birds from the far left of the screen when the CGI of the helicopter in the process of landing (Frame A) we can match that up with the CGI of the helicopter taking off (Frame C) and see that the bird entry on the left of the screen in both the scene of the landing (Frame A) and the scene of the take off of the helicopter (Frame C) match. PBS's attempted coverup has failed.

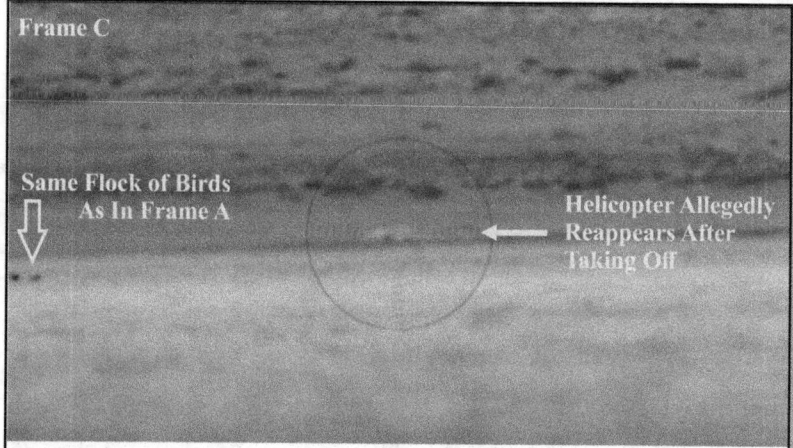

As the helicopter is allegedly taking off from below the horizon, the same flock of Birds appear (above in Frame C) in an identical formation as when the helicopter allegedly disappeared below the horizon moments earlier in Frame A. That indicates that the same video was used for the helicopter's alleged landing as was used for the helicopter's alleged take off. That means that the helicopter is CGI being inserted into a common looped video to falsely portray the earth as a sphere.

PBS tried and failed to prove that the earth is a sphere by using video trickery. When they were busted, they attempted to cover up their fraud, but their coverup also failed. Yet, the scientific community still touts the altered PBS video of that experiment as proof that the earth is a sphere. It is very much like the scam run by Alfred Russel Wallace at the Bedford Canal, which modern scientists still tout as proof that the earth is a sphere.

32 Propaganda Misfire by National Geographic

The PBS sham experiment demonstrates that the scientific skulduggery of the kind orchestrated by Alfred Russel Wallace at the Bedford Canal in 1870 continues today. Such sham experiments are regularly being conducted today and presented as proof that the earth is a sphere. The National Geographic documentary, which was discussed earlier in this book, involved just such an experiment designed to hoodwink the public into believing that the earth is a globe.[1031] They conducted an experiment to prove that the earth is a sphere. But their experiment is provably fallacious.

Sometimes the most convincing proof of the flat earth actually comes from those who promote the heliocentric model. "How so?" you might ask. In the effort of heliocentric "scientists" to attack the evidence of the flat earth, they necessarily must engage in all manner of sophistry, obfuscation, and deception. When that deception is revealed, the logical question in the minds of men of reason is "why engage in such deception if the earth were truly a moving globe?" The ineluctable conclusion is that there would be no reason for deception if the earth were a globe as the "scientists" portray it. The earth, therefore, must be flat.

As mentioned earlier in this book, the National Geographic documentary carried the clear message that belief in a flat earth is a dangerous threat to science and society. Of course, the National Geographic had to portray some semblance of scientific proof to slam the door on what they viewed as the dangerous theory of flat earth. They turned to a group known as the *Independent Investigations Group*. That organization set up an experiment on the Salton Sea Lake in California to prove that the earth is a sphere.

The commentator (Mariana van Zeller) interviewed James Underdown, who is the founder and chairman of the *Independent Investigations Group*. Underdown is an entertainer; he is not a scientist. Underdown has a B.A. degree in English, not science. He has toured comedy clubs under the moniker "Jim U-Boat."[1032] He has written, directed, and acted in films. He was the lead singer in the rock and roll group, The Heathens. He also writes a column, *Ask The Atheist*.[1033] Think about that for a moment. The esteemed National Geographic turns not to a scientist to prove that the earth is a globe. No, they choose an entertainer. It seems that Underdown was selected based on his philosophy of life and skill in persuasion, rather than his scientific acumen. The experiment had more to do with being convincing than being scrupulous.

Underdown explained to van Zeller that "this is the boat base target. It's [got] horizontal stripes. We're going to launch a small boat out into the water here with a striped target. And as it gets farther and farther out you'll start to lose the stripes."[1034]

Closeup shot of the banner on the beach with James Underdown and Mariana van Zeller showing the straight red and black horizontal lines. Notice the trick? The testing crew used an artifice of fashioning a banner that did not have a uniform number of stripes above and below the black stripe. When looking from a distance, a person would naturally think that the black stripe was the middle stripe. But that was not the case. That gave the false impression that the bottom was being obscured to a greater extent than was really the case. Indeed, the cameraman was thus able to misleadingly explain that more stripes were obscured than was in fact the case.

Van Zeller then explains that "as a boat approaches the horizon, it appears to slowly dip down into the water before disappearing completely. That's got everything to do with the curvature of the earth. If the planet was flat, the entire boat would remain visible. So, it'll be a very visual depiction of the curvature of the earth."[1035]

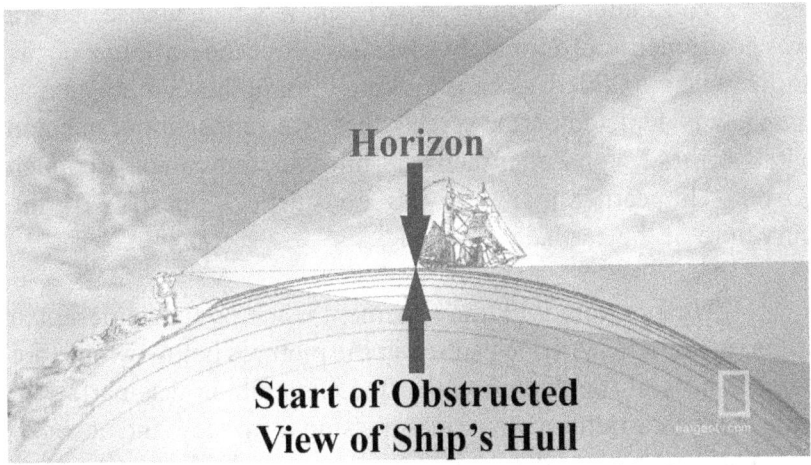

Annotated graphic shown during National Geographic documentary depicting how a ships hull is blocked from view because it is allegedly dropping below the horizon of a spherical earth. The spherical earth theory requires that the horizon be in front of the obstructed view of the ship's hull.

The narrator indicated that the experiment proved that the earth is a sphere. But what is seen proves no such thing. Van Zeller begins her misleading narration by explaining that "at first all the stripes are clearly visible. But, sure enough, as the boat reaches the horizon, the stripes begin to disappear one by one." Hearing that statement a listener would have the impression that many stripes had been obscured by the horizon. In fact, only one half of a stipe was obscured. And, as we will see, that disappearance was not due to it dropping below the horizon. Van Zeller claimed that the red stripe had "completely disappeared and it's now getting closer to sort of the middle green stripe." That was a false narration. Only part of the red stripe had disappeared and the entire white stripe below the black stripe (she called it green) was still visible. The obscuring of the banner did not come close to the middle black (green) stripe as claimed by Van Zeller. Notice that she called the dark stripe "the middle green stripe." That stripe was not the middle of the banner. The fact that it was closer to the bottom of the banner than the top was part of the planned optical illusion.

Van Zeller then interviewed a cameraman, whose camera was positioned approximately 12 inches above the waterline on the shore, who explained, as he is looking through his camera, and as his view is depicted on the screen, that "we've lost about one and a half stripes." Van Zeller then asks him "so, this can only happen why?" The cameraman answers on queue: "because of the curvature of the earth."[1036]

The problem with the statement made by the cameraman is that it was a lie. As one can see in the pictures below, which are screen-shots of the depiction that the cameraman was narrating, only half of the bottom red strip is missing from view and not "one and a half stripes" as the cameraman he alleged. The testing crew used a trick of creating a banner that did not have a uniform number of stripes above and below the black stripe. The top of the banner above the black stripe, there was one red stripe separated by two white stripes. But the bottom of the banner had only one white stripe and one red stripe. That gave the false impression when looking at the banner from a distance that more of the banner was being obscured than was the case. That is why the cameraman announced that "we've lost about one and a half stripes," when in fact, only half of the bottom red stripe was obscured.

The banner was being held by hand from a small boat. There was no mechanical device that was used to affix the banner to the boat. The banner was not even displayed until the boat was at a great distance away from shore. There was no way to verify whether the bottom of the banner was being submerged in the water either purposely or inadvertently. There was no reported measurement of the distance the boat was from shore. There were no real controls, and the experimenters had an agenda. The experiment proved nothing.

Furthermore, we can see the distortion due to light refraction by the misshapen horizontal stripes on the banner. That is the reason the cameraman crouched down as close to the waterline as possible. Light refraction is most prevalent close to the waterline.

Banner as seen through the camera lens during the National Geographic documentary showing the lines on the banner distorted by light refraction.

Van Zeller explained that the phenomenon that was being observed was due to the curvature of the earth. She narrated that fact as a graphic (depicted above) was being displayed on the screen showing a ship dipping below the horizon. Under the orthodox view of a spherical earth, the horizon is the point at which the bottom of the banner is supposed to disappear. The problem with that theory is that it is not born out by the observed events. Indeed, when the banner is viewed we find that the disappearance of part of the red stripe takes place in front of the horizon and not at the juncture of the horizon as predicted by van Zeller. The horizon is behind the banner. The banner cannot be blocked by something behind it.

The red stripe on the bottom of the banner is not blocked from view due to it dropping below the horizon on a spherical earth. We know that because the bottom of the banner cannot be obstructed by something that is behind it. The horizon must be in front of the banner for it to be the cause of the visual obstruction. That can mean only one thing. The bottom of the banner is not disappearing from view due to the curvature of the earth. It is being obscured by a combination of perspective and light refraction.

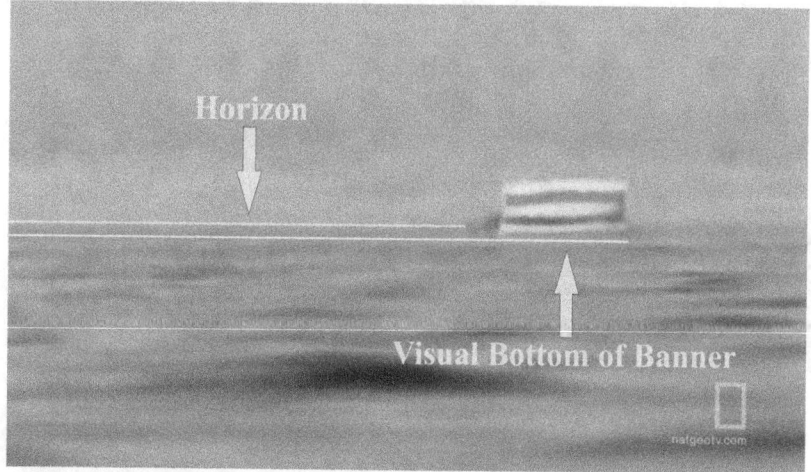

Annotated screen shot of the National Geographic documentary depicting the bottom of the banner disappearing from view in front of the horizon, which can be seen in the background. Thus, the red stripe on the bottom of the banner is not blocked from view due to it dropping below the horizon on a spherical earth because the bottom of the banner cannot drop behind something when it is in front of it. The banner must be behind the horizon in order for the horizon to be the cause of the visual obstruction of the banner. That means that the bottom of the banner is not being blocked from view by the alleged curvature of the earth. It is being obscured due to perspective and light refraction.

  The principal cause of the disappearance of the bottom of the National Geographic banner was light refraction. By crouching down closer to the water, the cameraman enhanced the effect of light refraction. Crouching down also caused his perspective to draw closer to the bottom of the banner, which further augmented the bottom-up vanishing effect. Areas that are equidistant in elevation from the eye-level converge at a point at eye level. But when a person lowers his perspective, that causes objects that move away from the observer to become cut-off from view beginning from the bottom-up.

The maximum angular resolution of a person who has 20/20 Snellen acuity is .98 arcminutes.[1037] That is roughly one arcminute, which is 1/60th of one degree (.017°). When the angular resolution reaches its limit, the object cannot be seen beyond that point. That vanishing point takes place at eye level. For example, in the case of a U.S. penny, which is 3/4 (.75) of an inch in diameter, the penny will disappear from a person's vision when it gets to approximately 214 feet away from the observer. That is because at 214 feet away, the penny's diameter will have reached one arcminute (.017°). Of course, a large object, like the banner in the National Geographic experiment, can be seen at a longer distance before it disappears from sight.

But not all objects that travel away from an observer on a flat plane will be seen to vanish uniformly from top-to-bottom. That is because if the observer is closer to the bottom of the viewed object, he will see the bottom of the object become cut off from view before seeing the top of the object disappear.[1038] The disappearance of a distant object from the bottom-up occurs because the person's eyes are closer to the elevation of the object's bottom. This is caused by the maximum angular resolution of the person's eyes being reached first by the object's bottom. Once that happens, the object begins to disappear from the bottom-up.

The effect of visual disappearance due to angular resolution is much reduced when a telephoto lens is used, as was the case in the National Geographic experiment. A telephoto lens acts to bring the object closer and thus allow a vanished object to reappear because it is brought back within the limits of the angular resolution of the viewer. But the effect on angular resolution by the use of a telephoto lens can be countered regarding the bottom of the observed object by bringing the telephoto lens closer to the surface of the water or ground, as the cameraman did in the National Geographic video. When the cameraman crouched down to within one foot of the surface of the water, the lowered view from the camera enhanced the bottom-up disappearance of the banner.

Rowbotham explains that because a typical observer onshore is closer to the hull of a ship than he is to the masthead when the ship is sailing away from him "[t]he hull of a ship is nearer to the water--the surface on which it moves--than the masthead. Ergo, the hull of an outward bound ship must be the first to disappear."[1039] The phenomenon is well known among scientists, and the Independent Investigations Group, who performed the banner experiment for the National Geographic, certainly knew about that phenomenon. That is why they chose that experiment, and that is why the cameraman made certain to crouch down close to the water's surface.

Add to the laws of perspective the phenomenon of light refraction, and we have a recipe for the disappearance of the bottom of the banner. But that disappearance has nothing to do with the sphericity of the earth. The fact that the horizon can be clearly seen behind the banner is proof that the banner's bottom is not being cut off from view due to the earth's alleged curvature. The banner cannot be blocked by something that is behind it. The National Geographic tried constructing an elaborate experiment to hoodwink the public to believe that the earth is a globe. But the pesky evidence that the earth is flat could not be hidden.

Van Zeller punctuates her scientific charade with the ominous warning of danger, which really was the unstated theme of the National Geographic documentary. With an impassioned inflection in her voice, she states that "thousands of years of empirical scientific evidence is now being dismissed as a mere conspiracy, and that's where I think it really starts getting dangerous for all of us."[1040] According to van Zeller and her ilk, those who believe in the biblical flat earth are "dangerous." The devil and his minions consider the issue of a flat and stationary earth a serious matter; perhaps you should too.

33 NASA Christians?

Dr. Danny Falkner portrays himself as a Christian. He buys (or pretends to buy) hook-line-and-sinker the lies of NASA. He takes umbrage at anyone who would question the integrity of Christians who are NASA astronauts. Dr. Faulkner emotes:

> Christians who think that the earth is flat or that men never set foot on the moon are effectively accusing several Christian brothers of lying about one of the biggest things that ever happened in their lives. Are the Apollo moon landing deniers prepared to make this accusation?[1041]

This author will answer his question in the affirmative. All NASA astronauts are liars. And that includes those who claim to be Christians. God admonishes us not to place any trust in men. "Shall mortal man be more just than God? shall a man be more pure than his maker? Behold, he put no trust in his servants; and his angels he charged with folly:" (Job 4:17-18)

Notice that God mentions "his angels he charged with folly." Those are the fallen angels, i.e., devils. Beware, both Satan and his minions can appear as angels of light.

And no marvel; for Satan himself is transformed into an angel of light. Therefore it is no great thing if his ministers also be transformed as the ministers of righteousness; whose end shall be according to their works. (2 Corinthians 11:14-15)

We, as Christians, are called on to have discernment; we are to be harmless as doves, but also to be wise as serpents. "Behold, I send you forth as sheep in the midst of wolves: be ye therefore wise as serpents, and harmless as doves." (Matthew 10:16)

One of the NASA astronauts identified by Dr. Faulkner as an upstanding Christian was James Irwin (1930-1991). He was the Lunar Module Pilot for Appollo 15, and as such, he was alleged to have been the eighth person to walk on the moon. A little known fact is that James Irwin was a Freemason.[1042] Irwin belonged to Tajon Masonic Lodge, No. 104, in Colorado Springs, Colorado.[1043]

Freemasonry is a religion, whose occult doctrines flow from the Kabbalah. The god of Freemasonry is Lucifer.[1044] The hidden truth that is ultimately revealed to the higher adepts who have proven themselves worthy of knowing is that Freemasonry is the worship and service of the fallen angel, Satan.[1045] In this author's book *The Greatest Lie on Earth*, I document that Masonic astronauts and administrators control NASA.[1046]

God can save anyone out of any false religion, even Freemasonry. It is possible that Irwin was saved. Irwin claimed to be a Christian and was giving his Christian testimony in Nashville, Tennessee. At that time, he met a fellow Christian, Lee Gelvani, who had almost convinced James Irwin, to confess to the moon landing hoax. Later, Irwin telephoned Bill Kaysing, who was a senior technical writer and engineer who worked for Rocketdyne, a company that designed and built the Apollo rocket engines.[1047] Kaysing was famous for having written a book, *We Never Went to the Moon: America's Thirty Billion Dollar Swindle*, which revealed the moon landing hoax.[1048] Why would Irwin, a NASA astronaut, call someone known to have evidence that the moon landings were a hoax? Because Irwin was going to blow the whistle.

James Irwin told Kaysing during the phone call that he was concerned that the phone he was using was tapped. He gave Kaysing his home phone number and asked Kaysing to call him back that coming Friday at his home in Colorado Springs, Colorado. When Kaysing called him as scheduled that Friday, Kaysing found out that Irwin had died of a heart attack.[1049] James Irwin died on Thursday, August 8, 1991, the day before Kaysing was scheduled to call him. Irwin knew that his phone calls were tapped, which speaks volumes about the kind of pervasive surveillance the astronauts are under. While there is no definite proof that Irwin was murdered, his sudden death the day before he was expected to confess to the moon landing hoax is undoubtedly suspicious.

Another NASA astronaut that Dr. Danny Faulkner portrays as an upstanding Christian who is beyond reproach is Charles M. Duke, who was the Apollo 16 Lunar Module Pilot. Duke was alleged to have joined Commander John W. Young on the moon. Dr. Faulkner "asked Charles Duke to respond to those who think that the earth is flat and those who think that we faked the Apollo moon landing. This is what he wrote:"[1050]

> I was the lunar module pilot on the Apollo 16 mission to the moon. We launched from KSC (Kennedy Space Center) in Florida on April 16, 1972. We left earth orbit for our three day trip to the moon about three hours later. As we maneuvered our spacecraft to dock with our lunar module, the earth came into view about 20,000 miles away. It was an awesome sight. As you can

see in the photo, it is obviously a sphere and not a flat circle. As we journeyed to the moon, we would look out our windows and see a smaller earth, and each time we would see different landmasses, so it was obviously rotating on its axis.[1051]

Charlie Duke, the alleged "Christian" astronaut, is a liar. The fraud of his trip to the moon and his alleged moon excursion was inadvertently revealed in a documentary film produced by NASA.

In a documentary film produced by NASA about the Apollo 16 moon mission, two videos, each allegedly taken from the moon, were displayed and narrated. NASA claims that one video was taken from the moon showing John Young at the rim of a moon crater on April 21, 1972.[1052] The NASA narrator explains that the astronauts traveled approximately one kilometer west of the LEM landing site to get to the moon crater where John Young can be seen standing.[1053] The simultaneous radio transmission of the conversation between Young and Duke, in pertinent part, went as follows:

> Charlie Duke: "God you're just beautiful. That is the most beautiful sight."
>
> John Young: "What's that?"
>
> Charlie Duke: "You standing there on the rim of that crater."

Notice that Charlie Duke, the "Christian," begins his explanation by taking God's name in vain. *See* Exodus 20:7. The NASA documentary explains that the next day, April 22, 1972, the astronauts traveled over 4 kilometers south of the landing site in the lunar rover and climbed up the side of Stone Mountain to a crater 700 feet in elevation above the LEM landing site. The two astronauts, John Young and Charles Duke, can be seen standing near the rim of the alleged moon crater. Again there is heard a simultaneous radio transmission from Duke where he explains:

> Charlie Duke: "Wow! What a place. What a view isn't it John?"
>
> John Young: "It's absolutely unreal."
>
> Charlie Duke: "... It's just spectacular ... all I can say is it's spectacular."

When viewing the two videos, supposedly taken one day apart and many miles distance from one another, one can see clearly that the astronauts are in the same location in both videos. In each video, Charlie Duke can be heard simultaneously narrating the excursion. But when the videos of the two excursions, which were represented by NASA to be at two different locations separated by several miles, are viewed together, it can be seen that the excursions are hoaxes because they are being filmed from the same place.

Notice that John Young calls the place he is observing "unreal." Could he be giving us a cryptic hint that the moonscape where he is being filmed is "unreal" in the sense that it is not really the moon? The scenery certainly indicates it is a film set and not the moon. In each video, the foregrounds are identical, right down to every rock and pebble. Not only is the location identical, but the shadows cast by the rocks are identical, which indicates that an artificial, stationary light source is illuminating the area. Further, the camera from which the two videos were taken was positioned at the same place and was shooting from precisely the same angle. This is clear evidence that the moon landings were videotaped on Earth, using artificial lighting.

Identical foreground, with identical shadows, videotaped from precisely the same distance, at precisely the same angle, portrayed by NASA to have been taken at two separate locations on two separate days on the moon.

Portrayed by NASA to be one kilometer west of the moon landing site on April 21, 1972.

Portrayed by NASA to be four kilometers south of the moon landing site on April 22, 1972.

"Christian" astronaut Charlie Duke is up to his eyeballs in a massive deception to conceal from the world the truth of God's creation. The Bible warns us about such servants of the devil who will appear as ministers of righteousness. *See* 2 Corinthians 11:14-15. NASA has never explained the videos. Instead, it has tried to conceal the evidence. This author has searched the NASA website video library of the Apollo 16 moon mission for the original video footage used in the NASA Apollo 16 film documentary.[1054] The original videos of the two excursions discussed above are not posted on the NASA internet video library, which is supposed to contain a complete library of the Apollo 16 videos. Nonetheless, the two videos have been represented by NASA to be official videos of the Apollo 16 moon mission.

The NASA space missions have been hoaxes from the beginning. There is no such thing as the vacuum of space. In Genesis, it states that God made the firmament and he called the firmament Heaven. Genesis 1:7-19. The firmament, as the name suggests, is something hard. It is not a vacuum of nothingness. God set the sun, moon, and stars in the firmament of the heaven. The firmament divides the waters beneath the firmament on the earth from the waters above the firmament. Genesis 1:6-9. That is why the sky is blue; there is water above the firmament.

Charlie Duke, promoted by Faulkner as a paragon of Christian virtue is, in fact, a lying shill for NASA. And, as we have seen, Dr. Danny Faulkner has credibility issues of his own. Faulkner and Duke are two peas in a pod, who both continue to promote the lie that the earth is a spinning and orbiting globe in a vacuum of space. We have one con artist (Faulkner) vouching for the credibility of another con artist (Duke).

34 All or Nothing

Jesus stated: "So then because thou art lukewarm, and neither cold nor hot, I will spue thee out of my mouth." (Revelation 3:16) The lukewarm creation scientists play fast and loose with God's word. They adhere to the literal creation by God of man and the world in a literal six days, but when it comes to God's description of a flat, stationary earth, suddenly that part of the Bible is to be taken poetically. The creation scientists take every single passage that describes a flat, stationary earth poetically. When their poetic scheme does not do the trick, they simply redefine inconvenient words.

This stratagem of the creation scientists has not gone unnoticed by the world. An atheist known as the Sensuous Curmudgeon has taken these creation scientists to task for their hypocrisy. In one article titled *Is Jason Lisle a Flat Earther?*[1055], the Sensuous Curmudgeon concludes that Jason Lisle must be a flat earther if he is to be consistent in claiming that one must take all of the Bible as one's final authority, including Genesis. It is all or nothing. The Curmudgeon points out the Bible passages that clearly illustrate that the Bible is stationary and flat. Dr Lisle states:

> It's a very slippery slope when you decide that there are some sections of the Bible that you are

going to allow the secular scientist to tell you what it really means. ... You've opened a very dangerous door. ... Some people will say they can live with the inconsistencies. They'll tell me: 'Well, it's just Genesis that I allow the scientists to tell me what it meant,' ... But, what we've found is that children will see that inconsistency, and they will be more consistent, they will reject all of the Bible. They'll say, 'Well, mom and dad don't really believe in the Bible because they don't believe in the first few chapters. Why should I believe in the Gospel?' We've seen that happen. The statistics are just alarming. We see the students walking away from church in droves.[1056]

The Curmudgeon concludes that "Jason is right — it's gotta be all or nothing."[1057] The Curmudgeon then exposes the hypocrisy of Dr. Lisle to on the one hand advocate that the Bible should be the final authority over contrary secular science, but at the same time to reject the primacy of the Bible when its depiction of a flat and stationary earth conflicts with the heliocentric model.

He's right again. So where does flat-Earth come into this? In a sense, our title is unfair, because Jason didn't discuss it. But if the question were put to him, he'd have to answer that it's flat. We've previously given you a large list of scripture passages that clearly say so — see The Earth Is Flat! And Jason must also believe that The Earth Does Not Move! That's why he's our favorite creation scientist.[1058]

Based upon what he has said, Dr. Lisle must either believe in the flat earth or be a hypocrite. Since Dr. Lisle has come out on the side of the secular scientific view of heliocentrism as having primacy over the biblical depiction of a flat, stationary earth, that makes him a hypocrite.

The atheist Sensuous Curmudgeon will suffer an eternal comeuppance if God does not turn him from his rebellion to a saving knowledge of Jesus Christ. Many atheists, like the Curmudgeon, enjoy running around in their comfort, blaspheming God and pronouncing their conviction that there is no God. But they change their tune when they find their lives threatened. The old saying that there are no atheists in foxholes is true. This author spoke to an atheist soldier who when threatened with impending death admitted that he prayed to God for deliverance. Sadly, after the danger passed, he went back to his atheism. He attributed his sudden plea to God to a moment of weakness and vowed never again to repeat that prayer. Samuel Rowbotham describes what he witnessed when atheists found themselves at death's door:

> In 1841 the author was on board a steamer sailing along the western shores of Scotland, when suddenly the vessel struck upon an unseen rock; all hands were called to aid in working the pumps, but the water gradually gained upon them. After a few hours the captain announced that all hope of safety had passed away, and, being evidently a religious man, he exhorted all on board to shape their thoughts and feelings for a future life. Immediately every knee was bent, and every eye and face upcast towards Heaven. Among the--over one hundred--passengers, male and female, young and old, were several apostles of atheism, who for a time bravely bore the prospect of death, but, as the ship sank deeper and deeper, a calm reflective aspect came over them, and shortly afterwards no eye or face could be seen higher and more imploringly gazing upwards than those who for years had treated with contempt all ideas of Heaven or God or anything other than a boundless

universe filled with material globular worlds, and their godless, soulless, hopeless inhabitants.[1059]

Notice that all on the ship, including the avowed atheists, prayed to God for deliverance by looking up to heaven above. They knew that God's abode was in heaven above. They seemed to know that creation is as God described it; the flat earth is below and God's throne in heaven is above. Even the atheists, in their heart of hearts, when their life was in the balance, seemed to know that truth. The atheists imploring God in heaven for deliverance reveals the stark truth that men are without excuse. Deep down, all men know who God is and where God is. They know the invisible things of God because, as God explains in his Bible, he has revealed himself to man through his creation. "For the invisible things of him from the creation of the world are clearly seen, being understood by the things that are made, even his eternal power and Godhead; so that they are without excuse." Romans 1:20.

Atheism is one form of rebellion against God; hypocrisy is another. Dr. Lisle tries to cover his hypocrisy by arguing that the sections of the Bible that describe a flat, stationary earth should be taken poetically or by redefining the words in the passages. But those arguments are unconvincing work-arounds. They are premised on the assumption that science (falsely so-called) is correct that the earth is a spinning sphere revolving around the sun in space. There is really little difference between accepting the lies of science over the truths in the Bible on the one hand and claiming that the Bible has authority over science but then interpreting the Bible to change its plain language into poetry so that it conforms to the lies of science.

Dr. Lisle is concerned that children will see that their mom and dad don't really believe what is written in the Bible, and think to themselves, then "why should I believe in the Gospel?" How is that any different from what Dr. Lisle is doing. He hypocritically does the very thing of which he warns. He takes a little truth that there are "some" poetic passages in the Bible, and he applies that truth deceptively to every Bible passage that describes a flat, stationary earth. That is not an honest reading of the Bible, that is someone with a heliocentric agenda twisting the meaning of the Bible.

If all of the passages in the Bible that describe a flat, stationary earth are to be read poetically, as advised by Dr. Lisle, why not subject the other passages to that poetic license? Lisle argues that the Genesis account should be interpreted to mean the creation was in six literal, 24-hour days. But that interpretation runs counter to Lisle's poetic rubric. Under Lisle's poetic license, the creation in six days could be interpreted poetically to mean millions of years; Noah's ark could be poetically interpreted as not a real event; the parting of the Red Sea could be poetically interpreted as not a real event; the miracles of Jesus could be poetically interpreted as not real events; the death and resurrection of Jesus could be poetically interpreted as not real events. There is simply no end to the damage that can be done by Dr. Lisle's prejudicial rendering the Bible as a book of poetry. He knows it. Dr. Lisle warns against giving science primacy over the Bible, but giving a poetic reading to every flat earth Bible passage has the effect of doing that very thing.

The only reason Dr. Lisle is turning the flat earth Bible passages into poetry is that he has a preconceived notion that the earth is a spinning ball in space. He, thus, must find a way to undermine the authority of the flat earth Bible passages. Enter Lisle the poet. He takes off his science hat, puts on his poetry hat, and presto-chango, he becomes modern day Shakespeare. With his new-found expertise in poetry, he issues an edict that all passages in the Bible referring to a flat earth do not, in fact, refer to a flat earth. Those passages shall, hereafter, be considered mere poetry. Do not dare to question that edict, because it is coming from Creation Science Hall of Famer Dr. Jason Lisle. He reconciles the biblical text with the heliocentric model by reducing the Bible to poetry; he does so on no authority but his say so. But the dirty secret is that Dr. Lisle is not a very good scientist, and he is a terrible poet.

It is people like Dr. Lisle who push "science falsely so called" whom we are warned about in the Bible. "O Timothy, keep that which is committed to thy trust, avoiding profane and vain babblings, and oppositions of science falsely so called: Which some professing have erred concerning the faith. Grace be with thee. Amen." 1 Timothy 6:20-21.

The Curmudgeon correctly chides the creation science phonies like Dr. Lisle. "All creationists who are not also flat-earthers are hereby declared to be hypocrites."[1060] The Curmudgeon states that if the Bible is to be believed accurate, those who adhere to it must accept that the earth is flat. The language in the Bible allows for no other interpretation. The Curmudgeon concludes that "there can be no confusion regarding mention of the earth's 'edges' or 'ends' or 'pillars' or 'corners' or 'borders.' Those terms are incompatible with a spherical shape."[1061] The Curmudgeon cites more than 20 Bible passages that clearly indicate that the earth is flat and stationary. He concludes from those passages that "[t]here's nothing more to be said. The earth is flat, and that's that."[1062]

Keep in mind that the Curmudgeon does not believe the truth of what the Bible states; he is just reading it for what it says. He is attacking the credibility of the creation scientists by pointing out that if they are going to give the Bible primacy over science, they must accept that the earth is flat. The Curmudgeon states:

> Our plan from now on will be to chide creationists for the hypocrisy of their belief in creationism while they simultaneously refuse to believe in the scriptural doctrines of not only the flat earth but also the unmoving earth and the geocentric

universe.[1063]

The Curmudgeon is an atheist and believes, as do the creation scientists, that the earth is a spinning sphere. Of course, being an atheist, he disputes the creation scientists' view of creation by God in six literal days. And so he attacks the biblical creation story as being untrue. His attack is premised on his belief that the Bible inaccurately portrays the earth as being flat. He concludes that if the Bible is wrong about the earth being flat, it is also wrong about creation in six literal days. They both hang together. The Curmudgeon concludes that if the creation scientists insist on accepting as authoritative the description in Genesis of creation in six literal days, to be consistent, they must also accept as authoritative the description in Genesis of a flat earth. The Curmudgeon explains that there can be no middle ground:

> Our point, in case anyone somehow missed it, is that if one insists on creationism because it's scriptural, notwithstanding the findings of science to the contrary, then it's utterly and inexplicably inconsistent to deny that the earth is flat, doesn't move, rests on pillars, and the sun, moon, and stars revolve around it. If a creationist can reject an unscientific teaching like the flat earth or the geocentric universe, then why can't creationism also be rejected? If one is going to be a creationist, he should go all the way. There's nothing more to be said.[1064]

The analysis by the Curmudgeon is correct regarding the hypocrisy of the creation scientists. To be clear, both the Curmudgeon and the creation scientists are wrong about the existence of a spherical earth. But the Curmudgeon is correct that the Bible depicts a flat earth; he is incorrect that the Bible is wrong about that. On the other hand, the creation scientists are correct about creation in six literal days, but they are wrong that the Bible does not depict a flat earth. In the end, the Curmudgeon correctly describes creation scientists as hypocrites.

That hypocrisy has not gone unnoticed. Paul Rosenberg is a California-based writer/activist, senior editor for Random Lengths News, and a columnist for Al Jazeera English. He was puzzled why progressives (i.e., socialists) don't go on the attack against creationists by calling them out for using biblical arguments similar to adherents of the flat earth.

> It's obvious why creationists would not want to be associated with flat-earthers, but it's not at all obvious why we should let them get away with it, given how similar their arguments, assumptions and purposes are. ... [I]t seems high time that progressives stop playing defense and start going on offense. Asking Christian conservatives to defend flat-earthism any time they open their mouths would be an excellent place to start. The Bible, after all, is far, far clearer in supporting a flat earth than it is in opposing abortion.[1065]

Robert Schadewald was an atheist and former board member and president of the National Center for Science Education. He was a famous leader in the fight against creationism. One of Schadewald's primary strategies in attacking creationism as pseudoscience was to compare it with belief in a flat earth. He viewed the Bible as describing a flat earth.[1066] And he would examine the parallels between the two beliefs. He used that to bludgeon the creation science hypocrites who rejected the truth of what the Bible clearly stated about the earth being flat. The charlatan creation scientists tried to defend God's account of creation by rejecting what the Bible clearly said about God creating a flat and stationary earth. Schadewald was successful only because the creation science hypocrites abandoned "the sword of the Spirit, which is the word of God." Ephesians 6:17. They were thus left without a spiritual weapon with which to do battle. The battle was lost before it even started.

Rather than embrace the truth of the Bible in its depiction of a flat earth, heliocentric creation scientists reject the truth of the Bible and open themselves up to being exposed as hypocrites. Heliocentric creation scientists are hypocrites. They claim to take God's account in the Bible of creation literally. But when it comes to God's account in the Bible of his creation of a flat and stationary earth, they say that God did not really mean what he said. Karl Giberson, Ph.D., reveals the flawed reasoning of the creation scientists.

Karl Giberson is a professor of science and religion at Stonehill College. He is a renowned science and religion scholar who has lectured throughout the world at the most prestigious institutions of higher learning, including, but not limited to, the Vatican, Oxford University, London's Thomas Moore Institute, Brigham Young University, and Columbia University. He has written, co-authored, or edited 11 books, which have been translated into Spanish, Polish, Italian, and Romanian. He is viewed by the world as an expert in the interaction of science and religion.

Dr. Giberson correctly states that the Bible clearly describes the centrality of the stationary earth in God's creation. But he nonetheless thinks that the churches today are correct to have capitulated and accepted the heliocentric model of science. He criticizes the ultraconservative Missouri Synod of the Lutheran Church for being dilatory after Galileo's infamous trial and taking almost three centuries to accept the truth (as he sees it) of heliocentricity.[1067]

> The motion of the earth was threatening in 1633 when Galileo was on trial. The Bible was quite clear that the earth was fixed and said so in so

many words: "The earth is fixed and cannot be moved" wrote the Psalmist with unfortunate clarity in chapter 93. And there were theological issues. The earth-centered universe made theological sense. If humanity was the focus of God's creation, then it followed that the earth would be located in a special place. In the worldview of the times, however, the center of the universe was special in that hell was located there. Things improved as one moved out toward the stars, in the general direction of heaven, and away from the earth.[1068]

Dr. Giberson draws an accurate parallel between the controversy over the heliocentric model promoted by Galileo in 1633 and the controversy today where modern science, armed with its theory of evolution, denies that Adam and Eve were real historical persons. Dr. Giberson poses a logical question. If the passages in the Bible that state that the earth is immovable can be so easily dismissed as figurative language by the churches in order to make peace with science after the middle ages, why cannot the passages regarding Adam and Eve not also be dismissed as being figurative language to make peace with science over evolution?

> The controversy over Adam and Eve is much the same. There are biblical references to Adam and Eve that, if taken literally, suggest they were real people. But these references are no more compelling than those made by the Psalmist to a fixed earth. And Adam essentially disappears from the Old Testament after his brief cameo in the Garden of Eden. The real issue, however, is theological. St. Paul, in the New Testament, speaks of Christ as a "Second Adam," undoing the damage created by the first Adam. If we don't have Adam to explain where sin came from, then Christianity supposedly collapses. The intertwined

> biblical and theological problems of the Adam controversy are strikingly analogous to their Galilean predecessors. The Adam issue is more significant, however, since it deals with humanity and connects to Christ.[1069]

Dr. Giberson hits the nail on the head. There is no difference in the reasoning behind the capitulation in the churches in interpreting as metaphors the Bible passages describing a flat and stationary earth and metaphorizing the passages in Genesis regarding the creation of Adam and Eve. Once you go down the road of dismissing the literal truth of Bible passages regarding God's creation in one area, the entire foundation of the gospel is undermined.

Dr. Giberson is correct that undermining the literal truth of the creation account of Adam and Eve directly attacks the account of Jesus Christ. They stand or fall together. If one falls, so does the other. But what he misses is that undermining the literal truth of God's creation of a fixed and flat earth is also an attack on the account of Jesus Christ. It is also true that if the stationary, flat earth falls, so does the incarnation of Jesus Christ. Dr. Giberson misses the point that Jesus emphatically states that Moses wrote of him.

> Do not think that I will accuse you to the Father: there is one that accuseth you, even Moses, in whom ye trust. For had ye believed Moses, ye would have believed me: for he wrote of me. But if ye believe not his writings, how shall ye believe my words? (John 5:45-47)

Moses wrote Genesis about Jesus as the creator of all things, both seen and unseen. Colossians 1:16. Genesis not only describes the creation of Adam and Eve, but also the flat and stationary earth. If one attacks any point of God's creation, it is an attack on Jesus. Indeed, Jesus made the point that if one does not believe what Moses wrote about him (including his creation of a flat earth, Adam, and Eve) then they would not believe him. One must take the Bible as a package. Either you believe all of it or none of it. "If I have told you earthly things, and ye believe not, how shall ye believe, if I tell you of heavenly things?" John 3:12. You cannot pick and choose. If you don't believe Genesis then you also don't believe Jesus. It is that plain and simple.

Dr. Giberson does not even try to treat the passages describing a stationary and flat earth as metaphors; he simply thinks that they are fiction. Indeed, since Dr. Giberson dismisses the account of a stationary earth in the Bible as fiction, he can easily conclude that it "is far from obvious that this [creation of Adam and Eve] should be read as literal history."[1070]

Dr. Giberson acknowledges that according to the rubric set up to overrule the Bible and welcome the science of heliocentrism into Christian theology, he sees no reason why the creation account for Adam and Eve should be taken literally. But while Dr. Giberson has no problem making that argument himself he seems to bristle when atheists make that same argument. Atheists criticize Christian theologians for cherry-picking certain passages to take as fiction (creation of a flat, stationary earth), but then others they interpret literally (creation of Adam and Eve). The atheists argue that there is no way to know which Bible passages are to be read literally and which are to be read figuratively.

Against that argument by atheists, Dr. Giberson presents an answer for those who want to accept as true the creation account of Adam and Eve but still reject as fiction the depiction in the Bible of a stationary earth. Dr. Giberson argues that "[t]he assumption that identifying one part as fiction undermines the factual character of another part is ludicrous."[1071] Dr. Giberson likens the Bible to a library that is full of both fiction and nonfiction books. He states that Christians can argue that just because one of the books in the library is fiction (stationary, flat earth) that does not mean that all the other books in the library are also fiction. The nonfiction books (Adam and Eve) should be read as nonfiction without regard to the fact that there are other fiction books (flat, stationary earth) in the library.

Oddly, Dr. Giberson admits that he has no basis for determining whether the Bible passages describing a stationary earth are fiction and, on the contrary, the other Bible passages describing the creation of Adam and Eve are literally true historical accounts. He only offers that library analogy as an argument that can be made by Christians against the atheist argument that they are being arbitrary and capricious in deciding which Bible passages to take literally and which to dismiss as fiction.

It seems that the basis for assessing the truth of a Bible passage by the churches is the relative strength of the science that is in opposition to the Bible passage. Churches seem to find the science behind heliocentricity is compelling, whereas the science behind evolution is less so. Almost all of the churches of the world seem to think that the Bible must yield to science. They have done that regarding heliocentricity. But many churches today do not "yet" think that science has done a very good job of refuting Adam and Eve and proving evolution.

Albert B. Collver, Ph.D., is Director of Church Relations, Assistant to the President of the Missouri Synod, and Executive Secretary for the International Lutheran Council. He criticizes Dr. Giberson's equation of the authority of the Bible passages describing a stationary earth with the Bible passages describing the creation of Adam and Eve. Dr. Collver does not think that they are equally dismissible. Dr. Collver's approach is typical. The Lutheran Church must treat those passages differently because it long ago gave up the battle against the error of heliocentricity.

While Dr. Giberson considers the debate of whether Adam and Eve were historical people on par with the Reformation era debate over whether or not the earth orbited the sun, it is not an apple to apple comparison. The Copernican Revolution did not challenge Christology or diminish Christ unlike the denial of the historicity of Adam and Eve.[1072]

Dr. Collver claims that the retreat from the biblical description of the creation of a literal flat and stationary earth is not on par with the retreat from the creation of a literal Adam and Eve. He seems to think that it is only a retreat from the truth of a literal Adam and Eve that calls into question the truth of the incarnation of Jesus Christ. Dr. Collver is wrong. In fact, the retreat from the reality of God's creation of a flat and stationary earth is on par with a retreat from the reality of the creation of Adam and Eve. Retreating from either truth calls into question the gospel of Jesus Christ.

Dr. Elizabeth Mitchell also takes umbrage at Dr. Giberson's equation of the Bible accounts of a stationary earth and Adam and Eve being on the same footing. She defends the Genesis account of a literal Adam and Eve. But when it comes to the account in Psalms 93 of an immovable earth, she changes the rules and states that the passage does not mean what it says. She claims that "[t]he passage does not mean the earth does not move unless the careless reader removes it from context."[1073]

Dr. Mitchell, M.D., in an article posted on the creation science website *Answers in Genesis,* claims that Psalm 93 means only that "neither the world God made nor His sovereignty can be disturbed or destroyed by outside forces."[1074] That is false. Dr. Mitchell is just making things up. The passage, read in context, means exactly what it says. Dr. Mitchell's statement is erroneous. The entirety of Psalm 93 is only 5 verses. When reading Psalm 93 in context, we find that it means that the world is immovable:

> The LORD reigneth, he is clothed with majesty; the LORD is clothed with strength, wherewith he hath girded himself: **the world also is stablished, that it cannot be moved.** Thy throne is established of old: thou art from everlasting. The floods have lifted up, O LORD, the floods have lifted up their voice; the floods lift up their waves. The LORD on high is mightier than the noise of many waters, yea, than the mighty waves of the sea. Thy testimonies are very sure: holiness becometh thine house, O LORD, for ever. (Psalms 93:1-5)

The context of the passage indicates that the world is immovable. The passage is describing the strength with which God is girded and his eternally established throne and juxtaposing that with God's creation of an immovable world. Just as the world is fixed, so also is God strong, and his throne is immovable. The god of heliocentrity is not the God of the Bible. If the earth can be moved, as required by the heliocentric model, then the god of heliocentrism and his throne can also be moved. But Psalm 93 impeaches the heliocentric model. The context explains that both the world and God are immovable. Dr. Mitchell's interpretation is pure eisegesis.

35   Houston Has a Problem

The charlatan "Christian" pastors and creation science shills rely heavily on NASA and the other national space agencies for their doctrine. They reject the biblical model of a fixed, flat earth because NASA rejects the model of a fixed, flat earth. But NASA is not really a space agency; it is actually an intelligence agency that spews religious dogma cloaked in scientific jargon. The religious charlatans simply parrot the party line.

"Houston, we have a problem" is a popular rendition of a statement made over the radio from Apollo 13 moon-mission astronaut Jack Swigert and the NASA Mission Control Center at Houston, Texas during the emergency plagued (and mythical) spaceflight of Apollo 13. Incidently, Swigert actually said: "Okay, Houston, we've had a problem here." When NASA Mission Control Center at Houston asked him to repeat his statement, Swigert said: "Houston, we've had a problem." But Houston today has a real problem with its heliocentric science fiction. It simply does not comport with real science.

From time to time, NASA and the other space agencies must adjust their doctrine to conceal the conflict between their religious dogma and true science. For example, on February 20,

2019, the European Space Agency (ESA) announced a discovery that the moon is within the earth's atmosphere.[1075] "'The Moon flies through Earth's atmosphere,' says Igor Baliukin of Russia's Space Research Institute, lead author of the paper presenting the results."[1076] The space agencies are not saying that the moon is close to the earth; they are saying that the earth's atmosphere encompasses a distant moon. That discovery was alleged by ESA to be based upon data that came from the ESA/NASA spacecraft known as the Solar and Heliospheric Observatory (SOHO). The SOHO data allegedly "shows that the gaseous layer that wraps around Earth reaches up to 630,000 km (391,000 miles) away, or 50 times the diameter of our planet."[1077] ESA explains that the "outermost part of our planet's atmosphere extends well beyond the lunar orbit – almost twice the distance to the Moon."[1078]

The suspicious thing about the announcement is that the SOHO data was obtained more than 20 years ago. ESA's explanation for the delay was that "[w]e were not aware of it until we dusted off observations made over two decades ago by the SOHO spacecraft."[1079] That explanation is incredible. In fact, no such data exists because there is no SOHO, and there is no outer space.

The established dogma of science is that there is no atmosphere in space, and there is no atmosphere around the moon. Outer space is always portrayed as a black void. A perfect vacuum. There is no atmosphere in space. Why are NASA and ESA suddenly coming up with this curious announcement that contradicts more than 50 years of space exploration propaganda? That is because space agencies have a physics problem with their premise of space travel using rockets in the vacuum of space. That problem is solved by the new "discovery" of the earth's expansive atmosphere extending beyond the moon.

NASA, ESA, and all space agencies have created a mythology of space travel based upon rockets in the vacuum of space. The problem the space agencies face is that people are becoming aware that rockets require a fulcrum to push against to move.[1080] On the earth, the fulcrum is initially the ground, and after a rocket lifts off the launching pad, the atmosphere becomes the fulcrum. Space is supposed to be an empty vacuum. In a vacuum, there is nothing to act as a fulcrum for a rocket to push against. A rocket in the vacuum of space would be useless.[1081] But if the space agencies can introduce an atmosphere into outer space that solves their problem. They can explain that the fulcrum upon which the rockets push is the expanded atmosphere that goes beyond the moon.

Another problem space agencies have is the orthodox scientific model for radio communications. That scientific model has painted the scientific community into a corner. The fact of long-distance radio communications proves that the earth is flat with a firmament over it. The scientific community has come up with theories for radio communications that make no sense on a globular earth. The makeshift theories are so contradictory and impossible that they implicitly suggest that there is no outer space and the earth must have a firmament over it. The distant moon within the expanded atmosphere explanation is the solution that ESA/NASA has come up with to refute the inference that the earth is flat and covered by a firmament.

Modern science has come up with several convoluted theories to explain long-distance radio transmissions because they cannot allow it to be known that the earth is flat. The most prevalent theory is the ionosphere bounce theory.[1082] Under that mythology, radio operators can talk to people on the other side of the supposed spherical earth, not because the earth is flat, but because their radio signal bounces off the thin upper atmosphere, called the ionosphere. Think about it logically. Under the ionosphere bounce theory, radio waves have no problem traveling through the atmosphere, but when the radio waves reach the thinnest part of the atmosphere (it is then called the ionosphere), those same radio waves bounce off that thin ionosphere and return to earth. That is nonsense.

The firmament is the surface upon which long-distance radio transmissions are bounced. This author explains that concept in detail in *The Greatest Lie on Earth (Expanded Edition)*, which was published in September 2018. The book further explains how the modern theory of bouncing radio signals off of the ionosphere is impossible if there had been, as supposed, radio communications with the Apollo astronauts on the moon. Indeed, under the orthodox theory of ionosphere bounce, all radio communications with spacecraft anywhere in space would be impossible. Radio signals cannot both bounce off and also pass through the ionosphere. It is that impossibility that has caused NASA and ESA to come up with the mythology that the earth's atmosphere reaches out to 391,000 miles, which is approximately 152,100 miles past the moon.

Elizabeth Howell, writing for Space.com, explains the generally accepted scientific theory that "Earth's magnetic field and atmosphere shields the planet from 99.9 percent of the radiation from space."[1083] That scientific theory poses a problem for the mythology of the moon being 238,900 miles away in outer space. Modern scientific theory has the earth's atmosphere acting as a giant Faraday cage to protect the earth from the allegedly dangerous radiation made up of gamma rays, x-rays, and cosmic rays. There is not agreement among scientists whether cosmic radiation is made up of electromagnetic waves or subatomic particles.[1084] NASA categorizes cosmic rays as part of the electromagnetic spectrum.[1085] Just below cosmic rays on the electromagnetic spectrum are gamma rays and x-rays. Radio waves are also considered electromagnetic waves.

Everybody who has had medical or dental x-rays knows that they are dangerous, and typically, vital organs are covered by a lead shield. The x-ray technician will usually stand behind a lead-lined wall when activating the x-ray machine. That is done because it is understood that the atmosphere is no barrier to x-rays. But modern scientists would have us believe that the same atmosphere that offers no impediment to x-rays in a medical facility, magically becomes an impenetrable barrier when the x-rays are trying to reach earth from outer space.[1086] It is impossible for the atmosphere to block x-rays. That means that there cannot be any x-rays coming from outer space. Indeed, x-rays cannot emanate from outer space because there is no outer space.

If Earth's atmosphere is actually able to block dangerous gamma rays, x-rays, and cosmic rays supposedly bombarding earth from outer space, it can certainly block radio waves. How could astronauts, seemingly in outer space, and even on the moon, use electromagnetic radio waves to communicate through that purportedly impenetrable atmospheric shield to NASA mission control back on earth?

The scientific community does not have a good explanation for the radio signal anomaly for how the earth's atmosphere can block gamma rays, x-rays, and cosmic rays, but it cannot block radio waves. They contradict themselves when they say the atmosphere (ionosphere) can in fact block and reflect radio waves back to earth when they travel upward from earth, while at the same time NASA has no problem with radio waves passing through the allegedly impenetrable ionosphere as they supposedly communicate with astronauts in outer space. Also, the astronauts have no problem sending transmissions of radio communications from outer space through the atmosphere that is supposed to act as an impenetrable barrier to all electromagnetic waves, whether they be gamma rays, x-rays, cosmic rays, or radio waves.

Why does the scientific community have such illogical and opposing theories? Because the high priests of science need the ionosphere bounce phenomenon to explain long-distance radio communications on the supposed spherical earth. And at the same time, they need to allow for radio communications from Earth with astronauts who are supposed to be in outer space. The new paradigm constructed by the expanded atmosphere that extends beyond the moon solves the problem of the heretofore scientific construct that has the atmosphere nonsensically both blocking radio waves and conducting radio waves at the same.

Outer space, as portrayed by modern science, is a subtle and blasphemous attack on God. Only the chosen high priests of science (called astronauts), can venture into the devilish black void of space. They must wear special ceremonial protective suits before they enter into the godless void of space. The chosen astronauts come back to earth to report that instead of finding God, they found an empty, hostile, and blackest of black voids. Of course, outer space as portrayed by NASA is not real; it is religious mythology. Indeed, NASA has never explained how the special ceremonial garb, called space suits, that have no lead linings, can protect their astronauts (priests) from the dangerous x-rays, gamma rays, and cosmic rays that are alleged to exist in outer space. The new expanded atmosphere extending outward from earth for 391,000 miles offers some plausible explanation for why astronauts are not fried alive by the dangerous gamma rays, x-rays, and cosmic rays of space.

As we have learned, the ionosphere bounce theory requires radio waves to travel through the atmosphere until the atmosphere gets extremely thin (the ionosphere), and when those radio waves reach that thinnest part of the atmosphere, they bounce off and return to Earth. The modern scientists are not sure where the bouncing takes place, because the height of the ionosphere is thought to range from 50 miles to 600 miles in altitude. Does that make sense? No.

The modern myth of the ionosphere-bounce theory is completely impeached by the practice of what is known as moon-bounce or earth-moon-earth (EME) communication.[1087] Moonbounce communication or EME is where radio operators, including amateur radio (ham) operators, bounce radio signals off the moon.[1088] The moon is supposed to be approximately 238,900 miles from Earth. Think about this logically; if the ionosphere, which is the atmosphere that is at a height of 50 to 600 miles from the earth's surface is supposed to reflect radio signals back to earth, how can those same radio signals pass through the ionosphere and travel all the way to the moon, which is supposed to be approximately 238,900 miles from earth, to facilitate EME communications? Indeed, how can the alleged protection offered by the atmosphere in blocking out the supposedly powerful and dangerous electromagnetic waves, at the same time allow exponentially weaker electromagnetic transmissions from amateur radio operators to pass back and forth through that supposedly impassable atmosphere as they bounce off the distant moon?

Obviously, the ionosphere bounce theory has a problem. Scientists cannot have a theory whereby radio waves bounce off the ionosphere and also have those same radio waves pass through the ionosphere to bounce off the distant moon supposedly located beyond the ionosphere in outer space to facilitate the EME communications. The moon must be closer than the alleged 238,900 miles from Earth, and it cannot be above what scientists call the ionosphere. The only way the same radio signals that are supposed to bounce off the ionosphere can also bounce off the moon for EME communications would be if both the moon and ionosphere were in the same place. The ineluctable conclusion is that radio signals bounce off the firmament. Scientists are deceptively describing what is actually a firmament bounce as being, instead, an ionosphere bounce.

In order for radio signals to both bounce off the firmament and the moon means that the moon must necessarily be in the firmament. That perfectly explains how radio signals can be reflected from both the moon and every other area in the sky. Indeed, the evidence of radio signal reflection from both the sky and the moon confirms God's word; the moon is in the firmament.

> And God said, **Let there be lights in the firmament** of the heaven to divide the day from the night; and let them be for signs, and for seasons, and for days, and years: And let them be for **lights in the firmament** of the heaven to give light upon the earth: and it was so. And God made two great lights; the greater light to rule the day, and the lesser light to rule the night: he made the stars also. And **God set them in the firmament of the heaven** to give light upon the earth, And to rule over the day and over the night, and to divide the light from the darkness: and God saw that it was good. And the evening and the morning were the fourth day. (Genesis 1:14-19)

Obviously, the ionosphere bounce theory poses a problem for outer space radio communications. There is simply no way for the radio signals to reach outer space if they purportedly bounce off the ionosphere. For radio signals to reach outer space would require the ionosphere to have an on/off switch that turns off the ionosphere reflector and allow waves through it when NASA wants to communicate with astronauts in space and on the moon during the Apollo moon missions. The on/off switch would also come in handy in allowing radio signals through the ionosphere when ham radio operators want to bounce their signals off the purportedly distant moon.

It sounds ridiculous, but it is a fact, that modern scientific theories have the ionosphere being both a reflector and a conductor of radio waves. Modern "science" uses the ionosphere bounce theory to explain the long-distance radio communications that otherwise would be impossible on a globular earth. And then, presto-chango, the formerly impenetrable ionosphere reflector suddenly allows the radio waves to pass right through when they need to explain radio communications to and from the earth and the mythical vacuum of space. Indeed, these radio communications are supposed to have passed back and forth through the ionosphere between earth and the alleged astronauts 238,900 miles away on the moon.

The theory that radio waves both bounce off the ionosphere and pass through the ionosphere are mutually exclusive and thus impossible nonsense. Houston realized it had a problem. NASA and ESA were not going to trash the heliocentric model and admit that the moon is in the firmament as revealed in the Bible. Indeed, they are not going to acknowledge the existence of the firmament at all. So, they decided to modify their heliocentric model by expanding the ionosphere 391,000 miles out from earth past the moon. That modification seems to be laying the groundwork for later arguing that their ionosphere bounce theory could exist and still make sense alongside the claim that they can communicate via radio with the astronauts in outer space and even those who were on the moon during the Apollo moon missions. The new distant atmosphere theory certainly obfuscates the issue and allows for some plausible workaround for the problems with the ionosphere bounce theory.

Indeed, giving any real thought to the heliocentric model for our atmosphere reveals the heliocentric model as impossible, even under the recent theory of a massive expanse of the atmosphere. Atmospheric pressure alone refutes the existence of the vacuum of outer space abutting the atmosphere. Atmospheric pressure is real and cannot be denied. That leaves science with a problem because scientists allege that the earth's atmosphere abuts a vacuum. Vacuums, by definition, suck. The priests of science solve that problem with ... wait for it ... "gravity." According the priests of science, "[a]tmospheric pressure is caused by the gravitational attraction of the planet on the atmospheric gases above the surface, and is a function of the mass of the planet, the radius of the surface, and the amount and composition of the gases and their vertical distribution in the atmosphere."[1089]

But gravity cannot solve the problem of atmospheric pressure because that same atmosphere abuts the supposed vacuum of outer space. To put the atmosphere under pressure, the atmosphere must be in a container. The atmosphere is a gas. The Department of Chemistry at Elmhurst College explains that for there to be gas pressure, the gas must be in a container.

> Pressure is a force exerted by the substance per unit area on another substance. **The pressure of a gas is the force that the gas exerts on the walls of its container.** When you blow air into a balloon, the balloon expands because the pressure of air molecules is greater on the inside of the balloon than the outside.[1090]

Under the heliocentric model, the atmosphere is not in a container but is abutted to the vacuum of outer space. The heliocentric model is wrong. Indeed, it is physically impossible, since to have atmospheric pressure, there must be a container. The Bible explains that there is a container; it is called the firmament. But science rejects the existence of the firmament.

Even with the recent adjustment in their mythology to have a great expanse of the atmosphere, the heliocentric model has a powerful force of gravity preventing the massive vacuum of outer space from sucking air from the atmosphere. David Weiss uses a simple example of a drinking straw to refute that nonsense. He explains that with his weak lungs sucking on a drinking straw, he can create a slight low-pressure vacuum and pull water and air up and away from earth at any altitude. He can defeat the alleged gravity by sucking on a straw to create a vacuum. If the mythology of the powerful gravity model that defeats the massive vacuum of outer space were true, we would not be able defeat that same gravity with the weak vacuum of our lungs to drink liquids out of straws.

The existence of atmospheric pressure is evidence of a firmament containing the atmosphere. Since the earth is not a sphere, it is a misnomer to call the air above it atmosphere; the air should more appropriately be called atmosplane.

Scientists are going to have to do some rewriting of their space science mythology. That is because the Karman line, which is where the atmosphere is supposed to end and space is supposed to begin is thought to be 50 miles (80 kilometers) above Earth, according to NASA and U.S. Air Force[1091], and 100 kilometers (62 miles) above the earth, according to the Federation Aeronautique Internationale.[1092] The fact that the U.S. (50 miles) and Europe (100 kilometers) have determined that space begins at nice round numbers according to their respective measuring scales, and that those elevations are different, indicates that space is mythological.

This new massive expanse of the atmosphere reaching 391,000 miles in space past the moon is not a new scientific discovery; it is just another doctrinal modification in "science falsely so called." 1 Timothy 6:20. It is merely the latest tweak in a satanic religious dogma, masquerading as science, being used to keep a lid on the true nature of God's creation. Rockets do not travel to space. Man never landed on the moon. There was no radio communication with them. Indeed, there is no radio communication with anyone in space because there is no vacuum of space. The moon is close; it is in the firmament. When radio waves are being reflected back down to earth, they are being bounced off the firmament.

NASA is not an agency of science; it is an agency of spiritual disinformation. NASA portrays science fiction as though it is science fact. Heliocentricity is an evil religious superstition masquerading as science. The heathen mythology of heliocentricity is a spiritual attack by Satan and his minions on the authority of

God and his Holy Bible. Sadly, that occult mythology has infiltrated most churches.

God commands us not to equate holy things with profane things. The mainstream "churches" today have committed the sin of the corrupt priests in Israel. God upbraided the priests of Israel for putting "no difference between the holy and profane." Ezekiel 22:26. "Profane" is defined as something that is not sacred. "Profane" things are worldly things. "Profane" denotes irreverence to things sacred or proceeding from contempt of sacred things.[1093] Modern "churches" have put no difference between the profane science of heliocentricity and the holy things of the gospel. We are to "avoiding profane and vain babblings, and oppositions of science falsely so called." (1 Timothy 6:20) But the mainstream churches have embraced the profanity of heliocentricity and made it part of a corrupted gospel. "A little leaven leaveneth the whole lump." (Galatians 5:9)

The adoption by the churches of the cursed doctrine of heliocentricity has caused them to preach a perverted gospel.

> I marvel that ye are so soon removed from him that called you into the grace of Christ unto another gospel: Which is not another; but there be some that trouble you, and would pervert the gospel of Christ. But though we, or an angel from heaven, preach any other gospel unto you than that which we have preached unto you, let him be accursed. As we said before, so say I now again, If any man preach any other gospel unto you than that ye have received, let him be accursed. (Galatians 1:6-9)

If one believes in the heliocentric creation, he will necessarily believe in a heliocentric creator. A heliocentric creation does not exist. So also, a heliocentric creator does not exist. A heliocentric creator is a false god. We have been warned to avoid the preaching of a false gospel, which presents a false Jesus.

> But I fear, lest by any means, as the serpent beguiled Eve through his subtilty, so your minds should be corrupted from the simplicity that is in Christ. For if he that cometh preacheth **another Jesus**, whom we have not preached, or if ye receive another spirit, which ye have not received, or **another gospel**, which ye have not accepted, ye might well bear with him. (2 Corinthians 11:3-4)

Endnotes

1. Hardcover Book ISBN: 978-1-943056-05-7; Paperback Book ISBN: 978-1-943056-03-3; Ebook ISBN: 978-1-943056-04-0.

2. T. Winship (a.k.a. Rectangle), Zetetic Cosmogony, Second Edition-Enlarged, at 135 (1899), quoting Lucifer, Dec. 23rd, E.M. 287 (1887) (all capital letters in original).

3. Paul Sutter, Going Bananas: The Real Story of Kepler, Copernicus and the Church, February 21, 2017, https://www.space.com/35772-copernicus-vs-catholic-church-real-story.html.

4. Paul Sutter, Going Bananas: The Real Story of Kepler, Copernicus and the Church, February 21, 2017, https://www.space.com/35772-copernicus-vs-catholic-church-real-story.html.

5. Paul Sutter, Going Bananas: The Real Story of Kepler, Copernicus and the Church, February 21, 2017, https://www.space.com/35772-copernicus-vs-catholic-church-real-story.html.

6. Paul Sutter, Going Bananas: The Real Story of Kepler, Copernicus and the Church, February 21, 2017, https://www.space.com/35772-copernicus-vs-catholic-church-real-story.html.

7. Paul Sutter, Going Bananas: The Real Story of Kepler, Copernicus and the Church, February 21, 2017, https://www.space.com/35772-copernicus-vs-catholic-church-real-story.html.

8.Heresy, American Dictionary of the English Language (1828), http://webstersdictionary1828.com/Dictionary/heresy.

9.Heresy, American Dictionary of the English Language (1828), http://webstersdictionary1828.com/Dictionary/heresy.

10.Heresy Against The State, part 2, Christian Flat Earth Ministry, June 19, 2019, https://christianflatearthministry.org/2019/06/19/heresy-against-the-state-part-2/.

11.Heresy Against The State, part 2, Christian Flat Earth Ministry, June 19, 2019, https://christianflatearthministry.org/2019/06/19/heresy-against-the-state-part-2/.

12.Heresy Against The State, part 2, Christian Flat Earth Ministry, June 19, 2019, https://christianflatearthministry.org/2019/06/19/heresy-against-the-state-part-2/.

13.February 9, 2019, 2:25 p.m. email from the professor to Edward Hendrie.

14.February 9, 2019, email from Edward Hendrie to the professor containing the following information: Jenny Lea, December 10, 2011 Lunar Eclipse at Sunrise: Selenelion Viewed from Cahokia Mounds, Posted December 14, 2011, https://www.youtube.com/watch?v=QUkjb4bbjpc. John Kees, Partial Lunar Eclipse, Madison Wisconsin 12-10-2011, https://www.youtube.com/watch?v=mn6WrC_30IM. Impossible "Selenelion" eclipse, Dec 2011, Southern New Mexico, https://www.youtube.com/watch?v=jIyw6xuEJxk, uploaded December 10, 2011.

15. February 9, 2019, 7:56 p.m. email from the professor to Edward Hendrie.

16. NASA Eclipse Website, Eclipses During 2011, Published in Observer's Handbook, Royal Astronomical Society of Canada, https://eclipse.gsfc.nasa.gov/OH/OH2011.html#LE2011Dec10T.

17. Madison, Wisconsin, Sunrise, December 10, 2011, https://www.timeanddate.com/sun/usa/madison?month=12&year=2011.

18. Madison, Wisconsin, Eclipse, December 10, 2011, https://www.timeanddate.com/eclipse/in/usa/madison?iso=20111210.

19. Madison, Wisconsin, Sunrise, December 10, 2011, https://www.timeanddate.com/sun/usa/madison?month=12&year=2011.

20. Total Lunar Eclipse On Wednesday Will Be a Rare 'Selenelion', October 5, 2014, https://www.space.com/27338-total-lunar-eclipse-rare-sunrise-selenelion.html. See also, Lunar Eclipse Provides an Extra Twist for Skywatchers: Selenelion, NBC News, April 14, 2014, https://www.nbcnews.com/science/space/lunar-eclipse-provides-extra-twist-skywatchers-selenelion-n219586.

21. Joe Rao, Saturday's Lunar Eclipse Will Include 'Impossible' Sight, December 7, 2011, https://www.space.com/13856-total-lunar-eclipse-rare-senelion.html.

22. Joe Rao, Simon and Schuster, https://www.simonandschuster.com/authors/Joe-Rao/487539430 (last visited on March 15, 2019).

23. Joe Rao, Saturday's Lunar Eclipse Will Include 'Impossible' Sight, December 7, 2011, https://www.space.com/13856-total-lunar-eclipse-rare-senelion.html.

24. Joe Rao, Saturday's Lunar Eclipse Will Include 'Impossible' Sight, December 7, 2011, https://www.space.com/13856-total-lunar-eclipse-rare-senelion.html.

25. Joe Rao, Saturday's Lunar Eclipse Will Include 'Impossible' Sight, December 7, 2011, https://www.space.com/13856-total-lunar-eclipse-rare-senelion.html.

26. February 11, 2019, 2:41 p.m., email from the professor to Edward Hendrie.

27. February 15, 2019 email from the professor to Edward Hendrie.

28. February 15, 2019, 3:56 p.m. email from Edward Hendrie to the professor.

29. February 20, 2019, 5:56 p.m., email from Edward Hendrie to the professor sending the following link: Impossible "Selenelion" Eclipse, Dec 2011, Published December 10, 2011, https://www.youtube.com/watch?v=jIyw6xuEJxk.

30. February 20, 2019, 10:37 p.m., email from he professor to Edward Hendrie.

31. February 16, 2019, email from Edward Hendrie to the professor.

32. May 17, 2019, email from the professor to Edward Hendrie, et. al.

33. June 25, 2019, 2:44 p.m., email from professor to Edward Hendrie, et. al.

34. Is the Bible a Geocentric Book? Heliocentrism v. Geocentricity, November 20, 2015, https://www.youtube.com/watch?v=V90v8_51agE.

35. Is the Bible a Geocentric Book? Heliocentrism v. Geocentricity, November 20, 2015, https://www.youtube.com/watch?v=V90v8_51agE.

36. Is the Bible a Geocentric Book? Heliocentrism v. Geocentricity, November 20, 2015, https://www.youtube.com/watch?v=V90v8_51agE.

37. Is the Bible a Geocentric Book? Heliocentrism v. Geocentricity, November 20, 2015, https://www.youtube.com/watch?v=V90v8_51agE.

38. Flat Earth Folly: Heliocentrism v. Geocentricity, December 16, 2015, https://www.youtube.com/watch?v=IC3grambpI0.

39. About Math is Fun, https://www.mathsisfun.com/aboutmathsisfun.html (last visited on March 26, 2019).

40. Curriculum, https://www.mathsisfun.com/links/index-curriculum.html (last visited on March 26, 2019).

41. About Math is Fun, https://www.mathsisfun.com/aboutmathsisfun.html (last visited on March 26, 2019).

42. About Math is Fun, https://www.mathsisfun.com/aboutmathsisfun.html (last visited on March 26, 2019).

43. Face, https://www.mathsisfun.com/definitions/face.html (last visited on March 25, 2019).

44. Sphere Facts, https://www.mathsisfun.com/geometry/sphere.html (last visited on March 25, 2019).

45. Face, Merriam-Webster, https://www.merriam-webster.com/dictionary/face (last visited on March 25, 2019).

46. Face, Merriam-Webster, http://www.webster-dictionary.org/definition/face (last visited on March 25, 2019)

47. Faces, Edges, and Vertices of Solids, https://www.ck12.org/geometry/Faces-Edges-and-Vertices-of-Solids/lesson/Faces-Edges-and-Vertices-of-Solids-MSM6/ (last visited on March 25, 2019).

48. Atul Kumar Kuthiala, MSc Hons School Physics, Panjab University, Chandigarh (1972), https://www.quora.com/Geometry-How-many-faces-does-a-sphere-have (last visited on March 25 2019).

49. The Creation Account in Genesis Describes a Flat Earth and Teaches True Science, September 25, 2018, https://flatearthscienceandBible.com/2018/09/25/the-creation-account-in-genesis-describes-the-flat-earth-and-t

eaches-true-science/.

50. The Creation Account in Genesis Describes a Flat Earth and Teaches True Science, September 25, 2018, https://flatearthscienceandBible.com/2018/09/25/the-creation-account-in-genesis-describes-the-flat-earth-and-teaches-true-science/.

51. A Lake at the Bottom of the Ocean: Mike deGruy on the Ocean Floor, October 6, 2015, https://www.youtube.com/watch?v=-juTelJbsxE.

52. Circle, https://www.merriam-webster.com/dictionary/circle.

53. he Biblical Flat Earth Series: Philip Stallings Vs. Kent Hovind, May 21, 2016, https://www.youtube.com/watch?v=_MVhnCAVupg.

54. Circle, https://www.merriam-webster.com/dictionary/circle. Basic Information About Circles, Math Planet, https://www.mathplanet.com/education/geometry/circles/basic-information-about-circles (last visited on March 30, 2019).

55. Face, https://www.mathsisfun.com/definitions/face.html (last visited on March 25, 2019).

56. Atul Kumar Kuthiala, MSc Hons School Physics, Panjab University, Chandigarh (1972), https://www.quora.com/Geometry-How-many-faces-does-a-sphere-have (last visited on March 25 2019).

57. The, https://www.merriam-webster.com/dictionary/the.

58. Of, https://www.merriam-webster.com/dictionary/of.

59. Verity Baptist Church, What We Believe, https://www.veritybaptist.com/whatwebelieve.html (last visited on June 25, 2019).

60. Flat Earth Debunked by Christian Mathematician Isaiah 40 22, Conspiracy, Geocentric, Heliocentric, June 4, 2018, https://www.youtube.com/watch?v=P4qkTnw3uIA.

61. Flat Earth Debunked by Christian Mathematician Isaiah 40 22, Conspiracy, Geocentric, Heliocentric, June 4, 2018, https://www.youtube.com/watch?v=P4qkTnw3uIA.

62. Flat Earth Debunked by Christian Mathematician Isaiah 40 22, Conspiracy, Geocentric, Heliocentric, June 4, 2018, https://www.youtube.com/watch?v=P4qkTnw3uIA.

63. Flat Earth Debunked by Christian Mathematician Isaiah 40 22, Conspiracy, Geocentric, Heliocentric, June 4, 2018, https://www.youtube.com/watch?v=P4qkTnw3uIA.

64. Flat Earth Debunked by Christian Mathematician Isaiah 40 22, Conspiracy, Geocentric, Heliocentric, June 4, 2018, https://www.youtube.com/watch?v=P4qkTnw3uIA.

65. Compass, American Dictionary of the English Language, 1828, http://1828.mshaffer.com/d/word/compass.

66. Image: Flat Earth versus Spherical Earth (Matthew 4 - 8 and Luke 4 - 5), for RW.PNG,

http://rationalwiki.org/wiki/File:Flat_Earth_versus_Spherical_Earth_%28Matthew_4_-_8_and_Luke_4_-_5%29,_for_RW.PNG. Copyright for image was released by its author into the public domain.

67. Turn, Noah Webster American Dictionary of the English Language, 1828, http://webstersdictionary1828.com/Dictionary/turn.

68. Turn, Noah Webster American Dictionary of the English Language, 1828, http://webstersdictionary1828.com/Dictionary/turn.

69. Turn, Merriam Webster Dictionary, https://www.merriam-webster.com/dictionary/turn.

70. Turn, Noah Webster American Dictionary of the English Language, 1828, http://webstersdictionary1828.com/Dictionary/turn.

71. Turn, Merriam Webster Dictionary, https://www.merriam-webster.com/dictionary/turn.

72. Celebrate Truth, Pastor Preaching Flat Earth Truth from the Bible, June 4, 2018, https://www.youtube.com/watch?v=V6yHPRsxyRo&t=1710s.

73. Amelia Saintonge, How Many Stars Are Born and Die Each Day?, Ask an Astronomer, June 27, 2015, http://curious.astro.cornell.edu/about-us/83-the-universe/stars-and-star-clusters/star-formation-and-molecular-clouds/400-how-many-stars-are-born-and-die-each-day-beginner.

74. Steadfast Baptist Church, The Flat Earth Heresy Exposed - Bro. Jesse Michael, August 3, 2018, https://www.youtube.com/watch?v=OCXQMyy-n30.

75. Frank Hall, Sovereign Grace Assembly, Kannapolis, NC, http://www.calvaryslamb.com/archived-articles.html (last visited on January 17, 2019).

76. R.B. YERBY, THE ONCE AND FUTURE ISRAEL, p. 73-75 (1977).

77. See R.B. YERBY, THE ONCE AND FUTURE ISRAEL, p. 47 (1977).

78. Frank Hall, Sovereign Grace Assembly, Kannapolis, NC, http://www.calvaryslamb.com/archived-articles.html (last visited on January 17, 2019).

79. Frank Hall, Sovereign Grace Assembly, Kannapolis, NC, http://www.calvaryslamb.com/archived-articles.html (last visited on January 17, 2019).

80. Frank Hall, Sovereign Grace Assembly, Kannapolis, NC, http://www.calvaryslamb.com/archived-articles.html (last visited on January 17, 2019).

81. Samuel Birley Rowbotham (Parallax), Zetetic Astronomy, Earth Not a Globe (1881), Chapter 15, http://www.sacred-texts.com/earth/za/za66.htm.

82. Vatican Considers Possibility of Aliens, November 11, 2009, https://www.cbsnews.com/news/vatican-considers-possibility-of-aliens/.

83. Adam Withnall, Pope Francis Says He Would Baptise Aliens: 'Who Are We to Close Doors?', 13 May 2014,

https://www.independent.co.uk/news/world/europe/pope-francis-says-he-would-baptise-aliens-9360632.html.

84. Samuel Birley Rowbotham (Parallax), Zetetic Astronomy, Earth Not a Globe (1881), Chapter 15, http://www.sacred-texts.com/earth/za/za66.htm.

85. Samuel Birley Rowbotham (Parallax), Zetetic Astronomy, Earth Not a Globe (1881), Chapter 15, http://www.sacred-texts.com/earth/za/za66.htm.

86. Samuel Birley Rowbotham (Parallax), Zetetic Astronomy, Earth Not a Globe (1881), Chapter 15, http://www.sacred-texts.com/earth/za/za66.htm.

87. Dennis Bratcher, *The Canons of Dordt (1618-1619)*, http://www.crivoice.org/creeddordt.html (last visited on October 13, 2011).

88. Dennis Bratcher, *"TULIP" Calvinism Compared to Wesleyan Perspectives*, http://www.crivoice.org/tulip.html (last visited on October 13, 2011).

89. Dennis Bratcher, *The Five Articles of the Remonstrants (1610)*, http://www.crivoice.org/creedremonstrants.html (last visited on October 13, 2011).

90. Stephen Tomkins, John Wesley, A Biography, at 168 (2003) (emphasis added).

91. Kenneth Talbot, Gary W. Crampton, D. James Kennedy, *Calvinism, Hyper-Calvinism, & Arminianism: A Workbook*, at 38 (2007).

92. Society of Evangelical Arminians, http://evangelicalarminians.org/ (last visited on November 28, 2011).

93. Micael Horton, Evangelical Arminians, Option or Oxymoron?, November 28, 2011, http://www.reformationonline.com/arminians.htm.

94. Franklin Graham, *Expect Suffering, But Not Forever*, April 27, 2011, Billy Graham Evangelistic Association, http://www.billygraham.org/articlepage.asp?articleid=1162.

95. Ken Johnson, The Gnostic Origins of Calvinism, at 69-70 (2013).

96. Ken Johnson, The Gnostic Origins of Calvinism, at 69-70 (2013).

97. George William Rutler, Nicolaus Copernicus, Catholic Education Resource Center, http://www.catholiceducation.org/en/science/faith-and-science/nicolaus-copernicus.html (last visited on September 17, 2015).

98. Nicolaus Copernicus (1543), Dedication of the Revolutions of the Heavenly Bodies to Pope Paul III, http://www.bartleby.com/39/12.html.

99. Nicolaus Copernicus (1543), Dedication of the Revolutions of the Heavenly Bodies to Pope Paul III, http://www.bartleby.com/39/12.html.

100. Jessica Wolf, The Truth about Galileo and His Conflict with the Catholic Church, UCLA Newsroom, December 22, 2016, http://newsroom.ucla.edu/releases/the-truth-about-galil

eo-and-his-conflict-with-the-catholic-church.

101. Jessica Wolf, The Truth about Galileo and His Conflict with the Catholic Church, UCLA Newsroom, December 22, 2016, http://newsroom.ucla.edu/releases/the-truth-about-galileo-and-his-conflict-with-the-catholic-church.

102. Patrick Reilly, *Assessing the Catholic Campaign for Human Development, Human Events,* November 20, 1998.

103. *Id.*

104. *Id.*

105. *Id.*

106. *Id.*

107. Katheryn Jean Lopez, *Catholic Campaign for Human Development: Still Entranced by Leftist Activism, Despite Growing Unrest, Human Events,* November 10, 2000.

108. *Id.*

109. *Id.*

110. *Id.*

111. *Id.*

112. KERRI HOUSTON AND PATRICIA FAVA, ALL GORE, AMERICA IN THE BALANCE, p. 59 (2000).

113. Africa, at 403, citing J. Kepler, letter to Michael Mastlin, 11 June 1598, Gesammelte Werke, ed. Max Caspar (Munich: Beck'sche, 1955), XIII, 219.

114. Africa, at 404.

115. Africa, at 404.

116. Eric Dubay, The Flat Earth Conspiracy, at 149 (2015).

117. Eric Dubay, The Flat Earth Conspiracy, at 149 (2015).

118. Eric Dubay, The Flat Earth Conspiracy, at 149 (2015).

119. Jose Wudka, The Pythagoreans, http://physics.ucr.edu/~wudka/Physics7/Notes_www/node32.html (last visited on December 8, 2016).

120. The Divine Origin of the Kabbalah, Jewish Alchemy: the Kabbalah, http://www.alchemylab.com/jewish_alchemy.htm (last visited on January 5, 2016).

121. The Divine Origin of the Kabbalah, Jewish Alchemy: the Kabbalah, http://www.alchemylab.com/jewish_alchemy.htm (last visited on January 5, 2016).

122. Albert Pike, Morals and Dogma of the Ancient and Accepted Scottish Rite of Freemasonry, P. 741 (1871).

123. Albert Mackey, Encyclopedia of Freemasonry, http://www.phoenixmasonry.org/mackeys_encyclopedia/c.htm (last visited on January 1, 2016).

124. Protocols of the Learned Elders of Zion, Protocol 4, http://www.Biblebelievers.org.au/przion3.htm#PROTOCOL%20No.%204 (last visited on August 31, 2012). See also Des Griffin, Fourth Reich of the Rich, p. 216 (1993).

125. Texe Marrs, Masonic Jews Plot to Control World, Power of Prophecy, April 2003, http://www.texemarrs.com/masonic_jews_plot_world_control.htm (website address current as of April 4, 2003).

126. Texe Marrs, Masonic Jews Plot to Control World, Power of Prophecy, April 2003, http://www.texemarrs.com/masonic_jews_plot_world_control.htm (website address current as of April 4, 2003).

127. Texe Marrs, Masonic Jews Plot to Control World, Power of Prophecy, April 2003, http://www.texemarrs.com/masonic_jews_plot_world_control.htm (website address current as of April 4, 2003).

128. Albert Pike, "Instructions to the 23 Supreme Councils of the World" (July 14, 1889), as recorded by Abel Clarin de La Rive, La Femme et l'Enfant dans la Franc-Maçonnerie Universelle (1894): 588, http://amazingdiscoveries.org/S-deception-Freemason_Lucifer_Albert_Pike#footnotevii. See also Occult Theocrasy, pp. 220-21.

129. Albert Pike, Morals and Dogma of the Ancient and Accepted Scottish Rite of Freemasonry Prepared for the Supreme Council of the Thirty-Third Degree, for the Southern Jurisdiction of the United States, and

Published by Its Authority (Richmond, Virginia: L.H. Jenkins, 1871, New and Revised Edition 1950), 321.

130. Manly Palmer Hall, "The Fellow Craft," The Lost Keys of Freemasonry (Richmond, Virginia: Macoy Publishing, 1931), http://www.manlyphall.org/text/the-lost-keys-of-freemasonry/chapter-iv-the-fellow-craft/.

131. Blanche Barton, The Secret Life of a Satanist: The Authorized Biography of Anton Szandor LaVey, at 55 (1992).

132. Anton Szandor LaVey, Jew Age, http://www.jewage.org/wiki/en/Article:Anton_LaVey_-_Biography (last visited on August 31, 2018). See also Matt Lebovic, in Haunted Salem, a Jewish Church Founder Preaches the Art of 'Satanic' Social Change, The Times of Israel, October 20, 2016, https://www.timesofisrael.com/in-haunted-salem-a-jewish-church-founder-preaches-the-art-of-satanic-social-change/.

133. Anton Szandor LaVey, Jew Age, http://www.jewage.org/wiki/en/Article:Anton_LaVey_-_Biography (last visited on August 31, 2018). See also Jews Control U.S.A., Therefore the World – Is That a Good Thing?, at 8, http://www.solargeneral.org/wp-content/uploads/library/jews-control-usa-therefore-the-world-is-that-a-good-thing.pdf (last visited on August 31, 2018).

134. Matt Lebovic, in Haunted Salem, a Jewish Church Founder Preaches the Art of 'Satanic' Social Change, The Times of Israel, October 20, 2016, https://www.timesofisrael.com/in-haunted-salem-a-jewish-church-founder-preaches-the-art-of-satanic-social-c

hange/.

135. E.g., Lodge Copernicus No. 505, New Zealand; Lodge Copernicus No. 246, Australia.

136. See generally Athol Bloomer, *The Eucharist and The Jewish Mystical Tradition • Part 1*, Association of Hebrew Catholics, *at* http://hebrewcatholic.org/PrayerandSpirituality/eucharistjewishm.html, (last visited on February 12, 2010) (originally published in The Hebrew Catholic #77, pp 15-18.).

137. Fortescue, A. (1910). Liturgy. In The Catholic Encyclopedia. New York: Robert Appleton Company. Retrieved February 19, 2010 from New Advent: http://www.newadvent.org/cathen/09306a.htm.

138. Barbara Aho, *Mystery, Babylon the Great - Catholic or Jewish?*, Watch Unto Prayer, *at* http://watch.pair.com/mystery-babylon.html (last visited on February 8, 2010).

139. HEEDING Bible PROPHECY, Understanding Satan's Plan To Counterfeit the Second Coming of Christ & the Restoration of All Things, *at* http://watch.pair.com/new-israel.html, quoting Pinay, Maurice. THE PLOT AGAINST THE CHURCH, LA: St. Anthony Press, 1967, (last visited on February 11, 2010).

140. Rebecca Weiner, *The Virtual Jewish History Tour Rome, The Christian Empire*, Jewish Virtual Library, *at* http://www.jewishvirtuallibrary.org/jsource/vjw/Rome.html (last visited on February 11, 2010).

141. NESTA WEBSTER, SECRET SOCIETIES AND SUBVERSIVE MOVEMENTS, http://web.archive.org/web/20021005055527/http://www.plausiblefutures.com/text/SS.html (website address current as of 2-28-05) (citing Lexicon of Freemasonry, p. 323).

142. Edith Starr Miller, Occult Theocrasy, pp. 77 (1933) (quoting Flavien Brenier. Source: Lt. Gen. A. Netchvolodow, Nicolas II et les Juifs, p. 139.).

143. Edith Starr Miller, Occult Theocrasy, pp. 78-79 (1933) (quoting Flavien Brenier. Source: Lt. Gen. A. Netchvolodow, Nicolas II et les Juifs, p. 139.).

144. Edith Starr Miller, Occult Theocrasy, p. 80 (1933).

145. Edith Starr Miller, Occult Theocrasy, p. 81 (1933).

146. Michael Hoffman, *Judaism Discovered*, at 785 (2008).

147. Lawrence Fine, Chapter on Kabbalistic Texts, From: *Back to the Sources: Reading the Classic Jewish Texts* ("The First Complete Modern Guide to the Great Books of the Jewish Tradition: What They Are and How to Read Them"), at p. 337 (2006) (bold emphasis added, italics in original).

148. Lawrence Fine, Chapter on Kabbalistic Texts, From: *Back to the Sources: Reading the Classic Jewish Texts* ("The First Complete Modern Guide to the Great Books of the Jewish Tradition: What They Are and How to Read Them"), at p. 337 (2006) (quoting Zohar III, 152a).

149. Blavatsky, Theosophical Glossary, p. 168 (quoted by Barbara Aho, Mystery, Babylon the Great Catholic

or Jewish?, at http://watch.pair.com/mystery-babylon.html#cabala (last visited on April 17, 2010)).

150. Jewish Encyclopedia, Cabala, at http://www.jewishencyclopedia.com/view.jsp?artid=1&letter=C#4 (last visited on April 18, 2010).

151. MICHAEL A. HOFFMAN, JUDAISM'S STRANGE GODS, at p. 88, (2000).

152. MICHAEL A. HOFFMAN, JUDAISM'S STRANGE GODS, at p. 88, (2000). See also Michael Hoffman, *Judaism Discovered*, at 779 (2008) (quoting Gershom Scholem, *Kabbalah* pp.183-84).

153. MICHAEL A. HOFFMAN, JUDAISM'S STRANGE GODS, at p. 91, (2000).

154. Michael Hoffman, *Judaism Discovered*, at 780 (2008) (quoting Helen Jacaobus, *Eye Jinx*, Jewish Chronicle, May 7, 1999).

155. MICHAEL A. HOFFMAN, JUDAISM'S STRANGE GODS, at p. 92, (2000).

156. Michael Hoffman, *The Truth About the Talmud*, at http://www.revisionisthistory.org/talmudtruth.html (last visited on March 10, 2010) (excerpted from MICHAEL A. HOFFMAN, JUDAISM'S STRANGE GODS (2000)).

157. Robert Goldberg, *Talmud, Back to the Sources: Reading the Classic Jewish Texts* (New York: Simon and Schuster, 1984), p. 130 (quoted by Michael Hoffman, *Judaism Discovered*, at 187 (2008)).

158. Michael Hoffman, *Judaism Discovered*, at 189 (2008).

159. Rabbi Ben Zion Bokser, *Judaism and the Christian Predicament* (1966), pp. 59 and 159 (quoted by Michael Hoffman, *Judaism Discovered*, at 190 (2008)).

160. Michael Hoffman, *The Truth About the Talmud*, at http://www.revisionisthistory.org/talmudtruth.html (excerpted from MICHAEL A. HOFFMAN, JUDAISM'S STRANGE GODS (2000)).

161. Michael Hoffman, *The Truth About the Talmud*, at http://www.revisionisthistory.org/talmudtruth.html (excerpted from MICHAEL A. HOFFMAN, JUDAISM'S STRANGE GODS (2000)) (quoting Ari Goldman, New York Times, April 10, 1993, p. 38).

162. Michael Hoffman, *The Truth About the Talmud*, at http://www.revisionisthistory.org/talmudtruth.html (excerpted from MICHAEL A. HOFFMAN, JUDAISM'S STRANGE GODS (2000)).

163. Michael Hoffman, *The Truth About the Talmud*, at http://www.revisionisthistory.org/talmudtruth.html (excerpted from MICHAEL A. HOFFMAN, JUDAISM'S STRANGE GODS (2000)).

164. Marshall Hall, Kabbala, Part VII, The Concept of a Rotating Earth Orbiting the Sun Is Both the Pseudo-Scientific Foundation and The Achilles Heel of Modern Kabbala-based Cosmology, http://www.fixedearth.com/kabbala-7.html (last visited on September 17, 2015).

165. Marshall Hall, Kabbala, Part VII, The Concept of a Rotating Earth Orbiting the Sun Is Both the Pseudo-Scientific Foundation and The Achilles Heel of Modern Kabbala-based Cosmology, http://www.fixedearth.com/kabbala-7.html (last visited on September 17, 2015).

166. Marshall Hall, Kabbala, Part VII, The Concept of a Rotating Earth Orbiting the Sun Is Both the Pseudo-Scientific Foundation and The Achilles Heel of Modern Kabbala-based Cosmology, http://www.fixedearth.com/kabbala-7.html (last visited on September 17, 2015).

167. Marshall Hall, Kabbala, Part VII, The Concept of a Rotating Earth Orbiting the Sun Is Both the Pseudo-Scientific Foundation and The Achilles Heel of Modern Kabbala-based Cosmology, http://www.fixedearth.com/kabbala-7.html (last visited on September 17, 2015).

168. Edgar B. Herwick III, Big Bang Theory: A Roman Catholic Creation, March 20, 2014, http://wgbhnews.org/post/big-bang-theory-roman-catholic-creation.

169. The Divine Origin of the Kabbalah, Jewish Alchemy: the Kabbalah, http://www.alchemylab.com/jewish_alchemy.htm (last visited on January 5, 2016).

170. The Divine Origin of the Kabbalah, Jewish Alchemy: the Kabbalah, http://www.alchemylab.com/jewish_alchemy.htm (last visited on January 5, 2016).

171. Sir Isaac Newton and the Jews, Jewish Currents, July 4, 2015, http://jewishcurrents.org/july-5-sir-isaac-newton-and-the-jews-37605.

172. Sir Isaac Newton and the Jews, Jewish Currents, July 4, 2015, http://jewishcurrents.org/july-5-sir-isaac-newton-and-the-jews-37605.

173. Sarah, Dry, Saving Isaac Newton: How a Jewish Collector Brought the Physicist's Papers to America, May 5, 2014, http://www.tabletmag.com/jewish-arts-and-culture/books/170960/saving-isaac-newton.

174. Sarah, Dry, Saving Isaac Newton: How a Jewish Collector Brought the Physicist's Papers to America, May 5, 2014, http://www.tabletmag.com/jewish-arts-and-culture/books/170960/saving-isaac-newton.

175. The Religious Background and Religious Beliefs of Albert Einstein, http://www.adherents.com/people/pe/Albert_Einstein.html, citing Dr. Arthur J. Deikman, who noted that Einstein echoed Isaac Newton's belief in the reality of the mystical (source: "A Functional Approach to Mysticism" in Journal of Consciousness Studies, Vol. 7, No. 11-12, November/December 2000; special issue: 'Cognitive Models and Spiritual Maps'; URL: http://www.deikman.com/functional.html).

176. Sarah, Dry, Saving Isaac Newton: How a Jewish Collector Brought the Physicist's Papers to America, May 5, 2014, http://www.tabletmag.com/jewish-arts-and-culture/boo

ks/170960/saving-isaac-newton.

177. Sarah, Dry, Saving Isaac Newton: How a Jewish Collector Brought the Physicist's Papers to America, May 5, 2014, http://www.tabletmag.com/jewish-arts-and-culture/books/170960/saving-isaac-newton.

178. Marshall Hall, Sola Scriptura - IV, Kabbala Phariseeism or Bible Christianity?, http://www.fixedearth.com/sola-scriptura-4.html (last visited on December 8, 2015).

179. Gershom Scholem, The Kabbalah, Meridian Books, New York 1978, http://www.mishkan.com/kbltalk1.html.

180. Migene Gonzalez-Wippler, The Kabbalah & Magic of Angels, at 95-96 (2013).

181. Dennis, at 199.

182. Dan Cohn-Sherbok and Lavinia Cohn-Sherbok, Jewish and Christian Mysticism: An Introduction, at 167 (1994).

183. Rabbi Eli Mallon, M.Ed., LMSW, Shir ha-Shirim: The Song of Songs, April, 23, 2011, http://rabbielimallon.wordpress.com/2011/04/23/4-23-11-shir-ha-shirim-the-song-of-songs/, quoting, Schochet, J. Immanuel, transl. and ed.; Tzva'at ha-Rivash (The Ethical Will of the Baal Shem Tov); section 68; Kehot Publication Society.

184. Rabbi Eli Mallon, M.Ed., LMSW, Shir ha-Shirim: The Song of Songs, April, 23, 2011, http://rabbielimallon.wordpress.com/2011/04/23/4-23-11-shir-ha-shirim-the-song-of-songs/.

185. Francis and the Shekinah, Call Me Jorge, May 25, 2014, http://callmejorgebergoglio.blogspot.com/2014/05/francis-shekinah.html. See also, Brother Nathaniel Enlightens Us: Satan at the "Wailing Wall," http://givingpsychologyaway.com/?tag=davening and http://www.realjewnews.com/?p=798.

186. Brother Nathaniel Kapner, Satan at the Wailing Wall, February 13, 2013, http://www.realjewnews.com/?p=798.

187. Rabbi Michael Leo Samuel, Davening at Victoria's Secret, San Diego Jewish Herald, 27 December 2013, http://www.sdjewishworld.com/2013/12/27/davening-at-victorias-secret/, quoting Jacob I. Schochet, Tzavat HaRivash (Brooklyn, NY: Kehot Publication, 1998), pp.54-55.

188. Michael Hoffman, *Judaism Discovered*, at 239 (2008).

189. Michael Hoffman, *Judaism Discovered*, at 240 (2008).

190. Michael Hoffman, *Judaism Discovered*, at 240 (2008).

191. Todd Starnes, Fox News, Christian Bakers Face Government Wrath for Refusing to Make Cake for Gay Wedding, February 3, 2015, http://www.foxnews.com/opinion/2015/02/03/christian-bakers-face-government-wrath-for-refusing-to-make-cake-for-gay.html.

192. New Mexico Supreme Court: Wedding Photographer May Not Decline Business from Same-Sex Couple's Commitment Ceremony, The Federalist Society, January 31, 2014, https://fedsoc.org/commentary/publications/new-mexico-supreme-court-wedding-photographer-may-not-decline-business-from-same-sex-couple-s-commitment-ceremony.

193. Nicholas K. Geranios, Court: No Religious Rancor in Flowers for Gay Wedding Case, Associated Press, June 6, 2019, https://apnews.com/article/95f4dcf023764c4caf56101d3233af98.

194. Nicholas K. Geranios, Court: No Religious Rancor in Flowers for Gay Wedding Case, Associated Press, June 6, 2019, https://apnews.com/article/95f4dcf023764c4caf56101d3233af98.

195. Todd Starnes, Fox News, Christian Bakers Face Government Wrath for Refusing to Make Cake for Gay Wedding, February 3, 2015, http://www.foxnews.com/opinion/2015/02/03/christian-bakers-face-government-wrath-for-refusing-to-make-cake-for-gay.html.

196. Nico Lang, Masterpiece Cakeshop Owner in Court Again for Denying Lgbtq Customer, NBC News, April 15, 2020, https://www.nbcnews.com/feature/nbc-out/masterpiece-cakeshop-owner-court-again-denying-lgbtq-customer-n1184656.

197. Trailer Park Entirely Inhabited by Paedophiles and Sex Offenders, 60 Minutes Australia,

https://www.youtube.com/watch?v=OiquubYVbWQ&t=722s, November 2, 2019.

198. TEDx tries to Normalise Pedophilia, July 22, 2018, https://www.youtube.com/watch?v=Wn4ok_W-7d4. TEDx Talk under Review, June 19, 2018, https://blog.ted.com/tedx-talk-under-review/.

199. U.S. House of Representatives, 8th District of Wisconsin, Press Release, U.S. House Passes Rep. Green "Two Strikes Bill," http://www.house.gov/markgreen/PRESS/2000/July00News/NR072500TwoStrikesPassage.htm (website address current as of August 16, 2003). See also http://www.geocities.com/Wellesley/2726/Molester.html (website address current as of August 16, 2003); Jon Donenberg, Keller Attacks Johnson's Vote On 1987 Bill, The Daily Illini Online, October 3, 2000, http://www.dailyillini.com/oct00/oct03/news/printer/news01.shtml (website address current as of August 16, 2003).

200. James M. Cantor, PhD, American Psychological Association, June 2009, Vol 40, No. 6, https://www.apa.org/monitor/2009/06/random.

201. Steve Baldwin, Child Molestation and the Homosexual Movement, 14 REGENT L. REV. 267, 278 (2002), http://www.mega.nu/ampp/baldwin_pedophilia_homosexuality.pdf.

202. Baldwin, supra, at 271, 278 citing W.D. Erickson et al., *Behavior Patterns of Child Molesters*, 17 ARCHIVES SEXUAL BEHAV., at 83 (1988).

203. Baldwin, supra, at 278.

204. Baldwin, supra, at 274.

205. Baldwin, supra, at 268.

206. Baldwin, supra, at 272-73, 277.

207. Mackey's Encyclopedia of Freemasonry, http://www.masonicdictionary.com/ordoabchao.html (last visited on May 30, 2019).

208. Mackey's Encyclopedia of Freemasonry, http://www.masonicdictionary.com/lux.html (last visited on May 30, 2019).

209. Orwell Today, Big Brother Events, https://www.orwelltoday.com/stagedevents.shtml (last visited on May 30, 2019).

210. The Friends of Charles Darwin, Marx of Respect, http://friendsofdarwin.com/articles/marx/ (last visited on November 1, 2015).

211. Michael StGeorge, The Survival Of A Fitting Quotation, http://anonpress.org/spencer/ (last visited on December 26, 2017).

212. Media Bio for Dr. James White, http://www.aomin.org/aoblog/about/media-bios/ (last visited on June 28, 2019).

213. James White @DrOakley1689, 27 March 2017, https://twitter.com/DrOakley1689/status/846368438238928897.

214. Micah Doulos @Mdoulos, 28 Mar 2017, https://twitter.com/DrOakley1689/status/84636843823

8928897.

215. James White @DrOakley1689, 27 March 2017, https://twitter.com/DrOakley1689/status/846368438238928897.

216. James White @DrOakley1689, 27 March 2017, https://twitter.com/DrOakley1689/status/846368438238928897.

217. SHOCKING - Minister FIRED from his Church for Seeking Truth, September 15, 2018, https://www.youtube.com/watch?v=DIfhWO5XHp0.

218. Gary Shogren, Is the Earth a flat disc after all?, https://openoureyeslord.com/2016/06/21/is-the-earth-a-flat-disc-after-all/ (last visited on April 5, 2019).

219. Robert C. Newman, http://www.arn.org/authors/newman.html (last visited on April 5, 2019).

220. Robert C. Newman, Evangelicals and Crackpot Science, Interdisciplinary Biblical Research Institute Biblical Theological Seminary, http://www.leaderu.com/science/crackpot.html (last visited on April 4, 2019).

221. Robert Carter and Jonathan Sarfati, A Flat Earth, and Other Nonsense, Debunking Ideas That Would Not Exist Were it Not for the Internet, Creation Ministries International, 13 September 2016, updated 26 October 2018, https://creation.com/refuting-flat-earth.

222. Robert Carter and Jonathan Sarfati, A Flat Earth, and Other Nonsense, Debunking Ideas That Would Not Exist Were it Not for the Internet, Creation Ministries

International, 13 September 2016, updated 26 October 2018, https://creation.com/refuting-flat-earth.

223. National Geographic, Flat Earth vs. Round Earth | Explorer, January 16, 2019, https://www.youtube.com/watch?v=06bvdFK3vVU.

224. National Geographic, Flat Earth vs. Round Earth | Explorer, January 16, 2019, https://www.youtube.com/watch?v=06bvdFK3vVU.

225. National Geographic, Flat Earth vs. Round Earth | Explorer, January 16, 2019, https://www.youtube.com/watch?v=06bvdFK3vVU.

226. National Geographic, Flat Earth vs. Round Earth | Explorer, January 16, 2019, https://www.youtube.com/watch?v=06bvdFK3vVU.

227. National Geographic, Flat Earth vs. Round Earth | Explorer, January 16, 2019, https://www.youtube.com/watch?v=06bvdFK3vVU.

228. Why the Flat-earth Movement Is the Best Symbol of the Increasingly Diminished Value of Truth and Intelligence, https://nationalpost.com/life/why-the-flat-earth-movement-is-the-best-symbol-of-the-increasingly-diminished-value-of-truth-and-intelligence (last visited on April 5, 2019).

229. Madison Malone Kircher, Can You Believe YouTube Caused the Rise in Flat-Earthers?, New York Intelligencer, February 19, 2019, https://nymag.com/intelligencer/2019/02/can-you-believe-youtube-caused-the-rise-in-flat-earthers.html.

230. Madison Malone Kircher, Can You Believe YouTube Caused the Rise in Flat-Earthers?, New York Intelligencer, February 19, 2019, https://nymag.com/intelligencer/2019/02/can-you-believe-youtube-caused-the-rise-in-flat-earthers.html.

231. Madison Malone Kircher, Can You Believe YouTube Caused the Rise in Flat-Earthers?, New York Intelligencer, February 19, 2019, https://nymag.com/intelligencer/2019/02/can-you-believe-youtube-caused-the-rise-in-flat-earthers.html.

232. Kaitlyn Tiffany, If a Scientific Conspiracy Theory Is Funny, That Doesn't Mean It's a Joke, October 9, 2017, https://www.theverge.com/2017/10/9/16424622/reddit-conspiracy-theories-memes-irony-flat-earth.

233. Kaitlyn Tiffany, If a Scientific Conspiracy Theory Is Funny, That Doesn't Mean It's a Joke, October 9, 2017, https://www.theverge.com/2017/10/9/16424622/reddit-conspiracy-theories-memes-irony-flat-earth.

234. Kaitlyn Tiffany, If a Scientific Conspiracy Theory Is Funny, That Doesn't Mean It's a Joke, October 9, 2017, https://www.theverge.com/2017/10/9/16424622/reddit-conspiracy-theories-memes-irony-flat-earth.

235. Alex Wong, What a Filmmaker Learned from Taking Flat Earthers Seriously, Gentlemen's Quarterly, GQ Magazine, June 4, 2018, https://www.gq.com/story/behind-the-curve-flat-earth-director-interview.

236. CIA Document #1035-960, RE: Concerning Criticism of the Warren Report, http://www.jfklancer.com/CIA.html (last visited on April 16, 2019).

237. CIA Document #1035-960, RE: Concerning Criticism of the Warren Report, http://www.jfklancer.com/CIA.html (last visited on April 16, 2019).

238. Alex Wong, What a Filmmaker Learned from Taking Flat Earthers Seriously, Gentlemen's Quarterly, GQ Magazine, June 4, 2018, https://www.gq.com/story/behind-the-curve-flat-earth-director-interview.

239. Alex Wong, What a Filmmaker Learned from Taking Flat Earthers Seriously, Gentlemen's Quarterly, GQ Magazine, June 4, 2018, https://www.gq.com/story/behind-the-curve-flat-earth-director-interview.

240. How the Internet Made Us Believe in a Flat Earth (And Put the Planet in Danger?), December 10, 2018, https://www.youtube.com/watch?v=Lw4JMl1sErY.

241. Neil deGrasse Tyson: Flat Earth, Fake Science & Space Exploration, June 6, 2016, https://www.youtube.com/watch?v=CuwjWZV8EA0.

242. Flat Earth - Dear Pastor, April 4, 2019, https://www.youtube.com/watch?v=VDVt392y2LM&feature=youtu.be.

243. David Wise, supra, at 200-201.

244. Alex Constantine, The Depraved Spies and Moguls of the CIA's Operation MOCKINGBIRD,

www.whatreallyhappened.com (last visited on April 24, 2016), citing Deborah Davis, Katharine The Great, New York: Sheridan Square Press, at 119-132, 1991, and Carl Bernstein, The CIA and the Media, October 20, 1977.

245. Carl Bernstein, supra.

246. Carl Bernstein, supra.

247. Don Fortner, In Christ (Romans 16:7), September 23, 2018, at 20:00, https://www.youtube.com/watch?v=RKDB26EN64w&feature=youtu.be.

248. Michael StGeorge, The Survival Of A Fitting Quotation, http://anonpress.org/spencer/ (last visited on December 26, 2017).

249. Email from Don Fortner to Frank Hall and others on September 11, 2017.

250. Email from Don Fortner to Frank Hall and others on September 11, 2017.

251. Brett Molina, Apollo Moon Samples Have Gone Untouched for 50 Years Now NASA Plans to Study Them, USA Today, March 13, 2019, https://www.usatoday.com/story/tech/news/2019/03/13/nasa-study-apollo-moon-samples-untouched-50-years/3148810002/

252. Brett Molina, Apollo Moon Samples Have Gone Untouched for 50 Years Now NASA Plans to Study Them, USA Today, March 13, 2019, https://www.usatoday.com/story/tech/news/2019/03/13/nasa-study-apollo-moon-samples-untouched-50-years/3148810002/

253. Email from Don Fortner to Frank Hall and others on September 11, 2017.

254. Robert Carter and Jonathan Sarfati, a Flat Earth, and Other Nonsense, 13 September 2016, https://creation.com/refuting-flat-earth.

255. "Science Falsely So Called (Evolution, Flat Earth, Global Warming)" | Pastor Jason Robinson, Mountain Baptist Church, August 12, 2018, https://www.youtube.com/watch?v=D1J6KgVt6Iw.

256. "Science Falsely So Called (Evolution, Flat Earth, Global Warming)" | Pastor Jason Robinson, Mountain Baptist Church, August 12, 2018, https://www.youtube.com/watch?v=D1J6KgVt6Iw.

257. "Science Falsely So Called (Evolution, Flat Earth, Global Warming)" | Pastor Jason Robinson, Mountain Baptist Church, August 12, 2018, https://www.youtube.com/watch?v=D1J6KgVt6Iw.

258. The Flat Earth from an Engineering Perspective (Pastor Jason Robinson), June 11, 2018, https://www.youtube.com/watch?v=BOQQkwoc88Q.

259. Pastor Robinson Schooling Flattards (the stupidity of the Flat Earth), June 14, 2018, https://www.youtube.com/watch?v=10xQO_aNkYk&t=179s.

260. Science Falsely So Called (Evolution, Flat Earth, Global Warming)" | Pastor Jason Robinson, Mountain Baptist Church, August 12, 2018, https://www.youtube.com/watch?v=D1J6KgVt6Iw, at 39:15.

261. Basic Information About Circles, Math Planet, https://www.mathplanet.com/education/geometry/circles/basic-information-about-circles (last visited on March 30, 2019). Sphere, https://en.oxforddictionaries.com/definition/us/circle (last visited on April 22, 2019).

262. Science Falsely So Called (Evolution, Flat Earth, Global Warming)" | Pastor Jason Robinson, Mountain Baptist Church, August 12, 2018, https://www.youtube.com/watch?v=D1J6KgVt6Iw, at 39:40.

263. Sphere, https://www.mathsisfun.com/definitions/sphere.html (last visited on April 22, 2019). Sphere, https://en.oxforddictionaries.com/definition/us/sphere (last visited on April 22, 2019).

264. Sphere, https://www.mathsisfun.com/definitions/sphere.html (last visited on April 22, 2019). Sphere, https://en.oxforddictionaries.com/definition/us/sphere (last visited on April 22, 2019).

265. The Flat Earth from an Engineering Perspective (Pastor Jason Robinson), June 11, 2018, https://www.youtube.com/watch?v=BOQQkwoc88Q.

266. Kent Hovind OFFICIAL, 5-4-18 Dr. Kent Hovind Divide and Conquer & The Flat Earth, May 4, 2018, https://www.youtube.com/watch?v=aTVkrvkPIvU&t=2457s.

267. Strong Hold Baptist Church, Flat Earth Foolishness, August 7, 2019, https://www.youtube.com/watch?v=xa8Aj7HGcf4&t=

2134s.

268. Strong Hold Baptist Church, Flat Earth Foolishness, August 7, 2019, https://www.youtube.com/watch?v=xa8Aj7HGcf4&t=2134s.

269. Strong Hold Baptist Church, Flat Earth Foolishness, August 7, 2019, https://www.youtube.com/watch?v=xa8Aj7HGcf4&t=2134s.

270. Strong Hold Baptist Church, Flat Earth Foolishness, August 7, 2019, https://www.youtube.com/watch?v=xa8Aj7HGcf4&t=2134s.

271. Strong Hold Baptist Church, Flat Earth Foolishness, August 7, 2019, https://www.youtube.com/watch?v=xa8Aj7HGcf4&t=2134s.

272. Strong Hold Baptist Church, Flat Earth Foolishness, August 7, 2019, https://www.youtube.com/watch?v=xa8Aj7HGcf4&t=2134s.

273. Strong Hold Baptist Church, Flat Earth Foolishness, August 7, 2019, https://www.youtube.com/watch?v=xa8Aj7HGcf4&t=2134s.

274. Strong Hold Baptist Church, Flat Earth Foolishness, August 7, 2019, https://www.youtube.com/watch?v=xa8Aj7HGcf4&t=2134s.

275. Hold, American Dictionary of the English Language, 1828, http://webstersdictionary1828.com/Dictionary/hold.

276. Don Fortner, In Christ (Romans 16:7), September 23, 2018, at 20:00, https://www.youtube.com/watch?v=RKDB26EN64w&feature=youtu.be.

277. Wyatt Houtz, John Calvin on Nicolaus Copernicus and Heliocentrism, October 28, 2014, https://biologos.org/articles/john-calvin-on-nicolaus-copernicus-and-heliocentrism/, quoting John Calvin, "Sermon on 1 Corinthians 10:19-24", Calvini Opera Selecta, Corpus Refomatorum, Vol 49, 677, trans. by Robert White in "Calvin and Copernicus: the Problem Reconsidered", Calvin Theological Journal 15 (1980), p233-243, at 236-237.

278. Gospel, Webster's Revised Unabridged Dictionary, 1913 Edition, https://www.webster-dictionary.org/definition/gospel (last visited on June 14, 2019).

279. Gospel, Oxford English Dictionary (Unabridged).

280. Harper's Bible Dictionary, at 354 (1985).

281. Harper's Bible Dictionary, at 354 (1985).

282. The New International Dictionary of the Bible, at 398 (1984).

283. Gospel, Oxford English Dictionary (Unabridged).

284. Gospel, Oxford English Dictionary (Unabridged).

285. Spell, American Dictionary of the English Language (1828), http://webstersdictionary1828.com/Dictionary/spell.

286. The New International Dictionary of the Bible, at 398 (1984).

287. Gospel, Oxford English Dictionary (Unabridged).

288. Gospel, Oxford English Dictionary (Unabridged).

289. Gail Riplinger, The Language of the King James Bible, at 49-50 (1998), http://nashpublications.com/wp-content/uploads/2013/10/King_James_Bible/Riplinger_Books/Language-of-the-KJB.pdf, quoting Kittel, The Theological Dictionary of the New Testament (p. 660, Vol. 10).

290. Gail Riplinger, The Language of the King James Bible, at 49-50 (1998), http://nashpublications.com/wp-content/uploads/2013/10/King_James_Bible/Riplinger_Books/Language-of-the-KJB.pdf.

291. Gospel, Oxford English Dictionary (Unabridged).

292. Gospel, Oxford English Dictionary (Unabridged).

293. Gospel, Oxford English Dictionary (Unabridged).

294. E.g., Gospel, Online Etymology Dictionary, https://www.etymonline.com/word/gospel (last visited on June 19, 2019).

295. Gail Riplinger, Hazardous Materials, at 1140-41.

296. FlatEarthDoctrine, Kent Hovind FINALLY Admits that the Bible... (FLAT EARTH), June 4, 2018,

https://www.youtube.com/watch?v=n5bRSp-kueM. Don Fortner, In Christ (Romans 16:7), September 23, 2018, at 20:00, https://www.youtube.com/watch?v=RKDB26EN64w&feature=youtu.be.

297. Dr. Neelak S. Tjernagel, Holy Scripture Is the Word of God (1984).

298. Gospel, Oxford English Dictionary (Unabridged).

299. Gospel, Oxford English Dictionary (Unabridged).

300. Gail Riplinger, The Language of the King James Bible, at 50 (1998), http://nashpublications.com/wp-content/uploads/2013/10/King_James_Bible/Riplinger_Books/Language-of-the-KJB.pdf.

301. Gail Riplinger, The Language of the King James Bible, at 49-50 (1998), http://nashpublications.com/wp-content/uploads/2013/10/King_James_Bible/Riplinger_Books/Language-of-the-KJB.pdf.

302. Gospel, Oxford English Dictionary (Unabridged).

303. Gail Riplinger, The Language of the King James Bible, at 49-50 (1998), http://nashpublications.com/wp-content/uploads/2013/10/King_James_Bible/Riplinger_Books/Language-of-the-KJB.pdf, citing Webster's Encyclopedic Dictionary.

304. Gospel, Webster's Dictionary of the English Language, 1828, http://webstersdictionary1828.com/Dictionary/gospel.

305. Euaggelion, https://biblehub.com/str/greek/2098.htm (last visited on June 16, 2019).

306. Tidings, American Dictionary of the English Language (1828), http://webstersdictionary1828.com/Dictionary/tidings; Tidings, Webster's 1913 Dictionary, https://www.webster-dictionary.org/definition/tidings.

307. Tidings, American Dictionary of the English Language (1828), http://webstersdictionary1828.com/Dictionary/tidings.

308. Intelligence, American Dictionary of the English Language (1828), http://webstersdictionary1828.com/Dictionary/intelligence.

309. Intelligence, American Dictionary of the English Language (1828), http://webstersdictionary1828.com/Dictionary/intelligence.

310. Good, American Dictionary of the English Language (1828), http://webstersdictionary1828.com/Dictionary/good.

311. Tidings, American Dictionary of the English Language (1828), http://webstersdictionary1828.com/Dictionary/tidings; Tidings, Webster's 1913 Dictionary, https://www.webster-dictionary.org/definition/tidings.

312. Intelligence, American Dictionary of the English Language (1828), http://webstersdictionary1828.com/Dictionary/intellige

nce.

313.Big Think, 3 Proofs That Debunk Flat-earth Theory | NASA's Michelle Thaller, May 23, 2018, https://www.youtube.com/watch?v=CGjFAe018oA.

314.Big Think, 3 Proofs That Debunk Flat-earth Theory | NASA's Michelle Thaller, May 23, 2018, https://www.youtube.com/watch?v=CGjFAe018oA.

315.Big Think, 3 Proofs That Debunk Flat-earth Theory | NASA's Michelle Thaller, May 23, 2018, https://www.youtube.com/watch?v=CGjFAe018oA.

316.Email from Frank Hall to Edward Hendrie, January 13, 2019.

317.YouTube Demotes Flat-Earthers, Conspiracy Theorists, Space Daily, January 25, 2019, http://www.spacedaily.com/afp/190125185823.24zhsgo7.html.

318.Sat, Sep 16, 2017, 11:28 a.m., email from pastor.

319.Sep 18, 2017, 11:56 a.m., email sent out to church members.

320.August 22-25, 20018, Take on the World Conference, Vermilion Ohio, https://www.facebook.com/TakeOnTheWorldConferences/ (last visited on January 26, 2018).

321.SHOCKING - Minister FIRED from his Church for Seeking Truth, September 15, 2018, https://www.youtube.com/watch?v=DIfhWO5XHp0.

322.Pastor Preaches 1st FLAT EARTH SERMON After Getting FIRED from Church, October 1, 2018, https://www.youtube.com/watch?time_continue=451&v=D9OWe0bgclk.

323.Chad Talyor, FIRED FOR TRUTH - Nate Wolfe full interview, September 16, 2018, https://www.youtube.com/watch?v=KoILGsBpVQw&t=82s.

324.Chad Talyor, FIRED FOR TRUTH - Nate Wolfe full interview, September 16, 2018, https://www.youtube.com/watch?v=KoILGsBpVQw&t=82s.

325.Fired for Truth, https://www.gofundme.com/firedfortruth (last visited on January 27, 2019).

326.About Louie Giglio, https://www.louiegiglio.com/about/ (last visited on April 12, 2019).

327.God's Universe, August 22, 2016, https://www.youtube.com/watch?v=6-nLyPtbSSA.

328.God's Universe, August 22, 2016, https://www.youtube.com/watch?v=6-nLyPtbSSA.

329.God's Universe, August 22, 2016, https://www.youtube.com/watch?v=6-nLyPtbSSA.

330.God's Universe, August 22, 2016, https://www.youtube.com/watch?v=6-nLyPtbSSA.

331.God's Universe, August 22, 2016, https://www.youtube.com/watch?v=6-nLyPtbSSA.

332.God's Universe, August 22, 2016, https://www.youtube.com/watch?v=6-nLyPtbSSA.

333. Ferocious, https://en.oxforddictionaries.com/definition/ferocious (last visited on April 13, 2019).

334. Ferocious, https://www.merriam-webster.com/dictionary/ferocious (last visited on April 13, 2019).

335. God's Universe, August 22, 2016, https://www.youtube.com/watch?v=6-nLyPtbSSA.

336. God's Universe, August 22, 2016, https://www.youtube.com/watch?v=6-nLyPtbSSA.

337. EVANGELICAL APOSTASY - Louie Giglio Embraces Antichrist Pope Exposed!, June 16, 2016, https://www.youtube.com/watch?v=EbVk7_J_UG8&app=desktop.

338. Africa, at 404.

339. E.g., Lodge Copernicus No. 505, New Zealand; Lodge Copernicus No. 246, Australia.

340. Hank Hanegraaff, Flat Earth, https://www.lightsource.com/ministry/Bible-answer-man/flat-earth-608850.html (last visited on April 16, 2019).

341. Jay Howard Exposes Hank Hanegraaff, December 16, 2018, https://m.youtube.com/watch?v=J8k53KcghRY.

342. Jay Howard, Hard Questions for the Bible Answer Man: Hank Hanegraaff and His Takeover of the Christian Research Institute, 2009, ISBN-13: 978-0615311678.

343. Jay Howard Exposes Hank Hanegraaff, December 16, 2018, https://m.youtube.com/watch?v=J8k53KcghRY.

344. Plagiarism, Oxford English Dictionary, https://en.oxforddictionaries.com/definition/plagiarism (last visited on April 18, 2019).

345. Robert M. Bowman, Jr., Is the Good News Bear a Copycat? Hank Hanegraaff and Plagiarism, http://web.archive.org/web/20060619081529/http://www.atlantaapologist.org/COPYCAT.html (last visited on April 16, 2019).

346. Robert M. Bowman, Jr., Is the Good News Bear a Copycat? Hank Hanegraaff and Plagiarism, http://web.archive.org/web/20060619081529/http://www.atlantaapologist.org/COPYCAT.html (last visited on April 16, 2019).

347. D. JAMES KENNEDY ON HANK HANEGRAAFF'S PLAGIARISM, AND MORE, April 26, 2010, https://www.youtube.com/watch?v=JfZODpbAUk4&app=desktop.

348. D. JAMES KENNEDY ON HANK HANEGRAAFF'S PLAGIARISM, AND MORE, April 26, 2010, https://www.youtube.com/watch?v=JfZODpbAUk4&app=desktop.

349. Tim Funk, How a photo of radio's 'Bible Answer Man' in church lost him thousands of listeners, Miami Herald, June 2, 2017, https://www.miamiherald.com/news/nation-world/national/article154139454.html.

350. Emmanuel Hatzidakis (Eastern Orthodox Priest), The Heavenly Banquet. Understanding the Divine Liturgy, http://saintandrewgoc.org/home/2018/10/1/faith-and-science (last visited on April 17, 2019).

351. Emmanuel Hatzidakis (Eastern Orthodox Priest), The Heavenly Banquet. Understanding the Divine Liturgy, http://saintandrewgoc.org/home/2018/10/1/faith-and-science (last visited on April 17, 2019).

352. Emmanuel Hatzidakis (Eastern Orthodox Priest), The Heavenly Banquet. Understanding the Divine Liturgy, http://saintandrewgoc.org/home/2018/10/1/faith-and-science (last visited on April 17, 2019).

353. Emmanuel Hatzidakis (Eastern Orthodox Priest), The Heavenly Banquet. Understanding the Divine Liturgy, http://saintandrewgoc.org/home/2018/10/1/faith-and-science (last visited on April 17, 2019).

354. Praying to the Saints, http://www.saintbarbara.org/growing_in_christ/praying_to_the_saints (last visited on April 16, 2019).

355. Tim Funk, How a Photo of Radio's 'Bible Answer Man' in Church Lost Him Thousands of Listeners, Miami Herald, June 2, 2017, https://www.miamiherald.com/news/nation-world/national/article154139454.html.

356. Orthodox Catechism, http://www.ocf.org/OrthodoxPage/reading/catechism.html (last visited on April 18, 2019).

357. Orthodox Catechism, http://www.ocf.org/OrthodoxPage/reading/catechism.html (last visited on April 18, 2019).

358. Volume II - Worship, The Divine Liturgy, Eucharistic Canon: Anaphora, https://oca.org/orthodoxy/the-orthodox-faith/worship/the-divine-liturgy/eucharistic-canon-anaphora (last visited on April 18, 2019).

359. Holy Communion, The Monastery of St. Tikhon of Zadonsk, https://sttikhonsmonastery.org/article.php?id=38 (last visited on April 18, 2019).

360. Holy Communion, The Monastery of St. Tikhon of Zadonsk, https://sttikhonsmonastery.org/article.php?id=38 (last visited on April 18, 2019).

361. Holy Communion, The Monastery of St. Tikhon of Zadonsk, https://sttikhonsmonastery.org/article.php?id=38 (last visited on April 18, 2019).

362. Holy Communion, The Monastery of St. Tikhon of Zadonsk, https://sttikhonsmonastery.org/article.php?id=38 (last visited on April 18, 2019).

363. Holy Communion, The Monastery of St. Tikhon of Zadonsk, https://sttikhonsmonastery.org/article.php?id=38 (last visited on April 18, 2019).

364. Holy Communion, The Monastery of St. Tikhon of Zadonsk,

https://sttikhonsmonastery.org/article.php?id=38 (last visited on April 18, 2019).

365. Longer Catechism of the Orthodox, Catholic, Eastern Church by St. Philaret (Drozdov) of Moscow (1830), https://blogs.ancientfaith.com/orthodoxyandheterodoxy/2013/08/14/the-doctrine-of-transubstantiation-in-the-orthodox-church/ (last visited on April 18, 2019).

366. Orthodox Confession of Dositheus, Patriarch of Jerusalem (1672), https://blogs.ancientfaith.com/orthodoxyandheterodoxy/2013/08/14/the-doctrine-of-transubstantiation-in-the-orthodox-church/ (last visited on April 18, 2019).

367. Orthodox Confession of Faith, Peter Mogila, Metropolitan of Kiev (1633-1647), https://blogs.ancientfaith.com/orthodoxyandheterodoxy/2013/08/14/the-doctrine-of-transubstantiation-in-the-orthodox-church/ (last visited on April 18, 2019).

368. WILLIAM AND SHARON SCHNOEBELEN, LUCIFER DETHRONED, p. 56-58 (1993).

369. *Id.* at p.141.

370. WILLIAM AND SHARON SCHNOEBELEN, LUCIFER DETHRONED, p. 259-66 (1993).

371. *Id.* at p. 264.

372. Sacrifice of the Mass, Orthodox Church in America, https://oca.org/questions/romancatholicism/sacrifice-of-the-mass (last visited on April 18, 2019).

373. Tim Funk, How a Photo of Radio's 'Bible Answer Man' in Church Lost Him Thousands of Listeners, Miami Herald, June 2, 2017, https://www.miamiherald.com/news/nation-world/national/article154139454.html.

374. Tim Funk, How a Photo of Radio's 'Bible Answer Man' in Church Lost Him Thousands of Listeners, Miami Herald, June 2, 2017, https://www.miamiherald.com/news/nation-world/national/article154139454.html.

375. Q&A #27 - Does the Bible Teach the Earth Is Flat?, April 24, 2018, https://www.youtube.com/watch?v=IBm9wy0LjDU.

376. Q&A #27 - Does the Bible Teach the Earth Is Flat?, April 24, 2018, https://www.youtube.com/watch?v=IBm9wy0LjDU.

377. Q&A #27 - Does the Bible Teach the Earth Is Flat?, April 24, 2018, https://www.youtube.com/watch?v=IBm9wy0LjDU.

378. Christian Pastor, David O'Steen, rebukes FLAT EARTH DOCTRINE, May 2, 2018, https://www.youtube.com/watch?v=FGKizZ4EH5U&t=1153s.

379. Michael Hoggard, Flat Earth Education for the Globally Challenged, https://geofrisbee.com/ (last visited on January 27, 2019).

380. Michael Hoggard, Bible Answers To Honest Questions About The Shape of the Earth, Novermber 22, 2018, https://www.youtube.com/watch?v=gkqz3F_3crM&t=

811s.

381. Pastor Mike Hoggard, Flat Earth: Does the Bible Say if Men Went To Space?, https://pastormikehoggard.com/2018/11/19/flat-earth-does-the-Bible-say-if-men-went-to-space/?utm_source=feedburner&utm_medium=email&utm_campaign=Feed%3A+mikehoggard+%28The+Hog+Blog%29 (last visited on January 27, 2019).

382. Michael Hoggard, Live Broadcast of my Interview of a Former Flat Earth Promoter, December 13, 2018, https://www.youtube.com/watch?v=mTYFGeV5Anw.

383. Michael Hoggard, Former Flat Earther Reveals the Truth, Flat Earth Is a Psy-Op!!, December 12, 2018, https://www.youtube.com/watch?v=RmY8jGxwtWI&t=211s.

384. Michael Hoggard, Live Broadcast of my Interview of a Former Flat Earth Promoter, December 13, 2018, https://www.youtube.com/watch?v=mTYFGeV5Anw, at 1:20:15.

385. Michael Hoggard, FLAT EARTH: Are Freemasons Helping Satan Cover Up the Shape of the Earth, October 10, 2018, https://www.youtube.com/watch?v=tlL_78pts6s.

386. Michael Hoggard, FLAT EARTH: Are Freemasons Helping Satan Cover Up the Shape of the Earth, October 10, 2018, https://www.youtube.com/watch?v=tlL_78pts6s.

387. Michael Hoggard, Former Flat Earther Reveals the Truth, Flat Earth Is a Psy-Op!!, December 12, 2018, https://www.youtube.com/watch?v=RmY8jGxwtWI&t

=211s.

388. Does the Bible teach that the Earth is round or flat?, https://www.versebyverseministry.org/Bible-answers/does-the-Bible-teach-that-the-earth-is-round-or-flat/.

389. Steve Van Nattan, Flat Earth Heretics, http://www.blessedquietness.com/journal/theworld/Flat_Earth_Heretics.htm (last visited on April 4, 2019).

390. Steve Van Nattan, Flat Earth Heretics, http://www.blessedquietness.com/journal/theworld/Flat_Earth_Heretics.htm (last visited on April 4, 2019).

391. Fable, Merriam-Webster Dictionary, https://www.merriam-webster.com/dictionary/fable (last visited on April 22, 2019).

392. Basic Information About Circles, Math Planet, https://www.mathplanet.com/education/geometry/circles/basic-information-about-circles (last visited on March 30, 2019). Sphere, https://en.oxforddictionaries.com/definition/us/circle (last visited on April 22, 2019).

393. Sphere, https://www.mathsisfun.com/definitions/sphere.html (last visited on April 22, 2019). Sphere, https://en.oxforddictionaries.com/definition/us/sphere (last visited on April 22, 2019).

394. Sphere, https://www.mathsisfun.com/definitions/sphere.html (last visited on April 22, 2019). Sphere, https://en.oxforddictionaries.com/definition/us/sphere (last visited on April 22, 2019).

395. Trapp, John. "Commentary on Isaiah 40:22". John Trapp Complete Commentary. https://www.studylight.org/commentaries/jtc/isaiah-40.html (last visited on April 21, 2019).

396. Gill's Exposition, Isaiah 40, https://Biblehub.com/commentaries/gill/isaiah/40.htm (last visited on April 21, 2019).

397. Basic Information About Circles, Math Planet, https://www.mathplanet.com/education/geometry/circles/basic-information-about-circles (last visited on March 30, 2019).

398. Barnes' Notes, Isaiah 40, https://Biblehub.com/commentaries/barnes/isaiah/40.htm (last visited on April 21, 2019).

399. Jamieson-Fausset-Brown Bible Commentary, Isaiah 40, https://Biblehub.com/commentaries/jfb/isaiah/40.htm (last visited on April 21, 2019).

400. Whedon, Daniel. "Commentary on Isaiah 40:22". "Whedon's Commentary on the Bible". https://www.studylight.org/commentaries/whe/isaiah-40.html (last visited on April 21, 2019).

401. Cambridge Bible for Schools and Colleges, Isaiah 40, https://Biblehub.com/commentaries/cambridge/isaiah/40.htm (last visited on April 21, 2019).

402. Scofield, C. I. "Scofield Reference Notes on Isaiah 40:22". "Scofield Reference Notes (1917 Edition)". https://www.studylight.org/commentaries/srn/isaiah-40.html (lat visited on April 21, 2019).

403. JOHN L. BRAY, MILLENNIUM - THE BIG QUESTION, P. 58 (1984).

404. WILLIAM R. KIMBALL, THE RAPTURE, A Question of Timing, p. 51 (1985).

405. C.E. Carlson, The Zionist Created Scofield "Bible," http://christianparty.net/scofield.htm (website address current as of August 9, 2003).

406. C.E. Carlson, The Zionist Created Scofield "Bible," http://christianparty.net/scofield.htm (website address current as of August 9, 2003).

407. C.E. Carlson, The Zionist Created Scofield "Bible," http://christianparty.net/scofield.htm (website address current as of August 9, 2003).

408. C.E. Carlson, The Zionist Created Scofield "Bible," http://christianparty.net/scofield.htm (website address current as of August 9, 2003).

409. CYRUS SCOFIELD -- WHO WAS HE? Excerpt from "The Unified Conspiracy Theory," http://www.sweetliberty.org/issues/hoax/scofield.htm (website address current as of August 9, 2003).

410. CYRUS SCOFIELD -- WHO WAS HE? Excerpt from "The Unified Conspiracy Theory," http://www.sweetliberty.org/issues/hoax/scofield.htm (website address current as of August 9, 2003).

411. C.E. Carlson, The Zionist Created Scofield "Bible," http://christianparty.net/scofield.htm (website address current as of August 9, 2003).

412. CYRUS SCOFIELD -- WHO WAS HE? Excerpt from "The Unified Conspiracy Theory,"

http://www.sweetliberty.org/issues/hoax/scofield.htm (website address current as of August 9, 2003).

413.CYRUS SCOFIELD -- WHO WAS HE? Excerpt from "The Unified Conspiracy Theory," http://www.sweetliberty.org/issues/hoax/scofield.htm (website address current as of August 9, 2003).

414.CYRUS SCOFIELD -- WHO WAS HE? Excerpt from "The Unified Conspiracy Theory," http://www.sweetliberty.org/issues/hoax/scofield.htm (website address current as of August 9, 2003). Scofield: The Christian Leader With Feet of Clay, http://www.virginiawater.co.uk/christchurch/articles/scofield1.html (website address current as of August 9, 2003).

415.CYRUS SCOFIELD -- WHO WAS HE? Excerpt from "The Unified Conspiracy Theory," http://www.sweetliberty.org/issues/hoax/scofield.htm (website address current as of August 9, 2003).

416.CYRUS SCOFIELD -- WHO WAS HE? Excerpt from "The Unified Conspiracy Theory," http://www.sweetliberty.org/issues/hoax/scofield.htm (website address current as of August 9, 2003).

417.Scofield: The Christian Leader With Feet of Clay, http://www.virginiawater.co.uk/christchurch/articles/scofield1.html (website address current as of August 9, 2003).

418.Scofield: The Christian Leader With Feet of Clay, http://www.virginiawater.co.uk/christchurch/articles/scofield1.html (website address current as of August 9, 2003).

419. G.A. RIPLINGER, NEW AGE Bible VERSIONS, p. 405 (1993).

420. Nicolaitans Meaning and Etymology, http://www.abarim-publications.com/Meaning/Nicolaitans.html#.XE4HRIgvz9c (last visited on January 27, 2019).

421. Nicolaitans Meaning and Etymology, http://www.abarim-publications.com/Meaning/Nicolaitans.html#.XE4HRIgvz9c (last visited on January 27, 2019).

422. Nicolaitans Meaning and Etymology, http://www.abarim-publications.com/Meaning/Nicolaitans.html#.XE4HRIgvz9c (last visited on January 27, 2019).

423. Joseph-Nicolas Robert-Fleury, Vatican Admits Galileo Was Right, 7 November 1992, https://www.newscientist.com/article/mg13618460-600-vatican-admits-galileo-was-right/.

424. Brother Cloud, I Have a Question, Way of Life Literature, http://www.wayoflife.org/wayoflife/questions.html (last visited on November 11, 2011).

425. Brother Cloud, I Have a Question, Way of Life Literature, http://www.wayoflife.org/wayoflife/questions.html (last visited on November 11, 2011).

426. What Is Way of Life Literature?, http://www.wayoflife.org/wayoflife/whatiswayoflife.html (last visited on November 11, 2011).

427. What Is Way of Life Literature?, http://www.wayoflife.org/wayoflife/whatiswayoflife.html (last visited on November 11, 2011).

428. What Is Way of Life Literature?, http://www.wayoflife.org/wayoflife/whatiswayoflife.html (last visited on November 11, 2011). See also, Hidup Adalah Kristus, What Is Way of Life Literature?, https://dancesuatBibleclass.wordpress.com/2011/12/17/what-is-way-of-life-literature/ (last visited on February 2, 2019).

429. David Cloud, A Flat Earth, Nuttiness, and the Lunar Eclipse, January 9, 2018, https://www.wayoflife.org/reports/a_flat_earth_nuttiness_and_the_lunar_eclipse.php?awt_l=7lFOU&awt_m=3fj2a1ujgCNpjkC.

430. David Cloud, A Flat Earth, Nuttiness, and the Lunar Eclipse, January 9, 2018, https://www.wayoflife.org/reports/a_flat_earth_nuttiness_and_the_lunar_eclipse.php?awt_l=7lFOU&awt_m=3fj2a1ujgCNpjkC.

431. David Cloud, A Flat Earth, Nuttiness, and the Lunar Eclipse, January 9, 2018, https://www.wayoflife.org/reports/a_flat_earth_nuttiness_and_the_lunar_eclipse.php?awt_l=7lFOU&awt_m=3fj2a1ujgCNpjkC.

432. David Cloud, A Flat Earth, Nuttiness, and the Lunar Eclipse, January 9, 2018, https://www.wayoflife.org/reports/a_flat_earth_nuttiness_and_the_lunar_eclipse.php?awt_l=7lFOU&awt_m=3fj2a1ujgCNpjkC.

433. David Cloud, A Flat Earth, Nuttiness, and the Lunar Eclipse, January 9, 2018, https://www.wayoflife.org/reports/a_flat_earth_nuttiness_and_the_lunar_eclipse.php?awt_l=7lFOU&awt_m=3fj2a1ujgCNpjkC.

434. What Is Way of Life Literature?, http://www.wayoflife.org/wayoflife/whatiswayoflife.html (last visited on November 11, 2011). See also, Hidup Adalah Kristus, What Is Way of Life Literature?, https://dancesuatBibleclass.wordpress.com/2011/12/17/what-is-way-of-life-literature/ (last visited on February 2, 2019).

435. David Cloud, Way of Life Literature, https://www.wayoflife.org/whois/ (last visited on February 2, 2019).

436. David Cloud, A Flat Earth, Nuttiness, and the Lunar Eclipse, January 9, 2018, https://www.wayoflife.org/reports/a_flat_earth_nuttiness_and_the_lunar_eclipse.php?awt_l=7lFOU&awt_m=3fj2a1ujgCNpjkC.

437. Satellite 2018, March 12-18, 2018, http://2018.satshow.com/.

438. Satellite 2018, March 12-18, 2018, http://2018.satshow.com/.

439. Pastor Charles Lawson Sermons and Teaching from the KJB, http://pastorcharleslawson.org/ (last visited on June 10, 2018).

440. Angry Christian Pastor Speaks Out Against Flat Earth!! Never Question Men, NASA & SpaceX, April

30, 2018, https://www.youtube.com/watch?v=Kk0p8hAKs6k&t=3s. See also The "Pastor Charles Lawson" FLAT EARTHER Challenge, May 1, 2018, https://www.youtube.com/watch?v=RHhTT7txBRM&t=70s.

441. Flat Earth Debunked by Christian Mathematician (Isaiah 40:22, Conspiracy, Geocentric, Heliocentric), June 3, 2013, https://www.youtube.com/watch?v=HuItq1apHaE.

442. "The Flat Earth Debunked" (KJV Baptist Preaching), June 3, 2018, https://www.youtube.com/watch?v=Uwj6AQBUukE.

443. Steve Van Nattan, Flat Earth Heretics, http://www.blessedquietness.com/journal/theworld/Flat_Earth_Heretics.htm (last visited on April 4, 2019).

444. Resume of Steve Van Nattan, http://www.balaams-ass.com/journal/resume.htm (last visited on April 4, 2019).

445. Steve Van Nattan, Flat Earth Heretics, http://www.blessedquietness.com/journal/theworld/Flat_Earth_Heretics.htm (last visited on April 4, 2019).

446. Steve Van Nattan, Flat Earth Heretics, http://www.blessedquietness.com/journal/theworld/Flat_Earth_Heretics.htm (last visited on April 4, 2019).

447. Steve Van Nattan, Flat Earth Heretics, http://www.blessedquietness.com/journal/theworld/Flat_Earth_Heretics.htm (last visited on April 4, 2019).

448. Steve Van Nattan, Flat Earth Heretics, http://www.blessedquietness.com/journal/theworld/Fla

t_Earth_Heretics.htm (last visited on April 4, 2019).

449. Steve Van Nattan, Flat Earth Heretics, http://www.blessedquietness.com/journal/theworld/Flat_Earth_Heretics.htm (last visited on April 4, 2019).

450. Steve Van Nattan, Flat Earth Heretics, http://www.blessedquietness.com/journal/theworld/Flat_Earth_Heretics.htm (last visited on April 4, 2019).

451. Steve Van Nattan, Flat Earth Heretics, http://www.blessedquietness.com/journal/theworld/Flat_Earth_Heretics.htm (last visited on April 4, 2019).

452. Steve Van Nattan, Flat Earth Heretics, http://www.blessedquietness.com/journal/theworld/Flat_Earth_Heretics.htm (last visited on April 4, 2019).

453. Chad Wagner, Flat Earth Refutation (Part 2) - A Biblical and Scientific Refutation, April 9, 2017, https://www.youtube.com/watch?v=9zjf_Vyd6BA.

454. Flat Earth Refutation (Part 1) - A Biblical Refutation, April 2, 2017, https://www.youtube.com/watch?v=T0DZrGUqe-k.

455. Flat Earth Refutation (Part 1) - A Biblical Refutation, April 2, 2017, https://www.youtube.com/watch?v=T0DZrGUqe-k.

456. Flat Earth Refutation (Part 1) - A Biblical Refutation, April 2, 2017, https://www.youtube.com/watch?v=T0DZrGUqe-k.

457. Michael Newton Keas, https://stream.org/author/michaelnewtonkeas/ (last visited on April 7, 2019).

458. Michael Newton Keas, Don't Believe the Flat (Earth) Myth. It's Anti-Christian Bias Disguised as History, February 1, 2019, https://stream.org/dont-believe-flat-earth-myth/.

459. Michael Newton Keas, Don't Believe the Flat (Earth) Myth. It's Anti-Christian Bias Disguised as History, February 1, 2019, https://stream.org/dont-believe-flat-earth-myth/.

460. Testimonies, In Awe of Thy Word, http://www.avpublications.com/avnew/testimonies/hinton.html (last visited on June 11, 2019).

461. Faculty, Christian Life School of Theology, https://clstglobal.org/about/faculty/. But see Dr Grady McMurtry - What are his qualifications and scientific expertise?, December 16, 2008, http://www.ecalpemos.org/2008/12/dr-grady-mcmurtry-what-are-his.html.

462. Grady S. McMurtry, https://www.creationworldview.org/about-us/ (last visited on April 6, 2019). But see Dr Grady McMurtry - What are his qualifications and scientific expertise?, December 16, 2008, http://www.ecalpemos.org/2008/12/dr-grady-mcmurtry-what-are-his.html.

463. Faculty, Christian Life School of Theology, https://clstglobal.org/about/faculty/. But see Dr Grady McMurtry - What are his qualifications and scientific expertise?, December 16, 2008, http://www.ecalpemos.org/2008/12/dr-grady-mcmurtry-what-are-his.html.

464.Faculty, Christian Life School of Theology, https://clstglobal.org/about/faculty/. But see Dr Grady McMurtry - What are his qualifications and scientific expertise?, December 16, 2008, http://www.ecalpemos.org/2008/12/dr-grady-mcmurtry-what-are-his.html.

465.Faculty, Christian Life School of Theology, https://clstglobal.org/about/faculty/. But see Dr Grady McMurtry - What are his qualifications and scientific expertise?, December 16, 2008, http://www.ecalpemos.org/2008/12/dr-grady-mcmurtry-what-are-his.html.

466.Faculty, Christian Life School of Theology, https://clstglobal.org/about/faculty/. But see Dr Grady McMurtry - What are his qualifications and scientific expertise?, December 16, 2008, http://www.ecalpemos.org/2008/12/dr-grady-mcmurtry-what-are-his.html.

467.Faculty, Christian Life School of Theology, https://clstglobal.org/about/faculty/. But see Dr Grady McMurtry - What are his qualifications and scientific expertise?, December 16, 2008, http://www.ecalpemos.org/2008/12/dr-grady-mcmurtry-what-are-his.html.

468.Grady S. McMurtry, https://www.creationworldview.org/about-us/ (last visited on April 6, 2019). Mensa, https://www.mensa.org/ (last visited on April 6, 2019).

469.Grady S. McMurtry, The Myth of the Flat Earth Concept, Creation World View Ministries, https://www.creationworldview.org/about-us/ (last visited on April 6, 2019).

470. Face, https://www.mathsisfun.com/definitions/face.html (last visited on March 25, 2019).

471. Compass, Noah Webster American Dictionary of the English Language, 1828, http://webstersdictionary1828.com/Dictionary/compass.

472. Face, https://www.mathsisfun.com/definitions/face.html (last visited on March 25, 2019).

473. Turn, Noah Webster American Dictionary of the English Language, 1828, http://webstersdictionary1828.com/Dictionary/turn.

474. Turn, Noah Webster American Dictionary of the English Language, 1828, http://webstersdictionary1828.com/Dictionary/turn.

475. Turn, Merriam Webster Dictionary, https://www.merriam-webster.com/dictionary/turn.

476. Turn, Noah Webster American Dictionary of the English Language, 1828, http://webstersdictionary1828.com/Dictionary/turn.

477. Turn, Merriam Webster Dictionary, https://www.merriam-webster.com/dictionary/turn.

478. Grady S. McMurtry, The Myth of the Flat Earth Concept, Creation World View Ministries, https://www.creationworldview.org/about-us/ (last visited on April 6, 2019).

479. Calvary Chapel Tri-Cities, "Flat Earth, Real Or Not?" Truth Set Free Q&A, November 30, 2019,

https://www.youtube.com/watch?v=uywUHpGo2us.

480. Calvary Chapel Tri-Cities, "Flat Earth, Real Or Not?" Truth Set Free Q&A, November 30, 2019, https://www.youtube.com/watch?v=uywUHpGo2us.

481. Basic Information About Circles, Math Planet, https://www.mathplanet.com/education/geometry/circles/basic-information-about-circles (last visited on March 30, 2019).

482. Testimony of John Todd, http://www.av1611.org/crock.html (web address current as of 9-26-05).

483. The Free Gift Gospel Mission, Pastor Vern Hall- Flat Earth Doctrine and Pagan Origins (Dec. 18, 2019), https://www.youtube.com/watch?v=aWhTzARpu3s&t=433s.

484. The Free Gift Gospel Mission, Pastor Vern Hall- Flat Earth Doctrine and Pagan Origins (Dec. 18, 2019), https://www.youtube.com/watch?v=aWhTzARpu3s&t=433s.

485. The Free Gift Gospel Mission, Pastor Vern Hall- Flat Earth Doctrine and Pagan Origins (Dec. 18, 2019), https://www.youtube.com/watch?v=aWhTzARpu3s&t=433s.

486. The Free Gift Gospel Mission, Pastor Vern Hall- Flat Earth Doctrine and Pagan Origins (Dec. 18, 2019), https://www.youtube.com/watch?v=aWhTzARpu3s&t=433s.

487. Pastor's Perspective 7/26/2016 - Flat Earth, Cherubim and More, July 26, 2016, https://www.youtube.com/watch?v=EWxAeR4KGho&

t=2620s.

488. Pastor's Perspective 7/26/2016 - Flat Earth, Cherubim and More, July 26, 2016, https://www.youtube.com/watch?v=EWxAeR4KGho&t=2620s.

489. Hold, American Dictionary of the English Language, 1828, http://webstersdictionary1828.com/Dictionary/hold.

490. Terry Watkins, *Joel Osteen True or False*, http://www.av1611.org/osteen.html (web address current as of October 15, 2005).

491. Luisa Kroll, Megachurches, Megabusinesses, Forbes, September 17, 2003.

492. Terry Watkins, *Joel Osteen True or False*, http://www.av1611.org/osteen.html (web address current as of October 15, 2005).

493. Joel Osteen MOCKS JESUS - PRAISES POPE!, February 17, 2018, https://www.youtube.com/watch?v=-NO0sT-AGxo.

494. Steadfast Baptist Church, The Flat Earth Heresy Exposed - Bro. Jesse Michael, August 3, 2018, https://www.youtube.com/watch?v=OCXQMyy-n30.

495. Q&A #27 - Does the Bible Teach the Earth Is Flat?, April 24, 2018, https://www.youtube.com/watch?v=IBm9wy0LjDU.

496. Angry Christian Pastor Speaks Out Against Flat Earth!! Never Question Men, NASA & SpaceX, April 30, 2018, https://www.youtube.com/watch?v=Kk0p8hAKs6k&t=

3s. See also The "Pastor Charles Lawson" FLAT EARTHER Challenge, May 1, 2018, https://www.youtube.com/watch?v=RHhTT7txBRM&t=70s.

497. "The Flat Earth Debunked" (KJV Baptist Preaching), June 3, 2018, https://www.youtube.com/watch?v=Uwj6AQBUukE.

498. Jesus is Savior, Traffic Overview, https://www.similarweb.com/website/jesus-is-savior.com#overview (last visited on March 29, 2019).

499. David J. Stewart, The Tower Of Babel Today, http://www.jesus-is-savior.com/False%20Religions/Illuminati/tower_of_babel.htm (last visited on March 29, 2019).

500. David J. Stewart, The Flat Earth Heresy, April 2018, https://www.jesus-is-savior.com/False%20Doctrines/flat_earth.htm.

501. David J. Stewart, The Flat Earth Heresy, April 2018, https://www.jesus-is-savior.com/False%20Doctrines/flat_earth.htm.

502. David J. Stewart, The Flat Earth Heresy, April 2018, https://www.jesus-is-savior.com/False%20Doctrines/flat_earth.htm.

503. David J. Stewart Exposed!, August 22, 2013, https://davidjstewartexposed.blogspot.com.

504. David J. Stewart, The Tower Of Babel Today, www.jesus-is-savior.com, Wayback Machine, July 28,

2013, https://web.archive.org/web/20130728001955/http://www.jesus-is-savior.com/False%20Religions/Illuminati/tower_of_babel.htm. See also David J. Stewart Exposed!, https://davidjstewartexposed.blogspot.com/ (last visited on March 29, 2019).

505. David J. Stewart, The Tower Of Babel Today, http://www.jesus-is-savior.com/False%20Religions/Illuminati/tower_of_babel.htm (last visited on March 29, 2019).

506. David J. Stewart, The Tower Of Babel Today, www.jesus-is-savior.com, Wayback Machine, July 28, 2013, https://web.archive.org/web/20130728001955/http://www.jesus-is-savior.com/False%20Religions/Illuminati/tower_of_babel.htm. See also David J. Stewart Exposed!, https://davidjstewartexposed.blogspot.com/ (last visited on March 29, 2019).

507. Stephen Tomkins, John Wesley, A Biography, at 168 (2003) (emphasis added).

508. Celebrate Truth, Pastor Preaching Flat Earth Truth from the Bible, June 4, 2018, https://www.youtube.com/watch?v=V6yHPRsxyRo&t=1710s.

509. Celebrate Truth, Pastor Preaching Flat Earth Truth from the Bible, June 4, 2018, https://www.youtube.com/watch?v=V6yHPRsxyRo&t=1710s.

510. Celebrate Truth, Pastor Preaching Flat Earth Truth from the Bible, June 4, 2018, https://www.youtube.com/watch?v=V6yHPRsxyRo&t

=1710s.

511. Rick Jacoby, Pastor David Hoffman believes in flat earth (Common Man's Reference Bible), January 30, 2016, https://www.youtube.com/watch?v=lP6v9S1zw1o.

512. To Pastors Against Flat Earth: WATCH. Weigh the Fruit..., May 7, 2017, https://www.youtube.com/watch?v=wYQsf5dAVVQ&t=153s.

513. Rick Jacoby, Pastor David Hoffman believes in flat earth (Common Man's Reference Bible), January 30, 2016, https://www.youtube.com/watch?v=lP6v9S1zw1o.

514. MEGA church, Andy Stanley, preaches MEGA HERESIES on God's FLAT EARTH, August 8, 2019, https://www.youtube.com/watch?v=iaZWCTVpoBg&t=2251s.

515. Atheist, now CHRISTIAN...FLAT EARTH!, August 11, 2018, https://www.youtube.com/watch?v=rfU9_92zQ18.

516. The $5,000 Challenge, https://challengetheflatearth.com/ (last visited on March 31, 2019).

517. The $5,000 Challenge, https://challengetheflatearth.com/ (last visited on March 31, 2019).

518. Living Waters, Believe in a Flat Earth? You Must Watch This, November 7, 2019, https://www.youtube.com/watch?v=9RfSPoxh96g.

519. Living Waters, Believe in a Flat Earth? You Must Watch This, November 7, 2019, https://www.youtube.com/watch?v=9RfSPoxh96g.

520. Polaris Star Trails, All Night, Posted January 2, 2010, https://www.youtube.com/watch?v=PhVGKKEMk4g.

521. License for Camera Image: emoji_u1f4f7.svg, noto-emoji/LICENSE, Apache License 2.0, https://github.com/googlefonts/noto-emoji/blob/f931bea0efd67aefdf6beae404e1f3150c90314e/LICENSE.

522. Dr. Neville Thomas Jones, Ph.D., Airy's Experiment, http://www.geocentricuniverse.com/Airy.htm (last visited on August 24, 2012).

523. MARSHAL HALL, THE EARTH IS NOT MOVING, p. 97 (1991)

524. Flat Earth Belief and Salvation!!!, June 20, 2018, https://www.youtube.com/watch?v=e7ZxeS9yc8M.

525. Flat Earth Belief and Salvation!!!, June 20, 2018, https://www.youtube.com/watch?v=e7ZxeS9yc8M.

526. Basic Information About Circles, Math Planet, https://www.mathplanet.com/education/geometry/circles/basic-information-about-circles (last visited on March 30, 2019).

527. About David Platt, https://radical.net/about-david-platt/ (last visited on April 7, 2019).

528. David Platt, Founder of Secret Church, says "FLAT EARTH!", September 21, 2017,

https://www.youtube.com/watch?v=olpaKv7k28I.

529.David Platt, Founder of Secret Church, says "FLAT EARTH!", September 21, 2017, https://www.youtube.com/watch?v=olpaKv7k28I.

530.David Platt, Founder of Secret Church, says "FLAT EARTH!", September 21, 2017, https://www.youtube.com/watch?v=olpaKv7k28I.

531.David Platt, Founder of Secret Church, says "FLAT EARTH!", September 21, 2017, https://www.youtube.com/watch?v=olpaKv7k28I.

532.David Platt, Founder of Secret Church, says "FLAT EARTH!", September 21, 2017, https://www.youtube.com/watch?v=olpaKv7k28I.

533.From Misconceptions to the Real Jesus: Do Christians Think the Earth Is Flat?, July 19, 2018, https://www.navigators.org/from-misconceptions-to-the-real-jesus-do-christians-think-the-earth-is-flat/.

534.Parnell McCarter, The Navigators: an Assessment, Puritan News Weekly, February 20, 2007, http://www.puritans.net/news/navigators022007.htm.

535.FlatEarthDoctrine, Kent Hovind FINALLY Admits that the Bible... (FLAT EARTH), June 4, 2018, https://www.youtube.com/watch?v=n5bRSp-kueM.

536.FlatEarthDoctrine, Kent Hovind FINALLY Admits that the Bible... (FLAT EARTH), June 4, 2018, https://www.youtube.com/watch?v=n5bRSp-kueM.

537.Where Major Religious Groups Stand on Abortion, June 21, 2016, Pew Research Center, http://www.pewresearch.org/fact-tank/2016/06/21/whe

re-major-religious-groups-stand-on-abortion/.

538. Daniel Schiff, Abortion in Judaism, at 40 (2002).

539. Daniel Schiff, Abortion in Judaism, at 40 (2002).

540. Statements and Resolutions Regarding Freedom of Choice, Sixteenth General Synod, 1987, United Church of Christ, http://assets.nationbuilder.com/unitedchurchofchrist/legacy_url/2038/GS-Resolutions-Freedon-of-Choice.pdf?1418425637.

541. Resolution Number:1994-A054, Reaffirm General Convention Statement on Childbirth and Abortion, Concurred As Substituted and Amended, The Acts of Convention, The Archives of the Episcopal Church, https://episcopalarchives.org/cgi-bin/acts/acts_resolution.pl?resolution=1994-A054.

542. Dr. A.L.Barry, President, Lutheran Church, Missouri Synod, What About Abortion.

543. Dr. A.L.Barry, President, Lutheran Church, Missouri Synod, What About Abortion.

544. Justin Cannon, The Bible, Christianity and Homosexuality, https://www.gaychurch.org/homosexuality-and-the-Bible/the-Bible-christianity-and-homosexuality/ (last visited on March 10, 2019).

545. Record Breaking Astronaut Shares Faith in God, Christian Concern, September 2, 2016, https://www.christianconcern.com/our-concerns/not-ashamed/record-breaking-astronaut-shares-faith-in-god.

546. Southern Seminary, A Conversation with Astronaut, Col. Jeff Williams, August 30, 2016, https://www.youtube.com/watch?time_continue=38&v=7x84nK2z2Ng.

547. Southern Seminary, A Conversation with Astronaut, Col. Jeff Williams, August 30, 2016, https://www.youtube.com/watch?time_continue=38&v=7x84nK2z2Ng.

548. Valentin Vasilyevich, I am proud to be accused of having introduced Yury Gagarin to Orthodoxy, 12 April 2006, http://www.interfax-religion.com/?act=interview&div=24.

549. Valentin Vasilyevich, I am proud to be accused of having introduced Yury Gagarin to Orthodoxy, 12 April 2006, http://www.interfax-religion.com/?act=interview&div=24.

550. Astronaut Jeff Williams Talks About Flat Earth, February 2, 2018, https://www.youtube.com/watch?v=Kcx5qXaF4os.

551. Is the Earth Flat? A Christian Astronaut Answers, March 1, 2017, https://www.youtube.com/watch?v=BxB4lckfKLA. Astronaut Jeff Williams Talks About Flat Earth, February 2, 2018, https://www.youtube.com/watch?v=Kcx5qXaF4os.

552. Ken Ham, Creation Science Hall of Fame, http://creationsciencehalloffame.org/inductees/living/ken-ham/ (last visited on February 18, 2019).

553. IS THE EARTH FLAT - Christian Astronaut Barry Wilmore ANSWERS - Ken Ham, July 2, 2017, https://www.youtube.com/watch?v=c9yaToss5X0.

554. IS THE EARTH FLAT - Christian Astronaut Barry Wilmore ANSWERS - Ken Ham, July 2, 2017, https://www.youtube.com/watch?v=c9yaToss5X0.

555. IS THE EARTH FLAT - Christian Astronaut Barry Wilmore ANSWERS - Ken Ham, July 2, 2017, https://www.youtube.com/watch?v=c9yaToss5X0.

556. Awe130 a Journey Towards the Truth Apollo Hoax, http://www.awe130.com/apollo-hoax-explained/178-apollo-12-astronaut-conrad-this-is-the-blackest-black-i-ever-saw (last visited on April 9, 2018).

557. Charlotte Lytton, Secrets of a Spaceman: Meet Eugene Cernan, the Last Man to Ever Walk on the Moon, The Telegraph, 17 January 2017, https://www.telegraph.co.uk/men/the-filter/secrets-of-a-spaceman-meet-eugene-cernan-the-last-man-to-ever-wa/.

558. The Strange Truth Project. Winner! Best Truth documentary of all time. TEAMYAHAWASHI #TheSTP, at 00:29:00, December 19, 2017, https://www.youtube.com/watch?v=kj-W5jB1Nv4.

559. The Strange Truth Project. Winner! Best Truth documentary of all time. TEAMYAHAWASHI #TheSTP, at 00:29:00, December 19, 2017, https://www.youtube.com/watch?v=kj-W5jB1Nv4.

560. Valentin Vasilyevich, I am proud to be accused of having introduced Yury Gagarin to Orthodoxy, 12

April 2006, http://www.interfax-religion.com/?act=interview&div=24.

561. IS THE EARTH FLAT - Christian Astronaut Barry Wilmore ANSWERS - Ken Ham, July 2, 2017, https://www.youtube.com/watch?v=c9yaToss5X0.

562. Profane, American Dictionary of the English Language.

563. Ken Ham, Creation Science Hall of Fame, http://creationsciencehalloffame.org/inductees/living/ken-ham/ (last visited on February 18, 2019).

564. Ken Ham, Did Jesus Say He Created in Six Literal Days?, Answers In Genesis, December 2007, https://answersingenesis.org/days-of-creation/did-jesus-say-he-created-in-six-literal-days/.

565. Ken Ham, Answers in Genesis, Does the Bible Teach a Flat Earth?, April 6, 2015, https://www.youtube.com/watch?time_continue=51&v=it8JkhzjAVw.

566. Dr. Robert W. Carter, https://creation.com/dr-robert-carter (last visited on February 18, 2019). See also https://creation.com/dr-robert-carter-cv (last visited on February 18, 2019).

567. Robert Carter, Creation Science Hall of Fame, http://creationsciencehalloffame.org/inductees/living/robert-carter/ (last visited on February 18, 2019).

568. Robert Carter and Jonathan Sarfati, A Flat Earth, and Other Nonsense, Debunking Ideas That Would Not Exist Were it Not for the Internet, Creation Ministries

International, 13 September 2016, updated 26 October 2018, https://creation.com/refuting-flat-earth.

569. Chris Hardy and Robert Carter, The Biblical Minimum and Maximum Age of the Earth, Journal of Creation, August 2014, https://creation.com/biblical-age-of-the-earth.

570. Gary Zeolla, Why are These Books in the Bible and Not Others?, https://books.google.com/books?id=6Lh4DQAAQBAJ&pg=PT26&lpg=PT26&dq=robert+carter+genesis+literal&source=bl&ots=nl0KuvaZJt&sig=ACfU3U0els3fskCnEFeA_4mSL4C1rpvIeg&hl=en&sa=X&ved=2ahUKEwiWkevp_8XgAhUSpFkKHaK3Ahk4ChDoATACegQIBBAB#v=onepage&q=robert%20carter%20genesis%20literal&f=false (last visited on February 18, 2019).

571. Lita Cosner and Robert Carter, Where Was Eden? Part 1—examining Pre-flood Geographical Details in the Biblical Record, Journal of Creation, December 2013, https://creation.com/eden-1.

572. Robert Carter and Jonathan Sarfati, A Flat Earth, and Other Nonsense, Debunking Ideas That Would Not Exist Were it Not for the Internet, Creation Ministries International, 13 September 2016, updated 26 October 2018, https://creation.com/refuting-flat-earth.

573. Robert Carter and Jonathan Sarfati, A Flat Earth, and Other Nonsense, Debunking Ideas That Would Not Exist Were it Not for the Internet, Creation Ministries International, 13 September 2016, updated 26 October 2018, https://creation.com/refuting-flat-earth.

574. Robert Carter and Jonathan Sarfati, A Flat Earth, and Other Nonsense, Debunking Ideas That Would Not Exist Were it Not for the Internet, Creation Ministries International, 13 September 2016, updated 26 October 2018, https://creation.com/refuting-flat-earth.

575. Robert Carter and Jonathan Sarfati, A Flat Earth, and Other Nonsense, Debunking Ideas That Would Not Exist Were it Not for the Internet, Creation Ministries International, 13 September 2016, updated 26 October 2018, https://creation.com/refuting-flat-earth.

576. Robert Carter and Jonathan Sarfati, A Flat Earth, and Other Nonsense, Debunking Ideas That Would Not Exist Were it Not for the Internet, Creation Ministries International, 13 September 2016, updated 26 October 2018, https://creation.com/refuting-flat-earth.

577. Robert Carter and Jonathan Sarfati, A Flat Earth, and Other Nonsense, Debunking Ideas That Would Not Exist Were it Not for the Internet, Creation Ministries International, 13 September 2016, updated 26 October 2018, https://creation.com/refuting-flat-earth.

578. Can Christianity and Science Coexist?, ABC News, June 11, 2009, https://www.youtube.com/watch?v=M5sMva2ydoU.

579. Robert Carter, The Non-Mythical Adam and Eve!, 20 August 2011, https://creation.com/historical-adam-biologos.

580. Robert Carter, The Non-Mythical Adam and Eve!, 20 August 2011, https://creation.com/historical-adam-biologos.

581. Robert Carter, The Non-Mythical Adam and Eve!, 20 August 2011, https://creation.com/historical-adam-biologos.

582. Jonathan D. Sarfati, Creation Science Hall of Fame, http://creationsciencehalloffame.org/inductees/living/jonathan-sarfati/ (last visited on February 19, 2019).

583. Robert Carter and Jonathan Sarfati, A Flat Earth, and Other Nonsense, Debunking Ideas That Would Not Exist Were it Not for the Internet, Creation Ministries International, 13 September 2016, updated 26 October 2018, https://creation.com/refuting-flat-earth.

584. Robert Carter and Jonathan Sarfati, A Flat Earth, and Other Nonsense, Debunking Ideas That Would Not Exist Were it Not for the Internet, Creation Ministries International, 13 September 2016, updated 26 October 2018, https://creation.com/refuting-flat-earth.

585. Robert Carter, Creation Ministries International, Flat Earth? The Bible And Science Say No!, September 5, 2018, https://www.youtube.com/watch?v=rSTdZvs8upI&t=387s.

586. Robert Carter, Creation Ministries International, Flat Earth? The Bible And Science Say No!, September 5, 2018, https://www.youtube.com/watch?v=rSTdZvs8upI&t=387s.

587. Robert Carter, Creation Ministries International, Flat Earth? The Bible And Science Say No!, September 5, 2018, https://www.youtube.com/watch?v=rSTdZvs8upI&t=3

87s.

588.Robert Carter and Jonathan Sarfati, A Flat Earth, and Other Nonsense, Debunking Ideas That Would Not Exist Were it Not for the Internet, Creation Ministries International, 13 September 2016, updated 26 October 2018, https://creation.com/refuting-flat-earth.

589.Paul H. Seely, The Geographical Meaning of "Earth" and "Seas" in Genesis 1:10, Westminster Theological Journal 59 (1997) 231-55, https://www.godawa.com/chronicles_of_the_nephilim/Articles_By_Others/Seely-3-Geo_Meaning_Earth_Sea.pdf.

590.Paul H. Seely, The Geographical Meaning of "Earth" and "Seas" in Genesis 1:10, Westminster Theological Journal 59 (1997) 23-55, https://www.godawa.com/chronicles_of_the_nephilim/Articles_By_Others/Seely-3-Geo_Meaning_Earth_Sea.pdf.

591.Paul H. Seely, The Geographical Meaning of "Earth" and "Seas" in Genesis 1:10, Westminster Theological Journal 59 (1997) 23-55, https://www.godawa.com/chronicles_of_the_nephilim/Articles_By_Others/Seely-3-Geo_Meaning_Earth_Sea.pdf.

592.Paul H. Seely, The Geographical Meaning of "Earth" and "Seas" in Genesis 1:10, Westminster Theological Journal 59 (1997) 23-55, https://www.godawa.com/chronicles_of_the_nephilim/Articles_By_Others/Seely-3-Geo_Meaning_Earth_Sea.pdf.

593. Paul H. Seely, Is the 'Erets (Earth) Flat?, August 1, 2001, https://answersingenesis.org/astronomy/earth/is-the-erets-earth-flat-seely-response/.

594. James Patrick Holding, https://creation.com/james-patrick-holding (last visited on April 4, 2019).

595. The Legendary Flat-Earth Bible By James Patrick Holding, https://www.oneplace.com/ministries/Bible-answer-man/read/articles/the-legendary-flatearth-Bible-16691.html (last visited on April 4, 2019).

596. How the Bible must Be Read If We Consider it to Be an Authoritative Text, July 10, 2018, https://www.youtube.com/watch?v=fQtEwY9Tl1c.

597. John Stump, Interpreting Adam: An Interview with John Walton, April 8, 2014, https://biologos.org/articles/interpreting-adam-an-interview-with-john-walton.

598. John Stump, Interpreting Adam: An Interview with John Walton, April 8, 2014, https://biologos.org/articles/interpreting-adam-an-interview-with-john-walton.

599. Naked Bible, Old Testament Cosmology Michael S Heiser NEW, January 26, 2016, https://www.youtube.com/watch?v=AbPtym0NboU.

600. Michael S. Heiser, Christians Who Believe the Earth is Really Flat — Does It Get Any Dumber Than This?, February 8, 2016, http://drmsh.com/christians-who-believe-the-earth-is-r

eally-flat-does-it-get-any-dumber-than-this/.

601. Michael S. Heiser, Christians Who Believe the Earth is Really Flat — Does It Get Any Dumber Than This?, February 8, 2016, http://drmsh.com/christians-who-believe-the-earth-is-really-flat-does-it-get-any-dumber-than-this/.

602. Michael S. Heiser, Christians Who Believe the Earth is Really Flat — Does It Get Any Dumber Than This?, February 8, 2016, http://drmsh.com/christians-who-believe-the-earth-is-really-flat-does-it-get-any-dumber-than-this/.

603. Mike Heiser, Modern Flat Earth Theory Exposed, Part I, September 9, 2016, http://drmsh.com/modern-flat-earth-theory-exposed-part-i/.

604. Paul H. Seely, Is the 'Erets (Earth) Flat?, August 1, 2001, https://answersingenesis.org/astronomy/earth/is-the-erets-earth-flat-seely-response/.

605. Paul H. Seely, Is the 'Erets (Earth) Flat?, August 1, 2001, https://answersingenesis.org/astronomy/earth/is-the-erets-earth-flat-seely-response/.

606. Flat Earth Creation Ministries Rob Carter Gospel MSG, September 2, 2018, at the 1:10 mark of the video, https://www.youtube.com/watch?v=O0LTcKD5ZUk. See also Flat Earth? The Bible And Science Say No!, September 5, 2018, https://www.youtube.com/watch?v=rSTdZvs8upI&t=2418s.

607.Flat Earth Creation Ministries Rob Carter Gospel MSG, September 2, 2018, at the 2:00 mark of the video, https://www.youtube.com/watch?v=O0LTcKD5ZUk. See also Flat Earth? The Bible And Science Say No!, September 5, 2018, https://www.youtube.com/watch?v=rSTdZvs8upI&t=2418s.

608.Flat Earth Creation Ministries Rob Carter Gospel MSG, September 2, 2018, at the 3:45 mark of the video, https://www.youtube.com/watch?v=O0LTcKD5ZUk. See also Flat Earth? The Bible And Science Say No!, September 5, 2018, https://www.youtube.com/watch?v=rSTdZvs8upI&t=2418s.

609.FlatEarthDoctrine, Dr Robert Coward's (Carter) and Creation Ministries International's anti-Biblical shenanigans, September 5, 2018, https://www.youtube.com/watch?v=D4_rpw4Ou_Y.

610.Flat Earth? The Bible And Science Say No!, September 5, 2018, https://www.youtube.com/watch?v=rSTdZvs8upI&t=2418s.

611.Robert J. Schadewald, Scientific Creationism, Geocentricity, and the Flat Earth, 1981, https://www.lockhaven.edu/~dsimanek/crea-fe.htm.

612.Citing, In Everybody's Political What's What, quoted by martin Gardner in Fads and Fallacies in the Name of Science (New York: Dover, 1957), p. 14.

613.Citing, Zetetic, v. 2, n. 5, (July 1873), p. 39.

614. Robert J. Schadewald, Scientific Creationism, Geocentricity, and the Flat Earth, 1981, https://www.lockhaven.edu/~dsimanek/crea-fe.htm. Citing, The Earth: Scripturally, Rationally, and Practically Described. A Geographical, Philosophical, and Educational Review, Nautical Guide, and General Student's Manual, n. 17 (November 1, 1887), p. 7.

615. Flate Earth Doctrine, Creation Ministries International HIDES God's TRUTH (FLAT EARTH), July 19, 2018, https://www.youtube.com/watch?v=W6xYIc_A31E.

616. Robert J. Schadewald, Scientific Creationism, Geocentricity, and the Flat Earth, 1981, https://www.lockhaven.edu/~dsimanek/crea-fe.htm.

617. Duane T. Gish, Creation Science Hall of Fame, http://creationsciencehalloffame.org/inductees/deceased/duane-t-gish/ (last visited on March 24, 2019).

618. Robert J. Schadewald, Scientific Creationism, Geocentricity, and the Flat Earth, 1981, https://www.lockhaven.edu/~dsimanek/crea-fe.htm.

619. Robert J. Schadewald, Scientific Creationism, Geocentricity, and the Flat Earth, 1981, https://www.lockhaven.edu/~dsimanek/crea-fe.htm.

620. Robert J. Schadewald, Scientific Creationism, Geocentricity, and the Flat Earth, 1981, https://www.lockhaven.edu/~dsimanek/crea-fe.htm.

621. E.g., Duane T. Gish, Ph.D., More Creationist Research (14 Years) Part 1: Geological Research, CRS Quarterly, Volume 25, Number 4 March, 1989, https://creationresearch.org/creationist-research-14-yea

rs-part-1-geological-research/?hilite=%27gish%27.

622. Statement of Belief, https://creationresearch.org/statement-of-belief/ (last visited on March 24, 2019).

623. What We Believe, Creation Ministries International, http://creation.com/about-us#what_we_believe.

624. Jason Lisle, Creation Science Hall of Fame, http://creationsciencehalloffame.org/inductees/living/jason-lisle/ (last visited on February 19, 2019).

625. Kerrigan Kelly, Dr. Jason Lisle DESTROYS Flat Earth NONSENSE! | ICR - Christian Creationism, August 30, 2016, https://www.youtube.com/watch?v=KbYbCB5Zj_E&t=5s.

626. Dr. Jason Lyle, Refuting the Critics #2, August 18, 2017, https://biblicalscienceinstitute.com/apologetics/refuting-the-critics-2/.

627. Kerrigan Kelly, Dr. Jason Lisle DESTROYS Flat Earth NONSENSE! | ICR - Christian Creationism, August 30, 2016, https://www.youtube.com/watch?v=KbYbCB5Zj_E&t=5s.

628. Compass, American Dictionary of the English Language, 1828, http://1828.mshaffer.com/d/word/compass.

629. Dr. Danny R. Faulkner, Honorable Mention, Creation Science Hall o Fame, http://creationsciencehalloffame.org/inductees/honorab

le-mention/ (last visited on March 24, 2019).

630. Danny Faulkner, Is the Earth Flat?, Answers in Genesis, May 24, 2016, https://answersingenesis.org/astronomy/earth/is-the-earth-flat/.

631. About Creation Today, https://creationtoday.org/author/creationtoday/ (last visited on May 6, 2019).

632. Flat Earth vs Creationism – A Biblical Perspective, Creation Today, https://creationtoday.org/flat-earth-vs-creationism-a-biblical-perspective/ (last visited on May 6, 2019).

633. Danny Faulkner, Does the Bible Teach That the Earth Is Flat?, April 4, 2017, https://answersingenesis.org/astronomy/earth/does-Bible-teach-earth-flat/.

634. Danny Faulkner, Does the Bible Teach That the Earth Is Flat?, April 4, 2017, https://answersingenesis.org/astronomy/earth/does-Bible-teach-earth-flat/.

635. Danny Faulkner, Does the Bible Teach That the Earth Is Flat?, April 4, 2017, https://answersingenesis.org/astronomy/earth/does-Bible-teach-earth-flat/.

636. Danny Faulkner, Does the Bible Teach That the Earth Is Flat?, April 4, 2017, https://answersingenesis.org/astronomy/earth/does-Bible-teach-earth-flat/.

637. Danny Faulkner, Does the Bible Teach That the Earth Is Flat?, April 4, 2017,

https://answersingenesis.org/astronomy/earth/does-Bible-teach-earth-flat/.

638. Danny Faulkner, Does the Bible Teach That the Earth Is Flat?, April 4, 2017, https://answersingenesis.org/astronomy/earth/does-Bible-teach-earth-flat/.

639. Danny Faulkner, Does the Bible Teach That the Earth Is Flat?, April 4, 2017, https://answersingenesis.org/astronomy/earth/does-Bible-teach-earth-flat/.

640. Danny Faulkner, Does the Bible Teach That the Earth Is Flat?, April 4, 2017, https://answersingenesis.org/astronomy/earth/does-Bible-teach-earth-flat/.

641. Firmament, Merriam Webster Dictionary, https://www.merriam-webster.com/dictionary/firmament.

642. Firmament, Online Etymology Dictionary, https://www.etymonline.com/word/firmament (last visited on February 17, 2019).

643. Danny Faulkner, Does the Bible Teach That the Earth Is Flat?, April 4, 2017, https://answersingenesis.org/astronomy/earth/does-Bible-teach-earth-flat/.

644. Danny Faulkner, Does the Bible Teach That the Earth Is Flat?, April 4, 2017, https://answersingenesis.org/astronomy/earth/does-Bible-teach-earth-flat/.

645. G. A. RIPLINGER, NEW AGE Bible VERSIONS, p. 141-148 (1993).

646. Frank Logsdon Denounces New American Standard Version (Transcript), https://www.defendproclaimthefaith.org/dr_frank_logsdon.html (last visited on March 27, 2019).

647. Frank Logsdon Denounces New American Standard Version, http://fmh-child.org/NewAgeVersions/FrankLogsdon.html (last visited on March 27, 2019).

648. G.A. Riplinger, New Age Bible Versions, p. 435 (1993).

649. Samuel C. Gipp, An Understandable History of the Bible, p. 116-130 (1987).

650. *Id.*

651. *Id.* at 126-29.

652. *Id.* at 131-68.

653. *Id.*

654. *Id.*

655. *Id.*

656. *Id.*

657. *Id.*

658. *Id.* at p. 405.

659. *Id.* at p. 400.

660. *Id.*

661. *Id.* at p. 406.

662. *Id.* at p. 432.

663. G. A. Riplinger, The Language of the King James Bible, p. 66 (1998).

664. *Id.* at p. 132 (quoting *Carlo Martini, In the Thick of the Ministry,* p. 42, the Liturgical Press, Collegeville, Minn., 1990).

665. G.A. RIPLINGER, BLIND GUIDES, p. 19.

666. G.A. RIPLINGER, BLIND GUIDES, p. 19.

667. G.A. RIPLINGER, BLIND GUIDES, p. 19.

668. Danny R. Faulkner, Geocentrism and Creation, August 1, 2001, https://answersingenesis.org/creationism/arguments-to-avoid/geocentrism-and-creation/.

669. Danny R. Faulkner, Geocentrism and Creation, August 1, 2001, https://answersingenesis.org/creationism/arguments-to-avoid/geocentrism-and-creation/.

670. Danny R. Faulkner, Geocentrism and Creation, August 1, 2001, https://answersingenesis.org/creationism/arguments-to-avoid/geocentrism-and-creation/.

671. P.H. Seely, The firmament and the water above. Part I: The meaning of raqiya' in Gen. 1:6–8, Westminster Theological Journal 53:227–240, 1991, https://faculty.gordon.edu/hu/bi/ted_hildebrandt/otesources/01-genesis/text/articles-books/seely-firmament-wtj.pdf.

672. P.H. Seely, The firmament and the water above. Part I: The meaning of raqiya' in Gen. 1:6–8, Westminster Theological Journal 53:227–240, 1991, at 239, https://faculty.gordon.edu/hu/bi/ted_hildebrandt/otesources/01-genesis/text/articles-books/seely-firmament-wtj.pdf.

673. P.H. Seely, The firmament and the water above. Part I: The meaning of raqiya' in Gen. 1:6–8, Westminster Theological Journal 53:227–240, 1991, at 236, https://faculty.gordon.edu/hu/bi/ted_hildebrandt/otesources/01-genesis/text/articles-books/seely-firmament-wtj.pdf.

674. P.H. Seely, The firmament and the water above. Part I: The meaning of raqiya' in Gen. 1:6–8, Westminster Theological Journal 53:227–240, 1991, at 239, https://faculty.gordon.edu/hu/bi/ted_hildebrandt/otesources/01-genesis/text/articles-books/seely-firmament-wtj.pdf.

675. Alex Murashko, The Christian Post, October 13, 2013, Letting Science 'Interpret' Scripture Is Slippery Slope, Says Young Earth/Universe Creationist, https://www.christianpost.com/news/letting-science-interpret-scripture-is-slippery-slope-says-young-earth-universe-creationist-106525/.

676. English Standard Version (ESV), https://www.esv.org/ (last visited on February 17, 2019).

677. Dr. Terry Watkins, The Truth About the English Sub-Standard Version,

http://www.av1611.org/kjv/ESV_Fruit.html (last visited on February 17, 2019), quoting Mark L. Strauss, The Gender-Neutral Language of the English Standard Version (ESV).

678. Kent Hovind, Creation Science Hall of Fame, http://creationsciencehalloffame.org/inductees/living/kent-hovind/ (last visited on February 22, 2019).

679. Kent Hovind, Creation Science Hall of Fame, http://creationsciencehalloffame.org/inductees/living/kent-hovind/ (last visited on February 22, 2019).

680. The Kent Hovind Flat Earth Challenge, August 2, 2015, https://www.youtube.com/watch?v=gqYqs2R4wDA.

681. The Kent Hovind Flat Earth Challenge, August 2, 2015, https://www.youtube.com/watch?v=gqYqs2R4wDA.

682. FlatEarthDoctrine, Kent Hovind FINALLY Admits that the Bible... (FLAT EARTH), June 4, 2018, https://www.youtube.com/watch?v=n5bRSp-kueM.

683. FlatEarthDoctrine, Kent Hovind FINALLY Admits that the Bible... (FLAT EARTH), June 4, 2018, https://www.youtube.com/watch?v=n5bRSp-kueM.

684. FlatEarthDoctrine, Kent Hovind FINALLY Admits that the Bible... (FLAT EARTH), June 4, 2018, https://www.youtube.com/watch?v=n5bRSp-kueM.

685. FlatEarthDoctrine, Kent Hovind FINALLY Admits that the Bible... (FLAT EARTH), June 4, 2018, https://www.youtube.com/watch?v=n5bRSp-kueM.

686. FlatEarthDoctrine, Kent Hovind FINALLY Admits that the Bible... (FLAT EARTH), June 4, 2018, https://www.youtube.com/watch?v=n5bRSp-kueM.

687. FlatEarthDoctrine, Kent Hovind FINALLY Admits that the Bible... (FLAT EARTH), June 4, 2018, https://www.youtube.com/watch?v=n5bRSp-kueM.

688. The Flat Earth Deception, http://flatearthdeception.com/ (last visited on April 3, 2019).

689. Biblical Proofs Of The Geocentric Globe Earth, http://flatearthdeception.com/biblical-proofs-of-the-globe-earth/ (last visited on April 3, 2019).

690. David Nikao, Nathan Roberts of FlatEarthDoctrine What is the Flat Earth Gospel?, December 15, 2018, http://flatearthdeception.com/nathan-roberts-of-flateart hdoctrine-what-is-the-flat-earth-gospel/.

691. David Nikao, https://www.facebook.com/david.nikao (last visited on April 2, 2019).

692. Flat Earther Nathan Roberts of flatearthdoctrine.com DEBUNKED, http://flatearthdeception.com/flat-earther-nathan-roberts-of-flatearthdoctrine-com-debunked/ (last visited on April 3, 2019).

693. Kent Hovind Official, Dr. Kent Hovind with Edrique Visser - Debunking the Flat Earth Model - Part B, April 13, 2016, https://www.youtube.com/watch?v=oYNoqqUy_YE.

694. Kent Hovind Official, 5-4-18 Dr. Kent Hovind Divide and Conquer & The Flat Earth, May 3, 2018,

https://www.youtube.com/watch?v=aTVkrvkPIvU.

695. Kent Hovind Official, 5-4-18 Dr. Kent Hovind Divide and Conquer & The Flat Earth, May 3, 2018, https://www.youtube.com/watch?v=aTVkrvkPIvU.

696. Kent Hovind Official, Dr. Kent Hovind with Edrique Visser - Debunking the Flat Earth Model - Part C, August 13, 2016, https://www.youtube.com/watch?v=r9tApfDdZow&feature=youtu.be.

697. Dr. Kent Hovind and Robert Sungenis on "Flat Earth, Flat Wrong!", July 6, 2018, https://www.youtube.com/watch?v=1Ak7Qy_dHmk.

698. Dr. Kent Hovind and Robert Sungenis on "Flat Earth, Flat Wrong!", July 6, 2018, https://www.youtube.com/watch?v=1Ak7Qy_dHmk.

699. Rob Skiba vs. Dr. Robert Sungenis | Flat Earth Biblical Debate 2018, November 28, 2018, https://www.youtube.com/watch?v=AqbiwtRKrtg.

700. John Morris, Honorable Mention, Creation Science Hall of Fame, http://creationsciencehalloffame.org/inductees/honorable-mention/ (last visited on March 24, 2019).

701. Matt Schudel, The Seattle Times, Obituary: Henry M. Morris, Father of "Creation Science", March 5, 2006, http://community.seattletimes.nwsource.com/archive/?date=20060305&slug=morrisobit05.

702. Henry M. Morris, Creation Science Hall of Fame, http://creationsciencehalloffame.org/inductees/deceased/henry-m-morris/ (last visited on March 24, 2019).

703. John D. Morris, Ph.D., Is Earth Really Round?, Institute for Creation Research, March 1, 2006, , https://www.icr.org/article/2703/.

704. Circle, https://www.merriam-webster.com/dictionary/circle.

705. Sphere, https://www.merriam-webster.com/dictionary/sphere.

706. John D. Morris, Ph.D., Is Earth Really Round?, Institute for Creation Research, March 1, 2006, , https://www.icr.org/article/2703/.

707. John D. Morris, Ph.D., Is Earth Really Round?, Institute for Creation Research, March 1, 2006, , https://www.icr.org/article/2703/.

708. John D. Morris, Ph.D., Is Earth Really Round?, Institute for Creation Research, March 1, 2006, , https://www.icr.org/article/2703/.

709. Robert J. Schneider, Does the Bible Teach a Spherical Earth?, Berea College, September 2001, https://www.asa3.org/ASA/PSCF/2001/PSCF9-01Schneider.html, citing Henry M. Morris, Biblical Creationism: What Each Book of the Bible Teaches about Creation and the Flood (Green Forest, AR: Master Books, 2000), 113.

710. Dr. Henry M. Morris, The Defender's Study Bible, King James Version, Defending the Faith from a Literal Creationist Viewpoint, at 754 (1995), ISBN: 9780529104441.

711. Compass, American Dictionary of the English Language, 1828, http://1828.mshaffer.com/d/word/compass.

712. Compass, Merriam-Webster Dictionary, https://www.merriam-webster.com/dictionary/compass (last visited on April 27, 2019).

713. Compass, Merriam-Webster Dictionary, https://www.merriam-webster.com/dictionary/compass (last visited on April 27, 2019).

714. Circle, Merriam-Webster Dictionary, https://www.merriam-webster.com/dictionary/circle (last visited on April 27, 2019).

715. Jonathan Sarfati, The Flat Earth Myth, April 2013, https://creation.com/flat-earth-myth.

716. Jonathan Sarfati, The Flat Earth Myth, April 2013, https://creation.com/flat-earth-myth.

717. Jack McElroy, Which Bible Would Jesus Use? The Bible Version Controversy Explained and Resolved, ISBN: 978-0986026515 (2013).

718. Robert J. Schneider, Does the Bible Teach a Spherical Earth?, Berea College, September 2001, https://www.asa3.org/ASA/PSCF/2001/PSCF9-01Schneider.html.

719. Robert J. Schneider, Does the Bible Teach a Spherical Earth?, Berea College, September 2001, https://www.asa3.org/ASA/PSCF/2001/PSCF9-01Schneider.html.

720. Robert J. Schneider, Does the Bible Teach a Spherical Earth?, Berea College, September 2001, https://www.asa3.org/ASA/PSCF/2001/PSCF9-01Schneider.html.

721. Dennis Bratcher, "The Circle of the Earth" Translation and Meaning in Isaiah 40:22, http://www.crivoice.org/circle.html (last visited on April 26, 2019).

722. Dennis Bratcher, "The Circle of the Earth" Translation and Meaning in Isaiah 40:22, http://www.crivoice.org/circle.html (last visited on April 26, 2019).

723. Dennis Bratcher, "The Circle of the Earth" Translation and Meaning in Isaiah 40:22, http://www.crivoice.org/circle.html (last visited on April 26, 2019).

724. Dennis Bratcher, "The Circle of the Earth" Translation and Meaning in Isaiah 40:22, http://www.crivoice.org/circle.html (last visited on April 26, 2019).

725. Steadfast Baptist Church, The Flat Earth Heresy Exposed - Bro. Jesse Michael, August 3, 2018, https://www.youtube.com/watch?v=OCXQMyy-n30.

726. Basic Information About Circles, Math Planet, https://www.mathplanet.com/education/geometry/circles/basic-information-about-circles (last visited on March 30, 2019).

727. Gail Riplinger, Hazardous Materials: Greek and Hebrew Study Dangers, ISBN: 978-0979411762 (2008).

728. Creation Ministries International, Is The Earth Flat?, January 27, 2020, https://www.youtube.com/watch?v=NJw5mz4BseY&t=558s.

729. Creation Ministries International, Is The Earth Flat?, January 27, 2020, https://www.youtube.com/watch?v=NJw5mz4BseY&t=558s.

730. Ethan Siegel, These Are The Most Distant Objects We've Ever Discovered In The Universe, October 23, 2018, https://medium.com/starts-with-a-bang/these-are-the-most-distant-objects-weve-ever-discovered-in-the-universe-2be54e384eb6.

731. Jason Lisle, Does Distant Starlight Prove the Universe Is Old?, December 13, 2007, https://answersingenesis.org/astronomy/starlight/does-distant-starlight-prove-the-universe-is-old/.

732. Jason Lisle, Does Distant Starlight Prove the Universe Is Old?, December 13, 2007, https://answersingenesis.org/astronomy/starlight/does-distant-starlight-prove-the-universe-is-old/.

733. E.g., Tichomir Tenev, John Baumgardner, M.F. Horstemeyer, A Solution for the Distant Starlight Problem Using Creation Time Coordinates, International Conference on Creationism, http://creationicc.org/2018_papers/11%20Tenev%20starlight%20final.pdf (last visited on June 29, 2019); Jason Lisle, Anisotropic Synchrony Convention—A Solution to the Distant Starlight Problem, September 22, 2010, https://answersingenesis.org/astronomy/starlight/anisotropic-synchrony-convention-distant-starlight-problem/.

734. Jason Lisle, Does Distant Starlight Prove the Universe Is Old?, December 13, 2007, https://answersingenesis.org/astronomy/starlight/does-distant-starlight-prove-the-universe-is-old/.

735. Robert Newton, Distant Starlight and Genesis: Conventions of Time Measurement, April 1, 2001, https://answersingenesis.org/astronomy/starlight/distant-starlight-and-genesis-conventions-of-time-measurement/.

736. Dr Jason Lisle, Ph.D., Creationist Astrophysicist, https://creation.com/dr-jason-lisle (last visited on June 29, 2019).

737. Brian Mullin, Official Launch! Force the Line Is On, July 16, 2016, https://www.youtube.com/watch?v=iu1t0jBBuTI.

738. Brian Mullin, Official Launch! Force the Line Is On, July 16, 2016, https://www.youtube.com/watch?v=iu1t0jBBuTI.

739. Flat Earth Debate George Hnatiuk & Brian Mullin - Nathan Oakley MIRROR, July 27, 2018, https://www.youtube.com/watch?v=AD49ue1l5Uo. Brian Mullin Vs Globe Zealot George Hnatiuk Flat Earth Hypocrisy, July 30, 2018, https://www.youtube.com/watch?v=wTRgOzFBeNg.

740. Robert Newton, Distant Starlight and Genesis: Conventions of Time Measurement, April 1, 2001, https://answersingenesis.org/astronomy/starlight/distant-starlight-and-genesis-conventions-of-time-measurement/.

741. Robert Newton, Distant Starlight and Genesis: Conventions of Time Measurement, April 1, 2001, https://answersingenesis.org/astronomy/starlight/distant-starlight-and-genesis-conventions-of-time-measurement/.

742. Robert Newton, Distant Starlight and Genesis: Conventions of Time Measurement, April 1, 2001, https://answersingenesis.org/astronomy/starlight/distant-starlight-and-genesis-conventions-of-time-measurement/.

743. Robert Newton, Distant Starlight and Genesis: Conventions of Time Measurement, April 1, 2001, https://answersingenesis.org/astronomy/starlight/distant-starlight-and-genesis-conventions-of-time-measurement/.

744. E.g., Tichomir Tenev, John Baumgardner, M.F. Horstemeyer, A Solution for the Distant Starlight Problem Using Creation Time Coordinates, International Conference on Creationism, http://creationicc.org/2018_papers/11%20Tenev%20starlight%20final.pdf (last visited on June 29, 2019); Jason Lisle, Anisotropic Synchrony Convention—A Solution to the Distant Starlight Problem, September 22, 2010, https://answersingenesis.org/astronomy/starlight/anisotropic-synchrony-convention-distant-starlight-problem/.

745. Robert Newton, Distant Starlight and Genesis: Conventions of Time Measurement, April 1, 2001, https://answersingenesis.org/astronomy/starlight/distant-starlight-and-genesis-conventions-of-time-measurement/.

746. Robert Newton, Distant Starlight and Genesis: Conventions of Time Measurement, Journal of Creation 15(1): 80-85, April 2001, https://creation.com/distant-starlight-and-genesis-conventions-of-time-measurement.

747. Dr Jason Lisle, Ph.D., Creationist Astrophysicist, https://creation.com/dr-jason-lisle (last visited on June 29, 2019).

748. The Bible Sceptic, What the Bible Got Wrong: A Flat Earth, Part 1, June 3, 2011, https://www.youtube.com/watch?v=MS78uT8j3ok&list=PL5F34CF577900491D&index=1; Part 2, September 26, 2013, https://www.youtube.com/watch?v=YUpiz6d8Yys&list=PL5F34CF577900491D&index=5; Part 3, June 15, 2011, https://www.youtube.com/watch?v=ilr-m1BxTgc&list=PL5F34CF577900491D&index=3; Part 4, June 22, 2011, https://www.youtube.com/watch?v=6h5K5PrEMzU&list=PL5F34CF577900491D&index=4.

749. The Bible Sceptic, What the Bible Got Wrong: A Flat Earth, Part 2, Part 2, September 26, 2013, https://www.youtube.com/watch?v=YUpiz6d8Yys&list=PL5F34CF577900491D&index=5.

750. The Bible Sceptic, What the Bible Got Wrong: A Flat Earth, Part 2, Part 2, September 26, 2013, https://www.youtube.com/watch?v=YUpiz6d8Yys&list=PL5F34CF577900491D&index=5.

751. The Bible Sceptic, What the Bible Got Wrong: A Flat Earth, Part 3, June 15, 2011, https://www.youtube.com/watch?v=ilr-m1BxTgc&list

=PL5F34CF577900491D&index=3.

752. The Bible Sceptic, What the Bible Got Wrong: A Flat Earth, Part 4, June 22, 2011, https://www.youtube.com/watch?v=6h5K5PrEMzU&list=PL5F34CF577900491D&index=4.

753. Bruce J. Malina, John J. Pilch, Social-science Commentary on the Book of Revelation, at 77 (2000).

754. Ray Comfort and the Flat Earth, May 27, 2014, https://www.youtube.com/watch?v=SsFz5orH7Ng.

755. Dr. Robert W. Carter, https://creation.com/dr-robert-carter (last visited on February 18, 2019). See also https://creation.com/dr-robert-carter-cv (last visited on February 18, 2019).

756. Robert Carter and Jonathan Sarfati, A Flat Earth, and Other Nonsense, Debunking Ideas That Would Not Exist Were it Not for the Internet, Creation Ministries International, 13 September 2016, updated 26 October 2018, https://creation.com/refuting-flat-earth.

757. Jonathan Sarfati, The Moon: the Light That Rules the Night, September 1998, https://creation.com/the-moon-the-light-that-rules-the-night.

758. Jonathan Sarfati, The Moon: the Light That Rules the Night, September 1998, https://creation.com/the-moon-the-light-that-rules-the-night.

759. Enno Logic eT650D Dual Laser Infrared Thermometer.

760. Chad Wagner, Flat Earth Refutation (Part 2) - A Biblical and Scientific Refutation, April 9, 2017, https://www.youtube.com/watch?v=9zjf_Vyd6BA.

761. Chad Wagner, Flat Earth Refutation (Part 2) - A Biblical and Scientific Refutation, April 9, 2017, https://www.youtube.com/watch?v=9zjf_Vyd6BA.

762. Chad Wagner, Flat Earth Refutation (Part 2) - A Biblical and Scientific Refutation, April 9, 2017, https://www.youtube.com/watch?v=9zjf_Vyd6BA.

763. Danny Faulkner, Testing a Flat-Earth Prediction: Is the Moon's Light Cooling?, Answers in Genesis, January 9, 2019, https://answersingenesis.org/astronomy/earth/testing-flat-earth-prediction-moonlight-cooling/.

764. Danny Faulkner, Testing a Flat-Earth Prediction: Is the Moon's Light Cooling?, Answers in Genesis, January 9, 2019, https://answersingenesis.org/astronomy/earth/testing-flat-earth-prediction-moonlight-cooling/.

765. Danny Faulkner, Testing a Flat-Earth Prediction: Is the Moon's Light Cooling?, Answers in Genesis, January 9, 2019, https://answersingenesis.org/astronomy/earth/testing-flat-earth-prediction-moonlight-cooling/.

766. Danny Faulkner, Testing a Flat-Earth Prediction: Is the Moon's Light Cooling?, Answers in Genesis, January 9, 2019, https://answersingenesis.org/astronomy/earth/testing-flat-earth-prediction-moonlight-cooling/.

767. Danny Faulkner, Testing a Flat-Earth Prediction: Is the Moon's Light Cooling?, Answers in Genesis, January 9, 2019, https://answersingenesis.org/astronomy/earth/testing-flat-earth-prediction-moonlight-cooling/.

768. What Is Thermal Conductivity?, https://www.khanacademy.org/science/physics/thermodynamics/specific-heat-and-heat-transfer/a/what-is-thermal-conductivity (last visited on April 24, 2019).

769. What Is Thermal Conductivity?, https://www.khanacademy.org/science/physics/thermodynamics/specific-heat-and-heat-transfer/a/what-is-thermal-conductivity (last visited on April 24, 2019).

770. Danny Faulkner, Testing a Flat-Earth Prediction: Is the Moon's Light Cooling?, Answers in Genesis, January 9, 2019, https://answersingenesis.org/astronomy/earth/testing-flat-earth-prediction-moonlight-cooling/.

771. Danny Faulkner, Testing a Flat-Earth Prediction: Is the Moon's Light Cooling?, Answers in Genesis, January 9, 2019, https://answersingenesis.org/astronomy/earth/testing-flat-earth-prediction-moonlight-cooling/.

772. Thermal Mass, http://www.greenspec.co.uk/building-design/thermal-mass/ (last visited on April 24, 2019). See also Thermal Conductivity of common Materials and Gases, https://www.engineeringtoolbox.com/thermal-conductivity-d_429.html (last visited on April 24, 2019).

773. Thermal Mass, http://www.greenspec.co.uk/building-design/thermal-m

ass/ (last visited on April 24, 2019). See also Thermal Conductivity of Metals, Metallic Elements and Alloys, https://www.engineeringtoolbox.com/thermal-conductivity-metals-d_858.html (last visited on April 24, 2019).

774.Danny Faulkner, Testing a Flat-Earth Prediction: Is the Moon's Light Cooling?, Answers in Genesis, January 9, 2019, https://answersingenesis.org/astronomy/earth/testing-flat-earth-prediction-moonlight-cooling/.

775.Danny Faulkner, Testing a Flat-Earth Prediction: Is the Moon's Light Cooling?, Answers in Genesis, January 9, 2019, https://answersingenesis.org/astronomy/earth/testing-flat-earth-prediction-moonlight-cooling/.

776.Danny Faulkner, Testing a Flat-Earth Prediction: Is the Moon's Light Cooling?, Answers in Genesis, January 9, 2019, https://answersingenesis.org/astronomy/earth/testing-flat-earth-prediction-moonlight-cooling/.

777.Danny Faulkner, Testing a Flat-Earth Prediction: Is the Moon's Light Cooling?, Answers in Genesis, January 9, 2019, https://answersingenesis.org/astronomy/earth/testing-flat-earth-prediction-moonlight-cooling/.

778.Thermal Mass, http://www.greenspec.co.uk/building-design/thermal-mass/ (last visited on April 24, 2019).

779.Thermal Mass, http://www.greenspec.co.uk/building-design/thermal-mass/ (last visited on April 24, 2019).

780. Danny Faulkner, Testing a Flat-Earth Prediction: Is the Moon's Light Cooling?, Answers in Genesis, January 9, 2019, https://answersingenesis.org/astronomy/earth/testing-flat-earth-prediction-moonlight-cooling/.

781. Danny Faulkner, Testing a Flat-Earth Prediction: Is the Moon's Light Cooling?, Answers in Genesis, January 9, 2019, https://answersingenesis.org/astronomy/earth/testing-flat-earth-prediction-moonlight-cooling/.

782. R. Henry Noad, "Lectures on Chemistry," p. 334, quoted in Samuel Rowbotham, Zetetic Astronomy, at 145 (1881).

783. R. Henry Noad, "Lectures on Chemistry," p. 334, quoted in Samuel Rowbotham, Zetetic Astronomy, at 145 (1881).

784. Danny Faulkner, Testing a Flat-Earth Prediction: Is the Moon's Light Cooling?, Answers in Genesis, January 9, 2019, https://answersingenesis.org/astronomy/earth/testing-flat-earth-prediction-moonlight-cooling/.

785. Danny Faulkner, Testing a Flat-Earth Prediction: Is the Moon's Light Cooling?, Answers in Genesis, January 9, 2019, https://answersingenesis.org/astronomy/earth/testing-flat-earth-prediction-moonlight-cooling/.

786. Danny Faulkner, Testing a Flat-Earth Prediction: Is the Moon's Light Cooling?, Answers in Genesis, January 9, 2019, https://answersingenesis.org/astronomy/earth/testing-flat-earth-prediction-moonlight-cooling/.

787. Danny Faulkner, Testing a Flat-Earth Prediction: Is the Moon's Light Cooling?, Answers in Genesis, January 9, 2019, https://answersingenesis.org/astronomy/earth/testing-flat-earth-prediction-moonlight-cooling/.

788. Danny Faulkner, Testing a Flat-Earth Prediction: Is the Moon's Light Cooling?, Answers in Genesis, January 9, 2019, https://answersingenesis.org/astronomy/earth/testing-flat-earth-prediction-moonlight-cooling/.

789. Danny Faulkner, Testing a Flat-Earth Prediction: Is the Moon's Light Cooling?, Answers in Genesis, January 9, 2019, https://answersingenesis.org/astronomy/earth/testing-flat-earth-prediction-moonlight-cooling/.

790. Danny Faulkner, Testing a Flat-Earth Prediction: Is the Moon's Light Cooling?, Answers in Genesis, January 9, 2019, https://answersingenesis.org/astronomy/earth/testing-flat-earth-prediction-moonlight-cooling/.

791. Dr. Danny Faulkner, https://answersingenesis.org/bios/danny-faulkner/ (last visited on April 25, 2019).

792. Danny Faulkner, Flat Earth Proof—Just a Mirage, Answers In Genesis, January 16, 2017, https://answersingenesis.org/astronomy/earth/flat-earth-proof-just-a-mirage/.

793. Samuel Birley Rowbotham (Parallax), Zetetic Astronomy, Earth Not a Globe, at 11-12 (1881).

794. Joshua Nowicki, https://joshuanowicki.smugmug.com/search/?q=chicago&c=photos (last visited on October 22, 2015).

795. Allison Eck, the Perfectly Scientific Explanation for Why Chicago Appeared Upside Down in Michigan, Nova, May 8, 2015, https://www.pbs.org/wgbh/nova/article/the-perfectly-scientific-explanation-for-why-chicago-appeared-upside-down-in-michigan/.

796. Danny Faulkner, Flat Earth Proof—Just a Mirage, Answers In Genesis, January 16, 2017, https://answersingenesis.org/astronomy/earth/flat-earth-proof-just-a-mirage/.

797. Danny Faulkner, Flat Earth Proof—Just a Mirage, Answers In Genesis, January 16, 2017, https://answersingenesis.org/astronomy/earth/flat-earth-proof-just-a-mirage/.

798. Danny Faulkner, Flat Earth Proof—Just a Mirage, Answers In Genesis, January 16, 2017, https://answersingenesis.org/astronomy/earth/flat-earth-proof-just-a-mirage/.

799. Humphreys, W.J., Physics Of The Air Second Edition, 451 (1929).

800. Danny Faulkner, Flat Earth Proof—Just a Mirage, Answers In Genesis, January 16, 2017, https://answersingenesis.org/astronomy/earth/flat-earth-proof-just-a-mirage/.

801. Strange Ships, Superior Mirages, Atmospheric Optics, https://www.atoptics.co.uk/fz150.htm (last visited on May 2, 2019).

802. Strange Ships, Superior Mirages, Atmospheric Optics, https://www.atoptics.co.uk/fz150.htm (last visited on May 2, 2019).

803. Danny Faulkner, Flat Earth Proof—Just a Mirage, Answers In Genesis, January 16, 2017, https://answersingenesis.org/astronomy/earth/flat-earth-proof-just-a-mirage/.

804. Danny Faulkner, Flat Earth Proof—Just a Mirage, Answers In Genesis, January 16, 2017, https://answersingenesis.org/astronomy/earth/flat-earth-proof-just-a-mirage/.

805. Pekka Parviainen, http://www.twanight.org/newTWAN/photographers_about.asp?photographer=Pekka%20Parviainen (last visited on May 3, 2019).

806. Pekka Parviainen, Mirages in Finland, December 2001, https://finland.fi/life-society/mirages-in-finland/. See also Polar Image, http://www.polarimage.fi/mirages/superi01.htm (last viewed on May 3, 2019).

807. Pekka Parviainen, Mirages in Finland, December 2001, https://finland.fi/life-society/mirages-in-finland/. See also Polar Image, http://www.polarimage.fi/mirages/superi01.htm (last viewed on May 3, 2019).

808. Polar Image, http://www.polarimage.fi/mirages/superi01.htm (last viewed on May 3, 2019).

809. Polar Image, http://www.polarimage.fi/mirages/superi01.htm (last

viewed on May 3, 2019).

810. Danny Faulkner, Flat Earth Proof—Just a Mirage, Answers In Genesis, January 16, 2017, https://answersingenesis.org/astronomy/earth/flat-earth-proof-just-a-mirage/.

811. Danny Faulkner, Flat Earth Proof—Just a Mirage, Answers In Genesis, January 16, 2017, https://answersingenesis.org/astronomy/earth/flat-earth-proof-just-a-mirage/.

812. Danny Faulkner, Flat Earth Proof—Just a Mirage, Answers In Genesis, January 16, 2017, https://answersingenesis.org/astronomy/earth/flat-earth-proof-just-a-mirage/.

813. Atmospheric Refraction, http://hyperphysics.phy-astr.gsu.edu/hbase/atmos/mirage.html (last visited on May 2, 2019).

814. Danny Faulkner, Flat Earth Proof—Just a Mirage, Answers In Genesis, January 16, 2017, https://answersingenesis.org/astronomy/earth/flat-earth-proof-just-a-mirage/.

815. Atmospheric Refraction, http://hyperphysics.phy-astr.gsu.edu/hbase/atmos/mirage.html (last visited on May 2, 2019).

816. Atmospheric Refraction, http://hyperphysics.phy-astr.gsu.edu/hbase/atmos/mirage.html (last visited on May 2, 2019).

817. Atmospheric Refraction, http://hyperphysics.phy-astr.gsu.edu/hbase/atmos/mirage.html (last visited on May 2, 2019).

818. Atmospheric Refraction, http://hyperphysics.phy-astr.gsu.edu/hbase/atmos/mirage.html (last visited on May 2, 2019).

819. Atmospheric Refraction, http://hyperphysics.phy-astr.gsu.edu/hbase/atmos/mirage.html (last visited on May 2, 2019).

820. Pekka Parviainen, Mirages in Finland, December 2001, https://finland.fi/life-society/mirages-in-finland/. See also Polar Image, http://www.polarimage.fi/mirages/superi01.htm (last viewed on May 3, 2019).

821. Danny Faulkner, Flat Earth Proof—Just a Mirage, Answers In Genesis, January 16, 2017, https://answersingenesis.org/astronomy/earth/flat-earth-proof-just-a-mirage/.

822. Danny Faulkner, Flat Earth Proof—Just a Mirage, Answers In Genesis, January 16, 2017, https://answersingenesis.org/astronomy/earth/flat-earth-proof-just-a-mirage/.

823. Danny Faulkner, Flat Earth Proof—Just a Mirage, Answers In Genesis, January 16, 2017, https://answersingenesis.org/astronomy/earth/flat-earth-proof-just-a-mirage/.

824. Danny Faulkner, Flat Earth Proof—Just a Mirage, Answers In Genesis, January 16, 2017, https://answersingenesis.org/astronomy/earth/flat-earth-proof-just-a-mirage/.

825. Samuel Birley Rowbotham (Parallax), Zetetic Astronomy, Earth Not a Globe (1881), Chapter 15, http://www.sacred-texts.com/earth/za/za66.htm.

826. Samuel Birley Rowbotham (Parallax), Zetetic Astronomy, Earth Not a Globe (1881), Perspective on the Sea, http://www.sacred-texts.com/earth/za/za33.htm.

827. Samuel Birley Rowbotham (Parallax), Zetetic Astronomy, Earth Not a Globe (1881), Chapter 15, http://www.sacred-texts.com/earth/za/za66.htm.

828. Samuel Birley Rowbotham (Parallax), Zetetic Astronomy, Earth Not a Globe (1881), at 201-213, http://www.sacred-texts.com/earth/za/za32.htm.

829. Samuel Birley Rowbotham (Parallax), Zetetic Astronomy, Earth Not a Globe (1881), at 201-213, http://www.sacred-texts.com/earth/za/za32.htm.

830. Samuel Birley Rowbotham (Parallax), Zetetic Astronomy, Earth Not a Globe (1881), Perspective on the Sea, http://www.sacred-texts.com/earth/za/za33.htm.

831. Samuel Birley Rowbotham (Parallax), Zetetic Astronomy, Earth Not a Globe (1881), Chapter 15, http://www.sacred-texts.com/earth/za/za66.htm.

832. Samuel Birley Rowbotham (Parallax), Zetetic Astronomy, Earth Not a Globe (1881), at 201-213, http://www.sacred-texts.com/earth/za/za32.htm.

833. Samuel Birley Rowbotham (Parallax), Zetetic Astronomy, Earth Not a Globe (1881), Chapter 15, http://www.sacred-texts.com/earth/za/za66.htm.

834. Samuel Birley Rowbotham (Parallax), Zetetic Astronomy, Earth Not a Globe (1881), Perspective on the Sea, http://www.sacred-texts.com/earth/za/za33.htm.

835. Samuel Birley Rowbotham (Parallax), Zetetic Astronomy, Earth Not a Globe (1881), Perspective on the Sea, http://www.sacred-texts.com/earth/za/za33.htm.

836. Samuel Birley Rowbotham (Parallax), Zetetic Astronomy, Earth Not a Globe (1881), Perspective on the Sea, http://www.sacred-texts.com/earth/za/za33.htm.

837. Samuel Birley Rowbotham (Parallax), Zetetic Astronomy, Earth Not a Globe (1881), Perspective on the Sea, http://www.sacred-texts.com/earth/za/za33.htm.

838. Samuel Birley Rowbotham (Parallax), Zetetic Astronomy, Earth Not a Globe (1881), Perspective on the Sea, http://www.sacred-texts.com/earth/za/za33.htm.

839. Yanoff, Myron; Duker, Jay S. (2009). Ophthalmology 3rd Edition. MOSBY Elsevier. p. 54.

840. Samuel Birley Rowbotham (Parallax), Zetetic Astronomy, Earth Not a Globe (1881), at 201-213, http://www.sacred-texts.com/earth/za/za32.htm.

841. Samuel Birley Rowbotham (Parallax), Zetetic Astronomy, Earth Not a Globe (1881), at 201-213, http://www.sacred-texts.com/earth/za/za32.htm.

842. Samuel Birley Rowbotham (Parallax), Zetetic Astronomy, Earth Not a Globe (1881), at 201-213, http://www.sacred-texts.com/earth/za/za32.htm.

843. Samuel Birley Rowbotham (Parallax), Zetetic Astronomy, Earth Not a Globe (1881), at 201-213, http://www.sacred-texts.com/earth/za/za32.htm.

844. Samuel Birley Rowbotham (Parallax), Zetetic Astronomy, Earth Not a Globe (1881), at 201-213, http://www.sacred-texts.com/earth/za/za32.htm.

845. Danny Faulkner, Flat Earth Proof—Just a Mirage, Answers In Genesis, January 16, 2017, https://answersingenesis.org/astronomy/earth/flat-earth-proof-just-a-mirage/.

846. The Alfred Russel Wallace Website, http://wallacefund.info/faqs-myths-misconceptions (last visited on June 1, 2019).

847. Charles Darwin & Alfred Wallace, On the Tendency of Species to form Varieties; and on the Perpetuation of Varieties and Species by Natural Selection, August 1858, http://wallaceletters.info/sites/wallaceletters.info/files/1858_PAPER.pdf.

848. Letter from the Royal Society to Wallace, November 6, 1890. Copyright Wallace Literary Estate, The Natural History Museum, Fred Edwards, http://wallacefund.info/faqs-myths-misconceptions (last visited on June 1, 2019).

849. The Bedford Level Experiment, https://en.wikipedia.org/wiki/Bedford_Level_experiment#cite_ref-garwood_1-0, citing "The Association for Science Education". School Science Review. London: John Murray. 24: 120. 1942; Richards-Jones, P (1968). "Astronomy at O level". Physics Education. 3 (1): 35–39.

850. Alfred Russel Wallace, My Life, A Record of Life and Opinions, 1905, at 53, http://darwin-online.org.uk/content/frameset?viewtype

=side&itemID=A237.2&pageseq=1.

851. Alfred Russel Wallace, My Life, A Record of Life and Opinions, 1905, at 275-350 (in particular 327-337), http://darwin-online.org.uk/content/frameset?viewtype=side&itemID=A237.2&pageseq=1.

852. Alfred Russel Wallace, My Life, A Record of Life and Opinions, 1905, at 327, http://darwin-online.org.uk/content/frameset?viewtype=side&itemID=A237.2&pageseq=1.

853. Alfred Russel Wallace, My Life, A Record of Life and Opinions, 1905, at 275, http://darwin-online.org.uk/content/frameset?viewtype=side&itemID=A237.2&pageseq=1.

854. Alfred Russel Wallace, My Life, A Record of Life and Opinions, 1905, at 295, http://darwin-online.org.uk/content/frameset?viewtype=side&itemID=A237.2&pageseq=1.

855. Alfred Russel Wallace, My Life, A Record of Life and Opinions, 1905, at 274, http://darwin-online.org.uk/content/frameset?viewtype=side&itemID=A237.2&pageseq=1.

856. Warlock, Merriam-Webster Dictionary, https://www.merriam-webster.com/dictionary/warlock (last visited on June 7, 2019).

857. Warlock, https://www.etymonline.com/word/warlock (last visited on June 7, 2019).

858. Parallax (Samuel Rowbotham), Experimental Proofs that the Surface of Standing Water Not Convex

But Horizontal, at 1-2, 1870, https://archive.org/details/parallax-experimental_proofs_that_the_surface_of_water_is_not_convex_but_horizontal.

859. Parallax (Samuel Rowbotham), Experimental Proofs that the Surface of Standing Water Not Convex But Horizontal, at 4, 1870, https://archive.org/details/parallax-experimental_proofs_that_the_surface_of_water_is_not_convex_but_horizontal.

860. Bobe Schadewald, The Plane Truth, https://www.cantab.net/users/michael.behrend/ebooks/PlaneTruth/pages/Chapter_02.html (last visited on June 2, 2019).

861. Alfred Russel Wallace, Encyclopedia Britannica, https://www.britannica.com/biography/Alfred-Russel-Wallace (last visited on June 2, 2019).

862. Parallax (Samuel Rowbotham), Experimental Proofs that the Surface of Standing Water Not Convex But Horizontal, at 14, 1870, https://archive.org/details/parallax-experimental_proofs_that_the_surface_of_water_is_not_convex_but_horizontal.

863. Basic Surveying - Theory and Practice, Oregon Department of Transportation, Ninth Annual Seminar, at 10-1, February 15-17, 2000. See Differential Leveling, Purdue University, https://engineering.purdue.edu/~asm215/topics/difflevl.html. See also Section 2: Differential Leveling, TxDOT Survey Manual, April 1, 2016, http://onlinemanuals.txdot.gov/txdotmanuals/ess/differential_leveling.htm.

864. Chapter 3 Surveying Measurements, Survey Manual, Department of Transportation, State of New Jersey, http://www.state.nj.us/transportation/eng/documents/survey/Chapter3.shtm (last visited on March 19, 2018).

865. Alfred Russel Wallace, My Life, A Record of Life and Opinions, 1905, at 368-69, http://darwin-online.org.uk/content/frameset?viewtype=side&itemID=A237.2&pageseq=1.

866. Jesse Kozlowski, Chris Van Matre Talking About His Surveying Career And His Flat Earth Beliefs, at 0:34:00, March 3, 2018, https://www.youtube.com/watch?v=JCVY9yvyFBE.

867. Parallax (Samuel Rowbotham), Experimental Proofs that the Surface of Standing Water Not Convex But Horizontal, at 13, 1870, https://archive.org/details/parallax-experimental_proofs_that_the_surface_of_water_is_not_convex_but_horizontal.

868. The Earth Not a Globe Review, 1893-1897, https://ia801203.us.archive.org/23/items/earth_not_a_globe_review_1893-1897/earth_not_a_globe_review_1893-1897.pdf.

869. Bobe Schadewald, The Plane Truth, https://www.cantab.net/users/michael.behrend/ebooks/PlaneTruth/pages/Chapter_02.html (last visited on June 2, 2019).

870. Bobe Schadewald, The Plane Truth, https://www.cantab.net/users/michael.behrend/ebooks/PlaneTruth/pages/Chapter_02.html (last visited on June 2, 2019).

871. The Earth Not a Globe Review, 1893-97, at 87, https://ia801203.us.archive.org/23/items/earth_not_a_globe_review_1893-1897/earth_not_a_globe_review_1893-1897.pdf.

872. Bobe Schadewald, The Plane Truth, https://www.cantab.net/users/michael.behrend/ebooks/PlaneTruth/pages/Chapter_02.html (last visited on June 2, 2019).

873. Bobe Schadewald, The Plane Truth, https://www.cantab.net/users/michael.behrend/ebooks/PlaneTruth/pages/Chapter_02.html (last visited on June 2, 2019).

874. Bobe Schadewald, The Plane Truth, https://www.cantab.net/users/michael.behrend/ebooks/PlaneTruth/pages/Chapter_02.html (last visited on June 2, 2019).

875. J. H. Walsh, The Convexity of Water, March 18, 1870, https://people.wku.edu/charles.smith/wallace/zCarpenter1870Field1.pdf.

876. Bobe Schadewald, The Plane Truth, https://www.cantab.net/users/michael.behrend/ebooks/PlaneTruth/pages/Chapter_02.html (last visited on June 2, 2019).

877. William Carpenter, The Old Bedford Level, March 26, 1894, Earth Not a Globe Review, May 1894, https://ia801203.us.archive.org/23/items/earth_not_a_globe_review_1893-1897/earth_not_a_globe_review_1893-1897.pdf

878. Parallax (Samuel Rowbotham), Experimental Proofs that the Surface of Standing Water Not Convex But Horizontal, at 15-16, 1870, https://archive.org/details/parallax-experimental_proofs_that_the_surface_of_water_is_not_convex_but_horizontal.

879. Parallax (Samuel Rowbotham), Experimental Proofs that the Surface of Standing Water Not Convex But Horizontal, at 15-16, 1870, https://archive.org/details/parallax-experimental_proofs_that_the_surface_of_water_is_not_convex_but_horizontal.

880. J. H. Walsh, The Convexity of Water, March 18, 1870, https://people.wku.edu/charles.smith/wallace/zCarpenter1870Field1.pdf.

881. James Naylor, Bedford Canal Not Convex, The Earth Not a Globe, 1873.

882. James Naylor, Bedford Canal Not Convex, The Earth Not a Globe, 1873.

883. James Naylor, Bedford Canal Not Convex, The Earth Not a Globe, 1873.

884. J. H. Walsh, The Convexity of Water, March 18, 1870, https://people.wku.edu/charles.smith/wallace/zCarpenter1870Field1.pdf.

885. J. H. Walsh, The Convexity of Water, March 18, 1870, https://people.wku.edu/charles.smith/wallace/zCarpenter1870Field1.pdf.

886. The Earth Not a Globe Review, 1893-97, at 265, https://ia801203.us.archive.org/23/items/earth_not_a_globe_review_1893-1897/earth_not_a_globe_review_1893-1897.pdf.

887. James Naylor, Bedford Canal Not Convex, The Earth Not a Globe, 1873.

888. James Naylor, Bedford Canal Not Convex, The Earth Not a Globe, 1873.

889. Alfred Russel Wallace, My Life, A Record of Life and Opinions, 1905, at 368, http://darwin-online.org.uk/content/frameset?viewtype=side&itemID=A237.2&pageseq=1.

890. J. H. Walsh, The Convexity of Water, March 18, 1870, https://people.wku.edu/charles.smith/wallace/zCarpenter1870Field1.pdf.

891. J. H. Walsh, The Convexity of Water, March 18, 1870, https://people.wku.edu/charles.smith/wallace/zCarpenter1870Field1.pdf.

892. J. H. Walsh, The Convexity of Water, March 18, 1870, https://people.wku.edu/charles.smith/wallace/zCarpenter1870Field1.pdf.

893. Parallax (Samuel Rowbotham), Experimental Proofs that the Surface of Standing Water Not Convex But Horizontal, at 16-18, 1870, https://archive.org/details/parallax-experimental_proofs_that_the_surface_of_water_is_not_convex_but_horizontal.

894. Parallax (Samuel Rowbotham), Experimental Proofs that the Surface of Standing Water Not Convex But Horizontal, at 16-18, 1870, https://archive.org/details/parallax-experimental_proofs_that_the_surface_of_water_is_not_convex_but_horizontal.

895. Parallax (Samuel Rowbotham), Experimental Proofs that the Surface of Standing Water Not Convex But Horizontal, at 16-18, 1870, https://archive.org/details/parallax-experimental_proofs_that_the_surface_of_water_is_not_convex_but_horizontal.

896. Parallax (Samuel Rowbotham), Experimental Proofs that the Surface of Standing Water Not Convex But Horizontal, at 4-7, 1870, https://archive.org/details/parallax-experimental_proofs_that_the_surface_of_water_is_not_convex_but_horizontal.

897. Samuel Birley Rowbotham (Parallax), Zetetic Astronomy, Earth Not a Globe, at 11-12 (1881).

898. Parallax (Samuel Rowbotham), Experimental Proofs that the Surface of Standing Water Not Convex But Horizontal, at 4-7, 1870, https://archive.org/details/parallax-experimental_proofs_that_the_surface_of_water_is_not_convex_but_horizontal.

899. Bobe Schadewald, The Plane Truth, https://www.cantab.net/users/michael.behrend/ebooks/PlaneTruth/pages/Chapter_03.html (last visited on June 2, 2019).

900. Bobe Schadewald, The Plane Truth, https://www.cantab.net/users/michael.behrend/ebooks/PlaneTruth/pages/Chapter_02.html (last visited on June 2, 2019). Alfred Russel Wallace, My Life, A Record of Life and Opinions, 1905, at 370, http://darwin-online.org.uk/content/frameset?viewtype=side&itemID=A237.2&pageseq=1.

901. Alfred Russel Wallace, My Life, A Record of Life and Opinions, 1905, at 370, http://darwin-online.org.uk/content/frameset?viewtype=side&itemID=A237.2&pageseq=1.

902. Bobe Schadewald, The Plane Truth, https://www.cantab.net/users/michael.behrend/ebooks/PlaneTruth/pages/Chapter_02.html (last visited on June 2, 2019).

903. Bobe Schadewald, The Plane Truth, https://www.cantab.net/users/michael.behrend/ebooks/PlaneTruth/pages/Chapter_02.html (last visited on June 2, 2019).

904. Alfred Russel Wallace, My Life, A Record of Life and Opinions, 1905, at 372-76, http://darwin-online.org.uk/content/frameset?viewtype=side&itemID=A237.2&pageseq=1.

905. John Timmer, Why Do Flat Earth Believers Still Exist? | Ars Technica, November 7, 2018, https://www.youtube.com/watch?v=mYB1JP-gfLE.

906. John Timmer, Senior Science Editor, Ars Technica, https://arstechnica.com/author/john-timmer/ (last visited on July 4, 2021).

907. E.g., John Timmer, Our Ancestors Left Africa Both with and Without Modern Brains, Ars Tecnica, April 9, 2021, https://arstechnica.com/science/2021/04/our-ancestors-left-africa-both-with-and-without-modern-brains/.

908. E.g., John Timmer, Climate-driven Coastal Flooding in the US Likely to Get Worse Suddenly, Ars Technica, June 22, 2021, https://arstechnica.com/science/2021/06/climate-driven-coastal-flooding-in-the-us-likely-to-get-worse-suddenly/.

909. E.g., John Timmer, We Have Another Highly Effective Covid Vaccine, Based on Different Tech, Ars Technica, June 14, 2021, https://arstechnica.com/science/2021/06/we-have-another-highly-effective-covid-vaccine-based-on-different-tech/.

910. Eleanor McBean, The Poisoned Needle, at 29 (1957), http://www.whale.to/a/mcbean.html, quoting "Lecture Memoranda," XVII International Congress of Medicine, London, 1913.

911. Raymond Obomsawin, Ph.D., Immunity, Infectious Disease, and Vaccination. Video Re-Posted by Edward Hendrie Under Article Heading: The History of Vaccines Proving They Are Ineffective and Dangerous, May 26, 2021, https://greatmountainpublishing.com/2021/05/26/the-history-of-vaccines-proving-they-are-ineffective-and-dangerous/. See also, Ida Honorof and Eleanor McBean, Vaccination, The Silent Killer: A Clear and Present Danger (1977), https://archive.org/details/vaccinationsilen00hono, and Eleanor McBean, The Poisoned Needle (1957),

http://www.whale.to/a/mcbean.html.

912. Edward Hendrie, Study Shows That Vaccinated Children Are Significantly Less Healthy Than Unvaccinated Children, December 20, 2020, https://greatmountainpublishing.com/2020/12/20/study-shows-that-vaccinated-children-are-significantly-less-healthy-than-unvaccinated-children/.

913. James Lyons-Weiler and Paul Thomas, Relative Incidence of Office Visits and Cumulative Rates of Billed Diagnoses Along the Axis of Vaccination, 22 November 2020, https://www.mdpi.com/1660-4601/17/22/8674/htm.

914. James Lyons-Weiler, et al., Relative Incidence of Office Visits and Cumulative Rates of Billed Diagnoses Along the Axis of Vaccination, 14 November 2020, https://www.mdpi.com/1660-4601/17/22/8674.

915. Lessons from the Lockdown—Why Are So Many Fewer Children Dying?, Children's Health Defense, June 18, 2020, https://childrenshealthdefense.org/news/lessons-from-the-lockdown-why-are-so-many-fewer-children-dying/.

916. Lessons from the Lockdown—Why Are So Many Fewer Children Dying?, Children's Health Defense, June 18, 2020, https://childrenshealthdefense.org/news/lessons-from-the-lockdown-why-are-so-many-fewer-children-dying/.

917. Santoli, Jeanne M et al. Effects of the COVID-19 Pandemic on Routine Pediatric Vaccine Ordering and Administration — United States, 2020. cdc.gov. https://www.cdc.gov/mmwr/volumes/69/wr/mm6919e

2.htm#F1_down.

918. Lessons from the Lockdown—Why Are So Many Fewer Children Dying?, Children's Health Defense, June 18, 2020, https://childrenshealthdefense.org/news/lessons-from-the-lockdown-why-are-so-many-fewer-children-dying/.

919. Bill Gates and His Friends and Their Plan to Vaccinate the World: One of the Biggest Frauds in Human History, May 3, 2020, https://flatearthperspectives.wordpress.com/2020/05/03/bill-gates-and-his-friends-and-their-plan-to-vaccinate-the-world-one-of-the-biggest-frauds-in-human-history/.

920. Deaths by Vaccination Status, England, Office for National Statistics, Dataset, https://www.ons.gov.uk/peoplepopulationandcommunity/birthsdeathsandmarriages/deaths/datasets/deathsbyvaccinationstatusengland (last visited on November 22, 2021).

921. Lazarus, Ross, et al., Grant ID: R18 HS 017045, Final Report, Electronic Support for Public Health–Vaccine Adverse Event Reporting System (ESP:VAERS), at 6, 2/01/07 - 09/30/10, Submitted to: The Agency for Healthcare Research and Quality (AHRQ) U.S. Department of Health and Human Services, https://digital.ahrq.gov/sites/default/files/docs/publication/r18hs017045-lazarus-final-report-2011.pdf.

922. Kimberly Blumenthal, Acute Allergic Reactions to mRNA COVID-19 Vaccines, Journal of the American Medical Association, March 8, 2021, https://jamanetwork.com/journals/jama/fullarticle/2777417.

923. Megan Redshaw, Latest VAERS Data Show Reports of Blood Clotting Disorders After All Three Emergency Use Authorization Vaccines, The Defender, April 16, 2021, https://childrenshealthdefense.org/defender/vaers-reports-clotting-disorders-all-three-emergency-use-authorization-vaccines/?itm_term=home. See also Tyler Durden, What The CDC's VAERS Database Reveals About "Adverse" Post-Vaccine Reactions, April 18, 2021, https://www.zerohedge.com/covid-19/what-cdcs-vaers-database-reveals-about-adverse-post-vaccine-reactions.

924. Open VEARS, https://www.openvaers.com/ (last visited on July 28, 2022).

925. The Expose, COVID Vaccines are at least 75x deadlier than all other Vaccines combined according to Medicine Regulators, August 19, 2022, https://expose-news.com/2022/08/19/covid-jabs-75x-deadlier-than-all-vaccines/.

926. The Expose, COVID Vaccines are at least 75x deadlier than all other Vaccines combined according to Medicine Regulators, August 19, 2022, https://expose-news.com/2022/08/19/covid-jabs-75x-deadlier-than-all-vaccines/.

927. Outbreak of SARS-CoV-2 Infections, Including COVID-19 Vaccine Breakthrough Infections, Associated with Large Public Gatherings — Barnstable County, Massachusetts, July 2021, CDC, August 6, 2021, https://www.cdc.gov/mmwr/volumes/70/wr/mm7031e2.htm.

928. Nina Pierpont, Covid-19 Vaccine Mandates Are Now Pointless: Covid-19 Vaccines Do Not Keep

People from Catching the Prevailing Delta Variant and Passing it to Others, September 9, 2021, https://theexpose.uk/wp-content/uploads/2021/09/Pierpont-Why-mandated-vaccines-are-pointless-final-1.pdf.

929. https://www.instagram.com/tv/CYpnmfioB2K/?utm_medium=copy_link.

930. https://www.instagram.com/tv/CYpnmfioB2K/?utm_medium=copy_link.

931. Jeff Faraudo, Cal Football: Bears Expecting Everyone Back From COVID-19 for the Big Game, Sports Illustrated, November 13, 2021, https://www.si.com/college/cal/news/cal-covid-update-111321.

932. University of California 2021 Football Roster, https://calbears.com/sports/football/roster.

933. Carol Rosenberg and Aishvarya Kavi, a U.S. Navy Combat Ship Is Stranded in Guantánamo Bay with a Virus Outbreak, The New York Times, December 25, 2021, https://www.nytimes.com/2021/12/25/world/navy-ship-covid-guantanamo-bay.html.

934. Darling v. Sacred Heart Health System, 3:21-CV-1787/TKW, (N.D. Fl. 2021), ruling from the bench of U.S. District Court Judge T. Kent Wetherell, II denying motion for preliminary injunction.

935. COVID-19 Vaccine Breakthrough Infections Reported to CDC — United States, January 1–April 30, 2021, CDC, May 28, 2021, https://www.cdc.gov/mmwr/volumes/70/wr/mm7021e3.htm.

936. Letter from Seanator Edward J. Markey to Dr. Dr. Rochelle P. Walletnsky, Director, CDC, July 22, 2021, https://www.markey.senate.gov/imo/media/doc/cdc_breakthrough_cases_letter.pdf.

937. Letter from Seanator Edward J. Markey to Dr. Dr. Rochelle P. Walletnsky, Director, CDC, July 22, 2021, https://www.markey.senate.gov/imo/media/doc/cdc_breakthrough_cases_letter.pdf.

938. Deaths by vaccination status, England. Office for National Statistics, https://www.ons.gov.uk/peoplepopulationandcommunity/birthsdeathsandmarriages/deaths/datasets/deathsbyvaccinationstatusengland, Release date: 06 July 2022.

939. Guy Page, 76% of September COVID-19 Deaths Are Vax Breakthroughs, Vermont Daily Chronicle, September 30, 2021, https://vermontdailychronicle.com/2021/09/30/76-of-september-covid-19-deaths-are-vaxxed-breakthroughs/.

940. Protect Yourself & Others, Vermont Department of Public Health, https://www.healthvermont.gov/covid-19/protect-yourself-others (last visited on October 14, 2021).

941. Hall Turner Radio Show, Newsdesk, November 9, 2021, https://halturnerradioshow.com/index.php/en/news-page/world/hospitals-in-antwerp-belgium-75-6-vaxxed-are-now-reporting-100-of-their-covid-cases-are-double-vaccinated.

942. EXCLUSIVE – 89% of COVID-19 Deaths in the past 4 Weeks Were among the Fully Vaccinated According to the Latest Public Health Data, The

Expose, November 11, 2021, https://theexpose.uk/2021/11/11/89-percent-of-covid-19-deaths-were-among-the-fully-vaccinated-in-the-past-month/.

943. Public Health Scotland, COVID-19 & Winter Statistical Report, As at 17 January 2022, Publication Date: 19 January 2022, https://publichealthscotland.scot/media/11223/22-01-19-covid19-winter_publication_report.pdf.

944. Public Health Scotland, COVID-19 & Winter Statistical Report, As at 17 January 2022, Publication Date: 19 January 2022, https://publichealthscotland.scot/media/11223/22-01-19-covid19-winter_publication_report.pdf.

945. Public Health Scotland, COVID-19 & Winter Statistical Report, As at 17 January 2022, Publication Date: 19 January 2022, https://publichealthscotland.scot/media/11223/22-01-19-covid19-winter_publication_report.pdf.

946. Compare COVID-19 epidemiology update, July 29, 2022, https://health-infobase.canada.ca/covid-19/, with COVID-19 epidemiology update, June 17, 2022, https://web.archive.org/web/20220622061056/https://health-infobase.canada.ca/covid-19/.

947. Trudeau's Government confirms the Quadruple/Triple Vaccinated have accounted for 90% of Covid-19 Deaths across Canada since the beginning of June, The Expose, July 29, 2022, https://expose-news.com/2022/07/29/trudeau-90percent-covid-deaths-vaccinated-canada/?cmid=60835409-a89a-4896-82cd-c51b2d11c704.

948. Trudeau's Government confirms the Quadruple/Triple Vaccinated have accounted for 90% of Covid-19 Deaths across Canada since the beginning of June, The Expose, July 29, 2022, https://expose-news.com/2022/07/29/trudeau-90percent-covid-deaths-vaccinated-canada/?cmid=60835409-a89a-4896-82cd-c51b2d11c704.

949. Trudeau's Government confirms the Quadruple/Triple Vaccinated have accounted for 90% of Covid-19 Deaths across Canada since the beginning of June, The Expose, July 29, 2022, https://expose-news.com/2022/07/29/trudeau-90percent-covid-deaths-vaccinated-canada/?cmid=60835409-a89a-4896-82cd-c51b2d11c704.

950. Cahterine Brown, et al., Outbreak of SARS-CoV-2 Infections, Including COVID-19 Vaccine Breakthrough Infections, Associated with Large Public Gatherings - Barnstable County, Massachusetts, July 2021, August 6, 2021, https://pubmed.ncbi.nlm.nih.gov/34351882/.

951. Nguyen Van Vinh Chau, et al., Transmission of SARS-CoV-2 Delta Variant Among Vaccinated Healthcare Workers, Vietnam, Volume 41, November 2021, 11043, https://doi.org/10.1016/j.eclinm.2021.101143, and also at: https://papers.ssrn.com/sol3/papers.cfm?abstract_id=3897733.

952. Carla Saade, et al., Live virus neutralization testing in convalescent patients and subjects vaccinated against 19A, 20B, 20I/501Y.V1 and 20H/501Y.V2 isolates of SARS-CoV-2, December 2021, https://pubmed.ncbi.nlm.nih.gov/34176436/.

953. Kasen K. Riemersma, et al., Shedding of Infectious SARS-CoV-2 Despite Vaccination, August 24, 2021, https://www.medrxiv.org/content/10.1101/2021.07.31.21261387v4.full.pdf.

954. The United Kingdom Health Security Agency COVID-19 Vaccine Surveillance Report, Publishing Reference: GOV-10227, at 12, October 21, 2021, https://assets.publishing.service.gov.uk/government/uploads/system/uploads/attachment_data/file/1027511/Vaccine-surveillance-report-week-42.pdf.

955. Latest UK Health Security Agency report Shows the COVID-19 Vaccines Have NEGATIVE Effectiveness As Low As MINUS 124%, The Expose, October 22, 2021, https://theexpose.uk/2021/10/22/covid-19-vaccines-have-negative-effectiveness-as-low-as-minus-124-percent/.

956. Official Government Reports Suggest the Fully Vaccinated Will Develop Acquired Immunodeficiency Syndrome by Christmas, The Expose, Ocober 27, 2021, https://theexpose.uk/2021/10/27/official-government-reports-suggest-the-fully-vaccinated-will-develop-acquired-immunodeficiency-syndrome-by-christmas/.

957. COVID-19 Vaccine Surveillance Report, Week 42, UK Health Security Agency, Publishing reference: GOV-10227, 21 October 2021, https://assets.publishing.service.gov.uk/government/uploads/system/uploads/attachment_data/file/1027511/Vaccine-surveillance-report-week-42.pdf.

958. Sally Fallon Morell, Dr. Thomas Cowan, and Dr. Andrew Kaufman, Statement on Virus Isolation (SOVI). "SARS-CoV-2 Has Never Been Isolated or Purified", Global Research, May 17, 2022.

959. Sally Fallon Morell, Dr. Thomas Cowan, and Dr. Andrew Kaufman, Statement on Virus Isolation (SOVI). "SARS-CoV-2 Has Never Been Isolated or Purified", Global Research, May 17, 2022.

960. Affidavit of Christine Massey, November 30. 2021, https://drive.google.com/file/d/1axe-YpJIFlV0NRtm47XvYzhQAski_oac/view.

961. Christine Massey, FOIs reveal that health/science institutions around the world (208 and counting!) have no record of SARS-COV-2 isolation/purification, anywhere, ever, https://www.fluoridefreepeel.ca/fois-reveal-that-health-science-institutions-around-the-world-have-no-record-of-sars-cov-2-isolation-purification/ (last visited on September 2, 2022).

962. Pieter Borger, et al., Review report Corman-Drosten et al. Eurosurveillance 2020, November 27, 2020, https://cormandrostenreview.com/report/.

963. Kary B. Mullis, The Nobel Prize, https://www.nobelprize.org/prizes/chemistry/1993/mullis/facts/ (last visited on September 27, 2022).

964. Inventor of COVID test calls Fauci a liar, says it 'doesn't tell you that you're sick'. Narural News,

March 17, 2021, https://www.naturalnews.com/2021-03-17-inventor-calls-fauci-a-liar.html#.

965. Inventor of COVID test calls Fauci a liar, says it 'doesn't tell you that you're sick'. Narural News, March 17, 2021, https://www.naturalnews.com/2021-03-17-inventor-calls-fauci-a-liar.html#.

966. Amandha Vollmer, PCR Tests Show Positive Because They Respond to Genetic Material Present in All Humans, G. Edward Griffin's Need to Know, August 28, 2020, https://needtoknow.news/2020/08/pcr-tests-show-positive-because-they-respond-to-genetic-material-present-in-all-humans/?utm_source=rss&utm_medium=rss&utm_campaign=pcr-tests-show-positive-because-they-respond-to-genetic-material-present-in-all-humans.

967. Protocol: Real-time RT-PCR assays for the detection of SARS-CoV-2 Institut Pasteur, Parishttps://www.who.int/docs/default-source/coronaviruse/real-time-rt-pcr-assays-for-the-detection-of-sars-cov-2-institut-pasteur-paris.pdf?sfvrsn=3662fcb6_2 (last visited on September 2, 2022).

968. Homo sapiens chromosome 8, GRCh38.p14 Primary Assembly, https://www.ncbi.nlm.nih.gov/nucleotide/NC_000008.11?report=genbank&log%24=nuclalign&from=63648346&to=63648363 (last visited on September 2, 2022).

969. CDC 2019-Novel Coronavirus (2019-nCoV) Real-Time RT-PCR Diagnostic Panel, Instructions for Use, at page 35, 7/21/2021, https://www.fda.gov/media/134922/download.

970. Edward Hendrie, The PCR Test is Generating False-Positive COVID-19 Results, November 19, 2020, https://greatmountainpublishing.com/2020/11/19/the-pcr-test-is-generating-false-positive-covid-19-results/.

971. Peter Andrews, *Landmark Legal Ruling Finds That Covid Tests Are Not Fit for Purpose. So What Do the MSM Do? They Ignore It*, RT, 27 November 2020, https://www.rt.com/op-ed/507937-covid-pcr-test-fail/.

972. Id.

973. Potential for False Positive Results with Antigen Tests for Rapid Detection of SARS-CoV-2 - Letter to Clinical Laboratory Staff and Health Care Providers, https://www.fda.gov/medical-devices/letters-health-care-providers/potential-false-positive-results-antigen-tests-rapid-detection-sars-cov-2-letter-clinical-laboratory (last visited on September 2, 2022).

974. Potential for False Positive Results with Antigen Tests for Rapid Detection of SARS-CoV-2 - Letter to Clinical Laboratory Staff and Health Care Providers, https://www.fda.gov/medical-devices/letters-health-care-providers/potential-false-positive-results-antigen-tests-rapid-detection-sars-cov-2-letter-clinical-laboratory (last visited on September 2, 2022).

975. Edward Hendrie, Authoritative Study Shows Zero Transmission of COVID-19 by Asymptomatic Carriers, December 22, 2020, https://greatmountainpublishing.com/2020/12/22/authoritative-study-shows-zero-transmission-of-covid-19-by-asymptomatic-carriers/.

976. Edward Hendrie, Proof that COVID-19 Statistics are Being Padded With Influenza Cases, February 3, 2021, https://greatmountainpublishing.com/2021/02/03/proof-that-covid-19-statistics-are-being-padded-with-influenza-cases/.

977. Edward Hendrie, Proof that COVID-19 Statistics are Being Padded With Influenza Cases, February 3, 2021, https://greatmountainpublishing.com/2021/02/03/proof-that-covid-19-statistics-are-being-padded-with-influenza-cases/.

978. Edward Hendrie, Proof that COVID-19 Statistics are Being Padded With Influenza Cases, February 3, 2021, https://greatmountainpublishing.com/2021/02/03/proof-that-covid-19-statistics-are-being-padded-with-influenza-cases/.

979. Edward Hendrie, World Council For Health Calls for Immediate Recall of All COVID-19 Vaccines, July 30, 2022, https://greatmountainpublishing.com/2022/07/30/world-council-for-health-calls-for-immediate-recall-of-all-covid-19-vaccines/.

980. Coronavirus Task Force Press Breifing, White House, April 7, 2020, https://www.whitehouse.gov/briefings-statements/remarks-president-trump-vice-president-pence-members-coronavirus-task-force-press-briefing-april-7-2020/.

981. Coronavirus Task Force Press Breifing, White House, April 7, 2020, https://www.whitehouse.gov/briefings-statements/rema

rks-president-trump-vice-president-pence-members-coronavirus-task-force-press-briefing-april-7-2020/.

982. Illinois Department of Public Health Director Dr. Ngozi Ezike Explains How Covid Deaths Are Classified, Published August 14, 2021, https://www.bitchute.com/video/vsEScGB2ifHx/.

983. Patrick Howley, BUSTED: CDC Inflated COVID Numbers, Accused of Violating Federal Law, March 8, 2021, National File, https://nationalfile.com/busted-cdc-inflated-covid-numbers-accused-of-violating-federal-law/.

984. Henry Ealy, et al., COVID-19 Data Collection, Comorbidity & Federal Law: A Historical Retrospective, Public Health Policy Initiative, October 12, 2020, https://jdfor2020.com/wp-content/uploads/2020/11/adf864_165a103206974fdbb14ada6bf8af1541.pdf

985. 2003 CDC Medical Examiner's and Coroner's Handbook on Death Registration, https://www.cdc.gov/nchs/data/misc/hb_me.pdf.

986. 2003 CDC Medical Examiner's and Coroner's Handbook on Death Registration, https://www.cdc.gov/nchs/data/misc/hb_me.pdf.

987. Steven Schaartz, Ph.D., Director - Division of Vital Statistics, National Center for Health Statistics, COVID-19 Alert No. 2, National Vital Statistics System, March 24, 2020, https://www.cdc.gov/nchs/data/nvss/coronavirus/Alert-2-New-ICD-code-introduced-for-COVID-19-deaths.pdf.

988. Greg Piper, Lawmakers seek federal grand jury investigation for COVID-19 statistical manipulation, Just the News, October 10, 2021, https://justthenews.com/government/federal-agencies/lawmakers-seek-federal-grand-jury-investigation-covid-19-statistical.

989. Oregon Senators Kim Thatcher and Dennis Linthicum, Formal Federal Grand Jury Petition Rights To Petition Protected By 18 USC §3332 & Case Law, August 16, 2021, https://standforhealthfreedom.com/wp-content/uploads/2021/09/0-Senate-Letterhead-Grand-Jury-Petition-AUSA.pdf.

990. CDC 2019-Novel Coronavirus (2019-nCoV) Real-Time RT-PCR Diagnostic Panel, Instructions for Use, at page 35, 7/21/2021, https://www.fda.gov/media/134922/download.

991. COVID-19 Breakthrough Case Investigations and Reporting (dropdown menu for state health departments) CDC, April 17, 2021 archived page, https://web.archive.org/web/20210417101408/https://www.cdc.gov/vaccines/covid-19/health-departments/breakthrough-cases.html.

992. Kit Knightly, How the CDC is manipulating data to prop-up "vaccine effectiveness", Off-Guardian, May 18, 2021, https://off-guardian.org/2021/05/18/how-the-cdc-is-manipulating-data-to-prop-up-vaccine-effectiveness/.

993. COVID-19 Vaccine Breakthrough Case Investigation and Reporting, CDC, archived page dated August 1, 2021, https://web.archive.org/web/20210801000527/https://

www.cdc.gov/vaccines/covid-19/health-departments/breakthrough-cases.html.

994. Joseph Mercola, Shockingly, CDC Now Lists Vaccinated Deaths as Unvaccinated, September 15, 2021, https://flybynews.wordpress.com/2021/09/15/shockingly-cdc-now-lists-vaccinated-deaths-as-unvaccinated/.

995. Joseph Mercola, Shockingly, CDC Now Lists Vaccinated Deaths as Unvaccinated, September 15, 2021, https://flybynews.wordpress.com/2021/09/15/shockingly-cdc-now-lists-vaccinated-deaths-as-unvaccinated/.

996. Joseph Mercola, Shockingly, CDC Now Lists Vaccinated Deaths as Unvaccinated, September 15, 2021, https://flybynews.wordpress.com/2021/09/15/shockingly-cdc-now-lists-vaccinated-deaths-as-unvaccinated/.

997. Weekly Updates by Select Demographic and Geographic Characteristics, Comorbidities and other conditions, CDC, https://www.cdc.gov/nchs/nvss/vsrr/covid_weekly/index.htm#Comorbidities.

998. Tyler Durden, Florida Man Who Died In Motorcycle Wreck Labeled As COVID-19 Death By State, July 19, 2020, https://www.zerohedge.com/political/florida-man-20s-who-died-motorcycle-wreck-labeled-covid-19-death-state.

999. Danielle Lama, FOX 35 INVESTIGATES: Questions raised after fatal motorcycle crash listed as COVID-19 death, July 18, 2020,

https://www.fox35orlando.com/news/fox-35-investigates-questions-raised-after-fatal-motorcycle-crash-listed-as-covid-19-death.

1000. Edward Hendrie, How the Federal Government Has Turned Hospitals into Death Chambers, February 25, 2022, https://greatmountainpublishing.com/2022/02/25/how-the-federal-government-has-turned-hospitals-into-death-chambers/.

1001. Mortality rate of COVID-19 patients on ventilators, March 30, 2020, https://www.physiciansweekly.com/mortality-rate-of-covid-19-patients-on-ventilators.

1002. Mortality rate of COVID-19 patients on ventilators, March 30, 2020, https://www.physiciansweekly.com/mortality-rate-of-covid-19-patients-on-ventilators.

1003. Martin Gould, EXCLUSIVE: 'It's a horror movie.' Nurse working on coronavirus frontline in New York claims the city is 'murdering' COVID-19 patients by putting them on ventilators and causing trauma to the lungs, Daily Mail, 14 May 2020, https://www.dailymail.co.uk/news/article-8262351/Nurse-New-York-claims-city-killing-COVID-19-patients-putting-ventilators.html.

1004. Michelle Rogers, Fact check: Hospitals get paid more if patients listed as COVID-19, on ventilators, USA Today, April 24, 2020, https://www.usatoday.com/story/news/factcheck/2020/04/24/fact-check-medicare-hospitals-paid-more-covid-19-patients-coronavirus/3000638001/.

1005. Official Government Reports Suggest the Fully Vaccinated Will Develop Acquired Immunodeficiency Syndrome by Christmas, The Expose, Ocober 27, 2021, https://theexpose.uk/2021/10/27/official-government-reports-suggest-the-fully-vaccinated-will-develop-acquired-immunodeficiency-syndrome-by-christmas/.

1006. Nobel Prize Winner French Virologist Luc Montagnier Explains How COVID-19 Vaccines Are Creating Variants, March 21, 2021, https://greatgameindia.com/covid-19-vaccines-creating-variants/.

1007. Pfizer admits in Confidential Documents that its Covid-19 Vaccine may cause Vaccine-Associated Enhanced Disease; and real-world data now proves it definitely does, The Expose, February 3, 2022, https://dailyexpose.uk/2022/02/03/pfizer-admits-covid-vaccine-causes-ade/.

1008. 5.3.6 CUMULATIVE ANALYSIS OF POST-AUTHORIZATION ADVERSE EVENT REPORTS OF PF-07302048 (BNT162B2) RECEIVED THROUGH 28-FEB-2021, https://drtrozzi.org/wp-content/uploads/2022/01/Pfizer-Cumulative-Analysis-of-Post-authorization-Adverse-Event-Reports.pdf.

1009. Larry Johnson, Inventor of mRNA Vaccine: Some Covid Vaccines Make the Virus More Dangerous, Gateway Pundit, July 28, 2021, https://www.thegatewaypundit.com/2021/07/inventor-mrna-vaccine-covid-vaccines-make-virus-dangerous/.

1010. Yen-Der Li, et. al., Coronavirus Vaccine Development: from SARS and MERS to COVID-19,

NIH, 20 December 2020,
https://www.ncbi.nlm.nih.gov/pmc/articles/PMC7749790/.

1011. Nobel Prize Winner French Virologist Luc Montagnier Explains How COVID-19 Vaccines Are Creating Variants, March 21, 2021, https://greatgameindia.com/covid-19-vaccines-creating-variants/.

1012. Wen Shi Lee, et. al., Antibody-dependent Enhancement and SARS-CoV-2 Vaccines and Therapies, NIH, September 9, 2020, https://pubmed.ncbi.nlm.nih.gov/32908214/.

1013. Ann M. Arvin, A Perspective on Potential Antibody-Dependent Enhancement of SARS-CoV-2, 2020 July 13, https://pubmed.ncbi.nlm.nih.gov/32659783/.

1014. Beattie, Kyle. (2021). Worldwide Bayesian Causal Impact Analysis of Vaccine Administration on Deaths and Cases Associated with COVID-19: A BigData Analysis of 145 Countries. 10.13140/RG.2.2.34214.65605, https://www.researchgate.net/publication/356248984_Worldwide_Bayesian_Causal_Impact_Analysis_of_Vaccine_Administration_on_Deaths_and_Cases_Associated_with_COVID-19_A_BigData_Analysis_of_145_Countries.

1015. Beattie, Kyle. (2021). Worldwide Bayesian Causal Impact Analysis of Vaccine Administration on Deaths and Cases Associated with COVID-19: A BigData Analysis of 145 Countries. 10.13140/RG.2.2.34214.65605, https://www.researchgate.net/publication/356248984_

Worldwide_Bayesian_Causal_Impact_Analysis_of_Vaccine_Administration_on_Deaths_and_Cases_Associated_with_COVID-19_A_BigData_Analysis_of_145_Countries.

1016. Medication Health Fraud, FDA, https://www.fda.gov/drugs/buying-using-medicine-safely/medication-health-fraud (last visited on September 24, 2022).

1017. Henna Maria, The Ten Stages of Genocide, Dawn of Peace, https://blog.dawnofpeace.org/2021/04/06/the-ten-stages-of-genocide/ (last visited on September 25, 2022).

1018. Mary Vilareal, COVID-19 vaccines are genocide, legendary doctor says, Nautural News, August 20, 2021, https://www.naturalnews.com/2021-08-20-covid-19-vaccines-equal-to-genocide.html.

1019. Mary Vilareal, COVID-19 vaccines are genocide, legendary doctor says, Nautural News, August 20, 2021, https://www.naturalnews.com/2021-08-20-covid-19-vaccines-equal-to-genocide.html.

1020. Get Vaccinated, COVID-19 Vaccination Posters, New York State Office of Mental Health, https://omh.ny.gov/omhweb/covid-19-resources/cv-19-vaccination-posters.pdf (last visited on September 25, 2022). See also David Montgomery, How to Sell the Coronavirus Vaccines to a Divided, Uneasy America, Washington Post, April 2021, https://www.washingtonpost.com/magazine/2021/04/26/coronavirus-vaccines-ad-council/.

1021. Anthony Lantian, et. al., "I Know Things They Don't Know!" The of Need for Uniqueness in Belief in Conspiracy Theories, Social Psychology, 48, (3), pp. 160-173, ISSN 1864-9335, 2017, https://kar.kent.ac.uk/62060/1/Manuscript%20Lantian%20et%20al.%20ACC.pdf. See also, https://doi.org/10.1027/1864-9335/a000306.

1022. John Timmer, Why Do Flat Earth Believers Still Exist? | Ars Technica, November 7, 2018, https://www.youtube.com/watch?v=mYB1JP-gfLE.

1023. J. Clendinning, The Principles of Surveying, at 98, Second Edition (1960).

1024. Taboo Conspiracy, There's No Curvature ... Let's Just Fake It! - Re-uploaded, May 2, 2021, https://www.youtube.com/watch?v=ft_zPawjnc0. See also, Taboo Conspiracy, There's No Curvature ... Let's Just Fake It! - Re-uploaded, May 2, 2021, https://odysee.com/@TabooConspiracy:c/there's-no-curvature-...-let's-just-fake:7.

1025. Taboo Conspiracy, There's No Curvature ... Let's Just Fake It! - Re-uploaded, May 2, 2021, https://www.youtube.com/watch?v=ft_zPawjnc0. See also, Taboo Conspiracy, There's No Curvature ... Let's Just Fake It! - Re-uploaded, May 2, 2021, https://odysee.com/@TabooConspiracy:c/there's-no-curvature-...-let's-just-fake:7.

1026. Alex Chertnik, Flat Earth CRUSHED by Discovery Channel, August 23, 2016, https://web.archive.org/web/20170801164338if_/https://www.youtube.com/watch?v=QVa2UmgdTM4.

1027. Alex Chertnick Reposting of Discovery Channel Version of PBS Video Unavailable, https://www.youtube.com/watch?v=QVa2UmgdTM4. See also, Original Discovery Channel Posting of PBS Video Unavailable, https://www.youtube.com/watch?v=zgZgoWfZb6c.

1028. Where Are We? Ch. 1 The Circumference of the Earth | Genius by Stephen Hawking, PBS, Genius by Steve Hawking, https://www.pbslearningmedia.org/resource/hawking_genius_ep06_clip01/where-are-we-ch-1-the-circumference-of-the-earth-genius-by-stephen-hawking/ (last visited on July 9, 2021).

1029. Alex Chertnik, Flat Earth CRUSHED by Discovery Channel, August 23, 2016, https://web.archive.org/web/20170801164338if_/https://www.youtube.com/watch?v=QVa2UmgdTM4.

1030. Where Are We? Ch. 1 The Circumference of the Earth | Genius by Stephen Hawking, PBS, Genius by Steve Hawking, https://www.pbslearningmedia.org/resource/hawking_genius_ep06_clip01/where-are-we-ch-1-the-circumference-of-the-earth-genius-by-stephen-hawking/ (last visited on July 9, 2021).

1031. Flat Earth vs. Round Earth | Explorer, National Geographic, January 16, 2019, https://www.youtube.com/watch?v=06bvdFK3vVU.

1032. James Underdown, https://wikivisually.com/wiki/James_Underdown (last visited on October 11, 2020).

1033. About Jim Underdown, Center for Inquiry, https://centerforinquiry.org/blog/authors/underdown-jim/ (last visited on October 11, 2020).

1034. Flat Earth vs. Round Earth | Explorer, National Geographic, January 16, 2019, https://www.youtube.com/watch?v=06bvdFK3vVU.

1035. Flat Earth vs. Round Earth | Explorer, National Geographic, January 16, 2019, https://www.youtube.com/watch?v=06bvdFK3vVU.

1036. Flat Earth vs. Round Earth | Explorer, National Geographic, January 16, 2019, https://www.youtube.com/watch?v=06bvdFK3vVU.

1037. Yanoff, Myron; Duker, Jay S. (2009). Ophthalmology 3rd Edition. MOSBY Elsevier. p. 54.

1038. Samuel Birley Rowbotham (Parallax), Zetetic Astronomy, Earth Not a Globe (1881), at 201-213, http://www.sacred-texts.com/earth/za/za32.htm.

1039. Samuel Birley Rowbotham (Parallax), Zetetic Astronomy, Earth Not a Globe (1881), at 201-213, http://www.sacred-texts.com/earth/za/za32.htm.

1040. National Geographic, Flat Earth vs. Round Earth | Explorer, January 16, 2019, https://www.youtube.com/watch?v=06bvdFK3vVU.

1041. Danny Faulkner, Is the Earth Flat?, Answers in Genesis, May 24, 2016, https://answersingenesis.org/astronomy/earth/is-the-earth-flat/.

1042. Masonic Astronauts, http://freemasoninformation.com/masonic-education/fa

mous/masonic-astronauts/ (last visited on April 28, 2019).

1043. Masonic Astronauts, http://freemasoninformation.com/masonic-education/famous/masonic-astronauts/ (last visited on April 28, 2019).

1044. Albert Pike, "Instructions to the 23 Supreme Councils of the World" (July 14, 1889), as recorded by Abel Clarin de La Rive, La Femme et l'Enfant dans la Franc-Maçonnerie Universelle (1894): 588, http://amazingdiscoveries.org/S-deception-Freemason_Lucifer_Albert_Pike#footnotevii. See also Occult Theocrasy, pp. 220-21.

1045. Manly Palmer Hall, "The Fellow Craft," The Lost Keys of Freemasonry (Richmond, Virginia: Macoy Publishing, 1931), http://www.manlyphall.org/text/the-lost-keys-of-freemasonry/chapter-iv-the-fellow-craft/.

1046. The Dark Side of NASA, May 28, 2008, http://primarysources.newsvine.com/_news/2008/05/28/1513441-the-dark-side-of-nasa.

1047. Bart Sibrel, Bill Kaysing Interview (Never Broadcast), April 14, 2013, https://www.youtube.com/watch?v=IJxHnpa90w4.

1048. Bart Sibrel, Bill Kaysing Interview (Never Broadcast), April 14, 2013, https://www.youtube.com/watch?v=IJxHnpa90w4.

1049. Bart Sibrel, Bill Kaysing Interview (Never Broadcast), April 14, 2013, https://www.youtube.com/watch?v=IJxHnpa90w4.

1050. Danny Faulkner, Is the Earth Flat?, Answers in Genesis, May 24, 2016, https://answersingenesis.org/astronomy/earth/is-the-earth-flat/.

1051. Danny Faulkner, Is the Earth Flat?, Answers in Genesis, May 24, 2016, https://answersingenesis.org/astronomy/earth/is-the-earth-flat/.

1052. International Astronautical Federation, 1972: Apollo 16 (NASA), March 8, 2009, https://www.youtube.com/watch?v=vsuBd0nUKZw.

1053. International Astronautical Federation, 1972: Apollo 16 (NASA), March 8, 2009, https://www.youtube.com/watch?v=vsuBd0nUKZw.

1054. Apollo 16 Video Library, https://www.hq.nasa.gov/alsj/a16/video16.html#lrvdeploy (last visited on January 3, 2016).

1055. Sensuous Curmudgeon, Is Jason Lisle a Flat Earther, 13 October 2013, https://sensuouscurmudgeon.wordpress.com/2013/10/13/is-jason-lisle-a-flat-earther/.

1056. Sensuous Curmudgeon, Is Jason Lisle a Flat Earther, 13 October 2013, https://sensuouscurmudgeon.wordpress.com/2013/10/13/is-jason-lisle-a-flat-earther/, quoting Alex Murashko, The Christian Post, October 13, 2013, Letting Science 'Interpret' Scripture Is Slippery Slope, Says Young Earth/Universe Creationist, https://www.christianpost.com/news/letting-science-interpret-scripture-is-slippery-slope-says-young-earth-universe-creationist-106525/.

1057. Sensuous Curmudgeon, Is Jason Lisle a Flat Earther, 13 October 2013, https://sensuouscurmudgeon.wordpress.com/2013/10/13/is-jason-lisle-a-flat-earther/.

1058. Sensuous Curmudgeon, Is Jason Lisle a Flat Earther, 13 October 2013, https://sensuouscurmudgeon.wordpress.com/2013/10/13/is-jason-lisle-a-flat-earther/.

1059. Samuel Birley Rowbotham (Parallax), Zetetic Astronomy, Earth Not a Globe (1881), Chapter 15, http://www.sacred-texts.com/earth/za/za66.htm.

1060. The Earth Is Flat!, 7 May 2011, https://sensuouscurmudgeon.wordpress.com/2011/05/07/the-earth-is-flat/.

1061. The Earth Is Flat!, 7 May 2011, https://sensuouscurmudgeon.wordpress.com/2011/05/07/the-earth-is-flat/.

1062. The Earth Is Flat!, 7 May 2011, https://sensuouscurmudgeon.wordpress.com/2011/05/07/the-earth-is-flat/.

1063. The Earth Does Not Move!, 20 May 2011, https://sensuouscurmudgeon.wordpress.com/2011/05/20/the-earth-does-not-move/.

1064. The Earth Does Not Move!, 20 May 2011, https://sensuouscurmudgeon.wordpress.com/2011/05/20/the-earth-does-not-move/.

1065. Paul Rosenberg, Creationists Endure Rough Few Weeks: Why the Flat-earth Crowd Is in Trouble, Salon, April 3, 2014, https://www.salon.com/2014/04/03/creationists_endure

_rough_few_weeks_why_the_flat_earth_crowd_is_in_trouble/.

1066. Robert Schadewald, The Flat Earth Bible, 1995, https://www.theflatearthsociety.org/library/newspaperandmagazine/Flat%20Earth%20Bible,%20The%20(Schadewald).pdf.

1067. Karl Giberson, The Bible Is a Library, Not a Book, Huffington Post, October 15, 2011, https://www.huffpost.com/entry/the-Bible-is-a-library-no_b_923690.

1068. Karl Giberson, The Bible Is a Library, Not a Book, Huffington Post, October 15, 2011, https://www.huffpost.com/entry/the-Bible-is-a-library-no_b_923690.

1069. Karl Giberson, The Bible Is a Library, Not a Book, Huffington Post, October 15, 2011, https://www.huffpost.com/entry/the-Bible-is-a-library-no_b_923690.

1070. Karl Giberson, The Bible Is a Library, Not a Book, Huffington Post, October 15, 2011, https://www.huffpost.com/entry/the-Bible-is-a-library-no_b_923690.

1071. Karl Giberson, The Bible Is a Library, Not a Book, Huffington Post, October 15, 2011.

1072. Albert B Collver, Copernicus and the Church, Lutherans and the Missouri Synod, https://www.academia.edu/12723823/Copernicus_and_the_Church_Lutherans_and_the_Missouri_Synod (last visited on April 19, 2019).

1073. Dr. Elizabeth Mitchell, The Bible: Library or Book?, August 27, 2011, https://answersingenesis.org/the-word-of-god/Bible-library-or-book/.

1074. Dr. Elizabeth Mitchell, The Bible: Library or Book?, August 27, 2011, https://answersingenesis.org/the-word-of-god/Bible-library-or-book/.

1075. Earth's Atmosphere Stretches Out to the Moon - And Beyond, 20 February 2019, https://www.esa.int/Our_Activities/Space_Science/Earth_s_atmosphere_stretches_out_to_the_Moon_and_beyond.

1076. Earth's Atmosphere Stretches Out to the Moon - And Beyond, 20 February 2019, https://www.esa.int/Our_Activities/Space_Science/Earth_s_atmosphere_stretches_out_to_the_Moon_and_beyond.

1077. Earth's Atmosphere Stretches Out to the Moon - And Beyond, 20 February 2019, https://www.esa.int/Our_Activities/Space_Science/Earth_s_atmosphere_stretches_out_to_the_Moon_and_beyond.

1078. Earth's Atmosphere Stretches Out to the Moon - And Beyond, 20 February 2019, https://www.esa.int/Our_Activities/Space_Science/Earth_s_atmosphere_stretches_out_to_the_Moon_and_beyond.

1079. Earth's Atmosphere Stretches Out to the Moon - And Beyond, 20 February 2019, https://www.esa.int/Our_Activities/Space_Science/Eart

h_s_atmosphere_stretches_out_to_the_Moon_and_bey ond.

1080. Brian Mullin, Ball's Out Physics Episode 5.0: Propulsion in Space, April 1, 2016, https://www.youtube.com/watch?v=q8C0mStHdV0. Brian Mullin, Ball's Out Physics Episode 5.1: Propulsion in a Vacuum Chamber, April 4, 2016, https://www.youtube.com/watch?v=Mq4fGmYoiqs. Mirrored at https://www.youtube.com/watch?v=rrNeuOhjBh4 and https://www.youtube.com/watch?v=JyPb5DByIPY. See also Flat Earth - Physics 101 - Newton's 3rd Law, October 11, 2017, https://www.youtube.com/watch?v=1X86guBXWfo.

1081. Scientist Shows Proof That Rockets Do Not Work In The Vacuum of Space, October 11, 2017, https://www.youtube.com/watch?v=Fnf_f4rogtg&index=2&list=WL.

1082. Sir Edward Appleton, The Discovery of the Properties of the Ionosphere, Nortown Amateur Radio Club of Toronto, http://www.ve3nar.org/meetings_files/Presentations/Appleton.pdf (last visited on June 11, 2018).

1083. Elizabeth Howell, What Are Cosmic Rays?, April 21, 2016, https://www.space.com/32644-cosmic-rays.html.

1084. Cosmic Rays, http://astronomy.swin.edu.au/cosmos/C/Cosmic+Rays (last visited on April 7, 2018).

1085. Electromagnetic Spectrum, October 30, 2012, https://www.nasa.gov/directorates/heo/scan/spectrum/t

xt_electromagnetic_spectrum.html.

1086. Radio Waves to Gamma-rays, https://www.e-education.psu.edu/astro801/content/l3_p4.html (last visited on April 7, 2018).

1087. How to Use Amateur Radio Moonbounce, EME Propagation, https://www.electronics-notes.com/articles/ham_radio/amateur-propagation/moonbounce-propagation-eme.php (last visited on April 7, 2018).

1088. Get ready for 2m MoonBounce Communications, https://www.dxmaps.com/jt65bintro.html (last visited on April 7, 2018). See also VE2ZAZ - First EME (Moonbounce) Radio Contact with HB9Q - Higher Quality Vidéo, April 2, 2017, https://www.youtube.com/watch?v=nfrPwdmmky4.

1089. Atmospheric Pressure, https://en.wikipedia.org/wiki/Atmospheric_pressure#cite_note-3, citing Atmospheric Pressure, National Geographic, https://www.nationalgeographic.org/encyclopedia/atmospheric-pressure/ and Department of Physics, University of Illinois at Urbana-Champaign, https://van.physics.illinois.edu/qa/listing.php?id=2232 (last visited on February 15, 2020).

1090. Department of Chemistry at Elmhurst College, Gas Pressure, http://chemistry.elmhurst.edu/vchembook/180pressure.html (last visited on February 15, 2020).

1091. Paul Voosen, Outer Space May Have Just Gotten a Bit Closer, July 24, 2018, https://www.sciencemag.org/news/2018/07/outer-space

-may-have-just-gotten-bit-closer?r3f_986=https://en.wikipedia.org/.

1092. Dr. S. Sanz Fernández de Córdoba, Presentation of the Karman Separation Line, Used as the Boundary Separating Aeronautics and Astronautics, 21 -06-2004, https://www.webcitation.org/618QHms8h?url=http://www.fai.org/astronautics/100km.asp.

1093. Profane, American Dictionary of the English Language.

Other books available from Great Mountain Publishing®

Hoax of Biblical Proportions
Edward Hendrie
ISBN: 978-1-943056-18-7

Satan knows that God has promised to preserve his words found in the Holy Scriptures, so it would be futile for him to try to destroy them. Thus, Satan's strategy is to obscure God's words by flooding the world with counterfeit Bibles. That way, he can flimflam people into reading his corrupt Bibles instead of God's infallible Scriptures. The devil can then lead men astray from the true gospel. This book will prove that the Authorized (King James) Version of the Holy Bible is given by inspiration of God. It will reveal how Satan is using profane Bible versions to divert the world away from God's inspired Holy Scriptures. The changes in the new Bible versions are not merely cosmetic for ease of reading, as claimed by the publishers; they change doctrine. The new Bible versions confuse churches and demoralize the world by proclaiming a different Jesus and a different gospel from what is in God's inspired King James Holy Bible.

Vaccine Danger: Quackery and Sin
Edward Hendrie
ISBN: 978-1-943056-17-0

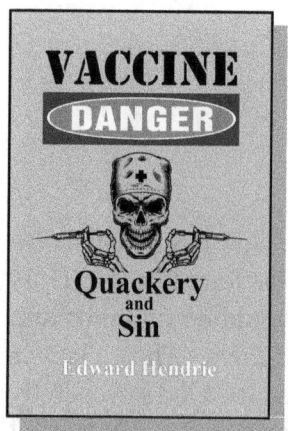

This book reveals the most significant medical fraud in history. The theory that you can prevent illness by injecting poisons into the bodies of healthy people is dangerous quackery and sin. All true science has proven the practice of vaccination to be ineffective and unsafe. But the medical establishment has been lured into the superstitious practice, hook, line, and sinker. It is not merely a matter of ignorance that the debilitating practice flourishes. It is, at its core, being promoted by those who know it is unsafe and ineffective. There is a malevolent spirit behind the practice. It is part of a conspiracy against God and man. While most doctors are unwitting, some are willing minions of that old serpent, called the Devil, and Satan, who are quite happy to kill people for profit. Jesus describes such men: "Ye are of your father the devil, and the lusts of your father ye will do. He was a murderer from the beginning, and abode not in the truth, because there is no truth in him. When he speaketh a lie, he speaketh of his own: for he is a liar, and the father of it." John 8:44.

The Greatest Lie on Earth
Proof That Our World Is Not a Moving Globe
Edward Hendrie
ISBN-13: 978-1-943056-01-9

This book reveals the mother of all conspiracies. It sets forth biblical proof and irrefutable evidence that will cause the scales to fall from your eyes and reveal that the world you thought existed is a myth. The most universally accepted scientific belief today is that the earth is a globe, spinning on its axis at a speed of approximately 1,000 miles per hour at the equator, while at the same time it is orbiting the sun at approximately 66,600 miles per hour. All of this is happening as the sun, in turn, is supposed to be hurtling through the Milky Way galaxy at approximately 500,000 miles per hour. The Milky Way galaxy, itself, is alleged to be racing through space at a speed ranging from 300,000 to 1,340,000 miles per hour. What most people are not told is that the purported spinning, orbiting, and speeding through space has never been proven. In fact, every scientific experiment that has ever been performed to determine the motion of the earth has proven that the earth is stationary. Yet, textbooks ignore the scientific proof that contradicts the myth of a spinning and orbiting globe. Christian schools have been hoodwinked into teaching heliocentrism, despite the clear teaching in the Bible that the earth is not a sphere and does not move. This book reveals the evil forces behind the heliocentric deception, and why scientists and the Christian churches have gone along with it.

The Greatest Lie on Earth (Expanded Edition)
Proof That Our World Is Not a Moving Globe
Edward Hendrie
ISBN-13: 978-1943056-03-3

This book is an expanded edition of *The Greatest Lie on Earth*. It contains more than 1,000 pages of authoritative evidence with more than 1,300 endnotes that document proof beyond any doubt that the earth is flat and stationary. The book reveals the mother of all conspiracies. It sets forth biblical proof and irrefutable evidence that will cause the scales to fall from your eyes and reveal that the world you thought existed is a myth. The most universally accepted scientific belief today is that the earth is a globe, spinning on its axis at a speed of approximately 1,000 miles per hour at the equator, while at the same time it is orbiting the sun at approximately 66,600 miles per hour. All of this is happening as the sun, in turn, is supposed to be hurtling through the Milky Way galaxy at approximately 500,000 miles per hour. The Milky Way galaxy, itself, is alleged to be racing through space at a speed ranging from 300,000 to 1,340,000 miles per hour. What most people are not told is that the purported spinning, orbiting, and speeding through space has never been proven. In fact, every scientific experiment that has ever been performed to determine the motion of the earth has proven that the earth is stationary. Yet, textbooks ignore the scientific proof that contradicts the myth of a spinning and orbiting globe. Christian schools have been hoodwinked into teaching heliocentrism, despite the clear teaching in the Bible that the earth is not a sphere and does not move. This book reveals the evil forces behind the heliocentric deception, and why scientists and the Christian churches have gone along with it.

Antichrist: The Beast Revealed
Edward Hendrie
ISBN-13: 978-0-9832627-8-7

The antichrist is among us, here and now. This book proves it by comparing the biblical prophecies about the antichrist with the evidence that those prophecies have been fulfilled. This book documents the man of sin's esoteric confession that he is the antichrist. You will learn how the antichrist has changed times and laws as prophesied by Daniel, and how he is today sitting in the temple of God, "shewing himself that he is God," in fulfillment of Paul's prophecy in 2 Thessalonians 2:4. The beast of Revelation has come into the world, "after the working of Satan with all power and signs and lying wonders, and with all deceivableness of unrighteousness," as prophesied in 2 Thessalonians 2:10. The antichrist's adeptness as a hypocrite is the reason for his evil success. Indeed, to be the antichrist, his evil character must be concealed beneath a facade of piety. "And no marvel; for Satan himself is transformed into an angel of light. Therefore it is no great thing if his ministers also be transformed as the ministers of righteousness; whose end shall be according to their works." 2 Corinthians 11:14-15. The key to revealing the identity of the antichrist is to uncover his hypocrisy. Because the hypocrisy of the antichrist is so extreme, those who have been hoodwinked by his religious doctrines will be shocked to learn of it. This book exposes the concealed iniquity of the antichrist and juxtaposes it against his publicly proclaimed false persona of righteousness, thus bringing into clear relief that man of sin, the son of perdition, who is truly a ravening wolf in sheep's clothing, speaking lies in hypocrisy. See Matthew 7:15 and 1 Timothy 4:1-3.

9/11-Enemies Foreign and Domestic
Edward Hendrie
ISBN-13: 978-0983262732

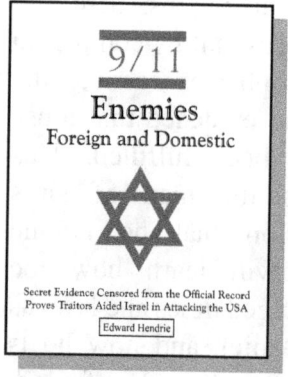

9/11-Enemies Foreign and Domestic proves beyond a reasonable doubt that the U.S. Government's conspiracy theory of the attacks on September 11, 2001, is a preposterous cover story. The evidence in 9/11-Enemies Foreign and Domestic has been suppressed from the official government reports and censored from the mass media. The evidence proves that powerful Zionists ordered the 9/11 attacks, which were perpetrated by Israel's Mossad, aided and abetted by treacherous high officials in the U.S. Government. 9/11-Enemies Foreign and Domestic identifies the traitors by name and details their subversive crimes. There is sufficient evidence in 9/11-Enemies Foreign and Domestic to indict important officials of the U.S. Government for high treason. The reader will understand how the U.S. Government really works and what Sir John Harrington (1561-1612) meant when he said: "Treason doth never prosper: what's the reason? Why if it prosper, none dare call it treason." There are millions of Americans who have taken an oath to defend the U.S. Constitution against all enemies foreign and domestic. The mass media, which is under the control of a disloyal cabal, keeps those patriotic Americans ignorant of the traitors among them. J. Edgar Hoover, former Director of the FBI, explained: "The individual is handicapped by coming face-to-face with a conspiracy so monstrous-he simply cannot believe it exists." 9/11-Enemies Foreign and Domestic erases any doubt about the existence of the monstrous conspiracy described by Hoover and arms the reader with the knowledge required to save our great nation. "My people are destroyed for lack of knowledge." Hosea 4:6.

Solving the Mystery of BABYLON THE GREAT
Edward Hendrie
ISBN-13: 978-0983262701

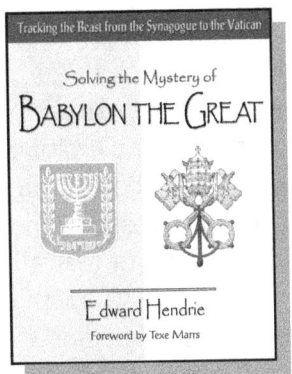

"Attorney and Christian researcher Edward Hendrie investigates and reveals one of the greatest exposés of all time. . . . a book you don't want to miss. Solving the Mystery of Babylon the Great is packed with documentation. Never before have the crypto-Jews who seized the reins of power in Rome been put under such intense scrutiny." Texe Marrs, Power of Prophecy. The evidence presented in this book leads to the ineluctable conclusion that the Roman Catholic Church was established by crypto-Jews as a false "Christian" front for a Judaic/Babylonian religion. That religion is the core of a world conspiracy against man and God. That is not a conspiracy theory based upon speculation, but rather the hard truth based upon authoritative evidence, which is documented in this book. Texe Marrs explains in his foreword to the book: "Who is Mystery Babylon? What is the meaning of the sinister symbols found in these passages? Which city is being described as the 'great city' so full of sin and decadence, and who are its citizens? Why do the woman and beast of Revelation seek the destruction of the holy people, the saints and martyrs of Jesus? What does it all mean for you and me today? Solving the Mystery of Babylon the Great answers these questions and more. Edward Hendrie's discoveries are not based on prejudice but on solid evidence aligned forthrightly with the 'whole counsel of God.' He does not condone nor will he be a part of any project in which Bible verses are taken out of context, or in which scriptures are twisted to mean what they do not say. Again and again you will find that Mr. Hendrie documents his assertions, backing up what he says with historical facts and proofs. Most important is that he buttresses his findings with scriptural understanding. The foundation for his research is sturdy because it is based on the bedrock of God's unshakeable

Word."

The Anti-Gospel
Edward Hendrie
ISBN-13: 978-0983262749

Edward Hendrie uses God's word to strip the sheep's clothing from false Christian ministers and expose them as ravening wolves preaching an anti-gospel. The anti-gospel is based on a myth that all men have a will that is free from the bondage of sin to choose whether to believe in Jesus. The Holy Bible, however, states that all men are spiritually dead and cannot believe in Jesus unless they are born again of the Holy Spirit. Ephesians 2:1-7; John 3:3-8. God has chosen his elect to be saved by his grace through faith in Jesus Christ. Ephesians 1:3-9; 2:8-10. God imbues his elect with the faith needed to believe in Jesus. Hebrews 12:2; John 1:12-13. The devil's false gospel contradicts the word of God and reverses the order of things. Under the anti-gospel, instead of a sovereign God choosing his elect, sovereign man decides whether to choose God. The calling of the Lord Jesus Christ is effectual; all who are chosen for salvation will believe in Jesus. John 6:37-44. The anti-gospel has a false Jesus, who only offers the possibility of salvation, with no assurance. The anti-gospel blasphemously makes God out to be a liar by denying the total depravity of man and the sovereign election of God. All who preach that false gospel are under a curse from God. Galatians 1:6-9.

Bloody Zion
Edward Hendrie
ISBN-13: 978-0983262763

Jesus told Pontius Pilate: "My kingdom is not of this world." John 18:36. God has a spiritual Zion that is in a heavenly Jerusalem. Hebrews 12:22; Revelation 21:10. Jesus Christ is the chief corner stone laid by God in Zion. 1 Peter 2:6. Those who believe in Jesus Christ are living stones in the spiritual house of God. 1 Peter 2:5; Ephesians 2:20-22. Believers are in Jesus and Jesus is in believers. John 14:20; 17:20-23. All who are elected by God to believe in Jesus Christ are part of the heavenly Zion, without regard to whether they are Jews or Gentiles. Romans 10:12. Satan is a great adversary of God, who has created his own mystery religions. During the Babylonian captivity (2 Chronicles 36:20), an occult society of Jews replaced God's commands with Satan's Babylonian dogma. Their new religion became Judaism. Jesus explained the corruption of the Judaic religion: "Howbeit in vain do they worship me, teaching for doctrines the commandments of men." Mark 7:7. Jesus revealed the Satanic origin of Judaism when he stated: "Ye are of your father the devil, and the lusts of your father ye will do." John 8:44. Babylonian Judaism remains the religion of the Jews today. Satan has infected many nominal "Christian" denominations with his Babylonian occultism, which has given rise to "Christian" Zionism. "Christian" Zionism advocates a counterfeit, earthly Zion, within which fleshly Jews take primacy over the spiritual church of Jesus Christ. This book exposes "Christian" Zionism as a false gospel and subversive political movement that sustains Israel's war against God and man.

Murder, Rape, and Torture in a Catholic Nunnery
Edward Hendrie
ISBN-13: 978-1-943056-00-2

There has probably not been a person more maligned by the powerful forces of the Roman Catholic Church than Maria Monk. In 1836 she published the famous book, *Awful Disclosures of the Hotel Dieu Nunnery of Montreal*. In that book, she told of murder, rape, and torture behind the walls of the cloistered nunnery. Because the evidence was verifiably true, the Catholic hierarchy found it necessary to fabricate evidence and suborn perjury in an attempt to destroy the credibility of Maria Monk. The Catholic Church has kept up the character assassination of Maria Monk now for over 175 years. Even today, there can be found on the internet websites devoted to libeling Maria Monk. Edward Hendrie has examined the evidence and set it forth for the readers to decide for themselves whether Maria Monk was an impostor, as claimed by the Roman Catholic Church, or whether she was a brave victim. An objective view of the evidence leads to the ineluctable conclusion that Maria Monk told the truth about what happened behind the walls of the Hotel Dieu Nunnery of Montreal. The Roman Catholic Church, which is the most powerful religious and political organization in the world, has engaged in an unceasing campaign of vilification against Maria Monk. Their crusade against Maria Monk, however, can only affect the opinion of the uninformed. It cannot change the evidence. The evidence speaks clearly to those who will look at the case objectively. The evidence reveals that the much maligned Maria Monk was a reliable witness who made awful but accurate disclosures about life in a cloistered nunnery.

What Shall I Do to Inherit Eternal Life?
Edward Hendrie
ISBN-13: 978-0983262770

A certain ruler posed to Jesus the most important question ever asked: "Good Master, what shall I do to inherit eternal life?" (Luke 18:18) The man came to the right person. Jesus is God, and therefore his answer to that question is authoritative. This book examines Jesus' surprising answer and definitively explains how one inherits eternal life. This is a book about God's revelation to man. Except for the Holy Bible, this is the most important book you will ever read.

The Damnable Heresy Of Salvation by Dead Faith (Expanded Edition)
Edward Hendrie
ISBN 13: 978-1943056118

Good works follow salvation; they do not earn salvation. Good works do not save us. The works of faith are those works ordained and performed by God through the believer. They are the result of faith. It is that perfect faith that justifies the believer. "For by grace are ye saved through faith; and that not of yourselves: it is the gift of God: Not of works, lest any man should boast. For we are his workmanship, created in Christ Jesus unto good works, which God hath before ordained that we should walk in them. For we are his workmanship, created in Christ Jesus unto good works, which God hath before ordained that we should walk in them." Ephesians 2:8-10. In Romans, chapters 6 and 8, Paul explains faith without good works cannot save. Paul says that God's elect "walk not after the flesh, but after the Spirit." Romans 8:1. He states that those who do not walk in the Spirit but instead walk in the flesh "shall not inherit the kingdom of God." Galatians 5:15-25. John explains: "If we say that we have fellowship with him, and walk in darkness, we lie, and do not the truth: But if we walk in the light, as he is in the light, we have fellowship one with another, and the blood of Jesus Christ his Son cleanseth us from all sin." 1 John 1:6-7. James asks a rhetorical question: "What doth it profit, my brethren, though a man say he hath faith, and have not works? can faith save him?" James 2:14. James succinctly explains that "faith without works is dead." James 2:20. The pronouncement in James that true faith bears the fruit of good works is a theme found in the gospel. But some perniciously preach that God saves a person by faith that has no good works. That is one of the "damnable heresies" about which Peter warned. See 2 Peter 2:1-22.

Rome's Responsibility for the Assassination of Abraham Lincoln, With an Appendix Containing Conversations Between Abraham Lincoln and Charles Chiniquy
Thomas M. Harris
ISBN-13: 978-0983262794

The author of this book, General Thomas Maley Harris, was a medical doctor, who recruited and served as commander of the Tenth West Virginia Volunteers during the Civil War. He rose in rank through meritorious service to become a brigadier general in the Union Army. General Harris established a reputation for faithfulness, industriousness, intelligence, and efficiency. He was noted for his leadership in preparing his troops and leading them in battle. He was brevetted a major general for "gallant conduct in the assault on Petersburg." After the Civil War, General Harris served one term as a representative in the West Virginia legislature, and was West Virginia's Adjutant General from 1869 to 1870. General Harris was a member of the Military Commission that tried and convicted the conspirators who assassinated President Abraham Lincoln. He had first hand knowledge of the sworn testimony of the witnesses in that trial. This book summarizes the salient evidence brought out during the military trial and adds information from other sources to present before the public the ineluctable conclusion that the assassination of Abraham Lincoln was the work of the Roman Catholic Church. The Roman Catholic Church has been largely successful in suppressing the circulation of this book. This book has never been given a place on bookstore shelves, as it exposed too much for the Roman Catholic hierarchy to tolerate. Any display of this book would bring an instant boycott of the bookstore. It is only now, in the age of the internet, where the marketplace of ideas has been opened wide, that this book can be found by those searching for the truth of who was behind the assassination of Abraham Lincoln.

The above books can be ordered from bookstores and from internet sites, including, but not limited to:

www.antichristconspiracy.com
https://greatmountainpublishing.com
www.911enemies.com
www.mysterybabylonthegreat.net
www.antigospel.com
https://play.google.com
www.barnesandnoble.com
www.amazon.com

Edward Hendrie
edwardhendrie@gmail.com